JAVA 5
OBJECTS FIRST

BARRY I. SOROKA

CALIFORNIA STATE POLYTECHNIC UNIVERSITY

JONES AND BARTLETT PUBLISHERS

Sudbury, Massachusetts

BOSTON   TORONTO   LONDON   SINGAPORE

World Headquarters
Jones and Bartlett Publishers
40 Tall Pine Drive
Sudbury, MA 01776
978-443-5000
info@jbpub.com
www.jbpub.com

Jones and Bartlett Publishers Canada
6339 Ormindale Way
Mississauga, Ontario L5V 1J2
CANADA

Jones and Bartlett Publishers International
Barb House, Barb Mews
London W6 7PA
UK

Jones and Bartlett's books and products are available through most bookstores and online booksellers. To contact Jones and Bartlett Publishers directly, call 800-832-0034, fax 978-443-8000, or visit our website www.jbpub.com.

Substantial discounts on bulk quantities of Jones and Bartlett's publications are available to corporations, professional associations, and other qualified organizations. For details and specific discount information, contact the special sales department at Jones and Bartlett via the above contact information or send an email to specialsales@jbpub.com.

Production Credits
Acquisitions Editor: Tim Anderson
Production Director: Amy Rose
Marketing Manager: Andrea DeFronzo
Editorial Assistant: Kate Koch
Composition: Northeast Compositors
Cover Design: Kristin E. Ohlin
Cover Image: © Alejandro Lapuerta Mediavilla/ShutterStock, Inc.
Printing and Binding: Courier Westford
Cover Printing: Courier Westford

Library of Congress Cataloging-in-Publication Data
Soroka, Barry.
  Java 5 : objects first / Barry Soroka. — 1st ed.
    p. cm.
  Includes index.
  ISBN-13: 978-0-7637-3720-7 (pbk.)
  1. Java (Computer program language)   I. Title.
  QA76.73.J38S67 2006
  005.13'3—dc22
  6048   2005032131

Printed in the United States of America
10 09 08 07 06 10 9 8 7 6 5 4 3 2 1

Dedication

For Gary and Harvey and for my students,
who have taught me so much.

Preface for the Student

Welcome to the world of Computer Science (CS) and Java programming! You have probably come to this text because you're taking CS 1, the first course in Computer Science.

This preface starts by discussing what I expect of you and what you can expect of this text. Next, I discuss the need for lifelong learning. One of my main goals is to prepare you to learn other languages during the course of your career. Finally, I suggest some behaviors that will help you succeed in this course. Good luck!

What Is Computer Science?

High school students are often confused about what Computer Science is and is not. Many students enter CS only to discover that they actually prefer another computer specialty. Historically and nationally, about one-third of those who begin as CS majors will end up in some other major. There are three related fields that are often confused:

- *Computer programming* is writing the instructions that tell computers to perform useful work. This is what Computer Science is centered around.
- *Designing physical computers* is the field known as Computer Engineering. Programming is only peripheral to this field.
- *Bringing computer systems into organizations* is known as Management Information Systems (MIS), or Computer Information Systems (CIS).

Computer Science students spend a lot of time working with computers, trying to convert English-language specifications into the program that gets the computer to do the assigned task. Typically, the working program is the end product of many incorrect programs. Some students feel awful when they make mistakes. CS students, and professors, make many mistakes! You need resilience.

Computer Science requires good communication skills. It will be rare for you to work alone on a project of your own choice. In your career, you'll need to communicate with three groups:

- *Your boss*—You need to describe what you have been doing, what remains to be done, and what resources are required. You must always be prepared to *justify your job*.
- *Your client*—Sometimes, you must help the client write a definitive specification of what they want. Next, your firm must compete for business against other firms, and you must demonstrate that your group can do the work. Finally, you must demonstrate that your product (a program) does what the client wants.
- *Your team*—In industry, most programs are written by *teams* of programmers, and teams are being used more and more in university CS courses. First, you'll need to learn how to divide a project and assign the pieces to programmers or teams of programmers. Finally, you'll need to evaluate the contributions of team members.

Not everyone enjoys Computer Science. Some students feel frustrated because they can't get a program right on the first try. They feel bad when they make mistakes. Others come to CS because they like to work alone. They are annoyed that CS requires so much communication and interaction with others. Computer Science also requires lifelong learning because computers, their uses, and their languages are constantly changing.

What I Assume You Know

I presume that you are familiar with some pertinent concepts from mathematics, typical uses of computers, and with computers as entertainment devices.

Mathematics

I expect that you have seen binary numbers and complex numbers in math courses you have taken before coming to CS 1. Binary numbers are the basis of computer arithmetic, and complex numbers will provide a rich test bed for programming problems. I expect that you have encountered a few concepts from number theory including remainders, modulus, and prime numbers. From logic, I expect that you have seen the logical concepts of **and**, **or**, and **not**. When we begin using any of these topics, I present a quick review of the material.

Applications

I assume that you have used common personal computer (PC) applications, including word processors and spreadsheets. Some of you will have used database applications; these will be studied in detail in a later CS course devoted entirely to databases.

Entertainment

In recent years, most of the students entering my CS 1 classes have had extensive experience using computers for entertainment purposes. Many high school graduates have far more experience with such applications than I do. Here are some of the ways in which PCs facilitate entertainment:

- *Video games*—running on both general-purpose computers and on special-purpose, dedicated hardware.
- *Audio*—burning CDs and downloading music as well as using the computer to record and edit your own music.
- *Video*—seeing the results of computers in movie-making, including computer graphics and motion control.

None of these experiences is a skill required for CS 1, but I mention them from time to time because computer programming underlies them all.

What I Am Trying to Teach

CS 1 is an introduction to Computer Science. It uses Java, but it's not a Java course. There will always be parts of Java that CS 1 can't cover, but your training in this course should prepare you to learn on your own those parts of Java that we will not study together.

Java is the language we will be using in this course, but my goal is to teach you the fundamentals of computer programming that will apply to any language you will be asked to use. I hope to teach you skills that will be useful in learning new programming languages. This is what you will be doing for the rest of your career. Two of these skills are how to learn a new language in small increments, and how to write small programs to test novel constructs you encounter in Java or any other new language.

Lifelong Learning

I can't teach you everything you will need for your entire working life. (Some of it hasn't been invented yet!) You must be open-minded and ready to learn new things as they come along.

Paradigms

For our purposes, a paradigm is a systematic approach to programming. We have had three major programming paradigms in the past 60 years. If history repeats itself, then over the course of your working life (say 35 years), you will see *two* shifts in programming paradigms. This will require that you learn to change the way you program, despite the fact that your prior methods may have been very productive and successful.

Languages

This book will not teach you all of Java. I will teach you the basics that let you write substantial programs, and you will be prepared to learn other parts of Java as you need them.[1]

You will also be prepared to learn new languages as they are developed. No matter what language we teach in CS 1, you will be using a different language ten years from now. However, I hope to teach you techniques that will make it easier to learn new languages as they come along. You will learn how to write *small programs*:

- in order to get a handle on *fundamental capabilities* you need in any language, including reading and writing to a file.
- in order to *reinforce* your knowledge of language features that you find in a book or at a workshop.
- in order to test language features that you find *unclear*.

---

[1] There's a relevant proverb: "Give a man a fish and you feed him for a day. Teach a man to fish and you feed him for a lifetime."

Resources for Java

This text is the principal Java resource in the course you're now taking, but there are other resources available to help you explore, in greater depth, concepts and constructs that are introduced here.

Additional Books

The market offers many books and references for Java, each with a different approach. Good sources for additional books are:

- *Libraries*—both college and public.
- *Bookstores*—especially technical bookstores.
- *Online bookstores*—many offer reviews of every book they sell, reviews by people who have bought the book and used it, and reviews by people who have *tried* to use it.

Java and the API

Sun Microsystems, Inc., offers Java, free of charge, for several platforms. Check *http://java.sun.com/j2se/*. Using this website, you can install Java on your personal computer.

Sun Microsystems, Inc., also provides a library of capabilities for Java. This is called the Applications Programming Interface (API). This is documented at the website *http://java.sun.com/docs/index.html.* You can also download this documentation to your PC.

Be careful in using the Java libraries. Your instructor may ask you to write a program with capabilities that are already available in the API—a sorting program, for instance. If you use the API instead of writing the program from scratch, then you have cast yourself in the role of a tool-*user* rather than a tool-*builder*, and you may be penalized for your "initiative." Computer Science students must learn how to implement almost all the API capabilities from scratch.

The World Wide Web

The World Wide Web (www) offers many resources for the student of Java. For instance, many individuals and companies have published Java *tutorials* on the Web. So, if you need more information or examples about the `switch` statement in Java, ask your favorite search engine to find

```
"java tutorial" and "switch"
```

This will link you to many useful pages, as well as some that are not so useful. Look at the hits and you will probably find what you are looking for.

Another online resource involves the Web pages connected with Java courses around the world. Try these approaches:

- Search for `java` and `syllabus` on the Web. This will find pages for college courses that use Java. Some are CS 1 courses, and others are more advanced courses that *use* Java, but don't teach it.
- Select a college and go to its website. Go to the page for the Computer Science department, and then go to the introductory course. Most likely it uses Java, and you may find useful pointers to lecture notes, labs, and exercises. Remember the URLs of pages you find useful.

Deprecation

From time to time you will encounter the word "deprecated" regarding a class or method in the Java API. Java is a growing language, and each new version adds new capabilities. There's a downside to this. If a new version of Java makes a preexisting class or method invalid, then some preexisting code will *break*—it won't compile or run any more. Java never kills off prior methods or classes. It marks them as *deprecated,* meaning that there's a newer method or class with the same capabilities. There's also a veiled threat that code that uses the deprecated method may not compile in future versions of Java.

How to Succeed in This Course

To survive, succeed, or excel in this course, you need to do three things: listen, read, and practice.

Listen

You need to attend class and hear what your instructor says. The text is usually only an approximation to what your instructor wants you to learn:

- Some sections will be ignored.
- Some sections will be emphasized.
- Some material will be taught that is not in the text.
- Some terminology will be changed.

In addition, your instructor may approach some topics differently than I do.

Read

Read the book. Generally, the lecture and the book will explain the same concept, but in different ways. You will benefit from seeing both approaches. Read other books to supplement this one; for a particular topic, their treatment may speak to you better than I do. Websites may also provide tutorial information and exercises regarding the topic of this lecture.

You should engage in active reading. Never read a computer book without having a computer in front of you. You can test new programming concepts and features as you encounter them. Typical tests are:

- Does this really work the way I expect it to?
- What happens to the example program if I tweak it a little?
- What would Java do if I tried *this*?

This book is punctuated with exercises designed to get you to try things on the computer as you read along.

Practice

Just as you can't learn a *natural* language—for example, French—without practicing it, you can't learn a *programming* language without practicing it. You can read all you want, but only practice will cement your understanding. Successful students love to program. When homework is assigned, they start thinking about it right away. They do not wait until the night before it is due.

Language Learning Is Progressive

Progressive means that each lecture and concept builds on the one before it. You can't skip the first half of the term and expect to pick up what you missed. If you haven't done the reading and you don't understand the material from class N, then you probably won't understand class $N + 1$. If you're not going to keep up with the reading and the homework, then you should drop the course and find a better way to spend your time. Attendance isn't worth much if you haven't prepared.

How to Study

Exams and homework will often take one of the following forms:

- Write a program that solves the given problem.
- Write a Java program that tests how Java handles a particular situation.

- Write a Java program that demonstrates that Java acts in a specific way in a given situation.

I assume that you are doing the homework on your own, unless otherwise specified, but exams you will certainly do on your own. A good way to *prepare* for exams is to work with a partner. Each student should invent a problem, solve it, and send the problem to his or her partner to be solved. Then, the partners should discuss and compare their solutions. By looking at multiple solutions to the same problem, you will learn new ways of approaching Java exercises, and you will be a better programmer. You will be better prepared for the questions posed on an exam, and you may even have guessed some of the problems!

Supplements

The following supplements are available through the book's website, *http://www.jbpub.com/catalog/0763737208/supplements.htm*:

- PowerPoint lecture slides for each chapter.
- Code for all of the programs in each chapter.

In addition, a Student Lecture Companion is available.

Bon Voyage!

Have a fruitful and exciting journey into Computer Science and Java!

Preface for the Instructor

Since 1999, California State Polytechnic University, Pomona has used Java in its CS 1 offerings, and I have taught roughly a quarter of them. I enjoy being my students' first college CS instructor. It gives me the opportunity to teach my students good programming habits at the beginning of their careers. Our department chose to use an objects-first approach because we found that our students didn't seem to adopt object-oriented design principles when objects were presented after a standard imperative-first coverage of Java's structured programming concepts. None of the texts then available was entirely satisfactory for an objects-first course, and I soon had developed many lecture notes and sample programs and exercises. *Java 5: Objects First* is the result of my teaching experience.

In the sections that follow, I describe the principal features of the text, including a chapter-by-chapter summary and an overview of the supplemental materials for instructors using this text in their courses.

Objects First

This book uses objects from the very beginning. Chapter 2 discusses how object-oriented programming involves the identification and elaboration of classes, which are natural to a given programming problem. Students don't become expert object-oriented designers, but they get the message that objects are important and primary. Students see objects used in almost all the algorithms and examples in the text:

- When I teach them to find the *average value* of an array, I teach them to find the average of an array of Students—objects.
- When I teach them to compute the *sum* of an array, I teach them to compute the sum of an array of complex numbers—objects again!

UML diagrams reinforce the significance of classes, objects, and methods.

Objects are not just a new-fangled doodad added to an imperative language. If we teach objects at the end of the course, students get the message that objects are unimportant. I have encountered many students who succeeded at CS 1 and could write nice loops but had not learned that object-oriented design could save them time and make their code more readable. As educators, it is imperative that we actually use the software technology that is currently thought to be most beneficial to programmers and users alike.

Note: This text is not as objects-first as possible. There are courses for which inheritance and polymorphism are covered within the first four weeks, and selection and iteration are covered in the last four weeks.[1]

Conversational Writing Style

The book is written in a conversational style, and I use the pronouns "I," "you," and "we" as appropriate. The student is a partner in the learning experience, not merely the target of a lecture. The text is accessible and user friendly.

I try to be a co-learner more than an authority. A programming language is an awesome thing, and one must be humble in approaching it. The way Java does things could be, has been, and will be done differently in other languages. In writing the sample chapters, I learned more than once that my model of Java is not perfect. I try to convey an attitude of experimentation and active learning.

My approach is experimental rather than authoritarian. Students should be near a computer when reading this book. They should pose questions and use the computer to get the answers:

- Does this really work?
- Is this really how Java does this?
- What if …?

Sometimes the text will suggest experiments. Other times, I expect that experiments will suggest themselves as the students read about Java's capabilities and mechanics. A good student is an experimenter, and I hope to encourage those experiments.

---

[1] Carl Alphonce & Phil Ventura, Object orientation in CS1-CS2 by design. *7th Annual SIGCSE Conference on Innovation and Technology in Computer Education.* Aarhus, Denmark, June 2002.

Learning to Learn

Working in CS is a commitment to a lifetime of learning new things. In 10 years, our students will be using another language. In 20 years, they'll be using a paradigm other than object-oriented programming.

Students must learn to study on their own. I'm always saddened when a student asks a question such as, "What does Java do in such-and-such a situation?" Students must be encouraged to imagine Java's possible behaviors, and they must learn how to write a targeted program that will tell them which behavior Java's designers actually selected. Most language features can be implemented in a variety of ways (think of the two-argument `substring` method, for example). Our students need to discover which way works best in a given situation. My book discusses many language options and gives examples of small programs that can disambiguate a language at hand.

We won't be present when students are writing a program in the middle of the night, the night before it's due. They need to learn how to test novel language constructs without an instructor or student partner to tell them how things work. They must learn to use all available resources for understanding Java.

Style Counts

Computing is an art, not a science. A program is like an English composition: there are many programs that solve the same problem, but they're not all equally readable or extensible. My main metric for code is *readability*. I often present alternative pieces of code that have the same effect, but that are not equally readable or maintainable. I encourage you to use in-class exercises, whereby the class is divided into small groups, each of which solves the same problem. As a whole, we examine the different solutions and quickly see the importance of style and readability.

Patterns

I use this term in its traditional sense, not in the "design patterns" sense of software engineering. "Algorithm" is often a synonym.

I emphasize patterns because most of the programs we write are *variants* of those we've seen or written before. We rarely write a program that is completely novel. We spend more time doing pattern recognition than problem-solving. Most programming involves recognizing a problem (pattern) we've seen before and modifying a known solution (program) to solve the current problem.

Example 1   We know the pattern:

Find the highest number in an array.

A similar problem modifies the *collection* to get:

Find the highest grade in a *file*.

Another problem modifies the *datatype* to get:

Find the largest *complex number* in an array.

Example 2   We know how to open a disk file for reading. We're asked to open two files so that we can compare them, element-by-element. We recognize the pattern and we adjust the code to fit the new problem.

My text exposes students to numerous patterns and programs. They must learn the patterns and the associated solutions. They must recognize the pattern when it appears again, and they must modify the solution to fit the new circumstances.

I don't expect students to discover all the algorithms on their own, but I do expect them to learn the patterns and to apply the patterns when they're appropriate.

Exercises

I try to *show* code before I ask the students to *write* something comparable.[2] I give drivers and ask students to design and implement classes that match my drivers. I use objects as much as possible.

I give many small exercises rather than a few big ones. Each homework assignment should exercise a single new part of the material. Students do their homework the night before it's due. Frequent assignments mean they will study more, and thus have more exposure to the material. Big homeworks often encourage plagiarism and poor design. In my CS 1 courses, I try to assign at least two programming homeworks per week. If students program less than

---

[2] This is another way in which programming is like English composition: we read much more than we write.

that, they simply can't be actively learning the material. Most of the exercises are also suitable for closed-lab settings.

Nonexhaustive

I don't attempt to teach everything about Java, but students will have learned how to use many resources to understand new language features. It's more important that they learn *how to learn* than that I teach them everything I can cram into the available pages. A number of optional topics are covered in the appendices.

Graphics/Graphical User Interface (GUI) Optional

These topics are presented in supplements at the end of each chapter, forming a GUI track that is parallel to the main development of the text. The graphics/GUI material is not critical to the main line of the text.

Command-Line Java

I teach the students to compile and run Java from a command-line, as used by Sun's SDK software packages. As an instructor, you must teach them how to use your particular operating system, including files, directories, and editors. You may want to teach and require a particular IDE.

Chapters

Preface for the Student. Please encourage your students to read this. I describe Computer Science in relation to similar majors, and I set forth my expectations of the student and my advice for succeeding in the CS 1 course.

Chapter 1 develops a common vocabulary for the parts of a computer system, both hardware and software. I introduce the software life cycle, noting that maintenance is extremely expensive, and this cost has motivated the trend toward object-oriented programming.

Chapter 2 presents an overview of object-oriented design. I develop classes, instance variables, and methods for a Bank. Students are not expected to be able to produce good designs at this stage, but they have, at least, been exposed to the technology.

Chapter 3 presents a first Java program, printing `Hello` to the monitor. Students learn the required parts of even a simple Java program, including boilerplate, action statements, comments, and white space. We learn the capitalization conventions for the names of classes and methods. Students learn overloading because the `println` command of class `PrintStream` is overloaded.

Chapter 4 uses class `String` to illustrate declaration, assignment, methods, parameters, and return types. This class presents methods such as `trim`, `concat`, and `toUpperCase`. Cascading and composition are ways of using multiple methods. Students learn that there's more than one way to achieve the same output from a program.

Chapter 5 describes character input/output using Java's `Scanner` and `PrintStream` classes. We *read* from disk files and the keyboard; we *write* to disk files and the monitor. Students learn to decompose a specification into the individual Java statements. Using the basic i/o statements of Java, students learn to write code to accomplish compound tasks.

In Chapter 6 we write our first new classes, `Teacher` and `Animal`. Students learn about constructors, accessors (getters), and mutators (setters). We write methods that use our own class `Animal` as parameter and return type. This shows that user-defined classes have the same status as built-in classes. The `toString` method is our way of getting Java to print our objects in a reasonable fashion. We learn to "read objects" with `static` read methods that read and assemble the instance variables. These disciplined `read` methods will be important later when we develop loops that read through files of objects stored as text.

Chapter 7 introduces integers, the first of four primitive datatypes. Each primitive is presented in its own chapter because each enables new and substantially different programming capabilities. Integers are used as instance variables within object definitions. We learn basic arithmetic operations and precedence. An `EggShipment` example uses gross-dozen-unit to exercise modulus arithmetic. A `Complex` class models complex numbers. Class variables (`static` variables) allow us to count the number of instances we have created of a particular class.

Chapter 8 introduces the `boolean` datatype along with logical operators and DeMorgan's laws. Students write the predicates `odd`, `even`, and `isPassing`.

Chapter 9 introduces `chars` and students learn `String` methods involving `chars`. We write predicates that determine the case of a `char` and whether it's a vowel or a consonant.

Chapter 10 presents floating-point numbers. Methods from class `Math` permit us to compute square roots and trigonometric functions. Instances of class `Circle` have a `radius`, `circumference`, and `area`. Students learn to format decimal numbers using `printf`.

Chapter 11 introduces conditional execution. Students use `if-else` statements to validate the parameters in object constructors and to write code for computing pay with overtime. Multiway branching presents an elegant way to convert a numeric grade to a letter grade. Class `ZooShipment` contains a `toString` method that distinguishes singular from plural and "a" from "an." Other interesting uses of conditional statements are assigned as exercises.

Chapter 12 begins with a discussion of test cases and automatic testing. We then get some tips on coding and debugging and how to document errors in order to seek help. By this point in the course, the students have written enough code that they are able to benefit from some practical advice.

Chapter 13 introduces `while` and `for` loops in the context of reading and processing objects from files. Students learn basic algorithms, such as computing the sum and finding extrema of a collection. By learning these patterns in the context of files, we are able to isolate looping from the additional complexity required by arrays.

Chapter 14 presents one-dimensional arrays and adapts prior algorithms to work on arrays. Students learn arrays in the context of their use with objects. Class `MyString` represents `Strings` as arrays of `chars`. Class `Section` represents college class rosters as arrays of `Students`. Numerous additional algorithms are presented for working with arrays. We introduce the syntax and uses of two-dimensional arrays.

Chapter 15 discusses interfaces. We begin with Java's `Comparable` interface, using it to enable sorting of arrays of objects by built-in sort methods. We then develop the `Talker` interface and learn polymorphism using arrays of objects from classes that implement `Talker`. Finally, we see how interfaces can be used to pass methods as arguments to other methods, which enable the printing of tables and bar graphs.

Chapter 16 presents inheritance. The first example is an extension of `PrintStream`. Then, I discuss class hierarchies and abstract classes. Examples include a hierarchy of `Animals` and a hierarchy of `Persons` within an organization.

Chapter 17 presents `Exceptions` and exception handling in Java.

Chapter 18 discusses recursion. Recursive versions are now presented for the `MyString` methods such as `length`, `equals`, and `concat`. Students write further recursive methods as exercises.

Chapter 19 is an album of additional algorithms for working with numbers and `Strings`. Linear and binary search are discussed. Selection sort is implemented.

The appendices present reference material, as well as special topics that you may want to teach. Several appendices describe features introduced in Java 5.

Appendix 1 is the style sheet I use for the code in the text. Your style may differ.

Appendix 2 lists Java's reserved words.

Appendix 3 gives the Unicode and ASCII values for Java's printable characters.

Appendix 4 is a complete table of operator precedence.

Appendix 5 gives full details of the increment and decrement operators.

Appendix 6 describes the conditional operator (`?:`).

Appendix 7 presents the enhanced `for` loop.

Appendix 8 describes the varargs feature, introduced in Java 5, which allows methods to take variable length argument lists.

Appendix 9 describes enumerated types.

Appendix 10 describes the use of `ArrayLists`.

Appendix 11 describes wrapper classes and boxing and unboxing.

Appendix 12 presents `javadoc`.

Supplements

Instructors who have adopted this text have access to the following materials through the book's website, *http://www.jbpub.com /catalog/0763737208/ supplements.htm*:

- PowerPoint lecture slides for each chapter.
- Code for all of the programs in each chapter.
- An *Instructor's Solutions Manual* that presents solutions to all of the exercises in the text. Most of the exercises are suitable for closed-lab settings.

Acknowledgments

Publishing a book requires the skills and efforts of many individuals, and I would like to thank everyone involved in the preparation of this text.

At many stages in its development, reviewers' comments have improved this book. I thank:

Seth D. Bergmann, Rowan University

Donald L. Muench, St. John Fisher College

Sridhar Narayan, University of North Carolina, Wilmington

Mikhail Brikman, Salem State College

Jamie Doll, Foothill College

Kevin Burger, Rockhurst University

Steven Andrianoff, Saint Bonaventure University

The folks at Jones and Bartlett have been tireless, and they cheerfully initiated me into the mysteries of publishing. I particularly thank Tim Anderson, Amy Rose, Kate Koch, and Jenny Bagdigian.

I also thank my students in CS 140 and CS 141 at Cal Poly Pomona. They suffered through early versions of the manuscript (without an index!), and they contributed many items of "erratica."

Contents

Chapter 7   **Integer Datatypes   211**

Chapter 12   Testing, Coding, and Debugging   449

Chapter 13   Loops and Files   485

Chapter 16   Inheritance and Class Hierarchies   765

Introduction

Chapter Objectives

- Develop a common vocabulary regarding computer systems.
- Identify the parts of a computer system, both hardware and software.
- Use the prefixes kilo-, mega-, and giga-.
- Learn how computers are joined into networks.
- Differentiate the levels of programming languages.
- Identify the edit-compile-run loop for writing and running a computer program.
- Learn the phases of software development and the importance of the maintenance phase.
- Understand programming paradigms.

Computer systems are composed of *hardware* and *software*. The hardware is the physical computer, composed of metal, plastic, chips, and wires. Software is the set of instructions that makes the hardware become a lively, responsive partner that can react to the commands we give in order to perform a variety of useful tasks.

This chapter provides a common vocabulary describing the hardware and software of a typical computer system. A computer interacts with other computers by means of *networks* and the *World Wide Web (WWW)*. Software can be of various *levels*, depending on how it interacts with a particular computer.

Programming involves the edit-compile-run cycle. Software has a *life cycle*, ranging from *design* through *implementation* to *maintenance*, which is the costliest phase. Since the mid-1940s, the software industry has embraced three models (*paradigms*) for cutting costs and rationalizing programming; the latest is *object-oriented programming*. *Java* is a good example of a *programming language*.

By the end of this chapter, you will have a workable overview of computers and programming.

1.1 A Single Computer

Figure 1–1 shows the block diagram of a general computer. The three pieces are memory, CPU, and peripherals. Memory is where information is stored, the CPU performs the actual computations, and peripherals enable a computer to interact with the user and with external devices.

The *memory* is where the computer stores data that it's actively processing. Memory consists of a set of *cells* or *words*, each of which has a unique *address*. Usually, all the cells have the same *width* (in bits), which we call the *word size*.

Memory can be either *RAM* or *ROM*—*random access memory* or *read-only memory*. When powered off, the data in RAM is lost; thus we say RAM is

Figure 1–1
The Parts of a
Computer

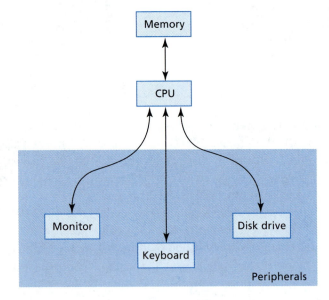

volatile. The information in ROM is eternal and nonvolatile. When a computer is powered on, it consults its ROM for its first instructions upon "waking."

Memory cells contain both data and instructions. *Machine language* is a numeric code that tells the computer what to do.

Most modern computers have a word size of *eight bits*, called a *byte*. For large numbers of bytes, we use the prefixes *kilo-*, *mega-*, and *giga-*, described here:

1 kilobyte	2^{10} bytes	1,024	~ 10^3 bytes	~ thousand
1 megabyte	2^{20} bytes	1,048,576	~ 10^6 bytes	~ million
1 gigabyte	2^{30} bytes	1,073,741,824	~ 10^9 bytes	~ billion

The abbreviations are K, M, and G. For bytes, these become KB, MB, and GB. A typical computer has 512 MB of memory.

The *central processing unit (CPU)* is the heart of the computer. It fetches instructions and data from memory and returns to memory the results of requested operations. The CPU has three components:

- *Registers* are where data is stored when it's brought to the CPU for processing. They're like memory cells, but they can be accessed and changed much more quickly. Data must be brought to the CPU in order to be used in computation.
- The *program counter* is a pointer to the next instruction to be executed.
- The *arithmetic-logic unit (ALU)* decodes the instruction at the location where the program counter is pointing, grabs the required operands from registers or memory, and performs the operation, perhaps returning a value to a register or a memory cell.

The speed of a computer—its *clock speed*—is usually reported as the number of instructions it performs in a second. The unit of measurement is *Hertz (Hz)*, which means *per second*. As for bytes, the prefixes K, M, and G are used with Hertz to produce KHz, MHz, and GHz. A typical computer has a speed of 2.6 GHz or higher.

Peripherals are devices that attach to the CPU for a variety of purposes. Some peripherals permit interaction with users and programmers; typical of this is a *terminal*, comprising a *keyboard* and a *monitor*. Some peripherals are designed for data storage: for example, hard disks, floppy disk drives, CD drives, DVD drives, and magnetic tape drives. Memory is *primary storage*; these other devices are *secondary storage*. A typical computer has a hard disk of 80 GB or more. The information on a disk is organized into *files*, and the thousands of files on a disk form a *file system*.

Other peripherals permit communication with external computers and devices. One of these is a *modem*, which is short for "modulate and demodulate." A modem allows computers to interact over cables or via wireless technology. When a modem connects computers via telephone lines, we call it a *dial-up* modem.

1.2 Networks

As soon as two computers are hooked together, they form a network. A *local area network (LAN)* connects the computers in a single home or office. The network allows the computers to share resources such as printers or a modem connection. A *file server* is a computer that acts as a gateway so that other computers can access a large hard drive, which might contain a *database*. Computers that share a network must exchange messages using a specified format that all of them can understand; a *protocol* is an agreement about how these computers will communicate over the network.

A *wide area network (WAN)* is formed when several LANs are joined. Such a network would be formed when a company links all of its offices in a given city or when a supermarket links all of its stores.

The *Internet* is the network that links millions of computers around the globe. It evolved from a Department of Defense prototype called the *ARPANET*, which originally linked a few dozen universities and research centers. Computers on the Internet use a protocol known as *TCP/IP*—Transmission Control Protocol/Internet Protocol. Each machine has a unique *IP address*. The typical form is 192.168.1.100, representing four bytes of address information, where each byte has a value in the range 0 to 255.

Many home computers connect to the Internet by dial-up, *cable modem*, or *DSL* (Digital Subscriber Line) through an *Internet service provider (ISP)*. A *domain name* specifies the location of a variety of *host* machines. For example, *csupomona.edu* specifies California State Polytechnic University Pomona), where your author works. Hosts may offer a variety of services:

- *Telnet* allows users to log in to a distant computer and turns the user's computer into a terminal of the distant computer. The user can then use the distant computer's various computational resources.
- *FTP (File Transfer Protocol)* allows users to exchange files with a distant computer. *Downloading* is the process of bringing a file from the distant machine to the local computer. *Uploading* is the reverse.

1.3 The World Wide Web

Perhaps the principal use of the Internet today involves the World Wide Web, whereby information is offered and consumed, and goods and services are bought and sold. A program called a *browser* is directed to a resource by means of a *Uniform resource locator* (*URL*, sometimes pronounced "Ural"). Common browsers are Internet Explorer, Mozilla Firefox, Opera, and Safari. An example of a URL is http://www.csupomona.edu/~cs/, which connects the user to the Computer Science Department at Cal Poly Pomona.

Information is presented on *Web pages*. Web pages contain *links* which, when clicked, take the reader to other related pages. Instead of text, we have *hypertext*, where pages are connected by links, allowing—hopefully—for swift connection to the information or service we want. Web pages are constructed using a language called *HTML*, or *Hypertext Markup Language*. If your browser is pointed at a Web page, you can see the corresponding HTML by asking to View | Source.

1.4 Software

We have examined computer hardware and how computers are linked to the Internet, which hosts the World Wide Web. Now let's turn our attention back to an individual computer and consider its *software*.

Like a car, a computer consists of metal, wires, plastic, and other physical elements. Unlike a car, however, a computer is *versatile*: it can be used to lay out a budget, write a term paper, record and play music, or perform a host of other tasks. A car cannot become a plane, a boat, or an orchestra. What differentiates a computer from a car is that a computer's hardware can be specialized by means of software to make the computer perform a variety of very different tasks. We say that a computer can be *programmed*.

We divide software into two types: *operating system (OS)* and *applications programs* (or simply, *applications*).

An operating system provides basic capabilities required by all tasks. For example, an OS:

- provides a file system and its commands for creating, deleting, and renaming files.
- enforces the protocols whereby we can add peripherals (e.g., a mouse or a printer) to the system.
- maintains a list of users, logins, and permissions.

- provides security so that one user's data can be kept private, or so that common files can be shared.

Common operating systems are Windows, Unix, Linux, and Tiger.

An application allows us to use the computer for a single specific task. Common applications include:

- word processors
- browsers
- spreadsheets
- databases
- games
- audio and video editing programs.

The next part of the text will examine the nature of programming.

1.5 Levels of Programming

We get computers to do useful work by programming them. We give them instructions which, when executed, accomplish the work we want. An *algorithm* is the set of conceptual instructions that solves the problem at hand. *Pseudo-code* is a textual way of discussing an algorithm without committing ourselves to a particular programming language.

Computer programs are *text files* that must be translated into the machine language of the computer before the computer can execute them. A program is written in a *programming language (PL)* which, like a natural language, has

- syntax—rules for determining whether or not a text file is a correct program and;
- semantics—rules for interpreting a program (i.e., what does the program do?).

A program is also called *source code*. Most programs contain *comment statements* (or simply, *comments*) along with *executable statements*. The comments serve to *document* the program so that a future reader can understand the code more easily. Comments are often used to describe the following:

- the purpose of the program;
- how to run it; and
- why the program has this particular design.

Some programming languages are *low-level*. They are said to be *close* to the actual computer hardware because the instructions reference specific registers and specific memory cells. Low-level programs are *not portable* from one type of computer to another because different computers have different numbers of registers and different width memory cells. Low-level programs have lots of small instructions, each of which does only a small amount of work. Low-level programs are hard for *people* to understand, but they're easily converted into a form that a computer can run.

High-level languages (HLLs) are not tied to the architecture of a single kind of computer. They are fairly universal and portable. Each instruction expands to a set of low-level language statements. A *compiler* translates the high-level program into lower-level statements, which a specific target computer can actually run.

Here is a chart comparing low-level and high-level languages:

Low-Level Language	High-Level Language
Many statements	Fewer statements
Tied to a particular computer architecture	Universal and portable
Hard for people to understand	Easier for people to understand

An Alphabet Soup of High-Level Languages

Since the spread of computers in the early 1950s, there have been more than a hundred HLLs. The following table discusses some of the more important ones.

Name	Date of First Use	Comments
Fortran	1950s	"Formula translator." Used extensively in science and engineering.
Lisp	1958	"List processor." Used in artificial intelligence and natural language processing.
COBOL	1959	"Common Business-Oriented Language." The first language widely used in the nonscientific community. Used for business programs such as inventory and payroll.
APL	1963	"A Programming Language." Designed by IBM. Interactive.
BASIC	1964	"Beginner's All-purpose Symbolic Instruction Code." Interactive—the computer responded almost immediately to what you typed. Designed for college students.

Name	Date of First Use	Comments
Prolog	~1972	"Programming in Logic." Used in artificial intelligence.
Smalltalk	1970s	An object-oriented language invented at Xerox PARC, Palo Alto, CA.
C++	1979	Bell Laboratories was the research arm of what was once the monopoly company in the U.S. telephone business. They developed C, a low-level language that was extended into C++ by incorporating some aspects of object-oriented programming.
Ada	1980	Named after Lady Ada Augusta Byron, daughter of Lord Byron, the poet. She is widely accepted as the first programmer because of her work with Charles Babbage's analytical engine, a mechanical computer. The Ada language was commissioned by the U.S. Department of Defense (DoD), which hoped to require that all its software vendors write in a single language. At the time, the DoD was the largest purchaser of software in the U.S., but the end of the Cold War and the rise of PCs and the Internet cut DoD's standards-making power. Ada is rarely used today.
Java	1995	Sun Microsystems, Inc. produced and maintained this language, which is grounded in object-oriented programming.
C#	~2000	Partly because Sun Microsystems has retained total control over Java, Microsoft developed the comparable and competing language C# (pronounced "see sharp").

In your career, you may have to modify programs written in "dead" languages. We call such programs *legacy code*. If a program is working, most organizations are hesitant to change it without good reason. Translating a program from one language to another is a major effort, which may "break" the existing code. This is a good example of the adage: *If it isn't broken, don't fix it.*

Over your working lifetime, even more languages will be invented, and you must be prepared to learn new languages and extend your skills continually. You won't be able to rely solely on what you learn during your undergraduate studies.

In the course of your college studies, you will probably take a course—often called *Programming Languages*—which compares a variety of languages so that you can see the different ways people have chosen to implement language features. Most languages are *equivalent* in the sense that any program in language X can also be written in language Y. In natural language terms, Chinese is equivalent to English because, in general, we can express the same ideas in either language, but translating between the two can be difficult.

A Sample Statement

Consider the statement:

```
a ← b + c
```

Assuming that b and c have somehow been given actual values, this statement assigns to a the sum of the current values of b and c. In the following sections, we'll examine how this statement would be written at each of three levels:

- high-level language;
- assembly language; and
- machine language.

1.6   a ← b + c in a High-Level Language

In Java, our sample statement would be written as

```
a = b + c;
```

The "=" means "gets" or "is assigned" rather than "equals." This is an example of an *assignment statement*. (We'll study these in more detail in Chapter 4.) Other high-level languages express our sample statement in other ways:

Languages	Expression of Our Sample Statement
Java, C++, C#	`a = b + c;`
Pascal, Ada	`a := b + c;`
APL	`a ← b + c`
Sail	`a ← b + c;`
COBOL	`add b to c giving a.`

The virtue of a high-level language is that you can move a program from one computer to another as long as both computers have a compiler for that high-level language.

1.7   a ← b + c in Assembly Language

Assembly language is a low-level language because it references the specific registers of the target machine, a property called *machine-dependence*. Assembly language programs won't transfer from one type of computer to another if the two computers have different *architectures* (i.e., different numbers of registers, different word sizes, and so forth).

Our sample statement, a ← b + c, might translate into the following statements in a typical assembly language:

```
load r1,b
add r1,c
store r1,a
```

We can explain these in English like this:

take whatever's in location b and put it in register r1

add whatever's in location c to the contents of r1

move the contents of r1 to location a.

Notice:

- The verbs {load, add, store}. We call these *mnemonics* because they are easier to remember than their machine language (numerical) equivalents.
- The single high-level statement has been converted into three assembly-language statements. Assembly language is low-level.

You will take a course on assembly language at some point in your undergraduate studies. That course will give you an appreciation of computer hardware and how a language translator must work in order to translate higher-level languages into sets of hardware-specific statements.

1.8   a ← b + c in Machine Language

Machine language is the lowest level of programming. It's machine-dependent because we can't move a program from one type of computer to another. Instead of mnemonics, a machine language program uses binary numbers to represent both data and instructions. Sometimes the instructions are expressed in *octal* or *hexadecimal* notation. Machine language programs are very hard for people to write and understand; each instruction requires considerable thought. On the other hand, machine language programs are computer-ready and they can be loaded directly into the computer without translation.

A Model Machine and Its Machine Language

Let's make three assumptions about the computer for which we're preparing our sample statement:

- The computer has eight possible operations it can perform, such as addition and subtraction. Each operation has a numerical *opcode*—an operation code—and each opcode is represented by a binary number in the range [000,111]. We need three bits to specify an opcode.
- There are two registers, r0 and r1, which can hold operands on which the ALU can operate. We need one bit to specify a register. Each register is one byte wide.
- There are 16 memory locations, each holding one byte (eight bits). We need four bits to specify a memory location.

Thus, an instruction will be one byte (eight bits) wide:

Opcode	Register	Memory Address
3 bits	1 bit	4 bits

Translating Our Sample Statement

Let's solve our problem by loading b into register r1, then adding c into r1, then storing r1 into a.

Suppose that the variables are laid out in memory like this:

Variables	Location (binary)	Location (decimal)
a	1000	8
b	0110	6
c	0011	3

Suppose that the operations have the following opcodes:

Operation	Opcode (binary)
load	011
add	100
store	101

Then this is what our program would look like in machine language:

Assembly Language Instruction	Opcode	Register	Operand	Instruction (binary)	Instruction (hexadecimal)
load r1,b	011	1	0110	01110110	76
add r1,c	100	1	0011	10010011	93
store r1,a	101	1	1000	10111000	B8

So the final program would be: 76, 93, B8. I think you will agree that this code is nontrivial for people to write, read, and modify.

In a future course, you will study machine language in more detail, because it's the bread and butter of those who design computers and networks.

1.9   The Edit-Compile-Run Loop

Much of programming involves the following actions:

1. **Edit**—Enter a program or modify one that isn't working correctly.
2. **Compile**—Submit the code to the compiler. The code may or may not contain a *compile-time error* (either a *syntax error* or a *semantic error*).
3. **Run**—Our code has compiled correctly, and we ask the computer to run it. We may observe correct behavior, or the program may bomb because of a *run-time* error or because it contains a *logical error*.

Baking a Cake

We will examine these steps in the context of baking a cake, where *we* write the instructions and our *helper* does the actual baking. To make this more like the computer situation, let's assume that the helper doesn't understand English—only *Elvish*—but we have a translator for English to Elvish. Also, the helper will mechanically follow the instructions we give, without applying common sense. Computers, likewise, do what we *tell* them to do, which is not necessarily what we *intended* them to do.

Step 1: Edit

First we write an English-language program with our instructions for baking a cake. We use an *editor*, which, in the context of programming, is a second-rate word-processor: It has only one font, no automatic indenting, and no attributes such as color.[1] And remember that our helper can't understand the program we've written, because it's in English rather than Elvish. So we go to the next step.

Step 2: Compile

In this step we translate the program from English to Elvish. The program may contain compile-time errors such as invalid English. The statement

```
Preheat the oven to 300F
```

is acceptable, but

```
300F oven Preheat the to
```

is nonsensical, and

```
Preheat the oven
```

is unacceptable because it doesn't specify a temperature. Syntax errors are bad English (or Java), which make no sense to the translator/compiler.

If our program compiles correctly, then we have an Elvish version of our instructions, and we go to the next step, Run.

If our program *doesn't* compile, then we need to fix whatever error the compiler discovered. We say that the program contains a *bug* or *bugs*, and *debugging* is the process of eliminating the bugs. When debugging, we don't

---

[1] Recently, Integrated Development Environments (IDEs) have become available to aid in Java programming. These tools include editors that use color and automatic indent to help the user see the structure of the program being written.

just randomly permute or mutate the instructions in a program[2]—we know English (or Java) and about the task at hand, so we have a head start at locating and fixing the error.

Step 3: Run

When we reach this step, we know that the translator (compiler) is satisfied with our program, so we hand the Elvish program to our helper. If all is well, then the helper produces the cake we wanted, but it's possible that run-time errors might occur. For example, our program might contain the statement

```
Preheat the oven to 300F
```

but the oven might not be able to go above 250°F. In this case, the program will abort or, perhaps, wait indefinitely for the oven to reach an unreachable temperature. If such an error occurs, we go back to Step 1 (Edit) and we intelligently approach the revision of our program.

Logical Errors

Suppose our program contained the instruction:

```
add the juice of three onions
```

The compiler would accept the program and produce an Elvish version. The helper would perform the requested operations without error. But the resulting cake would taste awful! This is a case where our program is correct English, and the Elvish code executes without problem, but the program doesn't solve the problem we were given, namely to bake an edible cake. We analyze the code and the problem, and we return to Step 1 (Edit). Again, to emphasize: We don't just randomly change the program. If you find yourself doing it, then you need to take a break, study the language some more, and return to editing only when you understand what went wrong.[3]

---

[2] Some students *do* randomly change their programs until they compile. This is not an efficient way to debug a program, and it shows a lack of understanding of Java and the task at hand.

[3] If you rely on the compiler to validate a sequence of randomly altered programs, then you may, in fact, succeed in producing an acceptable program. However, you won't be able to write a program on a written exam, because you won't have the compiler to weed out your errors.

Figure 1–2
The Edit-Compile-
Run Cycle

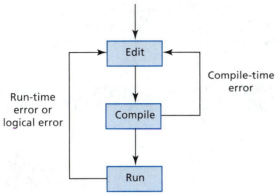

A Diagram

Figure 1–2 shows a *flowchart* of the edit-compile-run loop and the activities we have described in this section.

1.10 Levels of Users and Programmers

From the viewpoint of programming, we can divide the world's population into three groups:

- *Tool-builders* write the base-level code used by all others. They are trained in departments of Computer Science (CS). They design the languages, write the compilers and run-time systems, and write program libraries that enable others to work with files, graphics, calendars, and so on.
- *Tool-users* are those who build the large software systems that use our languages and libraries to computerize the activities of individuals, corporations, and organizations. Tool-users are trained in departments of Management Information Systems (MIS) and Computer Information Systems (CIS).
- *End-users* are nonprogrammers who use the software systems to accomplish or facilitate their daily activities, both work and play.

Please note the difference between CS and CIS. The two disciplines require different kinds of students. CS people program; CIS people work with organizations to determine and fill their computer needs. Sometimes the difference is sharp, and sometimes it's fuzzy.

We need more tool-users than tool-builders, just as we need more automobile drivers than auto designers or car builders or car service and repair people. So CS *ought* to have many fewer majors than MIS-CIS.

1.11   The Software Life Cycle

The software life cycle is the set of activities involved in producing and maintaining a software system. The activities can be overlapped and repeated. In general, however, the order of activities that follows is a rough approximation of the stages of a typical software project. You will probably take a course in software engineering, which treats these topics in much greater detail.

Analyze

A software engineer interviews the client to determine the parameters of the project. At a minimum, the following questions should be answered:

- What must this software do?
- Who will be using it?
- What system, if any, does it replace?
- What are the boundaries on cost and delivery time?
- Does the client have other requirements?

This responsibility is often divided or shared between CS and CIS personnel.

Design

Experienced software engineers next look at the requirements and design the internals of the product. Typically, a software system contains many pieces that must interact in a coordinated fashion. The design often permits a divide and conquer strategy, whereby parts of the product can be developed by different programming groups working in parallel. This saves time in development. A plan is produced, which details the software modules, the human resources required, and the tests that will be used to verify fulfillment of the client's needs and to test for errors.

Code/Implement

Programming teams take the specifications of the designers and produce code that meets the requirements and passes the prescribed tests. This activity is where computer programming is mostly used. As you can see, the coding activity is only one of many other activities involved in producing software systems. As a CS graduate, you may find that programming does not occupy the majority of your time at work. Nonetheless, no one gets a CS degree without demonstrating mastery of computer programming.

Test

Each individual software module must pass rigorous tests to verify that it performs correctly in isolation before it's assembled into the final product.

The completed system must also be tested to verify that it performs according to specifications and that it fulfills the client's needs. It is essential to maintain good lines of communication with the client.

Deploy

The completed software system must be delivered to the client and started in execution. Often, there is a prior system that is being replaced or upgraded. Sometimes the new system and the old system are run in parallel for a while.

Deployment also requires *training* the client's personnel on the new system. This requires documentation such as user's guides.

Maintain

Work remains for the software developer even after delivery of the system to the client. Errors are found and must be corrected. Enhancements are requested and the code must be modified. The next section will discuss the maintenance activity in more detail.

Never Done

In the early days of programming, we were taught that the software development activities are done in a fixed order, from analysis to delivery. More experience with software has shown that developers must often return to earlier activities in the development of a software system. For example:

- Testing may show a fault, which requires that modules be recoded.
- Design may show that the client's specifications are inconsistent or cannot be met as originally written.

1.12 Change Is Inevitable: Maintenance Is the Costliest Activity

Maintenance is the most costly phase of software development. Programs are always being changed:

- Bugs need fixing. You can show that a bug is present, but you can't prove that a program is bug-free.
- New capabilities may be added. At Cal Poly Pomona, the registration system was recently altered to add waiting lists for students who tried to add courses that were full.
- Systems may need porting to a new natural language. This author's bank's ATMs started out English-only, but they now offer Spanish and Chinese as well. All of the phrases—such as "Type your password and press ENTER"—had to be provided in a second and third language.

Maintenance is expensive for a variety of reasons:

- Often, the person who modifies the code is not the person who wrote the code, so the new programmer has to understand what the first programmer did. Make your code readable to the people who come next— those who will maintain your code—and include clear and concise documentation. You may not appreciate this right now, but one day *you* will be asked to fix or extend someone else's code, and you'll appreciate the need for good documentation.
- It is often easier to write complete programs from scratch than to modify existing code. One day you'll find that you can't understand a piece of code that you wrote only six months earlier, and you'll decide to trash it and start over. The new version often contains considerably better comments and documentation than the version it replaces.

Keep in mind, though, that one way to cut maintenance costs is to write code that is commented and well-documented to begin with; this will make it easier for programmers who come to it later to understand how the code works.

Programs can be assessed on a variety of criteria. Historically, speed and size were used as metrics. In this book, *readability* will be the prime criterion for evaluating programs.

Figure 1–3 shows how software costs have become the dominant costs in computer systems. Cost is computed by totaling hardware expenses and software expenses over the lifetime of a computer, from the time it's purchased to the time it's scrapped.

Figure 1-3
Relative Cost of
Hardware and
Software

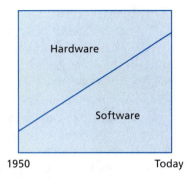

Hardware

Software

1950   Today

In the 1950s, computers were the size of entire rooms, and many users worked on the same computer. There were few applications. The physical cost of the computer overshadowed the cost of software.

Today, computers are the size of a high school yearbook, and they are packed with applications. The hardware is now cheap, and the programs constitute the major expense.

1.13 Programming Paradigms

Thomas Kuhn, a historian and philosopher of science, introduced the notion of a scientific paradigm in his book *The Structure of Scientific Revolutions*, first published in 1962. A paradigm is the generally accepted approach to a craft or a body of knowledge. Kuhn's major example concerned two different paradigms for understanding the motion of the planets and the stars: The geocentric paradigm held that the earth was the center of the universe and that the sun and planets revolved around the earth. The heliocentric paradigm holds that the earth and planets revolve around the sun. In the west, the geocentric paradigm held sway from the time of Ptolemy of Alexandria (100–170 A.D.) to the time of Nicolaus Copernicus (1473–1543). Explaining and predicting the motions of the heavenly bodies is extremely complicated under the geocentric paradigm, yet it was generally accepted for thirteen centuries! Copernicus showed that the heliocentric paradigm made astronomical calculations much simpler, and as a result that paradigm has been dominant ever since. The change from one paradigm to another is called a paradigm shift, and these shifts are uncomfortable because we need to change our customary way of thinking. Kuhn described paradigm shifts as *scientific revolutions*.

A *programming paradigm* is a generally accepted approach to programming. It's not a specific language, but rather a general approach as to how we will program and what kinds of languages will be acceptable. Programming in high-level languages has gone through three paradigms in the last 60 years. Because programming is expensive, software developers are constantly seeking ways to make the process less costly. Changes in paradigm occur because the industry believes it will save money by programming in a different fashion. New paradigms spread because companies fear that competitors who use the new paradigm will gain a cost advantage. Shifts in programming paradigm are uncomfortable for programmers who are asked to change their fundamental approach to work they've been performing successfully without the new paradigm.

The next three sections describe the paradigms through which computer programming has moved since its inception.

1.14 The First Paradigm: Spaghetti Code (1945–1975)

In the earliest days of programming, control within a program would jump arbitrarily from any statement to any other statement. The result was a tangled web—like a bowl of cooked spaghetti—and it was often difficult to follow the course of a program or to modify it. Such *spaghetti code* programs lacked *locality*, the property whereby related statements are close together in the code. Fortran, BASIC, and assembly language are examples of languages created while this first paradigm ruled.

1.15 The Second Paradigm: Structured Programming (1970–1995)

Industrial and academic personnel noticed the high cost to produce and maintain programs produced by undisciplined coding practices, but what was to be done? Edsger W. Dijkstra[4] (1930–2002), a Dutch computer scientist, crystallized the debate: His paper "Go To Statement Considered Harmful" blamed

---

[4] Dijkstra is hailed as the father of computer science, which he always called *computing* science in order to emphasize that CS is the study of *the nature of computation*, not the study of *particular hardware devices*.

software unreadability on the use of undisciplined jumps—gotos—from one part of a program to another.

Dijkstra proved that any program whatsoever could be written using only a small set of programming constructs. Arbitrary jumps—gotos—were abolished, and *structured programs* were restricted to only a few safe constructs. In the course of later chapters, we will encounter the following constructs allowed by structured programming:[5]

Construct	Description
Sequence	One statement directly follows another.
Alternation	Execute one statement out of a set of statements. (if-then)
Repetition	Repeat a group of statements until some criterion is reached. (while)
Subroutines	Group a set of statements into a unit that can be invoked, as needed, in several locations of a program.

The following languages obeyed the tenets of structured programming: ALGOL, Pascal, PL/I, C, and Ada.

One of the goals of structured programming was to develop a theory and methodology for *proving* that programs meet their specifications. By restricting programmers to a small set of control constructs, the task of formal proof would be easier. The proof-of-correctness thrust of structured programming was not fully successful, but some aspects survive today in the form of *preconditions* and *postconditions*. You will study formal program proof techniques in more detail in advanced CS courses.

Personal Anecdote: The Author's Reaction to Paradigm Change

I remember well the paradigm shift from spaghetti code to structured programming. For several years I had programmed in spaghetti languages like Fortran and BASIC. Suddenly, I was told to switch to ALGOL, a language that had no goto statement. I was annoyed. Why did I have to change my habits? Why couldn't I use goto? I doubted that the limited constructs of structured

---

[5]   Another name for structured programming is procedural programming.

programming would allow me to write all the programs I'd previously written. My resistance to change wasn't based on logic; I just didn't want to surrender the old habits, which had served me well. But I survived this paradigm shift, and I came to use, enjoy, and teach structured programming.

1.16 The Third Paradigm: Object-Oriented Programming (1995–present)

Over the past decade, a new paradigm has become dominant: object-oriented programming (OOP) and object-oriented (OO) design. The goal of designing with objects is to make the program correspond more visibly to the real world. Programs should be easier to read and modify because their pieces will correspond to natural entities, actions, and properties of the problem being solved. Given a piece of the code, it should be easy to identify the corresponding real-world entities. Understanding and maintaining code should be easier and less expensive.

Some Languages for Object-Oriented Programming

The first OO language was Smalltalk, designed and implemented by programmers at the Xerox Palo Alto Research Center (Xerox PARC) in the 1970s. It was not commercialized.[6]

The C++ language was initially designed at Bell Labs in 1979, building on C. C++ contains object-oriented constructs, but these are only loosely bound to the language. By 1991, there were 400,000 users of C++ worldwide.[7]

Java was introduced by Sun Microsystems, Inc. in 1995, and it developed into a language for use with networks of computers, including, most promi-

[6] Xerox PARC invented many seemingly indispensable products and ideas: the personal computer, the tablet computer, the computer mouse, the graphical user interface (GUI), "What You See Is What You Get" (WYSIWYG), the laser printer, and Ethernet, to name a few—but Xerox did not seize the opportunity to benefit from the commercialization of these products.

[7] Bjarne Stroustrup, A History of C++: 1979–1991; in Thomas J Bergin Jr & Richard G Gibson Jr, *History of Programming Languages—II*. Reading, MA: Addison-Wesley, 1996, pp. 699–769.

nently, the World Wide Web. Object-orientation is deeply entwined in the foundations of the Java language. Java provides a large number of built-in capabilities for a programmer to use, which can be found in the *API (Application Programming Interface)*.

Inertia

Object-oriented programming has been around for a long time, but industry has only recently embraced it. Software is too expensive, and software companies hope that OOP will make them more competitive.

Schools also took a long time to embrace OOP. Until May 2003, the Advanced Placement Test for Computer Science was given using, for the most part, the structured programming aspects of C++. In 2004, the exam began to test Java, which is fundamentally object-oriented.

1.17   Human Reactions to Paradigm Change

People don't like change, and as such many programmers resist paradigm change. They're expert or competent at programming in the current paradigm, but the new paradigm will require that they learn something new, and learning a new paradigm is much harder than learning a new language. Moreover, programmers are skeptical of the power and ease of the new paradigm.

Students who know structured programming may actually have a harder time learning OOP than students who have no prior programming experience.[8] They have to *unlearn* many habits that served them well under the prior paradigm.

Many teachers resist paradigm change, just as programmers do. Teachers can be quite eloquent in explaining why a new paradigm is not an improvement over the current one.

Many Java textbooks are not really object-oriented. Many are basically translations of Pascal texts into Java, and as a result they don't embrace the new paradigm. Some texts have a longer history: a Pascal book became a C

---

[8]   John Minor Ross & Huazhong Zhang, Structured programmers learning object-oriented programming: Cognitive considerations. *SIGCHI Bulletin*, 29(4):93–99, October 1997. Association for Computing Machinery (ACM).

book became a C++ book became a Java book. It is easier to change the language of a book than to change its paradigm. The text you are reading was designed, from scratch, to use Java and object-oriented programming.

Chapter Summary

- A physical computer consists of a central processing unit (CPU), memory, and peripherals.
- "Kilo-" means 2^{10}, or roughly one thousand. "Mega-" means 2^{20}, or roughly one million. "Giga-" means 2^{30}, or roughly one billion.
- The CPU consists of registers, a program counter, and the arithmetic-logic unit (ALU).
- Local area networks (LANs) are composed of overall computers linked in one location, such as an office.
- Wide area networks (WANs) are aggregations of LANs.
- The Internet is a global computer network.
- The World Wide Web (WWW) is software that makes the Internet usable by nonprogrammers.
- Web pages are written in Hypertext Markup Language (HTML).
- Software consists of systems programs and applications.
- Machine language is the lowest level of programming. It consists of numbers and it relies on the architecture of a particular computer.
- Assembly language is a human-friendly form of machine language, using mnemonics and symbols instead of numbers.
- Programs written in high-level languages (HLLs) can be run on any computer system that includes the appropriate compiler.
- There are many high-level languages.
- Java is a fairly new HLL, dating from 1995.
- Programming involves the edit-compile-run loop. We use an editor to write the code. We compile the code into a lower-level language. We run the program to get results.
- Compile-time errors occur when a program does not obey the rules of the programming language being used.
- Syntax errors and semantic errors are two types of compile-time errors.
- Run-time errors occur when a program fails when we try to run it.
- Logical errors occur when a program runs but does not produce correct results.
- Computer users include tool-builders, tool-users, and end-users.
- The software life cycle includes the phases of analysis, design, coding, testing, deployment, and maintenance.

- Program maintenance is never finished. Bugs are found and fixed, and new features are added to existing programs.
- Maintenance is the most expensive part of the programming life cycle.
- A programming paradigm is a generally accepted approach to programming.
- Spaghetti code was the first programming paradigm. It allowed arbitrary jumps from one part of the code to another.
- Structured programming was the second programming paradigm. It restricted the flow of control to only a few well-chosen patterns.
- Object-oriented programming (OOP) is the current paradigm. Programs neatly model the objects involved in real-world situations.
- Most people are reluctant to learn a new programming paradigm. They resist change.

Terminology Introduced in This Chapter

address	edit-compile-run loop	memory
algorithm	executable statements	mnemonic
API (application	file	modem
programming	file server	monitor
interface)	file system	network
application program	FTP (File Transfer	object-oriented
(application)	Protocol)	programming
arithmetic-logic unit	giga-	opcode (operation code)
(ALU)	hardware	operating system (OS)
assembly language	Hertz (Hz)	paradigm
browser	high-level language (HLL)	peripheral
byte	HTML (Hypertext Markup	primary storage
cable modem	Language)	program counter
cell	hypertext	programming
clock speed	Internet	programming language
comment statements	IP address	(PL)
(comments)	ISP	protocol
compiler	keyboard	pseudo-code
compile-time error	kilo-	RAM
CPU (central processing	legacy code	register
unit)	link	ROM
dial-up	LAN (local area network)	run-time error
documentation	logical error	secondary storage
domain name	machine language	semantic error
downloading	machine-dependent	software
DSL	mega-	software life cycle

source code	uploading	word size
spaghetti code	URL (uniform resource	World Wide Web
structured programming	locator)	
syntax error	volatile	
TCP/IP	Web page	
telnet	WAN (wide area network)	
terminal	word	

Exercises

Exercise 1–1.   What are the basic parts of a physical computer?

Exercise 1–2.   What are the parts of the central processing unit (CPU)?

Exercise 1–3.   Give three examples of peripherals.

Exercise 1–4.   What is the purpose of computer networks?

Exercise 1–5.   Name some functions of systems software.

Exercise 1–6.   Give examples of application programs.

Exercise 1–7.   Label the following 1, 2, and 3, with 1 being the lowest-level language and 3 being the highest-level language:

_____ assembly language
_____ high-level language
_____ machine language

Exercise 1–8.   What possible values can a bit have?

Exercise 1–9.   How many bits are in a byte?

Exercise 1–10.   What possible values can a byte have?

Exercise 1-11. How many bits are in a kilobyte?

Exercise 1-12. How do high-level languages differ from machine language?

Exercise 1-13. Would you prefer to program in a high-level language or a machine language? Why?

Exercise 1-14. Research the history of a high-level computer language. When was it invented? By whom? For what sorts of applications is or was it used?

Exercise 1-15. What are the three steps in the edit-compile-run loop? Explain them.

Exercise 1-16. Give an example of a syntax error.

Exercise 1-17. Give an example of a logical error.

Exercise 1-18. Why are CS majors considered tool-*builders* whereas CIS majors are considered tool-*users*?

Exercise 1-19. What are the phases of the software life cycle?

Exercise 1-20. Why is software maintenance a never-ending process?

Exercise 1-21. What is a programming paradigm?

Exercise 1-22. What are the programming paradigms seen so far?

Exercise 1-23. Why do programmers resist paradigm change?

Exercise 1-24. Why does a CS career require lifelong learning?

Exercise 1–25.   Spell out the full terms for each of the following acronyms and then define them.

    a. ALU

    b. API

    c. CPU

    d. DSL

    e. FTP

    f. HLL

    g. HTML

    h. ISP

    i. LAN

    j. OS

    k. RAM

    l. ROM

    m. URL

    n. WAN

    o. WWW

Exercise 1–26.   Explain each of the following prefixes.

    a. giga-

    b. kilo-

    c. mega-

Exercise 1–27.   Which of the terms below concerns hardware? Which concern software?

    a. address

    b. arithmetic-logic unit

    c. browser

    d. clock speed

    e. compile-time error

    f. Hertz

    g. hypertext

    h. legacy code

    i. memory

    j. program counter

    k. volatile

Exercise 1-28. For each term in column A, identify the related term in column B. Terms may be related as part–whole, part–part, opposites, and so forth. Explain each answer.

	Column A		Column B
1.	arithmetic-logic unit	a.	comments
2.	clock speed	b.	dial-up
3.	compile-time error	c.	giga-
4.	downloading	d.	Hertz
5.	executable statements	e.	mouse
6.	keyboard	f.	register
7.	LAN	g.	run-time error
8.	mega-	h.	structured programming
9.	modem	i.	uploading
10.	OOP	j.	WAN

Exercise 1-29. In your local newspaper, find advertisements for three computer systems. For each system, identify the processor speed, memory size, hard disk capacity, and other peripherals. Which is the better system? Why?

Exercise 1-30. In your local newspaper, find three advertisements for comparable computer systems. For each system, identify the processor speed, memory size, hard disk capacity, and other peripherals. Which is the best buy? Why?

CHAPTER TWO

Classes and Objects

Chapter Objectives

- Appreciate object-oriented analysis and design.
- Identify the objects and methods involved in a typical banking (finance) situation.
- Use UML diagrams.
- Understand the features of the object-oriented paradigm: classes, objects, methods, and instance variables.
- Identify the inheritance involved in classes `Person` and `Employee`.
- Model a `Section` of `Students`.
- Understand instance variables.
- Model `Complex` numbers.
- Learn Java conventions for identifiers and capitalization.

Object-oriented programming (OOP) attempts to produce programs that closely model the real world. For example, if a program concerns films and theatres, then we expect to see parts of the program that clearly model films and theatres. This correspondence between program and problem makes the code easier to understand and to maintain, and this cuts programming costs over the lifetime of the program. In this chapter, we'll study some examples of going from problems to classes, and we'll learn the major features of the OO paradigm. We'll also learn the universal Java conventions for capitalization of the names of classes and instances and methods.

2.1 Modeling a Bank

The first step in modeling a real-world problem is to identify the major *classes* of objects that it involves. For a bank, these classes would include `Account`, `Person`, and `Employee`. A full analysis of the bank scenario would, no doubt, yield more classes, but these are sufficient for our current discussion.

> **Object** An identifiable piece, significant to the problem at hand.
>
> **Class** A template for a set of objects.
>
> **Instance** An object. Every object is an instance of some class or other.
>
> **Instance variable** Data slots which differentiate one instance of a class from another.
>
> **Instantiation** The act of creating an object from a class template.
>
> **Method, Behavior, Message** Legal operations for a given class.

Each class is a template or blueprint that describes many possible *instances* of the class, each of which is called an *object*. As a template, the definition of class `Account` would state that every instance of the class has slots for `owner`, `balance`, and `accountNumber`. These slots are called *instance variables*. Each instance of a class is an object created from the template by the process of *instantiation*—filling in the instance variables for that particular instance. For example, a particular `Account` would have a specific `owner`, `balance`, and `accountNumber`.[1]

The next step in modeling is to identify the *methods* or *behaviors* that apply to each specific class. What operations are legal for a bank `Account`? The methods `getBalance`, `deposit`, `withdraw`, and `addInterest` are applicable. These can also be viewed as *messages*. For example, when the message `getBalance` is sent to an `Account` object, the current balance is returned.

We will return to the definition of `Account` shortly. For the moment, we will use this introductory description of `Account` to introduce the next topic.

UML Diagrams

> **UML diagram** A graphical representation of classes and objects.

In recent years, it has become customary to represent classes and instances by means of diagrams in the *Unified Modeling Language (UML)*.[2] Such diagrams can be used to represent both classes and instances.

---

[1] Note the capitalization scheme being used: Class names begin with a capital letter, and slot names begin with a lowercase letter, but words after the first are capitalized. We'll return to these conventions later in the chapter.

[2] Grady Booch, James Rumbaugh, & Ivar Jacobson, *The Unified Modeling Language User Guide*. Reading, MA: Addison-Wesley, 1999.

Schematically, a *UML diagram* for a class looks like this:

ClassName
data
methods

The name of the class is at the top, and then comes a rectangle split horizontally. The top part specifies the instance variables, which must be provided for each instance. The bottom part describes the methods—behaviors—which are applicable to instances of this class.

Based on our discussion above, we would have the following UML diagram for class `Account`:

Account
owner balance accountNumber
getBalance deposit withdraw addInterest

A single instance of class `Account` would be similar, but the instance variables would be filled with the appropriate values:

Account	
owner	*Pointer to a* Person *object, perhaps the* Person *representing John Smith of 1804 Dandelion Lane*
balance	1500.00
accountNumber	"034-5902"

Given a group of `Accounts`, note that each instance has different values for the instance variables, but the *methods apply to all instances of the class*. Thus, we don't need to list methods in the UML boxes that represent objects.

Also, note that each instance variable has a specific *type*:

- `owner` points to a `Person` object;
- `balance` is a number with a decimal point; and
- `accountNumber` is a `String` of characters. (Our example includes punctuation; it's not really a number.)

When we have learned more about Java, we will revisit UML diagrams to see how the types of the variables can be specified.

Let's examine the methods we've sketched for class `Account`:

```
getBalance
deposit
withdraw
addInterest
```

For each method, we could specify more detail:

> **Parameter, Argument** A detail sent, in parentheses, with a method call.

- Some methods require *parameters* or *arguments*, which specify details of the operation being performed. For example, we can't `deposit` or `withdraw` unless we have a specific amount to `deposit` or `withdraw`. On the other hand, `getBalance` requires no parameters; it merely returns to us the current balance in the `Account`.
- Each parameter must have a specified type. We can `deposit` a numeric amount, but not a `Person` or the `String` "hello".
- Some methods return values whereas others do not. `getBalance` returns the number that is the current balance of the `Account`, but `deposit` has only the task of incrementing the `balance`, so it needn't return a value.

In Chapter 4, we will study how to specify types for parameters and return values of methods.

Account

Here is a more complete description of the class `Account`:

```
Account
owner
balance
accountNumber

Account(...)—constructor
getBalance
deposit
withdraw
addInterest
```

Constructor A method that creates an instance of a given class.

Notice the method `Account(...)`. This is a *constructor*—a special method used to create a new `Account`. We'll learn more about constructors in Chapter 3.

2.2 Person **and** Employee

Here is the UML diagram for class `Person`:

Person
name ssn dateOfBirth address
Person(...)—*constructor* setName setAddress

Each piece of this diagram is also underspecified. Let's analyze:

- name—Initially, we might think of making this a single `String`, such as `"Susan B Anthony"`, but names have structure, and we may want to specify `firstName`, `middleName`, and `lastName`. Then we could recognize people with the same `lastName`. Alas, it's still more complicated: We could have `"John James van Dien Jr"`. We might end up with a class just for names, where each instance variable is a distinct piece of the name. Let's assume that we use a simple `String`.
- ssn—We might want to represent the Social Security Number as a `String` rather than a number: `"012-34-5678"` is easier to understand than `012345678`.
- dateOfBirth—This has three pieces: year, month, and day. There are many alternatives for representing dates. You may recall the Y2K problem, when all code that used only a two-digit year in dates had to be rewritten when the century turned. Perhaps we should create a class for `Date` itself. In fact, the Java API provides exactly such a class.
- address—Addresses come in a variety of flavors, but `String` is the simplest way to represent them.
- Person(...)—Given appropriate arguments, the constructor creates an instance of class `Person`.
- setName—This method takes a `String` and changes the name of the `Person` object to which it is sent.

- setAddress—This message takes a String and changes the address of the Person—the object to which it is sent.

Employee

Every Employee is also a Person. We can represent this situation with the following coupled diagrams:

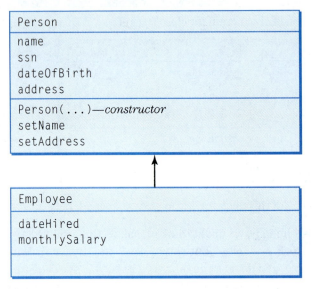

Every Employee has all the instance variables of Person, and all the methods affecting Persons will also affect Employees. We say:

Employee is a subclass of Person

or

Person is a superclass of Employee

or

Employee inherits from Person.

We don't need to do the double work of defining the exact same instance variables and methods in two separate classes. *Inheritance* allows a subclass to use the instance variables and methods that have already been defined in the superclass. Inheritance promotes code reuse because we can adapt existing classes for new, but related, purposes. Note that Employee has some instance variables that *don't* occur in class Person: dateHired and monthlySalary.

> **Inheritance** One class inherits instance variables and methods from the definition of another class.

Relations has-a and is-a

has-a The instance variable of one class is an object from another class. **is-a** An inheritance relationship between two classes.

The bank example illustrates two important relations among classes:

- An `Account` *has-a* slot `owner`, of type `Person`.
- An `Employee` *is-a* `Person`, meaning that all the slots and methods of `Person` are also applicable to `Employee`.

We will study inheritance in more detail in Chapter 19.

2.3 Features of the OO Paradigm

This section will summarize some points discussed previously and will introduce further characteristics of object-oriented programming.

A *class* is a template or blueprint that describes (1) the slots that will appear in each *instance* of that class, and (2) the common behaviors applicable to each instance.

An instance is an object created according to a class template. Different instances may have different values of the instance variables described in the template. For example, every `Person` will have a different `ssn`.

Methods describe the behavior of all instances of the classes. Each method is a *message*, which can be sent to an object. A method may take *parameters* (*arguments*), and a method may return a *value*.

In object-oriented programming, *work is accomplished when a message is sent to an object*. For example, if a is an `Account`, then the expression

```
a.getBalance()
```

returns the current balance of a, and

```
a.withdraw(200.00)
```

withdraws $200 from a.

In a future chapter, we'll see that we can print "`hello`" by sending the message `println("hello")` to the built-in object `System.out`[3], where `System.out` is an instance of class `PrintStream`.

Not every message is appropriate for every object. If a is an `Account`, then

```
a.println("hello")
```

---

[3] `System.out` is an exception to the rule that objects begin with a lowercase letter.

is an error, and if `outputFile` is a `PrintStream`, then

```
outputFile.getBalance()
```

is an error. Defining a class specifies exactly which methods are and are not legal for instances of that class.

2.4 Modeling a `Section` of `Students`

A `Student` is like a `Person`, with instance variables as shown here:

Student
name
ssn
dateOfBirth
gpa

Now let's model a `Section` of `Students` at a university. A given `Course` may have several `Sections`, each with its own details. What instance variables and methods might a `Section` have?

Instance Variables

> **Collection**   An aggregation of same-type objects.

- `roster`—This is a *collection* of `Students`. Some Sections will have many `Students`; some will have few; some will have none. We'll use the generic term collection to refer to a data structure that can hold a variable number of items, all of the same type. We can have a *collection* of numbers, or a collection of `Students`. We can even have a collection of Sections, which would be a collection of collections. Later in this text we'll examine a variety of types of collections, and your CS2 course will spend much of its time defining and studying more complicated types of collections.
- `instructor`—This will refer to an instance of class `Instructor`, which will be a subclass of `Person`. Note that `instructor`—lowercase—refers to an instance, and `Instructor`—uppercase—denotes a class.
- `room`—This will refer to the room in which the `Section` meets. A `room` might be a number, or it might be an object with slots for `location`, `capacity`, and `technologyOffered`.
- `timeSlot`—This will specify the time slot (e.g., MWF 10:30–11:35).

Methods

Now that we've looked at the instance variables of a Section, let's examine the capabilities (methods) that are likely to apply to it:

- Add a Student to the Section.
- Remove a Student from the Section.
- Determine if a given Student is in the Section.
- Given two Sections, return a new Section of those Students who are in *both* Sections.

The following table provides a formal summary of the parameters and return types of these methods:

Method Name	Type of Parameters/Arguments	Return Type
add	Student	none/void
remove	Student	none/void
contains	Student	true or false
intersect	Section	Section

UML Diagram

Here is the final UML diagram for Section:

Section
roster instructor room timeSlot
Section(...)—*constructor* addStudent(Student) remove(Student) contains(Student) intersect(Section)

The Lesson

Object-oriented design requires that we brainstorm the problem in order to learn as much as possible about classes and methods that have not yet been implemented. It's cheaper to fix an error during the design phase than during the coding phase. Once we've written the code for a class, we may have to rewrite large portions of the code to fix a newly-found error. So the lesson you should take away is: Brainstorm! Brainstorm! Brainstorm!

> **Test your skill with Exercises 2-1 through 2-3.**

2.5   Modeling Complex Numbers

Complex numbers were invented in order to represent solutions of equations that involve the square roots of negative numbers. Mathematically, the complex number $z = a + bi$ has a real part a and an imaginary part b. These become the instance variables of objects of class `Complex`. Methods include the following:

Method Name	Type of Parameters, If Any	Return Type	Description
add	Complex	Complex	Add two `Complex` numbers.
sub	Complex	Complex	Subtract one `Complex` number from another.
mul	Complex	Complex	Multiply one `Complex` number by another.
magnitude	none	number	Returns the magnitude of a `Complex` number, namely $\sqrt{a^2 + b^2}$.
power	number n	Complex	Computes the nth power of a `Complex` number, z^n.

Here's the UML diagram for class `Complex`:

Complex
real
imaginary
add
sub
mul
magnitude
power

We will write the complete Java code for class `Complex` in Chapter 7.

> **Test your skill with Exercises 2-4 through 2-8.**

2.6   Conventions

Convention   A general agreement.

A *convention* is a general agreement about how things
should be done. Some Java conventions specify standards
for capitalization of names. When you are paid to program,
you will be told exactly what conventions and style your
employer/client/customer demands. When a community of
programmers abides by the same conventions, the code written by one programmer will be more easily readable by other programmers. This will result
in lower software costs and higher software reliability. This section presents
some of the conventions that are observed by the worldwide Java programming community.

Identifiers

Identifier   A name for a class,
variable, or method.

An *identifier* is a word that can be used as the name of a
class, variable, or method. Identifiers may be composed
from letters, digits, and the underscore ("_").

Identifiers must begin with a letter. Java is case-sensitive:
a and A are considered different, as are a1 and A1.

Identifiers may be arbitrarily long, but be careful: If a name is very long, you're
liable to mistype it. Here are some valid identifiers: `timeToLive`, `bistro99`, `U2`,
`MAXIMUM_VALUE`.

Capitalization

An uppercase letter is used for the first letter in every word in a class name.
Examples of class names are `Account`, `BankAccount`, `ClosedCurve`, and
`Matrix3By3`.

The first word of an instance is lowercase. The first letter of the subsequent
word(s) is capitalized. Examples are: `cs1`, `numberOfStudents`, `averageAge`,
and `taxRate`.

Categories of Identifiers

Any given identifier falls into one of the following categories:

Reserved words   Names that
only Java is permitted to define
and use.

- Reserved words—These have special meaning to Java,
  and we're not allowed to use them in any other way.
  Examples are `class`, `public`, `private`, and `static`.
  Appendix 2 lists Java's reserved words.

- Names defined by other programmers—These names were used by programmers who wrote code we plan to use. Much of the code in the Java API falls into this category. Examples are: `System.out`, `println`, and `PrintStream`.
- Names *we* select—We use these to name the classes, variables, and methods of the code we're writing for a given project.

> **Test your skill with Exercises 2-9 and 2-10.**

2.7   The Road Ahead

The remainder of this text will explain how to use Java to implement object-oriented designs. In Chapter 3, we'll examine how to use predefined classes for writing to the monitor. Chapter 4 discusses the methods presented by the predefined `String` class. Chapter 5 presents the classes that enable us to read `Strings` from the keyboard and from text files. Chapter 6 teaches how to define classes of our own devising. Chapters 7 through 10 describe Java's primitive datatypes, which can be incorporated as the types of instance variables in classes we define. Chapters 10 and 11 describe *control structures*, which allow us to define more complicated methods. Chapter 12 takes a breather to examine how better to code and test our programs. Chapters 13 and 14 examine the two simplest collections: files and arrays. Chapters 15 through 17 present two major ways in which classes can be related: interface and inheritance. The remainder of the text presents numerical algorithms and some advanced Java topics: exceptions and recursions. *Bon voyage!*

Chapter Summary

- Programs in object-oriented languages closely model the real world.
- A class is a template for a large number of similar objects.
- Each object is an instance of some class.
- Instance variables are data that differentiate one object from another when both are instances of the same class.
- A method is an operation that pertains to an object.
- The Unified Modeling Language (UML) is a convenient graphic notation for classes, objects, instance variables, and methods.

- An `Account` is a useful class for modeling a `Bank`.
- The `Employee` class inherits data and methods from the `Person` class.
- A `Section` object references a collection of `Student` objects.
- The `Complex` class models complex numbers, each of which has a real part and an imaginary part.
- Java identifiers must begin with a letter, and may contain letters, digits, and the underscore ("_").
- Conventions are general agreements about how to select identifier names and how to use capital letters.
- In class names, all words begin with a capital letter: `BankAccount`, `Closed-Curve`.
- In variable names, the first word is *not* capitalized, but the first letter of the remaining word(s) is: `numberOfStudents`, `averageAge`, `taxRate`.
- Reserved words have special meaning to Java, and we can't use them for names of classes, variables, or methods.

Terminology Introduced in This Chapter

argument	inheritance	object
behavior	inherits	parameter
class	instance	reserved word
collection	instance variables	UML diagram
constructor	instantiation	Unified Modeling
convention	is-a	Language (UML)
has-a	message	
identifier	method	

Exercises

Exercise 2-1. Brainstorm the classes and methods required to model a car dealership, class `CarDealership`. Several classes are required.

Exercise 2-2. Brainstorm the classes and methods required to model a tropical fish store involving `Fish` and `Tanks`.

Exercise 2-3. Brainstorm the classes and methods required to model an airline.

Exercise 2-4.   Recall the definition of mathematical sets, particularly sets of integers. Recall the following operations:

Operation	Mathematical Symbol	Definition
Membership	$n \in s$	Is integer n in the set s?
Add	$s \cup \{n\}$	Add integer n to set s.
Union	$s_1 \cup s_2$	Compute the union of two sets.
Intersect	$s_1 \cap s_2$	Compute the intersection of two sets.
Difference	$s_1 - s_2$	Compute the difference of two sets: $n \in s_1 - s_2$ if and only if $n \in s_1$ and $n \notin s_2$.
Remove	$s - \{n\}$	Remove an element n from a set.

Consider how these mathematical operations would be transformed into classes and methods. Describe the method names, parameters, and return types.

Exercise 2-5.   Think about a file system including `File` and `Directory` classes. What are the methods involved in a file system? What are their parameters? Describe the methods that permit us to read and write files. What about methods that involve the size and properties of files? Brainstorm this problem with other class members.

Exercise 2-6.   What classes and methods would be involved in modeling an `ApartmentBuilding` with many `Apartments`?

Exercise 2-7.   What classes, instance variables, and methods would be involved in modeling a rental car company that rents `Cars` and `Trucks`?

Exercise 2-8.   What classes, instance variables, and methods would be involved in modeling `Movies`, `Actors`, and `Directors`?

Exercise 2-9.   Which of the following are valid identifiers? For those that aren't, explain why.

```
counter
2stars
counter2
counter_2
counter-2
a++
#21
21
```

Exercise 2-10.   Consider the class `Student`, which represents a student at a university. Give its UML diagram. Describe each instance variable and method.

CHAPTER THREE

Using Predefined Classes and Objects

Chapter Objectives

- Become familiar with methods of class `PrintStream` and its predefined instance `System.out`.
- Use the `print` and `println` methods to write to the monitor.
- Compile and run a Java program.
- Recognize required boilerplate statements in a Java program.
- Document a program using comments.
- Use white space to make programs more readable.
- Learn Java's graphics coordinate system.
- Use Java's graphics color system.
- Write simple GUI programs that display geometrical shapes.

In Chapter 2, we introduced the methodology of object-oriented programming, and we saw how to analyze a problem into classes and instances. In the coming chapters, we'll see how to implement our designs using Java. Our approach is this:

- In this chapter, we'll use classes and objects that are predefined by Java. This will give us experience in invoking methods—sending messages—with various parameters.
- In Chapters 4 and 5 we'll write programs in which we define *new instances* of Java's predefined classes. This will give us experience in

using constructors to create new objects that have specific qualities—qualities that we require in order to solve new problems.

- Finally, in Chapter 6, we will write *classes of our own* to solve problems for which Java's built-in classes are not sufficient.

At the end of these learning experiences, we will have a firm grounding in how Java connects with object-oriented programming.

3.1   What Java Provides

Java provides a host of predefined classes, as well as a number of predefined instances of those classes. These built-in classes provide facilities that are useful to many, if not most, Java programmers. Facilities that are useful only to a few special projects will be implemented in special classes targeted at those particular problems. Java's Application Programming Interface (API) describes the built-in classes. You can find the API online at

> **Application Programming Interface (API)**   Java's library of predefined classes and methods.

http://java.sun.com/j2se/1.5.0/docs/api/overview-summary.html

Here is a brief taxonomy of Java's built-in capabilities:

- Classes to enable reading and printing.
- Classes to manage files and directories.
- Classes for Date, Time, and Calendar.
- Classes for drawing graphics on the screen and for a GUI system.

In the following chapters we will work with predefined classes, which allow us to write to the monitor and read from the keyboard. This is generally the first capability you must acquire when you encounter a new language or a new computer system.

3.2   Class `PrintStream` and Instance `System.out`

Class `PrintStream` models printing to the monitor and to files. `System.out` is a predefined instance of `PrintStream`, and it always points to the terminal/monitor.

Suppose we want to write the `String` "hello" to the monitor. The appropriate Java statement is

```
System.out.println("hello");
```

which we can analyze into three pieces:

> **Receiver** The recipient (object) of a method call.

- `System.out` is the *receiver* of a message. `System.out` is an instance of class `PrintStream`, which means that it can accept only a predefined set of messages.
- `println` is a *method*, which is applicable to `PrintStream`s. Its purpose is to print something to the monitor. It may also be viewed as a *message* being sent to the receiver.
- "hello" is the *parameter* or *argument* of the call to `println`. "hello" is also a user-defined instance of predefined class `String`; we'll learn more about this topic later in this chapter.

This statement will be the heart of our first Java program, which we'll write in the next section.

3.3 Using Java

Figure 3–1 shows a block diagram of how to use the Java compiler and run-time system.

> **Byte code** Output of the Java compiler; input to the JVM.
> **Java Virtual Machine (JVM)**
> Program that interprets byte code and actually runs a Java program.

We start with a file of Java *source code* (extension `.java`). This is a text file containing a Java program in human-readable form.

The Java *compiler* reads the source code and produces a file of Java *byte code* (extension `.class`), which is readable by the machine but makes no sense to humans. Sometimes the compiler detects *errors*, which prevent successful compilation.

The Java byte code is then given to a Java *run-time system* that understands the byte code and executes the program. The run-time system is also called the *Java Virtual Machine (JVM)*.

The next section will take our first Java program through the steps illustrated in Figure 3–1.

Figure 3–1
Using Java

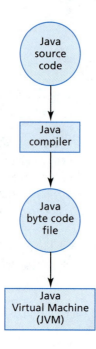

3.4   A First Java Program

Our first Java program will print "hello" to the monitor. Such a program, often called the "Hello World" program, is usually the first program we write when we move to a new language or computer system. If we can't do this task, then we probably can't program anything else.

Java source code files should be created without the formatting commands of a word processor. In Windows, use an editor such as Notepad or WordPad. In Unix, use an editor such as vi or pico.

The file First.java contains the relevant code, which we'll discuss in detail in the remaining sections of this chapter. The extension .java is required for Java source code files. First let's see how to compile and run this program.

First.java   A First Java Program

```
/// Written by Barry Soroka
//
// A first Java program.
//
////////////////////////////////////////////////////////////////////////////////
class First
```

```
{
//-------------------------------------------------------------------------
   public static void main ( String [] args ) throws Exception
   {
   System.out.println("hello");
   }
//-------------------------------------------------------------------------
} // end class First
/////////////////////////////////////////////////////////////////////////
```

Compiling the Program

We order Java to compile our program within a command prompt or terminal window. We enter the command line

```
% javac First.java
```

where % is the prompt provided by the command processor.

If all goes well, then we'll next see the command prompt:

```
%
```

and a new file, First.class, will have been created. The extension .class indicates a file of byte code that has been created by the Java compiler. Often, however, our file will generate a compile-time error and Java will print a more-or-less useful message.

Running the Program

Once we've achieved a successful compile and produced a file First.class, we can run our program by giving the command line

```
% java First
```

Note that I haven't used a file extension on the First. The program produces the output

```
hello
```

If our code was incorrect, we may have encountered run-time errors, which halt the program prematurely, or our program may have run but given the wrong results—a logical error.

Now let's examine the contents of file `First.java`.

 Test your skill with Exercise 3-1.

3.5   Action Statements

The program `First.java` contains just one single action statement:

```
System.out.println("hello");
```

The other 12 statements are required to enable this `println` statement to do its work. We'll discuss those surrounding statements in the next few sections.

3.6   Boilerplate

Boilerplate   Java statements that we must use, often without completely understanding them.

Boilerplate is the standardized text that we must include with every Java program that we write. We won't understand it all right away, so we just use it as given. Must you memorize it? Yes.

Every new language you learn will require a certain amount of boilerplate that, at first, you must use by rote, without full understanding.

Two back slashes—//—indicate that the rest of the line is a *comment*. A comment is text that helps the reader understand the program, but isn't itself Java code. A program begins with five lines of comment:

```
// Written by Barry Soroka
//
// A first Java program.
//
////////////////////////////////////////////////////////////////////////////
```

The top line includes the name of the person who wrote the program. The third line describes the purpose of the file. The line of slashes is part of the style rule: Every class is surrounded by a row of slashes. This helps the reader understand where classes begin and end.

Next comes

```
class First
   {
```

which announces that a new class, First, begins here and extends from the open brace (() until the matching close brace (}).

The line of dashes announces the main method and fulfills the style rule: Every method is surrounded by a row of dashes.

// -

The main method begins with the boilerplate

```
public static void main ( String [] args ) throws Exception
{
```

We'll understand all of this by the end of CS 1, but for the moment we need to memorize it. Some students remember

```
public static void main
```

by using the sentence

Please stop violent movies.

Every Java program requires a main method—it's what the JVM looks for when it tries to start execution of the compiled code.

Next comes our action statement

```
System.out.println("hello");
```

and the close of the main method:

```
    }
```
// -

Then we close the class First:

```
} // end class First
```
///

After the closing brace, notice that the comment

```
// end class First
```

has been inserted. This helps the reader understand which class is being ended by the brace and by the line of slashes.

You may have noted the use of indentation in `First.java`. Some lines are at the left edge, and others are indented by three or six spaces. The purpose of indentation is to make the code easier to read, and we will use indentation consistently according to the style sheet (Appendix 1). Every employer or client will require a style of its own, and we will be judged—or fired—on the basis of how well we obey the style required.

3.7   Comments

We've seen the use of `//`:

```
// comments out the rest of the line
```

which can be used at the beginning of a line or any other place in the line. Suppose, however, that we need *five* lines of comments. If we use `//`, then our code will be:

```
// comment line 1
// comment line 2
// comment line 3
// comment line 4
// comment line 5
```

Java provides a second way to create comments: It treats anything between `/*` and `*/` as a comment. Thus, the five-line comment could be:

```
/*
    comment line 1
    comment line 2
    comment line 3
    comment line 4
    comment line 5
*/
```

Some writers would use

```
/*
 *    comment line 1
 *    comment line 2
```

```
*    comment line 3
*    comment line 4
*    comment line 5
*/
```

where the vertical row of *s helps the reader see the unity of the comment.

Comments are needed so that later readers can understand your code. Inevitably, someone will need to read your code in order to maintain the program by adding features, fixing bugs, and so forth. Your employer will save money if that programmer can understand your code with minimal effort. You won't fully appreciate the value of comments until (1) you have to read someone else's uncommented code, or (2) you return to your own code six months later and you find that you can't understand how it works. One day you will have to rewrite your own code because it's easier to write it again than to try and understand what you previously wrote.

We've seen two special types of comments:

- a row of slashes surrounds a class, and
- a row of dashes surrounds a method.

These are the conventions of *this* textbook. Your employers/clients will tell you the specific styles they want for each specific programming project.

Don't Overdo It!

It's possible to put too many comments into your code. Consider this example:

```
// Print the first name:
System.out.println(firstName);
// Print the middle name:
System.out.println(middleName);
```

The comments are unnecessary; they don't tell me more than I could learn by simply reading the code.

3.8   White Space

Java code is free-form. Statements may begin at any place in a line, and they can spread over multiple lines.

Java programs contain *tokens*, which cannot be split:

c lass is not the same as class

"h e ll o" is not the same as "hello"

Programs are unchanged if we insert white space—spaces, tabs, or blank lines—anywhere we want *between* tokens.

> **White space**   Spaces, indents, and blank lines used to make code more readable.

A program is unchanged when we delete or insert comments, or when we delete or insert white space.

We can convert our program First.java into the program FirstBad.java. It's easier to read and understand the program where white space has been used intelligently.

FirstBad.java   **A Less Legible Version of First.java**

```
// Program FirstBad
          class
First          {                    public
                                    static
void
     main(String[
                             ]
                             args
                             )
     throws Exception{
                        System
       .
out
       .
         println(
"hello");}}
```

Blank Lines

When a program has many lines, we can use blank lines to achieve a visual grouping. Visual grouping cues the reader that certain lines belong together and perform a single task. We'll use this feature when our programs get more complicated.

3.9   File Names and Class Names

In previous sections we had a file named First.java containing code for a class named First. We can represent this as follows:

First.java

```
class First
{
    ...
}
```

We compile this file with the command

```
% javac First.java
```

which produces a new file, `First.class`.[1] We run our program with the command

```
% java First
```

which tells the operating system to look for a `main` method in file `First.class`. Note the inconsistency:

Compile   `% javac First.java`
Run   `% java First`

For the compiler, we're required to specify the file's extension, `.java`. For runtime, we're forbidden to use the file's extension, `.class`. Most programmers have made their share of errors by using or omitting extensions; both of the following statements are erroneous:

```
% javac First (Wrong!)
% java First.class (Wrong!)
```

Test your skill with Exercise 3-2.

NOTE   I usually use the same name for both the file name and the class name, but it's not required by Java.

---

[1]   Actually, we'll see in Chapter 6 that a source file can contain code for more than one class. The compiler produces a `.class` file for each class defined in the source file.

Consider a file `Foo.java` containing a class named `Bar`:

Foo.java

```
class Bar
{
    ...
}
```

When Java compiles this file with the `javac` command, it produces the file `Bar.class`! The class file takes its name from the `class` statement inside the file, *not* from the name of the source code file.

3.10   Using a Template File—`Blank.java`

The boilerplate for a Java program is pretty lengthy, but there's a way to avoid having to type it in from scratch for every new program: create a file `Blank.java`, which can serve as a template for routine Java files.

Blank.java   **A Template for Java Programs**

```
// Written by Barry Soroka
//
// description of this program
//
import java.io.*;
//////////////////////////////////////////////////////////////////////////
class Blank
{
//-------------------------------------------------------------------------
    public static void main ( String [] args ) throws Exception
    {
    }
//-------------------------------------------------------------------------
} // end class Blank
//////////////////////////////////////////////////////////////////////////
```

   Test your skill with Exercise 3-3.

Suppose we want to create a file `Print99.java`, which prints "99" to the monitor. We copy `Blank.java` to `Print99.java` and we edit the file appropriately:

• Change `Blank` to `Print99` every place it occurs.

- Change the description of the file:
  ```
  // Prints 99 to the monitor.
  ```
- Insert the action statement inside the main method:
  ```
  System.out.println(99);
  ```

This produces the final program. Using the template saved a lot of typing!

Print99.java   **Print 99 to the Monitor**

```
// Written by Barry Soroka
//
// Prints 99 to the monitor.
//
import java.io.*;
/////////////////////////////////////////////////////////////////////////////
class Print99
{
//-----------------------------------------------------------------------------
    public static void main ( String [] args ) throws Exception
    {
        System.out.println(99);
    }
//-----------------------------------------------------------------------------
} // end class Print99
/////////////////////////////////////////////////////////////////////////////
```

 | **Test your skill with Exercise 3-4.**

Recall that Blank.java compiles without error, and runs without error, even though it does nothing. If we create Print99.java from Blank.java, and it doesn't compile, then we know that the error must be in the code we added to Blank.java. This is an example of good programming practice:

NOTE   Start with code that compiles and runs. Modify it. If it no longer compiles and runs, then the error is due to the code you added or changed.

Always start with a working program and modify it to give it the capabilities required for the problem at hand.

NOTE

Keep checkpoints of working programs as you gradually bring the program into full compliance with its requirements. If you accidentally mangle the code, you can fall back on the last working version—you won't have to start from scratch.

NOTE

3.11   Methods for Class `PrintStream`

Every class has a set of methods that it recognizes, and `PrintStream` is no exception. There are three methods available, which are described in the following table:

Method Name	Parameters	Example	Description
`println`	`String`	`println("hello")`	Prints its argument and goes to the next line.
`println`	Ø	`println()`	Terminates the current line and goes to the next. Useful for inserting a blank line.
`print`	`String`	`print("hello")`	Prints its argument but doesn't move to the next line.

One way to characterize a method is by its *signature*—its name plus its parameters. By this definition, the three methods above have signatures

```
println(String)
println()
print(String)
```

Signatures are important for distinguishing one method from another method. We'll use this capability in the sections that follow.

Don't forget that a complete Java statement with these methods must include `System.out` as the receiver of the message. For example:

```
System.out.println("hello");
```

3.12   Overloading

Overloading   Occurs when methods have the same name but different numbers or types of parameters.

When two methods have the same name but different arguments, we say that the method name is *overloaded*. Thus, `println` is overloaded because we have the methods

```
println()
```

and

```
println(String)
```

The name `println` refers to two completely different methods. If a program contains the statements

```
System.out.println("hello");
System.out.println();
```

then the compiler can determine which `println` refers to which method by looking at the arguments in the call to `println`.

We will encounter many more examples of overloading in the chapters ahead.

3.13   There's More Than One Way to Solve a Problem

Given the `print` and `println` methods, we can write many programs. For example, `Prog0301` prints

```
abc
```

using the statement

```
System.out.println("abc");
```

But we can get the same output from

```
System.out.print("ab");
System.out.println("c");
```

or

```
System.out.print("abc");
System.out.println();
```

or

```
System.out.print("a");
System.out.print("bc");
System.out.println();
```

Prog0301.java   Write Out abc

```
// Written by Barry Soroka
//
// Write out
//                 abc
//
import java.io.*;
/////////////////////////////////////////////////////////////////////////////
class Prog0301
{
//- - - - - - - - - - - - - - - - - - - - - - - - - - - - - - - - - - - - - - -
   public static void main ( String [] args ) throws Exception
   {
      System.out.println("abc");
   }
//- - - - - - - - - - - - - - - - - - - - - - - - - - - - - - - - - - - - - - -
} // end class Prog0301
/////////////////////////////////////////////////////////////////////////////
```

> **Test your skill with Exercise 3-5.**

3.14   GUI: Java's Graphics Libraries

This is the first of a sequence of chapter supplements that demonstrate Java's graphics capabilities. Using these capabilities, we can develop graphical user interfaces (GUIs) to our programs.

Abstract Windowing Toolkit (AWT)   Java's first graphics library.

Java's API contains two different libraries of graphics components. *AWT*—the Abstract Windowing Toolkit—was developed first. To use it, we must include the statement

```
import java.awt.*;
```

| **Swing** Java's second graphics library. | in our programs. Later, the *Swing* library was added to Java to provide enhanced functionality, and we include the statement |

```
import javax.swing.*;
```

in order to use it. (Note the `javax` rather than `java`!) You will often see these statements in the programs in the graphic supplements.

3.15 GUI: Coordinates and Colors

| **Picture Element (Pixel)** The smallest dot on a graphics screen. **Applet** A graphics program that requires a browser. **Application** A stand-alone graphics program. **RGB** The red-green-blue color system. **Color channels** The red, green, and blue that comprise the RGB color system for a computer screen display. | The image on your computer screen is formed by a grid of picture elements—pixels—with different locations and colors. The complete image can be specified by assigning a color to each location on the screen. Usually, we draw on the screen by specifying graphics primitives (such as rectangles and ovals) with their corresponding locations (dimensions and colors). |

Java can do graphics in two different ways. An *applet* is graphics code that requires a browser or equivalent in order to run. An *application* is a stand-alone Java program containing graphics commands. We will be concerned only with applications. An application works by opening graphical windows (`JFrames`) on the screen and by drawing in the `JFrames`.

By the end of this chapter's GUI supplement, you will be able to draw simple scenes using `JFrames` and the graphics primitives.

Java uses the coordinate system shown in Figure 3–2. The dot marks the location $(100, 50)$. The axes are x and y. (Note that the orientation of the axes is different from the xy-axes you used in analytical geometry and calculus.) We will often refer to x as width and y as height.

Each color is described by a triple of numbers, with each number in the range 0 to 255. These numbers represent the intensity of red, green, and blue, respectively. This is called an RGB color system, and we sometimes refer to the red, green, and blue *color channels*. In the RGB system, red corresponds to $(255,0,0)$, green to $(0,255,0)$, and blue to $(0,0,255)$. Using the colors red,

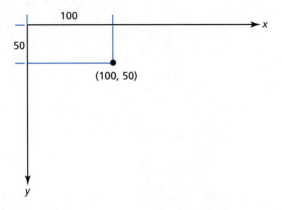

Figure 3–2
Java's Coordinate
System for
Graphics

green and blue, Java can approximate any color we want.[2] Here is a table that shows the correspondence of built-in colors to RGB triples:

Color	Java's Built-In Color Name	RGB Values
Black	Color.BLACK	(0,0,0)
Blue	Color.BLUE	(0,0,255)
Cyan	Color.CYAN	(0,255,255)
Gray	Color.GRAY	(128,128,128)
Dark gray	Color.DARK_GRAY	(64,64,64)
Light gray	Color.LIGHT_GRAY	(192,192,192)
Green	Color.GREEN	(0,255,0)
Magenta	Color.MAGENTA	(255,0,255)
Orange	Color.ORANGE	(255,200,0)
Pink	Color.PINK	(255,175,175)
Red	Color.RED	(255,0,0)
White	Color.WHITE	(255,255,255)
Yellow	Color.YELLOW	(255,255,0)

Note that black corresponds to *no light* in any of the three color channels, and that white corresponds to *maximum intensity* in all three channels. This agrees with the observation that a glass prism breaks white light into a mixture

---

[2] If you use a magnifying glass to observe the screen of a liquid crystal display, you can see that each dot is actually a triple of red-green-blue, and you can see how an arbitrary color is formed by various intensities of the three basic colors.

of all the colors in the spectrum. Levels of gray have all three basic colors at equal intensity.

3.16 GUI: Opening a `JFrame`

Prog0302 is an application that opens a `JFrame` with the following specifications:

Width	200 pixels
Height	400 pixels
Upper-left corner	`(200,100)`
Color	`Color.CYAN`

Try it.

This program contains a lot of boilerplate, which will be described in the following paragraphs. After that, you should be able to take this code and vary it in order to write other Java graphics programs.

Prog0302.java Open a JFrame

```java
// Written by Barry Soroka
//
// Open a JFrame with a specified location, dimensions, and color.
//
import java.io.*;
import javax.swing.*;
import java.awt.*;
/////////////////////////////////////////////////////////////////////////////
class Prog0302
{
//--------------------------------------------------------------------------
    public static void main ( String [] args ) throws Exception
    {
        MyFrame f = new MyFrame();
        f.setVisible(true);
    }
//--------------------------------------------------------------------------
} // end class Prog0302
/////////////////////////////////////////////////////////////////////////////
class MyFrame extends JFrame
{
//--------------------------------------------------------------------------
```

```
    public MyFrame()
    {
        setTitle("Our First JFrame");
        setSize(200,400);
        setLocation(200,100);
        setDefaultCloseOperation(EXIT_ON_CLOSE);

        Container c = getContentPane();
        c.setBackground(Color.CYAN);
    }
//-------------------------------------------------------------------------
} // end class MyFrame
///////////////////////////////////////////////////////////////////////////
```

Prog0302.java contains two classes: Prog0302 and MyFrame. Prog0302 is a driver, and MyFrame is a supporting class definition. In Chapter 6 we'll learn how to write our own new classes. For the moment, you'll be safe by copying and varying the given code.

The main program creates a MyFrame object by calling its constructor and then making the MyFrame visible:

```
    MyFrame f = new MyFrame();
    f.setVisible(true);
```

These statements are responsible for opening the JFrame onto the computer screen.

The header of class MyFrame declares that MyFrame is a class derived from the class JFrame:

```
    class MyFrame extends JFrame
```

This is an example of *inheritance*, which we'll study in detail in Chapter 16. The effect of this statement is that the methods of class JFrame are all applicable to instances of class MyFrame.

Within class MyFrame we find a constructor with the header

```
    public MyFrame()
```

The statements within this constructor are responsible for giving each instance of MyFrame its characteristics. The statement

```
    setTitle("Our First JFrame");
```

puts the String "Our First JFrame" in the title bar of the MyFrame and in the tab in the task bar at the bottom of a Windows screen. The statement

```
    setSize(200,400);
```

causes the MyFrame to have a width of 200 pixels and a height of 400 pixels. The location of its upper-left corner is set to (200,100) by the statement

```
setLocation(200,100);
```

The statement

```
setDefaultCloseOperation(EXIT_ON_CLOSE);
```

tells Java that closing the MyFrame should result in exiting the application that opened it. The next two statements set the color of the MyFrame:

```
Container c = getContentPane();
c.setBackground(Color.CYAN);
```

You should use and vary these lines as required.

Java graphics work by placing interactive elements onto JFrames visible to the user. Such elements include buttons, panels for graphical display, and fields for text entry and display. Applications sometimes use more than one JFrame for user interaction.

   Test your skill with Exercises 3-6 through 3-8.

3.17   GUI: Drawing Geometrical Shapes

Program Prog0303 draws the simple "race car" shown in Figure 3–3. The driver, Prog0303, begins by creating a new JFrame in variable frame. Then it creates a new MyPanel via

```
MyPanel mp = new MyPanel();
```

Figure 3–3
A Race Car

adds the `MyPanel` to `frame`, packs the `JFrame`, and then makes it visible. We can copy this sequence of actions to draw scenes of any complexity.

Prog0303.java **Drawing a Race Car**

```java
// Written by Barry Soroka
//
// A simple drawing -- a race car.
//
import java.awt.*;
import javax.swing.*;
import java.io.*;
/////////////////////////////////////////////////////////////////////////////
class Prog0303
{
//---------------------------------------------------------------------------
    public static void main (String[] args) throws Exception
    {
        JFrame frame = new JFrame ("Race Car");
        frame.setDefaultCloseOperation (JFrame.EXIT_ON_CLOSE);

        MyPanel mp = new MyPanel();

        frame.getContentPane().add(mp);
        frame.pack();
        frame.setVisible(true);
    }
//---------------------------------------------------------------------------
} // end class Prog0303
/////////////////////////////////////////////////////////////////////////////
class MyPanel extends JPanel
{
//---------------------------------------------------------------------------
    public MyPanel()
    {
        setBackground(Color.WHITE);
        setPreferredSize(new Dimension(700,450));
    }
//---------------------------------------------------------------------------
    public void paintComponent ( Graphics page )
    {
        super.paintComponent(page);
        page.drawRect(100,150,500,150);
```

```
    page.fillOval(150,250,100,100);
    page.fillOval(450,250,100,100);
  }
//--------------------------------------------------------------------------
} // end class MyPanel
////////////////////////////////////////////////////////////////////////////
```

Class `MyPanel` contains a constructor `MyPanel()`, which sets the background and size of the panel. (The `JFrame` will flex to fit the added `MyPanel`.) The actual work of drawing the race car is done in method `paintComponent`, which contains four statements. The first is

```
    super.paintComponent(page)
```

and this is boilerplate—copy it in every `paintComponent` method you write. This is followed by the statement

```
    page.drawRect(100,150,500,150);
```

which draws a 500×150 rectangle with upper-left corner at (100, 150). Note that the rectangle is drawn in outline; the method `fillRect` would have drawn a solid black rectangle.

The left wheel is a solid circle produced by the statement

```
    page.fillOval(150,250,100,100);
```

Bounding box A rectangle, aligned with the xy-axes, which encloses an oval or other geometric shape.

The oval is drawn inside a rectangle with upper-left corner at (150, 250), with both width and height 100. This rectangle is sometimes called the *bounding box* of the oval. `fillOval` will draw *ellipses* if the bounding box is not square. Also, the method `drawOval` will draw the *outline* of an oval, not a solid (filled-in) shape. The second wheel of the race car is drawn with the statement

```
    page.fillOval(450,250,100,100);
```

A Java application initially draws objects using the color `Color.BLACK`. If you'd rather draw in a different color—say, red—you would issue a statement such as

```
    page.setColor(Color.RED);
```

All drawing from that point on would be in red, until the program ends or you execute a different setColor statement.

> **Test your skill with Exercise 3-9.**

Drawings like that of our race car require that we specify the graphics coordinates of every geometrical shape in the scene. A good way to plan for a diagram is to sketch the drawing on graph paper and extract the required coordinates from the drawing. Figure 3–4 shows the race car laid out on graph paper.

> **Test your skill with Exercises 3-10 through 3-16.**

drawLine

A line has two end-points, and the method drawLine takes four integer parameters:

x1—the x-coordinate of the first end-point;

y1—the y-coordinate of the first end-point;

x2—the x-coordinate of the second end-point;

y2—the y-coordinate of the second end-point.

Figure 3–4
Layout of the
Race Car on
Graph Paper

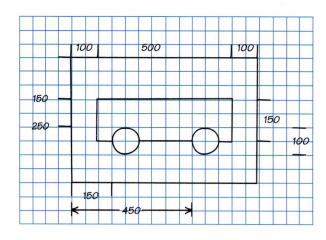

Thus, `drawLine(50,100,150,200)` draws a line from $(50, 100)$ to $(150, 200)$.

 Test your skill with Exercises 3-17 through 3-18.

drawArc

Arc   A portion of a circle's border.

An arc of a circle or ellipse is a connected portion of the boundary. For example, a semicircle is 180° of the full 360° circumference of a circle. Java permits us to draw arcs of ovals by specifying six integers:

`x`—the x-coordinate of the upper-left corner of the bounding box;

`y`—the y-coordinate of the upper-left corner of the bounding box;

`width`—the width of the bounding box;

`height`—the height of the bounding box;

`start`—the angular position at which the arc begins, specified in degrees;

`stop`—the angular position at which the arc ends, specified in degrees.

The 0 angular position is a horizontal line going from the center of the oval out and to the right. Positive angles are measured counterclockwise from the 0 position:

90° is pointing straight up from the center of the oval;

180° is pointing to the left from the center of the oval;

270° is pointing straight down from the center of the oval.

Figure 3–5 shows how `start` and `stop` are interpreted for a variety of angles.

 Test your skill with Exercises 3-19 through 3-21.

3.18   GUI: Displaying a JPEG Image

JPEG   A popular scheme for storing images on computers; an image stored in JPEG format.

The Joint Photographic Experts Group created a standard for compressing digital images to be stored and used on computers. Many images conform to this JPEG standard, including many produced by digital cameras or found on

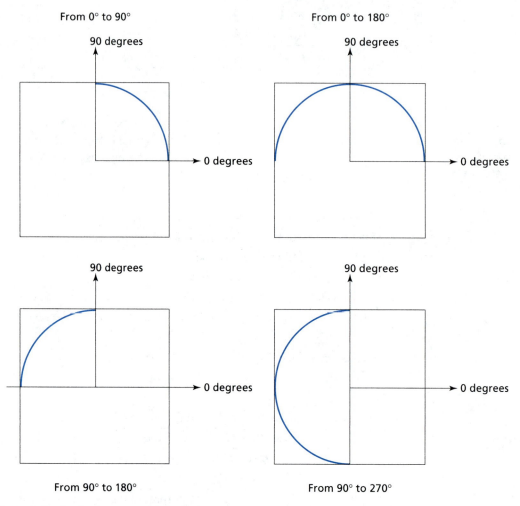

Figure 3–5 Arc Angles

the Web. Prog0304.java shows how a Java program can display a JPEG image on the screen. The statement

```
Image image = new ImageIcon("bacon.jpg").getImage();
```

creates an Image object from the disk file bacon.jpg. This Image is displayed by the statement

```
page.drawImage(image,50,50,this);
```

where (50, 50) is the location of the upper-left corner of the image.

Prog0304.java   Display a JPEG Image

```
// Written by Barry Soroka
//
// Display a jpeg image.
//
import java.io.*;
import java.awt.*;
import javax.swing.*;
//////////////////////////////////////////////////////////////////////////////
class Prog0304
{
//------------------------------------------------------------------------------
    public static void main (String[] args) throws Exception
    {
        JFrame frame = new JFrame ("Display a JPEG File");
        frame.setDefaultCloseOperation (JFrame.EXIT_ON_CLOSE);

        MyPanel mp = new MyPanel();

        frame.getContentPane().add(mp);
        frame.pack();
        frame.setVisible(true);
    }
//------------------------------------------------------------------------------
} // end class Prog0304
//////////////////////////////////////////////////////////////////////////////
class MyPanel extends JPanel
{
//------------------------------------------------------------------------------
    public MyPanel()
    {
        setBackground(Color.WHITE);
        setPreferredSize(new Dimension(400,300));
    }
//------------------------------------------------------------------------------
    public void paintComponent ( Graphics page )
    {
        super.paintComponent(page);
        Image image = new ImageIcon("bacon.jpg").getImage();
        page.drawImage(image,50,50,this);
    }
```

```
//-------------------------------------------------------------------
} // end class MyPanel
////////////////////////////////////////////////////////////////////
```

 Test your skill with Exercises 3-22 through 3-23.

3.19   GUI: Diagonals

When applied to a JPanel, getWidth() and getHeight() return its current
dimensions. Prog0305.java draws a window with diagonals. As the window is
resized, the diagonals are redrawn appropriately.

Prog0305.java   Diagonal Crosshairs

```java
// Written by Barry Soroka
//
// Draws diagonal cross-hairs across a window.
//
import java.awt.*;
import javax.swing.*;
////////////////////////////////////////////////////////////////////
class Prog0305
{
//-------------------------------------------------------------------
    public static void main (String[] args)
    {
        JFrame frame = new JFrame ("CrissCross");
        frame.setDefaultCloseOperation (JFrame.EXIT_ON_CLOSE);

        MyPanel mp = new MyPanel();

        frame.getContentPane().add(mp);
        frame.pack();
        frame.setVisible(true);
    }
//-------------------------------------------------------------------
} // end class Prog0305
////////////////////////////////////////////////////////////////////
class MyPanel extends JPanel
{
//-------------------------------------------------------------------
```

```
    public MyPanel()
    {
        setBackground(Color.BLACK);
        setPreferredSize(new Dimension(400,100));
    }
//----------------------------------------------------------------
    public void paintComponent ( Graphics page )
    {
        super.paintComponent(page);

        int width = getWidth();
        int height = getHeight();

        page.setColor(Color.YELLOW);
        page.drawLine(0,0,width,height);
        page.drawLine(0,height,width,0);
    }
//----------------------------------------------------------------
} // end class MyPanel
////////////////////////////////////////////////////////////////////////
```

| **Test your skill with Exercise 3-24.** |

Chapter Summary

- The Java Application Programming Interface (API) describes the classes and methods that are built into Java.
- `System.out` is a predefined instance of class `PrintStream`. It's associated with the monitor.
- Java source code is stored in files with extension `.java`.
- The Java compiler converts a source code file into a byte-code file, with extension `.class`.
- The Java Virtual Machine (JVM) runs programs by interpreting `class` files.
- The `print` and `println` methods enable us to print `String`s via a `PrintStream`.
- Boilerplate statements are statements that are required by every Java program. We may not understand these statements right now, but we have to use them as a foundation.
- Single lines can be commented using "`//`".
- Multiline comments begin with "`/*`" and end with "`*/`".
- Judicious use of white space can make programs more readable.

- Programming is simplified if we start with a working program—e.g. `Blank.java`—and add statements. If an error occurs, we know it's due to the most recently added code.
- A method is overloaded if its name occurs with two different numbers or types of parameters.
- A given problem can usually be solved in more than one way.
- AWT and Swing are Java's two GUI libraries.
- Java's graphics coordinates are an xy-coordinate system. The origin is in the upper-left corner of the screen. X increases going downward. Y increases going to the right.
- Java colors are triples of the primitives red, green, and blue (RGB).
- GUI programs typically display graphics on a `JFrame` open to the monitor.
- Java provides GUI primitives for drawing a variety of geometric shapes.
- A GUI program can display JPEG images.

Terminology Introduced in This Chapter

Abstract Windowing Toolkit (AWT)	bounding box	pixel
applet	byte code	receiver
application	color channels	RGB color system
Application Programming Interface (API)	Java Virtual Machine (JVM)	Swing
arc	JPEG	white space
boilerplate	overloading	
	picture element	

Exercises

Exercise 3-1.   Give an example of a possible logical error for the program `First.java`.

Exercise 3-2.   Generate the errors associated with the following two erroneous command lines:
```
% javac First
% java First.class
```
Observe the messages given by your compiler and operating system.

Exercise 3-3.   Prove that `Blank.java` compiles without error. What does it do when it runs?

Exercise 3-4.   Verify that `Print99.java` compiles without error. When it runs, does it do what it's supposed to do?

Exercise 3-5.   Give six programs that print
```
Java
rules!
```

Try to make them as different as possible. Your answer need only be the statements that perform the printing; however, you should try each proposed solution with a compiled and running Java program.

Exercise 3-6.   Modify `Prog0302` by commenting out the lines for `setTitle`, `setSize`, `setLocation`, and `setBackground`. To what values do these items default? Measure the screen as needed.

Exercise 3-7.   Modify `Prog0302` so that you open two `JFrame`s. Adjust the parameters so that they have different colors and so that they don't overlap.

Exercise 3-8.   Experiment with `Prog0302` by changing the size and location of the `JFrame`. Do its size and location match our discussion of the Java graphics coordinate system?

Exercise 3-9.   Write an application that draws each of the following ovals:

Bounding Box			
Upper-Left x	Upper-Left y	Width	Height
100	100	100	100
100	100	100	200
100	100	100	300
300	100	100	100
300	100	200	100
300	100	300	100

Exercise 3-10.   Write an application that draws the scene shown in Figure 3-6. Draw the scene on graph paper first.

Figure 3-6
Rings

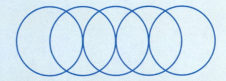

Exercise 3–11.   Write an application that draws the scene shown in Figure 3–7. Draw the scene on graph paper first.

Figure 3–7
Who? Me?

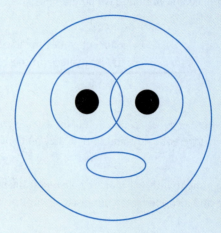

Exercise 3–12.   Write an application that draws the scene shown in Figure 3–8. Draw the scene on graph paper first.

Figure 3–8
Apologies to
Mondrian

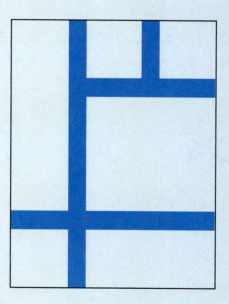

Exercise 3-13. Write an application that draws the scene shown in Figure 3-9. Draw the scene on graph paper first.

Figure 3-9
Circles

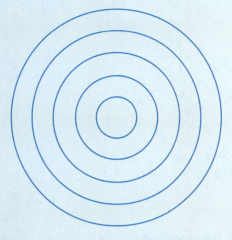

Exercise 3-14. Write an application that draws the scene shown in Figure 3-10. Draw the scene on graph paper first. To achieve the correct overlap of black and white, you'll need to draw the larger circles first.

Figure 3-10
Bull's Eye

Exercise 3–15. Write an application that draws the scene shown in Figure 3–11. Draw the scene on graph paper first.

Figure 3–11
Squares

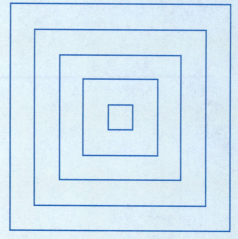

Exercise 3-16. Write an application that uses the setColor statement to draw geometric shapes in a variety of colors. Draw possible scenes on graph paper first.

Exercise 3-17. Write an application that draws the scene shown in Figure 3–12. Draw the scene on graph paper first.

Figure 3–12
Marks the Spot

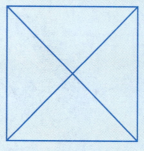

Exercise 3-18. Write an application that draws the scene shown in Figure 3–13. Draw the scene on graph paper first.

Figure 3–13
Many Lines

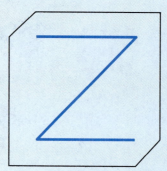

Exercise 3-19. Write an application that draws a snowman. Use an arc for the smile. Draw the scene on graph paper first.

Exercise 3-20. Write an application that draws the scene shown in Figure 3-14. Draw the scene on graph paper first.

Figure 3-14
Initial

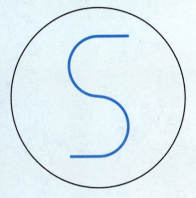

Exercise 3-21. Write an application that draws the scene shown in Figure 3-15. Draw the scene on graph paper first.

Figure 3-15
Yin and Yang

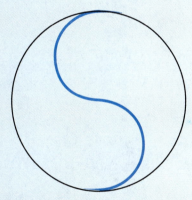

Exercise 3-22. Write an application that displays a JPEG image of your own choice.

Exercise 3-23. Write an application that displays two JPEG images. Create two `MyPanels`—`mp1` and `mp2`—and add both of them to `frame`.

Exercise 3-24. Write an application that displays a window with a white panel with a 10-pixel black border on all sides. As the window is resized, the border should adjust to the new size of the window.

CHAPTER FOUR

Using Class String

Chapter Objectives

- Declare variables and assign values.
- Use `String` literals.
- Send messages to variables and obtain result values.
- Learn the difference between `null` and the empty `String`.
- Understand method signatures and prototypes.
- Learn methods of the `String` class, including `toUpperCase`, `toLowerCase`, `trim`, and `concat`.
- Differentiate cascading and composition.
- Write GUI programs that read and display text.

This chapter uses the `String` class to examine a variety of features of Java, and of programming languages in general. We'll begin with a simple program that illustrates declaring a variable and assigning it a value, and we'll examine many variations. We'll study a few of the methods in the `String` class, and we'll learn how to combine them using composition and cascading. By the end of the chapter, you will know many different ways to solve problems that involve `String`s.

4.1 Declarations

Consider Prog0401, for which the following are the nonboilerplate statements:

```
String s;
s = "hello";
System.out.println(s);
```

Let's analyze these.

The statement

```
String s;
```

is a *declaration*. It says that

"s is a *variable* and it may only refer to objects of type String."

> **Declaration** A statement that formally creates a variable and specifies its type.
> **Variable** A name that can refer to different values during the run of a program.

As the program executes, s may refer to different instances of class String, but it may never refer to an object of any other type. The declaration does not give s a value—it merely declares its type. We can declare variables for any class. For example, the statement

```
PrintStream ps;
```

says that ps may only refer to objects of type PrintStream. We often say that s has *type* String or ps has *type* PrintStream.

Prog0401.java **Declaring, Assigning, and Printing a String Variable**

```
// Written by Barry Soroka
//
// Declaring, assigning to, printing a String variable.
//
import java.io.*;
/////////////////////////////////////////////////////////////////////////////
class Prog0401
{
//-----------------------------------------------------------------------------
    public static void main ( String [] args ) throws Exception
    {
        String s;
        s = "hello";
        System.out.println(s);
    }
```

```
//---------------------------------------------------------------
} // end class Prog0401
////////////////////////////////////////////////////////////////////
```

> **Block**   A group of statements contained within braces.

A pair of braces—{ ... }—creates a special environment called a *block*. Within a block, a variable may only be declared once, so it's illegal for a block to contain the following pair of statements:

```
String s;
String s;
```

Similarly, a block may not contain both of the following statements:

```
String s;
PrintStream s;
```

because a variable may not have two different types.

> **Test your skill with Exercises 4-1 and 4-2.**

The shorthand

```
String s1, s2, s3;
```

has the same effect as

```
String s1;
String s2;
String s3;
```

and declares three variables. Sometimes we will use the first version and sometimes we'll use the second version—it depends on which makes the code more readable.

4.2   String **Literals**

> **Literal**   A sequence of characters that specifies a particular instance of a class.

In a Java program, a *literal* is a set of characters that describes an instance of a class.[1] For example, "hello" is an instance of class String. So is "goodbye". We've seen these before in statements such as

```
System.out.println("hello");
```

---

[1]   In later chapters, we will encounter literals belonging to "primitive datatypes": -37 is an *integer* literal, and 1.25 is a *floating-point* literal.

We know that spaces are *allowed* inside `String` literals—"hello there" or "
"—and that spaces are *important* inside `String` literals. For example, "hello"
is not the same as "h ello".

> **Escape sequence**   A sequence of characters with special significance.

There is also a set of *escape sequences*, which are denoted by special symbols when they occur inside string literals. Each escape sequence begins with a backslash (\):

Escape Sequence	Effect
\t	Moves right, to the next tab position.
\n	Jumps to a new line.
\\	Inserts a backslash.
\"	Inserts a double-quote character.

We call these *escape* sequences because they are not interpreted literally as the characters themselves. Instead, they tell Java to take some special action.

4.3   Assignment Statements

In `Prog0401`, the second action statement is

```
s = "hello";
```

This is an *assignment statement*. It means

> **Assignment statement**
> Assigns a value to a variable.
> **Initialize**   To assign a first value to a variable.
> **Initialization**   The process of initializing a variable.

From this point on, s has the value "hello"

and we say that the statement *assigns* the value "hello" to the variable s. We say that s has been *initialized*—it's been given an *initial* value.

Once a value has been assigned to a variable, we can use the name of the variable to retrieve that value. For example, the statements

```
s = "hello";
System.out.println(s);
```

have the same effect as

```
System.out.println("hello");
```

except that s continues to have the value "hello".

Values of Variables Are . . . Well . . . Variable

Values of variables can change during the course of a program. Consider the code

```
String s;
s = "abc";
System.out.println(s);
s = "def";
System.out.println(s);
```

This prints out

```
abc
def
```

which shows that the value of s has changed from "abc" to "def". Each assignment to a variable wipes out the previous value of that variable.

Combining Declaration and Assignment

We can *combine declaration and assignment*: We can replace

```
String s;
s = "hello";
```

with

```
String s = "hello";
```

We can also make more complicated and mixed statements like this one:

```
String s1, s2 = "hello", s3;
```

but I think it's on the edge of being unreadable.

Right-Hand Sides

We have seen that the left-hand side of an assignment statement is a variable, and we've seen that one possible right-hand side is a *literal*:

```
s = "hello";
```

It is also possible to have a *variable* as the right-hand side:

```
String s1, s2;
s1 = "hello";
s2 = s1;
```

In the next few pages, we'll see that we can also use an *expression* on the right-hand side of an assignment.

Variables Can Receive Messages

Once we (1) declare a variable to be of a particular class, and (2) assign it a value, then the object to which the variable refers can accept any message that is appropriate to its class. For example, the following statement makes output into a PrintStream and makes it point to System.out:

```
PrintStream output = System.out;
```

Then output is a fully functional PrintStream, and it can process methods such as println:

```
output.println("Hello");
```

Declaration Must Precede Use

You have to declare a variable before you use it. The statements

```
String s;
s = "hello";
```

are legal, but the statements

```
s = "hello";
String s;
```

are not.

Test your skill with Exercise 4-3.

4.4   Objects and References

This section analyzes the following sequence of statements:

```
String s1, s2;
s1 = "hello";
s2 = s1;
s1 = "hi";
s2 = "bye";
```

Our goal is to understand exactly what is happening with the *objects*—"hello" and "hi" and "bye"—and the *references*—s1 and s2. Figures 4–1 and 4–2 show the evolution of the situation. These figures are two different ways to view the relations among references and objects.

The statement

```
String s1, s2;
```

Figure 4–1
Memory Diagram
(Format 1)

a.

b.

c.

d.

e.

Figure 4–2
Memory Diagram
(Format 2)

a.
S1 •
S2 •

b. S2 •

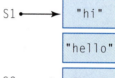

c. S2 •

S1 •⟶ "hi"

d. S2 •⟶ "hello"

S1 •⟶ "hi"

"hello"

e. S2 •⟶ "bye"

`null`   A reference without a value.

declares that s1 and s2 can refer only to `String` objects, but, initially, they don't refer to specific objects—their value is `null`. Figure 4–1(a) shows the two references, floating freely, unattached to any objects. Figure 4–2(a) also shows the references without objects.

The statement

```
s1 = "hello";
```

initializes s1. Figure 4–1(b) shows the reference s1 attached to the `String` "hello"—we may say that s1 is a *label* on the "hello" object. Note that the label s2 is still floating freely, unattached. Figure 4–2(b) shows the same situation, using an *arrow* from the reference s1 to the object "hello".

Next comes

```
s2 = s1;
```

The label s2 is now affixed to the object to which s1 refers. *We don't create a new object*—we have an object with two labels. Figures 4–1(c) and 4–2(c) display the situation.

We make `s1` refer to a new object `"hi"` by means of the statement

```
s1 = "hi";
```

We have the situation shown in Figures 4–1(d) and 4–2(d). Each label is on a different object.

Finally, we assign `s2` to a new object `"bye"`:

```
s2 = "bye";
```

> **Garbage**   Memory cells that are no longer referenced.
> **Garbage collection**   The action of reclaiming garbage cells for reuse.

Figures 4–1(e) and 4–2(e) display the situation. `"hello"` has no label—it cannot be referenced. In Java terms, it has become *garbage*—it occupies space in memory, but it cannot ever be referenced. Eventually, a process called *garbage collection* will reclaim this wasted space.

You should take the following lessons from this section:

- A single variable can refer to only one object at a time.
- A variable can refer to different objects over the course of a program.
- Two variables can refer to the same object.
- An object becomes garbage when no variable refers to it.

4.5   Java Is a Strongly Typed Language

> **Strongly typed**   A language in which a given variable may refer to objects only of the type specified when the variable is declared.

In a *strongly typed* language, a variable, once declared, has a single specific type, and it may only have values of that type.[2] So, in an assignment statement, the value on the right side of the = must be the same type as the variable on the left side. Thus, the following statement sets are legal

```
String s;
s = "hello";

PrintStream ps;
ps = System.out;
```

----

[2] On the other hand, *loosely typed* variables may take values of different types at different times. Lisp and APL are loosely typed languages.

and the statement sets below are *illegal*:

```
String s;
s = System.out;

PrintStream ps;
ps = "hello";

String s = "hello";
PrintStream ps;
ps = s;
```

HOLD YOUR HORSES

Later, we will learn that Java *sometimes* allows us to assign a value with a type different than that of the variable in an assignment statement. The conversions are not always allowed and are not always automatic.

4.6   The Empty String

Every String has a certain definite number of characters:

"hello" has 5 characters

"mom" has 3 characters

"x" has 1 character

"" has 0 characters

Empty String   A String that contains no characters.

That last String, "", is the *empty* String.

If we print it on a line by itself

```
System.out.println("");
```

we see an empty line.

The empty String can be put adjacent to any other Strings just as though it weren't there. For example,

```
System.out.println("abc");
```

is equivalent to

```
System.out.print("a");
System.out.print("");
System.out.println("bc");
```

and to

```
System.out.print("");
System.out.print("a");
System.out.print("");
System.out.println("bc");
```

and to

```
System.out.print("a");
System.out.print("");
System.out.print("b");
System.out.print("");
System.out.print("c");
System.out.println("");
```

 Test your skill with Exercises 4-4 and 4-5.

Consider the statements:

```
System.out.println("");
```

and

```
System.out.println(" ");
```

By themselves, each prints out an empty line, but we see a great difference if we surround the print version with the statements

```
System.out.print("abc");
...
System.out.println("def");
```

Here's a table:

Code	Output
System.out.print("abc"); System.out.print(""); System.out.println("def");	abcdef
System.out.print("abc"); System.out.print(" "); System.out.println("def");	abc def

> **Test your skill with Exercise 4-6.**

4.7 The Uninitialized String Variable and null

Suppose we declare a String variable s and we try to print it before we initialize it:

```
String s;
System.out.println(s);
```

What value does it have? My compiler won't compile these statements; it gives the error message

```
C:\>javac Prog9902.java
Prog9902.java:13: variable s might not have been initialized
        System.out.println(s);
                           ^
1 error
```

Java compilers often enforce the following rule:

> Don't reference a variable until you've initialized it.

Java has specific default values for uninitialized variables, but it's best to initialize variables explicitly before using them.[3]

---

[3] I've always wanted to write a compiler that assigned a random value to variables when they are declared. Any code that made assumptions about the values assigned to uninitialized variables would behave randomly, making debugging a nightmare!

In fact, upon declaration, a `String` is immediately initialized with the special value `null`. We can explicitly assign the value `null` with a statement of the form:

```
String s = null;
```

`null` is a reference that points nowhere. We can print it with the statements

```
String s = null;
System.out.println(s);
```

which prints out

```
null
```

We will soon see that a `String` variable can accept messages such as

> Return the length of the `String`

and

> Return a `String` that is like this one, but all letters are uppercase.

`null` cannot receive any of these messages because it's not pointing at a `String`—it's pointing nowhere. If we send a message to `null` or to a variable whose value is `null`, then we'll generate a `NullPointerException` and our program will halt.

`null` is not the same as the empty `String`. `null` points nowhere, but the empty `String` refers to a specific `String` that just happens to contain zero characters. The empty `String` can accept messages such as length, but `null` cannot.

`null` is not the same as the `String` `"null"`. The latter is a `String` of length four. The former is a reference pointing nowhere.

4.8 Signatures, Prototypes, and Return Types

> **Signature**   Method name + parameters.
> **Prototype**   Return type + method name + parameters.

Previously, we defined the *signature* of a method to be

> method name + parameters

and we learned that Java permitted *overloading*; that is, using the same method name more than once if the parameters were of different types.

Now we'll introduce the *prototype* of a method:

> return type + method name + parameters

The following table presents the methods we learned for class `PrintStream`:

Return Type	Method Name	Parameters
void	println	String
void	println	Ø
void	print	String

When the return type is `void`, the method does not return a value. We'll use Ø to indicate that a method takes no parameters. Here are the prototypes of the three methods in the table:

```
void println(String)
void println()
void print(String)
```

In Chapter 6, we'll use method prototypes when we're designing new classes and we want to describe the methods proposed for a new class.

4.9   Methods with a Non-`void` Return Type

For class `String`, `toUpperCase` is a typical method with a non-`void` return type. When applied to a `String`, the method `toUpperCase` returns a new `String`. This new `String` is the same as the receiving `String`, except that all alphabetical characters are now uppercase. `toUpperCase` takes no parameters, but returns a `String`. Here are three equivalent examples of how it's used:

```
String s1 = "hello";
String s2 = s1.toUpperCase();
System.out.println(s2);

String s = "hello";
System.out.println(s.toUpperCase());

System.out.println("hello".toUpperCase());
```

Expression   A value, such as one formed by an object followed by method calls.

Because the return type is non-`void`—`String`—we can use an *expression* involving `toUpperCase` as the parameter of another method:

```
System.out.println("hello".toUpperCase());
```

The underlined expression is the String that results from applying the method toUpperCase to the literal "hello".

Here's a good question: Does toUpperCase() change the String to which it's sent as a message? We can ask Java to answer this question for us:

```
String s = "hello";
System.out.println("s: " + s);
System.out.println("all caps: " + s.toUpperCase());
System.out.println("s: " + s);
```

The output of this code is:

```
s: hello
all caps: HELLO
s: hello
```

Notice that s begins as "hello" and ends as "hello" despite the fact that it's used to produce "HELLO" along the way. We can conclude that toUpperCase *uses* the receiving String but doesn't change it. This is one example of how Strings are *immutable*—they can act as receivers of methods, but they cannot be changed.

Immutable   Unchangeable.

4.10 Methods with a void Return Type

All of the PrintStream methods we've seen have a void return type:

Return Type	Method Name	Parameters
void	println	String
void	println	∅
void	print	String

Consider the statement

```
System.out.println("hello");
```

Side effect   An action performed by a method, but not its return value.

println takes a parameter, namely the String it's supposed to print, but it has no return type. println does all its work by taking an action—in this case, printing. We call such actions *side effects*.

Because `println` has `void` return type, we can't use an expression involving `println` as the parameter to another method. We can't say

```
System.out.println(System.out.println("hello"));
```

because

```
System.out.println("hello")
```

doesn't return a value; `println` does all its work with side effects.

4.11 Overloading Depends on the Signature, Not the Prototype

Recall the definitions:

signature = name + parameters

prototype = return type + name + parameters

A given class can contain both of the following methods:

```
PrintStream f()
PrintStream f(String)
```

The name `f` is overloaded. Given expressions

```
... PrintStream f() ...
... PrintStream f(String) ...
```

the compiler can look at the parameters and determine which method is being invoked by each statement.

On the other hand, a class cannot define both of these methods:

```
PrintStream g()
String g()
```

They use the name `g` but they differ only in the return type; their signatures are identical. When these methods are used, their occurrences look the same:

```
... g() ...
```

and the compiler cannot look at the code to determine which of the methods is intended.

In Chapter 6, we will define our own classes, and we'll be able to prove that overloading involves signatures and not prototypes. In particular, we'll be able to show that a class can't contain definitions of the following methods at the same time:

```
PrintStream g()
String g()
```

A class can have one or the other, but not both.

| Test your skill with Exercise 4-7. |

4.12   Class String—**Methods That Return** Strings

Class String provides many methods. We'll study some of them now, others later in the book, and some never. The API describes all of them.

The following table describes four String methods that return Strings:

Return Type	Method Name	Parameters
String	toUpperCase	∅
String	toLowerCase	∅
String	trim	∅
String	concat	String

The toUpperCase method returns a new String. This new String is the same as the receiving String, except that all characters have been changed to uppercase:

```
"hello".toUpperCase() → "HELLO"
```

Notice that the method name is followed by an empty pair of parentheses—(). This is the indicator that the method takes no parameters. You can check what Java's doing by writing a test driver containing the single line

```
System.out.println("hello".toUpperCase());
```

which will print out

```
HELLO
```

`toUpperCase` can also be applied to a `String` *variable*. The statements

```
String s = "hello";
System.out.println(s.toUpperCase());
```

will also print out

```
HELLO
```

Thus, a `String` method may be applied to a `String` literal or a `String` variable.

Note that a method invocation always requires parentheses for the parameter list *even if the method requires no parameters*. Thus,

```
"hello".toUpperCase()
```

is legal, but

```
"hello".toUpperCase
```

is not.

Test your skill with Exercises 4-8 through 4-10.

toLowerCase()

The method `toLowerCase()` behaves like `toUpperCase()`, except that the `String` returned is entirely lowercase rather than entirely uppercase.

Test your skill with Exercise 4-11.

trim()

When applied to a `String`, the method `trim()` returns a `String` that is based on the receiving `String`. Note, however, that *all leading and trailing spaces have been removed*. For example:

```
"   hello there ".trim() → "hello there"
```

The spaces embedded between nonspaces are not deleted.

Test your skill with Exercises 4-12 through 4-14.

```
concat()
```

The concat method takes two Strings—the receiving String and the parameter String—and returns their concatenation. For example:

```
"abc".concat("defg") → "abcdefg"
```

"Concatenate" comes from the Latin word for "chain," and concat is the action of *chaining* two Strings together.

 | **Test your skill with Exercises 4-15 through 4-17.** |

4.13   Cascading and Composition of Methods

In prior sections, we've constructed expressions by applying single methods to an object. For example:

```
"hello ".concat("there") → "hello there"
```

Cascading

| **Cascading**   Joining several method calls using ".". |

Cascading is a technique for applying several methods, one after another, by tacking each new method onto an expression that is already formed. For example, we can start with the expression

```
"hello ".concat("there")
```

and we can cascade another concat at the right end:

```
"hello ".concat("there").concat(", Java!")
```

which evaluates to "hello there, Java!". Or, we could tack on the method toUpperCase, getting

```
"hello ".concat("there").toUpperCase()
```

which evaluates to "HELLO THERE". Notice that the order of the methods in a cascade is very important:

Expression	Results In
"hello ".concat("there").toUpperCase()	"HELLO THERE"
"hello ".toUpperCase().concat("there")	"HELLO there"

Let's try to get a grasp on the order in which Java evaluates methods. Consider the expression

```
"hello ".toUpperCase().concat("there")
```

The first thing that Java can evaluate is the `toUpperCase` method. We'll indicate this by underlining the next subexpression to be evaluated:

```
"hello ".toUpperCase().concat("there")
```

which produces

```
"HELLO ".concat("there")
```

Java can now process the `concat` message, which we'll indicate by

```
"HELLO ".concat("there")
```

The final value of the expression is

```
"HELLO there"
```

 Test your skill with Exercise 4-18.

Composition

Composition   Using an expression as the parameter to a method.

Composition is another technique for combining methods in expressions, but it works by enlarging the parameters rather than by putting further methods at the end of expressions. For example, if we have the expression

```
"hello ".concat("there")
```

then we can compose another `concat` at the right end:

```
"hello ".concat("there".concat(", Java!"))
```

producing `"hello there, Java!"`. Notice how this differs from the corresponding cascade:

```
"hello ".concat("there").concat(", Java!")
```

We can use underlining to indicate the order in which methods are applied in the composed version:

```
"hello ".concat("there".concat(", Java!"))
"hello ".concat("there, Java!")
"hello there, Java!"
```

Cascading versus Composition

Suppose that we have four Strings—s1, s2, s3, and s4—and we want to create a new String result by concatenating them together in that order. We have two tools: cascading and composition.

For *cascading*, here's the order in which the methods are applied:

```
String result = s1.concat(s2).concat(s3).concat(s4);
                 - - - - - - - - - - - -
                 - - - - - - - - - - - - - - - - - - - - -
                 - - - - - - - - - - - - - - - - - - - - - - - - - - - - - - - -
```

For *composition*, the order is:

```
String result = s1.concat(s2.concat(s3.concat(s4)));
                                      - - - - - - - - - - - -
                                - - - - - - - - - - - - - - - - - - - - -
                 - - - - - - - - - - - - - - - - - - - - - - - - - - - - - - - -
```

Notice that the order of evaluation is different between cascading and composition. Sometimes one is appropriate, and sometimes the other is appropriate. Readability is the deciding factor.

4.14   Constructors and new

We have been using statements like the following to create instances of class String:

```
String s = "hello";
```

This is shorthand for

```
String s = new String("hello");
```

> **Constructor** A special method that creates instances of a class.

The phrase new String("hello") is an example of invoking a *constructor* for the String class: It returns an instance of String.

In general, every class has at least one constructor—a method that can be used to create an instance of that class. The constructor has the same name as the class: class String has a constructor named String; class PrintStream has a constructor named PrintStream; and so forth. When the keyword new precedes a constructor, it represents a call to the appropriate constructor, and an object of that class is created and returned.

Here is another example of the shorthand we've been using:

```
System.out.println("hello");
```

is shorthand for

```
System.out.println(new String("hello"));
```

The phrase new String("hello") is an example of invoking a constructor: It returns an instance of String, which we can send, as a parameter, to method println.

The String class has several constructors, but we can understand only two of them right now:

- String() returns the empty String.
- String("hello") returns a String representing "hello".

String methods use String constructors when they want to return a new String. Thus, inside the code for toUpperCase() we would find a call to the constructor new String(. . .).

Summary

Constructors have the same name as the class. For example, class Foo must have one or more constructors named Foo. If there's more than one constructor, then their parameters must differ, and we have an *overloaded constructor*. We invoke a constructor Foo(. . .) by saying new Foo(. . .), and the result is an instance of class Foo.

4.15   A Shortcut for String Concatenation

We've been using the following syntax to concatenate Strings:

```
"hello ".concat("there") → "hello there"
```

A shortcut allows us to use the plus sign ("+") to concatenate two Strings:

```
"hello " + "there" → "hello there"
```

   Test your skill with Exercise 4-19.

4.16   Right-Hand Side of an Assignment, Revisited

The right-hand side of an assignment can be one of three things:

- A *literal*, as in

  ```
  String s = "hello";
  ```

- A *variable*, as in

  ```
  String s1 = "hello";
  String s2 = s1;
  ```

- An *expression*, as in

  ```
  String s1 = "hello".toUpperCase();
  ```

In any case, the right-hand side must have the same type as the left-hand side.

4.17   Other Methods of the Class String

In the previous section, we studied methods of class String that returned Strings. In this section, we will take a quick glance at other String methods. These methods take *non-String parameters* or have *non-String return types*.

Class String contains a variety of methods that return non-Strings:

- length() returns an integer that is the length of the receiving String;
- indexOf(String) returns an integer that represents whether and where a parameter String occurs in the receiving String;
- equals(String) returns true or false depending on whether the receiving String and the parameter String are equal, character-by-character.

We will discuss these methods in later chapters once we've introduced Java's representation of integers and `true-false`.

Other `String` methods take non-`Strings` as parameters. In particular, class `String` contains methods involving integers:

- `substring(integer,integer)` and `substring(integer)` are methods that return a specified substring of the receiving `String`.
- `charAt(integer)` returns the *character* at a particular position in the receiving `String`.

We will study these methods in detail once we have introduced Java's representation of integers and characters.

4.18   GUI: `JLabels` and `JTextFields`

`Prog0402.java` is an application that accepts an entered `String` and echoes it. When started, we see a window such as the one shown in Figure 4–3. In addition to the frame label, we see four significant items:

- A `JLabel`—`inputLabel`—displaying `"Enter a String:"`
- A `JTextField`—`input`—an empty box that awaits our input
- A `JLabel`—`outputLabel`—displaying `"You entered"`
- A `JLabel`—`output`—currently displaying `"---"`

The program waits for us to enter a `String` in the `JTextField` input. When we do, it executes the code to accept the `String` and to display it in the `JLabel` output.

Prog0402.java   JTextField and JLabel

```
// Written by Barry Soroka
//
// Use a JTextField to read a String.
// Display it in a JLabel.
```

Figure 4–3
Initial Display

```
//
import java.io.*;
import java.awt.*;
import java.awt.event.*;
import javax.swing.*;
///////////////////////////////////////////////////////////////////////////////
class Prog0402
{
//----------------------------------------------------------------------------
   public static void main (String[] args) throws Exception
   {
      JFrame frame = new JFrame ("Using Labels & a TextField");
      frame.setDefaultCloseOperation (JFrame.EXIT_ON_CLOSE);

      frame.getContentPane().add(new MyPanel());
      frame.pack();
      frame.setVisible(true);
   }
//----------------------------------------------------------------------------
} // end class Prog0402
///////////////////////////////////////////////////////////////////////////////
class MyPanel extends JPanel
{
   private JTextField input;
   private JLabel inputLabel, outputLabel, output;
//----------------------------------------------------------------------------
   public MyPanel()
   {
      inputLabel = new JLabel("Enter a String: ");
      outputLabel = new JLabel("You entered ");
      output = new JLabel("---");

      input = new JTextField(5);
      input.addActionListener(new GetAndSet());

      add(inputLabel);
      add(input);
      add(outputLabel);
      add(output);

      setBackground(Color.YELLOW);
      setPreferredSize(new Dimension(300,40));
   }
```

```
//--------------------------------------------------------------
//////////////////////////////////////////////////////////////////////
private class GetAndSet implements ActionListener
{
//--------------------------------------------------------------
    public void actionPerformed ( ActionEvent event )
    {
        String text = input.getText();
        output.setText(text);
    }
//--------------------------------------------------------------
} // end class GetAndSet
//////////////////////////////////////////////////////////////////////
} // end class MyPanel
//////////////////////////////////////////////////////////////////////
```

The main method creates a `MyPanel` and adds it to the underlying `JFrame`.

The constructor for `MyPanel` sets up the `inputLabel` and the `outputLabel`, and initializes the `output` as "---". Then it sets up `input` as a `JTextField` with width 5, and it associates an `ActionListener` with `input`. It is the `ActionListener`—a `GetAndSet`—that watches `input` for activity. `ActionListeners` are part of Java's *event model*, requiring the statement

```
import java.awt.event.*;
```

When the user enters a `String`, the `ActionListener` is triggered and performs its action. After adding the `ActionListener` to input, the `MyPanel` constructor adds the four items to the `MyPanel` and sets the background color and default dimensions.

> **Inner class**   A class defined within another class.

`GetAndSet` is an *inner class*—a class defined inside another class. Its purpose is to allow easier access to the variables of the outer class. In the current case, the method `actionPerformed` gets the text from `input` and sets it into the `JLabel` output.

When we enter "abc" in the `JTextField`, we see the text echoed in the `JLabel` output, as shown in Figure 4–4.

When we enter "this is a very long string," we see Figure 4–5, where `output` has been shifted to a second line. The first three items are on the first line, but the fourth item spills onto a second line.

If we widen the window, as shown in Figure 4–6, we see that all the items are, once again, displayed on a single line.

Figure 4–4
A Short Entry

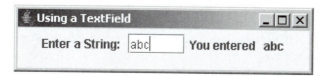

Figure 4–5
A Long Entry

Figure 4–6
After Widening

If we narrow the window, as shown in Figure 4–7, we force the second item—the JTextField input—onto the second line, and we force the fourth item—output—onto a third line.

> **Flow layout**   A GUI layout scheme wherein each new item is added to the end of a line of items, perhaps spilling over to a new line.

Our MyPanel uses *flow layout*, whereby items are added at the end of a current line until they spill over onto a next line. In Chapter 16 we will study how to use other layouts. For example, it is possible to dictate the strict position of each of the items on the MyPanel.

 Test your skill with Exercises 4-20 through 4-22.

Figure 4–7
After Narrowing

Chapter Summary

- Declaration statements create variables and specify their type.
- Java is a strongly typed language. A variable may reference only a value of the single type specified in its declaration.
- String literals are enclosed in double-quotes (e.g., `"this is a literal"`).
- Assignment statements use the equals sign ("=") to assign a value to a variable.
- Initialization is the process of assigning a first value to a variable.
- During the course of a program, a given variable may have many different values, but they must all be of the appropriate type.
- Variables must be declared before they are used.
- Memory diagrams show how variables reference values.
- `print` and `println` are methods applicable to `PrintStream`s.
- `print` puts its argument on the current output line.
- `println` puts its argument on the current output line and then finishes the line and moves onto the next line.
- The empty `String` (`""`) is a `String` that contains zero characters.
- If a `String` variable is declared but not initialized, then its value is `null`, a reference to no object.
- `null` is not the same as the empty `String`. `null` signifies that a variable has no reference value. The empty `String` is a full-fledged `String`, which just happens to be of length zero.
- The signature of a method is the method name + parameters.
- The prototype of a method is the return type + method name + parameters.
- Some methods have `void` return type. For example, `print` and `println` have `void` return type, but they have the side effect of printing their arguments.
- Methods like `toUpperCase` have non-`void` return type; they return a `String`.
- `toUpperCase` and `toLowerCase` apply to a `String` and return a new `String` in which every letter is upper- or lowercase, respectively.
- `trim` applies to a `String` and returns a new `String` for which all leading and trailing spaces have been deleted. If `trim` is applied to a `String` composed entirely of spaces, the result is the empty `String`.
- `concat` applies to a `String`; it takes a `String` and returns a new `String`, which is the concatenation of the receiver and the parameter.
- Methods are cascaded when an expression is followed by "." and a method that is to be applied to the expression.
- Methods are composed when an expression is the argument to a method.
- In general, we create an object by using "new" with a constructor.
- The literal `"hello"` is shorthand for `new String("hello")`.

- "+" can be used to command `String` concatenation. `"abc"+"def"` is the same as `"abc".concat("def")`.
- Other `String` methods, such as `length`, `indexOf`, and `equals`, will be studied in later chapters.
- A `JLabel` is a GUI object that displays a `String`.
- A `JTextField` is a GUI object that allows a program to input `Strings`.

Terminology Introduced in This Chapter

assignment statement	expression	literal
block	flow layout	null
cascading	garbage	prototype
composition	garbage collection	side effect
constructor	immutable	signature
declaration	initialize	strongly typed
empty `String`	initialization	variable
escape sequence	inner class	

Exercises

Exercise 4-1.   Try to compile a program containing the lines

```
String s;
String s;
```

Does Java allow this? If not, what message do you get?

Exercise 4-2.   Try to compile a program containing the lines

```
String s;
PrintStream s;
```

Does Java allow this? If not, what message do you get?

Exercise 4-3.   What message does the compiler give if we try to compile a program containing the statements:

```
s = "hello";
String s;
```

Exercise 4-4. Prove that the following sets of statements are equivalent. Insert them in a Java program. Compile and run the program.

```
System.out.println("abc");

System.out.print("a");
System.out.print("");
System.out.println("bc");

System.out.print("");
System.out.print("a");
System.out.print("");
System.out.println("bc");

System.out.print("a");
System.out.print("");
System.out.print("b");
System.out.print("");
System.out.print("c");
System.out.println("");
```

Exercise 4-5. Using the empty String, give six sets of statements that print out

```
Java
rules!
```

Exercise 4-6. If s1 and s2 are String variables, then how many characters are printed by the statements

```
System.out.print(s1);
System.out.print(s2);
```

Your answer should be in terms of the lengths of s1 and s2. Now consider the statements

```
System.out.print(s1);
System.out.print("");
```

How many total characters are printed? What does this imply about the length of the empty String?

Exercise 4-7. Suppose that a class defines a method with the prototype

```
String f(String)
```

Give two other methods that *can* be defined in the class.
Give two other methods that *can't* be defined in the class.

Exercise 4-8.   Write and run Java programs that prove that a `String` method may be applied to a `String` literal or to a `String` variable.

Exercise 4-9.   Give six sets of Java statements that print out `HELLO THERE`. Use Java to prove that they work.

Exercise 4-10.   What error message does Java give if a program contains the following line?

```
System.out.println("hello".toUpperCase);
```

Exercise 4-11.   Write a program that demonstrates that `toLowerCase()` does not affect the value of the receiving `String`.

Exercise 4-12.   Write a program that demonstrates what `trim()` does when the receiving `String` is empty.

Exercise 4-13.   Write a program that tests what `trim()` does when the receiving `String` consists entirely of spaces.

Exercise 4-14.   Give five expressions that produce the `String` `"Java"` using `trim()` and other methods.

Exercise 4-15.   Give five expressions that produce the `String` `"Java"` using `concat()` and other methods.

Exercise 4-16.   Write a program that proves that if we `concat` any `String` to the empty `String`, then we'll have the `String` we started with.

Exercise 4-17.   Write a program that proves that if we `concat` the empty `String` to any `String`, then we'll have the `String` we started with.

Exercise 4-18.   Show the order of evaluation for the expression:

```
"hello ".toUpperCase().concat("there")
```

Exercise 4-19. (*Also appropriate as an In-Class Exercise.*) Print

```
JAVA
rules!
```

to the monitor in as many significantly different ways as possible.

Exercise 4-20. According to the API, the argument to `JTextField` is the number of columns to display. This doesn't square with what we see in Figures 4–4 and 4–5. Experiment with `JTextField` to determine what its argument means.

Exercise 4-21. Modify `Prog0402` so that it accepts a `String` and displays it on the screen in three ways:

- as entered;
- all uppercase;
- all lowercase.

Label the outputs.

Exercise 4-22. Modify `Prog0402` so that it accepts *two* `String`s—a first name and a last name—and displays the combined name.

CHAPTER FIVE

Output and Input

Chapter Objectives

- Delete and rename files using Java programs.
- Write to a disk file using a `PrintStream`.
- Read from a disk file using a `Scanner`.
- Learn what happens when we try to read past the end of a disk file.
- Read from the keyboard using a `Scanner`.
- Write more complicated programs using the basic i/o operations.

This chapter teaches how to use Java to *read from* and *write to* disk files and the monitor. We will learn a variety of classes that Java provides for this purpose. Our goal is to learn four capabilities or patterns:

- Writing to the monitor. We've learned this already with `System.out`, `print`, and `println`.
- Writing to a disk file.
- Reading from a disk file.
- Reading from the monitor.

Additionally, we will learn how to delete and rename files.

Once we have acquired these capabilities, we will be able to use them together to solve problems such as the following:

- Read a file name from the keyboard and delete the corresponding file.
- Read a line from the keyboard and write it to a disk file.
- Read a line from a disk file and write it to the monitor.

So our approach is twofold: We'll acquire some i/o skills, and we'll assemble them to make programs that do useful work.

5.1 Characteristics of Disk Files

Disk files have a variety of characteristics that make them useful. To start with, disk files have *persistence*. They don't go away when you log off, or when you power-down your computer.

Disk files can be large. Today, a typical computer comes with 1 GB of main memory and 240 GB of hard disk space. Large files and documents are stored in hard disk files.

We use disk files to store many different types of data, including:

- Documents, such as a term paper, a letter, or the manuscript for this book.
- Spreadsheets, which represent a grade sheet, a budget, or a draft of an income tax return.
- Java source programs and files of Java byte code.
- Audio clips, such as telephone messages or popular songs.
- Image files, such as photographs or faxes.
- Video clips, such as movies or television segments.
- Email, both sent and received.
- Web page descriptors, which together comprise a website.
- Data files, which, for example, may represent data we collected for a lab course in the sciences.

In addition to its contents, a disk file has a set of attributes:

- The *name* of the file.
- *Properties*, such as *read-only* or *hidden*.
- *Permissions*, which specify the individual users or groups of users that can read or write to this file.

In this book, we will concentrate on *text files*, where file contents are *streams of characters* that people can understand. Text files can be viewed either with text editors or by using the Windows/DOS `type` command or the Unix `cat` command. We will read files line by line, and each line will be read as an individual `String`.

Which operations do we normally perform on text files?

- *Delete* the file.
- *Rename* the file.
- *Read* its contents.
- *Put* text into the file.
- *Copy* the file.
- *Edit* the file.

Some of these operations are easier than others. We'll study the file operations provided by the Java API, and we'll see that the other operations can be implemented as Java programs.

5.2   Methods of Class File

Java's class `File` represents disk files, providing constructors and other appropriate methods. `Prog0501` gives the Java program that deletes the file named `foo`. In order to access class `File` and its methods, we must put the statement

```
import java.io.*;
```

above class `Prog0501`. We'll need this so often that I recommend you put it in your `Blank.java`.

Prog0501.java   **Deleting a File**

```
// Written by Barry Soroka
//
// Delete the file named "foo"
//
import java.io.*;
///////////////////////////////////////////////////////////////////////////////
class Prog0501
{
//--------------------------------------------------------------------------------
```

```
public static void main ( String [] args ) throws Exception
{
    File f = new File("foo");
    f.delete();
}
```
```
//----------------------------------------------------------------------
} // end class Prog0501
////////////////////////////////////////////////////////////////////////
```

Test your skill with Exercise 5-1.

The statement

```
File f = new File("foo");
```

creates an instance of class `File`, and f points to a file named `foo`. Java doesn't require that the file already exist—`foo` may be the name of a file that we intend to *create*. On the other hand, Java *does* check the proposed file name to be sure that it obeys the rules of the operating system in use. Operating systems differ in terms of the allowed length of file names and the characters that are allowed in file names.

Test your skill with Exercise 5-2.

exists()

Java provides a method `exists()` that, when applied to a `File`, tells us whether the `File` exists or not. Its result is of type `boolean`—`true` or `false`—which we won't study until Chapter 8. At that time, we'll learn how to take different actions depending on whether or not the file exists.

Test your skill with Exercise 5-3.

delete()

The second statement in `Prog0501` does the deleting:

```
f.delete();
```

What might go wrong?

1. The file f might not exist.
2. We may not have permission to delete it.

The delete method actually returns a boolean value that indicates whether or not the delete was successful. Here we will use it only for its side effect, not for its result.

Test your skill with Exercise 5-4.

Renaming a File

Prog0502 shows the code that changes the name of a file from foo to bar. First, we must create *two* File objects: one representing the old file name, and the other representing the new file name:

```
File f = new File("foo");
File g = new File("bar");
```

Then we rename f by sending it a message renameTo(g):

```
f.renameTo(g);
```

What might go wrong?

1. File foo might not exist.
2. File bar might *already* exist, making it impossible to rename foo to bar.
3. File foo might be read-only or otherwise protected so that we can't rename it.

Prog0502.java   **Renaming a File**

```
// Written by Barry Soroka
//
// Rename the file "foo" to be "bar"
//
import java.io.*;
////////////////////////////////////////////////////////////////////////////
class Prog0502
```

```
{
//----------------------------------------------------------------------
    public static void main ( String [] args ) throws Exception
    {
        File f = new File("foo");
        File g = new File("bar");
        f.renameTo(g);
    }
//----------------------------------------------------------------------
} // end class Prog0502
///////////////////////////////////////////////////////////////////////
```

| **Test your skill with Exercise 5-5.** |

Review, and Some Shortcuts

Here are the methods we have learned for File so far:

Method Name	Parameters	Return Type
exists	∅	boolean
delete	∅	void
renameTo	File	void

The result of a new operation is an object, and it can be the receiver of messages. Thus, the lines

```
File f = new File("foo");
f.delete();
```

can be written as the single line

```
(new File("foo")).delete();
```

The lines

```
File f = new File("foo");
File g = new File("bar");
f.renameTo(g);
```

can be written as the single line

```
(new File("foo")).renameTo(new File("bar"));
```

5.3   Writing to the Monitor

This is the easiest form of output, and we've used it in previous chapters. `System.out` is a predefined instance of `PrintStream`, which points at the monitor. We can use the `PrintStream` methods

```
void print(String)
void println(String)
void println()
```

to write to `System.out`.

5.4   Writing to a Disk File

We'll approach this task in two stages, assuming that we are given a `String` that is the name of the target disk file:

- First, we'll associate a `PrintStream` with the given disk file.
- Next, we'll apply `PrintStream` methods to do the actual writing.

Once we have a `PrintStream` object pointing at the file, we know how to use the `print` and `println` methods to send the desired text to that destination.

`Prog0503` gives the code that writes a few lines to the file `foo`. The first action statement is:

```
PrintStream ps = new PrintStream(
                    new FileOutputStream(
                        new File("foo")));
```

Creating a `PrintStream` from a file name requires three steps:

- First, we create a `File` from the `String`.
- Second, we create a `FileOutputStream` from the `File`.
- Third, we create a `PrintStream` from the `FileOutputStream`.

It's best to memorize this code; you'll apply it many times in the future.

You should add the following lines at the bottom of your `Blank.java` file:

```
/*
        PrintStream ps = new PrintStream(
                            new FileOutputStream(
                                new File(filename)));
*/
```

Whenever you need to produce a `PrintStream` from a file name, you can uncomment, move, and edit these lines as required.

Prog0503.java   Writing to a File

```
// Written by Barry Soroka
//
// Write a few lines to the file "foo"
//
import java.io.*;
///////////////////////////////////////////////////////////////////////////
class Prog0503
{
//------------------------------------------------------------------------
    public static void main ( String [] args ) throws Exception
    {
        PrintStream ps = new PrintStream(
                            new FileOutputStream(
                                new File("foo")));
        ps.println("hello");
        ps.println("another line");
        ps.println();  // a blank line
        ps.println("this is the last line");
    }
//------------------------------------------------------------------------
} // end class Prog0503
///////////////////////////////////////////////////////////////////////////
```

To generate these lines from scratch, you can use the mnemonic

Please Stop Frying Our Small Fry

according to the following chart:

Please	
Stop	PrintStream
Frying	
Our	FileOutputStream
Small	
Fry	File

 Test your skill with Exercise 5-6.

Stylistic Considerations

Consider the problem of writing the String `"hello"` to the file `foo`. As usual, there's more than one way to write the code. Here's the original version:

```
PrintStream ps = new PrintStream(
                      new FileOutputStream(
                          new File("foo")));
ps.println("hello");
```

This code is concise and parsimonious. Note how each `new` lines up with a token in the line above.

Consider the code:

```
File f = new File("foo");
FileOutputStream fos = new FileOutputStream(f);
PrintStream ps = new PrintStream(fos);

ps.println("hello");
```

From Java's point of view, this code is equivalent to the previous version, but I'd criticize it because it introduces the unnecessary variables `f` and `fos`. They're declared here, but used only once and then forgotten.

Here's an even more bloated version of the code:

```
File f;
FileOutputStream fos;
PrintStream ps;

f = new File("foo");
fos = new FileOutputStream(f);
ps = new PrintStream(fos);

ps.println("hello");
```

Notice how the declarations for `f`, `fos`, and `ps` have been separated from the corresponding assignment statements. *Locality* is lost. We have to look higher up in the program to see the type of a variable being used below.

My style recommendations are these:

- Use composition to keep the code readable.
- Don't define variables that you only use once.

5.5 Reading from a Disk File

Writing required a special class `PrintStream`, which could point at either the monitor or a disk file. Once pointed, we could apply the methods `print` and `println` in order to output `String`s to the `PrintStream`.

Reading is similar: It requires a special class `Scanner`, which can point at either the keyboard or a disk file. Once pointed, we can apply the method `nextLine` in order to read `String`s from the `Scanner`.

Prog0504 reads the first line of file `foo` and writes it to the monitor. In order to use class `Scanner`, we need to include the statement

```
import java.util.Scanner;
```

The first action statement creates a `Scanner`, which points to the file named `foo`:

```
Scanner sc = new Scanner(new File("foo"));
```

The next line of `Prog0504` is

```
String line = sc.nextLine();
```

The method `nextLine` reads the next `String` from the `Scanner` to which it is applied, and the next statement

```
System.out.println(line);
```

prints that `String` to the monitor. We could combine those two lines into one:

```
System.out.println(sc.nextLine());
```

Prog0504.java   Reading from a File

```
// Written by Barry Soroka
//
// Read the first line of the file "foo" and print it to the monitor.
//
import java.io.*;
import java.util.Scanner;
///////////////////////////////////////////////////////////////////////////
class Prog0504
{
//-------------------------------------------------------------------------
    public static void main ( String [] args ) throws Exception
```

```
    {
        Scanner sc = new Scanner(new File("foo"));
        String line = sc.nextLine();
        System.out.println(line);
    }
//---------------------------------------------------------------------
} // end class Prog0504
//////////////////////////////////////////////////////////////////////////
```

Reading Three Lines from a File

Prog0505 is a program that reads three lines from the file Prog0505.java. Each invocation of nextLine reads the next line from the receiving Scanner.

Prog0505.java **Reading and Echoing Three Lines from a File**

```
// Written by Barry Soroka
//
// Read the first three lines of the file "Prog0505.java"
// and print them to the monitor.
//
import java.io.*;
import java.util.Scanner;
//////////////////////////////////////////////////////////////////////////
class Prog0505
{
//---------------------------------------------------------------------
    public static void main ( String [] args ) throws Exception
    {
        Scanner sc = new Scanner(new File("Prog0505.java"));
        System.out.println(sc.nextLine());
        System.out.println(sc.nextLine());
        System.out.println(sc.nextLine());
    }
//---------------------------------------------------------------------
} // end class Prog0505
//////////////////////////////////////////////////////////////////////////
```

NOTE A *Java source file*, such as Prog0505.java, is simply another text file. It can be read line by line using nextLine. Without this capability, how would the Java compiler process a Java source file?

You should add the following line in a comment at the bottom of your `Blank.java` file:

```
Scanner kb = new Scanner(File(filename));
```

Then you can copy and edit it to places in your programs where you need to create `Scanner`s pointing to specific files.

5.6   Reading Past the End of a File

Suppose we have a program that opens a `Scanner` to file `foo` and then reads the first two lines of the file:

```
Scanner sc = new Scanner(new File("foo"));
System.out.println(sc.nextLine());
System.out.println(sc.nextLine());
```

Suppose file `foo` is empty or contains a single line. What might happen when the Java program tries to read past the end of the file? What are the possibilities? Think about it before reading on.

STOP AND THINK

In cases such as these, where `nextLine` is asked to read beyond the end of a file, Java throws an `Exception`—a `NoSuchElementException`—giving the additional information `No line found`.

 Test your skill with Exercise 5-7.

In Chapter 13 we'll learn how to detect the end of a file before trying to apply `nextLine` to the corresponding `Scanner`. We'll use this knowledge to write programs that loop through *all* the lines of a file.

5.7   Reading from the Keyboard

The previous section presented the code that allows us to read `String`s from a *disk file*. Now we'll turn our attention to reading from the *keyboard*. Our approach will be to create a `Scanner` that points at the keyboard, and then to invoke the `nextLine` method to read a full line as a `String`.

Prog0506 reads a line from the keyboard and reports it to the monitor. We create the required Scanner with the line

```
Scanner kb = new Scanner(System.in);
```

I have named the Scanner kb because kb reminds me that this Scanner is pointed at the *keyboard*. System.in is a predefined object that points to the keyboard.

Prog0506.java   Reading a Line from the Keyboard

```java
// Written by Barry Soroka
//
// Read a line from the keyboard.
// Report it to the monitor.
//
import java.io.*;
import java.util.Scanner;
////////////////////////////////////////////////////////////////////////////
class Prog0506
{
//-------------------------------------------------------------------------
    public static void main ( String [] args ) throws Exception
    {
        Scanner kb = new Scanner(System.in);

        System.out.print("Enter a String: ");
        String line = kb.nextLine();
        System.out.println("You entered \"" + line + "\"");
    }
//-------------------------------------------------------------------------
} // end class Prog0506
////////////////////////////////////////////////////////////////////////////
```

You should add the following line in a comment at the bottom of your Blank.java file:

```
Scanner kb = new Scanner(System.in);
```

Whenever you need to produce a Scanner for the keyboard, you can copy and paste this line.

The next two statements in `Prog0506` are:

```
System.out.print("Enter a String: ");
String line = kb.nextLine();
```

Notice the first line:

```
System.out.print("Enter a String: ");
```

> **Prompt** A program output that tells the user what is requested.

This statement *prompts* the user, telling what sort of input is expected. We call such a statement a *prompt*.

You should always prompt before taking input. Otherwise, the program waits for input, and the user may not know what sort of input is required.

The line

```
String line = kb.nextLine();
```

fills variable `line` with the `String` entered by the user, and the line

```
System.out.println("You entered \"" + line + "\"");
```

prints out the `String` between double quotes. Note that these two lines could be combined into the single line

```
System.out.println("You entered \"" + kb.nextLine() + "\"");
```

 Test your skill with Exercises 5-8 through 5-10.

5.8 Patterns and Reuse

In this chapter, we've seen how to read and write from disk files and the terminal. These are *patterns* that we will adapt again and again for a wide variety of problems. We won't reinvent this code every time we need it; we remember it and recall it when it is needed.

You will need to develop three skills:

- Remember patterns and be able to reproduce and adapt them.
- Recognize which patterns are required for a given problem.
- Assemble and adapt the patterns into the appropriate order to solve the problem.

In order to avoid excess typing, you should take your `Blank.java` file and add, as a comment, the archetypal code for reading and writing. This is shown as the file `Blank.java`. When you need a statement for reading or writing, copy the appropriate template statement to the place where it's needed, and edit it so that it serves your purpose.

Blank.java   A Blank Template File for Java Programs

```
// Written by Barry Soroka
//
// description of this program
//
import java.io.*;
import java.util.Scanner;
/////////////////////////////////////////////////////////////////////////////
class Blank
{
//---------------------------------------------------------------------------

    public static void main ( String [] args ) throws Exception
    {
    }
//---------------------------------------------------------------------------

} // end class Blank
/////////////////////////////////////////////////////////////////////////////
/*
        Scanner kb = new Scanner(System.in);

        Scanner sc = new Scanner(new File(filename));

        PrintStream ps = new PrintStream(
                            new FileOutputStream(
                                new File(filename)));
*/
```

Example

Consider the following problem:

> From the keyboard, read the name of a file.
> Print the first line of that file to the monitor.

We begin by outlining the structure of the solution:

- Open a `Scanner`—`kb`—to the keyboard.
- Prompt for a file name.
- Read a file name.
- Open a `Scanner`—`sc`—to the specified file.
- Read a line from `sc`.
- Print the line to `System.out`.

We flesh out this skeleton using (1) adaptations of the appropriate i/o statements, and (2) other required statements. `Prog0507` shows the final version of the program.

Prog0507.java **A Complicated Program Using the Primitives**

```java
// Written by Barry Soroka
//
// Read the name of a file
// and print the first line of that file to the terminal.
//
import java.io.*;
import java.util.Scanner;
///////////////////////////////////////////////////////////////////////////////
class Prog0507
{
//--------------------------------------------------------------------------
    public static void main ( String [] args ) throws Exception
    {
        Scanner kb = new Scanner(System.in);

        System.out.print("Filename? ");
        String filename = kb.nextLine();

        Scanner sc = new Scanner(new File(filename));

        String line = sc.nextLine();
        System.out.println(line);
    }
//--------------------------------------------------------------------------
} // end class Prog0507
///////////////////////////////////////////////////////////////////////////////
```

5.9 Practice!

The contents of this chapter will enable you to solve numerous problems involving input to and output from files and the terminal. You will encounter these problems in homework assignments, in labs, and on exams. Solving such problems involves the same steps we used above: Identify the skeleton of the solution, and then flesh out that skeleton with the appropriate statements, including i/o statements.

There is no secret process for generating these problems. Each problem results from a combination of the capabilities we've acquired in this chapter:

- Deleting a file.
- Renaming a file.
- Writing to the monitor.
- Writing to a disk file.
- Reading from the keyboard.
- Reading from a disk file.

Once you've seen the exercises at the end of this chapter, you should be able to create problems similar to those that might appear on exams.

I recommend that students work in pairs. Each student should create problems for the other student to solve. If you practice enough, then you won't be surprised or puzzled by the problems you'll encounter on the exams.

Chapter Summary

- Disk files can store large quantities of persistent data.
- The `File` constructor creates `File` objects from `String`s that are file names.
- Method `delete` deletes the file associated with a `File` object.
- Method `exists` can determine whether or not a file exists.
- Method `rename` renames a file.
- `System.out` is the `PrintStream` associated with the monitor.
- We can associate `PrintStream` objects with disk files.
- We write to `PrintStream`s using the `print` and `println` methods.
- The first step in reading from the keyboard is to associate a `Scanner` with `System.in`.
- The first step in reading a disk file is to associate a `Scanner` with the file.
- Method `nextLine` applies to `Scanner`s and reads the next line from the associated file or keyboard.
- Complicated programs can be built up from the primitive i/o operations.

Terminology Introduced in This Chapter

prompt

Exercises

Exercise 5-1. Remove the `import` statement from `Prog0501`. Does it compile? What message does the compiler give?

Exercise 5-2. Alter `Prog0501` so that it specifies a file name that is illegal for your operating system. What message does the compiler give?

Exercise 5-3. The following lines will report `true` or `false`, depending on whether or not file `foo` exists.

```
File f = new File("foo");
System.out.println("foo exists? " + f.exists());
```

Run this code for two cases:

1. `foo` exists;
2. `foo` doesn't exist.

Exercise 5-4. Alter `Prog0501` so that it tries to delete

1. a file that exists;
2. a file that doesn't exist.

What is the difference in the way that Java handles the two cases?

Exercise 5-5. Try `Prog0502` on an acceptable case and on the following three special cases:

1. When the receiving `File` does not exist.
2. When the parameter `File` already exists.
3. When the receiving `File` is read-only or otherwise protected so that we can't rename it.

What messages does Java give when `renameTo` fails? Are the messages informative and reasonable?

Exercise 5-6. Write a program that writes the lines

```
hello
there
```

to a file named `myFirstFileOutput`.

Exercise 5-7. Write and run a program that demonstrates how Java behaves when we try to read past the end of a file.

Exercise 5-8.   What does `Prog0506` print when you press only `Enter` in response to the prompt?

Exercise 5-9.   What does `Prog0506` print when you enter just a space and press `Enter` in response to the prompt?

Exercise 5-10.   Write a program that reads two `String`s from the keyboard and then prints them—concatenated in both orders—on two lines. Here's an example where what the user types is underlined:

```
% java Prog99
Enter String 1: abc
Enter String 2: d e
abcd e
d eabc
```

Exercise 5-11.   Here is the specification of a program:
Write a program that reads a file name from the keyboard and then deletes that file. Here is the required i/o; what the user types is underlined:

```
% java Deleter
Enter a filename: foo
That file has now been deleted!
%
```

Show the hard copy you must give the instructor in order to demonstrate that your program works correctly. *Note:* You do not need to write the program.

Exercise 5-12.   Write a Java program `Renamer` that reads a file name from the user. This file contains two lines. The first line is the name of an existing file that we will rename. The second line is the new name to be given to the existing file. Thus, if the user enters the file name `foo`, and `foo` contains the lines

```
bar
bar.out
```

then the effect of `Renamer` would be to rename the file `bar` as `bar.out`.

Exercise 5-13.   Write a Java program that reads a file name from the keyboard and then writes the first line of that file to a new file. The new file should have the same name as the input file, except with ".out" appended to the name. For example, if the user enters the file name `foo`, then your program should copy the first line of file `foo` to file `foo.out`.

Exercise 5-14. Write a Java program that writes `hello` to both the monitor and to the file `foo`.

Exercise 5-15. Write a Java program that writes `hello` to the monitor and `goodbye` to the file `foo`.

Exercise 5-16. Write a Java program that reads a file name from the user and then writes the first two lines of that file to the monitor.

Exercise 5-17. Write a Java program that reads a file name from the user and then writes the first two lines of that file to the monitor, but in reverse order: second line first, then first line.

Exercise 5-18. Write a Java program `Cases` that reads a file name from the user, then reads the first line of that file, then writes it out to the monitor in three different ways: as found, all uppercase, and all lowercase.

Here is a typical test run, where what the user types is underlined:

```
% java Cases
Enter a filename: foo
Hello U2!
HELLO U2!
hello u2!
%
```

Obviously, this example assumes that the first line of the file `foo` is "Hello U2!".

Exercise 5-19. Write a Java program with the following behavior:

- Ask the user for the names of two files. Let's call these `filename1` and `filename2`.
- Read the first line of each of these files, and concatenate these lines to get the name of a third file.
- Write the `String` "hello" to the third file.

For instance, if the first line of `file1` is "still" and the first line of `file2` is "waiting", then your program must write the `String` "hello" to a new file named `stillwaiting`.

Exercise 5-20. Fill in the blanks in the following table. If a method name appears more than once, then the method is overloaded and you should give different signatures for the two lines on which it appears.

Method Name	Class to Which It Applies	Return Type	Parameters
concat			
delete			
exists			
length			
print			
println			
println			
renameTo			
substring			
substring			
trim			
toUpperCase			

Exercise 5–21. Give five different problems that use reading and writing on files.

Exercise 5–22. Give several pieces of code that solve a problem you select. Discuss the pros and cons of each solution.

CHAPTER SIX

Defining New Classes

Chapter Objectives

- Define new classes and methods.
- Define overloaded methods.
- Use instance variables.
- Learn visibility modifiers `public` and `private`.
- Define constructors for new classes.
- Write getters and setters.
- Learn the hazards of sharing data structure among multiple references.
- Use newly defined classes as parameters and result types.
- Use the `this` pointer inside constructors and methods.
- Define `toString` methods.
- Write `static read` methods for reading the components of an object and creating an instance.
- Learn the difference between class methods and instance methods.
- Learn a methodology for designing and writing new classes.
- Understand default constructors.
- Take in values from command line arguments.

C hapter 2 introduced the object-oriented paradigm, and we studied how to take a real-world problem and identify the appropriate classes, methods, and instances. Then we wrote programs that used the predefined object `System.out` to write `String`s to the monitor. In Chapter 4, we learned how to declare variables and how to assign them values. We also studied how methods are characterized by their signatures and prototypes. In Chapter 5 we used Java classes to read and write from disk files, read from the keyboard, and write to the monitor.

We have (1) used predefined objects, and (2) created instances of predefined classes. Now we'll define our own new classes in Java. We'll start with simple classes in order to grasp the relevant syntax and semantics. Then we'll design classes that use more of Java's capabilities. Finally, we will summarize the class design process.

6.1   Our First Class Definition

Our first example is a class Teacher containing a constructor and a simple method lecture(). Prog0601.java shows the code. Notice that the program contains two classes: class Prog0601 and class Teacher.

Prog0601.java   Initial Code for Class Teacher

```java
// Written by Barry Soroka
//
// Initial code for class Teacher.
//
/////////////////////////////////////////////////////////////////////////////
class Prog0601
{
//---------------------------------------------------------------------------
   public static void main ( String [] args ) throws Exception
   {
      Teacher t = new Teacher();
      t.lecture();
   }
//---------------------------------------------------------------------------
} // end class Prog0601
/////////////////////////////////////////////////////////////////////////////
class Teacher
{
//---------------------------------------------------------------------------
   public Teacher() {}
//---------------------------------------------------------------------------
   public void lecture()
   {
      System.out.println("do your homework!");
   }
```

```
//------------------------------------------------------------------
} // end class Teacher
//////////////////////////////////////////////////////////////////////////
```

Prog0601 is a *driver* containing the main method that tells the JVM where to grab and start this Java program. This class can be understood on its own even if we did not have access to the code of class Teacher. Consider the first statement:

```
Teacher t = new Teacher();
```

Teacher t tells us that Teacher is the name of a *class* and that variable t will be of type Teacher. The phrase new Teacher() tells us that class Teacher must contain a constructor that takes no parameters. The second statement is

```
t.lecture();
```

Since t is an instance of class Teacher, this statement tells us that class Teacher must contain a *method* lecture(), which takes no parameters.

If someone gives us a driver, we can determine the classes it uses and the methods defined in those classes. Correspondingly, when we are trying to design a class or set of classes, we will often write a driver *first*, in order to see what methods are required that we still need to write.

What does this program, Prog0601, do? Run it. You'll see that it prints

```
do your homework!
```

Let's now look at the code for class Teacher. Our file Prog0601.java shows the *completed* class, but let's begin by examining its general structure. We'll ignore the comments for the moment.

From high up, the class Teacher looks like this:

```
class Teacher
{
    . . .
}
```

Instance variable Private data of an object.
Visibility modifier A specifier of `public` versus `private`.

Class definitions begin with the word `class`, followed by the name of the class we're defining. Then comes a pair of braces[1]—{...}. Inside the braces we'll put method definitions and *instance variables*, which flesh out the class. For `Teacher`, we have two methods: a constructor `Teacher()` and a method `lecture()`. Let's examine the syntax and semantics of these two methods.

Consider the constructor

```
public Teacher() {}
```

The word `public` is a *visibility modifier*, which tells Java that we want this method to be visible outside the class `Teacher`. In general, methods are `public` because we define them *inside* one class, but they're intended to be used by other methods *outside* the class.

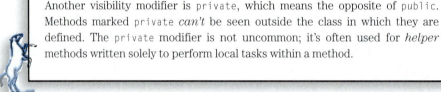

HOLD YOUR HORSES

Another visibility modifier is `private`, which means the opposite of `public`. Methods marked `private` *can't* be seen outside the class in which they are defined. The `private` modifier is not uncommon; it's often used for *helper* methods written solely to perform local tasks within a method.

The next word in the constructor is `Teacher`, which is *the name of the class*. When Java sees the phrase `public class-name` at the start of a method, it assumes that we are defining a constructor.

The next part of the constructor is an empty pair of parentheses—(). These parentheses enclose the *parameters* of the constructor. Because they're empty, it means that this constructor takes *no* parameters, and we are able to say

```
new Teacher()
```

---

[1] Some authors call them "*curly* brackets." Another example of paired punctuation is [...], which I call "*square* brackets."

to create an instance, but not

```
new Teacher("john")
```

because the constructor we're defining takes no parameters.

The last part of the constructor is an empty pair of braces—{}. These braces enclose the *body* of the constructor—the Java statements that represent the work to be done by this constructor. In the case of `Teacher`, the braces are empty because we simply want to *create* an instance of `Teacher`, but we aren't doing anything else. As we will see later, constructors often do quite a bit of work as they create an instance of their class.

TRY IT OUT   Can a class contain two constructors with no parameters? Write the code to test this. One such constructor might have an empty body. Another might contain a `println` statement. Is Java happy?

Let's look at the code for the `lecture` method. Here are its pieces:

- `public` means it's visible outside the class `Teacher`. We need this because `lecture` will be called from class `Prog0601`.
- `void` means that the method has no return value. Unlike a square-root function, for example, `lecture` doesn't return anything. To be useful, it must perform an action *inside* the method. In this case, the useful action will be printing. These nonreturn actions are called side effects.
- `lecture` is the name of the method.
- The empty parentheses—`()`—tell Java that this method takes no parameters.
- The braces—{...}—enclose the single statement in the *body* of the method, namely

```
System.out.println("do your homework!");
```

Now let's examine the *comments* that `Prog0601.java` has added to the basic structure of classes `Prog0601` and `Teacher`. These comments have been dictated by the style sheet (Appendix 1), and their purpose is to make the code more readable. At the top of the file we have written the name of the program's author and a brief comment that describes the purpose of the program. Other comments are used to show where classes and methods begin and end:

- Every *class* is surrounded by rows of *slashes*—//////////...
- Every *method* is surrounded by rows of *dashes*—//----------...

The end of each class is emphasized by a comment of the form

```
// end class class-name
```

Within each class, we define constructors (if any) *before* we write methods. Finally, each new level of code is indented by three spaces.

6.2 Overloading a Method

Prog0602.java is a minimal change from Prog0601.java—we overload the method named lecture. When we compile and run the program, we see the following output:

```
do your homework!
sara, do your homework!
```

In the driver, note that we have added the line t.lecture("sara"). This requires that the class Teacher contain a new method void lecture(String).

Prog0602.java   **Overloading Method lecture of Class Teacher**

```
// Written by Barry Soroka
//
// Overload the lecture method of class Teacher.
//
////////////////////////////////////////////////////////////////////////////////
class Prog0602
{
//---------------------------------------------------------------------------
   public static void main ( String [] args ) throws Exception
   {
      Teacher t = new Teacher();
      t.lecture();
      t.lecture("sara");
   }
//---------------------------------------------------------------------------
} // end class Prog0602
////////////////////////////////////////////////////////////////////////////////
class Teacher
{
//---------------------------------------------------------------------------
   public Teacher() {}
//---------------------------------------------------------------------------
```

```
   public void lecture()
   {
      System.out.println("do your homework!");
   }
//-------------------------------------------------------------------
   public void lecture ( String name )
   {
      System.out.println ( name + ", do your homework!");
   }
//-------------------------------------------------------------------
} // end class Teacher
/////////////////////////////////////////////////////////////////////
```

> **Coding and Debugging**
> Whenever you are learning a new programming language, you should test each new feature by making a minimal change to a program that already works.

Let's examine the new method, word by word. Its prototype is this:

```
public void lecture ( String name )
```

- `public` means that this method can be seen outside the class definition. Methods are usually `public`.
- `void` means that the method has no return value. The method is useful only because of its side effect, namely printing to `System.out`.
- `lecture` is the name of the method. Because the class already contains a method named `lecture`, this name is considered to be overloaded. As required, the methods that overload a name must have different signatures.
- `( String name )` tells Java that this method takes one argument, which must be of type `String`. I have selected `name` as the name of that variable; any unused variable name would have been equally legal. I chose `name` because its value will represent the *name* of a student in the class. As noted in the style sheet (Appendix 1), variable names should be meaningful, not random.

TRY IT OUT

Overloading involves only the signature and not the prototype. With respect to overloading, the return value is ignored. Prove this by trying to write a class that contains two methods that differ only in *return value*. Their signatures should be identical, but their prototypes should be different. Is Java happy with this?

TRY IT OUT   Does Java allow a method to have two parameters with the same name?

    Test your skill with Exercise 6-1.

6.3   Introducing Instance Variables

In the last two programs we defined a class `Teacher` and we demonstrated how to define methods and how to overload methods. Class `Teacher`, however, suffers from a significant limitation: Every instance of `Teacher` is identical. `Teacher`s share common methods, but they possess no feature—such as a name—that would make them distinguishable. Now we are going to introduce another class, `Animal`, and each instance of `Animal` will be distinguished by its *name* and the *sound* it makes. For example, we might have an `Animal` named

> **Slot**   A colloquial term for an instance variable.

`fluffy` that makes the sound `meow`, and we might have an `Animal` named `fido` that makes the sound `woof`. They will share common methods, but each `Animal` will have two private data *slots*—instance variables—that belong only to that `Animal`.

`Prog0603.java` presents the class `Animal` and a driver `Prog0603` that exercises it. Let's examine the first few statements of the driver. Initially, the program invokes a constructor to create an `Animal`:

```
Animal a1 = new Animal("fluffy","meow");
```

The phrase `Animal a1` signals that `Animal` is a class and `a1` is an instance of that class. The next phrase is

```
new Animal("fluffy","meow")
```

What does it tell us? First, it says that `Animal` is the name of a class (we knew this already from the earlier part of the statement). Second, the phrase calls a constructor with *two* parameters, both of them `String`s. Our program will not compile unless class `Animal` defines such a constructor. The first parameter is the name of the `Animal` and the second parameter is the sound made by that `Animal`. Overall, this statement creates `a1`, a reference to a new `Animal`.

Prog0603.java   **Initial Code for Class Animal**

```java
// Written by Barry Soroka
//
// Initial code for class Animal.
//
///////////////////////////////////////////////////////////////////////////////
class Prog0603
{
//------------------------------------------------------------------------------
    public static void main ( String [] args ) throws Exception
    {
        Animal a1 = new Animal("fluffy","meow");
        a1.speak();
        Animal a2 = new Animal("fido","woof");
        a2.speak();
        Animal a3 = a2;
        a3.speak();
        a1 = new Animal("bessie","moo");
        a1.speak();
    }
//------------------------------------------------------------------------------
} // end class Prog0603
///////////////////////////////////////////////////////////////////////////////
class Animal
{
    private String name;
    private String sound;
//------------------------------------------------------------------------------
    public Animal ( String theName, String theSound )
    {
        name = theName;
        sound = theSound;
    }
//------------------------------------------------------------------------------
    public void speak()
    {
        System.out.println ( name + " says " + sound );
    }
//------------------------------------------------------------------------------
} // end class Animal
///////////////////////////////////////////////////////////////////////////////
```

The second statement—a1.speak();—tells us that class `Animal` provides a method `speak` that takes no parameters. This is reminiscent of the `lecture()` method of class `Teacher`.

The next two statements are as follows:

```
Animal a2 = new Animal("fido","woof");
a2.speak();
```

and their effect is to create a new `Animal` to which `a2` will refer. These statements are similar to those we analyzed above *except that* this `Animal` has a different name (`fido`) and a different sound (`woof`) than the previous `Animal`.

Now let's examine the definition of the class `Animal`. (We'll return to the driver in a little while.) The class `Animal` has a slightly different structure than that of class `Teacher`. This difference is required because `Animal`s have instance variables and `Teacher`s do not. Seen "from above," class `Animal` can be described as:

```
class Animal
{
    instance variables
    constructor(s)
    method(s)
}
```

We've seen constructors before, and we've seen methods before, but class `Animal` shows us how to define instance variables. The relevant statements are:

```
private String name;
private String sound;
```

Notice the structure:

```
private type variable-name;
```

Instance variables are `private`, which means that they can be seen only inside the class. In particular, only methods of the class—including constructors—

can change or reference the instance variables. We don't allow methods outside the class to reference or modify the instance variables directly.

> In general, *instance variables* are `private` and *methods* are `public`.

NOTE

> **HOLD YOUR HORSES**
>
> It may seem counterproductive to make instance variables private. Objects outside the class can get access to the instance variables, but only via the methods of the class. Wouldn't it be more efficient to allow objects outside the class to reach in and get or set instance variables directly? At first, this argument seems convincing, but it ignores the fact that instance variables can't have just any arbitrary value. Most instance variables need to be *validated*: a person's weight can't be negative and a person's name can't be a string of punctuation symbols. Also, some variables may be *coupled*: for a `Circle`, the `radius`, `area`, and `perimeter` are not independent.[2] We can't allow an outside method to put an object into an *invalid state*. For example, we must prevent having a `Circle` with `radius 0.0` and `area 1.0`. We build the validation into the methods of the class, and we require that outsiders touch the variables only through the validating—and validated—methods we provide.

Validate   To verify that values are sensible and legal.

Now that we can specify instance variables in the class definition, we need to learn how to *fill* the instance variables for a particular instance (object). Let's examine the constructor for class `Animal`:

```
public Animal ( String theName, String theSound )
{
    name = theName;
    sound = theSound;
}
```

---

[2]   Some languages allow the declaration of *constraints*—couplings—and can generate code to update coupled variables when one variable changes, thereby enforcing the constraint. Java does not provide this capability.

Figure 6–1
When the
Construction Is
Called

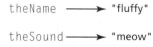

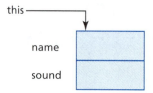

This method uses four variables: `theName`, `theSound`, `name`, and `sound`. What do they do? `name` and `sound` refer to the *slots* of the `Animal` object being created, and we selected these variable names when we defined the instance variables. `theName` and `theSound` refer to the parameters sent in a call to the constructor.[3] Figure 6–1 shows the situation. When a constructor is invoked, Java grabs ("allocates") the memory required to hold the instance variables—in our case, each `Animal` has a slot for `name` and a slot for `sound`. During construction, a special reference, `this`, refers to the object being constructed. The parameters of the constructor are matched to the actual arguments used in the call to the constructor. Now, the statements

```
name = theName;
sound = theSound;
```

cause the `name` slot to point wherever `theName` is pointing, and cause the `sound` slot to point wherever `theSound` is pointing. Figure 6–2 shows the situation *after* exiting the constructor. So, we understand our first example of constructors and instance variables.

HOLD YOUR HORSES

Only one of many schemes for naming constructor parameters has been shown. Other schemes will be shown in a later section.

---

[3]   We could have named these randomly, but it makes more sense to match `name` with `theName` and `sound` with `theSound`.

Figure 6–2
After Exiting the
Construction

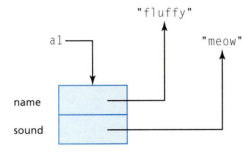

Now let's examine the `speak` method:

```
public void speak()
{
    System.out.println ( name + " says " + sound );
}
```

Question: How does this differ from the `lecture(String)` method of class `Teacher`? *Answer:* Instead of printing the method's *parameter*, it prints the *instance variables* of the object receiving the lecture message. Put another way, inside method `speak`, `name` refers to the `name` slot and `sound` refers to the `sound` slot of the receiver.

HOLD YOUR HORSES

You may be wondering what will happen if the parameter of a method has the same name as an instance variable. We'll discuss this later.

BY THE WAY

Our style sheet puts the instance variables at the top of the class definition. By seeing them *first*, we are primed to understand them when they appear later in constructors and methods.

Some authors put the instance variables at the end of the class, after the constructors and methods. I don't like that style. As we read down the method, we have to jump to the bottom to see the instance variables and then jump back up to where we were reading a method that uses them. I think it's better to present the instance variables first.

We've just learned the *syntax* used for instance variables:

- defining the variables at the top of the class,
- validating and assigning values passed via constructors, and
- using the instance variables in the methods of the class.

Now let's examine the *semantics* displayed in the driver class `Prog0603`. When we run this program, we see the following output:

```
fluffy says meow
fido says woof
fido says woof
bessie says moo
```

The first statement

```
Animal a1 = new Animal("fluffy","meow");
```

creates the memory structure shown in Figure 6–2, and the statement

```
a1.speak();
```

produces the expected output

```
fluffy says meow
```

Similarly, the statements

```
Animal a2 = new Animal("fido","woof");
a2.speak();
```

produce the memory structure shown in Figure 6–3 and the output

```
fido says woof
```

Figure 6–3 brings up an important rule of Java programming:

Do not use unnecessary instance variables in a class definition.

Every additional instance variable consumes an additional slot in every object created from the class definition. If we define one unnecessary instance variable, and we create 10,000 instances of the class, then we will have wasted 10,000 memory slots. This waste can incapacitate a program very quickly.

Figure 6–3
Memory Diagram
(1)

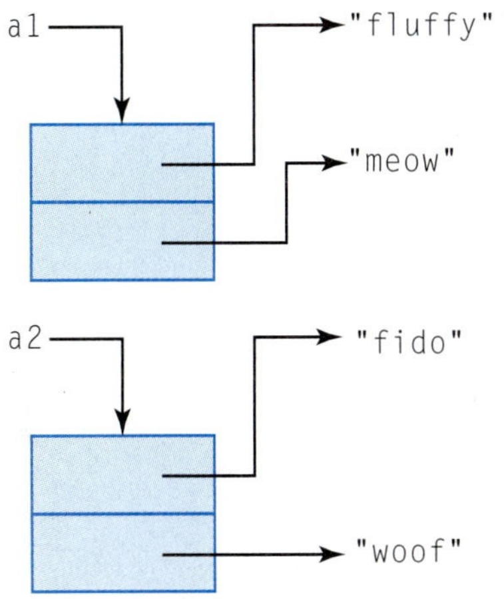

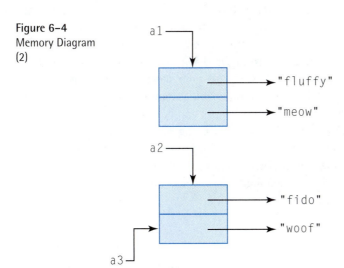

Returning to Prog0603, the next statement is

```
Animal a3 = a2;
```

Shared data structure
Memory cells that can be accessed by more than one reference.

which yields the memory map shown in Figure 6–4. Note that a2 and a3 refer to the same object: The fido-woof object is *shared*, and the phenomenon is called *sharing data structure*. Put another way, the fido-woof object has two names. The statement

```
a3.speak();
```

Figure 6–4
Memory Diagram
(2)

Figure 6–5
Memory Diagram
(3)

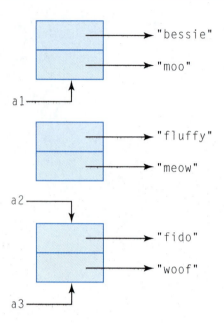

now produces the output

```
fido says woof
```

as expected. The next statement is

```
a1 = new Animal("bessie","moo");
```

Garbage Memory cells that are no longer referenced.

Garbage Memory cells that are no longer referenced. **Garbage collection** The action of reclaiming garbage cells for reuse.

and it causes a1 to refer to a new instance of Animal, as shown in Figure 6–5. Look at the memory holding the fluffy-meow object: Nothing is pointing at it anymore! This means that *no program statements can access this object in any way*. We call such orphaned memory *garbage*. From time to time, Java examines memory and reclaims the unreachable memory in a process called *garbage collection*. The reclaimed memory can be used for future objects. If garbage is allowed to accumulate without being reclaimed, then the program will eventually run out of memory. One symptom of this problem is that the program becomes slower and slower and eventually halts.

Getting back to Prog0603, the final executable statement

```
a1.speak();
```

results in the expected output

```
bessie says moo
```

6.4   Schemes for Naming Constructor Parameters

In the previous section, we saw a constructor for the class `Animal`. I mentioned that the names of the constructor parameters could be chosen *arbitrarily*, but that a *consistent naming scheme* would make our code more readable. Employers and clients will insist on your using their particular naming scheme. My goal in this section is to show you several popular approaches.

Here's the code we presented above:

```
public Animal ( String theName, String theSound )
{
    name = theName;
    sound = theSound;
}
```

Our naming scheme was this: We made the name of a parameter by prefixing `the` to the corresponding instance variable. A variant on this scheme is to use the prefix `a` or `an`, yielding parameters `aName` and `aSound`.

Another approach is to use an underscore as a suffix to the names of the instance variables:

```
public Animal ( String name_, String sound_ )
{
    name = name_;
    sound = sound_;
}
```

One variant on this scheme puts the underscore first—`_name`—and another variant puts the underscores on the names of the *instance variables* instead of the parameters. Our style sheet reserves underscores for separating the words of constants.

Here's an example of poorly chosen parameter names:

```
public Animal ( String a, String b )
{
    name = a;
    sound = b;
}
```

The variables `a` and `b` have no logical relation to the instance variables `name` and `sound`. The reader of the code seeks meaning in the `a` and `b`. Why were they chosen? What do they mean? If the constructor contained many state-ments, readers might forget what `a` and `b` stood for, and they would have to keep looking back up to the top of the constructor in order to know which parameter was which. If I were grading this code, the top line of the constructor would be marked BVN—Bad Variable Name—and the code, although correct, would not receive full credit.

Here's the scheme I prefer right now:[4]

```
public Animal ( String name, String sound )
{
    this.name = name;
    this.sound = sound;
}
```

What's new about this code? The variables name and sound appear in several contexts. Consider sound:

- We have the parameter variable sound.
- We have the phrase this.sound.
- We have the phrase . . . = sound;.

Let's first consider the *parameters* name and sound. As parameters, we know that they refer to the values being sent to the constructor by the caller. No problem.

What about name and sound in the body of the constructor? What might these refer to? There are two choices: They could refer to (1) the parameters coming in to the constructor, or (2) the instance variables of the object being constructed. Java resolves this ambiguity by dictating the following:

> If a name can refer to either a parameter or an instance variable,
> then that name refers to the parameter.

Unlike in the constructors we've seen before, name and sound do not refer to the instance variables because those variables are *blocked* by the parameter names that have higher priority. That's why we see the phrases this.name and this.sound. Consider the assignment statements

```
this.name = name;
this.sound = sound;
```

---

[4] I say "right now" because, as I write more and more Java code, my preferred style changes. This code reads the best and causes me the fewest problems, so it's currently preferred. Programming is an art, not a science.

> **this pointer**   A reference to the object being constructed or to the receiver of a method.

The left-hand sides refer to the *instance variables* of the object being constructed, and the right-hand sides refer to the values of the *parameters*.

Java provides the this mechanism to allow code to see past the parameters to the instance variables. We will often talk about "the this pointer" even though it sounds silly. In a constructor, the this pointer is always pointing to the instance being constructed.

In this section, four different ways of naming the variables used by the constructor for class Animal have been presented. To the compiler, these ways are all equivalent, but human readers will find some schemes easier to understand than others. When you program as a professional, your employer or client will specify the style you must use. *Why should they care what style you use?* Because your code will be read by others who will need to modify it, and it's easier to read code if all of the programmers obey the same conventions.

 Test your skill with Exercises 6-2 through 6-8.

6.5   Getters and Setters

In an earlier section, we talked about the rule that says that, in general, instance variables should be private, prohibiting methods outside the class from directly reading or changing their values. Now we will examine *methods* that can be called from outside the class to read and write values in a responsible fashion. To *read* the value of an instance variable, we can provide a *getter* (AKA *accessor* or *accessor method*). To *change* the value of an instance variable, we can provide a *setter* (AKA *mutator* or *mutator method*). Prog0604.java illustrates defining and using getters and setters for class Animal.

> **Accessor/Getter**   A method that returns the value of an instance variable.
> **Mutator/Setter**   A method that sets the value of an instance variable.

Prog0604.java   **Getters and Setters for Class Animal**

```
// Written by Barry Soroka
//
// Demonstrates getters & setters for class Animal.
//
//////////////////////////////////////////////////////////////////////////////
class Prog0604
{
//--------------------------------------------------------------------------
    public static void main ( String [] args ) throws Exception
```

```
   {
      Animal a1 = new Animal("fluffy","meow");
      System.out.println();
      System.out.println( a1.getName() + " says " + a1.getSound() );
      a1.speak();

      a1.setSound("hisss");
      System.out.println();
      System.out.println( a1.getName() + " says " + a1.getSound() );
      a1.speak();

      a1.setName("pretzel");
      System.out.println();
      System.out.println( a1.getName() + " says " + a1.getSound() );
      a1.speak();
   }
//----------------------------------------------------------------------
} // end class Prog0604
////////////////////////////////////////////////////////////////////////
class Animal
{
   private String name;
   private String sound;
//----------------------------------------------------------------------
   public Animal ( String theName, String theSound )
   {
      name = theName;
      sound = theSound;
   }
//----------------------------------------------------------------------
   public void speak()
   {
      System.out.println ( name + " says " + sound );
   }
//----------------------------------------------------------------------
   public String getName() { return name; }
//----------------------------------------------------------------------
   public void setName ( String newName ) { name = newName; }
//----------------------------------------------------------------------
   public String getSound() { return sound; }
//----------------------------------------------------------------------
   public void setSound ( String newSound ) { sound = newSound; }
//----------------------------------------------------------------------
} // end class Animal
////////////////////////////////////////////////////////////////////////
```

The getter for variable `sound` is:

```
public String getSound() { return sound; }
```

Let's dissect this:

- The getter is `public` so that it can be accessed by methods outside the class.
- The return type—`String`—matches the type of the variable being accessed: `sound` has type `String`.
- The method name `getSound` results from putting the word `get` in front of the name of the instance variable—`sound`. We capitalize the first letter of `sound` because it's the second word of a multiword method name. `getSound` is used here, but the method name could be *any* valid name.
- The getter has no arguments: It's a message sent directly to an `Animal`, and its sole job is to return the current value of `sound`.
- Finally, the body of the getter is the single `return` statement, enclosed in the required pair of braces.

I have written the entire `getSound` method on one line because `getSound` is a simple method and it fits on a single line. Here's another way it could be written:

```
public String getSound()
{
    return sound;
}
```

Let's look at the *setter* for variable `sound`:

```
public void setSound ( String newSound ) { sound = newSound; }
```

- The setter is `public` so that it can be accessed by methods outside the class.
- The return type is `void`. The setter's job is to change the current value of `sound`. It has a side effect— it has nothing to return.[5]

---

[5]   Some authors require that a setter return the old value that is being overwritten.

- `setSound` is the name of the setter. This comes by combining `set` and `sound`. We have to capitalize `Sound` because it's the second word of a multi-word method name.
- The setter takes a parameter, which is the new sound. The type of the parameter—`String`—is the same as the type of the instance variable it's updating. `newSound` is an excellent name for this parameter because it exactly describes the purpose of the parameter.
- Finally, the body of the method contains the single statement

```
sound = newSound;
```

- This is the action we want the setter to perform.

Again, I have written the method `setSound` on a single line because the method is simple and because it fits on one line.

The getter and setter for the variable `name` are analogous to those for `sound`.

Now let's see how getters and setters are used in the driver `Prog0604`. The first statement is

```
Animal a1 = new Animal("fluffy","meow");
```

which sets up an `Animal` object as shown in Figure 6–6(a). Then the statement

```
System.out.println( a1.getName() + " says " + a1.getSound() );
```

uses the getters to obtain the `name` and `sound` of the `Animal`:

- `a1.getName()` returns a `String` that is the `name`.
- `a1.getSound()` returns a `String` that is the `sound`.

Finally, three `Strings` are concatenated and then printed by `println`:

```
fluffy says meow
```

Note that this is the same output that we get from the next statement, `a1.speak()`. In one case a method of the class uses the instance variables directly. In the other case, getters bring the instance variables outside the object, where we can perform the appropriate work.

The next statement is

```
a1.setSound("hisss");
```

Figure 6–6
Using Getters and Setters

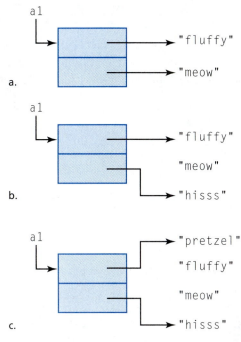

a.

b.

c.

and its effect is to change the value of sound in Animal a1. Figure 6–6(b) shows the situation. Note that the String "meow" is now garbage, because no object refers to it. The println statement now prints

```
fluffy says hisss
```

and we get the same result from the statement a1.speak().

Finally, the statement

```
a1.setName("pretzel");
```

changes the value of a1's name slot, resulting in the memory diagram of Figure 6–6(c). Now, as expected, both the println statement and the a1.speak() statement produce the output

```
pretzel says hisss
```

Test your skill with Exercises 6-9 through 6-10.

6.6 Problems with Sharing Data Structure

Prog0605.java illustrates some awkward behavior that can occur when we use setters with shared data structures. The file contains the class Animal as we've written it so far, and the driver is tailored to illustrate the surprising behavior.

Prog0605.java   Be Careful with Shared Data!

```java
// Written by Barry Soroka
//
// Be careful when using setters on shared data.
//
////////////////////////////////////////////////////////////////////////////
class Prog0605
{
//---------------------------------------------------------------------------
    public static void main ( String [] args ) throws Exception
    {
        Animal a1 = new Animal("fluffy","meow");

        Animal a2 = a1;    // Beware!  Memory structure is being shared.

        a1.speak();
        a2.speak();

        a2.setName("pretzel");

        System.out.println();
        a1.speak();
        a2.speak();
    }
//---------------------------------------------------------------------------
} // end class Prog0605
////////////////////////////////////////////////////////////////////////////
class Animal
{
    private String name;
    private String sound;
//---------------------------------------------------------------------------
    public Animal ( String theName, String theSound )
    {
        name = theName;
        sound = theSound;
    }
```

```
//----------------------------------------------------------------------
   public void speak()
   {
      System.out.println ( name + " says " + sound );
   }
//----------------------------------------------------------------------
   public String getName() { return name; }
//----------------------------------------------------------------------
   public void setName ( String newName ) { name = newName; }
//----------------------------------------------------------------------
   public String getSound() { return sound; }
//----------------------------------------------------------------------
   public void setSound ( String newSound ) { sound = newSound; }
//----------------------------------------------------------------------
} // end class Animal
//////////////////////////////////////////////////////////////////////
```

Consider the first two statements of the driver:

```
Animal a1 = new Animal("fluffy","meow");
Animal a2 = a1;
```

These statements set up the memory structure shown in Figure 6–7(a). Notice that a1 and a2 are referring to the same shared object. The two speak statements—a1.speak() and a2.speak()—result in the output:

```
fluffy says meow
fluffy says meow
```

Since both variables refer to the same object, we certainly expect the output to be the same. The next statement is

```
a2.setName("pretzel");
```

which seems to change only a2, but the memory structure becomes that shown in Figure 6–7(b).[6] We have explicitly changed a2, but a1 has also been changed, which you may not have expected. When we execute the statements

```
a1.speak();
a2.speak();
```

---

[6] The String "fluffy" is garbage, but that's not significant for the current discussion.

Figure 6–7
Shared Data
Structure

a.

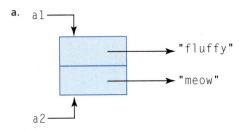

b.

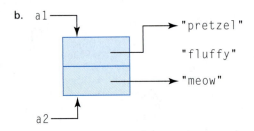

c.

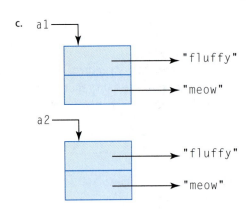

d.

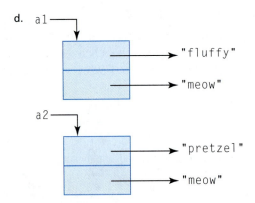

we get the output

```
pretzel says meow
pretzel says meow
```

Again, since a1 and a2 are referring to the same object, we expect the speak method to produce the same output for both references.

What's the problem? Well, we made a change to a2 and it caused a change to a1 as well. Whenever an object is shared, we run the risk of changing it via one reference and then being *surprised* when we access it via another reference. When things are shared, we need to take special care not to make changes unless all of the sharers expect things to change.

Here's a simple real-life example. Suppose John Smith lives at 1422 Meadow Avenue. If a bank's computer program executes the command

```
Deposit $1 million in the account of the customer
who lives at 1422 Meadow Avenue
```

then we may be surprised to discover that John Smith, formerly overdrawn, now has almost $1 million in his account. And it won't be easy to locate and fix this error, because there's no deposit statement that explicitly mentions *John Smith*. We must be careful when two names refer to the same object.

Copy Constructors

Recall the statements

```
Animal a1 = new Animal("fluffy","meow");
Animal a2 = a1;
```

Copy constructor   A constructor that produces a copy of an object.

which cause both a1 and a2 to refer to the same object in memory. If our intention was to have a2 refer to a *copy* of a1, then we need to use what is called a *copy constructor*. Prog0606.java shows the code. Our driver becomes this:

```
Animal a1 = new Animal("fluffy","meow");
Animal a2 = new Animal(a1);
```

where we have added a one-parameter constructor to class `Animal`. That parameter is the `Animal` object we want to copy. The code for the copy constructor is this:

```
public Animal ( Animal that )
{
    this.name = that.name;
    this.sound = that.sound;
}
```

We create a new `Animal` whose slots have the same values as those of the parameter. Figure 6–7(c) shows the memory diagram at this point. When we execute the statement

```
a2.setName("pretzel");
```

we get the memory diagram shown in Figure 6–7(d). The call to `setName` has changed only one of the `Animal`s because they don't point to the same object in memory.

Prog0606.java   Copy Constructor for Class Animal

```
// Written by Barry Soroka
//
// Copy constructor for class Animal.
//
/////////////////////////////////////////////////////////////////////////////
class Prog0606
{
//-------------------------------------------------------------------------
    public static void main ( String [] args ) throws Exception
    {
        Animal a1 = new Animal("fluffy","meow");

        Animal a2 = new Animal(a1);   // copy constructor

        a1.speak();
        a2.speak();

        a2.setName("pretzel");
```

```
         System.out.println();
         a1.speak();
         a2.speak();
      }
//-----------------------------------------------------------------------
} // end class Prog0606
/////////////////////////////////////////////////////////////////////////
class Animal
{
   private String name;
   private String sound;
//-----------------------------------------------------------------------
   public Animal ( String theName, String theSound )
   {
      name = theName;
      sound = theSound;
   }
//-----------------------------------------------------------------------
   public Animal ( Animal that )
   {
      this.name = that.name;
      this.sound = that.sound;
   }
//-----------------------------------------------------------------------
   public void speak()
   {
      System.out.println ( name + " says " + sound );
   }
//-----------------------------------------------------------------------
   public String getName() { return name; }
//-----------------------------------------------------------------------
   public void setName ( String newName ) { name = newName; }
//-----------------------------------------------------------------------
   public String getSound() { return sound; }
//-----------------------------------------------------------------------
   public void setSound ( String newSound ) { sound = newSound; }
//-----------------------------------------------------------------------
} // end class Animal
/////////////////////////////////////////////////////////////////////////
```

Figure 6–8
Deeper Sharing

a.

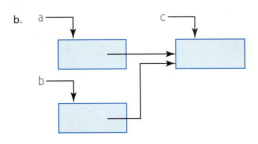

b.

HOLD YOUR HORSES

If the slots of an object point to other objects, there is a deeper form of sharing against which our naïve copy constructor has not protected us. Consider Figure 6–8(a), which shows object a with a slot pointing to object c. If we use a copy constructor to create object b from object a, we get the memory diagram in Figure 6–8(b). Both a and b have a slot pointing to object c. Several unexpected phenomena can occur:

- Using the reference c, a program could modify the object to which the slots in both objects a and b are pointing. This may or may not be what we want.
- Using either the reference a or b, a program could change the slots of object c. We run the risk of changing a slot of object a and discovering that a slot of object b has been changed unintentionally, and vice versa.

To make a copy of an object, we need to call for copies of all its slots and copies of all their slots.

Test your skill with Exercises 6-11 through 6-13.

6.7   Last Words on Setters and Getters

Setter methods have responsibilities beyond those we've discussed so far because not all values are valid for the variables being changed. Just like a constructor, a setter must *validate* the value it's given. For example, a Circle cannot have a negative radius.

Some instance variables may be *coupled*. If a Circle keeps track of both radius and area, then a change to either radius or area must affect the other variable as well, in order to keep the values consistent. This is the responsibility of the setter.

> **HOLD YOUR HORSES**
>
> Using coupled variables is not always a good idea. It allows for objects to have an inconsistent state.

Setters and getters are not difficult to write. In fact, it's a straightforward process to take an instance variable and generate the code for its setter and getter.[7] Of course, we can't automatically generate a setter if it involves validation or coupled variables.

Test your skill with Exercise 6-14.

6.8   What If a Parameter Is a User-Defined Object?

Let's add something new to class `Animal`. Suppose we want the output

```
fido is chasing fluffy
```

to be produced by the code

```
Animal a1 = new Animal("fido","woof");
Animal a2 = new Animal("fluffy","meow");
a1.chases(a2);
```

The novelty here is that the method `chases` is taking a parameter of type `Animal`, a class that we defined ourselves. We've written methods that take *predefined* objects (e.g., `String`) as parameters, but this new program will show that *user-defined* classes have the same status as predefined classes. In particular, objects from classes that *we* write can be passed as parameters to methods.

---

[7]   The C# language and the Eclipse interactive development environment can automatically generate simple getters and setters.

Consider program `Prog0607.java`, which produces the following output:

```
fido is chasing fluffy
fluffy is chasing fido
fido is chasing fido
```

Before reading on, look at the code and look at the output. Can you make sense of the code for the `chases` method?

 **AND THINK**

Prog0607.java   Using an **Animal** as a Parameter

```java
// Written by Barry Soroka
//
// chases is a method that takes an Animal as parameter.
//
////////////////////////////////////////////////////////////////////////////////
class Prog0607
{
//------------------------------------------------------------------------------
   public static void main ( String [] args ) throws Exception
   {
      Animal a1 = new Animal("fido","woof");
      Animal a2 = new Animal("fluffy","meow");
      a1.chases(a2);
      a2.chases(a1);
      a1.chases(a1);
   }
//------------------------------------------------------------------------------
} // end class Prog0607
////////////////////////////////////////////////////////////////////////////////
class Animal
{
   private String name;
   private String sound;
//------------------------------------------------------------------------------
   public Animal ( String theName, String theSound )
   {
      name = theName;
      sound = theSound;
   }
```

```
//--------------------------------------------------------------------
   public void chases ( Animal target )
   {
      System.out.println ( this.name + " is chasing " + target.name );
   }
//--------------------------------------------------------------------
   public void speak()
   {
      System.out.println ( name + " says " + sound );
   }
//--------------------------------------------------------------------
   public String getName() { return name; }
//--------------------------------------------------------------------
   public void setName ( String newName ) { name = newName; }
//--------------------------------------------------------------------
   public String getSound() { return sound; }
//--------------------------------------------------------------------
   public void setSound ( String newSound ) { sound = newSound; }
//--------------------------------------------------------------------
} // end class Animal
///////////////////////////////////////////////////////////////////////////
```

What complicates chases is that it involves two objects of type Animal. Consider the typical invocation, a1.chases(a2), where a1 is the *receiver* of the chases message, and a2 is the *parameter* being passed to chases. Inside chases, *the this pointer refers to the object that receives the message*, and we can get to an instance variable of the receiving object by prefixing its name with this. Similarly, we can get to an instance variable of any *parameter* object by prefixing its name with the name we chose for that parameter. In this case, I chose target for the name of the parameter. If we write *this*.name, then we're pointing at the name of the *receiving object*. If we write *target*.name, then we're pointing at the name of the *parameter object*. In other words, this is bound to the receiving object, and target is bound to the parameter object.

Inside a method, the this pointer refers to the receiver of the method.

Consider the statement a1.chases(a2). Figure 6–9(a) shows the situation as seen from *outside* the chases method: a1 and a2 are each referring to objects of type Animal. Figure 6–9(b) shows the situation as seen from *inside* the chases method while the statement a1.chases(a2) is being executed: this is pointing to the receiver (a1), and target is pointing to the parameter (a2). Any reference to this will be a reference to a1, and any reference to target will be a reference to a2. Thus, the statement

```
System.out.println ( this.name + " is chasing " + target.name );
```

Figure 6-9
Bindings inside a
Method

a.

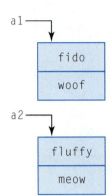

b.

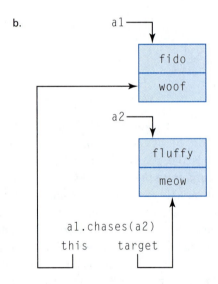

creates a String using:

- the name of the receiver (this),
- the literal String " is chasing ", and
- the name of the parameter (target).

Finally, chases prints that String to the terminal:

```
fido is chasing fluffy
```

 Test your skill with Exercises 6-15 through 6-18.

6.9   What If the Return Type Is a User-Defined Object?

We've written methods that returned objects from *predefined* classes:

```
public String getName() { return name; }
public String getSound() { return sound; }
```

Both `getName` and `getSound` returned `String`s. Now we'll write a method that returns an object of type `Animal`, a *user*-defined class that was not predefined by Java. We'll write a method `makeBig` that, when applied to an `Animal`, returns a new `Animal` object in which the `name` and `sound` are "bigger" than those of the receiving `Animal`. Here are two input/output examples of how `makeBig` should work:

Receiver Values		Result Values	
name	sound	name	sound
"fido"	"woof"	"big fido"	"WOOF"
"fluffy"	"meow"	"big fluffy"	"MEOW"

In English, we can describe `makeBig` by saying

- The `name` of the *result* is `"big"` + the `name` of the *receiver*.
- The `sound` of the *result* is the uppercase of the `sound` of the *receiver*.

Tables such as the one above are often helpful in designing and describing our methods.

`Prog0608.java` shows the code for `makeBig`. The driver, `Prog0608`, starts by creating and exercising an `Animal` object a1:

```
Animal a1 = new Animal("fido","woof");
a1.speak();
```

The output of the `speak` statement is this:

```
fido says woof
```

The driver then uses `makeBig` to create a new `Animal` object a2:

```
Animal a2 = a1.makeBig();
```

Figure 6–10
After `makeBig`

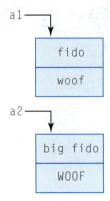

Notice two *unrelated* things:

- `makeBig` takes no parameters.
- It doesn't change its receiver.

The method `makeBig`, when applied to an `Animal` object, produces a new `Animal` object in which the slots have values that are based on the values of the receiving `Animal`. Put another way, the expression `a1.makeBig()` evaluates to an `Animal` object, enabling us to assign its result to the `Animal` reference `a2`. Figure 6–10 is a memory diagram after evaluation of `a2 = a1.makeBig()`. Note that `a1` and `a2` are completely different objects. The final statement of the driver is

```
a2.speak();
```

and it produces the output

```
big fido says WOOF
```

Prog0608.java   Using **Animal** as a Return Type

```
// Written by Barry Soroka
//
// makeBig is a method that returns an Animal
//
////////////////////////////////////////////////////////////////////////////
class Prog0608
{
//-------------------------------------------------------------------------
    public static void main ( String [] args ) throws Exception
    {
```

```
      Animal a1 = new Animal("fido","woof");
      a1.speak();

      Animal a2 = a1.makeBig();
      a2.speak();
   }
//----------------------------------------------------------------------
} // end class Prog0608
////////////////////////////////////////////////////////////////////////
class Animal
{
   private String name;
   private String sound;
//----------------------------------------------------------------------
   public Animal (String theName, String theSound )
   {
      name = theName;
      sound = theSound;
   }
//----------------------------------------------------------------------
   public Animal makeBig()
   {
      String resultName = "big " + name;
      String resultSound = sound.toUpperCase();
      return new Animal(resultName,resultSound);
   }
//----------------------------------------------------------------------
   public void speak()
   {
      System.out.println ( name + " says " + sound );
   }
//----------------------------------------------------------------------
} // end class Animal
////////////////////////////////////////////////////////////////////////
```

Let's examine the code for `makeBig`, starting with its prototype

```
      public Animal makeBig()
```

What do the pieces tell us?

- `public` means that this method can be invoked by methods outside the class. In general, methods are `public`.

- `Animal` says that this method returns an instance of class `Animal`. This is the significant feature of the example: It returns an instance of a *user-defined* class.
- `makeBig` is the name of the method.
- The empty parentheses mean that this method takes no arguments.

The method `makeBig` continues by computing the values of the slots of the `Animal` it must return. The first executable statement is

```
String resultName = "big " + name;
```

Local variable   A variable that exists only during execution of a method.
Scope   Statements that can "see" a particular variable.

The variable `name` refers to the instance variable of the receiver. The statement creates a *local variable*, `result-Name`, which is appropriately derived from the `name` slot of the receiver.

> **NOTE**
>
> Whenever you see a phrase of the form
>
> $$\langle type \rangle \ \langle variable\text{-}name \rangle$$
>
> you are witnessing the creation of a local variable. Such a variable is defined within a *scope* delimited by braces. The variable comes into existence when defined, and it vanishes when execution moves out of the scope. We have seen many instances of local variables in this and prior chapters.

The next statement in `makeBig` is

```
String resultSound = sound.toUpperCase();
```

which creates another local variable, `resultSound`. `resultSound` is appropriately transformed from the `sound` instance variable of the receiver. Finally, having created the temporaries `resultName` and `resultSound`, `makeBig` creates a new `Animal` object using the new values:

```
return new Animal(resultName,resultSound);
```

The phrase `new Animal(..., ...)` is a call to the constructor of class `Animal`. When a method returns an object, we will usually see calls to the constructor of that class. In makeBig, the Animal created will have the appropriate values of name and sound. When makeBig is finished, the local variables vanish; the memory they occupied becomes garbage.

Earlier, we saw:

> If a name can refer to either a parameter or an instance variable,
> then that name refers to the parameter.

A second rule is this:

> If a name can refer to either a local variable or a parameter,
> then that name refers to the local variable.

Test your skill with Exercise 6-19.

NOTE   The makeBig method doesn't change the slots of the receiving object. Its purpose was to create a new object that is appropriately derived from the receiver. However, nothing in Java syntax prevented us from intentionally or accidentally changing the instance variables of the receiver.[8] Thus, a programmer could produce a version of makeBig that appears to work, but that accidentally changes the slots of the receiver. That's one reason why testing is such an important part of the software design process.

BY THE WAY   Some languages contain syntactic constructs that tell the compiler *not* to permit changes to the receiver or to parameters.

TRY IT OUT   Prove that you can't have two local variables with the same name in the same scope.

Test your skill with Exercises 6-20 through 6-24.

---

8   All setters fall into this category: They change the slots of their receivers.

6.10 Schemes for Returning Objects from Methods

We've just seen one way to write the code for makeBig(), a method that, when applied to an Animal, returns another Animal. Here's the code we studied:

```
public Animal makeBig()
{
    String resultName = "big " + name;
    String resultSound = sound.toUpperCase();
    return new Animal(resultName,resultSound);
}
```

This method *invented names* for two local variables that we would use to create the values of the instance variable of the result. (The names were not chosen randomly: I got the names by prefixing "result" to the appropriate instance variable and capitalizing as required by our style sheet.) We'll now examine some other ways of writing this method.

Consider the following:

```
public Animal makeBig()
{
    String name = "big " + name;
    String sound = sound.toUpperCase();
    return new Animal(name,sound);
}
```

I've made local variables using the exact names of the instance variables, and this meant that I had to use the this pointer whenever I needed to access the instance variables themselves.

Here's another version:

```
public Animal makeBig()
{
    return new Animal ( "big " + this.name,
                        this.sound.toUpperCase() );
}
```

This used no local variables at all. Instead, I made a single call to new Animal, using as parameters the values I want in the returned object.

A final scheme:

```
public Animal makeBig()
{
    Animal result = new Animal("a","b");
    result.name = "big " + this.name;
    result.sound = this.sound.toUpperCase();
    return result;
}
```

This code begins by creating a "throw-away" Animal, which has gibberish in the instance variables. The next two statements fill the slots with the appropriate values, and the last statement returns the completely tailored object.

By seeing and understanding a variety of schemes for writing the same method, we gather a stockpile of patterns on which to draw when we write a method or read somebody else's.

> **Test your skill with Exercise 6-25.**

6.11   The toString **Method**

Java's print and println methods can print *any object they're given*, and Prog0609.java shows how Java prints instances from each of the following classes:

```
String
PrintStream
Scanner
Animal
```

The output is this:

```
hello
java.io.PrintStream@df6ccd
java.util.scanner@601bb1
Animal@ea2dfe
```

There's a pattern here: three cases fit, and one's an exception.

Prog0609.java   **Any Object Can Be Printed**

```
// Written by Barry Soroka
//
// Java can print any object, but not always meaningfully.
//
```

```
import java.io.*;
import java.util.*;
//////////////////////////////////////////////////////////////////////////////
class Prog0609
{
//-----------------------------------------------------------------------------
    public static void main ( String [] args ) throws Exception
    {
        System.out.println("hello");
        System.out.println(System.out);
        Scanner kb = new Scanner (System.in);
        System.out.println(kb);
        System.out.println(new Animal("fido","woof"));
    }
//-----------------------------------------------------------------------------
} // end class Prog0609
//////////////////////////////////////////////////////////////////////////////
class Animal
{
    private String name;
    private String sound;
//-----------------------------------------------------------------------------
    public Animal ( String theName, String theSound )
    {
        name = theName;
        sound = theSound;
    }
//-----------------------------------------------------------------------------
} // end class Animal
//////////////////////////////////////////////////////////////////////////////
```

In general, when Java prints an object, it prints the *name* of the object—
java.io.PrintStream, Animal, . . . —and a String of characters. The characters seem to come from the set of hexadecimal digits

$$0, 1, 2, 3, 4, 5, 6, 7, 8, 9, a, b, c, d, e, f,$$

and, indeed, the characters are the hexadecimal address of the object being
printed. So, in general, Java prints the name of the class and its address in
memory.

Now let's consider the exception. *Question:* For the String, why did Java
print hello instead of something like String@35af9? *Answer:* Because the def-

> **toString** A method that produces a printable representation of an object.

inition of class `String` contains a custom method *toString()*, which tells `print` and `println` how to print the `String`. If a class contains a `toString` method, then Java invokes it and then prints the result. Otherwise, Java uses a general `toString` method, inherited from class `Object`, which returns the concatenation of the class name and the hex address.

Let's write a `toString` method for class `Animal`. First we must decide how we want an `Animal` to print, since we don't want the default `Animal@hex-address`. Suppose our `Animal` has name `"fido"` and `sound` `"woof"`. Let's agree to print this as "fido (woof)". The program `Prog0610.java` shows the code for the appropriate `toString`:

```
public String toString()
{
    return name + " (" + sound + ")";
}
```

- `public` is required, or this method can't be seen outside class `Animal`.
- `String` is the required return type. It's the purpose of the whole method: Take the object and produce a `String` that represents it.
- `toString` is the method name that is recognized by `print` and `println`.
- The empty parentheses indicate that the method takes no arguments.

The statement

```
return name + " (" + sound + ")";
```

prepares the `String` on which we agreed above.

Prog0610.java   **Method toString() for class Animal**

```
// Written by Barry Soroka
//
// toString() method for class Animal
//
import java.io.*;
///////////////////////////////////////////////////////////////////////////////
class Prog0610
{
//------------------------------------------------------------------------------
    public static void main ( String [] args ) throws Exception
    {
```

```
       Animal a1 = new Animal("fido","woof");
       Animal a2 = new Animal("fluffy","meow");

       System.out.println(a1);
       System.out.println(a2);
       System.out.println(new Animal("leo","roar"));
       System.out.println("I think that " +
                          a1 +
                          " is more faithful than " +
                          a2 +
                          ".");
    }
//----------------------------------------------------------------------
} // end class Prog0610
////////////////////////////////////////////////////////////////////////
class Animal
{
   private String name;
   private String sound;
//----------------------------------------------------------------------
   public Animal ( String theName, String theSound )
   {
      name = theName;
      sound = theSound;
   }
//----------------------------------------------------------------------
   public String toString()
   {
      return name + " (" + sound + ")";
   }
//----------------------------------------------------------------------
} // end class Animal
////////////////////////////////////////////////////////////////////////
```

Prog0610 is the driver that tests our toString method. Let's examine its statements. We start with two statements, which create Animals for testing:

```
       Animal a1 = new Animal("fido","woof");
       Animal a2 = new Animal("fluffy","meow");
```

Then we call println on the Animals we've created:

```
       System.out.println(a1);
       System.out.println(a2);
```

Now, because we've defined a toString method for Animal, we get

```
fido (woof)
fluffy (meow)
```

instead of

```
Animal@whatever
Animal@whatever
```

Next comes

```
System.out.println(new Animal("leo","roar"));
```

which prints

```
leo (roar)
```

The purpose of that example was to show, once again, that the expression

```
new Animal("leo","roar")
```

is a perfectly valid Animal object, and it can be used anyplace that an Animal reference can go. I've broken the final statement over several lines:

```
System.out.println("I think that " +
                   a1 +
                   " is more faithful than " +
                   a2 +
                   ".");
```

and it prints

```
I think that fido (woof) is more faithful than fluffy (meow).
```

Because toString returns a String, I can use it the same way I use any other String. In particular, I can embed the printed representation of an Animal anywhere I want:

- At the front of a line.
- In the middle of a line.
- At the end of a line.

This is an example of the *Principle of Least Commitment*: Make methods as general as possible, so that they can be used as easily as possible, with the fewest restrictions.

When I first started programming in Java, I wrote many methods of the following form:

```
public void print()
{
    System.out.println( name + " (" + sound + ")" );
}
```

This statement printed, "leo (roar)", for example, but it always went to the next line after printing. My print() method was good only if I wanted the Animal to be printed at the end of the line, but I couldn't print the Animal in the *middle* of a line. Moreover, my print() method always printed to System.out: It couldn't be used to print to any other PrintStream—to a file, for example. So print() was very restricted in how it could be used. Then I started writing methods of the form print(PrintStream). These allowed me to write to any PrintStream I wanted. But once I mastered toString, I never wrote print(. . .) methods again. Also, note that toString can be used to implement both of my discarded methods

```
public void print()
{
    System.out.println(this.toString());
}

public void print(PrintStream ps)
{
    ps.println(this.toString());
}
```

but not vice versa. When designing methods, always pick methods with the fewest restrictions.

Let's look once more at the last statement in the driver Prog0610:

```
System.out.println("I think that " +
                    a1 +
                    " is more faithful than " +
                    a2 +
                    ".");
```

The code inside the parentheses produces a single String composed of five pieces. I chose to put each piece on its own line, leaving a plus sign (concatenation operator) at the end of all lines but the last. Each piece of the final

String appears at the same indentation level. Was this a waste of space? Should I have tried to jam the pieces closer together? I think not. By putting each piece of the String on its own line, I can easily move pieces around or add other pieces. From experience, I've learned that assembled Strings are often changed, and I've gravitated toward the preceding style.

> **Test your skill with Exercises 6-26 through 6-30.**

6.12   **Reading Objects Using** static read **Methods**

> **static read method**   A method that reads pieces of an object and assembles the object for use within a program.

This section presents the pattern to use when we want to *read* an Object, slot by slot, from the user or from a file. The pattern involves a read method that has the modifier static. We'll illustrate the pattern by writing a read method for class Animal and testing it with an appropriate driver.

When reading an Animal, the end user will see a dialog like this, where the user's input is underlined:

```
Reading an Animal ...
Enter name: fido
Enter sound: woof
```

Inside the program, a new Animal object will be created.

Prog0611.java shows the driver (class Prog0611) and the read method in class Animal. The driver defines a Scanner kb, which refers to the keyboard, and uses the read method in the following statement:

```
Animal a = Animal.read(System.out,kb);
```

Some of this statement is familiar, and some of it's new. Clearly, the expression Animal.read(..., ...) returns an Animal, and read must be the method that produces the end-user dialog shown above. The parameters make sense to us:

- The read method must *prompt* the user, so it needs a PrintStream as one of its parameters.
- The read method must *read* the user's choices for the values of the slots, so it must have a Scanner as one of its parameters.

In the call shown above, read will prompt to the PrintStream System.out and read from the Scanner kb. So much for the familiar!

Prog0611.java   A static read Method for Class Animal

```java
// Written by Barry Soroka
//
// static read method for class Animal
//
import java.io.*;
import java.util.Scanner;
//////////////////////////////////////////////////////////////////////////
class Prog0611
{
//---------------------------------------------------------------------
    public static void main ( String [] args ) throws Exception
    {
        Scanner kb = new Scanner(System.in);
        Animal a = Animal.read(System.out,kb);
        System.out.println();
        System.out.println(a);
    }
//---------------------------------------------------------------------
} // end class Prog0611
//////////////////////////////////////////////////////////////////////////
class Animal
{
    private String name;
    private String sound;
//---------------------------------------------------------------------
    public Animal ( String theName, String theSound )
    {
        name = theName;
        sound = theSound;
    }
//---------------------------------------------------------------------
    public static Animal read ( PrintStream ps, Scanner sc )
                                                    throws Exception
    {
        ps.println("Reading an Animal ...");
        ps.print("Enter name:  "); String name = sc.nextLine();
        ps.print("Enter sound: "); String sound = sc.nextLine();
        return new Animal(name,sound);
    }
//---------------------------------------------------------------------
```

```
    public String toString()
    {
       return name + " (" + sound + ")";
    }
//-------------------------------------------------------------------------
} // end class Animal
///////////////////////////////////////////////////////////////////////////
```

Now let's consider the phrase

```
Animal.read(..., ...)
```

The parameters are not important to our analysis. Something's new about this phrase: Up until now, all methods occurred in expressions of the form

```
objectName.methodName
```

where the method is applied to the object. Now we have an expression of the form

```
className.methodName
```

What's going on? Think about the statement

```
Animal a = Animal.read(..., ...);
```

Question: At this point in the program, is there an instance of class `Animal` to which we can send a `read` message? *Answer:* No. At this point, the only object we've created is `kb`, an instance of `Scanner`. The `read` method needs to be called *even though no instance of `Animal` has yet been created*. Indeed, the purpose of `read` is to *create* new instances of `Animal`, regardless of whether or how many `Animal` instances may exist. This situation is new to us, but it will occur again later.

Class Methods versus Instance Methods

Java allows two kinds of methods: instance methods and class methods (`static` methods). *Instance methods* are invoked by tacking them to the right of an appropriate receiver *object. Class methods* are invoked by tacking them to the right of the appropriate *class* name. *Instance methods* cannot be invoked unless an instance of the class has already been created. *Class methods*, on the other hand, may be invoked at any time in a program, regardless of whether any instances of the class have been created.

That's the semantics of the two kinds of methods. What about syntax? We already know how to write *instance* methods. Now let's see how to write a *class* method. Consider the `read` method in class `Animal` in `Prog0611.java`. The body presents nothing new:

```
ps.println("Reading an Animal ...");
ps.print("Enter name: "); String name = sc.nextLine();
ps.print("Enter sound: "); String sound = sc.nextLine();
return new Animal(name,sound);
```

As expected, the `print` statements use the `PrintStream` parameter, and the `nextLine` statements use the `Scanner` parameter. The `return` statement calls the constructor with the slot values that have been read. The novelty of the `read` method is in its *prototype*:

```
public static Animal read ( PrintStream ps,
                                    Scanner sc )
                     throws Exception
```

(I have rearranged the tokens so that the statement fits better here, but, to Java, it's the same statement that appears in `Prog0611.java`.) Let's analyze the header, starting with things we've already seen:

- `public` means that this method is accessible outside the class `Animal`.
- `Animal` is the return type of the method.
- `read` is the name of the method.
- `PrintStream ps` and `Scanner sc` are the parameters. Notice how the parameters are chosen to obey the *Principle of Least Commitment*. The `read` method can prompt to any `PrintStream` and read from any `Scanner`. Thus, we can use it to read a few `Animal`s from the keyboard or a long list of `Animal`s from a file.

Two phrases are *new*:

- `static` is the modifier that tells Java that this is a *class* method instead of an *instance* method. Only methods with the `static` modifier can be called without reference to a preexisting instance of the class.

- throws Exception is required because read uses the method nextLine, and nextLine can generate an Exception. For example, we could be reading from a file on disk, and the disk could halt unexpectedly. Or, we could be reading from the keyboard and the keyboard could come unplugged; or we could be reading from a distant website and our Internet connection could go down. Such situations produce an Exception, and Java requires that we acknowledge this possibility. The phrase throws Exception tells Java, "Yes, we know that this method uses nextLine, and we know that nextLine can throw an Exception, and we want such Exceptions to be handled outside this read method—by whatever method called read."

Now you should understand how the read method is made static and how we can invoke it as a *class* method rather than an *instance* method. The following table summarizes the differences:

Instance Method	Class Method (static Method)
Called by tacking to the right of an instance of the class.	Called by tacking to the right of the class name.
Requires an instance of the class.	Does not require an instance of the class.

Test your skill with Exercises 6-31 through 6-37.

Reading from a File

Suppose we have a file Animals that contains the text

```
rex
woof
pretzel
meow
spot
woof
```

representing two dogs and a cat and the sounds they make. Each Animal in the file consists of two lines: one for the name and one for the sound. Prog0612.java is a program that reads the name of a file and then reads and prints the *first two* Animals in the file. The driver Prog0612 reads a file name and creates a

Scanner sc to refer to it. The program reads Animals using the static read method like this:

```
Animal a1 = Animal.read(System.out,sc);
```

Note that we are reading from a file rather than from a keyboard. Here's the dialog we see:

```
G:\>java Prog0612
Enter the name of a file of Animals: Animals
Reading an Animal ...
Enter name: Enter sound: Reading an Animal ...
Enter name: Enter sound:
rex (woof)
pretzel (meow)
```

Note the following:

1. Fortunately, the program has read and printed the first two Animals in the file.
2. *Un*fortunately, the program has printed the prompts even though the data are coming from a file rather than from a human user.

In Chapter 11 we will study *conditional statements*, which will allow us to write a better static read method—one that can be commanded to omit the prompts when they aren't needed.

Prog0612.java   Reading **Animals** from a File

```java
// Written by Barry Soroka
//
// Reading Animals from a file.
//
import java.io.*;
import java.util.Scanner;
//////////////////////////////////////////////////////////////////////////////
class Prog0612
{
//--------------------------------------------------------------------------
   public static void main ( String [] args ) throws Exception
   {
      Scanner kb = new Scanner(System.in);
```

```
        System.out.print("Enter the name of a file of Animals: ");
        String filename = kb.nextLine();

        Scanner sc = new Scanner(new File(filename));

        Animal a1 = Animal.read(System.out,sc);
        Animal a2 = Animal.read(System.out,sc);

        System.out.println();
        System.out.println(a1);
        System.out.println(a2);
    }
//-----------------------------------------------------------------------
} // end class Prog0612
///////////////////////////////////////////////////////////////////////////
class Animal
{
    private String name;
    private String sound;
//-----------------------------------------------------------------------
    public Animal ( String theName, String theSound )
    {
        name = theName;
        sound = theSound;
    }
//-----------------------------------------------------------------------
    public static Animal read ( PrintStream ps, Scanner sc )
                                                    throws Exception
    {
        ps.println("Reading an Animal ...");
        ps.print("Enter name:  "); String name = sc.nextLine();
        ps.print("Enter sound: "); String sound = sc.nextLine();
        return new Animal(name,sound);
    }
//-----------------------------------------------------------------------
    public String toString()
    {
        return name + " (" + sound + ")";
    }
//-----------------------------------------------------------------------
} // end class Animal
///////////////////////////////////////////////////////////////////////////
```

    Test your skill with Exercise 6-38.

6.13 Aspects of static

When applied to a method, the static modifier can be understood in two ways:

- This method gets called with the class name and not with the name of an instance.
- This method can be called even if we have never created an instance of this class.

Predefined static Methods

We will see many other static methods in the chapters ahead. For example, the Java-supplied class Math provides a large set of mathematical functions:

- Math.abs(...) returns the absolute value of the parameter.
- Math.sin(...) returns the sine of the value of the parameter.
- Math.cos(...) returns the cosine of the value of the parameter.

Also, the class Integer provides a method parseInt, which converts a String to the integer it represents. For example, Integer.parseInt("273") will return the integer 273. Similar static methods can convert Strings into floating-point numbers. We'll learn more about these methods when we study numbers in later chapters.

public static void main

Every driver we've written contained a main method containing the phrase "public static void main". Three of these words are old:

- public means that the method can be seen from outside the class. This is crucial. If the main method is private, then the JVM won't be able to see it, and the driver won't run.
- void means that the method has no return value. This makes sense, since the purpose of the main method is to call a sequence of methods to accomplish the program's work. We aren't concerned with any result that main computes.[9]

---

[9] Some operating systems may check a code returned by a main method in order to decide what action to take next. This topic is dependent on the operating system and is beyond the scope of this text.

- `main` must name some method inside the driver class. If the operating system can't find a `main` method, then the driver won't run.

Now we can understand the word *static* in the phrase `public static void main`: It means that this method can be called even if we have never created an instance of the enclosing class. Consider `Prog0612.java`. It contains a class `Prog0612`, which in turn contains a method `main`. Clearly, we never create an instance of `Prog0612`—it's just a container for the `main` method. Thus, `main` must be `static`, so that the operating system can invoke it *even though we never create an instance of the enclosing class* `Prog0612`.

> **Test your skill with Exercises 6-39 through 6-41.**

6.14   Designing and Implementing Classes

In this chapter we have designed and implemented classes `Teacher` and `Animal`. Let's try to formalize the class design process. In particular, we'll examine the *activities* involved in class design. These are *activities* rather than *phases* or *steps* because class design and implementation is not a one-way process. During one activity, we often discover that the result of a prior activity needs to be revised. There are many models for analyzing and structuring the software design process. Trillions of dollars are spent on software each year, and any system that can cut the cost of software development will find a welcome audience. As a computer science major, you will take one or more courses that study the software life cycle and the process of software design.

The activities below are described for the case of designing a *single class*. In most cases, the implementation of a software system requires the coupled design of *many classes*. For such systems, the activities below are applied to multiple classes.

Activity 1—Write an Informal Description

This activity involves writing down the general purpose of the class we want to write. What data are stored in each instance? What behaviors do we want? This description will be presented to the client or customer for approval.

Activity 2—Write the Interface

Here we design the prototypes of the methods. Our first sketch may not be the interface we finally choose. Activity 3—writing sample programs—feeds back into Activity 2.

The interface becomes a formal contract between the class-writers and the class-users. Once the interface is made public ("published"), class-users will always be able to rely on this interface, no matter how much we may modify the code at a later time. Change is inevitable: Classes are modified in order to add additional capabilities and to improve the implementation, making the code more efficient or easier to read and maintain.

Activity 3—Write Sample Programs That Use the Interface

By writing sample programs, we can test the interface to see if it contains all of the capabilities required for our initial application. As noted earlier, we may modify the interface if we find that the methods we've sketched do not yield simple and elegant programs for typical tasks. Often, Activity 4 (selecting test cases) will mingle with Activity 3; an interface is not worth much if it can't support the test cases designed to validate the class.

Activity 4—Select Test Cases

Test cases should be selected before the code is designed. Even before the code is written, we ought to know what tests the code must pass: *If we don't know our target, how will get there?*

Some programmers defer test design until after coding is complete. They feel that testing is less challenging or less creative an activity than implementing the class. In fact, design and testing are two sides of the same coin, and early design of test cases will result in better design and better code.

Overconfident programmers often defer testing until all the code is written, and then reluctantly perform only a few obligatory tests. Their code tends to be buggy. If you test your own code, you will only test the cases that you anticipated. We can get better code by allowing the tests to come from people who were not involved in the actual implementation.

In industry, many companies have a *coding group* and a *testing group* that work in parallel, and you may find that your first job is in testing rather than coding. Sometimes the two groups are not permitted to talk to each other; this helps ensure that the tests are not dependent on any particular implementation decisions.

Activity 5—Write the Skeleton of the Class Definition

In this activity, we produce an outline of the final class. Here's the scheme:

```
class class-name
{
    instance-variables
    prototypes of constructor(s)
    prototypes of method(s)
}
```

For class `Animal`, the skeleton would look like this:

```
class Animal
{
    private String name;
    private String sound;

    public Animal ( String name, String sound)
    public void chases ( Animal target )
    public void speak()
    public String getName() { return name; }
    public void setName ( String newName )
    public String getSound()
    public void setSound ( String newSound )
    public Animal makeBig()
    public String toString()
    public static Animal read ( PrintStream ps,
                                    Scanner sc )

}
```

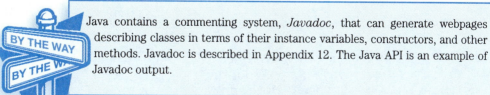

Java contains a commenting system, *Javadoc*, that can generate webpages describing classes in terms of their instance variables, constructors, and other methods. Javadoc is described in Appendix 12. The Java API is an example of Javadoc output.

Activity 6—Flesh Out the Skeleton

Now we write the code to flesh out the skeletons of the constructors and methods we identified earlier. Prog0613.java shows the complete code for class Animal.

Prog0613.java **Complete Code for Class Animal**

```java
// Written by Barry Soroka
//
// This is Prog0613.java
//
// Complete code for class Animal.
//
import java.io.*;
import java.util.Scanner;
//////////////////////////////////////////////////////////////////////////////
class Animal
{
   private String name;
   private String sound;
//------------------------------------------------------------------------------
   public Animal ( String name, String sound )
   {
      this.name = name;
      this.sound = sound;
   }
//------------------------------------------------------------------------------
   public void chases ( Animal target )
   {
      System.out.println ( this.name + " is chasing " + target.name );
   }
//------------------------------------------------------------------------------
   public void speak()
   {
      System.out.println ( name + " says " + sound );
   }
//------------------------------------------------------------------------------
   public String getName() { return name; }
//------------------------------------------------------------------------------
   public void setName ( String newName ) { name = newName; }
//------------------------------------------------------------------------------
   public String getSound() { return sound; }
//------------------------------------------------------------------------------
   public void setSound ( String newSound ) { sound = newSound; }
//------------------------------------------------------------------------------
```

```
    public Animal makeBig()
    {
        String resultName = "big " + name;
        String resultSound = sound.toUpperCase();
        return new Animal(resultName,resultSound);
    }
//------------------------------------------------------------------
    public String toString()
    {
        return name + " (" + sound + ")";
    }
//------------------------------------------------------------------
    public static Animal read ( PrintStream ps, Scanner sc ) throws Exception
    {
        ps.println("Reading an Animal ...");
        ps.print("Enter name:  "); String name = sc.nextLine();
        ps.print("Enter sound: "); String sound = sc.nextLine();
        return new Animal(name,sound);
    }
//------------------------------------------------------------------
} // end class Animal
//////////////////////////////////////////////////////////////////////
```

Activity 7—Run the Tests

Here we run the test cases that we designed earlier. In an efficient software design process, the code for testing will have been written before the classes themselves are coded. Testing can be done as soon as classes and methods are completed. The results of testing can be fed back to the implementation process in order to fix any errors that are detected.

> **Test your skill with Exercise 6-42.**

6.15   Default Constructors and `main` Methods

Default Constructors

In a class, if no constructor is given, then Java provides a *default constructor*, which takes no parameters and has an empty body. Recall our definition of class `Teacher` in `Prog01.java`. We defined only one constructor:

```
    public Teacher() {}
```

which is the same as the default constructor would have been. In truth, our definition was not necessary. Had we omitted it, Java would have provided it.

There's a flip side to the default constructor rule: If a class defines *any constructor whatsoever*, then Java does not provide the default constructor.

 | **Test your skill with Exercises 6-43 through 6-44.**

Any Class May Contain a `main` Method

We have been studying program files of the form

```
/////////////////////////////////////////////////////
class driver-name
{
//------------------------------------------
    public static void main ... { ... }
//------------------------------------------
    ...
} end class driver-name
/////////////////////////////////////////////////////
class class-name
{
    ...
} // end class class-name
/////////////////////////////////////////////////////
```

where only the driver class contains a `main` method. Actually, it is possible for *any* class to contain a `main` method.

Consider `Prog0614.java`, which contains three classes: `Prog0614` and `A` and `B`. Each of the classes contains a `public static void main` method. As expected, compiling `Prog0614.java` produces three `.class` files:

```
Prog0614.class
A.class
B.class
```

We can ask Java to *execute any one of these* by giving it as an argument to the `java` command. Java looks in the specified class file for a `main` method, and executes it. Here's hardcopy of a typical run, where what the user types is underlined:

```
G:\>java Prog0614
This is main from class Prog0614
G:\>java A
```

```
                   This is main from class A.
                   G:\>java B
                   This is main from class B.
```

So, *any class can contain a main method*. This is sometimes useful for testing classes.

Prog0614.java   Any Class May Contain a **main** Method

```java
// Written by Barry Soroka
//
// Any class may contain a main method.
//
/////////////////////////////////////////////////////////////////////////////
class Prog0614
{
//---------------------------------------------------------------------------
   public static void main ( String [] args ) throws Exception
   {
      System.out.println("This is main from class Prog0614.");
   }
//---------------------------------------------------------------------------
} // end class Prog0614
/////////////////////////////////////////////////////////////////////////////
class A
{
//---------------------------------------------------------------------------
   public static void main ( String [] args ) throws Exception
   {
      System.out.println("This is main from class A.");
   }
//---------------------------------------------------------------------------
} // end class A
/////////////////////////////////////////////////////////////////////////////
class B
{
//---------------------------------------------------------------------------
   public static void main ( String [] args ) throws Exception
   {
      System.out.println("This is main from class B.");
   }
//---------------------------------------------------------------------------
} // end class B
/////////////////////////////////////////////////////////////////////////////
```

6.16 Command-Line Arguments

This section introduces a new way of passing data values into programs. Consider a program that prints the length of a `String`. Previously, we could enter data values either by building them into the code or by reading them from the keyboard or a file. Now we will learn how to read these data values from the *command line*—the line on which we invoke the Java program. Consider `Prog0615.java`. This program uses the expression `args[0]`, which in turn refers to the phrase `String [] args`, which has graced every program we've written. The variable `args` refers to the complete list of arguments presented on the command line. For example, if we enter the line

```
G:\>java Prog0615 now is the time
```

then `args` is bound to the collection `now is the time`. The length of this collection is 4. Its elements can be accessed with expressions of the form `args[0]`, `args[1]`, `args[2]`, `args[3]`.[10]

Prog0615.java   Using Command-Line Arguments

```java
// Written by Barry Soroka
//
// Demonstrate command-line arguments.
//
import java.io.*;
/////////////////////////////////////////////////////////////////////////////
class Prog0615
{
//---------------------------------------------------------------------------
    public static void main ( String [] args ) throws Exception
    {
        System.out.println("args[0] = \"" + args[0] + "\"");
    }
//---------------------------------------------------------------------------
} // end class Prog0615
/////////////////////////////////////////////////////////////////////////////
```

---

[10] In future chapters, we'll see that $0, 1, 2, \ldots$ is the numbering scheme Java uses for positions in `String`s and positions in `array`s.

Let's examine a few examples of running `Prog0615`. To start, a single `String`, `"hello"`, is recognized as one `String`:

```
G:\>java Prog0615 hello
args[0] = "hello"
```

Most punctuation is recognized as normal characters:

```
G:\>java Prog0615 ...
args[0] = "..."
```

Anything within quote marks is recognized as a single `String`:

```
G:\>java Prog0615 "two words"
args[0] = "two words"
```

Numbers are seen as character strings:

```
G:\>java Prog0615 45
args[0] = "45"
```

Arithmetic expressions—to be covered in Chapter 7—are seen as `String`s of characters:

```
G:\>java Prog0615 5*18
args[0] = "5*18"
```

We have no problems if we supply more arguments than the program touches:

```
G:\>java Prog0615 a b
args[0] = "a"
```

However, we get an `Exception` if we provide *fewer* arguments than the program wants:

```
G:\>java Prog0615
Exception in thread "main" java.lang.ArrayIndexOutOfBoundsException
        at Prog0615.main(Prog0615.java:12)
```

Now consider program `Prog0616.java`, which expects *four* arguments on the command line. If we give it more arguments than it wants, then it ignores the extras:

```
G:\>java Prog0616 a 0.1 "two words" 4.5 extra arguments
args[0] = "a"
args[1] = "0.1"
args[2] = "two words"
args[3] = "4.5"
```

The program is happy if we give it the exact number of arguments it wants:

```
G:\>java Prog0616 a 0.1 "two words" 4+5
args[0] = "a"
args[1] = "0.1"
args[2] = "two words"
args[3] = "4+5"
```

But, if we give the program fewer arguments than it needs, it will process correctly until it asks for a nonexistent argument:

```
G:\>java Prog0616 a 0.1 "two words"
args[0] = "a"
args[1] = "0.1"
args[2] = "two words"
Exception in thread "main" java.lang.ArrayIndexOutOfBoundsException
        at Prog0616.main(Prog0616.java:15)
```

If we give it *no* arguments, then it will throw an `Exception` just as soon as the code touches a nonexistent argument:

```
G:\>java Prog0616
Exception in thread "main" java.lang.ArrayIndexOutOfBoundsException
        at Prog0616.main(Prog0616.java:12)
```

Prog0616.java   More Using Command-Line Arguments

```
// Written by Barry Soroka
//
// Demonstrate command-line arguments.
//
import java.io.*;
/////////////////////////////////////////////////////////////////////////////
class Prog0616
{
```

```
//-------------------------------------------------------------------------
    public static void main ( String [] args ) throws Exception
    {
        System.out.println("args[0] = \"" + args[0] + "\"");
        System.out.println("args[1] = \"" + args[1] + "\"");
        System.out.println("args[2] = \"" + args[2] + "\"");
        System.out.println("args[3] = \"" + args[3] + "\"");
    }
//-------------------------------------------------------------------------
} // end class Prog0616
//////////////////////////////////////////////////////////////////////////
```

 Test your skill with Exercises 6-45 through 6-46.

Chapter Summary

- A driver is a program that tests the methods of a class. From a driver, we can deduce part of the interface of the class.
- A class definition is a template for constructing objects.
- A constructor creates a new instance of a class.
- Within a constructor, the `this` pointer refers to the object under construction. Within a method, the `this` pointer refers to the receiver of the method call.
- Instance variables maintain the individual state of an object.
- In a class, instance variables are generally `private`, and methods are generally `public`.
- Overloading occurs when a class contains two methods with the same name, but with different numbers or types of parameters.
- Unnecessary instance variables cost space in every object created from a class template.
- Getters and setters allow controlled access to the `private` instance variables of a class.
- Data structure is shared when two or more variables reference the same structure in memory.
- A copy constructor creates a new object from an existing object. Corresponding instance variables have the same values.
- Constructors usually validate instance variables before creating an object.
- User-defined classes can be the parameter types and return types of methods, just as we have used predefined classes for these purposes.
- Objects have a `toString` method that is invoked when the object is printed or when it is used as a `String`.

- A `static read` method allows us to read the pieces of an object and return the constructed object.
- Instance methods are invoked by sending a message to an object of the appropriate class.
- Class methods are invoked by an expression of the form *className.methodName*. They can be invoked without reference to an object of the class.
- The `Math` class contains a variety of `static` methods for working with numbers.
- Class definition involves the following steps:
  1. Write an informal description.
  2. Write the interface.
  3. Write sample programs that use the interface.
  4. Select test cases.
  5. Write the skeleton of the class definition.
  6. Flesh out the skeleton.
  7. Run the tests.

Terminology Introduced in This Chapter

accessor	local variable	`static read` method
copy constructor	mutator	`this` pointer
garbage	scope	`toString`
garbage collection	shared data structure	validate
instance variable	slot	visibility modifier

Exercises

Exercise 6–1.   Using `Prog0601.java`, write a method `lecture(String)` that overloads the `lecture()` method. The driver code

```
Teacher t = new Teacher();
t.lecture("math");
t.lecture("philosophy");
```

should print out

```
do your math homework!
do your philosophy homework!
```

Write your own driver. Explain how your method works.

Exercise 6-2. Add another constructor to class `Animal`. This constructor takes one argument, the name of the `Animal`, and always uses the sound `"hey"`. Write an appropriate driver.

Exercise 6-3. For class `Animal`, write a method `sleeps()` that uses only one instance variable of `Animal`. The code

```
Animal a = new Animal("fido","woof");
a.sleeps();
```

causes the printout

```
fido is sleeping
```

Exercise 6-4. Define *overloaded method* and illustrate your definition with a concise and appropriate Java example of your own. Don't use a built-in method as your example; write one of your own.

Exercise 6-5. Write a class `Person` that models people and the colleges they attended. At the least, your class should have the following characteristics:

- Instance variables `lastName`, `firstName`, and `college`. All of them are `String`s.
- Two constructors that perform like this:
  ```
  Person p1 = new Person("George","Bush","Yale");
  Person p3 = new Person("Ralph","Nader");
  ```
  If no `college` is given, then that slot should default to `"some college"`.
- A method `speak()` that prints out sentences of the form:
  ```
  George Bush went to Yale.
  ```

Write and run an appropriate driver.

Exercise 6-6. Consider a class `Writer` with the following specifications:

- It has a constructor that takes one argument, a `String`, which it remembers as an instance variable.
- It has a method `writeToMonitor`, which takes no arguments and writes the remembered `String` to the monitor.
- It has a method `writeToFile` that takes one argument—a `String` that is a file name—and that writes the remembered `String` to that file.
- It has a method `writeToFile` that takes *no* arguments, but which prompts the user for a file name and then writes the remembered `String` to that file.

Give the Java code for class `Writer`.

Exercise 6-7.   Objects of the class `Doubler` have a method `repeat` that takes a `String` and prints it out *twice*, to the monitor. So, for example, the driver code

```
Doubler d = new Doubler();
d.repeat("hello")
```

produces the output

```
hello
hello
```

Give the Java code for the class `Doubler`. Write a driver to demonstrate it.

Exercise 6-8.   Enhance `Doubler` by adding methods

- `triple(String)`, which writes three lines of the given `String`;
- `sideBySide(String)`, which writes two copies of the given `String` on the same line.

Exercise 6-9.   Recall the class `Person`, which you wrote in a previous exercise. Add the following methods:

- A method `setCollege`, which changes the `college` slot of a `Person`.
- A method `getCollege`, which returns the value of the `college` slot of a `Person`.

Run your code against a driver containing the following code:

```
Person p1 = new Person("Jodie","Foster","Yale");
Person p2 = new Person("Matt","Damon","Harvard");
Person p3 = new Person("Susan","Sontag");
Person p4 = new Person ("Someone","Else");

System.out.println();

p1.speak();
p2.speak();
p3.speak();
p4.speak();

System.out.println();
```

```
p3.setCollege("Princeton");
p3.speak();

p3.setCollege(p1.getCollege());
p3.speak();
System.out.println(p3.getCollege());
```

Exercise 6-10.   Suppose that a class X has the following instance variables:

```
private Scanner sc;
private PrintStream ps;
private String label;
```

Write the getters and setters.

Exercise 6-11.   Write a copy constructor for the class Teacher. Write a driver that demonstrates that the result of your copy constructor is not pointing to the incoming Teacher.

Exercise 6-12.   Write a copy constructor for the class Person. Write a driver that demonstrates that the result of your copy constructor is not pointing to the incoming Person.

Exercise 6-13.   The following statements are executed in sequence, one after the other. Draw memory diagrams to show the state of the memory after execution of each statement.

```
Animal a1 = new Animal("fido","woof");
Animal a2 = a1;
Animal a3 = new Animal(a2);
Animal a1 = new Animal("fido","woof");
```

Exercise 6-14.   Write a Java program Ex99 that generates getters and setters automatically. Ex99 should prompt for the type and name of an instance variable and should output correct Java code for the appropriate getter and setter. Here's a sample run, with user input underlined:

```
G:\>java Ex99
I create getters and setters
    for an instance variable...
Enter the type of the variable: double
Enter the name of the variable: radius
```

Generated code:

```
//-------------------------------------------------------
//
// getter for variable radius
//
   public double getRadius()
   {
      return radius;
   }
//-------------------------------------------------------
//
// setter for variable radius
//
   public void setRadius(double newRadius)
   {
      radius = newRadius;
   }
//-------------------------------------------------------
```

Exercise 6-15. Consider the `Person` class, continuing from prior exercises. Write a method `hates` that takes one parameter, a `Person`. It prints a sentence of the form

name-of-receiver hates *name-of-parameter*

So, for example, driver code

```
Person p2 = new Person("Al","Gore","Harvard");
Person p3 = new Person("Ralph","Nader");
p2.hates(p3);
```

would produce the output

```
Al Gore hates Ralph Nader
```

Write the code for `Person`, including the `hates` method, and write and run a driver that exercises your method.

Exercise 6-16. Recall the class `Person`. Add a method `lovesUnrequited` that takes one parameter, a `Person`. The behavior is illustrated below. The driver code

```
Person p1 = new Person("bill","brock");
Person p2 = new Person("sue","smith");
```

```
p1.lovesUnrequited(p2);
p2.lovesUnrequited(p1);
p1.lovesUnrequited(p1);
```

produces the following output:

```
bill loves sue but sue doesn't love bill
sue loves bill but bill doesn't love sue
bill loves bill but bill doesn't love bill
```

Write the code for Person, including the method lovesUnrequited, and write and run a driver that exercises your method.

Exercise 6-17.   Recall the class Person. Add a method prefers that takes *two* parameters, both Persons, and writes out a sentence as illustrated by the code below. The driver code

```
Person p1 = new Person("George","Bush","Yale");
Person p2 = new Person("Al","Gore","Harvard");
Person p3 = new Person("Ralph","Nader");
p1.prefers(p3,p2);
```

produces the output:

```
Bush prefers Nader to Gore
```

Write the code for Person, including the method prefers, and write and run a driver that exercises your method.

Exercise 6-18.   Recall the class Person. Add a method cantStand that takes one parameter, an *Animal*, and writes out a sentence as illustrated by the code that follows. The driver code

```
Person p1 = new Person("George","Bush","Yale");
Animal a1 = new Animal("Fluffy","meow");
p1.cantStand(a1);
```

produces the output:

```
George Bush can't stand Fluffy's constant meow-ing.
```

Turn in your code for Person and Animal, and write and run a driver that exercises your method cantStand.

Exercise 6-19.   Write code that proves the following statement: If a name can refer to either a local variable or a parameter, then that name refers to the local variable.

Exercise 6-20.   Alter the driver Prog0608 so that it proves that the receiver, a1, is not changed by the call to makeBig.

Exercise 6-21.   Write a different method makeBig that, when applied to an Animal object, *changes* the values of the name and sound slots in the manner described for the makeBig method above. The method for this exercise has return type void. Write a driver to test your makeBig method.

Exercise 6-22.   If the class Animal includes *both* of the makeBig methods we've described in the text and in the exercises, will it compile? Why or why not? Run appropriate code to see Java's opinion. Explain.

Exercise 6-23.   Prove that the variables resultName and resultSound are not visible in the driver that calls makeBig().

Exercise 6-24.   Recall the class Person. Add a method cross that takes a Person as its argument and returns a new Person. The new Person's *first* name is to be the first name of the *receiver*; the *last* name of the new Person is to be the last name of the Person who is the *parameter*. The college of the new Person should be Penn. For example, the driver code

```
Person p1 = new Person("Jodie","Foster","Yale");
Person p2 = new Person("Matt","Damon","Harvard");

Person p5 = p1.cross(p2);
Person p6 = p2.cross(p1);
p5.speak();
p6.speak();
```

would produce the output:

```
Jodie Damon went to Penn.
Matt Foster went to Penn.
```

Write the code for Person, including the method cross, and write and run a driver that exercises your method.

Exercise 6-25.   Recall the class Person with variables firstName, lastName, and college. Add a method makeStateCollege() that, when applied to a Person, returns a *new* Person, which in turn is the same as the receiver *except* that the college is now

"StateCollege". Write `makeStateCollege` in the four different ways discussed in this section.

Exercise 6-26. Write and test a `toString` method for `Animal` that prints like this:

```
name: "fido"
sound: "woof"
```

Exercise 6-27. We've seen that `print` and `println` recognize `toString` methods where `toString` takes no parameters. Write a program that tests whether they also recognize `toString` methods that *do* take parameters.

Exercise 6-28. Recall the class `Person` with variables `firstName`, `lastName`, and `college`. Add a `toString` method that returns `String`s of the form

```
Al Gore (Harvard)
```

Write a driver that demonstrates your method.

Exercise 6-29. Recall the class `Person` with variables `firstName`, `lastName`, and `college`. Add a `toString` method that returns `String`s of the form

```
Harvard: Al Gore
```

Write a driver that demonstrates your method.

Exercise 6-30. Write and test a `toString` method for `Person` that prints like this:

```
firstName: "George"
lastName: "Bush"
college: "Yale"
```

Exercise 6-31. Experiment with the `read` method in `Prog0611.java` to determine exactly which statements require the phrase `throws Exception`.

Exercise 6-32. How does Java react if we omit the `static` modifier? Explain.

Exercise 6-33. How does Java react if we omit the phrase `throws Exception`? Explain.

Exercise 6-34. How does Java react if we use the phrase `throws IOException` instead of `throws Exception`? Explain.

Exercise 6-35.   How does Java react if we use `private` instead of `public`? Explain.

Exercise 6-36.   Write and test a method `redefine` that prompts the user for new values to replace the current values in an existing instance of `Animal`. The prototype should be

```
public void redefine(PrintStream,Scanner)
```

If this method were named `read`, could we include it in the class `Animal` with the `static read` method we wrote earlier? What does Java say?

Exercise 6-37.   Recall the class `Person` with variables `firstName`, `lastName`, and `college`. Write a `static read` method that will read a `Person` by reading all three instance variables. Don't forget to prompt. Write a driver that demonstrates your `read` method.

Exercise 6-38.   Suppose the file `Presidents3` contains the following lines:

```
Jimmy
Carter
Naval Academy
Richard
Nixon
Whittier College
Gerald
Ford
University of Michigan
```

Using the `static read` method you added to class `Person` in a previous exercise, write a driver that reads and prints the three `Persons` in file `Presidents3`. Indicate the unnecessary prompts.

Exercise 6-39.   Consider the following class:

```
////////////////////////////////////////////////////////////
class A
{
    private int var;
//----------------------------------------------------------
    public static void f()
    {
        System.out.println(var);
    }
//----------------------------------------------------------
}
////////////////////////////////////////////////////////////
```

It won't compile. Explain why.

Exercise 6-40. Some textbooks say that a `static` method cannot reference an instance variable. Why does this seem to be true?

Exercise 6-41. Consider the following class:

```
//////////////////////////////////////////////////////////
class A
{
    private int var;
//------------------------------------------------------------
    public static void g()
    {
        A a = new A();
        System.out.println(a.var);
    }
//------------------------------------------------------------
}
//////////////////////////////////////////////////////////
```

Does this compile? Does `static` method `g` reference an instance variable? Why is it allowed here?

Exercise 6-42. College students typically have at least the following properties: last name, first name, major, home city, and home state. Following the guidelines of this chapter, design a class `Student`. Write and run drivers that test and demonstrate the capabilities you have built into your class.

Exercise 6-43. Modify `Prog0601.java` to show that Java provides the default constructor if the class itself defines no constructors.

Exercise 6-44. Write code that proves that if a class provides any constructor, then Java does not provide the default constructor.

Exercise 6-45. Write an application `Twice.java` that reads the first `String` on the command line and prints it twice. Here's a typical session:

```
G:\>java Twice hi there
hi
hi
```

Exercise 6-46. Write an application `Reverse.java` that reads the first three `String`s on the command line and prints them in reverse order. Here's a typical session:

```
G:\>java Reverse am I here
here I am
```

Integer Datatypes

In prior chapters, we've acquired a variety of important skills:

- We can examine simple real-world problems and identify the classes and objects they require.
- We can use an assortment of Java's predefined classes.
- We can read `Strings` from the keyboard and from files.
- We can write `Strings` to the monitor and to files.
- We can declare variables and assign values.
- We know how methods are characterized by their signatures and prototypes.

Most recently, we learned how to define our own classes, including constructors and methods. We saw how the `static` modifier makes a method available even if no instances of the corresponding class have been defined—in particular, we used `static` on methods that `read` an object from the keyboard or from a file.

Up to this point, our programs have worked mostly with `Strings`. The current chapter will introduce *integer datatypes*, the first of a series of *primitive datatypes*—nonobjects—that we will study in the next few chapters. By the end of this chapter, you will know:

- How primitive datatypes differ from objects.
- How to convert between integers and `Strings`.
- How to create and evaluate complicated expressions using integers.
- How to use integers in classes such as `Complex` number, `Rectangle`, and `Fraction`.

HOLD YOUR HORSES

Feel free to read the Java API, but *don't use classes or methods that you haven't learned yet*. This book will teach you how to solve a variety of problems, and Java provides built-in answers for some of them. Our goal is not to use Java's solutions, but to write our own. This goal differentiates computer science majors (class *writers*) from other majors (class *users*).

7.1 Integers and Integer Types

Most programming languages divide numbers into two categories: integers and floating-point. Integers are *whole numbers*, which can be enumerated along a number line at equally spaced intervals:

```
..., -3, -2, -1, 0, 1, 2, 3, ...
```

Floating-point numbers are those that can be represented using a decimal fraction and a power of 10. Examples are

6.022×10^{23} Number of molecules in a mole

0.0825   Current sales tax rate for Los Angeles County

> **Integer datatypes**   Primitive datatypes that can represent integers: `byte`, `short`, `int`, and `long`.

This chapter considers only integers; we will return to floating-point numbers later.

Java provides *four* different integer types—`byte`, `short`, `int`, and `long`—which differ in the number of bits and bytes used to store them. Let's take a look at their sizes and the number of values each type can store:

	Bytes	Bits	No. of values	No. of Values	No. of Values
`byte`	1	8	2^8	256	$\sim 10^{2.4}$
`short`	2	16	2^{16}	65,536 = 64K	$\sim 10^{4.8}$
`int`	4	32	2^{32}	4,294,967,296 = 4G	$\sim 10^{9.6}$
`long`	8	64	2^{64}	18,446,744,073,709,551,616 = 16E*	$\sim 10^{19.3}$

Consider `byte`. Each `byte` has 8 bits, allowing for 2^8 values. Among these are 0 and 1 and 2 and . . . and also -1 and -2 and. . . . But a single byte can form only 256 bit patterns. How many of the bit patterns are reserved for positive numbers? for negative numbers? for zero? You'll learn more about these questions and their answers in courses on assembly language and logic design. In the meantime, here is a table that shows the most negative and most positive numbers each of the integer types can hold:

	Bytes	Bits	Most Negative Value and Most Positive Value	Using Magnitude Prefixes
`byte`	1	8	-128	
			127	
`short`	2	16	$-32,768$	$-32K$
			32,767	$32K - 1$
`int`	4	32	$-2,147,483,648$	$-2G$
			2,147,483,647	$2G - 1$
`long`	8	64	$-9,223,372,036,854,775,808$	$-8E$
			9,223,372,036,854,775,807	$8E - 1$

---

* *E* stands for the prefix *exa-*, where $1E = 2^{60} \sim 10^{18}$.

Overflow Getting an incorrect integer value because the true result is too large for the datatype being used.

Later in this chapter we will confront the *overflow* question regarding `byte`: What happens when you add 1 to 127, or when you subtract 1 from -128?

Integer Literals

When Java encounters an integer literal—say, 179—it interprets it as an `int`.

7.2 Read an `int` and Print Its Square

In Chapter 5, we wrote a program that read a `String` from the keyboard and then printed it to the monitor. That simple program is a good way to start mastering some fundamental skills on a new computer or with a new programming language. Each time you change computers or languages, you will have to remaster the skills you used routinely and mechanically on the last computer or language. Over time, you will develop a repertoire of simple programs that will test each of the fundamental skills of a complete programming language. The current section introduces a new set of skills regarding *integers*, and the basic program we will write is this: *Read an integer from the keyboard and write its square to the monitor*. This simple program will demonstrate fundamental skills with integers.

Prog0701.java is our first program involving integers. Here are two test runs, where what the user types is underlined:

```
G:\>java Prog0701
Enter an integer: 5
Its square is 25

G:\>java Prog0701
Enter an integer: -9
Its square is 81
```

Let's read and understand the Java code that lies behind these test runs.

Prog0701.java   **Read an int and Print Its Square**

```
// Written by Barry Soroka
//
// Reads an int and prints its square.
//
import java.io.*;
import java.util.Scanner;
```

```
/////////////////////////////////////////////////////////////////////////////
class Prog0701
{
//-----------------------------------------------------------------------------

    public static void main (String [] args ) throws Exception
    {
        Scanner kb = new Scanner(System.in);
        System.out.print("Enter an integer: ");
        int n = kb.nextInt();
        System.out.println("Its square is " + (n*n));
    }
//-----------------------------------------------------------------------------
} // end class Prog0701
/////////////////////////////////////////////////////////////////////////////
```

Prog0701 begins by creating the Scanner kb and pointing it to the keyboard. Then comes the statement

```
System.out.print("Enter an integer: ");
```

This is the prompt. Whenever we want the user to type something in, we need to tell the user what we want. Notice that this prompt is a print statement and not a println. This keeps the cursor on the same line as the prompt, so that we get both the prompt and the input on the same line:

```
Enter an integer: -9
```

Now the statement

```
String s = kb.nextInt();
```

reads an int from the user; when applied to a Scanner, the nextInt method reads and returns an int.

The final statement of Prog0701 is:

```
System.out.println("Its square is " + (n*n));
```

This uses *—the multiplication operator—to compute the square of n, namely n*n, an int. The parentheses group the n*n together. We concatenate a String ("Its square is ") with an int, and we print the result.

Given the task description—"read an int and print its square"—you should be able to produce code similar to that of Prog0701.

Errors

What if we enter a noninteger in response to the prompt? Here's a test run where we enter `hello` instead of an integer:

```
G:\>java Prog0701
Enter an integer: hello
Exception in thread "main" java.util.InputMismatchException
        at java.util.Scanner.throwFor(Unknown Source)
        at java.util.Scanner.next(Unknown Source)
        at java.util.Scanner.nextInt(Unknown Source)
        at java.util.Scanner.nextInt(Unknown Source)
        at Prog0701.main(Prog0701.java:15)
```

Java throws an `InputMismatchException` because the `String` "hello" cannot be interpreted as an `int`.

The largest `int` is approximately 2 billion. Let's enter *3* billion—an integer that is too large to fit in the 32 bits of an `int`:

```
G:\>java Prog0701
Enter an integer: 3000000000
Exception in thread "main" java.util.InputMismatchException:
For input string: "3000000000"
        at java.util.Scanner.nextInt(Unknown Source)
        at java.util.Scanner.nextInt(Unknown Source)
        at Prog0701.main(Prog0701.java:15)
```

Java objects appropriately.

If we enter the integer 2 billion, its *square* will be too large to fit inside an `int`. Here's what we observe:

```
G:\>java Prog0701
Enter an integer: 2000000000
Its square is -1651507200
```

The `int` datatype contains 32 bits. The square of 2,000,000,000 requires more than 32 bits in binary. Accordingly, some data are lost by the phenomenon of *overflow*. For `Prog0701`, the output is invalid, but Java doesn't warn us. Be careful:

> Arithmetic operations that produce overflow are usually not flagged as errors by Java.

 Test your skill with Exercise 7-1.

7.3 String **Methods Involving Integers**

In Chapter 4, we learned some methods from the class String. At that time, we didn't know integers, so we learned only methods involving Strings:

```
String concat(String)
String toUpperCase()
String toLowerCase()
String trim()
```

Now that we're studying integers, we can learn a host of other methods from the class String. First, let's consider length(), a method which, when applied to a String, returns its length—as an int. The code

```
String s = "hello";
int n = s.length();
System.out.println(n);
```

prints out 5, as expected. We ought to test this on a bunch of Strings, and Prog0702.java is a program that makes such extensive testing more feasible: It *repeatedly* reads a String and prints its length. Prog0702 takes the reading and writing code and puts it inside the code for an *infinite loop*:

```
while ( true )
{
    code
}
```

Consider this simply a *pattern* that provides infinite looping. We will use this pattern many times in this chapter and those ahead. In Chapter 13 we will learn about loops in general, and we'll understand *why* this code is an infinite loop. We'll also learn how to write loops that stop on a specified cue.

Prog0702.java   **Read a String and Print Its Length**

```
// Written by Barry Soroka
//
// Repeatedly:  Read a String and print its length.
//
import java.io.*;
import java.util.Scanner;
//////////////////////////////////////////////////////////////////////////
class Prog0702
```

```
{
//-----------------------------------------------------------------------------

   public static void main (String [] args ) throws Exception
   {
      Scanner kb = new Scanner(System.in);

      while ( true )
      {
         System.out.print("\nEnter a String:   ");
         String s = kb.nextLine();
         int n = s.length();
         System.out.println("String \"" + s + "\" has length " + n);
      }
   }
//-----------------------------------------------------------------------------
} // end class Prog0702
/////////////////////////////////////////////////////////////////////////////
```

Here is a typical run of Prog0702, where what the user types is underlined:

```
G:\>java Prog0702

Enter a String:   hello
String "hello" has length 5

Enter a String:   hello there
String "hello there" has length 11

Enter a String:
String "" has length 0

Enter a String:   ___
String "   " has length 3

Enter a String:   13
String "13" has length 2

Enter a String:          ← control-C typed here
Enter a String:   Exception in thread "main"
      java.util.NoSuchElementException: No line found
         at java.util.Scanner.nextLine(Unknown Source)
         at Prog0702.main(Prog0702.java:18)Exception in

G:\>
```

What's interesting about this? First, how do we break out of the infinite loop? That concerns our action at the last prompt—I typed *control-C* which, for my computer and my Java, causes a running program to halt. Java takes the control-C as an exceptional action, and it prints an appropriate message. Line 18 of the program involves `kb.nextLine()`. Since we entered control-C instead of a `String`, the `nextLine` method bombs, giving a `NoSuchElementException`. The program was looking for a line, but couldn't find one.

Now let's examine the five *normal* `String`s I typed into `Prog0702`:

String	length()	Remarks
`"hello"`	5	Obvious.
`"hello there"`	11	Embedded spaces are still part of the `String`.
`" "`	0	The empty `String` has length 0. We enter the empty `String` by typing only an `Enter` in response to the prompt.
`"   "`	3	This `String` contains 3 spaces. It's not the empty `String`. Its length is 3.
`"13"`	2	This `String` has length 2, even though it represents an integer.

Numbering String Positions

Within a `String`, the positions are numbered with integers, starting at 0. Consider the `String` `"hello there"`, which has length 11. Its characters are numbered like this:

0	1	2	3	4	5	6	7	8	9	10
h	e	l	l	o		t	h	e	r	e

where position 5 is the space character. Note the general principle: If a `String` has length n, then its positions are numbered 0, 1, . . ., n-1. So a `String` of length 11 has positions from 0 through 10.

> Not all languages number `String` positions beginning with 0. Many languages have used 1 as the starting index. I once thought that the designers of Java had made an error in their choice of 0 as the starting index, but I soon found myself writing a program[1] where a 1-start system would have yielded much more complicated code than Java's 0-start system. Moral: Don't be too hasty in judging the features of a language.

---

[1]   One simple program in which 0-start indexing shows its value is the code that copies several collections into a new collection. We'll see this code when we tackle arrays in Chapter 14.

substring

We know about integers, and we know how positions are numbered within Strings. Now we are ready for the substring methods, which take integer arguments and return Strings that are pieces of the receiving String. The String class of Java supplies *two* substring methods: one takes a single int parameter; the other takes *two* int parameters.

Consider the method substring(int). When applied to a String s, this method returns the String starting at the specified int position and ending at the end of the String. Consider the String "tiger":

0	1	2	3	4
t	i	g	e	r

Here are some examples of substring(int):

Expression	Result
"tiger".substring(0)	"tiger"
"tiger".substring(1)	"iger"
"tiger".substring(2)	"ger"
"tiger".substring(3)	"er"
"tiger".substring(4)	"r"
"tiger".substring(5)	""

Similar results would be realized if we had assigned "tiger" to a variable:

```
String s = "tiger";
System.out.println(s.substring(0));
. . .
```

Given a String s of length n, what are the legal values of the int n in a message of the form s.substring(n)? What are the smallest and largest legal values? For the smallest value, we reason like this: Since n is to be the first position in the substring, and the lowest-numbered position is 0, then n must be ≥ 0. For the largest value, we need to think a bit differently. We might have thought that n-1 is the last position at which a substring could start, but Java thinks differently:

- substring(n-1) yields a substring of length 1;
- substring(n) yields a substring of length 0—the empty String.

That's why `"tiger".substring(5)` or `s.substring(5)` evaluates to the empty `String` in the preceding table. This was a case where the designers of Java got to choose how a particular method would behave. Our intuition won't always match theirs, and Java is not entirely consistent, so you may need to check the API to determine exactly how a method works.

Test your skill with Exercise 7-2.

The second version of `substring` takes *two* int parameters:

- The first is the position at which the `substring` should begin.
- The second is *one past* where we want the `substring` to end.

For example,

        `"tiger".substring(1,4)`

yields `"ige"` because it includes the characters from index 1 to index 3. Similarly,

        `"tiger".substring(2,3)`

yields `"g"` because it includes the characters from index 2 to index 2.

Here's a table that illustrates the two-parameter `substring` method applied to the `String "tiger"`:

		Ending Position					
		0	1	2	3	4	5
Starting Position	0	`" "`	`"t"`	`"ti"`	`"tig"`	`"tige"`	`"tiger"`
	1	Illegal	`" "`	`"i"`	`"ig"`	`"ige"`	`"iger"`
	2	Illegal	Illegal	`" "`	`"g"`	`"ge"`	`"ger"`
	3	Illegal	Illegal	Illegal	`" "`	`"e"`	`"er"`
	4	Illegal	Illegal	Illegal	Illegal	`" "`	`"r"`
	5	Illegal	Illegal	Illegal	Illegal	Illegal	`" "`

You should try, at least once, to compute such a table using a `String` and viewing the result—possibly involving an error—for each possible *start* and *end* position.

From the table and from logical thinking, we can see the following rules, where *start*, *end*, and *length* have the obvious meanings:

- *start* must be ≥ 0.
- *end* must be ≥ *start*.
- *end* must be ≤ *length*.

You should check the API to see that it lists these same rules for method `substring(int,int)`. Note, also, that if *start* and *end* are equal, then the result is an empty `String`.

Not all languages specify the two-parameter `substring` method the way Java does. Some languages use a *starting position* and a *length* for the `substring`. Other languages use a *starting position* and the *ending position* of the substring, unlike Java's end-plus-one convention. When using a new language, be careful that you double-check how `substring` works in that language.

Test your skill with Exercises 7-3 through 7-5.

Indexing Methods

The `String` class provides two methods that report the position, if any, at which a given `String` occurs in a receiving `String`. For example, consider the String `"banana"` with the positions numbered here:

0	1	2	3	4	5
b	a	n	a	n	a

Then the following expressions and results illustrate the index methods `indexOf` and `lastIndexOf`:

- `"banana".indexOf("an")` evaluates to 1, which is the index of the *first* occurrence of the parameter `String` in the receiver.
- `"banana".lastIndexOf("an")` evaluates to 3, which is the index of the *last* occurrence of the parameter `String`.

Thus, `indexOf` searches from left to right, and `lastIndexOf` searches from right to left. We will find that both these methods can be useful.

Wait! What if the parameter `String` doesn't occur in the receiving `String`? For these cases, the designers of the `String` class decided that `indexOf` and `lastIndexOf` would return `-1`. Note that `-1` is not a legal position for a `String`, so it's a good indicator that the `String` we seek does not occur.

 Test your skill with Exercises 7-6 through 7-12.

HOLD YOUR HORSES

You may be wondering whether Java's `String` class offers a method that takes an `int` and returns the character at that specific position in a `String`. Don't worry. Once we learn the `char` datatype, we'll learn the method `charAt(int)`.

7.4   Arithmetic Operators for Integers

Operator   An action, such as +, -, or *.
Operand   What an operand acts upon.
Expression   A combination of operands and operators.

Java provides five arithmetic *operators* that work on integers:

```
+, -, *, /, %.
```

These operators work on data elements called *operands*. First we must clarify the terms *unary* and *binary*:

- Some operators work on *a single operand*, as in the expressions +n or -n. When an operator takes a single operand, we call it a *unary* operator.
- Some operators work on *two operands*, as in the expressions n+3, 5-n, 3*n, n/7, or 17%n. We call these *binary* operators.

Three of the operators work exactly as they do in mathematics: the addition operator (+), the subtraction operator (-), and the multiplication operator (*). We can treat these just as we have in the past.

On the other hand, the division operator (/) behaves differently in Java than in general mathematics:

When both operands are integers, the division operator commands *integer division*.

The result of the / operation will always be an *integer*. In our prior work in arithmetic, the fraction 2/3 yielded a real number with the approximate representation 0.6666666667. Not so in Java. To Java, 2/3 evaluates to 0 because 3 does not go into 2 even once. Similarly, 16/5 evaluates to 3. The fractional part of the result is simply discarded.

TRY IT OUT

You should be skeptical of what you've just read. Write a program that reads two integers and prints their quotient. How long does it take your intuition to agree with Java's behavior?

The remainder operator (%) takes two integer operands—a number and a divisor—and returns the *remainder* of an integer division of the number by the divisor. Here are a few examples:

10%3 → 1

11%3 → 2

12%3 → 0

13%3 → 1

The result will be 0 if the divisor evenly divides the number.

In a sense, Java has *two* integer division operators: "/" to find the quotient, and "%" to find the remainder.

 Test your skill with Exercises 7-13 and 7-14.

A Unary Method from the Math Class

The class Math provides the abs method, which computes the *absolute value* of its parameter. For example:

```
Math.abs(5) → 5
Math.abs(-7) → 7
Math.abs(0) → 0
```

In normal mathematical notation, we would write |n| using operator symbols that *surround* their argument. In Java, we place n as a parameter to the Math.abs(int) method. We can use this method in the midst of more complex expressions:

```
3*Math.abs(5-7) → 3*Math.abs(-2) → 3*2 → 6
```

When we learn about floating-point numbers, we'll discover a great many other useful methods in the Math class.

Test your skill with Exercise 7-15.

Don't Use / or % with Negative Numbers

The / and % operators are well-defined for positive operands, but it's not clear just what should be returned by expressions like 5/-3, -5%3, or 5%-3. Programming languages do not all agree on how to implement the divide and remainder operators for negative numbers. Each language provides theoretical reasons to justify its choice of algorithm. We can avoid a lot of problems if we simply refrain from using / and % with negative numbers.

Expressions

We have now seen operators used with integer variables and literals. An *expression* is built from variables, literals, and operators according to the following rules:

1. An integer variable is an expression.
2. An integer literal is an expression.
3. If e_1 and e_2 are expressions and *op* is a binary operator, then $e_1 \; op \; e_2$ is an expression.
4. If *e* is an expression, then (*e*) is an expression.

We say that this is a *recursive* definition of expression, and we can build more complex expressions from simpler expressions. Using these rules we can build expressions of any desired complexity.

7.5 Precedence and Parentheses

When expressions involve *more than one operator*, as in

    2+3*4

or

    2-4/3+2

or

17/8/3

we could logically argue for different results, depending on which of the operations is performed first. For example, 2+3*4 will yield either 14 or 20, depending on whether the * is performed *before* or *after* the +. Here is an illustration of those computations, where, in each expression, I've underlined the operands and operator that will be evaluated next:

2+<u>3*4</u> → <u>2+12</u> → 14

<u>2+3</u>*4 → <u>5*4</u> → 20

Precedence   Rules for evaluating expressions containing more than one operator.

All programming languages contain a set of rules for mechanically selecting which operator to evaluate next. These rules dictate the *precedence* of the different operations.

HOLD YOUR HORSES

Languages do not all agree about how to evaluate multioperator expressions. The rules of precedence are not self-evident. For the moment, we'll study how *Java* evaluates expressions, but over your working lifetime you will probably encounter languages that do it differently.

For Java, the first rule is:

The operators {*,/,%} are performed *before* the operators {+,-} if the operators are consecutive.

Thus, for Java, 2+3*4 will evaluate to 14, not to 20.

{*,/,%} are often called the *multiplicative operators* and {+,-} are called the *additive operators*. Thus, we can say that *multiplication has precedence over addition*. You may have been taught such a rule for arithmetic back in high school.

The second rule concerns expressions like 2-4+5, where we have *two operators of equal precedence*. This expression could yield either 3 or -18, depending on the order in which the operations are performed:

2-4+5 → -2+5 → 3

2-4+5 → 2-9 → -7

For Java, the second rule is:

> When two consecutive operators have equal precedence, the *leftmost* one is performed first.

Here are two expressions that involve the second rule:

2-4/3+2 → 2-1+2 → 1+2 → 3

17/8/3 → 2/3 → 0

NOTE   If you are ever uncertain about how an arithmetic expression will evaluate, you can ask Java to tell you the result by plugging the expression into the statement System.out.println(...).

Sometimes we have an expression where we don't want to use Java's natural precedence. Java's third rule for evaluating expressions is:

> An expression inside parentheses is evaluated on its own before being used by operators outside the parentheses.

For example, we can alter the results of the previous two expressions by using parentheses appropriately:

2-4/(3+2) → 2-4/5 → 2-0 → 2

17/(8/3) → 17/2 → 8

Operator precedence also applies between *Strings* and *numbers*. Consider how these three expressions evaluate under Java's rules of precedence:

`"hello"` + 3 + 2 → `"hello3"` + 2 → `"hello32"`

`"hello"` + (3 + 2) → `"hello"` + 5 → `"hello5"`

`"hello"` + 3 * 2 → `"hello"` + 6 → `"hello6"`

> **Test your skill with Exercises 7-16 and 7-17.**

7.6   Shortcuts for Arithmetic Expressions and Statements

The following kinds of expression occur frequently in Java programs:

```
n = n + 27;
n = n - 5;
n = n * 3;
n = n / 2;
```

and here is the model:

```
var = var operator operand
```

Because such statements occur frequently, Java provides a shortcut via the syntax

```
var operator = operand
```

with the following examples:

Expression	Shortcut
n = n + 27;	n += 27;
n = n - 5;	n -= 5;
n = n * 3;	n *= 3;
n = n / 2;	n /= 2;

Any binary operator can be used in this shortcut.

Note that this shortcut always evaluates the entire right-hand side of the assignment before performing the desired operation with the variable. So

```
n += j + 1;
```

is equivalent to

```
n = n + (j + 1);
```

Increment and Decrement Operators

Two other frequent operations are

```
n = n + 1;
```

and

```
n = n - 1;
```

Java provides the following shortcuts for these statements:

```
n++;
n--;
```

Always use these shortcuts as *single, independent statements*. Danger awaits those who use the shortcuts otherwise.

HOLD YOUR HORSES

Yes, Java, like C++, provides *four* such forms:

```
n++        ++n
n--        --n
```

In my experience, students—and veteran programmers—have difficulty using these properly. Everyone ends up getting them wrong in one program or another. Despite the danger, I'm willing to allow n++ and n-- when used as *statements*. See Appendix 5 for further details on these operators.

Test your skill with Exercise 7-18.

7.7 How Primitive Datatypes Differ from Objects

Primitive datatypes Datatypes that are not objects.

The previous section began our discussion of integer types, which are the first of the primitive datatypes we'll study; others will be floating-point numbers, characters, and true-false (`boolean`) values. *Primitive datatypes are not objects*, but we can use them as the types of *instance variables* of objects. For example, we can use an `int` value in an `age` slot for class `Animal` or class `Person` or class `Teacher`.

Primitive datatypes differ from objects in the following ways:

Objects	Primitive Datatypes

Created by `new` and a constructor:
 	
`new Animal("fido","woof")`
	Created by giving a literal or an expression:
	
	`37`
	
	`n+5`

Variables are *references* to objects:
 	
`Animal a = new Animal("fido","woof");`
 	
`String s = "hello";`
	Variables hold the value itself:
	
	`int n = 37;`

Have internal structure (instance variables).	Have no internal structure.

Do work by receiving messages (methods):
 	
`Animal a1, a2;`
 	
`...`
 	
`a1.speak();`
 	
`a2 = a1.makeBig();`
	Can be combined into expressions using primitive operators:
	
	`3+5`
	
	`3-n*2`

Are correlated with the problem our program is trying to solve.	Are correlated with the storage elements of the underlying computer hardware. Recall our discussion regarding `byte`, `short`, `int`, and `long`.
We can define new classes of objects.	We cannot define new primitive datatypes.

> **Test your skill with Exercise 7-19.**

7.8 `EggShipment`: **Gross, Dozen, Single**

The purpose of this example is to demonstrate how much we can compute using only the operators we've learned so far. We'll write a class `EggShipment`, which stores an integer number of eggs, and its `toString` method will produce a printed representation that separates the eggs into a triple: the number of *gross* (where 1 gross is 144), plus the number of *dozen* (where 1 dozen is 12), plus the number of *singles* (whatever's left).[2] Note that the

---

[2] The 144–12–1 ratio of gross–dozen–single is no more bizarre than having, for example, 16 ounces in a pound, 2000 pounds in a ton, 52 weeks in a year, 52 cards in a deck, or 60 minutes in an hour.

number of singles can never exceed 11, and the number of dozens can never exceed 11. We'll write a driver that will read a number of eggs, create an Egg-Shipment to store that number, and then print out the EggShipment displaying the correct triple.

We're going to study this problem, and others, in three steps:

1. First, we'll *sketch the hardcopy desired* from a program that performs the required task. Ideally, this provides us with an exhaustive set of test cases, which can be used to determine whether a proposed implementation is performing correctly.

2. Then we'll *write a test driver* that (a) produces the expected hardcopy, and (b) uses the proposed method(s). This will help us sharpen the prototypes and skeleton of the proposed new methods.

3. Finally, we'll *implement the new methods* and run the class with the test driver. This will allow us to verify that the implementation performs correctly on at least the test cases we have selected.

Step One

First, here's an example of the desired output from our target program:

```
Enter an int: 0
EggShipment:  0 gross + 0 dozen + 0 single

Enter an int: 1
EggShipment:  0 gross + 0 dozen + 1 single

Enter an int: 12
EggShipment:  0 gross + 1 dozen + 0 single
```

because 12 is one dozen and no remainder.

```
Enter an int: 15
EggShipment:  0 gross + 1 dozen + 3 single

Enter an int: 24
EggShipment:  0 gross + 2 dozen + 0 single
```

because 24 is two dozen and no remainder.

```
Enter an int: 72
EggShipment:  0 gross + 6 dozen + 0 single

Enter an int: 143
EggShipment:  0 gross + 11 dozen + 11 single

Enter an int: 144
EggShipment:  1 gross + 0 dozen + 0 single

Enter an int: 145
EggShipment:  1 gross + 0 dozen + 1 single

Enter an int: 156
EggShipment:  1 gross + 1 dozen + 0 single

Enter an int: 157
EggShipment:  1 gross + 1 dozen + 1 single
```

Verify these calculations.

Step Two

This step produces the driver in class `Prog0703`. It contains the usual infinite loop, which we often use when we test a simple new class or method. Within the loop, we have four statements:

```
System.out.print("\nEnter an int: ");
int n = kb.nextInt();
EggShipment es = new EggShipment(n);
System.out.println("EggShipment:  " + es);
```

The first statement prompts for an integer. It also inserts a blank line between each test case; this visually separates the test cases, making them easier to read. The second statement reads an `int` from the user. The third statement creates an `EggShipment` using the constructor and the `int`. The last statement invokes the `toString()` method of class `EggShipment`, printing out the triple of eggs: *gross–dozen–single*. Notice that enough spaces have been inserted in the `String` literals so that the input and output line up; this is often helpful in understanding test runs of a program.

Prog0703.java Using Class **EggShipment**

```java
// Written by Barry Soroka
//
// EggShipment -- Store a single int.
//              -- toString computes gross, dozen, single.
//
import java.io.*;
import java.util.Scanner;
//////////////////////////////////////////////////////////////////////////////
class Prog0703
{
//----------------------------------------------------------------------------
   public static void main (String [] args ) throws Exception
   {
      Scanner kb = new Scanner(System.in);

      while ( true )
      {
         System.out.print("\nEnter an int: ");
         int n = kb.nextInt();
         EggShipment es = new EggShipment(n);
         System.out.println("EggShipment:  " + es);
      }
   }
//----------------------------------------------------------------------------
} // end class Prog0703
//////////////////////////////////////////////////////////////////////////////
class EggShipment
{
   private int n;
//----------------------------------------------------------------------------
   public EggShipment ( int n )
   {
      this.n = n;
   }
//----------------------------------------------------------------------------
   public String toString()
   {
      int nGross = n / 144;
      int nDozen = (n % 144) / 12;
      int nSingle = (n % 144) % 12;
```

```
        return nGross + " gross + " +
               nDozen + " dozen + " +
               nSingle + " single";
   }
//----------------------------------------------------------------------------
} // end class EggShipment
////////////////////////////////////////////////////////////////////////////////
```

Step Three

Our final step involves implementing class `EggShipment`. It has one instance variable, `n`, which is `private` and `int`. The constructor takes an `int` and stores it. The `toString` method is a bit more complicated. It computes `nGross`, `nDozen`, and `nSingle`.[3] There's a pattern here that you should learn, because you'll use it again. The pattern relies on the fact that if `n` and `q` are integers,

- `n/q` tells us how many units of `q` are in `n`, and
- `n%q` tells us how many individuals are left over.

So the expression `n/144` computes the number of *gross* in `n`. That means that `n%144` is the number of eggs remaining past that number of gross. We compute the number of dozens with the expression `(n%144)/12`, and we compute the number of singles with `(n%144)%12`. Finally, the `toString` method assembles and returns the appropriate `String`.

Note that the conversion procedure is not meaningful when the number is negative. We want the user to enter a nonnegative number.[4] In Chapter 17, we'll learn how to detect unsuitable input and how to react in an appropriate fashion.

| **Test your skill with Exercises 7-20 through 7-26.** |

---

[3] Acceptable alternative names would be `n144`, `n12`, and `n1`, and `gross`, `dozen`, and `single`.

[4] We'll use the phrase "nonnegative number" a lot. It means positive or zero. In some mathematical courses, this might be called a natural number.

7.9   **Arithmetic with** EggShipments

In the previous section we introduced class EggShipment, and now we will define a method that will add two EggShipments and return the result. For example, if we have the following two EggShipments

	Gross	Dozen	Single
es1	7	7	5
es2	2	8	8

their sum would be:[5]

	Gross	Dozen	Single
sum	10	4	1

In modifying EggShipment, we will adhere to the same three steps we used in writing it initially:

1. Sketch the hardcopy desired.
2. Write a test driver.
3. Implement the new methods.

Our goal is this: Prog0704 will be a program that starts with a total of 0 eggs and then repeatedly asks the user to enter the number of eggs to add to the EggShipment. The triple of gross–dozen–single will be printed each time we go around the loop. Even before writing the code, we can show an annotated test run:

```
G:\1\book\programs>java Prog0704

The current total is 0 gross + 0 dozen + 0 single
```

The initial EggShipment contains 0 eggs.

```
Eggs to add? 11

          Adding 0 gross + 0 dozen + 11 single
```

---

[5] Check my arithmetic!

That added 11 eggs.

```
The current total is 0 gross + 0 dozen + 11 single

Eggs to add? 2

            Adding 0 gross + 0 dozen + 2 single

The current total is 0 gross + 1 dozen + 1 single
```

Two eggs cause us to push past the first dozen mark.

```
Eggs to add? 11

            Adding 0 gross + 0 dozen + 11 single

The current total is 0 gross + 2 dozen + 0 single
```

Eleven eggs pushed us to two dozen.

```
Eggs to add? 100

            Adding 0 gross + 8 dozen + 4 single

The current total is 0 gross + 10 dozen + 4 single
```

The program correctly converted 100 eggs to 0-8-4 and performed the correct egg arithmetic.

```
Eggs to add? 8

            Adding 0 gross + 0 dozen + 8 single

The current total is 0 gross + 11 dozen + 0 single
```

Eight eggs plus four eggs pushed us to the next dozen.

```
Eggs to add? 12

            Adding 0 gross + 1 dozen + 0 single

The current total is 1 gross + 0 dozen + 0 single
```

One full dozen pushed 11 dozen to the 1 gross mark.

Would this test run be sufficient to convince us that the code is correct? No, but it exercises three of the features we expect to see from the code: correct conversion from an `int` to a triple, increment when passing through the dozen mark, and increment when passing through the gross mark. Test cases should always try to push past every milestone possible.

Now let's consider the code for class `Prog0704`, the driver that tests the `add` method of `EggShipment`. The statement

```
EggShipment total = new EggShipment(0);
```

sets up our "egg counter" with an `EggShipment` with 0 eggs. Then, within the loop, we find five statements.

```
System.out.println("\nThe current total is " + total);
```

Each time around the loop, we're going to print the current `total`. Note that the new-line character is at the start of every printed line; this "double-spaces" the output so that the arithmetic is easier to see.

```
System.out.print("\nEggs to add? ");
EggShipment es = new EggShipment(kb.nextInt());
```

The program prompts for the number of eggs to add, and constructs the `Egg-Shipment`, which represents the new quantity.

```
System.out.println("\n            Adding " + es);
```

This statement prints out the `EggShipment` to be added, and we can see and verify the arithmetic. Notice that the blank spaces push the output so that the current and new `EggShipments` are roughly aligned.

```
total = total.add(es);
```

Now we use an `add` method to compute the new `total`.

We've studied the desired i/o and the test driver. Now let's actually implement the `add` method for class `EggShipment`. First, notice the header:

```
public EggShipment add ( EggShipment that )
```

Here's what the pieces mean:

- `public` makes this method visible outside the class. In general, methods are `public`.

- `EggShipment` is the return type. The purpose of this method is to return a new `EggShipment` that is the sum of two others.
- `add` is the name of the method.
- `EggShipment` is the type of the parameter. This `EggShipment` will be added to the receiver `EggShipment` to produce the result `EggShipment`.
- `that` is the name of the parameter. We'll refer to the receiver as `this`, so it seems appropriate to refer to the parameter as `that`. We thus have "`this` and `that`," an easy combination to remember.

Method `add` contains a single statement:

```
return new EggShipment ( this.n + that.n );
```

It sums the values of the `n` variable in `this` and `that`.

Prog0704.java   An add Method for EggShipment

```
// Written by Barry Soroka
//
// add for EggShipment
//
import java.io.*;
import java.util.Scanner;
//////////////////////////////////////////////////////////////////////////////
class Prog0704
{
//----------------------------------------------------------------------------
   public static void main (String [] args ) throws Exception
   {
      Scanner kb = new Scanner(System.in);

      EggShipment total = new EggShipment(0);

      while ( true )
      {
         System.out.println("\nThe current total is " + total);
         System.out.print("\nEggs to add? ");
         EggShipment es = new EggShipment(kb.nextInt());
         System.out.println("\n                 Adding " + es);
         total = total.add(es);
      }
   }
}
```

```
//-----------------------------------------------------------------
} // end class Prog0704
/////////////////////////////////////////////////////////////////////////
class EggShipment
{
   private int n;
//-----------------------------------------------------------------
   public EggShipment ( int n )
   {
      this.n = n;
   }
//-----------------------------------------------------------------
   public EggShipment add ( EggShipment that )
   {
      return new EggShipment ( this.n + that.n );
   }
//-----------------------------------------------------------------
   public String toString()
   {
      int nGross = n / 144;
      int nDozen = (n % 144) / 12;
      int nSingle = (n % 144) % 12;

      return nGross + " gross + " +
             nDozen + " dozen + " +
             nSingle + " single";
   }
//-----------------------------------------------------------------
} // end class EggShipment
/////////////////////////////////////////////////////////////////////////
```

There are two other ways to write method add. Obviously, both have the same prototype as the definition we've just seen. Here's one way:

```
public EggShipment add ( EggShipment that )
{
   int n1 = this.n;
   int n2 = that.n;
   return new EggShipment ( n1+n2 );
}
```

and here's the other:

```
public EggShipment add ( EggShipment that )
{
    EggShipment result = new EggShipment(0);
    result.n = this.n + that.n;
}
```

Think about these.

Test your skill with Exercises 7-27 through 7-30.

7.10   Complex Numbers: Mathematical Preliminaries

Complex numbers were invented to provide solutions to algebraic equations that did not have solutions among the real numbers. For example, the equation $x^2 - 4 = 0$ has solutions $x = +2$ and $x = -2$, but the equation $x^2 + 4 = 0$ has no solutions in the reals, since it requires that x^2 be negative, and the square of every real number is 0 or greater. To solve such equations, mathematicians invented complex numbers, which have two parts: a real part and an imaginary part. By convention, we use $i = \sqrt{-1}$ as the basis for the imaginary parts of complex numbers. ($i^2 = -1$). Each such number can be written as $a + ib$, where a is the real part and ib is the imaginary part. Sometimes we write $a + bi$. Also, by convention, the letter z is often used to represent a complex number:

$$z_1 = a_1 + ib_1,$$
$$z_2 = a_2 + ib_2, \ldots$$

Complex numbers are often used in electrical and mechanical design problems, and much computer code has been written for tasks involving complex numbers.

Starting with the two complex numbers, z_1 and z_2, we can examine the relevant arithmetic operations. Addition and subtraction are straightforward:

$$z_1 + z_2 = (a_1 + a_2) + i\,(b_1 + b_2)$$
$$z_1 - z_2 = (a_1 - a_2) + i\,(b_1 - b_2)$$

Multiplication derives as follows:

$$z_1 \cdot z_2 = (a_1 + ib_1)(a_2 + ib_2)$$
$$= a_1a_2 + ia_1b_2 + ia_2b_1 + i^2b_1b_2$$
$$= a_1a_2 + ia_1b_2 + ia_2b_1 - b_1b_2$$
$$= (a_1a_2 - b_1b_2) + i(a_1b_2 + a_2b_1)$$

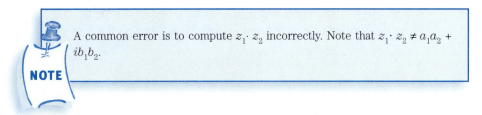

A common error is to compute $z_1 \cdot z_2$ incorrectly. Note that $z_1 \cdot z_2 \neq a_1 a_2 + i b_1 b_2$.

We will use integers for the real and imaginary parts of complex numbers.

Test your skill with Exercises 7-31 and 7-32.

7.11   Reading and Printing Complex Numbers

In this section we'll define the class Complex, and we'll write a driver that reads and prints complex numbers. We will follow the three-step procedure we've used before in writing classes and drivers.

Envision the Test Runs

Our program will be an infinite loop that reads and prints Complex numbers. Here is typical hardcopy:

```
Reading a complex number ...
Enter the real part:     3
Enter the imaginary part: 4
(3,4)
```

I have chosen to produce output of the form (3,4) to represent the complex number $3 + 4i$.

Write the Driver

Here is the code that repeatedly reads a Complex and prints it using toString:

```
Scanner kb = new Scanner(System.in);
while ( true )
{
    System.out.println();
    Complex z = Complex.read(System.out,kb);
    System.out.println(z);
}
```

We begin by creating a `Scanner` attached to the keyboard, and we follow with an infinite loop. The statement

```
System.out.println();
```

inserts a blank line between every test case in the loop. Then we read a `Complex` number with the statement

```
Complex z = Complex.read(System.out,kb);
```

Clearly, the intention is to write and use a standard `static read` method for class `Complex`. Finally, the statement

```
System.out.println(z);
```

calls on the `toString` method of class `Complex` to print out the object we've created.

Implement the Class

`Prog0705` shows the driver and the completed code for the class `Complex`. The implementation involves four pieces of code: (1) the instance variables, (2) the constructor, (3) the `toString` method, and (4) the `static read` method.

Prog0705.java   **Read and Print Complex Numbers**

```
// Written by Barry Soroka
//
// Read & print Complex numbers.
//
import java.io.*;
import java.util.Scanner;
//////////////////////////////////////////////////////////////////////
class Prog0705
{
//-------------------------------------------------------------------
    public static void main (String [] args) throws Exception
    {
        Scanner kb = new Scanner(System.in);

        while ( true )
        {
            System.out.println();
            Complex z = Complex.read(System.out,kb);
```

```
            System.out.println(z);
         }
      }
//-----------------------------------------------------------------------
} // end class Prog0705
/////////////////////////////////////////////////////////////////////////
class Complex
{
   private int real;
   private int imag;
//-----------------------------------------------------------------------
   public Complex ( int real , int imag )
   {
      this.real = real;
      this.imag = imag;
   }
//-----------------------------------------------------------------------
   public String toString ()
   {
      return "(" + real + "," + imag + ")";
   }
//-----------------------------------------------------------------------
   public static Complex read ( PrintStream ps, Scanner sc )
         throws Exception
   {
      ps.println("Reading a complex number ...");
      ps.print("Enter the real part:      ");
      int real = sc.nextInt();
      ps.print("Enter the imaginary part: ");
      int imag = sc.nextInt();
      return new Complex ( real, imag );
   }
//-----------------------------------------------------------------------
} // end class Complex
/////////////////////////////////////////////////////////////////////////
```

We start by selecting the instance variables:

```
            private int real;
            private int imag;
```

I chose real and imag because they are descriptive of the full terms, *real* and *imaginary*, but I didn't want to use the term *imaginary*. Why? First, it's too long (and I would be continually misspelling it). Two, I like related variables to be the same length. That way, they line up vertically, as we see in the *constructor*:[6]

```
this.real = real;
this.imag = imag;
```

The `toString` method composes parentheses, instance variables, and a comma to produce the `String` we specified above:

```
return "(" + real + "," + imag + ")";
```

The final piece of code is the `static read` method. Notice that we have merely adapted the pattern we've used before in class `Animal` and class `EggShipment`.

You should compile and test this program to verify that it's working as advertised.

 Test your skill with Exercise 7-33.

7.12   Arithmetic Operations on `Complex` **Numbers**

In this section, we will implement methods for addition, subtraction, and multiplication of complex numbers. These methods will have names `add`, `sub`, and `mul`. We'll implement `add` first, and, once it's debugged, we'll copy much of the code to methods `sub` and `mul`. A beginner's mistake is to type in all the code for all three methods, only to discover that the same basic error has been made three times. By debugging `add` first, we'll have a working template from which to implement the other methods.

Our first decision concerns the *prototype* for `add`. There are two choices:

```
public Complex add(Complex)
```

and

```
public void add(Complex)
```

---

[6] a and b would also be reasonable variable names here.

The first method adds two `Complex` numbers to obtain a third. The second adds a number to an existing `Complex`. Let's select the first method; it's more general than the second.

Envision Test Runs

Let's test our adder by repeatedly reading a `Complex` and adding it to a running total. Here is a typical test run:

```
Current total: (0,0)

Reading a complex number ...
Enter the real part:      3
Enter the imaginary part: 4

You entered:   (3,4)

Current total: (3,4)

Reading a complex number ...
Enter the real part:     -1
Enter the imaginary part: 2

You entered:   (-1,2)

Current total: (2,6)

Reading a complex number ...
Enter the real part:      0
Enter the imaginary part: 17

You entered:   (0,17)

Current total: (2,23)

Reading a complex number ...
Enter the real part:     -5
Enter the imaginary part: -5

You entered:   (-5,-5)

Current total: (-3,18)
```

Write the Driver

Here is a driver that will produce the test run shown above:

```
while ( true )
{
    System.out.println("\nCurrent total: " + total + "\n");
    Complex z = Complex.read(System.out,kb);
    System.out.println("\nYou entered:   " + z);
    total = total.add(z);
}
```

Each time around the loop, the driver performs the following activities, matched to the statements within the loop:

1. Write out the current total.
2. Read the next `Complex`.
3. Echo what we read.
4. Update the total.

Implement the Method

`Prog0706` contains the modified class `Complex` and the method `add`. Here's the relevant code:

```
public Complex add ( Complex that )
{
    return new Complex ( this.real + that.real,
                         this.imag + that.imag );
}
```

As before, to make them easier to remember, the two operands have been named `this` and `that`, and I have created a new `Complex` with components equal to the sum of the components of the two operands.

Prog0706.java   **Keep a Running Total of Complex Numbers**

```
// Written by Barry Soroka
//
// Read & keep a running total of Complex numbers.
//
import java.io.*;
import java.util.Scanner;
```

```
/////////////////////////////////////////////////////////////////////////
class Prog0706
{
//-----------------------------------------------------------------------
    public static void main (String [] args) throws Exception
    {
        Scanner kb = new Scanner(System.in);

        Complex total = new Complex(0,0);

        while ( true )
        {
            System.out.println("\nCurrent total: " + total + "\n");
            Complex z = Complex.read(System.out,kb);
            System.out.println("\nYou entered:    " + z);
            total = total.add(z);
        }
    }
//-----------------------------------------------------------------------
} // end class Prog0706
/////////////////////////////////////////////////////////////////////////
class Complex
{
    private int real;
    private int imag;
//-----------------------------------------------------------------------
    public Complex ( int real , int imag )
    {
        this.real = real;
        this.imag = imag;
    }
//-----------------------------------------------------------------------
    public Complex add ( Complex that )
    {
        return new Complex ( this.real + that.real,
                             this.imag + that.imag );
    }
//-----------------------------------------------------------------------
    public String toString ()
    {
        return "(" + real + "," + imag + ")";
    }
//-----------------------------------------------------------------------
    public static Complex read ( PrintStream ps, Scanner sc )
```

```
    {
        ps.println("Reading a complex number ...");
        ps.print("Enter the real part:      ");
        int real = sc.nextInt();
        ps.print("Enter the imaginary part: ");
        int imag = sc.nextInt();
        return new Complex ( real, imag );
    }
//--------------------------------------------------------------------
} // end class Complex
/////////////////////////////////////////////////////////////////////
```

Alternative Ways to Generate a `Complex` Result

There are two other ways to generate the `Complex` object that is returned by the add method. Consider this second approach:

```
        public Complex add ( Complex that )
        {
            int real = this.real + that.real;
            int imag = this.imag + that.imag;
            return new Complex(real,imag);
        }
```

We create two local variables—`real` and `imag`—and we fill them appropriately. Then we call the constructor `Complex(real,imag)` using the values we've put together, and we return the created object.

A third pattern for returning an object from a method is:

```
        public Complex add ( Complex that )
        {
            Complex result = new Complex(0,0);
            result.real = this.real + that.real;
            result.imag = this.imag + that.imag;
            return result;
        }
```

We create a local variable `result` of type `Complex`, the same type that we plan to return. It doesn't matter what values are in its slots, because the next two statements fill these with the appropriate values. Finally, we return the local variable `result`.

Finishing the Class

At this point, we should compile `Prog0706` and test it. Since the `add` method seems correct, we can write the methods `sub` and `mul`. `Prog0707` presents the complete code for class `Complex`. Notice that `sub` is almost the same as `add`, but that `mul` is more complicated, as befits multiplication of complex numbers. Notice the code for `mul`:

```
public Complex mul ( Complex that )
{
    int a1 = this.real;
    int b1 = this.imag;
    int a2 = that.real;
    int b2 = that.imag;
    return new Complex ( a1*a2 - b1*b2, a1*b2 + a2*b1 );
}
```

I have created four local variables—`a1`, `b1`, `a2`, and `b2`—and used them in computing the two integers that go into the `Complex` we're creating. My purpose in creating the local variables was to make the code more readable, and I think that

```
a1*a2 - b1*b2, a1*b2 + a2*b1
```

is more readable than

```
this.real*that.real - this.imag*that.imag,
this.real*that.imag + this.imag*that.real
```

Remember: Our highest priority is not speed or size of code, but *readability*.

Prog0707.java   **Complete Code for Class Complex**

```
// Written by Barry Soroka
//
// Prog0707 -- Complete code for class Complex.
//
import java.io.*;
import java.util.Scanner;
///////////////////////////////////////////////////////////////////////////
class Complex
{
    private int real;
    private int imag;
//-----------------------------------------------------------------------
    public Complex ( int real , int imag )
    {
```

```
            this.real = real;
            this.imag = imag;
        }
//---------------------------------------------------------------
    public Complex add ( Complex that )
    {
        return new Complex ( this.real + that.real,
                                this.imag + that.imag );
    }
//---------------------------------------------------------------
    public Complex sub ( Complex that )
    {
        return new Complex ( this.real - that.real,
                                this.imag - that.imag );
    }
//---------------------------------------------------------------
    public Complex mul ( Complex that )
    {
        int a1 = this.real;
        int b1 = this.imag;
        int a2 = that.real;
        int b2 = that.imag;
        return new Complex ( a1*a2 - b1*b2, a1*b2 + a2*b1 );
    }
//---------------------------------------------------------------
    public String toString ()
    {
        return "(" + real + "," + imag + ")";
    }
//---------------------------------------------------------------
    public static Complex read ( PrintStream ps, Scanner sc )
    {
        ps.println("Reading a complex number ...");
        ps.print("Enter the real part:      ");
        int real = sc.nextInt();
        ps.print("Enter the imaginary part: ");
        int imag = sc.nextInt();
        return new Complex ( real, imag );
    }
//---------------------------------------------------------------
```

```
} // end class Complex
//////////////////////////////////////////////////////////////////////
```

 Test your skill with Exercises 7-34 through 7-38.

7.13   **Class** Rectangle

This section uses integer types to define a class Rectangle, which models the familiar two-dimensional shape. Rectangle objects have instance variables length and width, and we will implement methods grow and shrink that increment and decrement the dimensions of the shape. We will follow the same three-step development procedure used in previous sections.

Envision Test Runs

Our sample dialog should demonstrate the use of all the methods of a Rectangle: construction, and the effect of the shrink and grow operations. The grow operation will increment both the length and width of the Rectangle. The shrink operation decrements both length and width. The getArea() method computes area as needed. Here's the desired program output:

```
Initially...
Rectangle r has length 5 width 10 area 50.
Let's grow it...
Rectangle r has length 6 width 11 area 66.
Let's shrink it...
Rectangle r has length 5 width 10 area 50.
Let's shrink it...
Rectangle r has length 4 width 9 area 36.
```

Write the Driver

The driver consists of groups of statements, each of which has the following structure:

1. Announce the action we're about to take.
2. Perform the action.
3. Report length, width, and area.

Here is a draft of the driver that would produce the sample dialog we've designed, where the required getters will be provided by class `Rectangle`:

```
public static void main (String [] args) throws Exception
{
   System.out.println("\nInitially...");
   Rectangle r = new Rectangle(5,10);
   System.out.println("Rectangle r has length " + r.getLength() +
                      " width " + r.getWidth() +
                      " area " + r.getArea() + "." );

   System.out.println("\nLet's grow it...");
   r.grow();
   System.out.println("Rectangle r has length " + r.getLength() +
                      " width " + r.getWidth() +
                      " area " + r.getArea() + "." );

   System.out.println("\nLet's shrink it...");
   r.shrink();
   System.out.println("Rectangle r has length " + r.getLength() +
                      " width " + r.getWidth() +
                      " area " + r.getArea() + "." );

   System.out.println("\nLet's shrink it...");
   r.shrink();
   System.out.println("Rectangle r has length " + r.getLength() +
                      " width " + r.getWidth() +
                      " area " + r.getArea() + "." );
}
```

The code above can be improved. Consider the statement

```
System.out.println("Rectangle r has length " + r.getLength() +
                   " width " + r.getWidth() +
                   " area " + r.getArea() + "." );
```

It's very long and is repeated four times. Repeated code is an invitation to difficulty in the maintenance phase of programming. When the code needs to be changed, it will need to be changed in *many* places, and we run the risk of overlooking some of the places we need to change. Suppose, for example, that a working program is to be ported into a different natural language—say, from English to French. Then the port is easier if we only need to replace each distinct English statement *once*.

I would improve our first draft by writing a method `report(Rectangle)` as a *helper function*:

```
private static void report ( Rectangle r )
{
    System.out.println("Rectangle r has length " + r.getLength() +
                    " width " + r.getWidth() +
                    " area " + r.getArea() + "." );
}
```

It gathers together the long statement I noted above, and it takes its `Rectangle` parameter and prints out the information we wanted in our sample dialog. If we ever need to change our wording or change the language, then we need only to make the changes in this one place.

Implement the Class

Refer to `Prog0708.java` to see the code. I have chosen instance variables `length` and `width`. The name `l`—the letter after `k`—is not appropriate because it looks too much like the number 1, and the reader would be confused.

Prog0708.java   **Testing Class Rectangle**

```
// Written by Barry Soroka
//
// Driver to test class Rectangle -- revised version.
//
import java.io.*;
////////////////////////////////////////////////////////////////////
class Prog0708
{
//------------------------------------------------------------------
    public static void main (String [] args) throws Exception
    {
        System.out.println("\nInitially...");
        Rectangle r = new Rectangle(5,10);
        report(r);

        System.out.println("\nLet's grow it...");
        r.grow();
        report(r);

        System.out.println("\nLet's shrink it...");
        r.shrink();
        report(r);

        System.out.println("\nLet's shrink it...");
```

```
        r.shrink();
        report(r);
    }
//-----------------------------------------------------------------
    private static void report ( Rectangle r )
    {
        System.out.println("Rectangle r has length " + r.getLength() +
                           " width " + r.getWidth() +
                           " area " + r.getArea() + "." );
    }
//-----------------------------------------------------------------
} // end class Prog0708
/////////////////////////////////////////////////////////////////
class Rectangle
{
    private int length;
    private int width;
//-----------------------------------------------------------------
    public Rectangle ( int length , int width)
    {
        this.length = length;
        this.width = width;
    }
//-----------------------------------------------------------------
    public int getLength() { return length; }
//-----------------------------------------------------------------
    public int getWidth() { return width; }
//-----------------------------------------------------------------
    public int getArea() { return length * width; }
//-----------------------------------------------------------------
    public void grow() { length++; width++; }
//-----------------------------------------------------------------
    public void shrink() { length--; width--; }
//-----------------------------------------------------------------
} // end class Rectangle
/////////////////////////////////////////////////////////////////
```

In designing the class Rectangle, we have two choices concerning the property *area*:

1. We can have a method getArea(), which *computes the area*, as needed, by multiplying length and width. This has the downside that, if we ask for the area many times without changing length and width, then we are doing many extra multiplications.

2. We can create an instance variable `area`, and we can maintain it as `length` and `width` change. The method `getArea()` would then merely return the value of this variable without having to perform multiplications on the spot. The upside of this approach is that we only compute the `area` when `length` or `width` changes. The downside is that we must be very careful to ensure that we always maintain `length`, `width`, and `area` in a valid state. This means that we must update the `area` variable every time either `length` or `width` changes. We have a hidden constraint,[7] which is not explicitly visible to someone who may maintain this code in the future. On a personal note, I have run into trouble by including such constraints and then forgetting them when I updated parts of my code.

Based on the arguments above, I opted for approach 1, which can be seen in `Prog0708`. The constructor for class `Rectangle` is consistent with my discussion of instance variables.

Three getters—`getLength()`, `getWidth()`, and `getArea()`—are provided.

As required, the `grow()` method increments both `length` and `width`. Similarly, the `shrink()` method decrements these variables. Our code does not notice when `length` or `width` drop into negative values.

> **Test your skill with Exercises 7-39 through 7-42.**

7.14 Counting Rectangles—static Again!

In the previous chapter, we saw a difference between instance methods and `static` methods (class methods):

- Instance methods are invoked by being sent, as messages, to objects.
- `static` methods are invoked by being attached to the name of the class.

You may recall class `Animal`. Here's a demonstration of some *instance* methods:

```
a1.speak();
a1.chases(a2);
Animal a3 = a1.makeBig();
String s = a3.toString();
```

---

[7] Some programming languages include a constraint feature, whereby the compiler can verify that dependencies among variables are being honored by the code. Java does not include such a constraint/dependency feature.

and here's an example of a `static` method:

```
Animal a = Animal.read(.. .,.. .);
```

A `static` method can be invoked *even if we have not created an instance of the class.*

> **Static variable** A variable that exists in only a single copy for an entire class.

Java provides similar capabilities for *variables*. When we define an *instance* variable, a slot for this variable is allocated in every object/instance that is constructed. That's why we avoid defining *unnecessary* instance variables: each one means a slot in every single object that is created from the class definition. On the other hand, Java offers *class* variables (AKA `static` variables) for use when we want to define *a single slot for the entire class*. Here are some cases where a class needs only a single slot:

- If the class needs to count how many instances have been created, then the class as a whole needs only one slot in which to keep this count.
- If a class needs to issue serial numbers to each instance that is created, then the class as a whole needs to maintain only one slot in which to store the next serial number to be issued.
- If we have a class `Item` that represents items for sale in a store, then we need to keep only one copy of the `taxRate` even though every `Item` will reference it. There's no need to put a copy of the `taxRate` in each `Item`. Moreover, by having only a single copy, we can change the `taxRate` by changing it in a single place.

I'll illustrate the use of `static` variables by adding to class `Rectangle` the capability of counting how many `Rectangles` have been created. `Prog0709.java` contains the modified `Rectangle` class and a driver that demonstrates the counting feature.

Prog0709.java   **Count How Many Rectangles Have Been Created**

```
// Written by Barry Soroka
//
// class Rectangle -- count how many are created
//
import java.io.*;
//////////////////////////////////////////////////////////////////////////////
```

```
class Prog0709
{
//-------------------------------------------------------------------
   public static void main (String [] args) throws Exception
   {
      report();
      Rectangle r1 = new Rectangle(5,10);
      report();
      Rectangle r2 = new Rectangle(7,2);
      report();
      r1 = r2;
      report();
      r2 = new Rectangle(1,1);
      report();
   }
//-------------------------------------------------------------------
   public static void report()
   {
      System.out.println ( "We have created " +
                           Rectangle.howMany() +
                           " Rectangles.");
   }
//-------------------------------------------------------------------
} // end class Prog0709
/////////////////////////////////////////////////////////////////////////
class Rectangle
{
   private int length;
   private int width;
   private static int nRectangles = 0;
//-------------------------------------------------------------------
   public Rectangle ( int length , int width)
   {
      this.length = length;
      this.width = width;
      nRectangles++;
   }
//-------------------------------------------------------------------
   public static int howMany() { return nRectangles; }
//-------------------------------------------------------------------
   public int getLength() { return length; }
//-------------------------------------------------------------------
   public int getWidth() { return width; }
```

```
//----------------------------------------------------------------------
   public int getArea() { return length * width; }
//----------------------------------------------------------------------
   public void grow() { length++; width++; }
//----------------------------------------------------------------------
   public void shrink() { length--; width--; }
//----------------------------------------------------------------------
} // end class Rectangle
//////////////////////////////////////////////////////////////////////////
```

Modifications to Class Rectangle

Let's start by examining class Rectangle. We have added a new variable to maintain a single count of how many Rectangles we've created:

```
   private static int nRectangles = 0;
```

Here's what the pieces mean:

- private—We don't want methods outside this class to touch the variable. All changes to the variable must be done by or through the methods provided by the class.
- static—This tells Java to create a single slot for this variable. This is different than instance variables, where a copy of the variable is inserted into every object created from the class definition.
- int—This is a reasonable type for a counter.
- nRectangles—This is the name of the variable. The name suggests a variable that counts Rectangles.
- = 0—This phrase initializes the class variable. *Class variables must be initialized in their declarations.* This differs from instance variables: according to the Style Sheet (Appendix 1), instance variables must not be initialized in their declarations; they must be initialized in the constructor.

Our next modification is to add the following statement to the constructor:

```
   nRectangles++;
```

Whenever a Rectangle is created, the counter nRectangles will be incremented.

Our final change is the definition of a method that can report nRectangles to the outside world:

```
public static int howMany() { return nRectangles; }
```

Notice that this method is static: We want to be able to ask "How many Rectangles?" *at any time*, even when no Rectangles have been created. The result is an int, and no parameters are needed. This method merely returns nRectangles.

Driver and Test Cases

The driver (class Prog0709) contains a helper function report:

```
public static void report()
{
    System.out.println ( "We have created " +
                          Rectangle.howMany() +
                          " Rectangles.");
}
```

The helper function allows us to insert report() statements into the driver instead of having to write a three-line println statement. Also, if we want to change the report or if we find a bug in the println statement, then we need only patch the offending code in one spot.

The driver itself tests several cases. Our discussion will intersperse lines from Prog0709 with lines from the program's output. The initial output is

Output: We have created 0 Rectangles.

which reports, as expected, that we have not yet created any Rectangles. The next two statements create Rectangles, and the output reports this:

Statement: Rectangle r1 = new Rectangle(5,10);
Output: We have created 1 Rectangles.
Statement: Rectangle r2 = new Rectangle(7,2);
Output: We have created 2 Rectangles.

The next statement is

Statement: r1 = r2;

and it generates the report

Output: We have created 2 Rectangles.

The `r1 = r2` statement doesn't create a `Rectangle`—it merely causes `r1` to refer to the same `Rectangle` as `r2`. Now, `r1` *used* to refer to a 5×10 `Rectangle`. What's happened to that `Rectangle`? Well, it's become *garbage* because nobody's referring to it, but the count of `Rectangles` is unaffected. The counter doesn't decrement when a `Rectangle` becomes garbage.[8] Finally, we make `r2` refer to a new `Rectangle`, and the counter is incremented appropriately.

Statement: r2 = new Rectangle(1,1);
Output: We have created 3 Rectangles.

The moral of the analysis is this: The counter is incremented only when the constructor is called.

> **Test your skill with Exercises 7-43 through 7-45.**

7.15 Generating Sequential ID Numbers

In this section, we'll study a `Student` class with a two-parameter constructor—`first` name and `last` name—that generates a unique `id` for each `Student`. The ID is formed by taking the first letters of the names and tacking on a three-digit sequence number. Here are the four examples tested in `Prog0710.java`:

In: first	In: name	Out: id
elfriede	jelinek	EJ000
pablo	neruda	PN001
gunter	grass	GG002
pearl	buck	PB003

The serial number is continuously increasing, and it doesn't belong to any single instance of `Student`. It belongs to the class as a whole. This means it will

---

8 This is not the end of the story. Some part of Java is targeted at actions to be taken when garbage objects are collected. However, this topic is beyond the scope of CS 1.

be a `static` variable rather than an instance variable. At the top of class `Student`, we find the lines:

```
private String first;
private String last;
private String id;
private static int serial = 0;
```

These create three instance variables, meaning that every `Student` object created will have a slot for the variables `first`, `last`, and `id`. We also create a *class* variable `serial`, which we initialize to 0. (We could, of course, have started the serial numbering at any other arbitrary value, such as 1 or 100.)

Prog0710.java   **Assign ID Numbers to Students**

```
// Written by Barry Soroka
//
// Assign ID numbers to Students as they are created.
//
import java.io.*;
//////////////////////////////////////////////////////////////////////////
class Prog0710
{
//-----------------------------------------------------------------------
    public static void main (String [] args) throws Exception
    {
        Student s1 = new Student("elfriede","jelinek");
        Student s2 = new Student("pablo","neruda");
        Student s3 = new Student("gunter","grass");
        Student s4 = new Student("pearl","buck");

        System.out.println ( "\n" + s1 + "\n" + s2 + "\n" + s3 + "\n" + s4 );
    }
//-----------------------------------------------------------------------
} // end class Prog0710
//////////////////////////////////////////////////////////////////////////
class Student
{
    private String first;
    private String last;
    private String id;
    private static int serial = 0;
```

```
//-----------------------------------------------------------------
   public Student ( String first, String last )
   {
      this.first = first;
      this.last = last;
      this.id = first.substring(0,1).toUpperCase() +
                last.substring(0,1).toUpperCase() +
                ("" + (1000 + serial)).substring(1);
      serial++;
   }
//-----------------------------------------------------------------
   public String toString()
   {
      return id + " " + first + " " + last;
   }
//-----------------------------------------------------------------
} // end class Student
/////////////////////////////////////////////////////////////////////
```

The next feature of interest is the constructor for `Student`:

```
public Student ( String first, String last )
{
   this.first = first;
   this.last = last;
   this.id = first.substring(0,1).toUpperCase() +
             last.substring(0,1).toUpperCase() +
             ("" + (1000 + serial)).substring(1);
   serial++;
}
```

The `id` slot is filled with a `String` composed of three parts:

1. uppercase of the first letter of the variable `first`,
2. uppercase of the first letter of the variable `last`,
3. a three-digit representation of the serial number, padded with 0s on the left.[9]

---

[9] If we had started `serial` at 1000, then we could get the three-digit leading-0 `String` representation simply by writing `(serial + "").substring(1)`.

We have seen these computations before. The last statement in the constructor increments the `serial` number so that it's ready for the next `Student`. The code for `toString` is obvious.

7.16 Fractions

A `Fraction` is an ordered pair of integers—a numerator and a denominator. `Prog0711.java` shows the basic class `Fraction` and a driver that repeatedly reads and prints `Fraction`s. The code is straightforward, but it doesn't do everything we might want. For example, it doesn't reduce 2/6 to 1/3 or 85/34 to 5/2, and it doesn't normalize 0/17 to 0/1.[10] We won't be able to make these fixes until we reach Chapter 11, on conditional statements, but the current code presents a test bed for method-defining exercises.

Prog0711.java   **Class Fraction**

```
// Written by Barry Soroka
//
// class Fraction
//
import java.io.*;
import java.util.Scanner;
/////////////////////////////////////////////////////////////////////////////////
class Prog0711
{
//---------------------------------------------------------------------------

   public static void main (String [] args ) throws Exception
   {
      Scanner kb = new Scanner(System.in);

      while ( true )
      {
         System.out.println();
         Fraction f = Fraction.read(System.out,kb);
```

[10] Normalization is an important concept in computer science. It means that equivalent values are all represented by the same value—the canonical form. This makes it easy to determine if two items are equivalent. For example, if 0/17 and 0/22 are both normalized to the canonical form 0/1, then a program can easily determine that they are equal. Ditto for 1/3, 2/6, and 10/30—they all reduce to the canonical form 1/3.

```
            System.out.println(f);
         }
      }
//----------------------------------------------------------------------
} // end class Prog0711
////////////////////////////////////////////////////////////////////////
class Fraction
{
   private int num;
   private int den;
//----------------------------------------------------------------------
   public Fraction ( int num, int den )
   {
      this.num = num;
      this.den = den;
   }
//----------------------------------------------------------------------
   public static Fraction read ( PrintStream ps, Scanner sc ) throws Exception
   {
      ps.println("Reading a Fraction ...");
      ps.print("Numerator:   ");
      int num = sc.nextInt();
      ps.print("Denominator: ");
      int den = sc.nextInt();
      return new Fraction(num,den);
   }
//----------------------------------------------------------------------
   public String toString()
   {
      return num + " / " + den;
   }
//----------------------------------------------------------------------
} // end class Fraction
////////////////////////////////////////////////////////////////////////
```

 | **Test your skill with Exercises 7-46 through 7-52.** |

7.17   Converting Strings to ints

Suppose we want to convert a String—say, "27"—to the corresponding int.
The naïve code is this:

```
        int n = "27";    //ILLEGAL!
```

but that's not legal because the items on either side of an assignment statement must be the same type. Java provides another way to do the desired conversion:

```
int n = Integer.parseInt("27");
```

Prog0712 reads a String, converts it to an int, and prints the square of that int. The novel parts of this code are these:

```
String s = kb.nextLine();
int n = Integer.parseInt(s);
```

The method Integer.parseInt takes a String as a parameter and returns the corresponding int if the String does, in fact, represent one. You can use parseInt whenever you have a String that must be converted to an int.

Prog0712.java   Convert a **String** to an Integer

```
// Written by Barry Soroka
//
// Read a String, convert it to an int, print its square.
//
import java.io.*;
import java.util.Scanner;
//////////////////////////////////////////////////////////////////////////////
class Prog0712
{
//----------------------------------------------------------------------------
    public static void main ( String [] args ) throws Exception
    {
        Scanner kb = new Scanner(System.in);
        System.out.print("Enter an int: ");
        String s = kb.nextLine();
        int n = Integer.parseInt(s);
        System.out.println("Its square is " + n*n);
    }
//----------------------------------------------------------------------------
} // end class Prog0712
//////////////////////////////////////////////////////////////////////////////
```

If the String does not represent a valid int, then parseInt throws a NumberFormatException:

```
G:\>java Prog0712
```

```
Enter an int: hello
Exception in thread "main" java.lang.NumberFormatException:
For input string: "hello"
at java.lang.NumberFormatException.forInputString(Unknown Source)
at java.lang.Integer.parseInt(Unknown Source)
at java.lang.Integer.parseInt(Unknown Source)
at Prog0712.main(Prog0712.java:16)
```

Notice that the `Exception` tells us that the problem occurred in line `16` of file `Prog0712.java`; this information can be helpful when debugging.

 Often, `Exceptions` send messages that are not very informative about the cause of the problem. Sometimes the messages are downright misleading! The good student learns to associate `Exceptions` with the problems they're trying to report. Learn from your mistakes. Sometimes you should make mistakes intentionally in order to see how Java will react.

Test your skill with Exercise 7-53.

The following table shows a few other `Strings` that `parseInt` rejects:

Invalid *String*	Why It's Invalid
`"+5"`	The minus sign is OK for `ints`, but the plus sign is not.
`"  5"`	Leading spaces are not allowed.
`"5  "`	Trailing spaces are not allowed.
`"5 7"`	Spaces are not allowed inside an `int`.
`"5a"`	`ints` cannot contain invalid characters.

 Java provides analogs to `parseInt` for each of the other integer datatypes:

```
Byte.parseByte(String)
Short.parseShort(String)
Long.parseLong(String)
```

7.18   **Converting ints to Strings**

The previous section taught how to convert Strings to ints. Now we'll study the reverse process: Given an int, we'll convert it to the corresponding String.

Our first thought might be to simply assign the int to the String, as shown here:

```
int i = 17;
String s = i;    // ILLEGAL!
```

As indicated, Java won't let us assign an int to a String. This would violate a fundamental rule concerning assignment: We are attempting to fill a String variable with a value that is *not* a String. (Java does not do many conversions automatically!) We'll need to find another way to achieve our goal.

Here is code that works:

```
int i = 17;
String s = i + "";
```

Consider the expression i + "". Because one of the operands is a String, the + sign calls for the *String concatenation* operator rather than the *arithmetic addition* operator. As we saw earlier, when Java concatenates a String with an int, the result is a String, and we're allowed to assign that String to the variable s. Now that we've converted an int to a String, we can apply any of the String methods.

HOLD YOUR HORSES

The Java API provides some much more complicated ways of converting an int to a String. We can achieve the same result using the simple technique described above, using the + operator. Don't use complicated code when simple code is sufficient.

Prog0713.java reads an integer in the range [0, 999], converts it to a String, and adds leading 0s to pad it out to width 3. Here are a few test cases:

```
Enter an int in the range [0,999]:  0
With leading 0s, that is: 000

Enter an int in the range [0,999]:  2
```

```
With leading 0s, that is: 002

Enter an int in the range [0,999]:   37
With leading 0s, that is: 037

Enter an int in the range [0,999]:   952
With leading 0s, that is: 952
```

Prog0713 uses a trick. Suppose the input is the integer 37. Here's the procedure:

1. Add 1000 to the int, getting 1037.
2. Convert this to the String "1037".
3. Use the substring method to drop the first character, getting "037".

Programmers use a lot of tricks like this. I don't expect you to invent or discover this solution on your own, but, once you see it, I expect you to be able to recall this pattern and apply it when appropriate. To be a successful programmer, you require *at least* three skills:

- Memory—You must be able to remember patterns after you've seen them.
- Recall—You must be able to recall patterns from memory.
- Indexing—You must recall patterns that are *appropriate* to the problem you're now trying to solve.

If you lack any of these skills—memory, recall, or indexing—then you will probably not be a very productive or happy programmer.

Prog0713.java   Print **ints** with Leading 0s

```java
// Written by Barry Soroka
//
// Print ints in range [0,999] with leading 0s.
//
import java.io.*;
import java.util.Scanner;
///////////////////////////////////////////////////////////////////////////
class Prog0713
{
//----------------------------------------------------------------------------
    public static void main (String [] args ) throws Exception
    {
        Scanner kb = new Scanner(System.in);
```

```
    while ( true )
    {
       System.out.print("\nEnter an int in the range [0,999]:  ");
       int n = kb.nextInt();
       String s = ((n + 1000) + "").substring(1);
       System.out.println("With leading 0s, that is: " + s);
    }
  }
//-----------------------------------------------------------------------
} // end class Prog0713
//////////////////////////////////////////////////////////////////////////
```

Let's examine some statements of Prog0713. Inside the infinite loop, we begin by prompting:

```
       System.out.print("\nEnter an int in the range [0,999]:  ");
```

Notice that we request an int in a particular range, [0, 999]. If the user enters an int outside this range, then we're not guaranteeing that the program will produce an intelligent result. In fact, here are two examples of what happens when the user violates the input specification:

```
       Enter an int in the range [0,999]:  -1
       With leading 0s, that is: 99

       Enter an int in the range [0,999]:  1234
       With leading 0s, that is: 234
```

In neither case have we added leading 0s.[11] Another interesting statement is:

```
       String s = ((n + 1000) + "").substring(1);
```

The basic arithmetic statement here is

```
       n + 1000 + ""
```

and I have inserted parentheses to ensure that the result will be the appropriate String. Consider an input of 37. Here are the steps in the computation:

$$(37 + 1000) + "" \rightarrow 1037 + "" \rightarrow "1037"$$

---

[11] This is a good example of GIGO—Garbage In, Garbage Out. For decades, programmers have used this acronym to describe the phenomenon whereby inappropriate input produces unexpected and inappropriate output.

Because of operator precedence, the parentheses are not needed here, but sometimes it's better to insert too many parentheses than too few.

 Test your skill with Exercise 7-54.

7.19   Pretty-Printing Integer Values

Prog0714 reads an int and prints the first five powers of that int. Here's a typical dialog:

```
G:\>java Prog0714
Enter an int: 5
1        5
2        25
3        125
4        625
5        3125
```

Notice how the numbers are staggered. Suppose we'd rather have the numbers line up like this:

```
1    5
2   25
3  125
4  625
5 3125
```

Java provides the printf method in class PrintStream to give us control over how numbers are printed.

Prog0714.java   **Print Powers of an int**

```java
// Written by Barry Soroka
//
// Prints powers of an int.
//
import java.io.*;
import java.util.Scanner;
/////////////////////////////////////////////////////////////////////////////
class Prog0714
{
//-------------------------------------------------------------------------
    public static void main ( String [] args ) throws Exception
    {
```

```
      Scanner kb = new Scanner(System.in);
      System.out.print("Enter an int: ");
      int n = kb.nextInt();
      System.out.println(1 + "\t" + n);
      System.out.println(2 + "\t" + n*n);
      System.out.println(3 + "\t" + n*n*n);
      System.out.println(4 + "\t" + n*n*n*n);
      System.out.println(5 + "\t" + n*n*n*n*n);
   }
//- - - - - - - - - - - - - - - - - - - - - - - - - - - - - - - - - - - - - - - - - - - - - - - - - - - - - - - - - - - - - -
} // end class Prog0714
//////////////////////////////////////////////////////////////////////////
```

printf is like print, but it has some special features. We can use it just like print in statements such as

```
      System.out.printf("hello\n");
```

to print hello on a line by itself.

Now let's add some special features. The statement

```
      System.out.printf("a%3db\n",25);
```

results in the line

```
      a 25b
```

printf took two arguments: a control string ("a%3db\n"), and an integer value (25). Some parts of the control string are taken literally—a and b. The \n is an escape sequence that produces a new line. The %3d is a field specifier; it tells printf to print the second argument *right-justified in a field of width 3.* Similarly, the statement

```
      System.out.printf("a%4db\n",25);
```

results in the line

```
      a   25b
```

where the 25 is right-justified in a field of width 4. In general, the control string %wd prints an integer in a field of width w. If we want a literal %, we must write the escape sequence %%.

A single control string can specify the printing of more than one value. The statement

```
System.out.printf("The square of%3d is%4d.\n",25,625);
```

results in the line

```
The square of 25 is 625.
```

The first field specifier (%3d) refers to the second argument and the next field specifier (%4d) refers to the next argument. Control strings may reference any number of arguments.

What if the number is too big for the field specified? The statement

```
System.out.printf("%3d\n%3d\n",999,1000);
```

results in the lines

```
999
1000
```

where *the second field has been expanded* so that the value can be fully printed.

Prog0715 uses `printf` and control strings to print the first five powers of an `int` where the values are right-justified:

```
G:\>java Prog0715
Enter an int: 5
1    5
2   25
3  125
4  625
5 3125
```

If we enter 8, then we observe the following dialog:

```
G:\>java Prog0715
Enter an int: 8
1    8
2   64
3  512
4 4096
5 32768
```

The last value was too big to fit in a field of width 4, so *the field was expanded to fit the value.*

Prog0715.java   **Print Powers of an int Formatted with printf**

```
// Written by Barry Soroka
//
// Prints powers of an int.
//
import java.io.*;
import java.util.Scanner;
///////////////////////////////////////////////////////////////////////////////
class Prog0715
{
//------------------------------------------------------------------------------
   public static void main ( String [] args ) throws Exception
   {
      Scanner kb = new Scanner(System.in);
      System.out.print("Enter an int: ");
      int n = kb.nextInt();
      System.out.printf("1 %4d\n",n);
      System.out.printf("2 %4d\n",n*n);
      System.out.printf("3 %4d\n",n*n*n);
      System.out.printf("4 %4d\n",n*n*n*n);
      System.out.printf("5 %4d\n",n*n*n*n*n);
   }
//------------------------------------------------------------------------------
} // end class Prog0715
///////////////////////////////////////////////////////////////////////////////
```

Class `String` contains a method `format` that accepts a control `String` and numeric arguments, and that produces a `String` representing the `printf` that would have printed. For example,

```
String.format("The square of%3d is%4d.",25,625)
```

results in the string `"The square of 25 is 625."`

   Test your skill with Exercise 7-55.

7.20 Casting

There are four integer datatypes—byte, short, int, and long—which hold different numbers of values. For example, a byte can hold only integers in the range [−128, +127], but an int can hold values roughly in the range [−2 billion, +2 billion]. This begs the question: What happens if we try to assign an int value to a byte? Clearly, some int values are too large to fit into a byte. How does Java handle this mismatch? Let's ask Java.

Consider:

```
byte b = 22;
```

Java has no problem with this statement.

Now let's try with a larger number:

```
byte b = 128;
```

Java balks:

```
Foo.java:12: possible loss of precision
found   : int
required: byte
      byte b = 128;
               ^
1 error
```

Java interprets the 128 as an int and warns that we're trying to jam it into a byte, where it will not fit. We get the same error when we try

```
int i = 37;
byte b = i;
```

even though the given number, 37, is clearly acceptable as a byte. Java tries to prevent the accidental loss of precision that would result from assigning a larger integer type to a smaller one.

> **Casting** Forcibly converting one datatype to another.

What if we really do want to perform such an assignment? We can use one of the *casting* operators: (byte), (short), (int), or (long). These operators explicitly take one integer datatype and return another, and, by using these operators, *we* accept responsibility for any loss of precision that may occur. Thus, we can fix the error we saw above by using the (byte) cast:

```
int i = 37;
byte b = (byte) i;
```

These statements compile without problems.

Let's try a cast that *does* lose data: Let's pick an int—say, 327—that is too large to fit in a byte. The following Java code compiles without problem:

```
int i = 327;
byte b = (byte) i;
System.out.println(b);
```

but it prints *71*. When the 32-bit int 327 is jammed into an 8-bit byte, we lose all of the int except for the rightmost 8 bits, leaving *71*.

The casting operators can cause a lot of trouble if they're used incorrectly. Casting tells Java to forget its protective instincts, and it enables statements that can lose information from our data. *Be careful!*

7.21 Integer Wraparound

Each of the four integer types—byte, short, int, and long—has a fixed number of bits and, therefore, a fixed number of bit patterns. A byte, for example, has 8 bits and can hold only 256 distinct bit patterns. Each of these bit patterns is assigned to a different integer, according to the following table:[12]

Bit Pattern	Integer Value
0000 0000	0
0000 0001	1
0000 0010	2
0000 0011	3
. . .	. . .
0111 1110	126
0111 1111	127
1000 0000	−128
1000 0001	−127
1000 0010	−126
. . .	. . .
1111 1110	−2
1111 1111	−1

---

[12] When you study machine arithmetic, you will discover that this particular assignment—*two's complement*—is not the only possible assignment. The dominant assignment is determined by the economics of alternative computer hardware designs.

This table is logical from a hardware point of view, but it seems a bit strange when viewed from a software perspective. Why should adding 1 to 127 result in -128? And why should subtracting 1 from -128 result in +127? How does Java handle this?

Consider Prog0716 which, in a byte, adds 1 to 127 and subtracts 1 from -128. We get the result:

$$127 + 1 \rightarrow -128$$
$$-128 - 1 \rightarrow 127$$

> **Wraparound**   When a simple action—e.g., adding 1—results in a huge change in value.

If our programs involve integer arithmetic, we must be very careful to avoid *wraparound* (also called *overflow*). If, for example, we're using a byte-sized variable to keep track of the number of sodas sold in a day, Java isn't going to tell us that we've suddenly gone from +127 to -128. In my humble opinion, Java should have thrown an Exception instead of wrapping around. A programming language should do everything it can to detect or prevent programmer error.

Prog0716.java   **Integer Wraparound**

```
// Written by Barry Soroka
//
// Demonstrates integer wraparound in a byte.
//
import java.io.*;
/////////////////////////////////////////////////////////////////////////////
class Prog0716
{
//-----------------------------------------------------------------
    public static void main (String [] args ) throws Exception
    {
        byte before;
        byte after;

        before = 127;
        after = before;
        after++;
        System.out.println("\n" + before + " + 1 --> " + after);

        before = -128;
        after = before;
```

```
      after--;
      System.out.println("\n" + before + " - 1 --> " + after);
   }
//------------------------------------------------------------------------
} // end class Prog0716
////////////////////////////////////////////////////////////////////////////
```

> When integer wraparound occurs, Java does not report it or throw an Exception.

7.22   How Scanner Works

This section explains some phenomena encountered when using Scanners, particularly *waiting* and *type-ahead*. First, we'll examine some code and hardcopy that present the phenomena. Then we'll describe how Scanner works, explaining what we observed. Finally, we'll discuss how to force the user to read just one input integer per line; this regimen is useful for files of input data.

Prog0717 reads two integers and prints their sum. Here's a simple run of this code where we enter the integers on separate lines:

```
G:\>java Prog0717
I compute the sum of two integers.
Enter the first integer:  3
Enter the second integer: 5
Their sum is 8
```

Java will wait for us if we enter white space before giving the numbers:

```
G:\>java Prog0717
I compute the sum of two integers.
Enter the first integer:        3
Enter the second integer:

5
Their sum is 8
```

Waiting   When a read operation waits past empty space until the value has been entered.

Notice that we entered spaces before the 3 and two new lines before the 5. Java waits for us to enter the number. This phenomenon is called *waiting*.

Prog0717.java **Read Two ints and Print Their Sum**

```
// Written by Barry Soroka
//
// Read two ints and print their sum.
//
import java.io.*;
import java.util.Scanner;
//////////////////////////////////////////////////////////////////////////////
class Prog0717
{
//-------------------------------------------------------------------------------
    public static void main (String [] args ) throws Exception
    {
        Scanner kb = new Scanner(System.in);

        System.out.println("I compute the sum of two integers.");
        System.out.print("Enter the first integer:  ");
        int n1 = kb.nextInt();
        System.out.print("Enter the second integer: ");
        int n2 = kb.nextInt();
        System.out.println("Their sum is " + (n1 + n2));
    }
//-------------------------------------------------------------------------------
} // end class Prog0717
//////////////////////////////////////////////////////////////////////////////
```

Successive nextInts accept both numbers if they're typed on a single line:

```
G:\>java Prog0717
I compute the sum of two integers.
Enter the first integer:  3 5
Enter the second integer: Their sum is 8
```

> **Type-ahead** Entering values before they are requested by the program.

Notice that the program read both the 3 and the 5, and it printed the second prompt even though the second response had already been entered. This phenomenon is called *type-ahead*.

The Explanation

> **Token** An indivisible unit seen by a Scanner.

A Scanner views its input as a sequence of *tokens* separated by *white space*—spaces, tabs, and new-lines. A token is a consecutive run of nonwhite space. At any given point in time, a Scanner has an associated pointer that points to the next character to be read. Initially, the pointer is at the beginning of the stream of characters that form the Scanner.

nextInt() "walks over" white space and grabs the next token. It tries to convert this token to an int. If the conversion is successful, then nextInt returns the value of the int produced and the pointer is left just past the end of the token read. If the conversion fails, then nextInt throws an Exception.

That explains *waiting*: nextInt keeps reading over white space until it gets a token to convert.

It also explains *type-ahead*, because nextInt leaves the pointer just after the first token read. The second call to nextInt proceeds from that pointer and grabs the second integer on the line.

When nextInt grabs a token, it grabs the entire token, not just that part that makes an int. For example, in

```
G:\>java Prog0717
I compute the sum of two integers.
Enter the first integer:  3a
Exception in thread "main" java.util.InputMismatchException
        at java.util.Scanner.throwFor(Unknown Source)
        at java.util.Scanner.next(Unknown Source)
        at java.util.Scanner.nextInt(Unknown Source)
        at java.util.Scanner.nextInt(Unknown Source)
        at Prog0717.main(Prog0717.java:17)
```

nextInt grabbed the entire token 3a and tried, but failed, to convert it into an int.

> nextInt() grabs the next token and tries to make an int from it.

Adding nextLine to the Mix

Prog0718 presents a call to nextInt, followed by a call to nextLine. Here are the relevant statements:

```
System.out.print("Enter an int: ");
int n = kb.nextInt();
System.out.println("int: " + n);
System.out.println("rest of the line: \"" +
                    kb.nextLine() + "\"");
```

Here is a typical run of this code:

```
G:\>java Prog0718
Enter an int: 35 hello there
int: 35
rest of the line: " hello there"
```

`nextInt` read the token 35 and `nextLine` grabbed all the rest of the line.

Prog0718.java   nextInt Followed by nextLine

```
// Written by Barry Soroka
//
// nextInt is followed by nextLine.
//
import java.io.*;
import java.util.Scanner;
//////////////////////////////////////////////////////////////////////////////
class Prog0718
{
//---------------------------------------------------------------------------
    public static void main (String [] args ) throws Exception
    {
        Scanner kb = new Scanner(System.in);

        System.out.print("Enter an int: ");
        int n = kb.nextInt();
        System.out.println("int: " + n);
        System.out.println("rest of the line: \"" + kb.nextLine() + "\"");
    }
//---------------------------------------------------------------------------
} // end class Prog0718
//////////////////////////////////////////////////////////////////////////////
```

> `nextLine` grabs all the characters from the current position to the end of the line and returns a single `String`.

Here's what we see when we enter just 35 on the input line:

```
G:\>java Prog0718
Enter an int: 35
int: 35
rest of the line: ""
```

Notice that the `nextLine` method did not request a new line of input; it was satisfied to grab the empty `String` between the 35 and the new-line character.

Foiling Type-Ahead

We can foil type-ahead and force the user to enter integers on *two separate lines* if we use a `nextLine` directly after a `nextInt`, in order to clear the remainder of the line containing the `int`. This is illustrated in `Prog0719`. The following is hardcopy of a typical run:

```
G:\>java Prog0719
I compute the sum of two integers.
Enter the first integer:  3 5
Enter the second integer: 7
Their sum is 10
```

Note that the typed-ahead 5 is ignored by the program because the `nextLine` method tosses away the rest of the line after the 3. By using the phrase

```
sc.nextInt(); sc.nextLine();
```

we can force the user to enter successive integers on successive lines.[13] At times we will use this technique to force Java to look at data on multiple lines.

Prog0719.java   **Read Two ints and Print Their Sum**

```
// Written by Barry Soroka
//
// Read two ints and print their sum.
//
import java.io.*;
import java.util.Scanner;
////////////////////////////////////////////////////////////////////////////
class Prog0719
{
//-----------------------------------------------------------------------
   public static void main (String [] args ) throws Exception
   {
      Scanner kb = new Scanner(System.in);

      System.out.println("I compute the sum of two integers.");
      System.out.print("Enter the first integer:  ");
```

---

[13] Those who are familiar with Pascal will recognize that this idiom in Java is similar to Pascal's `readln` procedure.

```
        int n1 = kb.nextInt(); kb.nextLine();
        System.out.print("Enter the second integer: ");
        int n2 = kb.nextInt();
        System.out.println("Their sum is " + (n1 + n2));
    }
//-------------------------------------------------------------------------
} // end class Prog0719
/////////////////////////////////////////////////////////////////////////////
```

7.23   GUI: Accept an `int` and Print Its Square

Prog0720.java is an application that accepts an integer in a JTextField and prints its square in a JLabel. This code is changed from Prog0402 in only two significant ways:

- It converts the String returned by input.getText() into an integer using Integer.parseInt.
- It sets the text of output to be the square of the integer. Note that we convert the number n*n into a String by concatenating it to the empty String.

Prog0720.java   **GUI: Read an int and Print Its Square**

```
// Written by Barry Soroka
//
// Use a JTextField to read an int; print its square.
// Uses an inner class for the event handler.
//
import java.awt.*;
import java.awt.event.*;
import javax.swing.*;
/////////////////////////////////////////////////////////////////////////////
class Prog0720
{
//--------------------------------------------------------------------------
    public static void main (String[] args)
    {
        JFrame frame = new JFrame ("Read int & square");
        frame.setDefaultCloseOperation (JFrame.EXIT_ON_CLOSE);

        frame.getContentPane().add(new MyPanel());
        frame.pack();
        frame.setVisible(true);
    }
```

```
//---------------------------------------------------------------------
} // end class Prog0720
/////////////////////////////////////////////////////////////////////////
class MyPanel extends JPanel
{
   private int n;
   private JTextField input;
   private JLabel inputLabel, outputLabel, output;
//---------------------------------------------------------------------
   public MyPanel()
   {
      inputLabel = new JLabel("Enter an int: ");
      outputLabel = new JLabel("Its square is ");
      output = new JLabel("---");

      input = new JTextField(5);
      input.addActionListener(new GetIntAndSquare());

      add(inputLabel);
      add(input);
      add(outputLabel);
      add(output);

      setBackground(Color.YELLOW);
      setPreferredSize(new Dimension(300,40));
   }
//---------------------------------------------------------------------
/////////////////////////////////////////////////////////////////////////
private class GetIntAndSquare implements ActionListener
{
//---------------------------------------------------------------------
   public void actionPerformed ( ActionEvent event )
   {
      int n = Integer.parseInt(input.getText());
      output.setText(n*n+"");
   }
//---------------------------------------------------------------------
} // end class GetIntAndSquare
/////////////////////////////////////////////////////////////////////////
} // end class MyPanel
/////////////////////////////////////////////////////////////////////////
```

 Test your skill with Exercises 7-56 and 7-57.

7.24 GUI: Adding Buttons to a JFrame

Prog0721.java adds two JButtons to a JFrame. For each button, we have three statements:

1. Create the button using the constructor for JButton and providing the text for the button.
2. Set the size of the button using the setBounds method.
3. Add the button to the ContentPane of the JFrame.

We end up with the window shown in Figure 7–1. We can click on the buttons, and they respond by momentarily darkening. In the next section, you'll learn how to attach actions to buttons.

Prog0721.java   Add Two Buttons to a MyFrame

```
// Written by Barry Soroka
//
// Add two buttons to a MyFrame.
//
import java.io.*;
import java.awt.*;
import javax.swing.*;
//////////////////////////////////////////////////////////////////////////
class Prog0721
{
```

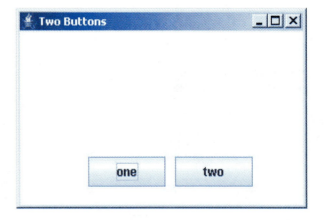

Figure 7–1
Two Buttons

```
//------------------------------------------------------------------
   public static void main ( String [] args ) throws Exception
   {
      MyFrame f = new MyFrame();
      f.setVisible(true);
   }
//------------------------------------------------------------------
} // end class Prog0721
////////////////////////////////////////////////////////////////////////////
class MyFrame extends JFrame
{
   private static final int WIDTH = 300;
   private static final int HEIGHT = 200;
   private static final int X_ORIGIN = 150;
   private static final int Y_ORIGIN = 250;

   private static final int BUTTON_WIDTH = 80;
   private static final int BUTTON_HEIGHT = 30;
//------------------------------------------------------------------
   public MyFrame()
   {
      setTitle("Two Buttons");
      setSize(WIDTH,HEIGHT);
      setLocation(X_ORIGIN,Y_ORIGIN);
      setDefaultCloseOperation(EXIT_ON_CLOSE);

      Container c = getContentPane();
      c.setLayout(null);
      c.setBackground(Color.WHITE);

      JButton button1 = new JButton("one");
      button1.setBounds(70,125,BUTTON_WIDTH,BUTTON_HEIGHT);
      c.add(button1);

      JButton button2 = new JButton("two");
      button2.setBounds(160,125,BUTTON_WIDTH,BUTTON_HEIGHT);
      c.add(button2);
   }
//------------------------------------------------------------------
} // end class MyFrame
////////////////////////////////////////////////////////////////////////////
```

 Test your skill with Exercise 7-58.

7.25 GUI: Add `ActionListener`s to the Buttons

`Prog0722.java` adds `ActionListener`s to the buttons. When we press a button, an appropriate message is written to `System.out`. `Handler` is an inner class that provides objects that watch for button clicks. The same instance of `Handler` is attached—as an `ActionListener`—to each button. When a button is clicked, the `actionPerformed` method is called with an `event` particular to the button that was pressed. The source of the `event` is the button, and the method `getText` retrieves the label of the button, which in turn gets printed.

Prog0722.java   **Print the Name of a Pressed Button**

```java
// Written by Barry Soroka
//
// Add an ActionListener to the buttons on a MyFrame.
// Prints the name of a pressed button to System.out.
//
import java.io.*;
import java.awt.*;
import java.awt.event.*;
import javax.swing.*;
//////////////////////////////////////////////////////////////////////////////
class Prog0722
{
//---------------------------------------------------------------------------

    public static void main ( String [] args ) throws Exception
    {
        MyFrame mf = new MyFrame();
        mf.setVisible(true);
    }
//---------------------------------------------------------------------------
} // end class Prog0722
//////////////////////////////////////////////////////////////////////////////
class MyFrame extends JFrame
{
    private static final int WIDTH = 300;
    private static final int HEIGHT = 200;
    private static final int X_ORIGIN = 150;
    private static final int Y_ORIGIN = 250;

    private static final int BUTTON_WIDTH = 80;
    private static final int BUTTON_HEIGHT = 30;
```

```
//--------------------------------------------------------------------------
   public MyFrame()
   {
       setTitle("Add ActionListeners");
       setSize(WIDTH,HEIGHT);
       setLocation(X_ORIGIN,Y_ORIGIN);
       setDefaultCloseOperation(EXIT_ON_CLOSE);

       Container c = getContentPane();
       c.setLayout(null);
       c.setBackground(Color.WHITE);

       JButton button1 = new JButton("one");
       button1.setBounds(70,125,BUTTON_WIDTH,BUTTON_HEIGHT);
       c.add(button1);

       JButton button2 = new JButton("two");
       button2.setBounds(160,125,BUTTON_WIDTH,BUTTON_HEIGHT);
       c.add(button2);

       Handler handler = new Handler();
       button1.addActionListener(handler);
       button2.addActionListener(handler);
   }
//--------------------------------------------------------------------------
} // end class MyFrame
/////////////////////////////////////////////////////////////////////////
class Handler implements ActionListener
{
//--------------------------------------------------------------------------
   public Handler() {}
//--------------------------------------------------------------------------
   public void actionPerformed ( ActionEvent event )
   {
       JButton button = (JButton) event.getSource();
       System.out.println("You pressed " + button.getText());
   }
//--------------------------------------------------------------------------
} // end class Handler
/////////////////////////////////////////////////////////////////////////
```

 Test your skill with Exercise 7-59.

7.26 GUI: Counting Button Clicks

Prog0723.java presents a button and a label. Each time the button is clicked, the text on the label is changed to the next integer. Note how the actionPerformed method of class ButtonListener does the work!

Prog0723.java Count Button Presses

```java
// Written by Barry Soroka
//
// Count button presses.
// Uses an inner class for the event handler.
//
import java.io.*;
import java.awt.*;
import java.awt.event.*;
import javax.swing.*;
/////////////////////////////////////////////////////////////////////////////
class Prog0723
{
//----------------------------------------------------------------------------
   public static void main (String[] args) throws Exception
   {
      JFrame frame = new JFrame ("Counting Button Clicks");
      frame.setDefaultCloseOperation (JFrame.EXIT_ON_CLOSE);

      frame.getContentPane().add(new PushCounterPanel());
      frame.pack();
      frame.setVisible(true);
   }
//----------------------------------------------------------------------------
} // end class Prog0723
/////////////////////////////////////////////////////////////////////////////
class PushCounterPanel extends JPanel
{
   private int count;
   private JButton button;
   private JLabel label;
//----------------------------------------------------------------------------
   public PushCounterPanel()
   {
      count = 0;

      button = new JButton("Push");
```

```
        button.addActionListener(new PushListener());

        label = new JLabel(count+"");

        add(button);
        add(label);

        setBackground(Color.YELLOW);
        setPreferredSize(new Dimension(125,35));
    }
//----------------------------------------------------------
////////////////////////////////////////////////////////////////////////
private class PushListener implements ActionListener
{
//----------------------------------------------------------
    public void actionPerformed ( ActionEvent event )
    {
        count++;
        label.setText(count+"");
    }
//----------------------------------------------------------
} // end class PushListener
////////////////////////////////////////////////////////////////////////
} // end class PushCounterPanel
////////////////////////////////////////////////////////////////////////
```

 | **Test your skill with Exercises 7-60 and 7-61.** |

Chapter Summary

- Integers are whole numbers (including 0), negative numbers, and positive numbers.
- Java provides four integer datatypes: `byte`, `short`, `int`, and `long`.
- `int` is used most frequently.
- `nextInt` is a method that applies to `Scanner`s, and that returns the next integer in the input stream.
- The `length` method of class `String` returns the integer length of the receiving `String`.
- Positions in a `String` are numbered 0, 1, 2, . . .
- The `substring(i)` method returns the substring of the receiver beginning at position `i` and continuing to the end of the `String`.
- The `substring(i,j)` method returns the substring of the receiver beginning at position `i` and continuing through the character just before position `j`.

- `indexOf(String)` returns the leftmost index at which the argument occurs in the receiving `String`. If the argument is not found, then −1 is returned.
- `lastIndexOf(String)` returns the rightmost index at which the argument occurs in the receiving `String`. If the argument is not found, then −1 is returned.
- Java provides five arithmetic operators for integers: +, -, *, /, and %.
- + and - are the familiar operations of addition and subtraction.
- * is the familiar operation of multiplication.
- / performs integer arithmetic, where the remainder is discarded.
- % returns the remainder when the left operand is divided by the right operand.
- `Math.abs` is Java's method for computing the absolute value of a number.
- Precedence determines how Java evaluates an expression containing multiple operators.
- The operators *, /, and % have precedence over the operators + and -; i.e., multiplication and division have precedence over addition and subtraction.
- If two consecutive operators have equal precedence, then the one on the left is performed first.
- An expression inside parentheses is evaluated on its own before being used by operators outside the parentheses.
- `n += 3;` is a shortcut for `n = n + 3;`
- `n++` is a shortcut for `n = n + 1`. This is the increment operator.
- `n--` is a shortcut for `n = n - 1`. This is the decrement operator.
- Primitive datatypes differ from objects in a variety of ways.
- Objects have internal structure. Primitive datatypes do not.
- Complex numbers can be represented by class `Complex`. Each instance has instance variables for the real part and the imaginary part.
- Rectangles can be represented by class `Rectangle`. Each instance has instance variables for `length` and `width`.
- We can count the number of `Rectangles` we create by maintaining a `static` variable for the count.
- We can use a `static` variable to aid in generating sequential ID numbers for objects created from a given class.
- `Integer.parseInt` is a `static` method of class `Integer`, which allows us to convert a `String` to an `int`.
- We can convert an `int` to a `String` by concatenating it with the empty `String`.
- `printf` allows us to "pretty-print" integer values by specifying the width of the output field in which the integer is right-aligned.

- printf takes one or more arguments. The first is a control String that tells how to format the values. The second and successive arguments are formatted according to the control String.
- Casting is the process of converting a value of one integer type into a different integer type. Information can be lost if the destination type has fewer bits than the origin type.
- Integer types wrap around from a large positive value to a large negative value if we continuously increment the value.
- A nextInt call to a Scanner will wait for the input stream to produce the next integer.
- Type-ahead means we type in values faster than the program is requesting them. The extra values are queued for later use unless a nextLine method call wipes out the entire current line.
- A JButton is a GUI object that, when clicked, can trigger an action such as counting clicks. An ActionListener, attached to the JButton, waits for clicks.

Terminology Introduced in This Chapter

casting	overflow	type-ahead
expression	precedence	waiting
integer datatypes	primitive datatypes	wraparound
operand	static variable	
operator	token	

Exercises

Exercise 7-1. Write a program that reads two ints and prints their sum.

Exercise 7-2. If a String s has length n, then what is the formula that tells us the length of s.substring(i)? Using that formula, what should be the length of s.substring(n)?

Exercise 7-3. If s has length 10, what is the value of s.substring(2,6).length()? What is the formula for s.substring(*i1*, *i2*).length()?

Exercise 7-4. Compute the table of two-int substrings for the String "hey". Write a Java program that reads the start and end positions and displays the computed substring. Sometimes the start and end positions will be illegal.

Exercise 7–5.   What `String`s do the following expressions return? Indicate those that generate errors.

a)   `"".substring(0,0)`

b)   `"a".substring(0,0)`

c)   `"a".substring(0,1)`

d)   `"a".substring(0,2)`

e)   `"a".substring(1,1)`

f)   `"a".substring(1,2);`

g)   `"a".substring(2,2);`

h)   `"abc".substring(0,0)`

i)   `"abc".substring(0,1)`

j)   `"abc".substring(0,2)`

k)   `"abc".substring(0,3)`

l)   `"abc".substring(0,4)`

m)   `"abc".substring(1,1)`

n)   `"abc".substring(1,2)`

o)   `"abc".substring(1,3)`

p)   `"abc".substring(1,4)`

q)   `"abc".substring(2,2)`

r)   `"abc".substring(2,3)`

s)   `"abc".substring(2,4)`

t)   `"abc".substring(3,3)`

u)   `"abc".substring(3,4)`

v)   `"abc".substring(4,4)`

Exercise 7–6.   Consider the `String "Mississippi River"`. Draw the table of positions and characters. Write down a list of test `String`s that would test every possible case of `indexOf` and `lastIndexOf`. For each test `String`, give the expected `int` results. Discuss your answer with your study partner.

Exercise 7–7.   [Don't do this problem until you have found a satisfactory answer to Exercise 7-6.] Write a program that repeatedly[14] reads `String`s and reports their index positions searching both from the left and from the right of the `String "Mississippi River"`. Verify that Java's answers match your predictions.

Exercise 7–8.   Write a program `Splitter`, which repeatedly reads `String`s and breaks them apart at the first space from the left. Use `indexOf(" ")` to locate the first space, and

---

[14] That means you should use the `while (true)` pattern for an infinite loop.

then use the appropriate `substring` method to get (1) the part of the `String` *before* the space, and (2) the part of the String *containing and after* the space. Here is a typical run:

```
G:\>java Splitter

Enter a String:  hello there
First part: "hello"
Remainder:  " there"

Enter a String:  a b c
First part: "a"
Remainder:  " b c"

Enter a String: __
First part: ""
Remainder:  "  "
```

Your program may fail if the input `String` does not contain a space. This is normal.

Exercise 7-9.   Repeat Exercise 7-8, but break the `String`s at the *last* space. Use `lastIndexOf` to find that last space.

Exercise 7-10.   Write a Java program `SplitFloat` that reads a `String` representing a floating-point number and separately prints the `String`s to the left and to the right of the decimal point. Here is a typical run:

```
G:\>java SplitFloat

Enter a floating-point number: 71.945
On the left is "71" and on the right is "945".
```

Hint: Use `indexOf` to locate the position of the decimal point.

Exercise 7-11.   Write an application `Initials` that reads a first name and a last name and computes the initials. Here's a typical session:

```
G:\>java Initials
I convert a name to its initials.
First name? John
Last name? Smith
John Smith's initials are JS.
```

Exercise 7-12. Write an application `Initials2` that reads a `String` containing a space. The program should extract a first name and a last name and compute the initials. Here's a typical session:

```
G:\>java Initials2
I convert a name to its initials.
Name (First Last) ? John Smith
John Smith's initials are JS.
```

Exercise 7-13. Write a program that reads two integers and prints the result of applying the remainder operator on them. Use this program to test your intuition about the remainder operator. Try enough test cases to cover all possibilities. Be sure that you understand how the remainder operator works. (For example, what if you are asked for `1%17` or `17%1` or `0%17`?)

Exercise 7-14. Write a Java program `Change` that repeatedly (1) reads an integer number of cents, and (2) uses Java's division and remainder operators to compute how to issue that amount using "large" coins—i.e., dollars, quarters, dimes, and nickels—in addition to pennies. Here's a typical session:

```
G:>java Change

Enter a number of cents: 138
That's 1 dollars + 38 cents.
That's 5 quarters + 13 cents.
That's 13 dimes + 8 cents.
That's 27 nickels + 3 cents.

Enter a number of cents: 369
That's 3 dollars + 69 cents.
That's 14 quarters + 19 cents.
That's 36 dimes + 9 cents.
That's 73 nickels + 4 cents.

Enter a number of cents: 18
That's 0 dollars + 18 cents.
That's 0 quarters + 18 cents.
That's 1 dimes + 8 cents.
That's 3 nickels + 3 cents.
```

Exercise 7-15. Is `abs` an instance method or a `static` method? Why?

Exercise 7-16. Evaluate the expressions below. Ask Java to check your work.

a) 8+6/4*2
b) (8+6)/4*2
c) 8+(6/4)*2
d) 8+6/(4*2)
e) (8+6/4)*2
f) 4-6*9/5*4-2
g) (4-6)*9/5*4-2
h) 4-6*(9/5)*4-2
i) (4-6)*9/5*4-2
j) 4-6*9/(5*4-2)
k) 4-6*9/5*(4-2)
l) (4-6*9)/5*4-2

Exercise 7-17. Insert parentheses, if necessary, into the following expressions in order to get the specified result:

Expression to Be Parenthesized	Result Required
3 + 4 / 7 * 2	2
3 + 4 / 7 * 2	6
3 + 4 / 7 * 2	3
17 / 7 * 5 - 3	4
17 / 7 * 5 - 3	7
17 / 7 * 5 - 3	0
17 / 7 * 5 - 3	-3

Use Java to check your work. Later in your undergraduate career you will learn how to write programs that can read arithmetic expressions and produce all possible parenthesizations. With such a program, the problem above would be a snap.

Exercise 7-18. Consider the program below, where *statement* will be filled in various ways:

```
public static void main (String [] args ) throws IOException
{
    int n = 20;

    while ( true )
    {
        System.out.println(n);
        statement
    }
}
```

This program is an infinite loop. For each of the following values of *statement*, give the first six values of n, which are printed:

a) `n *= 2;`
b) `n += 3;`
c) `n -= 4;`
d) `n /= 2;`
e) `n %= 3;`

Exercise 7-19. Run each of the following sets of statements by itself. They will give errors. In each case, what is Java trying to say?

a) `int n = new int(3);`
b) `int n = 5;`
   `System.out.println(n.toString());`

Exercise 7-20. Write a Java program `Change` that reads a nonnegative integer representing the number of cents change due to a customer. Your program should then print out the number of quarters, dimes, nickels, and pennies that should be dispensed. Here is a sample run:

```
G:\>java Change
How many cents change is due? 87
Coins due are:
   3 quarter(s)
   1 dime(s)
   0 nickel(s)
   2 penny(ies)
```

Don't worry about singular and plural of words like `quarter` and `penny`, or about omitting lines that specify 0 coins. We'll tackle these aspects of the problem in Chapter 11.

Exercise 7-21. Before 1971, British money was based on pounds, shillings, and pence: 12 pence made a shilling, and 20 shillings made a pound. Design and implement a class `UKMoney` that models old British money. Here is the driver you must match:

```
public static void main (String [] args ) throws IOException
{
    Scanner kb = new Scanner(System.in);

    while ( true )
```

```
        {
            System.out.print("\nEnter a number of pence: ");
            int n = kb.nextInt();
            UKMoney ukm = new UKMoney(n);
            System.out.println("                    UKMoney: " + ukm);
        }
    }
```

Here is an example of running the program:

```
G:\>java TestUK

Enter a number of pence: 25
                    UKMoney: 0 pounds + 2 shillings + 1 pence

Enter a number of pence: 311
                    UKMoney: 1 pounds + 5 shillings + 11 pence

Enter a number of pence: 600
                    UKMoney: 2 pounds + 10 shillings + 0 pence
...
```

Exercise 7-22.   Recall the linear expressions you learned in math:

$$f(x) = a_0 + a_1 x$$

Design and implement a class `Linear` that models a linear expression. Use the following driver to test your code:

```
public static void main (String [] args ) throws IOException
{
    Scanner kb = new Scanner(System.in);

    Linear lin = new Linear(2,3);

    while ( true )
    {
        System.out.print("\nValue at x = ? ");
        int x = kb.nextInt();
        System.out.println("The value of " +
                        lin +
                        " at x=" +
                        x +
                        " is " +
                        lin.valueAt(x));

    }
}
```

This particular driver uses only the expression $f(x) = 2 + 3x$. Typical output will be this:

```
G:\>java TestLinear

Value at x = ? 0
The value of 2 + 3*x at x=0 is 2

Value at x = ? 5
The value of 2 + 3*x at x=5 is 17
...
```

Test the program on a variety of values of `x`. Try other values for `a0` and `a1`.

The naïve `toString` method will produce *suboptimal* `String`s for some values of `a0` and `a1`. For example:

a0	a1	*Naïve Result of* `toString`	*Much Better Result of* `toString`
0	0	0 + 0x	0
0	3	0 + 3x	3x
2	0	2 + 0x	2
2	-3	2 + -3x	2 - 3x
0	1	0 + 1x	x
0	-1	0 + -1x	-x

Don't worry about this. We'll be able to produce the better `toString` results when we study conditional statements in Chapter 11.

Exercise 7-23.   Recall linear expressions, which we discussed in Exercise 7-22. We will now write a program that reads the coefficients—`a0` and `a1`—and then prints out the values of that linear expression for `x` taking the values $\{-2, -1, 0, 1, 2\}$. Here's most of the driver:

```
while ( true )
{
    System.out.println();

    Linear lin = Linear.read(System.out,kb);

    System.out.println("\nSome values of " +
                    lin +
                    " are:\n");
```

```
System.out.print(" x          ");
for ( int x = -2; x < 3 ;  x++ )
    System.out.print(x + "\t");
System.out.println();

System.out.print("f(x)        ");
for ( int x = -2; x < 3 ;  x++ )
    System.out.print(lin.valueAt(x) + "\t");
System.out.println();
}
```

We'll learn more about `for` statements in Chapter 13. For the moment, just think of the `for` statements as driving x through the values {-2, -1, 0, 1, 2}. Enhance your class `Linear` to fit this driver (you'll need a `static` `read` method). Typical output is:

```
Reading a Linear expression ...
Enter a0: 2
Enter a1: 3

Some values of 2 + 3*x are:

x         -2       -1        0        1        2
f(x)      -4       -1        2        5        8
```

Exercise 7-24. Consider a class `Person` that contains two instance variables, `name` of type `String` and `ageInMonths` of type `int`.

Write a constructor that takes a name, a number of *years*, and a number of *months*, and creates the appropriate `Person` object. Note that you will need to convert years and months to months. For example, if a new `Person` has age 5 years and 1 month, then the instance variable `ageInMonths` would get the value 61.

Write a `toString` method that returns `String`s like this:

```
Adam years 0 months 11
```

Write a driver that tests your class `Person`. Select appropriate test cases. Defend your choice of test cases.

Exercise 7-25. Write a program `First3Ints` that (1) reads the name of a file of `int`s, then (2) reads and prints the first three `int`s in the file, and then (3) computes and prints their average. Use integer arithmetic.

Exercise 7-26.   Design and implement a class `Student`. Each `Student` has a name and two grades: `exam1` and `exam2`. The name is a `String` and the grades are `int`s. Provide a `static read` method.

Write a program that reads three `Student`s and computes and prints the average of `exam1` and the average of `exam2`. Use integer arithmetic.

Exercise 7-27.   Take class `EggShipment` in `Prog0704` and add a method

```
public void increment()
```

which adds one egg to the receiving `EggShipment`. Write a driver that proves that your method works. Be sure that your driver tests moving upward past the border of a dozen or a gross.

Exercise 7-28.   In `Prog0704`, we implemented the method

```
public EggShipment add(EggShipment)
```

For this exercise, replace that method with

```
public void add(EggShipment)
```

Modify the driver to use the new `add` method. Java will not allow class `EggShipment` to contain both `add` methods. Why?

Exercise 7-29.   Modify class `EggShipment` so that it always maintains not the single `int n`, but a triple of `int`s: one for each of `nGross`, `nDozen`, and `nSingle`. Your modified class `EggShipment` should run through the driver with no difference.

Exercise 7-30.   Write a method `add` for the class `UKMoney` with the prototype

```
public UKMoney add ( UKMoney add )
```

Write a driver that enables sessions of the form:

```
C:\1\book\programs\07programs>java AddUK
The current total is 0 pounds + 0 shillings + 0 pence
Pence to add? 7
               Adding 0 pounds + 0 shillings + 7 pence
The current total is 0 pounds + 0 shillings + 7 pence
Pence to add? 15
               Adding 0 pounds + 0 shillings + 15 pence
The current total is 0 pounds + 1 shillings + 2 pence
Pence to add? 18
               Adding 0 pounds + 0 shillings + 18 pence
```

```
The current total is 0 pounds + 2 shillings + 0 pence
Pence to add? 199
            Adding 0 pounds + 9 shillings + 19 pence
The current total is 0 pounds + 11 shillings + 19 pence
Pence to add? 2
            Adding 0 pounds + 0 shillings + 2 pence
The current total is 1 pounds + 0 shillings + 1 pence
Pence to add?
```

Exercise 7-31.   Complete the following tables:

+	3 + 5i	2 - 3i	7	2i
3 + 5i				
2 - 3i				
7				
2i				

-	3 + 5i	2 - 3i	7	2i
3 + 5i				
2 - 3i				
7				
2i				

*	3 + 5i	2 - 3i	7	2i
3 + 5i				
2 - 3i				
7				
2i				

Exercise 7-32.   If $z = a + bi$ is an arbitrary complex number, then $z' = a - bi$ is called its *complex conjugate*. Prove that $z \times z'$ is always a *purely real* number.

Exercise 7-33.   A three-vector is an ordered list of three numbers. We'll use `ints` for the time being. Three-vectors can represent positions in three-space—the world around us. Write a class `Vector3` where each instance has instance variables x, y, and z. Here is part of a driver:

```
Vector3 v1 = new Vector3(5,2,7);
System.out.println(v1);
Vector3 v2 = new Vector3(1,4,2);
```

```
System.out.println(v2);
Vector3 v3 = Vector3.read(System.out,kb);
System.out.println(v3);
```

and here is the dialog where what the user types is underlined:

```
(5,2,7)
(1,4,2)
Reading a Vector3 ...
x? 7
y? 3
z? -2
(7,3,-2)
```

Write the code for `Vector3` and the driver.

Exercise 7-34.   Recall the class `Linear`, which we wrote in Exercise 7–22.

Write method `public Linear add(Linear)`, which takes a `Linear` and returns the element-by-element sum of the parameter and the receiver. Write a driver and test appropriately.

Exercise 7-35.   Recall the class `Vector3`, which we wrote in Exercise 7-33.

Write method `add`, which takes a `Vector3` and returns the element-by-element sum of the parameter and the receiver. Mathematically, if $v_1 = (x_1, y_1, z_1)$ and $v_2 = (x_2, y_2, z_2)$, then $v_1 + v_2 = (x_1 + x_2, y_1 + y_2, z_1 + z_2)$. The prototype is

```
public Vector3 add(Vector3)
```

Write a driver that reads two `Vector3`s from the keyboard and prints out their sum. Select and justify test cases before writing the code.

Exercise 7-36.   Write the `add` method for `Vector3` in three different ways, following the three ways described in Section 7.12 for writing `Complex add`.

Exercise 7-37.   Recall the class `Vector3`, which we wrote in Exercise 7-33.

Write method `sub`, which takes a `Vector3` and returns the element-by-element difference of the parameter and the receiver. Mathematically, if $v_1 = (x_1, y_1, z_1)$ and $v_2 = (x_2, y_2, z_2)$, then $v_1 - v_2 = (x_1 - x_2, y_1 - y_2, z_1 - z_2)$. The prototype is

```
public Vector3 sub(Vector3)
```

Write a driver that reads two `Vector3`s from the keyboard and prints out their difference. Select and justify test cases before writing the code.

Exercise 7-38.   Recall the class Vector3, which we wrote in Exercise 7-33.

Write method dot, which takes a Vector3 and returns the *dot product* of the two vectors. Mathematically, if $v_1 = (x_1, y_1, z_1)$ and $v_2 = (x_2, y_2, z_2)$, then $v_1 \cdot v_2 = (x_1x_2 + y_1y_2 + z_1z_2)$. The prototype is

```
public int dot(Vector3)
```

Write a driver that reads two Vector3s from the keyboard and prints out their dot product. Select and justify test cases before writing the code.

Exercise 7-39.   Write a version of class Rectangle that contains an instance variable for area. Update area whenever length or width changes. Run Prog0708 with your new class Rectangle. Your output should be unchanged. Add setters for length and width. (Can we write a setter for area?) Write a driver that tests the new methods.

Exercise 7-40.   Write a driver that starts with a valid Rectangle and then pushes it into a state with negative length or width.

Exercise 7-41.   Write a class Square that models geometrical squares. Your class should enable the following driver to run:

```
//- - - - - - - - - - - - - - - - - - - - - - - - - - - - - - - - - - - - - - - - - - - - - - - -
   public static void main (String [] args ) throws Exception
   {
      Square sq = new Square(5);

      System.out.println("\nside\tarea\tperimeter");

      report(sq);

      for ( int i = 0 ; i < 3 ; i++ )
      {
         sq.grow();
         report(sq);
      }

      System.out.println();

      for ( int i = 0 ; i < 12; i++ )
      {
         sq.shrink();
```

```
        report(sq);
    }
  }
//-------------------------------------------------------------
  private static void report(Square sq)
  {
      System.out.println(sq.getSide() + "\t" +
                          sq.getArea() + "\t" +
                          sq.getPerimeter()
                          );
  }
//-------------------------------------------------------------
```

We'll learn more about `for` statements in Chapter 13. For the moment, just think of the `for` statements as causing controlled repetition of the statements in the brackets that follow them—the statements they "govern."

Exercise 7-42. Write a `static read` method for class `Rectangle`. Test it with a driver that reads a `Rectangle` and then `grow`s it. Report the status of the `Rectangle` before and after the `grow` operation.

Exercise 7-43. Write a program that repeatedly reads `Rectangle`s from the user. After each `read`, your program should report how many `Rectangle`s have been created.

Exercise 7-44. Modify class `Complex` in `Prog0706.java` so that it counts and reports the number of `Complex` that have been created. Write an appropriate driver.

Exercise 7-45. In Exercise 7-33, we wrote a class `Vector3`. Modify that class so that it counts and reports the number of `Vector3`s that have been created. Write an appropriate driver.

Exercise 7-46. Modify the driver and class `Fraction` of `Prog0711` so that the program counts and reports the number of `Fraction`s created.

Exercise 7-47. Modify class `Fraction` by defining a method `add` that adds two `Fraction`s and returns their result. For example:

```
Fraction f1 = new Fraction(1,2);
Fraction f2 = new Fraction(3,5);
System.out.println(f1.add(f2));
```

would print 11/10. Write a driver that reads two Fractions from the user and prints their sum.

Exercise 7-48. Using the add method from Exercise 7–47, write a driver that maintains a running total of all the Fractions entered so far. Start with

```
Fraction total = new Fraction(0,1);
```

Exercise 7-49. Repeat Exercises 7-47 and 7–48 using the sub method, which subtracts two Fractions.

Exercise 7-50. Repeat Exercises 7-47 and 7–48 using the mul method, which multiplies two Fractions.

Exercise 7-51. Repeat Exercises 7-47 and 7–48 using the div method, which divides two Fractions.

Exercise 7-52. Try your Fraction arithmetic methods on the following code. Verify your results by hand.

```
Fraction f1 = new Fraction(1,2);
Fraction f2 = new Fraction(1,5);
Fraction f3 = new Fraction(7,3);
Fraction f4 = new Fraction(5,11);
System.out.println(f1.add(f2).sub(f3).mul(f4));
```

Exercise 7-53. Is parseInt an instance method or a static method? Why?

Exercise 7-54. Write a program that reads an int in the range [0, 99] and then prints out the reverse of the digits of the input number. For example:

```
Enter an int in the range [0,99]:   52
Reversed, that is: "25"

Enter an int in the range [0,99]:   8
Reversed, that is: "80"
```

Hint: Take the integer and create a String that adds leading 0s to make it width 2. Then print the appropriate pieces of that String in the appropriate order.

Exercise 7-55. Prog0724 prints out the multiplication table of $\{1, \ldots, 10\} \times \{1, \ldots, 10\}$, but the columns don't line up properly:

```
1 2 3 4 5 6 7 8 9 10
2 4 6 8 10 12 14 16 18 20
3 6 9 12 15 18 21 24 27 30
4 8 12 16 20 24 28 32 36 40
5 10 15 20 25 30 35 40 45 50
6 12 18 24 30 36 42 48 54 60
7 14 21 28 35 42 49 56 63 70
8 16 24 32 40 48 56 64 72 80
9 18 27 36 45 54 63 72 81 90
10 20 30 40 50 60 70 80 90 100
```

Change the `print` statement to the appropriate `printf` statement so that the columns line up to form a proper table.

Prog0724.java   **Print the Multiplication Table**

```java
// Written by Barry Soroka
//
// Prints the multiplication table.
//
import java.io.*;
/////////////////////////////////////////////////////////////////////////////
class Prog0724
{
//---------------------------------------------------------------------------
   public static void main ( String [] args ) throws Exception
   {
      for ( int r = 1 ; r <= 10 ; r++ )
      {
         for ( int c = 1 ; c <= 10 ; c++ )
            System.out.print(r*c + " ");
         System.out.println();
      }
   }
//---------------------------------------------------------------------------
} // end class Prog0724
/////////////////////////////////////////////////////////////////////////////
```

Exercise 7-56.   Modify `Prog0720` so that it prints both the square *and* the cube of the integer entered.

Exercise 7-57.   Modify `Prog0720` so that it accepts *two* integers and prints the sum and the product.

Exercise 7-58. What happens if the text for a button is larger than the button can display?

Exercise 7-59. Modify `Prog0722` so that it display three buttons—`alpha`, `beta`, and `gamma`—and prints an appropriate message when a button is clicked.

Exercise 7-60. Modify `Prog0723` so that it display three buttons—`inc`, `dec`, and `reset`—with the following meanings:

- When `inc` is pressed, the counter is incremented.
- When `dec` is pressed, the counter is decremented.
- When `reset` is pressed, the counter is reset to 0.

Exercise 7-61. Modify `Prog0723` so that the counter uses a `byte` instead of an `int`. Increment the counter until you pass 127, the most positive integer that can be held in a `byte`. What does it display after the 128th press?

Boolean Variables

In Chapter 7, we studied *integer* variables. These variables could hold integers from the set . . ., $-3, -2, -1, 0, 1, 2, 3, \ldots$ Now we will study *boolean* variables, which are allowed to hold only the values `true` or `false`. These "truth values" are the basis of logic, and they're called `boolean` in honor of the English mathematician George Boole (1815–1864), who contributed greatly to understanding how truth values can be combined and manipulated. This branch of mathematics is called Boolean algebra,[1] and it's the basis of how computers are designed. Indeed, one often encounters courses called *logic design*.

---

[1] One of Boole's books is entitled *An Investigation into the Laws of Thought*. Boolean logic is a reasonable first approximation of how the human mind processes information. Nowadays, artificial intelligence researchers are struggling to reconcile their models with the fact that humans are *not* terribly logical.

In this chapter, we'll examine the definition and manipulation of `boolean` variables. Our plan is three-fold:

- First we'll study the `boolean` *literals* `true` and `false`.
- Then we'll introduce *relational operators*, which produce `boolean` values by comparing numerical values.[2]
- Finally, we'll examine how *logical operators* can take `boolean` values and produce new values.

In Chapter 11 we will use logical tests to control conditional statements, and in Chapter 13 we'll use logical expressions to control loops.

8.1   Literals

There are only two `boolean` literals—`true` and `false`—and we can print them directly. The statements

```
System.out.println(true);
System.out.println(false);
```

produce the output

```
true
false
```

We can also print `boolean` *variables*. The statements

```
boolean b = true;
System.out.println(b);
b = false;
System.out.println(b);
```

produce

```
true
false
```

Java does not provide methods for *reading* `boolean` variables. There is no `Boolean.parseBoolean(String)` corresponding to `Integer.parseInt(String)` and there is no `nextBoolean` corresponding to `nextInt`.

---

[2] Relational operators can also be used to compare characters. We'll study this in Chapter 9.

8.2   Relational Operators and Numeric Types

Comparing numbers produces `booleans`:

- Is 3 less than 5? `true`.
- Is 3 less than 2? `false`.

Java provides six operators for comparing numbers, called *relational operators*:

> **Relational operators**   Relational operators compare two operands, producing a logical value.

<	less than
<=	less than or equal to
==	equal
!=	not equal
>=	greater than or equal to
>	greater than

`Prog0801` presents a program that reads two `ints` and reports (1) whether they are equal, and (2) whether the first `int` is smaller than the second. Here is hardcopy of a sample run:

```
Enter an int: 17
Enter an int: 99
i1 == i2? false
i1 < i2?  true
```

The code for reading the two `ints` is not novel, but the comparison statements are new to us:

```
System.out.println("\ni1 == i2? " + (i1 == i2));
System.out.println("\ni1 < i2?  " + (i1 < i2));
```

We can use a relational expression such as `i1 == i2` as though it were a `boolean` literal; it will print as `true` or `false` as appropriate.

Prog0801.java   **Relations Between Two ints**

```
// Written by Barry Soroka
//
// Read two ints and report their relations.
//
```

```
import java.io.*;
import java.util.Scanner;
//////////////////////////////////////////////////////////////////////////////
class Prog0801
{
//-----------------------------------------------------------------------------

   public static void main ( String [] args ) throws Exception
   {
      Scanner kb = new Scanner(System.in);

      System.out.print("\nEnter int 1: ");
      int i1 = kb.nextInt();

      System.out.print("Enter int 2: ");
      int i2 = kb.nextInt();

      System.out.println("\ni1 == i2? " + (i1 == i2));
      System.out.println("\ni1 < i2?  " + (i1 < i2));
   }
//-----------------------------------------------------------------------------

} // end class Prog0801
//////////////////////////////////////////////////////////////////////////////
```

Note the parentheses in the `println` statements above. If we omit these, we get an error. Consider the case of 17 and 99:

"\ni1 == i2? " + i1 == i2 *becomes*

<u>"\ni1 == i2? " + 17</u> == 99 *becomes*

"\ni1 == i2? 17" == 99

which results in an error: We're trying to compare a `String` to an `int`. This is an example of *precedence*, and we'll study this in more detail later in this chapter.

> BY THE WAY
>
> Most languages provide the six relational operators we find in Java, but different tokens are sometimes used to specify them. For example, Java uses "!=" to mean "not equal," but other symbols are used in other languages: "<>", "\=", and ".NE." are used in Pascal, Prolog and Ada, and FORTRAN. FORTRAN used the following symbols: .LT., .LE., .EQ., .NE., .GE., and .GT. You may one day find yourself working with code in one of these other languages.

8.3   Logical Operators

Logical operators   *and*, *or*, and *not* are represented by &&, ||, and !, respectively. These produce complex logical expressions.

Truth table   A tabular way of showing the values of a logical expression as a function of its inputs.

Inclusive-or   One or the other or both.

Logical operators—also called `boolean` operators—take one or more `boolean` values and compute a new `boolean` value. This is similar to how we generated and evaluated *numerical* expressions: With numbers, we used *numeric* operators to produce new numbers by combining existing numeric literals and variables. The numerical operators were +, -, *, /, and %. Now we must learn the *logical* operators so that we can generate new `boolean` values from existing `boolean` variables or literals. Java provides three logical operators.

The first logical operator is *and*, represented by the symbol &&. This is a binary operator that takes two `boolean` values and produces a third. Clearly, there are four possible input combinations to *and*: `true-true`, `true-false`, `false-true`, and `false-false`. We formally define *and* by means of a *truth table*, which shows what *and* produces for each possible input combination:

x	y	x && y
true	true	true
true	false	false
false	true	false
false	false	false

&& returns `true` only if both of its arguments are `true`. This is analogous to standard English usage.

The second logical operator is *or*, represented by the symbol ||. This binary operator returns `true` if either or both of its arguments is `true`:

x	y	x || y
true	true	true
true	false	true
false	true	true
false	false	false

Note that x || y returns `true` even when *both* its arguments are `true`; this is the *inclusive-or*. || does not mean "one or the other but not both"—that

> **Logical negation**   The *not* operator, !.

would be *exclusive-or*, which will be important in hardware design in later courses.

The third logical operator is *not*, represented by !. It's a *unary* operator, which takes a `boolean` variable and returns its *logical negation*:

x	!x
true	false
false	true

Note how the relational operator "!=l" ("not equal") uses the "!l" ("not") character.

8.4   Precedence

We have learned three kinds of operators that can be used to produce an expression:

Arithmetic operators	+, -, *, /, %
Relational operators	<=, <, ==, !=, >=, >
Logical operators	&&, ||, !

Here is a table that shows the precedence of the operators, from highest (at the top) to lowest (at the bottom):

$$!$$
$$*\quad/\quad\%$$
$$+\quad-$$
$$>\quad>=\quad<\quad<=$$
$$==\quad!=$$
$$\&\&$$
$$||$$

Operators on the same row have equal precedence.

Test your skill with Exercise 8-1.

8.5   Equality and Objects

Equality of objects can be interpreted in two ways:

- Two variables may refer to the exact same structure in memory. We denote this by ==, and this operation is available for all objects. It determines whether two references label the same object.
- Two similar objects may have all slots equal, but they may be located in different places in memory. We denote this by equals, and this operation is available only if it has been written for the specific class involved.

For example, consider the following code:

```
String s1 = "hello";
String s2 = s1;
String s3 = "he".concat("llo");
```

This results in the memory diagram shown in Figure 8–1. We have

```
s1 == s2 → true
s1 == s3 → false
```

because s1 and s2 refer to the same object, but s1 and s3 do not. The String class provides an equals method, so we have:

```
s1.equals(s2) → true
s1.equals(s3) → true
```

By default, a class inherits the equals method from the top of the object hierarchy, namely Object. This default equals is precisely the same as ==. So, if we want to test equality of instance variables for our own classes, we'll need to put our own equals method in the class itself.

Figure 8–1
Equals vs. --

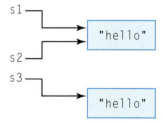

Figure 8–2
Two Equal
Instances of
Complex

z1   z2

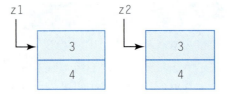

Consider the class Complex, which we defined in Chapter 7. The statements

```
Complex z1 = new Complex(3,4);
Complex z2 = new Complex(3,4);
```

result in the memory diagram shown in Figure 8–2. Because z1 and z2 do not refer to the same object,

z1 == z2 → false

Similarly, the default equals method will yield

z1.equals(z2) → false

If we want to consider the two objects equal, then we need to write our own equals method for class Complex.

Prog0802 reads two Complex numbers and determines whether they are slot-wise equal. Here is the code for the equals method:

```
//-------------------------------------------------------
    public boolean equals ( Complex that )
    {
        return this.real == that.real
               &&
               this.imag == that.imag;
    }
//-------------------------------------------------------
```

Notice how we explicitly test the slots and compute a boolean result that is true only if both slots are equal.

Prog0802.java   Method **equals** for Class **Complex**

```
// Written by Barry Soroka
//
// Method equals for class Complex
```

```java
//
import java.io.*;
import java.util.Scanner;
//////////////////////////////////////////////////////////////////////////////
class Prog0802
{
//----------------------------------------------------------------------------
   public static void main ( String [] args ) throws Exception
   {
      Scanner kb = new Scanner(System.in);

      System.out.println("I read two Complex numbers " +
                          "& report their equality or not.\n");
      Complex z1 = Complex.read(System.out,kb);
      System.out.println();
      Complex z2 = Complex.read(System.out,kb);
      System.out.println("\nz1.equals(z2) --> " + z1.equals(z2));
   }
//----------------------------------------------------------------------------
} // end class Prog0802
//////////////////////////////////////////////////////////////////////////////
class Complex
{
   private int real;
   private int imag;
//----------------------------------------------------------------------------
   public Complex ( int real , int imag )
   {
      this.real = real;
      this.imag = imag;
   }
//----------------------------------------------------------------------------
   public boolean equals ( Complex that )
   {
      return this.real == that.real
             &&
             this.imag == that.imag;
   }
//----------------------------------------------------------------------------
   public String toString ()
   {
      return "(" + real + "," + imag + ")";
   }
```

```
//- - - - - - - - - - - - - - - - - - - - - - - - - - - - - - - - - - - - - -
   public static Complex read ( PrintStream ps, Scanner sc )
   {
      ps.println("Reading a complex number ...");
      ps.print("Enter the real part:      ");
      int real = sc.nextInt();
      ps.print("Enter the imaginary part: ");
      int imag = sc.nextInt();
      return new Complex ( real, imag );
   }
//- - - - - - - - - - - - - - - - - - - - - - - - - - - - - - - - - - - - - -
} // end class Complex
///////////////////////////////////////////////////////////////////////////
```

= is the assignment operator and == is the test for equality.

Don't confuse them!

Test your skill with Exercises 8-2 through 8-5.

8.6 Predicates—Predefined and User-Defined

A *predicate* is a method that returns a `boolean` value—`true` or `false`. For class `String`, we've already seen the predicates

```
boolean equals(String)
```

and

```
boolean equalsIgnoreCase(String)
```

If you study the API, you'll discover some others: The methods

```
boolean endsWith(String)
```

and

```
boolean startsWith(String)
```

test one `String` against another to see if they're related as a prefix or a suffix. For class `File`, we have the predicates `canRead()`, `canWrite()`, `exists()`, and `isHidden()`.

We can write our own predicates, just as we wrote `equals` for class `Complex`. Let's add method

```
public boolean isLargerThan(Complex)
```

This method will compare the magnitudes (absolute values) of the receiver and the parameter. Mathematically, if $z = a + bi$ is a `Complex` number, then $|z| = \sqrt{a^2 + b^2}$ is its magnitude. We haven't yet studied square roots or floating-point numbers in Java, so our predicate will compare the *squares* of the magnitudes. `Prog0803` gives the code and a driver. Here's the code for our predicate:

```java
public boolean isLargerThan ( Complex that )
{
    int size1 = this.real*this.real + this.imag*this.imag;
    int size2 = that.real*that.real + that.imag*that.imag;
    return size1 > size2;
}
```

Prog0803.java   Method isLargerThan for Class Complex

```java
// Written by Barry Soroka
//
// Complex:  isLargerThan(Complex).
//
import java.io.*;
import java.util.Scanner;
//////////////////////////////////////////////////////////////////////////////
class Prog0803
{
//---------------------------------------------------------------------------
   public static void main ( String [] args ) throws Exception
   {
      Scanner kb = new Scanner(System.in);

      System.out.println("I read two Complex numbers " +
                         "& compare their magnitudes.\n");
      Complex z1 = Complex.read(System.out,kb);
      System.out.println();
      Complex z2 = Complex.read(System.out,kb);
```

```
                System.out.println("\nz1.isLargerThan(z2) --> " + z1.isLargerThan(z2));
    }
//--------------------------------------------------------------------------
} // end class Prog0803
////////////////////////////////////////////////////////////////////////////
class Complex
{
    private int real;
    private int imag;
//------------------------------------------------------------------
    public Complex ( int real , int imag )
    {
        this.real = real;
        this.imag = imag;
    }
//------------------------------------------------------------------
    public boolean isLargerThan ( Complex that )
    {
        int size1 = this.real*this.real + this.imag*this.imag;
        int size2 = that.real*that.real + that.imag*that.imag;
        return size1 > size2;
    }
//------------------------------------------------------------------
    public boolean equals ( Complex that )
    {
        return this.real == that.real
                &&
                this.imag == that.imag;
    }
//------------------------------------------------------------------
    public String toString ()
    {
        return "(" + real + "," + imag + ")";
    }
//------------------------------------------------------------------
    public static Complex read ( PrintStream ps, Scanner sc )
    {
        ps.println("Reading a complex number ...");
        ps.print("Enter the real part:      ");
        int real = sc.nextInt();
        ps.print("Enter the imaginary part: ");
        int imag = sc.nextInt();
        return new Complex ( real, imag );
    }
```

```
//------------------------------------------------------------------
} // end class Complex
//////////////////////////////////////////////////////////////////////////
```

   Test your skill with Exercises 8-6 through 8-9.

8.7   Odd and Even

Prog0804 reads an int from the user and reports its parity status (odd vs. even). Here's the relevant code:

```
System.out.println("Even? " + (0 == n%2));
System.out.println("Odd?  " + (0 != n%2));
```

After reading n, we use the expressions

```
0 == n%2
0 != n%2
```

to determine whether n is even or odd: Each evaluates to either true or false. Here's hardcopy for a typical run:

```
Enter an int: 13
Even? false
Odd?  true
```

Prog0804.java   **Even or Odd?**

```
// Written by Barry Soroka
//
// Read two ints and report their relations.
//
import java.io.*;
import java.util.Scanner;
//////////////////////////////////////////////////////////////////////////
class Prog0804
{
//---------------------------------------------------------------------
   public static void main ( String [] args ) throws Exception
   {
      Scanner kb = new Scanner(System.in);

      System.out.print("\nEnter an int: ");
```

```
    int n = kb.nextInt();

    System.out.println("Even? " + (0 == n%2));
    System.out.println("Odd?  " + (0 != n%2));
  }
//------------------------------------------------------------------------
} // end class Prog0804
////////////////////////////////////////////////////////////////////////
```

Remember Precedence and Parentheses

As noted earlier in this chapter, we can't omit the parentheses around the `boolean` expressions in `println` statements like this:

```
    System.out.println("Even? " + (0 == n%2));
```

If we do, then Java's precedence scheme will lead to a compile-time error.

Using a `boolean` Variable

Recall the statements we used in computing the parity of `int n`:

```
    System.out.println("Even? " + (0 == n%2));
    System.out.println("Odd?  " + (0 != n%2));
```

Notice that we compute `n%2` *twice*. There's a way to write the code so that we compute this expression only once:

```
    boolean isEven = ( 0 == n%2 );
    System.out.println("Even? " + isEven);
    System.out.println("Odd?  " + !isEven);
```

We compute the evenness of `n` and we store it in a `boolean` variable `isEven`. Then we use that variable to report even and odd: once in the positive sense `isEven`, and once in the negative sense `!isEven`.

I'm not saying that you should always write code this way, or that it's a terrible crime to compute `n%2` twice. I'm just presenting another way to write the program, and you may one day want to write code like this. The more alternatives you know, the more patterns you have to draw from when solving a new problem.

 Test your skill with Exercise 8-10.

8.8 static **Predicates**

Sometimes it's convenient to have *static* predicates. For example,

```
public static isEven ( int n ) { return 0 == n%2; }
```

tells us if an int is even, and

```
public static boolean isUpperCase ( String s )
{
    return s.equals(s.toUpperCase());
}
```

tells us if a String is entirely uppercase. In later chapters, we'll look at more complicated predicates such as

```
public static boolean isPrime ( int n )
```

and

```
public static boolean isPalindrome ( String s )
```

where a String is a palindrome if and only if it's the same forward and backward, like radar, madam, or toot.

> **Test your skill with Exercises 8-11 and 8-12.**

8.9 **DeMorgan's Laws**

We often need to negate boolean expressions like (a && b) or (a || b). The appropriate results are shown in the following table:

Expression	Its Negation
(a && b)	!a || !b
(a || b)	!a && !b

DeMorgan's Laws How to negate expressions using && or ||.

I present this here because, left on their own, many students use the wrong formulas. These rules are known as *DeMorgan's laws* and are named after the English mathematician Augustus DeMorgan (1806–1871).

8.10 Experiments to Test the Behavior of Logical Operators

Consider the expression `a && b` where `a` and `b` can be `boolean` expressions of arbitrary complexity. Which is evaluated first—`a` or `b`? `Prog0805` is an experimental approach to answering the question. We have two helper methods that return `boolean` values:

- `public boolean t(String)` prints the `String` and returns `true`;
- `public boolean f(String)` prints the `String` and returns `false`.

We can use these to construct expressions that tell us the order in which their components are evaluated.

Consider the expression

```
result = t("left operand of &&")
            &&
         t("right operand of &&");
```

We expect that both the left operand and right operand of `&&` will be evaluated, but which will be evaluated first? We get the printout

```
left operand of &&
right operand of &&
```

which indicates that `&&` evaluates its *left operand first*.

Test your skill with Exercise 8-13.

Consider the expression `a && b`. We know that `a` will be evaluated first, but what if `a` evaluates to `false`? Then the expression will evaluate to `false` *regardless of the value of* `b`. `Prog0805` contains the following statement, which asks what `&&` does when its left operand is `false`:

```
result = f("left operand of &&") && t("right operand of &&");
```

The output is this:

```
left operand of &&
```

Short-circuiting (lazy evaluation) Evaluating only as many operands as are absolutely required to compute the value of a logical expression.

which indicates that `&&` evaluates only as much as it must: Because the *left* operand is `false`, `&&` needn't evaluate its *right* operand at all. This tactic is know as *short-circuiting* or *lazy evaluation*—the operator evaluates only as much as it must.

Prog0805.java   **Demonstration of Short-Circuiting (Lazy Evaluation)**

```java
// Written by Barry Soroka
//
// Which operand do boolean operators evaluate first?
// Do boolean operators always evaluate ALL their operands?
//
import java.io.*;
////////////////////////////////////////////////////////////////////////////
class Prog0805
{
//-------------------------------------------------------------------------
    public static void main ( String [] args ) throws Exception
    {
        boolean result;

        result = t("left operand of &&") && t("right operand of &&");
        System.out.println(result);

        result = f("left operand of &&") && t("right operand of &&");
        System.out.println(result);

        System.out.println();
        result = f("left operand of &") & t("right operand of &");
        System.out.println(result);
    }
//-------------------------------------------------------------------------
//
// t(String) prints the String and returns true
//
    private static boolean t ( String s )
    {
        System.out.println(s);
        return true;
    }
//-------------------------------------------------------------------------
//
// f(String) prints the String and returns false
//
    private static boolean f ( String s )
    {
        System.out.println(s);
        return false;
    }
```

```
//-------------------------------------------------------------------------
} // end class Prog0805
/////////////////////////////////////////////////////////////////////////
```

 | **Test your skill with Exercises 8-14 through 8-16.** |

Chapter Summary

- Java's boolean literals are `true` and `false`.
- We can compare numeric values using the relational operators <, <=, =, !=, >=, and >. The result is a `boolean` value.
- `&&` and `||` are the `boolean` operators for *and* and *or*. They combine `boolean` expressions to yield another `boolean` expression.
- `!` is the `boolean` operator for *not*. It acts on a `boolean` expression to yield another `boolean` expression.
- `!` has very high precedence.
- `&&` and `||` have very low precedence, and `&&` has higher precedence than `||`.
- When comparing object references, `==` returns true if and only if the two references refer to the exact same structure in memory. This is shallow equality.
- Thus, two `Complex` numbers with the same real and imaginary parts may be deemed unequal using `==`.
- We can write an `equals` method for testing `Complex` numbers for equal instance variables. This is deep equality.
- An `equals` method is predefined for `String`s.
- Predicates are methods that return `true` or `false`.
- DeMorgan's laws tell how to negate expressions involving `&&` and `||`.
- `&&` and `||` implement short-circuit logic (lazy evaluation). They don't evaluate the right operand if the result can be inferred from evaluating just the left operand.

Terminology Introduced in This Chapter

DeMorgan's laws	logical negation	short-circuiting
inclusive-or	logical operator	truth table
lazy evaluation	relational operator	

Exercises

Exercise 8-1. Evaluate the expressions below. Indicate errors, if any. Remember: You can check your work by asking Java to evaluate the expressions for you!

a) `true && false || true`
b) `false && true || true`
c) `true || false && true`
d) `! false && true`
e) `! true && false`
f) `! (false && true)`
g) `5 = 2 + 3`
h) `5 == 2 + 3`
i) `! 5 == 2 + 3`
j) `2 + 3 > 3 + 4`
k) `2 < 3 && 4 < 3`

Exercise 8-2. Recall the class `Rectangle`, which we wrote in Section 7.13. Add a method `equals` that returns `true` only if the two `Rectangle`s—receiver and parameter—are slot-wise equal.

Exercise 8-3. Recall the class `Person`, which we wrote in Section 7.24. Add a method `equals` that returns `true` only if the two `Person`s—receiver and parameter—are slot-wise equal.

Exercise 8-4. Write the class `Student` with name and numerical grade. Add a method `equals` that returns `true` only if the two `Student`s—receiver and parameter—are slot-wise equal.

Exercise 8-5. Recall the class `Fraction` with slots for numerator and denominator. Two fractions, $\frac{a}{b}$ and $\frac{c}{d}$, should be considered equal if and only if $ad = bc$. Implement `equals` for class `Fraction`.

Exercise 8-6. Recall our code for class `Rectangle`. Add the predicate

```
public boolean isSquare()
```

so that it returns `true` if and only if the `length` and `width` of a `Rectangle` are equal.

Exercise 8-7. Recall our code for class `Rectangle`. Add the predicate

```
public boolean isThin()
```

so that it returns `true` if and only if the `length` is 8 or more times the `width`, or if the `width` is 8 or more times the `length`.

Exercise 8-8.   Recall our code for class `Rectangle`. Add the predicate

```
public boolean isLargerThan(int)
```

so that it returns `true` if and only if the area of the `Rectangle` is greater than the given `int`.

Exercise 8-9.   Write a class `Student` with slots `String name`, `int age`, and `int grade`. Write the following predicates:

a) `public boolean equals(Student)`
b) `public boolean canVote()`, so that it returns `true` if and only if the `Student`'s age ≥ 18.
c) `public boolean canDrink()`, so that it returns `true` if and only if the `Student`'s age ≥ 21.
d) `public boolean isPassing()`, so that it returns `true` if and only if the `Student`'s grade ≥ 60.
e) `public boolean scoresHigherThan(Student)`, so that it returns `true` if and only if the `grade` of the receiver > the `grade` of the parameter.

Exercise 8-10.   Write code that reads an `int` and reports whether it's positive, zero, or negative. Here is hardcopy of a typical run:

```
Enter an int: 77
Positive? true
Zero?     false
Negative? false
```

Exercise 8-11.   Write the predicate

```
public static boolean isOdd ( int n )
```

Exercise 8-12.   Write the predicate

```
public static boolean isBlank ( String s )
```

so that it returns `true` if and only if the `String s` contains no nonblank characters.

Exercise 8-13.   Using similar programming, determine whether || first evaluates its left operand or its right operand.

Exercise 8-14.   Using similar programming, determine whether || evaluates *both* operands if its left operand evaluates to true.

Exercise 8-15.   Java has variants of the && and || operators, namely & and |. Use our t and f methods to determine their behavior.

Exercise 8-16.   Suppose we have the method

```
private static int i(String,int)
```

that prints the given String and returns the given int.
Use i to determine the following:

- Does * evaluate its left operand or its right operand first?
- Does * evaluate both its operands if the first operand evaluates to 0?

CAUTION! The results of these experiments may not be the same for all Java compilers.

char

Chapter Objectives

- Use character literals, including escape sequences.
- Understand `String` methods involving `char`s.
- Appreciate the difference between `char`s and `String`s.
- Write predicates involving `char`s.
- Understand arithmetic operations on `char`s.

The primitive datatype `char` represents individual characters. Type `char` is somewhat like integer because:

- Characters have a definite order.
- Characters can be compared for equality and for order.
- We can perform some limited arithmetic with `char`s.
- `char`s can be cast into `int`s and vice versa.

9.1   Literals of Type `char`

A `char` is represented by a character between single quotation marks. Some examples are `'a'`, or `'A'`, `'1'`, and `','`.

Additionally, the type `char` includes a variety of *escape sequences*:

`'\t'`	Tab
`'\n'`	New line
`'\\'`	\
`...`	`...`

Note that `char` uses *single* quotes, not double quotes: `'a'` and `'\t'` are `chars`, but `"a"` and `"\t"` are `Strings`.

Except for escape sequences, single quotes may enclose only a single character: `'ab'` is not legal for Java.

Uppercase and lowercase are different: `'a'` is not the same `char` as `'A'`.

9.2   char **Size in Bits**

The English keyboard uses about 100 characters:

26 lowercase letters

26 uppercase letters

10 digits

1   space

1   tab

32 special characters

Seven bits—allowing for 128 values—are sufficient to represent all English characters. Twenty years ago, most computing involved the English alphabet, and the dominant character code was ASCII (pronounced "as-key"), which used 8 bits/character, allowing for 256 possibilities.

Over the past decade, computing with non-English alphabets has become significant, and a new character code, Unicode, has emerged. Unicode uses 16 bits per character, allowing for 65,536 possibilities. The Unicode Consortium[1] has devised codings for the alphabets of all known natural languages. Some are living languages (e.g., English, Chinese, Arabic, and Russian) and some are extinct (e.g., hieroglyphics and cuneiform).

ASCII is a subset of Unicode. Appendix 3 shows the relationship between printable characters and Unicode/ASCII values.

9.3   String **Methods Involving** chars

In previous chapters we've studied methods applicable to objects of type `String`, but these methods have involved parameters and return types only of type `String`, integer, and `boolean`. Now we can examine `String` methods that involve `chars`.

charAt(int)

This method returns the `char` at a specified position within a `String`. If a `String` has length n, then the positions are numbered 0, 1, . . ., n-1—an index

---

[1]   On the Web at www.unicode.org.

outside this range is illegal and will generate an Exception. The following table shows some examples of the charAt method:

"abc".charAt(0)	'a'
"abc".charAt(1)	'b'
"abc".charAt(2)	'c'
"abc".charAt(3)	*Illegal*
"abc".charAt(6)	*Illegal*
"abc".charAt(-1)	*Illegal*
"".charAt(0)	*Illegal*

Note that the code

```
String s = "hello";
System.out.println(s.charAt(1));
```

prints e.

Test your skill with Exercises 9-1 and 9-2.

indexOf(char)

This method returns the index of the *first* occurrence of the parameter char in the receiving String. If the char does not occur in the String, then indexOf returns -1. Here are a few examples:

"hello".indexOf('e')	1
"hello".indexOf('l')	2
"hello".indexOf('a')	-1
"".indexOf('a')	-1
"".indexOf('b')	-1
"mississippi".indexOf('i')	1
"mississippi".indexOf('s')	2
"mississippi".indexOf('p')	8
"mississippi".indexOf('g')	-1

In computing that last set of results, it helps to write out the chars and their positions:

0	1	2	3	4	5	6	7	8	9	10
m	i	s	s	i	s	s	i	p	p	i

 Test your skill with Exercise 9-3.

lastIndexOf(char)

This method returns the index of the *last* occurrence of the parameter char in the receiving String. If the char does not occur in the String, then indexOf returns -1. Here are a few examples:

```
"hello".lastIndexOf('e')              1
"hello".lastIndexOf('l')              3
"hello".lastIndexOf('a')             -1

"".lastIndexOf('a')                  -1
"".lastIndexOf('b')                  -1

"mississippi".lastIndexOf('i')       10
"mississippi".lastIndexOf('s')        6
"mississippi".lastIndexOf('p')        9
"mississippi".lastIndexOf('g')       -1
```

 Test your skill with Exercise 9-4.

Stylistic Considerations

To determine if the first character of a String is the letter 'a', use the statement

```
if ( s.charAt(0) == 'a' ) ...
```

rather than

```
if ( s.substring(0,1).equals("a") ) ...
```

The first statement is clear and direct. The second statement is bloated and harder to understand.

9.4   Strings and chars

Don't confuse them. Strings are objects, and chars are primitive datatypes. Strings accept messages—length, substring, and so forth—but chars do not. Strings use double quotes, and chars use single quotes.

Converting a char to a String

Suppose we have a char c and we want to make it into a String s. We can't say this:

```
String s = c;
```

because Java doesn't automatically convert chars to Strings. Instead, we'll concatenate c to the front of the empty String:

```
String s = c + "";
```

producing a String of length one.

Concatenating chars and Strings

We can concatenate a char to the front or the rear of a String:

```
's' + "pin" → "spin"
"pin" + 's' → "pins"
```

The result is a String.

Test your skill with Exercises 9-5 and 9-6.

9.5   Comparing chars with Relational Operators

char is a primitive datatype, and we use == to test two chars for equality. Similarly, we use != to test two chars for *in*equality.

Test your skill with Exercise 9-7.

> **Collating sequence** Alphabetical order defined over all characters.

The chars in Java obey a *collating sequence*, which specifies the order of the characters.[2] We can use the relational operators (<=, <, >, and >=) to determine which of two chars comes first in the sequence. For example,

```
'a' < 'b' → true
'b' < 'a' → false
```

 Test your skill with Exercises 9-8 and 9-9.

9.6 Is a char a Digit?

In this section we'll examine several ways of determining whether a given char is or is not a *digit*—one of '0', '1', . . ., '9'.

Prog0901 presents one solution to the problem. Here is the log of a typical run:

```
G:\>java Prog0901
Enter a char: a
digit?          false
Enter a char: 3
digit?          true
Enter a char: .
digit?          false
...
```

Prog0901.java   Is a char a Digit?

```
// Written by Barry Soroka
//
// Read chars & reports if they are digits
//
import java.io.*;
import java.util.Scanner;
//////////////////////////////////////////////////////////////////////////////
class Prog0901
{
//----------------------------------------------------------------------------
```

---

[2] Every language has a collating sequence, but not all languages use the *same* collating sequence. Often, not all of the *applications* on a computer use the same collating sequence!

```
public static void main ( String [] args ) throws Exception
{
    Scanner kb = new Scanner(System.in);

    while ( true )
    {
        System.out.print("Enter a char: ");
        char c = kb.nextLine().charAt(0);
        System.out.println("digit?        " + isDigit(c));
    }
}
//------------------------------------------------------------------------
private static boolean isDigit ( char c )
{
    return c == '0' || c == '1' || c == '2' || c == '3' || c == '4' ||
           c == '5' || c == '6' || c == '7' || c == '8' || c == '9';
}
//------------------------------------------------------------------------
} // end class Prog0901
//////////////////////////////////////////////////////////////////////////
```

Prog0901 uses a `static` helper method—`isDigit(char)`—to do the actual computation:

```
return c == '0' || c == '1' || c == '2' || c == '3' || c == '4' ||
       c == '5' || c == '6' || c == '7' || c == '8' || c == '9';
```

This clearly works, but it requires a lot of typing, and we could easily have omitted a required case if we hadn't been careful.

An alternate version uses *indexOf*:

```
return -1 != "0123456789".indexOf(c);
```

If c is in the `String` "0123456789", then the result of `indexOf` will *not* be -1.

Yet another version of `isDigit` uses *relational operators*:

```
return '0' <= c && c <= '9';
```

This relies on Java's collating sequence putting all the digits together in the ordering of `char`s.

Moral

There is often more than one way to solve a problem. It's useful to look at more than one way to solve a given problem; it increases the repertoire of techniques that we can bring to future problems.

Don't Grab Random Methods from the API!

A student once solved the problem above by using the statement

```
return Character(c).isDigit()
```

It works, but I hadn't ever used class `Character`, and I'd never seen this method. The student used a *canned method* to avoid having to solve the problem. Much of what we'll teach you as you study computer science is already implemented in one class or another of the Java API. Your goal is to solve the problem *on your own*, not to find a method that somebody wrote for you.

Computer scientists are the ones who write the methods in the Java API, and we're training you to write additional methods for Java, for applications, and for languages you'll encounter in future. I'm teaching you the tools you'll need to write new methods. Don't look for shortcuts or you'll end up not learning what you need to know.

Test your skill with Exercises 9-10 through 9-15.

9.7   Arithmetic with chars

Because `chars` are *ordered*, like integers, Java allows us to perform some arithmetic with them. The statements

```
char a1 = 'a' + 1;
System.out.println(a1);
```

print out

```
b
```

and the statement

```
System.out.println('c' - 'a');
```

prints

     2

which is the difference between the `char`s `'c'` and `'a'`.

   `char` arithmetic can be helpful, but use it cautiously. Test a small sample program before writing a large method that depends on it. It doesn't always work the way you expect.

9.8 Converting Between `char`s and `int`s

We can cast `char`s into `int`s and vice versa. Every `char` has a representation as an `int`, and many `int`s represent `char`s. We cast an `int` `n` to a `char` with `(char)n`, and we cast a `char c` to an `int` with `(int)c`.

 Test your skill with Exercises 9-16 and 9-17.

Chapter Summary

- `char` literals are enclosed within single-quotes (e.g., `'a'` or `'7'`).
- Escape sequences allow for special `char`s (e.g., `'\n'` for new line).
- Java characters are encoded in Unicode, with each `char` occupying 16 bits. This allows for `char`s in all known alphabets.
- The `String` method `charAt(int)` returns the `char` at a specified position of a `String`.
- The `String` method `indexOf(char)` returns the leftmost position of the given `char` within the receiving `String`.
- The `String` method `lastIndexOf(char)` returns the rightmost position of the given `char` within the receiving `String`.
- `String`s are enclosed in double quotes; `char`s are enclosed in single quotes.
- `"a"` is a `String`. `'a'` is a `char`. Don't confuse them.
- `char`s are ordered according to Java's collating sequence.
- `char`s can be compared with the relational operators.
- There are several ways to determine if a given `char` is a digit.
- The Java API contains methods for many common problems. Our goal is to code these algorithms without reference to the API.
- Java permits some arithmetic using `char`s. For example, `'a'+1` evaluates to `'b'`.
- We can cast `char`s to `int`s and vice versa.

Terminology Introduced in This Chapter

collating sequence

Exercises

Exercise 9-1. Write a Java program that reads a String, and then repeatedly prompts for an index and prints out the char at that index.

Exercise 9-2. Write a Java program that reads a String and prints out its first and last characters.

Exercise 9-3. Write a Java program that reads a String, and then repeatedly reads a char and prints the index of its first occurrence in the String. To read a char, use the following lines:

```
System.out.print("Enter a char: ");
char c = kb.nextLine().charAt(0);
```

Exercise 9-4. Write a Java program that reads a String, and then repeatedly reads a char and prints the index of its *last* occurrence in the String.

Exercise 9-5. Write a Java program that starts with an empty String and repeatedly reads a char, concatenates it to the *front* of the String, and prints the String.

Exercise 9-6. Write a Java program that starts with an empty String and repeatedly reads a char, concatenates it to the *rear* of the String, and prints the String.

Exercise 9-7. Write a Java program that repeatedly reads two chars and reports whether they are equal.

Exercise 9-8. Write a Java program that repeatedly reads two chars and reports the relation between them. Here is typical hardcopy:

```
Enter a char: f
Enter a char: x
'f' >  'x' ? false
'f' == 'x' ? false
'f' <  'x' ? true
```

Exercise 9-9. Determine the order of at least the following chars:

```
'0','1','2','a','b','c','A','B','C',' ','$'
```

Answer the following questions for Java:

(a) Are the digits next to each other?
(b) Are all the lowercase letters adjacent?
(c) Are all the uppercase letters adjacent?
(d) Are uppercase letters *above* the lowercase letters?

Exercise 9-10. Write a helper method

```
private static boolean inRange ( char c, char lo, char hi )
```

that returns `true` if and only if the `char c` is in the range from `lo` to `hi`.
Show the code for the `isDigit` method when we use `inRange`.

Exercise 9-11. Write the method

```
public static boolean isUpperCase ( char )
```

that returns `true` if and only if the given `char` is uppercase. Write this method in
several different ways. Write drivers and test your code.

Exercise 9-12. Write the method

```
public static boolean isVowel ( char )
```

that returns `true` if and only if the given `char` is a vowel. In English, the vowels are in
the set {a, e, i, o, u}. Both upper- and lowercases count. Write this method in several
different ways. Write drivers and test your code.

Exercise 9-13. Using `isVowel`, write the method

```
public static boolean beginsWithVowel ( String )
```

that returns `true` if and only if the given `String` begins with a vowel. Write a driver
and test your code.

Exercise 9-14. Write a method

```
public static boolean isLetter ( char )
```

that returns `true` if and only if the given `char` is a letter—A through Z, either upper-
or lowercase. Write this several ways. Write drivers and test your code.

Exercise 9-15.   Write a method

```
public static boolean isConsonant ( char )
```

that returns `true` if and only if the given char is a *consonant*, either upper- or lowercase. Use some of the methods you wrote for previous exercises. Write a driver and test your code.

Exercise 9-16.   Write an application that repeatedly reads a `char`, casts it to an `int`, and prints the `int`. What can you learn about Java's collating sequence?

Exercise 9-17.   Write an application that repeatedly reads an `int`, casts it to a `char`, and prints the `char`. What can you learn about Java's collating sequence?

Floating-Point Datatypes

Floating-point numbers correspond to numbers with *decimal points* (such as 4.73) and numbers in *scientific notation* (such as 6.023×10^{23}). This datatype can represent many more numbers than any integer type. Prior languages, such as FORTRAN, called these *real* numbers rather than *floating-point* numbers.

We can represent any floating-point number as the product of a *fraction* and a *multiplier*. Here's an example of numbers that have fraction 3.7 and various multipliers:

Number	Fraction	Multiplier
...	3.7	...
0.0037	3.7	10^{-3}
0.037	3.7	10^{-2}
0.37	3.7	10^{-1}
3.7	3.7	10^0
37.0	3.7	10^1
370.0	3.7	10^2
3700.0	3.7	10^3
...	3.7	...

Floating-points can hold a wider range of numbers than integers:

6.022×10^{23}   Number of molecules in a mole (Avogadro's number)

9.1×10^{-31}   Mass of an electron in kilograms

Sometimes the power of ten is omitted:

3.1415926535   An approximation to π

0.0825   Current sales tax rate for Los Angeles County

10.1   Java's Floating-Point Datatypes

Java provides two floating-point datatypes—`float` and `double`—which are described in the following table:

Type	Bits	From	To
`float`	32	-3.4×10^{38}	3.4×10^{38}
`double`	64	-1.8×10^{308}	1.8×10^{308}

`double`s have greater precision in the fraction. For most purposes, `double`s are preferred, and Java interprets floating-point literals (e.g., `2.71828`) as `double`s.

> For floating-point numbers, this text will use `double`s exclusively.

Test your skill with Exercises 10-1 and 10-2.

10.2   Floating-Point Literals

In general, Java assumes that floating-point literals are `double`s. The following statements are processed without complaint

```
double x;
x = 7.5;
x = 6.023e23;
x = 9.1e-31;
```

The latter two—`6.023e23` and `9.1e-31`—are examples of entering scientific notation to Java. Such numbers can also be negative: `-1.602e-19` represents the charge of an electron, in Coulombs, which we write in physics as -1.602×10^{-19}.

When Java sees the statements

```
float f;
f = 7.5;
```

we get an error: *possible loss of precision*. This is because Java sees `7.5` as a `double`, occupying 64 bits, and we're asking to store it in the `float` f, which only has 32 bits; therefore Java balks, citing the possible loss of precision in storing a 64-bit value in a 32-bit variable. We get the same error for the statement

```
f = 6.023e23;
```

In order to make Java see a floating-point literal as a *float*, we add the suffix `f`:

```
7.5f
6.023e23f
```

As discussed in the previous section, this text will use only `double`s.

Test your skill with Exercise 10-3.

10.3 Read a `double` and Print Its Square

`Prog1001` is a program that reads a `double` from the keyboard and prints its square. We begin by creating a `Scanner`, and we use the `nextDouble()` method to acquire a floating-point number from the user. `nextDouble` reads a `double` in the same way that `nextInt` reads an `int`. Here is a typical dialog:

```
C:\>java Prog1001
Enter a double: 2.5
Its square of 2.5 is 6.25.
```

We can also enter numbers in scientific notation:

```
C:\>java Prog1001
Enter a double: 1.5e1
Its square of 15.0 is 225.0.
```

`nextDouble` balks if we try to give it a non-`double`:

```
C:\>java Prog1001
Enter a double: hello
Exception in thread "main" java.util.InputMismatchException
        at java.util.Scanner.throwFor(Unknown Source)
        at java.util.Scanner.next(Unknown Source)
        at java.util.Scanner.nextDouble(Unknown Source)
        at Prog1001.main(Prog1001.java:16)
```

Suppose we enter a number that is too large to fit in a `double`:

```
C:\>java Prog1001
Enter a double: 1e400
The square of Infinity is Infinity.
```

If a floating-point number is too large to fit in a `double`, then Java has a way of calling it `Infinity`. You'll learn more about the peculiarities of floating-point arithmetic when you take a course on numerical methods. We also have

```
C:\>java Prog1001
Enter a double: 1e200
The square of 1.0E200 is Infinity.
```

where `1e200` can fit in a `double`, but its square cannot.

Prog1001.java   Read a double and Print Its Square

```java
// Written by Barry Soroka
//
// Read a double and print its square.
//
import java.io.*;
import java.util.Scanner;
/////////////////////////////////////////////////////////////////////////
class Prog1001
{
//---------------------------------------------------------------------------

    public static void main ( String [] args ) throws Exception
    {
        Scanner kb = new Scanner(System.in);

        System.out.print("Enter a double: ");
        double x = kb.nextDouble();
        System.out.println("The square of " + x +
                      " is " + x*x + '.');
    }
//---------------------------------------------------------------------------

} // end class Prog1001
/////////////////////////////////////////////////////////////////////////
```

10.4   Pretty-Printing Floating-Point Numbers

Consider the following dialog:

```
C:\>java Prog1001
Enter a double: 1.3
The square of 1.3 is 1.6900000000000002
```

What's happening here? Integers are represented exactly inside the computer, but floating-point numbers are stored as approximations. When the internal representation of a double is converted to a String, a slight error may be introduced; for example, 1.0 may print as 1.000000001 or 0.999999999. That's why the square of 1.3 appears as something other than exactly 1.69. Similarly, the fraction two-thirds has a decimal notation 0.666666..., and this cannot be printed in a finite representation without incurring some round-off error.

Round-off error   Error due to unavoidable imprecise representation of floating-point numbers.

In Chapter 7 we saw how `printf` allowed us to control the printing of integer values. Similarly, `printf` allows us to control how floating-point values are printed. Recall that the control string %4d put an integer right-aligned in a field of width 4. The control string %6.2f puts a floating-point value in a field of width 6, with 2 digits to the right of the decimal point. We represent this as $w.p$ where w is the width of the field and p is the precision, namely, the number of digits to the right of the decimal point.

Prog1002 gives an example of printing d=1.3*1.3 in eight different ways. The following table explains how d is printed for each of the different control strings:

Control String	Prints As	Comment
No format	1.6900000000000002	As before. No rounding.
6.0f	2	No decimal places. Rounds to the nearest unit. Five spaces before the 2.
6.1f	1.7	Rounds to the nearest 0.1. Three spaces before the 1.
6.2f	1.69	Rounds to the nearest 0.01. Two spaces before the 1
6.3f	1.690	Displays the 0.001 digit. One space before the 1.
6.4f	1.6900	Displays the 0.0001 digit. Entirely fills the allowed width of 6.
6.5f	1.69000	Too large to fit in a field of width 6, it pushes to width 7.
6.6f	1.690000	Too large to fit in a field of width 6, it pushes to width 8.

As we observed with the %d control string for integers, numbers expand beyond the field width if they are too large to fit.

Prog1002.java Using **printf** to "Pretty-Print" **doubles**

```
// Written by Barry Soroka
//
// Tests printf for doubles using "%6.2f%n".
//
import java.io.*;
//////////////////////////////////////////////////////////////////////////////
class Prog1002
{
//-------------------------------------------------------------------------
```

```
public static void main ( String [] args ) throws Exception
{
    double x = 1.3 * 1.3;
    System.out.println(x + " without a format");
    System.out.printf("%f in format %%f\n",x);
    System.out.printf("%6.0f in format %%6.0f\n",x);
    System.out.printf("%6.1f in format %%6.1f\n",x);
    System.out.printf("%6.2f in format %%6.2f\n",x);
    System.out.printf("%6.3f in format %%6.3f\n",x);
    System.out.printf("%6.4f in format %%6.4f\n",x);
    System.out.printf("%6.5f in format %%6.5f\n",x);
    System.out.printf("%6.6f in format %%6.6f\n",x);
}
//-------------------------------------------------------------------------
} // end class Prog1002
/////////////////////////////////////////////////////////////////////////////
```

The `String` class contains a `format` method that can format floating-point numbers according to the same control strings we saw for `printf`:

$$\text{String.format("\%6.3f",1.3*1.3)} \rightarrow \text{" 1.690"}$$

Feel free to use the `%w.pf` control string with `printf` and `format` to pretty-print floating-point values as required.

10.5   Arithmetic with Floating-Point Numbers

Java provides four arithmetic operators we can use with floating-point arguments:

$$+ \quad - \quad * \quad /$$

They have the obvious meaning, and when we add, subtract, multiply, or divide two floating-point numbers, the result also will be floating-point.

The remainder operator—%—cannot be applied to floating-point numbers.

Test your skill with Exercises 10-4 and 10-5.

10.6 Mixed-Mode Arithmetic

Mixed-mode arithmetic occurs when an arithmetic operator has an *integer* on one side and a *floating-point number* on the other. The result of such an operation is floating-point. For example, both

```
2 + 3.5
```

and

```
2.0 + 3
```

evaluate to `doubles`.

10.7 Precedence and Parentheses

As with integer arithmetic, the operators * and / have precedence over + and -. If two consecutive operators have the same precedence, then the one on the left is executed first. For example,

```
2.0 + 3.0 * 4.0
2.0 + 12.0
14.0

2.0 / 3.0 + 4.0
0.6666... + 4.0
4.6666...

2.0 / 3.0 * 5.0
0.6666... * 5.0
3.3333...
```

An expression within parentheses is evaluated *before* the result of the expression is used. For example:

```
(2.0 + 3.0) * 4.0
5.0 * 4.0
20.0
```

Mixed-mode arithmetic means that some of the intermediate results can be computed using integer arithmetic. *The presence of a floating-point number in an expression does not mean that every operation is performed as floating-point.*[1] Here are some examples:

```
2 / 4 * 5.0
0 * 5.0
0.0

2.0 / 3 * 5
0.6666... * 5
3.1666...
```

 | **Test your skill with Exercise 10-6.**

10.8   Shortcuts

The combined operators +=, -=, *=, and /= have the same meanings we saw for integers. For example,

```
d += 3.3;
```

is interpreted as

```
d = d + 3.3;
```

Mixed mode is allowed. If d is a `double`, then

```
d += 5;
```

means

```
d = d + 5;
```

10.9   Methods from Class Math

The `Math` class provides a variety of class methods (`static`) that apply to floating-point numbers.[2] I will use x to indicate a parameter that can be either a `double` or a `float`—all of these methods are overloaded.

---

[1]   There are languages for which the presence of even a single floating-point value in an expression "poisons" the expression so that *every* operation is done in floating-point. The designers of Java decided not to take that path.

[2]   Note that class `Math` is defined in package `java.lang`, *not* in package `java.math`.

- `Math.abs(x)` returns the absolute value of the parameter.
- `Math.sqrt(x)` returns the square root of the parameter.
- `Math.sin(x)` returns the sine of the parameter (interpreted as *radians*, not *degrees*).
- `Math.pow(x,y)` computes x^y.

Three methods can be used to convert a floating-point value to an integer:

- `Math.ceil(x)`—the *ceiling* function—returns the `double` value of the smallest integer that is not below x. For example,

      Math.ceil(4.7) → 5.0
      Math.ceil(4.0) → 4.0
      Math.ceil(-4.7) → -4.0

- `Math.floor(x)`—the *floor* function—returns the `double` value of the largest integer that is not above x. For example,

      Math.floor(4.7) → 4.0
      Math.floor(4.0) → 4.0
      Math.floor(-4.7) → -5.0

- Note that

      Math.floor(x) ≤ x ≤ Math.ceil(x).

- `Math.round(x)` returns the `long` that is closest to x. For example,

      Math.round(4.7) → 5
      Math.round(-4.7) → -5

- If x is midway between two integers, the larger is returned:

      Math.round(2.5) → 3
      Math.round(-2.5) → −2

> **Test your skill with Exercises 10-7 through 10-11.**

10.10 Floating-Point Constants

The keyword `final` can be used to make a variable *constant*, so that the variable can't be changed after its initial declaration and assignment:

    final double G = 9.8; // m/sec/sec

Note that the names of constants must be all uppercase letters.

The class `Math` contains two predefined constants: `Math.PI` and `Math.E`.

> **Test your skill with Exercises 10-12 and 10-13.**

10.11 Converting Between Integers and Floating-Point

Java has no problems converting an integer to floating-point:

```
int i = 3;
double x = i;    // accepted by Java
```

Another approach is to multiply the `int` by `1.0`:

```
double x = 1.0 * i;
```

The mixed-mode arithmetic produces a floating-point number from the integer.

You may recall class `Fraction`, which we introduced in Chapter 7, where each `Fraction` has two instance variables:

```
private int num;    // numerator
private int den;    // denominator
```

The following table shows a few `Fraction`s and the corresponding decimal representation:

num	den	floatValue
3	4	0.75
0	3	0.0
4	1	4.0
2	3	0.6666...

Here is the code for a method `floatValue` that returns the decimal value of the Fraction:

```
public double floatValue() { return 1.0 * num / den; }
```

Notice how multiplication by `1.0` allows us to get a floating-point quotient.

Floating-Point → Integer

Going this way is not automatic. The following sets of statements are refused by the compiler:

```
double x = 3.0;
int i = x;      //ILLEGAL!

double x = 2.5;
int i = x;      //ILLEGAL!
```

The error message is *possible loss of precision*. Java won't permit us to inadvertently lose precision when we do the conversions. Java even forbids the conversion of the int-like 3.0.

If we want to convert a double to an int, then we can use the statement

```
int i = (int) x;
```

The phrase "(int)" is called a *cast*, and indicates that we want to *cast* the double x into an int. In casting, *we* assume responsibility for possible loss of precision, and Java does the conversion as we request.

Casting a floating-point number to an int involves dropping the fractional part of the number, effectively rounding toward 0:

(int)3.4 $\rightarrow$ 3

(int)(-3.4) $\rightarrow$ -3

As noted earlier, Math.round, Math.floor, and Math.ceil are other ways of converting floating point numbers.

10.12 Testing for Equality of Floating-Point Numbers

Beware of using == with floating-point numbers! It tests for exact equality of the bit patterns, but this is not always what we want. Here are some examples:

- 2.78e-31 can be considered 0.0 in some, but not all, applications. For a bank, it's zero. For physics or chemistry, it may be quite significant and quite nonzero.
- 2.78 can be considered the same as 2.780000000001 for some, but not all, applications.
- In some hardware–software systems, 17.0*(1.0/17.0) is not equal to 1.0 because of round-off errors.

Approximate Equality

For many problems, we want to know if two numbers are *approximately* equal, not necessarily *exactly* equal. We select a tolerance—very small—and we say that two numbers are equal if they're within that tolerance. Here's the code that considers two `doubles` to be equal if they're within the tolerance 10^{-10}:

```
public static boolean almostEqual ( double x, double y )
{
    return Math.abs(x-y) <= 1e-10;
}
```

That's useful, but now let's see what price we pay for relaxing the definition of equality.

Transitivity

Here's an example of the property known as *transitivity*:

If

$$x = y$$

and

$$y = z$$

then

$$x = z$$

In math courses, we're taught that transitivity of equality is an important property possessed by certain sets, including integers and real numbers.

Suppose we allow for *approximate* equality, where we consider two variables, x and y, to be equal if they are sufficiently close, say, within a tolerance ϵ. We may lose transitivity:

- We can have $x = y$ because $x = y + \epsilon$ and
- we can have $y = z$ because $y = z + \epsilon$,
- but $x \neq z$ because $x = z + 2\epsilon$, which exceeds the tolerance for approximate equality!

We get into trouble if two mismatches align.

Carpenters observe the same phenomenon. If board1 is $\frac{1}{16}''$ longer than board2, and board2 is $\frac{1}{16}''$ longer than board3, then board1 is $\frac{1}{8}''$ longer than board3. An error of $\frac{1}{16}''$ may be negligible, but when *two* of these negligible errors line up we get the nonnegligible error of $\frac{1}{8}''$.

10.13 Class Circle

In this section, we'll define a class Circle that uses the capabilities of floating-point numbers. Prog1003.java contains the definition of two classes: the class Circle, and a driver class Prog1003. Note the order of the two classes:

```
class Prog1003
class Circle
```

We put the driver first, then follow it by the classes being tested.

Prog1003.java   **Class Circle**

```java
// Written by Barry Soroka
//
// class Circle
//
import java.io.*;
import java.util.Scanner;
////////////////////////////////////////////////////////////////////////////
class Prog1003
{
//--------------------------------------------------------------------------
   public static void main ( String [] args ) throws Exception
   {
      Scanner kb = new Scanner(System.in);

      System.out.print("\nEnter the radius for a circle: ");
      Circle c = new Circle(kb.nextDouble());

      System.out.printf("radius is %6.4f\n",c.getRadius());
      System.out.printf("area is   %6.4f\n",c.getArea());

      System.out.print("\nEnter a new radius for the circle: ");
      c.setRadius(kb.nextDouble());
```

```
        System.out.printf("radius is %6.4f\n",c.getRadius());
        System.out.printf("area is   %6.4f\n",c.getArea());
    }
//-----------------------------------------------------------------------
} // end class Prog1003
///////////////////////////////////////////////////////////////////////
class Circle
{
    private double radius;
//-----------------------------------------------------------------------
    public Circle ( double radius )
    {
        this.radius = radius;
    }
//-----------------------------------------------------------------------
    public double getRadius() { return radius; }
//-----------------------------------------------------------------------
    public void setRadius ( double newRadius ) { this.radius = newRadius; }
//-----------------------------------------------------------------------
    public double getArea() { return Math.PI * radius * radius; }
//-----------------------------------------------------------------------
} // end Circle
///////////////////////////////////////////////////////////////////////
```

Here is a typical run:

```
C:\>java Prog1003

Enter the radius for a circle: 1
radius is 1.0
area is   3.1416

Enter a new radius for the circle: 1.5
radius is 1.5
area is   7.0686
```

First we'll discuss the code for class Circle, and then we'll discuss the driver and the output. Note that we'll be working with both the radius and area of the Circles we define.

Class `Circle` defines a single instance variable, `radius`, which is a `double`. The current implementation does not define a separate instance variable for `area`; we'll examine that alternative approach in the next section of this chapter. The constructor is obvious:

```
public Circle ( double radius )
{
    this.radius = radius;
}
```

There are two getters. The method `getRadius` is obvious:

```
public double getRadius() { return radius; }
```

`getArea` computes the area by applying the formula πr^2:

```
public double getArea()
{
    return Math.PI * radius * radius;
}
```

Note the use of the constant `PI` from class `Math`; this is better than typing in a literal like `3.14159`. Note that we don't compute `area` until it's requested by a call to `getArea`.

We also provide a *setter*, which lets us change the `radius` of an existing `Circle`:

```
public void setRadius ( double newRadius )
{
    this.radius = newRadius;
}
```

Nothing new there.

Now let's examine the output of our test run.

```
Enter the radius for a circle: 1
radius is 1.0000
area is   3.1416
```

Note how we use `printf` to control the number of decimal places printed.

10.14   Unnecessary Instance Variables

`Prog1004` is equivalent to `Prog1003`, except that class `Circle` defines an instance variable for `area`. The two programs have identical input-output behavior, but creating a separate variable for `area` incurs certain costs: (1) the `area` variable must be updated every time the `radius` changes, and (2) the programmer must include code for this updating *every time a new method that changes the `radius` is introduced*. Thus, `radius` and `area` are *coupled*, and any change in `radius` affects `area` as well. This puts a considerable burden on the programmer, and errors are easy to make: We can add a method that changes `radius`, but forget to make the required change in `area`. Some languages (not Java) allow the programmer to declare constraints between variables. With constraints, the compiler can detect when one variable is changed but its partner is not.

Prog1004.java   **Maintaining an Instance Variable for area**

```java
// Written by Barry Soroka
//
// class Circle -- maintaining an instance variable for area
//
import java.io.*;
import java.util.Scanner;
/////////////////////////////////////////////////////////////////////////////
class Prog1004
{
//--------------------------------------------------------------------------
    public static void main ( String [] args ) throws Exception
    {
        Scanner kb = new Scanner(System.in);

        System.out.print("\nEnter the radius for a circle: ");
        Circle c = new Circle(kb.nextDouble());

        System.out.printf("radius is %6.4f\n",c.getRadius());
        System.out.printf("area is   %6.4f\n",c.getArea());

        System.out.print("\nEnter a new radius for the circle: ");
        c.setRadius(kb.nextDouble());

        System.out.printf("radius is %6.4f\n",c.getRadius());
        System.out.printf("area is   %6.4f\n",c.getArea());
    }
```

```
//---------------------------------------------------------------------------
} // end class Prog1004
/////////////////////////////////////////////////////////////////////////////
class Circle
{
   private double radius;
   private double area;
//---------------------------------------------------------------------------
   public Circle ( double radius )
   {
      this.radius = radius;
      this.area = Math.PI * radius * radius;
   }
//---------------------------------------------------------------------------
   public double getRadius() { return radius; }
//---------------------------------------------------------------------------
   public void setRadius ( double newRadius )
   {
      this.radius = newRadius;
      this.area = Math.PI * newRadius * newRadius;
   }
//---------------------------------------------------------------------------
   public double getArea() { return area; }
//---------------------------------------------------------------------------
} // end Circle
/////////////////////////////////////////////////////////////////////////////
```

Economics

Adding an instance variable for `area` adds an extra slot to every instance of `Circle`. If a program contains many `Circle` objects, then the penalty can be substantial.

Additionally, suppose that `setRadius` is called a thousand times before `area` is ever requested. Then `Prog1004` computes

```
Math.PI * radius * radius
```

999 times more than is necessary.

What if we wanted to add a method `getCircumference`? Would it pay to create and synchronize an instance variable `circumference`?

10.15   grow, shrink, report

Let's revert to the definition of class `Circle` in `Prog1003`. The only instance variable is `radius`, and we compute `area` with a method when it's required.

`Prog1005` adds methods `grow` and `shrink` to class `Circle`. The `grow` method increments `radius` by 10%, and the `shrink` method decreases it by 10%. If we had maintained a separate instance variable for `area`, we would have had to include code for updating it in both `grow` and `shrink`. We avoid this duplication of code by computing `area` only when required.

Prog1005.java   grow() and shrink()

```java
// Written by Barry Soroka
//
// class Circle -- add grow() and shrink()
//
import java.io.*;
import java.util.Scanner;
///////////////////////////////////////////////////////////////////////////////
class Prog1005
{
//--------------------------------------------------------------------------
   public static void main ( String [] args ) throws Exception
   {
      Scanner kb = new Scanner(System.in);

      System.out.print("\nEnter the radius for a circle: ");
      Circle c = new Circle(kb.nextDouble());

      System.out.println("\nInitially:");
      System.out.printf("radius is %6.4f\n",c.getRadius());
      System.out.printf("area is   %6.4f\n",c.getArea());

      c.grow();
      System.out.println("\nAfter grow:");
      System.out.printf("radius is %6.4f\n",c.getRadius());
      System.out.printf("area is   %6.4f\n",c.getArea());

      c.shrink();
      System.out.println("\nAfter shrink:");
      System.out.printf("radius is %6.4f\n",c.getRadius());
      System.out.printf("area is   %6.4f\n",c.getArea());

      c.shrink();
      System.out.println("\nAfter shrink:");
```

```
        System.out.printf("radius is %6.4f\n",c.getRadius());
        System.out.printf("area is   %6.4f\n",c.getArea());
    }
//-----------------------------------------------------------------
} // end class Prog1005
/////////////////////////////////////////////////////////////////////////
class Circle
{
    private double radius;
//-----------------------------------------------------------------
    public Circle ( double radius ) { this.radius = radius; }
//-----------------------------------------------------------------
    public double getRadius() { return radius; }
//-----------------------------------------------------------------
    public void setRadius ( double newRadius ) { radius = newRadius; }
//-----------------------------------------------------------------
    public double getArea() { return Math.PI * radius * radius; }
//-----------------------------------------------------------------
    public void grow() { radius *= 1.1; }
//-----------------------------------------------------------------
    public void shrink() { radius *= 0.9; }
//-----------------------------------------------------------------
}
/////////////////////////////////////////////////////////////////////////
```

However, Prog1005 does contain some unnecessary redundancy. The lines

```
        System.out.printf("radius is %6.4f\n",c.getRadius());
        System.out.printf("area is   %6.4f\n",c.getArea());
```

occur *four times* in the main method. Suppose we wanted to translate the i/o into French. We'd need to change the code in *four* places. Or, suppose we wanted to print the *circumference* as well as the radius and area; again, we'd need to change the code in *four* places.

Prog1006 shows a solution to the problem of code repetition. We define a method report, which does our reporting, and the only duplication of code is the use of the statement

```
        report(c)
```

in four places. Here's the code for report:

```
        private static void report ( Circle c )
        {
                System.out.printf("radius is %6.4f\n",c.getRadius());
                System.out.printf("area is   %6.4f\n",c.getArea());
        }
```

If we need to change the language to French, or if we want to add a line about circumference, then our changes are in a single spot in the method report.

Prog1006.java   **Helper Method report**

```
// Written by Barry Soroka
//
// class Circle --
// add static method report() in order to coalesce common print statements
//
import java.io.*;
import java.util.Scanner;
//////////////////////////////////////////////////////////////////////////////
class Prog1006
{
//-----------------------------------------------------------------------------
   public static void main ( String [] args ) throws Exception
   {
      Scanner kb = new Scanner(System.in);

      System.out.print("\nEnter the radius for a circle: ");
      Circle c = new Circle(kb.nextDouble());

      System.out.println("\nInitially:");
      report(c);

      c.grow();
      System.out.println("\nAfter grow:");
      report(c);

      c.shrink();
      System.out.println("\nAfter shrink:");
      report(c);

      c.shrink();
      System.out.println("\nAfter shrink:");
      report(c);
   }
```

```
//-----------------------------------------------------------------------
   private static void report ( Circle c )
   {
      System.out.printf("radius is %6.4f\n",c.getRadius());
      System.out.printf("area is   %6.4f\n",c.getArea());
   }
//-----------------------------------------------------------------------
} // end class Prog1006
/////////////////////////////////////////////////////////////////////////
class Circle
{
   private double radius;
//-----------------------------------------------------------------------
   public Circle ( double radius ) { this.radius = radius; }
//-----------------------------------------------------------------------
   public double getRadius() { return radius; }
//-----------------------------------------------------------------------
   public void setRadius ( double newRadius ) { radius = newRadius; }
//-----------------------------------------------------------------------
   public double getArea() { return Math.PI * radius * radius; }
//-----------------------------------------------------------------------
   public void grow() { radius *= 1.1; }
//-----------------------------------------------------------------------
   public void shrink() { radius *= 0.9; }
//-----------------------------------------------------------------------
}
/////////////////////////////////////////////////////////////////////////
```

Note the `static` modifier in the header of `report`. This is required so that `report` can be called even though we never create an instance of class `Prog1006`.

 Test your skill with Exercises 10-14 and 10-15.

10.16 Comparing `Circles`

In Section 10.12 we discussed using the `==` operator to test for equality of floating-point numbers. Most applications do not require exact equality; it's acceptable to call two numbers equal if they are within a small `TOLERANCE`.

Prog1007.java illustrates the use of approximate equality for numbers and Circles. The static final variable TOLERANCE determines how close two numbers must be in order to be considered equal:

```
private static final double TOLERANCE = 1e-10;
```

Prog1007.java   almostEqual

```java
// Written by Barry Soroka
//
// Prog1007 -- class Circle -- add equals with TOLERANCE
//
import java.io.*;
////////////////////////////////////////////////////////////////////////////////
class Circle
{
    private double radius;
    private static final double TOLERANCE = 1e-10;
//-----------------------------------------------------------------------------
    public Circle ( double radius ) { this.radius = radius; }
//-----------------------------------------------------------------------------
    public double getRadius() { return radius; }
//-----------------------------------------------------------------------------
    public void setRadius ( double newRadius ) { radius = newRadius; }
//-----------------------------------------------------------------------------
    public double getArea() { return Math.PI * radius * radius; }
//-----------------------------------------------------------------------------
    public void grow() { radius *= 1.1; }
//-----------------------------------------------------------------------------
    public void shrink() { radius *= 0.9; }
//-----------------------------------------------------------------------------
    private static boolean almostEqual ( double x, double y )
    {
        return Math.abs(x-y) < TOLERANCE;
    }
//-----------------------------------------------------------------------------
    public boolean equals ( Circle that )
    {
        return almostEqual(this.radius,that.radius);
    }
//-----------------------------------------------------------------------------
}
////////////////////////////////////////////////////////////////////////////////
```

The method

```
private static boolean almostEqual ( double x, double y )
```

tests two `double`s for approximate equality.

The method

```
public boolean equals ( Circle that )
```

uses the previous `equals` method to determine equality of instances of `Circle`.

> **Test your skill with Exercises 10-16 through 10-18.**

10.17 A `static` **Variable**—`taxRate`

In this section, we'll develop a program that models buying things from a store. Here are the items and their unit prices:

Item	Unit Price
tissue	1.22
soda	6.00
bread	2.59
applesauce	2.79

When we define class `Item`, we'll have instance variables `name` and `unitPrice`.

Now, let's assume that the sales tax rate is 10%. Then the purchase of three units of `tissue` might result in the following output:

```
Purchased 3 unit(s) of *tissue* at unit price 1.22
    net   3.66
    tax   0.37
  total   4.03
```

`Item`s have their individual `name`s and `unitPrice`s, but a single `taxRate` is common to *all* `Item`s. This means that `taxRate` should be a `static` variable in class `Item`. There will be a single class variable for `taxRate`:

- Every sale will reference that slot to find the current `taxRate`.
- A change in the `taxRate` will require a change in a *single* class variable.

`Prog1008.java` defines class `Item` and presents a driver that tests it. Let's examine the code. As expected, we find the variables:

```
                  private String name;
                  private double unitPrice;
                  private static double taxRate = 0.0;
```

We have set the initial taxRate to 0.0.

Now comes the method that allows us to change the taxRate:

```
            public static void setTaxRate ( double newTaxRate )
            {
                taxRate = newTaxRate;
            }
```

The method is static because it can be called without reference to any individual Item.

Prog1008.java   static taxRate

```
// Written by Barry Soroka
//
// class Item -- a single static taxRate applies to all Items
//
import java.io.*;
///////////////////////////////////////////////////////////////////////////////
class Prog1008
{
//-------------------------------------------------------------------------------
    public static void main (String [] args ) throws Exception
    {
        Item i1 = new Item("tissue",1.22);
        Item i2 = new Item("soda",6.00);
        Item i3 = new Item("bread",2.59);
        Item i4 = new Item("applesauce",2.79);

        i1.purchase(3);
        i4.purchase(1);

        System.out.println("\n*** Changing tax rate to 8.25%");
        Item.setTaxRate(0.0825);

        i1.purchase(3);
        i2.purchase(7);

        System.out.println("\n*** Changing tax rate to 10%");
        Item.setTaxRate(0.10);
```

```
        i2.purchase(7);
        i3.purchase(2);
    }
//------------------------------------------------------------------------------
} // end class Prog1008
////////////////////////////////////////////////////////////////////////////////
class Item
{
    private String name;
    private double unitPrice;
    private static double taxRate = 0.0;
//------------------------------------------------------------------------------
    public static void setTaxRate ( double newTaxRate )
    {
        taxRate = newTaxRate;
    }
//------------------------------------------------------------------------------
    public Item ( String name, double unitPrice )
    {
        this.name = name;
        this.unitPrice = unitPrice;
    }
//------------------------------------------------------------------------------
    public void purchase ( int quantity )
    {
        System.out.println("\nPurchased " +
                           quantity +
                           " unit(s) of *" +
                           name +
                           "* at unit price " +
                           unitPrice);
        double net = quantity * unitPrice;
        double tax = net * taxRate;
        System.out.printf("  net %6.2f\n",net);
        System.out.printf("  tax %6.2f\n",tax);
        System.out.printf("total %6.2f\n",net+tax);
    }
//------------------------------------------------------------------------------
} // end class Item
////////////////////////////////////////////////////////////////////////////////
```

The purchase method takes a quantity, computes the net, tax, and gross, and prints the appropriate output. We have used printf to achieve nicely formatted output.

Prog1008 is the driver. It starts by creating four Items:

```
Item i1 = new Item("tissue",1.22);
Item i2 = new Item("soda",6.00);
Item i3 = new Item("bread",2.59);
Item i4 = new Item("applesauce",2.79);
```

HOLD YOUR HORSES

In Chapter 14, we'll learn how to create an *array* of Items, so that we don't have to invent names like i1, i2, i3, and i4.

A typical purchase is triggered by a statement like this:

```
i1.purchase(3);
```

and we change the taxRate like this:

```
Item.setTaxRate(0.0825);
```

 Test your skill with Exercises 10-19 and 10-20.

10.18 Converting Strings to doubles

In Chapter 7, we learned how to convert a String to an int using Integer.parseInt(String), and we saw that some Strings cannot be successfully converted to ints:

```
"5a"
"+5"
" 5"
"5 "
```

In a similar fashion, we can convert a String to a double using Double.parseDouble(String). Using Prog1001, we can test a range of Strings for their suitability as doubles. Here are some Strings that *can* be converted successfully:

```
"4.5"
"4"
```

```
"-11.3"
"+11.3"
"2e-10"
"2.3e17"
"2.3e+17"
```

and here are some `String`s that *cannot* be converted into `double`s:

```
"ab"
"3..4"
"2e"
```

When `parseDouble` is called for such `String`s, it throws a `NumberFormatException`.

Test your skill with Exercise 10-21.

Java also provides `Float.parseFloat(String)`.

Before `parseDouble`

An earlier version of Java didn't have `Double.parseDouble`, but it provided a more long-winded way of converting `String`s to `double`s. Occasionally you will encounter some unusual conversion methods in older textbooks or in Java code. An earlier generation of Java programmers learned earlier techniques for converting `String`s to `double`s, and they may not appreciate that later versions of Java provide `parseDouble`.

`parseInt` and `parseDouble` **Are Not Consistent**

In Java version 1.5.0, we can find three cases where `String`s are rejected by `parseInt` but accepted by `parseDouble`:

String	Characteristic	parseInt	parseDouble
"27 "	Trailing space	Throws an Exception	ok
" 27"	Leading space	Throws an Exception	ok
"+27"	Leading plus sign	Throws an Exception	ok

The programming teams that implemented parseInt and parseDouble were not the same. Languages are very large systems, and it's difficult to ensure that they are consistent.

Test your skill with Exercise 10-22.

10.19 Converting doubles to Strings

Suppose we have a variable x:

```
double x = 17.4;
```

and we want to convert it to a String. Java won't do the conversion

```
String s = x;     //ILLEGAL!
```

but the following code will do the trick:

```
String s = x + "";
```

Of course, the format method of class String provides more flexible control over the width and number of decimal places in the String produced.

10.20 MIN_VALUE and MAX_VALUE

We have used Double.parseDouble and Integer.parseInt to convert Strings to doubles and ints, respectively. For each of the primitive datatypes there is a class that collects methods and constants relevant to that type. Among the constants are MIN_VALUE and MAX_VALUE, which are the smallest and largest numbers that can be represented in the class. Prog1009 is the code that prints out the extreme values for byte, short, int, long, float, and double. Here is its output:

```
byte:
-128
127
```

```
short:
-32768
32767

integer:
-2147483648
2147483647

long:
-9223372036854775808
9223372036854775807

float:
1.4E-45
3.4028235E38

double:
4.9E-324
1.7976931348623157E308
```

Prog1009.java   MIN_VALUE and MAX_VALUE

```
// Written by Barry Soroka
//
// Print out MIN_VALUE and MAX_VALUE for numeric types.
//
import java.io.*;
/////////////////////////////////////////////////////////////////////////////
class Prog1009
{
//--------------------------------------------------------------------------
   public static void main ( String [] args ) throws Exception
   {
      System.out.println("\nbyte:");
      System.out.println(Byte.MIN_VALUE);
      System.out.println(Byte.MAX_VALUE);

      System.out.println("\nshort:");
      System.out.println(Short.MIN_VALUE);
      System.out.println(Short.MAX_VALUE);

      System.out.println("\ninteger:");
      System.out.println(Integer.MIN_VALUE);
      System.out.println(Integer.MAX_VALUE);
```

```
    System.out.println("\nlong:");
    System.out.println(Long.MIN_VALUE);
    System.out.println(Long.MAX_VALUE);

    System.out.println("\nfloat:");
    System.out.println(Float.MIN_VALUE);
    System.out.println(Float.MAX_VALUE);

    System.out.println("\ndouble:");
    System.out.println(Double.MIN_VALUE);
    System.out.println(Double.MAX_VALUE);
  }
//------------------------------------------------------------------------------
} // end class Prog1009
////////////////////////////////////////////////////////////////////////////////
```

Chapter Summary

- A floating-point number contains a decimal point and, perhaps, a power-of-10 multiplier.
- Java provides two floating-point datatypes: `float` occupies four bytes, and `double` occupies eight bytes.
- `double`s provide greater range and precision than `float`s.
- When presented with a floating-point literal, such as `3.14`, Java assumes that the value is a `double`.
- Most code uses `double`s for floating-point values.
- `double` literals can contain a power-of-10 multiplier. For example, `9.1e-31` represents 9.1×10^{-31}.
- `nextDouble()` is the `Scanner` method for reading a `double`.
- `printf` provides the `f` directive to format floating-point numbers for printing. `6.2f` specifies a field of width six with two digits to the right of the decimal point.
- Java provides four arithmetic operators for working with floating-point numbers: `+`, `-`, `*`, and `/`.
- Mixed-mode arithmetic occurs when an operator has an integer on one side and a floating-point number on the other. The operation is performed in floating-point, and the result is a floating-point number.
- `x += 3.7` is a shortcut for `x = x + 3.7`.
- `Math.abs`, `Math.sqrt`, and `Math.sin` compute, respectively, the absolute value, square root, and sine of their floating-point arguments.

- `Math.pow(x,y)` computes x^y.
- `Math.ceil`, `Math.floor`, and `Math.round` are three different ways of converting a floating-point number to an integer.
- We convert from integer to floating-point by simple assignment.
- We can cast a `double` to an `int` if we're willing to accept a possible loss of precision.
- Two `double`s can be approximately equal if they differ by a very small tolerance.
- `==` is not a useful operator for determining if two `double`s are equal; it requires equality to the minutest decimal place.
- `Double.parseDouble` can be used to convert a `String` to a `double`.
- We can convert a `double` to a `String` by concatenating it with the empty `String`.
- `Double.MIN_VALUE` and `Double.MAX_VALUE` are, respectively, the smallest and largest possible values of `double`.

Terminology Introduced in This Chapter

round-off error

Exercises

Exercise 10-1.   Both `float` and `int` are 32-bit datatypes. Compare the range of numbers they can represent.

Exercise 10-2.   Both `double` and `long` are 64-bit datatypes. Compare the range of numbers they can represent.

Exercise 10-3.   Consider the literals `7.5f` and `6.023e23f`. Prove that Java accepts these as `float`s.

Exercise 10-4.   Use `Prog1001` to determine $\sqrt{2.0}$ to four places after the decimal point.

Exercise 10-5.   Given a function $f(x)$, a *root* of the function is a value of x for which $f(x) = 0$. Write a program that evaluates $f(x) = x^3 - 3x^2 - 4x + 12$ for a given value of x. Use this program to find a root of the function. Your answer should be correct to four places after the decimal point. (Note: This polynomial has *three* roots.)

Exercise 10-6. Evaluate the following expressions. You can use Java to verify your results.

(a) `2.0 + 3 / 4`
(b) `2 + 3.0 / 4`
(c) `(2 + 3.0) / 4`
(d) `2 / 3 * 4.0`
(e) `2 / 3.0 * 4`
(f) `2.0 / 3 * 4`

Exercise 10-7. What happens if you try calling `Math.sqrt` with a *negative* parameter?

Exercise 10-8. Write a program that compares `Math.pow(x,0.5)` with `Math.sqrt(x)`.

Exercise 10-9. Write a program that compares `Math.pow(x,-1.0)` with `1.0/x`.

Exercise 10-10. Write a program that computes

```
Math.ceil(x)
```

and

```
-Math.floor(-x)
```

Are the results the same? Test your program for a variety of values of `x`.

Exercise 10-11. Write a program that repeatedly reads an angle, in *degrees*, and prints its mathematical sine. What are good test cases?

Exercise 10-12. Write a Java program that prints out `Math.PI` and `Math.E`. Do they match the customary values?

Exercise 10-13. Can we declare a variable `final` without assigning it an initial value? Use Java to determine whether we can.

Exercise 10-14. What message does Java give if we try to compile `Prog1006` after removing the `static` modifier from method `report`?

Exercise 10-15. Add a `static read` method to class `Circle`. Your code should work with a driver containing the statements:

```
Circle c = Circle.read(System.out,kb);
report(c);
```

Exercise 10-16. Add a method to Prog1008

```
public boolean isLargerThan(Circle)
```

that returns true if and only if the radius of the receiving Circle is larger than the radius of the parameter Circle.

Exercise 10-17. Consider a class Circle with double instance variables xCenter, yCenter, and radius. Write a predicate

```
public boolean contains(Circle)
```

that returns true if and only if the receiving Circle fully contains the parameter Circle.

Exercise 10-18. Add a method to Prog1008

```
public int intersectionType(Circle)
```

that returns the number of points at which the Circles intersect. If the Circles are not the same, then return 0, 1, or 2 as appropriate. If the Circles *are* the same, then return -1 to signal the case where the Circles intersect in an infinite number of points.

Exercise 10-19. Starting with Prog1008, write and test a method doubleTaxRate that doubles the current taxRate.

Exercise 10-20. Starting with Prog1008, write and test a method incrementTaxRate that raises the current taxRate by the specified percent. For example, the statement

```
Item.incrementTaxRate(10.0)
```

would increase a taxRate from 5% to 5.5%, or from 6.5% to 7.15%.

Exercise 10-21. Use Prog1001 to test the limits of what Java considers a double.

Exercise 10-22. Test your Java. Have the inconsistencies between parseInt and parseDouble been removed?

CHAPTER ELEVEN

Conditional Execution

Chapter Objectives

- Learn the syntax and semantics of Java's conditional statements.
- Use `if` and `if-else` statements in a variety of problems.
- Use multiway branching as a structured form of nested `if` statements.
- Appreciate stylistic concerns regarding conditional statements.
- Use the `switch` statement.
- Learn how to program GUI check boxes and radio buttons.

In prior chapters we studied (1) classes, methods, and variables; (2) defining new classes; (3) input and output; and (4) primitive datatypes.

So far, we've written only straight-line code: For any given program, the flow of control—the order of statements—has always been the same for every run. However, for many problems, the behavior of a program should depend on its input. For example, we might be working with a class `Circle`, and it makes no sense to have a `Circle` with a negative value for `radius`. The constructor `Circle` should inspect the incoming `radius` and behave accordingly:

> **Straight-line code** Where statements are executed one after another.

- If the radius is `0` or greater, then the constructor should create the `Circle` as specified.
- If the radius is negative, then `Circle` should take some other action. It might print a message to the user, replace the illegal value, or throw an `Exception`.

> **Conditional execution** Executing only if certain specified conditions are met.

By the end of this chapter you will understand conditional execution, which is the process whereby data can determine which program statements will be executed. In Java, this mechanism involves a variety of syntactic constructs—`if`, `if-else`, and multiway branching. We will also study the stylistic considerations that are important in using these constructs to write maintainable programs.

11.1 Things to Validate

As noted in earlier chapters, a constructor does not just mechanically accept its parameters and plug them into the instance variables. Many instance variables have a limited range of legal, acceptable, or reasonable values, and one job of constructors is to verify that the incoming values are valid. This section will discuss a few such situations.

- Consider a class `Circle` with a one-parameter constructor that takes a desired `radius`. Negative values are not valid.
- Consider a class `Person` with a slot for `age`. Again, negative values are not acceptable. Also, it may be reasonable to reject an `age` that is too large—say, greater than 150.
- Consider the `name` slot for `Person`. Not all `Strings` are acceptable. The empty `String` is certainly not a valid name. Nor, most likely, is a `String` containing digits, such as `Neo22`.[1]

> **Validation** Ensuring that values are valid; i.e., legal and sensible.

What can a constructor do when it detects invalid parameters? Some subset of the following actions would be appropriate:

- Print a message to the user.
- Request a new value from the user.
- Replace the invalid value with some acceptable default value.
- Throw an `Exception` or an `Error`.

---

[1] There's an urban legend about a Mr. O. The computer at his state's Department of Motor Vehicles was programmed to require that names be length two or greater. After spending considerable time, money, and energy, Mr. O changed his name to Oh. Similarly, the name `Ng` might be rejected because it contains no vowel. We must be careful when we build such validation rules into our programs.

| **Test your skill with Exercise 11–1.** |

11.2   Our First if

This section presents a class `Circle` and introduces a conditional statement—an `if`—that detects an invalid value for `radius` and responds by throwing an `Error`.

> **Conditional statement**   A statement that executes only if certain specified conditions are met.

The Driver

Consider the driver in `Prog1101.java`. We will follow this driver throughout the first part of this chapter. The two action statements are

```
Circle c1 = new Circle(1.0);
```

and

```
Circle c2 = new Circle(-1.0);
```

The first statement is fine, but the second statement tries to create a `Circle` with a negative `radius`. Along with the constructor statements, we have two reporting statements:

```
System.out.println(c1);
```

and

```
System.out.println(c2);
```

These will allow us to see what value of `radius` the constructor has used in each case.

Prog1101.java   **Allow Circles with Negative radius**

```
// Written by Barry Soroka
//
// class Circle -- allows negative radius
//
import java.io.*;
import java.text.DecimalFormat;
```

```
//////////////////////////////////////////////////////////////////////////
class Prog1101
{
//--------------------------------------------------------------------------
   public static void main ( String [] args ) throws Exception
   {
      Circle c1 = new Circle(1.0);
      System.out.println(c1);

      Circle c2 = new Circle(-1.0);
      System.out.println(c2);
   }
//--------------------------------------------------------------------------
} // end class Prog1101
//////////////////////////////////////////////////////////////////////////
class Circle
{
   private double radius;
//--------------------------------------------------------------------------
   public Circle ( double radius )
   {
      this.radius = radius;
   }
//--------------------------------------------------------------------------
   public double area() { return Math.PI * radius * radius; }
//--------------------------------------------------------------------------
   public double circumference() { return 2.0 * Math.PI * radius; }
//--------------------------------------------------------------------------
   public String toString()
   {
      return "\nCircle:\n" +
             String.format("    Radius:           %6.2f\n",radius) +
             String.format("    Circumference:    %6.2f\n",circumference()) +
             String.format("    Area:             %6.2f\n",area());
   }
//--------------------------------------------------------------------------
} // end class Circle
//////////////////////////////////////////////////////////////////////////
```

Accept Invalid Values

Our first version of class Circle simply accepts a negative radius when it's offered. Here is hardcopy of a run of Prog1101:

```
G:\>java Prog1101

Circle:
    Radius:         1.00
    Circumference:  6.28
    Area:           3.14

Circle:
    Radius:        -1.00
    Circumference: -6.28
    Area:           3.14
```

Notice how the second `Circle` has a negative `radius` and a negative `circumference`. The code contains several items of interest:

1. `Math.PI` is used to bring out Java's best value for π. `Math.PI` is a better value than `3.14159`, or whatever else we might type in by ourselves.
2. The `toString` method uses `String.format` to produce numerical output with precisely two places to the right of the decimal point. We learned this technique in Chapter 10.

Throw an Error: **Our First** if

`Prog1102.java` detects a negative radius and responds by bringing the program to a halt. The relevant statement is found in the constructor:

```
public Circle ( double radius )
{
    if ( radius < 0.0 )
    {
        throw new Error("Illegal radius: " + radius);
    }
    this.radius = radius;
}
```

Condition A boolean expression that determines whether a statement is executed.

The phrase `radius < 0.0` is a condition that is true when the proposed `radius` is negative. When that happens—and *only* when that happens—the program executes the statement

```
throw new Error("Illegal radius: " + radius);
```

which causes the program to halt and display the following specified message:

```
G:\ >java Prog1102

Circle:
    Radius:         1.00
    Circumference:  6.28
    Area:           3.14
Exception in thread "main" java.lang.Error:
Illegal radius: -1.0
        at Circle.<init>(Prog1102.java:30)
        at Prog1102.main(Prog1102.java:16)
```

That is our first if statement. The next section will discuss if statements in more detail, and, in a future section, we will discuss other ways to handle invalid input for the class Circle.

Prog1102.java   throw an Error When radius Is Negative

```java
// Written by Barry Soroka
//
// class Circle -- throws an Error when radius is negative
//
import java.io.*;
import java.text.DecimalFormat;
//////////////////////////////////////////////////////////////////////////////
class Prog1102
{
//-----------------------------------------------------------------------------
    public static void main ( String [] args ) throws Exception
    {
        Circle c1 = new Circle(1.0);
        System.out.println(c1);

        Circle c2 = new Circle(-1.0);
        System.out.println(c2);
    }
//-----------------------------------------------------------------------------
} // end class Prog1102
//////////////////////////////////////////////////////////////////////////////
class Circle
{
    private double radius;
```

```
//-------------------------------------------------------------------
   public Circle ( double radius )
   {
      if ( radius < 0.0 )
      {
         throw new Error("Illegal radius: " + radius);
      }
      this.radius = radius;
   }
//-------------------------------------------------------------------
   public double area() { return Math.PI * radius * radius; }
//-------------------------------------------------------------------
   public double circumference() { return 2.0 * Math.PI * radius; }
//-------------------------------------------------------------------
   public String toString()
   {
      return "\nCircle:\n" +
             String.format("   Radius:          %6.2f\n",radius) +
             String.format("   Circumference:   %6.2f\n",circumference()) +
             String.format("   Area:            %6.2f\n",area());
   }
//-------------------------------------------------------------------
} // end class Circle
////////////////////////////////////////////////////////////////////
```

Test your skill with Exercise 11–2.

11.3   The if Statement

In this section we'll examine the definition of the if statement and alternative ways of writing it. The sections that follow examine the use of if in many programming contexts.

> **Guard**   A condition that determines whether a statement is executed.
> **Flowchart**   A graphical representation of the flow of control through statements of a program.

The if statement uses a boolean expression to "guard" a statement: If the condition is true, then the statement is executed; otherwise it is not. The syntax is

```
if ( cond ) stmt
```

where cond is the condition and stmt is the guarded statement. Figure 11–1 is a graphical representation—a flowchart—of this same logic. We can trace the flow of control two different ways,

Figure 11–1
Flowchart of if

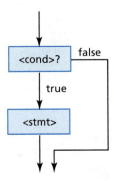

depending on whether *cond* is true. Some people find such diagrams helpful in understanding the flow of control. In the early days of programming, flow-charts were required; you had to get your flowchart approved before you were allowed to write any code. Flowcharts are no longer strictly required, but they are often useful in displaying the logic of programs with many if and if-else statements.[2]

Conditions

The condition in an if statement must be a boolean expression. These are formed according to the following rules:

1. A boolean *variable* is a boolean expression.
2. A boolean *literal* is a boolean expression.
3. The result of a *predicate*—a call to a boolean method—is a boolean expression.
4. The result of a *relational expression* is a boolean expression.
5. If *e* is a boolean expression, then !*e* is a boolean expression.
6. If e_1 and e_2 are boolean expressions, then so are e_1 && e_2 and e_1 || e_2.

---

[2] I once saw a program that could take a complete FORTRAN program and produce its flowchart. This capability was, presumably, useful for reverse engineering or for maintaining an underdocumented program.

Style

The most general form of an if statement is:

```
if ( ... )
{
    stmt
}
```

Because the guarded statements are between two vertical braces, we can add additional statements simply by adding another line. Some simple if statements are written like this:

```
if ( ... ) stmt
```

This format requires that the if, the condition, and the statement all fit on one line. Sometimes an if statement is too long for that form, and we have

```
if ( ... )
    stmt
```

where *stmt* is indented. You will see examples of all three forms in the remainder of this book.

Test your skill with Exercise 11–3.

11.4 Validating the radius of a Circle

In Section 11.2 we examined two ways in which the constructor for Circle could react to an invalid, negative radius:

- ignore the invalidity and create a Circle with a negative radius;
- throw a message with an Error, halting the program.

In Chapter 17, we'll learn how to throw an Exception in this same context. Meanwhile, the rest of this section examines how we can use the if statement to ensure that no Circle receives a negative radius.

Recall the driver that we're using:

```
Circle c1 = new Circle(1.0);
System.out.println(c1);

Circle c2 = new Circle(-1.0);
System.out.println(c2);
```

The `Circle` constructor in `Prog1103.java` can detect a negative `radius`, replace it with a default `1.0`, and notify the user about the replacement. Here's the code:

```
public Circle ( double radius )
{
   if ( radius < 0.0 )
   {
      System.out.println("\n*** Circle:" +
                         "\n*** Illegal radius: " + radius +
                         "\n*** Changed to:    1.0");
      radius = 1.0;
   }
   this.radius = radius;
}
```

Here's what the user sees when the program runs:

```
G:\>java Prog1103

Circle:
   Radius:          1.00
   Circumference:   6.28
   Area:            3.14

*** Circle:
*** Illegal radius: -1.0
*** Changed to:     1.0

Circle:
   Radius:          1.00
   Circumference:   6.28
   Area:            3.14
```

The first `Circle` is created silently, but the second `Circle` triggers the condition of the `if` statement.

Prog1103.java   Correct a Negative **radius**

```java
// Written by Barry Soroka
//
// class Circle -- corrects illegal radius & notifies the user
//
import java.io.*;
import java.text.DecimalFormat;
//////////////////////////////////////////////////////////////////////////////
class Prog1103
{
//----------------------------------------------------------------------------

    public static void main ( String [] args ) throws Exception
    {
      Circle c1 = new Circle(1.0);
      System.out.println(c1);

      Circle c2 = new Circle(-1.0);
      System.out.println(c2);
    }
//----------------------------------------------------------------------------
} // end class Prog1103
//////////////////////////////////////////////////////////////////////////////
class Circle
{
    private double radius;
//----------------------------------------------------------------------------
    public Circle ( double radius )
    {
      if ( radius < 0.0 )
      {
        System.out.println("\n*** Circle:" +
                           "\n*** Illegal radius: " + radius +
                           "\n*** Changed to:     1.0");
        radius = 1.0;
      }

      this.radius = radius;
    }
//----------------------------------------------------------------------------
```

```
   public double area() { return Math.PI * radius * radius; }
//-------------------------------------------------------------------

   public double circumference() { return 2.0 * Math.PI * radius; }
//-------------------------------------------------------------------

   public String toString()
   {
      return "\nCircle:\n" +
             String.format("    Radius:          %6.2f\n",radius) +
             String.format("    Circumference:   %6.2f\n",circumference()) +
             String.format("    Area:            %6.2f\n",area());

   }
//-------------------------------------------------------------------
} // end class Circle
////////////////////////////////////////////////////////////////////////
```

> **Magic number**   A number that appears without explanation.
> **Constant**   A variable that, once given a value, cannot be changed.

In the constructor, notice the 1.0—it occurs *twice*. We call this a magic number: If we change it in once place, then we must change it in the other place as well. Magic numbers are an invitation to problems during the maintenance phase of programming; it's very easy to change the number in some places and not in others.

The Circle constructor in Prog1104.java shows an improvement on the prior version. The magic number 1.0 has been replaced with the constant DEFAULT_RADIUS. The declaration is this:

```
final double DEFAULT_RADIUS = 1.0;
```

where the phrases have the following meanings:

- final means that this variable is a *constant*. It cannot be changed by subsequent statements.
- double is the datatype involved.
- DEFAULT_RADIUS is the name of the variable. As per the Style Sheet (Appendix 1), constants are in *capital letters*, and individual words are separated by underscores ("_").
- = 1.0; is the assignment of a value to this variable. You *must* assign values to constants when they are declared; you can't assign them values anywhere else.

Because 1.0 occurs only once, we can change the DEFAULT_RADIUS by changing the 1.0 in a single location.

MORAL	Avoid magic numbers.

Prog1104.java   Use a Constant, Not a Magic Number

```java
// Written by Barry Soroka
//
// class Circle -- replaces a magic number with a constant
//
import java.io.*;
import java.text.DecimalFormat;
/////////////////////////////////////////////////////////////////////////////
class Prog1104
{
//----------------------------------------------------------------------------

   public static void main ( String [] args ) throws Exception
   {
      Circle c1 = new Circle(1.0);
      System.out.println(c1);

      Circle c2 = new Circle(-1.0);
      System.out.println(c2);
   }
//----------------------------------------------------------------------------
} // end class Prog1104
/////////////////////////////////////////////////////////////////////////////
class Circle
{
   private double radius;
//----------------------------------------------------------------------------
   public Circle ( double radius )
   {
      final double DEFAULT_RADIUS = 1.0;

      if ( radius < 0.0 )
      {
         System.out.println("\n*** Circle:" +
                            "\n*** Illegal radius: " + radius +
                            "\n*** Changed to:     " + DEFAULT_RADIUS);
         radius = DEFAULT_RADIUS;
```

```
      }

     this.radius = radius;
  }
//-----------------------------------------------------------------------
  public double area() { return Math.PI * radius * radius; }
//-----------------------------------------------------------------------
  public double circumference() { return 2.0 * Math.PI * radius; }
//-----------------------------------------------------------------------
  public String toString()
  {
     return "\nCircle:\n" +
           String.format("   Radius:        %6.2f\n",radius) +
           String.format("   Circumference: %6.2f\n",circumference()) +
           String.format("   Area:          %6.2f\n",area());
  }
//-----------------------------------------------------------------------
} // end class Circle
///////////////////////////////////////////////////////////////////////
```

 | **Test your skill with Exercises 11–4 and 11–5.**

11.5 Properties of `ints`

In Chapter 8, we read integers and used boolean expressions to report their properties. Typical hardcopy was

```
Enter an integer: 17
Even? false
Odd?  true
```

and the relevant code was

```
System.out.println("Even? " + (n%2 == 0));
System.out.println("Odd?  " + (n%2 != 0));
...
```

In this section, we will rewrite that code to use `if` statements:

```
if ( n%2 == 0 ) System.out.println("even");
if ( n%2 != 0 ) System.out.println("odd");
```

`Prog1105.java` shows the final code. Typical hardcopy is

```
C:\>java Prog1105
Enter an int: 17
odd
positive
```

Prog1105.java   Report the Properties of an int

```java
// Written by Barry Soroka
//
// Read an int.  Compute & report its properties.
//
import java.io.*;
import java.util.Scanner;
////////////////////////////////////////////////////////////////////////////////
class Prog1105
{
//--------------------------------------------------------------------------------
   public static void main ( String [] args ) throws Exception
   {
      Scanner kb = new Scanner(System.in);

      while ( true )
      {
         System.out.print("\nEnter an int: ");
         int n = kb.nextInt();
         if ( n%2 == 0 ) System.out.println("even");
         if ( n%2 != 0 ) System.out.println("odd");
         if ( n > 0 ) System.out.println("positive");
         if ( n == 0 ) System.out.println("zero");
         if ( n < 0 ) System.out.println("negative");
      }
   }
//--------------------------------------------------------------------------------
} // end class Prog1105
////////////////////////////////////////////////////////////////////////////////
```

Notice that the lines directly above are somewhat redundant: Because *even* and *odd* are polar opposites, we are computing n%2 *twice*. One "improvement" is to introduce a local variable such as this:

```java
boolean isEven = (n%2 == 0);
if ( isEven )  System.out.println("even");
if ( !isEven ) System.out.println("odd");
```

That avoids duplicate computation. In Section 11.10 we will use the `if-else` statement to achieve the same savings but without introducing a local variable.

11.6 Classifying Temperature: Using `if`

In this section we will write a class `Person` that models a human being with temperature preferences: Some temperatures are `too cold`, some are `too hot`, and some are `ok`. We'll follow the three-step methodology we've used before.

Envision Test Runs

Behind the scenes, the program will create a `Person` with a specific `name`, `loThreshold`, and `hiThreshold`. When we invoke the program, the prompt will reflect that `Person`'s name and thresholds. In the case that follows, `Joe` has a `loThreshold` of 70 and a `hiThreshold` of 80. We'll enter a temperature, and the program will report the person's response. Here's a sample run:

```
Enter a temperature for Joe[70,80]: 65
That's too cold

Enter a temperature for Joe[70,80]: 70
That's ok

Enter a temperature for Joe[70,80]: 75
That's ok

Enter a temperature for Joe[70,80]: 80
That's ok

Enter a temperature for Joe[70,80]: 85
That's too hot
```

Notice that I have not chosen test temperatures randomly:

- I've chosen temperatures in all three ranges—`too cold`, `ok`, `too hot`.
- I've chosen temperatures on all the borders—`70`, `80`.

This is a good test plan, and it will tickle many likely coding errors. In Chapter 12 we'll learn more about testing and choosing test cases.

Some students always suggest using `hello` as a test case, as it generates the expected `InputMismatchException`. I don't agree. Our program isn't supposed to yield meaningful results except for integer inputs, so it doesn't prove anything no matter how a noninteger is treated.

Write the Driver

Prog1106.java contains the driver for this program. It's quite straightforward:

1. We open a Scanner so that we can read from the keyboard.
2. We create a Person for testing.
3. We open an infinite loop that reads an int and then calls p.judgeTemp(int) to get the Person's opinion of that temperature.

Prog1106.java   Classify an Integer Temperature

```java
// Written by Barry Soroka
//
// Using if statements to classify an integer temperature.
// No insurance that loThreshold <= hiThreshold.
//
import java.io.*;
import java.util.Scanner;
////////////////////////////////////////////////////////////////////////////////
class Prog1106
{
//---------------------------------------------------------------------------
   public static void main(String[] arg) throws Exception
   {
      Scanner kb = new Scanner(System.in);

      Person p = new Person ( "Joe", 70, 80 );

      while ( true )
      {
         System.out.print("\nEnter a temperature for " + p + ": ");
         int temp = kb.nextInt();
         System.out.println("That's " + p.judgeTemp(temp));
      }
   }
//---------------------------------------------------------------------------
} // end class Prog1106
////////////////////////////////////////////////////////////////////////////////
class Person
{
   private String name;
```

```
   private int loThreshold;
   private int hiThreshold;
//-------------------------------------------------------------------
   public Person ( String name, int loThreshold, int hiThreshold )
   {
      this.name = name;
      this.loThreshold = loThreshold;
      this.hiThreshold = hiThreshold;
   }
//-------------------------------------------------------------------
   public String judgeTemp ( int temp )
   {
      if ( temp < loThreshold ) return "too cold";
      if ( temp > hiThreshold ) return "too hot";
      return "ok";
   }
//-------------------------------------------------------------------
   public String toString()
   {
      return name + "[" + loThreshold + "," + hiThreshold + "]";
   }
//-------------------------------------------------------------------
} // end class Person
/////////////////////////////////////////////////////////////////////
```

Implement the Class

Prog1106.java implements the class Person as we specified:

- The instance variables are clear-cut.
- The constructor takes variables name, loThreshold, and hiThreshold and assigns them to the similarly named instance variables. (At this point, we ignore an obvious question: What if the user tries creating a Person with loThreshold greater than hiThreshold? We'll return to this question shortly.)
- The toString method is straightforward.
- The judgeTemp method uses if statements to detect too cold and too hot. Anything remaining must be ok. Note that when a return statement is executed inside a method, control leaves the method and returns to the point from which this method was called. Thus, if we return too cold, then we don't have to worry about any statements later in the judgeTemp method.

That concludes our initial solution to the judgeTemp problem.

Validation at the Constructor

What should we do if the constructor receives parameters such that `loThreshold` > `hiThreshold`? Think for a minute—there are several viable options.

 **AND THINK**

All right, here are a few options that I can see: If the `Person` constructor receives threshold values out of order, we can:

- throw an `Error` or `Exception` and send a message to the user.
- replace the thresholds with some defaults and send a message to the user.
- reverse the order of `loThreshold` and `hiThreshold` and send a message to the user.

I will implement the last of these options. The code is shown in `Prog1107.java`.

Prog1107.java   **Ensure That loThreshold ≤ hiThreshold**

```java
// Written by Barry Soroka
//
// Using if statements to classify an integer temperature.
// Ensures that loThreshold <= hiThreshold.
//
import java.io.*;
import java.util.Scanner;
////////////////////////////////////////////////////////////////////////////
class Prog1107
{
//----------------------------------------------------------------------------
   public static void main(String[] arg) throws Exception
   {
      Scanner kb = new Scanner(System.in);

      Person p = new Person ( "Joe", 80, 70 );

      while ( true )
      {
         System.out.print("\nEnter a temperature for " + p + ": ");
         int temp = kb.nextInt();
         System.out.println("That's " + p.judgeTemp(temp));
      }
   }
```

```java
//----------------------------------------------------------------------
} // end class Prog1107
/////////////////////////////////////////////////////////////////////
class Person
{
    private String name;
    private int loThreshold;
    private int hiThreshold;
//----------------------------------------------------------------------
    public Person ( String name, int loThreshold, int hiThreshold )
    {
        this.name = name;
        if ( loThreshold <= hiThreshold )
        {
            this.loThreshold = loThreshold;
            this.hiThreshold = hiThreshold;
        }
        if ( loThreshold > hiThreshold )
        {
            System.out.print("Reversed threshold [" +
                            loThreshold +
                            "," +
                            hiThreshold +
                            "] has been fixed for " +
                            name);
            this.loThreshold = hiThreshold;
            this.hiThreshold = loThreshold;
        }
    }
//----------------------------------------------------------------------
    public String judgeTemp ( int temp )
    {
        if ( temp < loThreshold ) return "too cold";
        if ( temp > hiThreshold ) return "too hot";
        return "ok";
    }
//----------------------------------------------------------------------
    public String toString()
    {
        return name + "[" + loThreshold + "," + hiThreshold + "]";
    }
//----------------------------------------------------------------------
} // end class Person
/////////////////////////////////////////////////////////////////////
```

Two cases are possible. In the first case, the thresholds are in the correct order, and we need merely copy the parameters over to the instance variables. Here is the relevant `if` statement:

```
if ( loThreshold <= hiThreshold )
{
   this.loThreshold = loThreshold;
   this.hiThreshold = hiThreshold;
}
```

In the second case, the thresholds must be reversed:

```
if ( loThreshold > hiThreshold )
{
   System.out.print("Reversed threshold [" +
                     loThreshold +
                     "," +
                     hiThreshold +
                     "] has been fixed for " +
                     name);
   this.loThreshold = hiThreshold;
   this.hiThreshold = loThreshold;
}
```

Notice that a given set of thresholds cannot activate *both* of the `if` statements: The conditions are mutually exclusive.

What if `loThreshold == hiThreshold`? This person is awfully finicky, because only one temperature is `ok`, but this is still a reasonable set of thresholds.

Test your skill with Exercises 11–6 through 11–8.

11.7   Improving the `static read` Method

In Chapter 6, we learned a pattern that produces a `static read` method for any given class. With this pattern, we can read instances of the class from an arbitrary `Scanner`. The prototype is

```
public classname read(PrintStream,Scanner)
                             throws Exception
```

where prompts are sent to the `PrintStream` and data is read from the `Scanner`.

In Chapter 7, we discovered a weakness in the method when we used it to read from a file. The reading went fine, but the method insisted on printing the prompts even though the data were coming from a file rather than a human user. Think for a moment: How might we modify the `read` method so that it doesn't always print the prompts?

STOP AND THINK

One solution would be to add a `boolean` third parameter—`promptWanted`—and then to test this parameter before printing the prompts. Here's how the code would look:

```
public static Complex read ( PrintStream ps,
                             Scanner sc,
                             boolean promptWanted )
          throws Exception
{
   if ( promptWanted ) ps.println("Reading a complex number ...");
   if ( promptWanted ) ps.print("Enter the real part:      ");
   int real = sc.nextInt();
   if ( promptWanted ) ps.print("Enter the imaginary part: ");
   int imag = sc.nextInt();
   return new Complex ( real, imag );
}
```

That's a reasonable fix to the problem of unwanted prompts.

Using `null`

Let's examine another solution, shown in `Prog1108.java`. The `read` method behaves as follows:

- If the `PrintStream` parameter is `null`, then no prompt is printed.
- Otherwise, the prompt is printed.

`null` is a special constant in Java. It is *the place a reference is pointing when the pointer isn't referring to an object*. We have seen `null` before in code such as this:

```
                        String s = null;
                        System.out.println(s.length());
```

where we get a NullPointerException.

Prog1108.java   Turn Off Unnecessary Prompts

```java
// Written by Barry Soroka
//
// Reads Complex numbers.
// Omits prompts when the PrintStream parameter is null.
//
import java.io.*;
import java.util.Scanner;
/////////////////////////////////////////////////////////////////////////////
class Prog1108
{
//-------------------------------------------------------------------------
    public static void main (String [] args) throws Exception
    {
        Scanner kb = new Scanner(System.in);

        Complex z1 = Complex.read(System.out,kb);
        System.out.println("The first complex number is:  " + z1);

        Complex z2 = Complex.read(null,kb); // omit prompt on second Complex
        System.out.println("The second complex number is: " + z2);

        System.out.println("Their sum is " + z1.add(z2));
    }
//-------------------------------------------------------------------------
} // end class Prog1108
/////////////////////////////////////////////////////////////////////////////
class Complex
{
    private int real;
    private int imag;
//-------------------------------------------------------------------------
    public Complex ( int real , int imag )
    {
        this.real = real;
        this.imag = imag;
    }
//-------------------------------------------------------------------------
```

```java
    public String toString ()
    {
       return "(" + real + "," + imag + ")";
    }
//-----------------------------------------------------------------
    public boolean equals ( Complex that )
    {
       return this.real == that.real
              &&
              this.imag == that.imag;
    }
//-----------------------------------------------------------------
    public static Complex read ( PrintStream ps, Scanner sc )
          throws Exception
    {
       if ( ps != null ) ps.println("Reading a complex number ...");
       if ( ps != null ) ps.print("Enter the real part:      ");
       int real = sc.nextInt();
       if ( ps != null ) ps.print("Enter the imaginary part: ");
       int imag = sc.nextInt();
       return new Complex ( real, imag );
    }
//-----------------------------------------------------------------
    public Complex add ( Complex that )
    {
       return new Complex ( this.real + that.real , this.imag + that.imag );
    }
//-----------------------------------------------------------------
    public Complex sub ( Complex that )
    {
       return new Complex ( this.real - that.real , this.imag - that.imag );
    }
//-----------------------------------------------------------------
    public Complex times ( Complex that )
    {
       int a1 = this.real, b1 = this.imag;
       int a2 = that.real, b2 = that.imag;
       return new Complex ( a1*a2-b1*b2, a1*b2+a2*b1 );
    }
//-----------------------------------------------------------------
} // end class Complex
/////////////////////////////////////////////////////////////////////////
```

null is a legitimate value for a reference to any type of object, but it *isn't* a legal value of a primitive datatype:

```
Animal a = new Animal(...);
a = null;
Complex c = new Complex(...);
c = null;

int n = 5;
n = null;          ← Illegal
```

We can also ask if a variable has the null value:

```
Animal a;
...
if ( a == null ) ...
```

Using null as discussed, we get the read method shown in Prog1108. The relevant statements are these:

```
if ( ps != null ) ps.println("Reading a complex number ...");
if ( ps != null ) ps.print("Enter the real part: ");
int real = sc.nextInt();
if ( ps != null ) ps.print("Enter the imaginary part: ");
int imag = sc.nextInt();
return new Complex ( real, imag );
```

If the PrintStream parameter is not null, then the println statements are executed. The nextInt methods are *always* called.

The driver of Prog1108 calls the read method twice—first with System.out as its first argument, and then with null as the first argument. Here's the output:

```
G:\>java Prog1108
Reading a complex number ...
Enter the real part: 3
Enter the imaginary part: 4
The first complex number is:  (3,4)
1                              ← Notice lack of prompt
2                              ← Notice lack of prompt
The second complex number is: (1,2)
Their sum is (4,6)
```

Reading Complex from a File

Let's consider this problem: Read the name of a file of Complex and then read two Complex objects from that file, and then print their sum. Assume that the file Complex2 contains the data

```
2
3
1
-5
```

which stands for the complex numbers $2 + 3i$ and $1 - 5i$. `Prog1109.java` demonstrates clean, successful reading from a file. By sending `null` as the `PrintStream` parameter to the `read` method, the driver requests that prompts be omitted. Here is the output of the run:

```
G:\>java Prog1109
Enter the name of a file of Complex: Complex2

  (2,3)
+ (1,-5)
- - - - - - - - - - - - - - - - - -
  (3,-2)
```

This hardcopy is not burdened with unnecessary prompts.

Prog1109.java   Sum the First Two Complex in a File

```java
// Written by Barry Soroka
//
// Read the name of a file of Complex numbers.
// Read and sum the first two Complex numbers in the file.
//
// Driver signals "Don't Prompt!"
//
import java.io.*;
import java.util.Scanner;
/////////////////////////////////////////////////////////////////////
class Prog1109
{
//-----------------------------------------------------------------
   public static void main (String [] args) throws Exception
   {
      Scanner kb = new Scanner(System.in);

      System.out.print("Enter the name of a file of Complex: ");
      String filename = kb.nextLine();

      Scanner sc = new Scanner(new File(filename));

      Complex z1 = Complex.read(null,sc);
      Complex z2 = Complex.read(null,sc);
```

```
      System.out.println("\n");
      System.out.println("   " + z1);
      System.out.println("+ " + z2);
      System.out.println("-------------------");
      System.out.println("   " + z1.add(z2));
   }
//-----------------------------------------------------------------
} // end class Prog1109
/////////////////////////////////////////////////////////////////////
class Complex
{
   private int real;
   private int imag;
//-----------------------------------------------------------------
   public Complex ( int real , int imag )
   {
      this.real = real;
      this.imag = imag;
   }
//-----------------------------------------------------------------
   public Complex add ( Complex that )
   {
      return new Complex ( this.real + that.real,
                           this.imag + that.imag );
   }
//-----------------------------------------------------------------
   public String toString ()
   {
      return "(" + real + "," + imag + ")";
   }
//-----------------------------------------------------------------
   public static Complex read ( PrintStream ps, Scanner sc )
         throws Exception
   {
      if ( ps != null ) ps.println("Reading a complex number ...");
      if ( ps != null ) ps.print("Enter the real part:      ");
      int real = sc.nextInt();
      if ( ps != null ) ps.print("Enter the imaginary part: ");
      int imag = sc.nextInt();
      return new Complex ( real, imag );
   }
//-----------------------------------------------------------------
} // end class Complex
/////////////////////////////////////////////////////////////////////
```

Out-of-Data Errors

Suppose we run `Prog1109` on the file `Complex1`, which contains only *one* `Complex` and is reflected in the lines:

```
2
3
```

Something bad will happen, because `Prog1109` expects to find *two* `Complex` numbers in its data file. What do you think will happen?

STOP AND THINK

Here's the hardcopy:

```
G:\>java Prog1109
Enter the name of a file of Complex: Complex1
Exception in thread "main" java.util.NoSuchElementException
        at java.util.Scanner.throwFor(Unknown Source)
        at java.util.Scanner.next(Unknown Source)
        at java.util.Scanner.nextInt(Unknown Source)
        at java.util.Scanner.nextInt(Unknown Source)
        at Complex.read(Prog1109.java:62)
        at Prog1109.main(Prog1109.java:24)
```

What, exactly, is Java trying to say? The program got a `NoSuchElementException` when executing a call to `nextInt` because we tried to read past the end of the file. In Chapter 13 we'll learn how to detect this situation, and we'll be able to loop through all the elements in a file of arbitrary length.

> **Test your skill with Exercises 11–9 through 11–11.**

11.8   Changing a `char` from Lowercase to Uppercase

This section presents two methods for changing a `char` from lowercase to uppercase. Both methods use `if`, and I'll assume we want a `static` method with the following prototype:

```
public static char toUpperCase ( char c )
```

The first method uses *brute force*. We'll have one `if` statement per character:

```
if ( c == 'a' ) return 'A';
...
if ( c == 'z' ) return 'Z';
```

On the positive side, this code is guaranteed to work—provided we make no errors in writing the lines. On the negative side, it's a lot of code to write.

The second method uses *character arithmetic*:

```
if ('a' <= c && c <= 'z') return (char)(c + 'A' - 'a');
```

Note that `'A'-'a'` is the integer difference between the uppercase and lowercase versions of any letter. Hence, if we add this difference to, say, `'m'`, we'll get `'M'`. However, we don't want to transform *all* chars this way—nonletters must *not* be transformed. Who knows what will happen to `'2'` or `'.'`? Nor do we want to change letters that are already uppercase. Hence we guard the transform statement with the clause

```
if ('a' <= c && c <= 'z')
```

so that it applies only to lowercase letters.

Test your skill with Exercise 11–12.

11.9 Computing Pay with Overtime

Here is a classic problem in computing:

> Given an hourly rate and a number of hours, compute an employee's pay, subject to the rule that time over 40 hours is paid at "time-and-a-half"— 150% of the regular rate.

You'll see this problem solved in every programming language you learn because it's an excellent exercise of conditional statements.

Prog1110.java shows our code. Here are the action statements of the driver:

```
System.out.print("\nEnter hourly rate: ");
double rate = kb.nextDouble();

Employee e = new Employee("sam",rate);
```

```
        while ( true )
        {
            System.out.print("\nHow many hours this week? ");
            int hours = kb.nextInt();
            System.out.printf("\nPay is %6.2f\n",e.calcPay(hours));
        }
```

We begin by reading an hourly rate and by creating an employee named sam, then continue with an infinite loop: We read a number of hours and print the pay, again and again and again.

Prog1110.java   Compute Pay with Overtime

```
// Written by Barry Soroka
//
// Compute pay with overtime
//
import java.io.*;
import java.util.Scanner;
//////////////////////////////////////////////////////////////////////////
class Prog1110
{
//-------------------------------------------------------------------------
    public static void main (String [] args) throws Exception
    {
        Scanner kb = new Scanner(System.in);

        System.out.print("\nEnter hourly rate: ");
        double rate = kb.nextDouble();

        Employee e = new Employee("sam",rate);

        while ( true )
        {
            System.out.print("\nHow many hours this week? ");
            int hours = kb.nextInt();
            System.out.printf("\nPay is %6.2f\n",e.calcPay(hours));
        }
    }
//-------------------------------------------------------------------------
} // end class Prog1110
//////////////////////////////////////////////////////////////////////////
```

```
class Employee
{
    private String name;
    private double rate;
//-------------------------------------------------------------------
    public Employee ( String name, double rate )
    {
        this.name = name;
        this.rate = rate;
    }
//-------------------------------------------------------------------
    public double calcPay ( int hours )
    {
        if ( hours <= 40 ) return rate * hours;

        return rate * 40 +
               rate * 1.5 * ( hours - 40 );
    }
//-------------------------------------------------------------------
} // end class Employee
///////////////////////////////////////////////////////////////////////
```

We've made some assumptions about class `Employee`. The constructor takes a `String name` and a `double rate`. A method `calcPay` takes an integer number of hours and returns the amount of pay. These assumptions are satisfied in the code for class `Employee`. The method of interest is `calcPay`:

```
public double calcPay ( int hours )
{
    if ( hours <= 40 ) return rate * hours;

    return rate * 40 +
           rate * 1.5 * ( hours - 40 );
}
```

We've divided the possibilities into those with `hours <= 40` and those with `hours > 40`. The former case is simple: `rate * hours`. The latter case requires that we recognize

- a block of 40 hours, payable at `rate`, and
- a block of the remaining hours (`hours - 40`), payable at `rate * 1.5`.

We have to be careful to apply the formula `rate * 1.5 * hours` only to the *excess* hours.

> **Test your skill with Exercises 11–13 and 11–14.**

> You can't end a non-`void` method with an `if` statement.

The purpose of this section is to show you an error you may encounter, and to explain Java's logic in this situation.

Consider the following method from `Prog1111.java`:

```
private static int abs ( int n )
{
    if ( n >= 0 ) return n;
    if ( n < 0 ) return -n;
}
```

Java won't compile this (at least *my* Java won't compile it). The hardcopy is:

```
G:\>javac Prog1111.java
Prog1111.java:10: missing return statement
    {
    ^
1 error
```

To Java, every non-`void` method must execute a `return` statement, and, when all your `returns` are guarded by `ifs`, Java worries that the method may not execute a `return`. We know that the `abs` method will *always* return because the conditions are *exhaustive* (i.e., one of them will always be true), but Java's reasoning powers are not as good as ours. Therefore, we must write:

```
private static int abs ( int n )
{
    if ( n >= 0 ) return n;
    return -n;
}
```

Remember this situation and its error message; you may see them again one day.

Prog1111.java   Can't End a Non-void Method with an if Statement

```
// Written by Barry Soroka
//
// Can't end a non-void method with an if statement.
//
/////////////////////////////////////////////////////////////////////////////
class Prog1111
{
//----------------------------------------------------------------------------
   private static int abs ( int n )
   {
      if ( n >= 0 ) return n;
      if ( n < 0 ) return -n;
   }
//----------------------------------------------------------------------------
} // end class Prog1111
/////////////////////////////////////////////////////////////////////////////
```

11.10   The if-else Statement

In Section 11.5, we looked at the task of taking an int n and printing "even" or "odd" depending on which was correct. We wrote the code

```
if ( n%2 == 0 ) System.out.println("even");
if ( n%2 != 0 ) System.out.println("odd");
```

which results in the flowchart shown in Figure 11–2. This code performs the task, but it computes n%2 twice. Clearly, once we know that n is *even*, we needn't bother to test if it is *odd*. The two conditions are mutually exclusive: One can be true or the other can be true, but *both* can never be true. The even–odd problem is amenable to the flowchart shown in Figure 11–3, which corresponds to the Java statement

```
if ( n%2 == 0 ) System.out.println("even");
else            System.out.println("odd");
```

Figure 11–2
Using two ifs

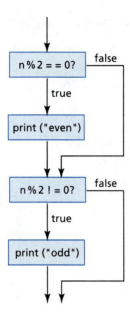

Figure 11–3
Using if-else

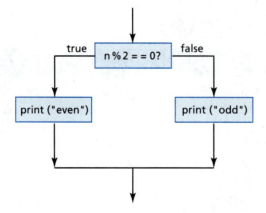

In general, the if-else statement has the form

```
if ( cond ) stmt1;
else        stmt2;
```

and the corresponding flowchart is shown in Figure 11–4. Note that I have written *stmt1* and *stmt2*, but we can use statements of any complexity, including sequences of statements enclosed by braces.

Figure 11-4
Flowchart for if-else

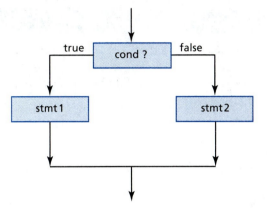

Style

The most general form of an if-else statement is:

```
if ( cond )
{
    stmt1
}
else
{
    stmt2
}
```

We can easily add more statements within the braces of the if or else actions. If all parts of the statement are small, we can write

```
if ( cond ) stmt1 else stmt2
```

Sometimes an if-else statement looks good like this:

```
if ( cond ) stmt1
else        stmt2
```

You will see a variety of these formats in the if-else examples in the remainder of this chapter.

11.11 Classifying Temperature: Using if-else

In Prog1107.java we modeled a person with temperature preferences, and we implemented a classifier—too hot, too cold, ok—using Java's if statement. Now we'll see what we can do with the additional power of the if-else statement. The final code is given as Prog1112.java.

Prog1112.java   **Classify a Temperature**

```java
// Written by Barry Soroka
//
// Using if-else statements to classify an integer temperature.
// Ensures that loThreshold <= hiThreshold.
//
import java.io.*;
import java.util.Scanner;
////////////////////////////////////////////////////////////////////////////
class Prog1112
{
//------------------------------------------------------------------------
    public static void main(String[] arg) throws Exception
    {
        Scanner kb = new Scanner(System.in);

        Person p = new Person ( "Joe", 80, 70 );

        while ( true )
        {
            System.out.print("\nEnter a temperature for " + p + ": ");
            int temp = kb.nextInt();
            System.out.println("That's " + p.judgeTemp(temp));
        }
    }
//------------------------------------------------------------------------
} // end class Prog1112
////////////////////////////////////////////////////////////////////////////
class Person
{
    private String name;
    private int loThreshold;
    private int hiThreshold;
//------------------------------------------------------------------------
    public Person ( String name, int loThreshold, int hiThreshold )
    {
        this.name = name;
```

```
        if ( loThreshold <= hiThreshold )
        {
           this.loThreshold = loThreshold;
           this.hiThreshold = hiThreshold;
        }
        else
        {
           System.out.print("Reversed threshold [" +
                         loThreshold +
                         "," +
                         hiThreshold +
                         "] has been fixed for " +
                         name);
           this.loThreshold = hiThreshold;
           this.hiThreshold = loThreshold;
        }
     }
//-------------------------------------------------------------------
   public String judgeTemp ( int temp )
   {
      if ( temp < loThreshold ) return "too cold";
      if ( temp > hiThreshold ) return "too hot";
      return "ok";
   }
//-------------------------------------------------------------------
   public String toString()
   {
      return name + "[" + loThreshold + "," + hiThreshold + "]";
   }
//-------------------------------------------------------------------
} // end class Person
/////////////////////////////////////////////////////////////////////
```

The obvious place to use the if-else statement is in the constructor, where we need to verify that loThreshold <= hiThreshold. In our first attempt we had a structure like this:

```
        if ( loThreshold <= hiThreshold )
        {
           various1
        }
        if ( loThreshold > hiThreshold )
        {
           various2
        }
```

We noted that the two conditions are mutually exclusive, and that we don't really need to compare the thresholds *twice*. In the new version, the structure has become

```
if ( loThreshold <= hiThreshold )
{
    various1
}
else
{
    various2
}
```

and we compare the thresholds only *once*.

We will *not* change the method `judgeTemp`, which has the statements

```
if ( temp < loThreshold ) return "too cold";
if ( temp > hiThreshold ) return "too hot";
return "ok";
```

because using `else` will not make this any more readable or efficient. We'll talk about this again when we get to Section 11.15, Stylistic Considerations.

 Test your skill with Exercises 11–15 through 11–17.

11.12   Multiway Branching: The Letter Grade Problem

Many problems require code that classifies an input according to a scale of decision points. At school, for example, we often convert a *numeric* grade to a *letter* grade, using the following rules:

- 90 and above is an A.
- 80 and above is a B.
- 70 and above is a C.
- 60 and above is a D.
- Below 60 is an F.

Multiway branching   Using `if-else` statements to select one of many statements.

This construction is so common that it has a name—*multiway branching*—and there's a standard way to convert it to Java code:

```
if         ( n >= 90 ) letter = 'A';
else if ( n >= 80 ) letter = 'B';
else if ( n >= 70 ) letter = 'C';
else if ( n >= 60 ) letter = 'D';
else                    letter = 'F';
```

Nested if   An if statement within another if statement.

The flowchart is shown as Figure 11–5. This is one of the few times you will be allowed to used *nested* if statements: if within if or else.

Let's examine another way—a naïve way—to implement the Letter Grade Problem:

```
if                      ( n >= 90 ) letter = 'A';
if (( n >= 80 ) && ( n < 90 )) letter = 'B';
if (( n >= 70 ) && ( n < 80 )) letter = 'C';
if (( n >= 60 ) && ( n < 70 )) letter = 'D';
if   ( n < 60 )                 letter = 'F';
```

Figure 11–5
Multiway Branching for the Letter Grade Problem

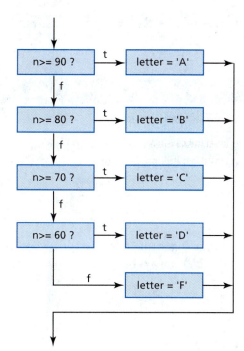

This code works, but it's *brittle*. If we accidentally change one of the relational operators (by omitting or inserting `'='`), the code will fail for a small number of cases. If we forget to test that case, we may find ourselves operating with faulty code. This code also makes it difficult to *change* the grading scale. The code currently gives an A to any grade in the range [90, 100], assuming that 100 is the largest possible numeric grade. If the professor wants to change the A range to be [89, 100], then we must change the literal 90 in *two* places. If we change only one of the 90s, we'll have either

```
if               ( n >= 89 ) letter = 'A';
if (( n >= 80 ) && ( n < 90 )) letter = 'B';
```

which gives a `'B'` to an 89, or we'll have

```
if               ( n >= 90 ) letter = 'A';
if (( n >= 80 ) && ( n < 89 )) letter = 'B';
```

which gives no grade at all to an 89.

We want to avoid the redundancy that can complicate the maintenance phase of programming.

 Test your skill with Exercises 11–18 and 11–19.

11.13 Properties of a char

Is a char a Vowel?

In English, the letters are divided into vowels and consonants. In general, the vowels are a, e, i, o, and u, and the consonants are the remaining letters. This section will examine a predicate that reports whether a char is a vowel:

```
private static boolean isVowel ( char c )
```

We'll look at a variety of code that could flesh out the body of this method. Let's start with a simple boolean expression:

```
return c == 'a' || c == 'A' ||
       c == 'e' || c == 'E' ||
       c == 'i' || c == 'I' ||
       c == 'o' || c == 'O' ||
       c == 'u' || c == 'U';
```

The char is compared to all of the possible vowels, and the results are *or*-ed together. If c matches any vowel, then the expression will have the value true.

Note that we can't say the following:

```
c == 'a' || 'e' || 'i' || 'o' || 'u' ||
     'A' || 'E' || 'I' || 'O' || 'U';
```

because '||'—the logical *or* operator—can only take operands of type boolean. Phrases like 'a' || 'e' are not legal in Java.

We could write the isVowel method using if statements:

```
if ( c == 'a' ) return true;
if ( c == 'e' ) return true;
if ( c == 'i' ) return true;
if ( c == 'o' ) return true;
if ( c == 'u' ) return true;

if ( c == 'A' ) return true;
if ( c == 'E' ) return true;
if ( c == 'I' ) return true;
if ( c == 'O' ) return true;
if ( c == 'U' ) return true;

return false;
```

You should always put tests in a reasonable order. The following code is *not* acceptable:

```
if ( c == 'e' ) return true;
if ( c == 'o' ) return true;
if ( c == 'U' ) return true;
if ( c == 'A' ) return true;
if ( c == 'E' ) return true;
if ( c == 'I' ) return true;
if ( c == 'i' ) return true;
if ( c == 'a' ) return true;
if ( c == 'O' ) return true;
if ( c == 'u' ) return true;
return false;
```

A maintainer would go mad trying to find an underlying but nonexistent order.

Multiway branching is another way to write isVowel:

```
if        ( c == 'a' ) return true;
else if ( c == 'e' ) return true;
else if ( c == 'i' ) return true;
else if ( c == 'o' ) return true;
else if ( c == 'u' ) return true;
else if ( c == 'A' ) return true;
else if ( c == 'E' ) return true;
else if ( c == 'I' ) return true;
else if ( c == 'O' ) return true;
else if ( c == 'U' ) return true;
else                 return false;
```

However, note that if any condition is true, then we return out of the method and we don't do any tests further down. In this case, else buys us nothing.

Finally, we can use the indexOf method of class String to see whether char c is in a list of vowels:

```
return -1 != "aeiouAEIOU".indexOf(c);
```

Experienced programmers can always tell you several different ways to solve a problem, as they have seen and used more programming patterns than novices. For those of us in CS 1, it's always good practice to think of several ways to solve a single problem.

Is a char Uppercase?

Let's examine several ways to determine whether a given char is uppercase. The prototype will be:

```
private static boolean isUpperCase ( char c )
```

- From Chapter 4, we know about Strings and uppercase, so we could convert the char to a String and then test the String for uppercase:
  ```
  return (c + "").toUpperCase().equals(c + "");
  ```
  Or, if we don't want to do c + "" twice:
  ```
  String s = c + "";
  return s.toUpperCase().equals(s);
  ```
- Using a boolean expression, we could write:
  ```
  return ( c == 'A') || ( c == 'B') || ... ( c == 'Z');
  ```

However, as noted before, we *can't* write:

```
return c == 'A' || 'B' || ... || 'Z';
```

- Using if statements, we have:

```
if ( c == 'A' ) return true;
...
if ( c == 'Z' ) return true;
return false;
```

- Using relational operators, we have:

```
return 'A' <= c && c <= 'Z';
```

- Using indexOf, we have:

```
return -1 != "ABCDEFGHIJKLMNOPQRSTUVWXYZ".indexOf(c);
```

Study all of these methods until you understand them. Code and test each of these techniques. By practicing them now, they'll be easier to remember when you need them later on.

Challenge Yourself

This exercise presents a problem with many solutions. Your class or study group should divide into groups of four or less. Each group should tackle the problem and write its answer on a separate piece of paper. At the end of the exercise, everyone should review each of the solutions and comment on correctness and style.

Here's the problem: There are four diseases that can be diagnosed according to two symptoms. The diagnostic logic is given in Figure 11–6. Write the body of the method

```
public static String diagnose ( boolean s1, boolean s2 )
```

For example, diagnose(true,true) returns the String "d1".

Figure 11–6
Two Symptoms,
Four Diseases

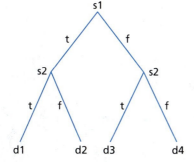

11.14 Nested `if`s and Dangling `else`s

This section investigates the interpretation of nested `if` statements and "ambiguous" `else` statements.

Use of unrestricted nested `if`s can lead to unreadable code. Consider the code

```
if (c1)
    if (c2) a1;
    else    a2;
```

where *c1* and *c2* are *conditions*, and *a1* and *a2* are *actions*. Because Java ignores white space outside of double quotes, this is the same as

```
if (c1)
    if (c2) a1;
else a2;
```

and is also the same as

```
if (c1) if (c2) a1; else a2;
```

Because we have an `if` statement inside an `if` statement, we have a situation called *nested `if`s*. The Java statement offers the possibility of an ambiguity: *to which `if` does the `else` belong?*

> **Dangling `else`** When an `else` clause appears to belong to several different `if`s.

There are two possibilities, illustrated in the flowcharts shown in Figure 11–7. In flowchart (a) the `else` belongs to the second `if`, and in flowchart (b) the `else` belongs to the first `if`. We call this situation a *dangling `else`*. Java resolves the dangling `else` by attaching it to the *closest* preceding `if`, that does not already have an `else`. Thus, our nested `if` statement is interpreted as (a) rather than (b), and the statement is interpreted as though it had been written as

```
if (c1) { if (c2) a1; else a2; }
```

instead of

```
if (c1) { if (c2) a1; } else a2;
```

 Test your skill with Exercise 11–20.

Figure 11–7
Disambiguating
Dangling else

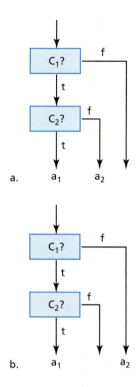

a.

b.

Nested ifs Can Be Hard to Understand

Prog1113.java presents a method mystery, which takes two ints and uses six ifs and six elses to compute and return an int in the set {1, 2, 3, 4, 5, 6, 7}. Here are typical questions we can ask about mystery:

- What value is returned for the call mystery(2,-9)?
- Give a value of m and a value of n such that mystery returns 5.

Code such as mystery is hard to understand, and the questions above are almost cruel. It's not good code. Some teachers—and many standardized tests—are keen on assigning problems such as mystery, I suspect due to ease of grading. I wish I could say that you will never see code like mystery in your professional life, but there is a lot of similar code out there. Perhaps skill at understanding such code is a reasonable measure of how well you'll do as a programmer.

Prog1113.java   mystery — Nested ifs Can Be Hard to Understand

```java
// Written by Barry Soroka
//
// Nested ifs can be hard to understand.
//
import java.io.*;
import java.util.Scanner;
////////////////////////////////////////////////////////////////////////////
class Prog1113
{
//-------------------------------------------------------------------------
    public static void main(String[] arg) throws Exception
    {
        Scanner kb = new Scanner(System.in);

        while ( true )
        {
            System.out.print("\nEnter m: ");
            int m = kb.nextInt();
            System.out.print("\nEnter n: ");
            int n = kb.nextInt();
            System.out.println("\nmystery(" + m + "," + n + ") = " + mystery(m,n));
        }
    }
//-------------------------------------------------------------------------
    private static int mystery ( int m, int n )
    {
        if ( m < 0 )
            if ( n < 5 )        return 1;
            else if ( n > 6 )   return 2;
                else            return 3;
        else if ( n > 8 )
                if ( m > 12 )   return 4;
                else            return 5;
        else if ( m > 20 )      return 6;
        else                    return 7;
    }
//-------------------------------------------------------------------------
} // end class Prog1113
////////////////////////////////////////////////////////////////////////////
```

➡ **Test your skill with Exercises 11–21 through 11–23.**

Humans Can't Process Deep Nesting

Nesting is a phenomenon of natural languages as well as computer languages. Consider the English sentence:

This is the dog that killed the cat.

This can be transformed into the equivalent:

This is the cat the dog killed.

That's easy to understand.

Let's add another relative clause to the sentence:

This is the dog that killed the cat that bit the rat.

That's equivalent to:

This is the rat the cat the dog killed bit.

This is just on the edge of understandability. Intoned correctly, it *can* be understood.

One more relative clause produces a comprehensible sentence:

This is the dog that killed the cat that bit the rat that ate the cheese.

The transformed sentence, although syntactically correct, cannot be understood:

This is the cheese the rat the cat the dog killed bit ate.

Progressions like these are used by linguists to demonstrate that humans depend on more than simple syntax to understand sentences. As programmers, we should learn the corresponding lesson: Just because a program compiles and runs correctly does not mean that humans will be able to easily comprehend it.

11.15 Stylistic Considerations

return **after** else

else is never needed directly after a return. The code

```
if ( cond ) return exp1;
else        return exp2;
```

is correct, but the reader may wonder if the writer understands the effect of `return`, or if something unusual is happening. This is better:

```
if ( cond ) return exp1;
return exp2;
```

if (cond == true)

You never need to test a boolean condition against `true` or `false`. The phrases

```
cond == true
```

and

```
cond == false
```

are never appropriate. Use the following guidelines:

Instead of writing this:	write this:
`if ( cond == true )`	`if ( cond )`
`if ( cond == false )`	`if ( !cond )`

For example,

Instead of writing this:	write this:
`if ( s1.equals(s2) == true )`	`if ( s1.equals(s2) )`
`if ( s1.equals(s2) == false )`	`if ( !s1.equals(s2) )`

boolean b = (cond == true);

Instead of writing this:	write this:
`boolean b = ( cond == true );`	`boolean b = cond;`
`boolean b = ( cond == false );`	`boolean b = !cond;`

```
if cond return true; else return false;
```

Instead of writing this:	write this:
if (*cond*) return true;	
else return false;	return *cond*;
if (*cond*) return false;	
else return true;	return !*cond*;

Alternative Code for the Predicate `even(int)`

The most direct code for the predicate `even` is this

```
public static boolean even ( int n )
{
   return 0 == n%2;
}
```

It didn't need `if` or `if-else`. Less direct is this

```
public static boolean even ( int n )
{
   if (0 == n%2) return true;
   else          return false;
}
```

which uses an `if-else` when none was needed. Another version is this

```
public static boolean even ( int n )
{
   if (0 == n%2) return true;
   return false;
}
```

which used the fact that we don't need an `else` after a `return`.

The preceding methods used the condition `0 == n%2` to detect divisibility by `2`. There's another technique you may sometimes encounter: The expression

```
n == 2*(n/2);
```

uses integer arithmetic to compute the same thing. Consider two cases, one even and one odd:

n	n/2	2*(n/2)	n == 2*(n/2)
6	3	6	true
5	2	4	false

If n is even, then n/2 is precisely half of n, and we get n back when we double it. If n is odd, then n/2 is *not* precisely half of n, and doubling it doesn't get n back for us. The formula n == 2*(n/2) is not as easy to read as the formula 0 == n%2, but it gives the same result.

11.16 An Improved toString for Class Complex

Recall the class Complex that we wrote in Chapter 7. We wrote a primitive toString method, which produced output of the form (0,0) and (0,5). In this section, we will improve the toString method so that we get output of the form 0 and 5i instead of (0,0) and (0,5). Before I present my version of the code, please solve Exercise 11–24.

 Test your skill with Exercise 11–24.

The Naïve Solution Doesn't Work

Consider the code

```
public String toString()
{
    return real + "+" + imag + "i";
}
```

which strings together the real part, a + sign, the imaginary part, and an i. This code fails on at least the following test cases:

real	imag	Result of Faulty toString	Should Be
3	-5	3+-5i	3-5i
3	1	3+1i	3+i
0	5	0+5i	5i
3	0	3+0i	3

We have to write something more complicated.

There are many ways to write toString correctly, but we will study the code presented in Prog1114.java.

Prog1114.java   Improved **toString** for Class **Complex**

```java
// Written by Barry Soroka
//
// Improved toString for class Complex.
//
import java.io.*;
import java.util.Scanner;
//////////////////////////////////////////////////////////////////////////
class Prog1114
{
//--------------------------------------------------------------------
    public static void main (String [] args) throws Exception
    {
        Scanner kb = new Scanner(System.in);

        while ( true )
        {
            System.out.println();
            Complex z = Complex.read(System.out,kb);
            System.out.println(z);
        }
    }
//--------------------------------------------------------------------
} // end class Prog1114
//////////////////////////////////////////////////////////////////////////
class Complex
{
    private int real;
    private int imag;
//--------------------------------------------------------------------
    public Complex ( int real, int imag )
    {
        this.real = real;
        this.imag = imag;
    }
//--------------------------------------------------------------------
    public static Complex read ( PrintStream ps, Scanner sc )
            throws Exception
```

```
      {
         if ( ps != null ) ps.println("Reading a complex number ...");
         if ( ps != null ) ps.print("Enter the real part:      ");
         int real = sc.nextInt();
         if ( ps != null ) ps.print("Enter the imaginary part: ");
         int imag = sc.nextInt();
         return new Complex ( real, imag );
      }
//------------------------------------------------------------------
   public String toString ()
      {
         if ( imag == 0 ) return real + "";

         String iString = Math.abs(imag) + "i";
         if ( Math.abs(imag) == 1 ) iString = "i";

         if ( real == 0 && imag > 0 ) return iString;
         if ( real == 0 && imag < 0 ) return "-" + iString;

         if ( imag > 0 ) return real + "+" + iString;

         return real + "-" + iString;
      }
//------------------------------------------------------------------
   public boolean equals ( Complex that )
      {
         return this.real == that.real
               &&
               this.imag == that.imag;
      }
//------------------------------------------------------------------
   public Complex add ( Complex z )
      {
         return new Complex ( real + z.real , imag + z.imag );
      }
//------------------------------------------------------------------
   public Complex sub ( Complex z )
      {
         return new Complex ( real - z.real , imag - z.imag );
      }
//------------------------------------------------------------------
   public Complex times ( Complex z )
```

```
{
    int a1 = real, b1 = imag;
    int a2 = z.real, b2 = z.imag;
    return new Complex ( a1*a2-b1*b2, a1*b2+a2*b1 );
}
//--------------------------------------------------------------
}
//////////////////////////////////////////////////////////////////////
```

We start with

```
if ( imag == 0 ) return real + "";
```

which handles the case where the number is purely real. Now the statements

```
String iString = Math.abs(imag) + "i";
if ( Math.abs(imag) == 1 ) iString = "i";
```

handle the case where imag is +1 or −1. In these cases, the 1 is omitted. We have also created iString, which represents the imaginary part of the Complex. We have 5i for both imag == 5 and imag == -5. We'll insert the proper sign in a later statement. Now we handle the case of purely imaginary numbers. We begin by printing iString with the appropriate sign:

```
if ( real == 0 && imag > 0 ) return iString;
if ( real == 0 && imag < 0 ) return "-" + iString;
```

At this point, we know that both real and imag are nonzero, so we need to print both of them using the appropriate sign:

```
if ( imag > 0 ) return real + "+" + iString;
return real + "-" + iString;
```

That completes my code for toString, but there are many other solutions to this problem. In general, we need to analyze the problem and locate the distinct cases involved. Then we write code to handle each of the cases. We test our code as we develop it, noting which cases the code handles correctly and which need further work.

11.17 The `switch` **Statement**

Java contains one more conditional statement: the `switch` statement. The `switch` statement is dangerous because it's much too easy to write code that compiles but isn't what you want. By the end of this section you'll see why it's so easy to misuse it.

The `switch` statement is like an alternative way to write a multiway branch with integer labels. Consider the following multiway branch:

```
if      ( n == 1 ) { s11; s12; }
else if ( n == 3 ) { s3; }
else if ( n == 0 ) { s01; s02; s03; }
else               { sA; sB; }
```

This is equivalent to the following `switch` statement:

```
switch (n)
{
    case 1 :  s11;
              s12;
              break;
    case 3 :  s3;
              break;
    case 0 :  s01;
              s02;
              s03;
              break;
    default : sA;
              sB;
}
```

Syntactically, the `switch` statement starts with an integer-valued expression that controls which actions are performed. In the preceding code that expression is n. A list of `cases` follows, each guarded by an integer value that is either a constant or a literal. Going down the list, the variable is compared to the value at each `case`. If the variable and the value match, then the actions in that `case` are performed. If `break` is encountered, then control leaves the `switch` statement. Otherwise, Java performs *all the actions in all the remaining cases* until we reach a `break` or we fall through the bottom of the `switch` statement. The keyword `default` matches any value, no two cases may have the same value, and the type of the variable can be any enumerated primitive type—byte, short, int, long, or char.

A case can be activated by multiple labels. The following code determines whether a given char is a vowel. Note that the case labels can be chars:

```java
public boolean isVowel ( char c )
{
    switch (c)
    {
        case 'a':
        case 'A':
        case 'e':
        case 'E':
        case 'i':
        case 'I':
        case 'o':
        case 'O':
        case 'u':
        case 'U':  return true;
        default:   return false;
    }
}
```

This is not the optimal code for the isVowel problem.

Let's look at some code that illustrates the dangers of the switch statement:

```java
switch ( n )
{
    case 1: System.out.println("action 1");
    case 2: System.out.println("action 2");
    case 3: System.out.println("action 3");
}
```

In this code, if n is 1, then the printout shows three actions:

```
action 1
action 2
action 3
```

If n is 2, then the printout shows two actions:

```
action 2
action 3
```

If n is 3, then the printout shows only one action:

```
action 3
```

In this code, control slides through all the actions from the point at which the variable matches the guard. There are situations when this sliding is appropriate and desired, but these situations are rare.

When writing code, if you forget a break in a switch statement, you may find your code executing many more statements than you intended. This is why the switch statement must be used with care.

As you move from language to language during your career, study carefully the switch statement or its equivalent. Language designers have been experimenting with guarded statements since Lisp in the 1950s, and constructs differ between languages.

11.18 GUI: Check Boxes and Three-Bit Integers

The application Prog1115.java uses JCheckBoxes. Each of these boxes can be either checked or unchecked (i.e., selected or not). The boxes are named b4, b2, and b1, and their labels are 4, 2, and 1, respectively. They correspond to the first three powers of 2: $2^0 = 1$, $2^1 = 2$, and $2^2 = 4$. An integer total is computed based on which boxes are checked, thus simulating a three-bit binary number. An ItemListener watches for checking and unchecking. The method itemStateChanged is called whenever the user checks or unchecks a box, at which time the number is recomputed based on which boxes are selected.

Prog1115.java   Check Boxes

```
// Written by Barry Soroka
//
// Tests check boxes -- binary to decimal.
//
import java.awt.*;
import java.awt.event.*;
import javax.swing.*;
/////////////////////////////////////////////////////////////////////////////
class Prog1115
{
//-------------------------------------------------------------------------
    public static void main (String[] args)
    {
        JFrame f = new JFrame("Binary numbers");
        f.setDefaultCloseOperation(JFrame.EXIT_ON_CLOSE);
```

```
      BinaryPanel bp = new BinaryPanel();

      f.getContentPane().add(bp);

      f.pack();
      f.setVisible(true);
   }
//-----------------------------------------------------------------------
} // end class Prog1115
/////////////////////////////////////////////////////////////////////////
class BinaryPanel extends JPanel
{
   private JLabel number, text;
   private JCheckBox b4, b2, b1;
   private int total;
//-----------------------------------------------------------------------
   public BinaryPanel()
   {
      total = 0;
      number = new JLabel(total+"");
      text = new JLabel(" in binary is ");
      b4 = new JCheckBox("4");
      b2 = new JCheckBox("2");
      b1 = new JCheckBox("1");

      BinaryPanelListener bpl = new BinaryPanelListener();
      b4.addItemListener(bpl);
      b2.addItemListener(bpl);
      b1.addItemListener(bpl);

      add(number);
      add(text);
      add(b4);
      add(b2);
      add(b1);

      setBackground(Color.YELLOW);
      setPreferredSize ( new Dimension(300,35) );
   }
//-----------------------------------------------------------------------
/////////////////////////////////////////////////////////////////////////
class BinaryPanelListener implements ItemListener
{
```

```
//----------------------------------------------------------------------
   public void itemStateChanged ( ItemEvent event )
   {
      total = 0;
      if ( b4.isSelected() ) total += 4;
      if ( b2.isSelected() ) total += 2;
      if ( b1.isSelected() ) total += 1;
      number.setText(total+"");
   }
//----------------------------------------------------------------------
} // end BinaryPanelListener
//////////////////////////////////////////////////////////////////////
} // end class BinaryPanel
//////////////////////////////////////////////////////////////////////
```

 Test your skill with Exercises 11–25 through 11–27.

11.19   GUI: Radio Buttons

The application Prog1116.java demonstrates radio buttons. These are button groups wherein only one button at a time can be selected, like those in car radios. In this program, the radio buttons choose between two Images: one of bacon and one of a cat named Sammy.

Prog1116.java   **Radio Buttons**

```
// Written by Barry Soroka
//
// Use radio buttons to display one of two jpeg images.
//
import java.awt.*;
import java.awt.event.*;
import javax.swing.*;
//////////////////////////////////////////////////////////////////////
class Prog1116
{
//----------------------------------------------------------------------
   public static void main (String[] args)
   {
      JFrame frame = new JFrame ("bacon v sammy");
      frame.setDefaultCloseOperation (JFrame.EXIT_ON_CLOSE);
```

```
      MyPanel mp = new MyPanel();

      frame.getContentPane().add(mp);
      frame.pack();
      frame.setVisible(true);
   }
//--------------------------------------------------------------------------
} // end class Prog1116
////////////////////////////////////////////////////////////////////////////
class MyPanel extends JPanel
{
   private Image image, imageBacon, imageSammy;
   private JRadioButton bacon, sammy;
//--------------------------------------------------------------------------
   public MyPanel()
   {
      setPreferredSize(new Dimension(400,300));
      imageBacon = new ImageIcon("bacon.jpg").getImage();
      imageSammy = new ImageIcon("sammy.jpg").getImage();
      image = imageBacon;

      bacon = new JRadioButton("bacon",true);
      sammy = new JRadioButton("sammy");
      ButtonGroup group = new ButtonGroup();
      group.add(bacon);
      group.add(sammy);

      RadioListener listener = new RadioListener();
      bacon.addActionListener(listener);
      sammy.addActionListener(listener);

      setBackground(Color.YELLOW);
      setPreferredSize ( new Dimension(425,325) );
      add(bacon);
      add(sammy);
   }
//--------------------------------------------------------------------------
   public void paintComponent ( Graphics page )
   {
      super.paintComponent(page);
      page.drawImage(image,50,50,this);
   }
//--------------------------------------------------------------------------
////////////////////////////////////////////////////////////////////////////
```

```
class RadioListener implements ActionListener
{
//----------------------------------------------------------------

   public void actionPerformed ( ActionEvent event )
   {
      Object source = event.getSource();
      if ( source == bacon ) image = imageBacon;
      else                   image = imageSammy;
      repaint();
   }
//----------------------------------------------------------------
} // end class RadioListener
/////////////////////////////////////////////////////////////////
} // end class MyPanel
/////////////////////////////////////////////////////////////////
```

We create two JRadioButtons—bacon and sammy—and add them to a But-tonGroup. We add an ActionListener to each button, and we add the buttons to a JPanel. The actionPerformed method is invoked whenever a button is clicked, and we use the source of the event to set image to be one of the two Images. When repaint is called, the appropriate Image is drawn on the screen.

Test your skill with Exercise 11–28.

Chapter Summary

- Until now, all our code has been straight-line—all statements were executed, one after another.
- Conditional statements permit code to be executed only in certain situations.
- Constructors must validate their parameters before assigning them to instance variables.
- Flowcharts are graphical representations of the flow of control through state-ments in a program.
- An if statement contains a boolean condition, which guards the execution of another statement.
- We can throw an Error to abort program execution.
- There's no need to prompt when values are read from a file.
- static read methods omit prompts when the PrintStream argument is null.
- Several techniques can be used to convert a char from lowercase to uppercase.

- Computing pay with overtime is a classic problem that can be solved with conditional statements.
- We can't end a non-`void` method with an `if` statement, because the compiler must be certain that a value is being returned from the method.
- The `if-else` construct allows control to pass to one or the other of two groups of statements.
- Multiway branching is a structured way of using `if-else` statements to select from a variety of alternative statements.
- Several techniques can be used to determine whether a given `char` is a vowel or is uppercase.
- When `if`s are nested, a dangling `else` is always grouped with the closest `if`.
- Nested `if` statements can be hard to understand.
- A variety of stylistic considerations can make `if-else` statements easier to understand.
- The `switch` statement allows an integer variable to select an action from a set of alternative statements.
- GUI check boxes allow the user to make binary selections.
- GUI radio buttons allow the user to make a single selection from a variety of alternatives.

Terminology Introduced in This Chapter

condition	dangling `else`	multiway branching
conditional execution	flowchart	nested `if`
conditional statement	guard	straight-line code
constant	magic number	validation

Exercises

Exercise 11–1. For each of the classes that follow, identify illegal or inappropriate values. Each class has been defined earlier in the book, either in the text itself or in the exercises.

a) `Animal`
b) `Complex`
c) `EggShipment`
d) `Fraction`
e) `Linear`
f) `Person`

g) Rectangle
h) Student
i) Teacher
j) UKMoney
k) Vector3

Exercise 11–2. Modify the following classes so that they throw an Error if the specified illegal condition occurs. Your Error should contain a descriptive String. Write a driver that causes the Error to occur.

a) Class Animal if the name is the empty String
b) Class Fraction if the denominator is 0
c) Class Rectangle if either length or width is set to a nonpositive value.

Exercise 11–3. Suppose a program has declarations

```
int n;
String s1, s2;
double x, y;
```

Give the if statement that writes "sweet" if each of the following conditions is met:

a) n is positive
b) n is in the range [2,10]
c) n is not in the range [2,10]
d) s1 occurs anywhere in s2
e) s1 is a prefix of s2
f) x is within 0.001 of y
g) x*y > 5.0
h) x*y > 5.0 and x is positive
i) x is positive and y is negative
j) n is not greater than x

Exercise 11–4. Modify class Fraction so that if the denominator ever becomes 0, then a message is printed to the user and the Fraction is set to 0/1. This condition can occur in the constructor or in the method div. Write a driver that triggers this condition.

Exercise 11–5. Modify class Rectangle so that if either length or width ever becomes 0 or negative, then a message is printed to the user and the offending dimensions are set to 1. This condition can occur in the constructor or in the method shrink. Write a driver that triggers this condition.

Exercise 11–6. Write a program that reads two integers and prints them out in ascending order. Use `if`.

Exercise 11–7. Some people believe that, for a `Rectangle`, the width must never be greater than the length. Modify the constructor of class `Rectangle` so that if the incoming `width >` `length`, then the instance variables will be assigned so that `length` gets the larger value.

Exercise 11–8. Write a main method that does each of the following:

- Reads an integer from the command line.
- If the integer is greater than 2, the method prints its square to a new file named `square`.
- If the integer is less than 2, the method prints its cube to the monitor.
- If the integer is 2, the method does both.

Produce hardcopy that demonstrates that your code works properly. Use the `if` statement.

Exercise 11–9. Modify the `read` method of class `Animal` so that sending `null` as the `PrintStream` parameter causes the omission of prompts. Write a driver and produce hardcopy that demonstrates that your code works properly.

Exercise 11–10. Modify the `read` method of class `EggShipment` so that sending `null` as the `PrintStream` parameter causes the omission of prompts. Write a driver that reads the name of a file containing `EggShipments`. Read and sum the first three `EggShipments` in the file.

Exercise 11–11. Modify the `read` method of class `Fraction` so that sending `null` as the `PrintStream` parameter causes the omission of prompts. Write a driver that reads the name of a file containing `Fractions`. Read and sum the first three `Fractions` in the file.

Exercise 11–12. Implement one of the `toUpperCase` methods described in Section 11.13. Write a driver that repeatedly requests `chars` from the user and prints them out in uppercase. Select test cases that show that your `toUpperCase` behaves properly.

Exercise 11–13. Write a program that computes `Employees`' pay based on the following formula:

- Employees are paid at their normal rate up to and including 40 hours per week.
- Hours past 40 but below 50 in a given week are paid at 150% of the normal rate.
- Hours past 50 in a given week are paid at 200% of the normal rate.

Exercise 11–14.   Write a program that computes Employees' pay based on the following formula:

- Overtime is always based on a window of two weeks.
- Hours past 80 in any two-week period are paid at 150% of the normal rate.

This problem requires that each Employee object remember the number of hours worked in the previous week. (What is a reasonable *initial* value for this instance variable?)

Exercise 11–15.   Write a class MyMath that contains a static method signum, which takes an int and returns one of three Strings—positive, zero, or negative—as appropriate. Write a driver that repeatedly reads ints from the user, passes them to signum, and prints the result.

Exercise 11–16.   Write the Java code for a class Student, which represents students in a class with three exams. Each object of the class Student has four instance variables:

- name of type String
- ex1Grade of type int
- ex2Grade of type int
- ex3Grade of type int

To begin, provide a constructor. Initially, a Student's exam grades should be zero. Second, provide a method setExamGrade. This method should take two parameters—an exam number and a grade, both ints—and set the appropriate exam grade. The method should do the following:

- If an illegal exam number is given, then reject the request and print an appropriate message.
- Require that exam grades be in the range [0,100].
- If a negative grade is encountered, then change it to 0 and print an appropriate message.
- If a grade above 100 is encountered, then change it to 100 and print an appropriate message.

Third, provide a method grade, which returns the average of a Student's three exam grades. This result should be a double. The exams have equal weight.
Finally, write a driver that demonstrates your compliance with the specifications above.

Exercise 11–17. Write a class `Student` that contains two instance variables—a `String name` and an `int age`. Include the following methods:

- A constructor of two arguments. If the `age` is negative, then print a message and change the `age` to 5.
- A method `canDrink` which, when applied to a `Student`, returns `true` or `false` depending on whether or not the `Student`'s age is 21 or above.
- A method `gradeLevel` which, when applied to a `Student`, returns the integer school grade level of the `Student` according to the following chart:

Age	≤5	6	7	8	9	10	11	12	13	14	15	16	17	≥18
Grade	0	1	2	3	4	5	6	7	8	9	10	11	12	99

Write a driver that repeatedly (1) reads a `Student`, (2) prints whether the `Student` has reached the legal drinking age, and (3) prints the `Student`'s appropriate school grade level. Select appropriate test cases.

Exercise 11–18. Lobsters are graded according to the following table:

Weight (oz.)	Grade
0–3	C
4–10	B
11–14	A
≥ 15	AA

Using multiway branching, write the code that reads a weight and prints out the corresponding grade.

Exercise 11–19. Boxers are divided into categories according to the following table of weights (in pounds):

Class	Weight(lbs.)
Heavyweight	> 190
Middleweight	≥ 154
Welterweight	≥ 140
Lightweight	≥ 130
Featherweight	≥ 122
Bantamweight	≥ 112
Flyweight	< 112

Using multiway branching, write the code that reads a weight and prints out the corresponding category.

Exercise 11–20. Write and run a program that demonstrates that Java resolves the dangling `else` problem in Section 11.14.

Exercise 11–21. Give the value of method `mystery` for each of the following parameters.

m	n	mystery(m, n)
-5	37	
0	0	
65	18	
1	9	
13	6	
7	5	
-5	5	
0	20	
13	9	
-5	-5	
65	0	

Exercise 11–22. Under what conditions of m and n does `mystery(m,n)` yield the following values?

	Conditions of m and n for which mystery(m, n) gives the value on the left
1	
2	
3	
4	
5	
6	
7	

Note: It is possible that some of these values cannot be reached! Consider the simple example

```
if ( n > 0 )
    if ( n < 0 ) return 8;
...
```

for which `return 8` cannot be reached.

Exercise 11–23. Give a set of values for m and n that causes `mystery(m,n)` to yield the value in the right column.

```
m       n       mystery(m, n)
                1
                2
                3
                4
                5
                6
                7
```

Exercise 11–24. Improve the `toString` method of the class `Complex` to generate code that obeys the rules illustrated in the following table:

real	imag	Result of `toString`
0	0	0
0	5	5i
3	0	3
3	5	3+5i
3	-5	3-5i
0	-5	-5i
3	1	3+i
3	-1	3-i
0	1	i
0	-1	-i

Test your code against the cases given in the table.

Exercise 11–25. Modify `Prog1115` to use *four* bits, thus producing integers in the range [0, 15].

Exercise 11–26. Write an application that has three check boxes—`big`, `red`, and `closed`—and that produces a sentence based on which buttons are selected.

Buttons Selected	Sentence Displayed
None	The door is open.
closed	The door is closed.
red	The red door is open.
red, closed	The red door is closed.
big	The big door is open.
big, closed	The big door is closed.
big, red	The big red door is open.
big, red, closed	The big red door is closed.

Exercise 11–27. Add a `plural` check box to the application in the previous exercise, which makes the sentence use the plural `doors` instead of the singular `door`. Thus, if the boxes `big`, `red`, `plural`, and `closed` are all selected, then the following sentence would be displayed: `The big red doors are closed.`

Exercise 11–28. Modify `Prog1116` so that radio buttons select one of two *shapes*—circle or square—and one of three *colors*—red, green, or blue. Draw the selected shape in the selected color on a white background.

Exercise 11–29. Consider class `ZooShipment`, which models shipments of animals. A `ZooShipment` is characterized by a `quantity` and a `species`. The `quantity` is an `int` and the `species` is a `String`.

The `quantity` cannot be negative. If it is, then write a message to the user and change the `quantity` to 0.

The behavior of the `toString` method is illustrated in the following table:

quantity	species	`toString()` returns
0	dog	no dogs
1	dog	a dog
2	dog	2 dogs
0	elephant	no elephants
1	elephant	an elephant
8	elephant	8 elephants
0	sheep	no sheep
1	sheep	a sheep
3	sheep	3 sheep

Many different conditions determine the result of `toString`. The `quantity` determines two things:

- which adjective will be at the front of the result: `"a"`, `"no"`, or a number;
- whether the singular or plural form of the `species` is used.

If the `quantity` is 1, then the first letter of the `species` determines whether `"a"` or `"an"` will be the adjective:

- `"an"` is used if the `species` begins with a vowel.
- `"a"` is used otherwise.

You may want to write helper methods such as

```
public static boolean beginsWithVowel(String)
```

and

```
public static boolean isVowel(char)
```

Most `species` are made plural by adding `"s"`, as in `lion-lions`, but there are many special cases. Your code must handle the following special singular–plural forms: `sheep-sheep`, `mouse-mice`, `ox-oxen`, and `goose-geese`. (We'll ignore other special cases.)

Test your code on all of the cases given in the preceding table.

You should facilitate the addition of new irregular plurals, keeping in mind that adding a new singular–plural pair should require as little new code as possible.

Your class `ZooShipment` should easily accommodate the addition of further methods. Typical methods to add would be:

- `public void increment()`—Adds one animal to the receiving `ZooShipment`.
- `public ZooShipment add(ZooShipment)`—Returns the result of adding animals to a `ZooShipment`. The program throws an `Error` if the `species` are not the same in the receiving and parameter `ZooShipment`s.
- `public double computeValue(double)`—The parameter is the price per animal.

Exercise 11–30[3] Consider class `Fraction` with integer instance variables `num` and `den`, which represent the numerator and denominator, respectively, of a fraction. When constructed, a `Fraction` is put into a *normal form* with the following specifications:

- The numerator and denominator must not have any common divisors. The following code computes the greatest common divisor (`gcd`) of two positive integers. (*Note:* The algorithm will not work if either argument is negative or 0.) In order to reduce a fraction to lowest terms, you should divide both the numerator and denominator by their `gcd`. Copy this code exactly:

```
//---------------------------------------------------------------
// Computes and returns the greatest common divisor of the two
// positive parameters. Uses Euclid's algorithm.
//---------------------------------------------------------------
```

---

[3] This exercise requests a `Fraction` class, which is an improvement over the class we wrote in Chapter 7.

```
private int gcd (int num1, int num2)
{
   while (num1 != num2)
      if (num1 > num2)
         num1 = num1 - num2;
      else
         num2 = num2 - num1;
   return num1;
}
```

- Fractions never have 0 in the denominator. If such a Fraction is about to be constructed, the constructor prints a warning message and changes the fraction to 0/1.
- Negative signs, if any, should appear only in the numerator. Thus, -1/2 is acceptable, but 1/-2 is not.
- Anything with 0 in the numerator and nonzero denominator, (such as, 0/-1 or 0/2) should reduce to 0/1.

These rules define a *normal form* or *canonical form*. This means that every fraction becomes a unique Fraction, and equality is easy to determine. For example, Fraction(2,3) and Fraction(4,6) produce the same Fraction with numerator 2 and denominator 3.

For this exercise you should:

a)   Write the code for class Fraction.
b)   Provide a two-argument constructor.
c)   Implement a public method toString that returns a String representation of a Fraction, such as "-2/3".

Fractions should *always* be normalized, from the moment they are constructed. Don't wait until printing to do the normalization.

Your Fraction class must include a static read method that takes two arguments—a PrintStream and a Scanner—and that prompts the user to enter the numerator and denominator of a Fraction. The method read *returns* the created Fraction. If the PrintStream is null, then you should not prompt; doing so indicates that the data is coming from a file or some other noninteractive source.

Your code must run with driver Prog1117.java. Here is some typical behavior:

```
G:\>java Prog1117

Reading a fraction ...
Enter numerator:   2
Enter denominator: 4
```

```
                          That fraction is: 1/2

                          Reading a fraction ...
                          Enter numerator:   -2
                          Enter denominator: -3
                          That fraction is: 2/3

                          Reading a fraction ...
                          Enter numerator:   0
                          Enter denominator: 17
                          That fraction is: 0/1
                          ...
```

Prog1117.java   **Driver for Class Fraction**

```java
// Written by Barry Soroka
//
// Driver for class Fraction.  Includes code for gcd.
//
import java.io.*;
import java.util.Scanner;
/////////////////////////////////////////////////////////////////////////////////
class Prog1117
{
//-------------------------------------------------------------------------------

   public static void main (String [] args) throws Exception
   {
       Scanner kb = new Scanner(System.in);

       while ( true )
       {
          System.out.println();
          Fraction f = Fraction.read(System.out,kb);
          System.out.println("That fraction is: " + f);
       }
   }
//-------------------------------------------------------------------------------
//  Computes and returns the greatest common divisor of the two
//  positive parameters. Uses Euclid's algorithm.
//
   private int gcd (int num1, int num2)
   {
      while (num1 != num2)
         if (num1 > num2)
            num1 = num1 - num2;
```

```
        else
            num2 = num2 - num1;
        return num1;
    }
//------------------------------------------------------------------------
} // end class Prog1117
/////////////////////////////////////////////////////////////////////////
```

Exercise 11–31. Implement and test methods `add`, `sub`, `mul`, and `div` for class `Fraction`.

CHAPTER TWELVE

Testing, Coding, and Debugging

Chapter Objectives

- Appreciate the need to test software thoroughly.
- Select appropriate test cases.
- Understand regression testing.
- Learn alternative methods of testing software.
- Learn tips for coding and debugging software.
- Report software glitches responsibly.
- Use style sheets to make programs more readable.

We're now at the midpoint of the text. You've learned how to define and use classes. You've learned about Java's primitive data types. In the chapters ahead, you'll learn how to process *collections* of objects—files and arrays.

At this point, let's take a breather to think about how to test our code. Also, because our programs are becoming more complicated, this chapter includes some advice about coding and debugging. You wouldn't have appreciated this advice any earlier in the course.

12.1 Why We Test

Faulty software can cause considerable damage. Two trains can be put on the same track, in danger of having a head-on collision. A hospital patient can be given the wrong medication, or the wrong dose of the right medication. A customer's credit limit can be accidentally set to zero.

Programs can kill. Consider the Therac-25 radiation therapy machine.[1] Under a particular set of conditions, it delivered a damaging or fatal dose of radiation to the patient. No one had ever anticipated or tested the particular conditions under which the Therac-25 changed from a tool of healing to a lethal weapon. A bug in the software cost the health and lives of half a dozen people.

The goal of testing is to verify that software performs according to its specifications. Given the ubiquity of software, testing justifies a major expense in the software development life cycle.

12.2 Select Test Cases *Before* You Write the Code

If you don't know your goals,
how will you know if you've achieved them?

Before you begin writing the code for a task, you should create a list of test cases and expected results. You want these test cases to touch a large subspace of possible inputs, and you want it to trigger a large subspace of statements firing within the program.

Ask others to look at your list of test cases. All of us have blind spots, especially when it comes to our own work. For example, in a numeric program, we might accidentally have restricted our test cases to *positive* numbers or *even* numbers. In a program that works with `String`s, we might have forgotten the following cases:

- An empty `String` as input for a name.
- A very long `String` that might bomb our code.[2]

It's possible for code to pass the tests *we've* written, but not those that a stranger would select.

Our code will almost certainly pass our own test cases—after all, those are the tests it must pass before we pronounce it suitable for others to use! But the same code that passes all of *our* tests may fail the first test handed it by a stranger. You will probably see this happen before we reach the end of CS 1.

---

[1] Nancy G Leveson & Clark S Turner. An investigation of the Therac-25 accidents. *Computer* 26(7):18-41, July 1993.

[2] This is the famous *buffer overflow problem*, which has enabled many viruses and worms to enter Unix systems. Unlike C and C++, Java does *not* permit buffer overflow.

It is common industrial practice to name a coding group and a corresponding *testing group* for a problem. These two groups work in parallel, and the job of the testers is to verify that the software meets its specifications without unexpected behavior. Indeed, your first industrial job after graduation may be in testing rather than in coding.

12.3   Selecting Good Test Cases

This section presents some rules-of-thumb for selecting test cases.

Decision Points and Cases in All Ranges

Recall the example involving *temperature* in Section 11.6, where a given `int` would be reported as one of {`too cold`, `ok`, `too hot`}. Suppose the dividing lines are `75` and `80`. We should test `75` and `80` because they are *boundary points* or *decision points*.

To do this, we should test something in each range. The set {60, 78, 82} has one point in each range. Some programmers like to test the integer values on both sides of the decision points; that would give the test set {74, 76, 79, 81}. Including the decision points in this set gives {74, 75, 76, 79, 80, 81}.

Test your skill with Exercise 12–1.

Extreme Values

Test the empty `String` for a program that reads names and such. For integers, test `0` and test a negative number. If a method takes an *object* as a parameter, try sending `null` to the method as that parameter.

Test All Regions of the Space of Cases

We can't test *all* possible cases, because the number of cases is practically infinite. However, we should attempt to *partition* the space of inputs into disjoint regions containing similar cases.

Consider class `Complex`. The following cases touch each test region of the `toString` method:

real	imag	Result of `toString()`
0	0	0
0	5	5i
3	0	3
3	5	3+5i
3	-5	3-5i
0	-5	-5i
3	1	3+i
3	-1	3-i
0	1	i
0	-1	-i

 Test your skill with Exercises 12–2 and 12–3.

Invalid Values

Objects represent things we encounter in the real world, and often we must write code to prevent objects from representing the impossible.

For a `Student`, the `age` may not be negative, and the `name` cannot be an arbitrary `String`, but must obey certain rules; for example, the empty `String` is not a valid `name`, and a `name` cannot contain digits.[3]

For a `Circle`, the `radius` cannot be negative. For a `Person`, with slots for `age` and `mother`, we must ensure that the `age` of the `Person` is less than the `age` of the `mother`.

 Test your skill with Exercise 12–4.

Beware of Inadequate Testing

Suppose you hire two classmates to write code for the function $f(x) = x^2$, but they accidentally program it as $f(x) = 2x$. If you test only the cases $x = 0$ and $x = 2$, you will pronounce their code correct even though it's not. It's important to use a wide range of disparate test cases when checking a program.

 Test your skill with Exercises 12–5 and 12–6.

---

[3] Note that some names contain *punctuation*, such as `O'Leary`.

12.4   Regression Testing

In Section 12.3, we discussed how to select test cases that give us confidence that our code is working correctly. In the next section we'll begin a study of several methods for using test cases so that we can compare *expected* output with *actual* output. Finally, we will assemble our choices into a regimen known as *regression testing*: Every time the implementation changes, we run the same set of test cases and we require that their output be the same as before.

> **Regression testing**   Running the same comprehensive test suite every time a given module is altered.

12.5   Testing Alternatives

Testing involves two activities:

- Entering data for a test case.
- Checking the output to see if it matches our expectations.

This structure allows for alternatives at several points:

- How will the data be entered?
- How will the output be checked?
- How will the results be reported?

In Section 12-3, we presented a minimal set of cases that exercised all aspects of the toString method of class Complex. In Sections 12.6 through 12.11 we will use various drivers to run these test cases against proposed implementations of Complex. For each approach, I will present the code for testing regardless of whether the toString method correctly handles the situations touched by the test cases. The exercises will then ask you to implement similar code for testing the classes Fraction and ZooShipment.

Class Complex

Prog1201 contains the code we'll be using as a correct implementation of class Complex. You will want to modify this code to obtain another version that compiles correctly, but which is logically flawed. Both the correct and flawed versions of Complex should contain the following methods:

- public Complex(int,int)—accepts the real and imaginary parts of a Complex.
- public String toString()—returns a String version of a Complex object. This should be the "improved" toString method developed in Chapter 11.
- public static Complex read(PrintStream,Scanner)—the standard static read method.

Prog1201.java   Class **Complex**

```
// Written by Barry Soroka
//
// Prog1201 -- class Complex
//
import java.io.*;
import java.util.Scanner;
/////////////////////////////////////////////////////////////////////////////
class Complex
{
   private int real;
   private int imag;
//------------------------------------------------------------------
   public Complex ( int real, int imag )
   {
      this.real = real;
      this.imag = imag;
   }
//------------------------------------------------------------------
   public static Complex read ( PrintStream ps, Scanner sc )
         throws Exception
   {
      if ( ps != null ) ps.println("Reading a complex number ...");
      if ( ps != null ) ps.print("Enter the real part:      ");
      int real = sc.nextInt();
      if ( ps != null ) ps.print("Enter the imaginary part: ");
      int imag = sc.nextInt();
      return new Complex ( real, imag );
   }
//------------------------------------------------------------------
   public String toString ()
   {
      if ( imag == 0 ) return real + "";
```

```
         String iString = Math.abs(imag) + "i";
         if ( Math.abs(imag) == 1 ) iString = "i";

         if ( real == 0 && imag > 0 ) return iString;
         if ( real == 0 && imag < 0 ) return "-" + iString;

         if ( imag > 0 ) return real + "+" + iString;

         return real + "-" + iString;
      }
//-------------------------------------------------------------
   public boolean equals ( Complex that )
   {
      return this.real == that.real
            &&
            this.imag == that.imag;
   }
//-------------------------------------------------------------
   public Complex add ( Complex z )
   {
      return new Complex ( real + z.real , imag + z.imag );
   }
//-------------------------------------------------------------
   public Complex sub ( Complex z )
   {
      return new Complex ( real - z.real , imag - z.imag );
   }
//-------------------------------------------------------------
   public Complex times ( Complex z )
   {
      int a1 = real, b1 = imag;
      int a2 = z.real, b2 = z.imag;
      return new Complex ( a1*a2-b1*b2, a1*b2+a2*b1 );
   }
//-------------------------------------------------------------
}
/////////////////////////////////////////////////////////////////////
```

We will be testing the toString method of class Complex. The flawed code should contain an incorrect version of toString.

 Test your skill with Exercise 12–7.

12.6 Type in Test Cases: Visually Check the Outputs

Prog1202 uses the methods read and toString in the simplest test driver: an infinite loop that repeatedly reads a Complex and then prints it out. Working down the list of test cases, the user types in each test case and then checks the *observed* output against the *expected* output.

Prog1202.java　Type in Test Cases: Visually Check the Output

```java
// Written by Barry Soroka
//
// Tests method toString of class Complex.
// Type in test cases.
// Visually check output.
//
import java.io.*;
import java.util.Scanner;
/////////////////////////////////////////////////////////////////////////////
class Prog1202
{
//-------------------------------------------------------------------------
    public static void main (String [] args) throws Exception
    {
        Scanner kb = new Scanner(System.in);

        while ( true )
        {
            System.out.println();
            Complex z = Complex.read(System.out,kb);
            System.out.println(z);
        }
    }
//-------------------------------------------------------------------------
} // end class Prog1202
/////////////////////////////////////////////////////////////////////////////
class Complex
{
// Same code as Prog1201
}
/////////////////////////////////////////////////////////////////////////////
```

There are two disadvantages to this approach. The first is that on the *input* side, the user has to type in the real and imaginary parts of every tested

`Complex` number every time the code is modified. So, for example, we might encounter the following testing behavior:

Type in case #1. Observe correct output.

Type in case #2. Observe correct output.

Type in case #3. Observe *incorrect* output.

Edit the code in hopes of fixing the error.

Run the modified program.

Now we have to type in the test cases starting at the beginning again. Every time you modify code, you have the upside that some of the cases that failed before will now *pass*, but you worry about the downside that some of the cases that passed before will now *fail*. So the naïve test driver will cause us a lot of typing!

A second disadvantage involves the *output* side of testing. We have to use our imperfect human visual system to determine whether a printed output matches the result we expect and require. The human visual system is subject to fatigue; sometimes we see things that *aren't* there, and sometimes we miss things that *are* there. In Section 12.9 we will see how to enlist the computer's near-perfect powers of comparison.

Test your skill with Exercises 12–8 through 12–10.

12.7 Driver Contains Inputs: Visually Check the Outputs

We can improve the testing scheme of Section 12.6 by building the test cases right into a test driver. We won't have to type in each test case when we need to test a new implementation of class `Complex`. `Prog1203` gives the code.

Prog1203.java   **Driver Contains Test Cases: Visually Check the Output**

```
// Written by Barry Soroka
//
// Tests method toString of class Complex.
// Driver contains the test cases.
// Visually check output.
//
import java.io.*;
import java.util.Scanner;
////////////////////////////////////////////////////////////////////////////
class Prog1203
{
```

```
//---------------------------------------------------------------
    public static void main (String [] args) throws Exception
    {
        testToString1(0,0);
        testToString1(0,5);
        testToString1(3,0);
        testToString1(3,5);
        testToString1(3,-5);
        testToString1(0,-5);
        testToString1(3,1);
        testToString1(3,-1);
        testToString1(0,1);
        testToString1(0,-1);
    }
//---------------------------------------------------------------
    private static void testToString1 ( int real, int imag )
    {
        System.out.println(real + "\t" +
                            imag + "\t" +
                            (new Complex(real,imag)));
    }
//---------------------------------------------------------------
} // end class Prog1203
////////////////////////////////////////////////////////////////
class Complex
{
// Same code as Prog1201
}
////////////////////////////////////////////////////////////////
```

Notice that each test case is entered as a brief invocation of the `test` method

```
testToString1(0,0);
testToString1(0,5);
testToString1(3,0);
testToString1(3,5);
testToString1(3,-5);
    . . .
```

Adding, deleting, or modifying a test case involves minimal typing. The code for the `testToString1` method uses the obvious statement for printing felicitous output lines. Here's the output from the full set of tests:

0	0	0
0	5	5i
3	0	3
3	5	3+5i
3	-5	3-5i
0	-5	-5i
3	1	3+i
3	-1	3-i
0	1	i
0	-1	-i

We can verify our code by checking each actual output against the expected output.

Note that our testing is still onerous because we must visually compare each actual output against the expected output. Moreover, in order to determine whether each test was satisfied, we need to consult a table of expected outputs.

Test your skill with Exercises 12–11 through 12–13.

12.8   Driver Contains I/O: Visually Check

Prog1204 shows the next stage in testing: The driver contains both the inputs and the expected result of each test case. This obviates the need to have a separate table of inputs and expected outputs. Notice how the method test-ToString1 takes *three* parameters:

1. The real part of the Complex being tested.
2. The imaginary part of the Complex being tested.
3. A String expected, which is the expected result of toString for the following case.

Prog1204.java   Driver Contains Input and Expected Output: Visually Check

```
// Written by Barry Soroka
//
// Tests method toString of class Complex.
// Driver contains input & expected output.
// Visually check output.
//
import java.io.*;
```

```java
import java.util.Scanner;
/////////////////////////////////////////////////////////////////////////////
class Prog1204
{
//---------------------------------------------------------------------------
    public static void main (String [] args) throws Exception
    {
        System.out.println("\nreal\timag\texp\tactual");
        testToString(0,0,"0");
        testToString(0,5,"5i");
        testToString(3,0,"3");
        testToString(3,5,"3+5i");
        testToString(3,-5,"3-5i");
        testToString(0,-5,"-5i");
        testToString(3,1,"3+i");
        testToString(3,-1,"3-i");
        testToString(0,1,"i");
        testToString(0,-1,"-i");
    }
//---------------------------------------------------------------------------
    private static void testToString ( int real, int imag, String expected )
    {
        System.out.println(real + "\t" +
                           imag + "\t" +
                           expected + "\t" +
                           (new Complex(real,imag)));
    }
//---------------------------------------------------------------------------
} // end class Prog1204
/////////////////////////////////////////////////////////////////////////////
class Complex
{
// Same code as Prog1201
}
/////////////////////////////////////////////////////////////////////////////
```

As before, the driver consists of a list of test cases:

```java
testToString(0,0,"0");
testToString(0,5,"5i");
testToString(3,0,"3");
testToString(3,5,"3+5i");
testToString(3,-5,"3-5i");
...
```

The output looks like this:

```
real    imag    exp      actual
0       0       0        0
0       5       5i       5i
3       0       3        3
3       5       3+5i     3+5i
3       -5      3-5i     3-5i
0       -5      -5i      -5i
3       1       3+i      3+i
3       -1      3-i      3-i
0       1       i        i
0       -1      -i       -i
```

In order to verify each test case, we need only compare the entries in the third and fourth columns; there's no need for a separate table of expected outputs.

Test your skill with Exercises 12–14 through 12–16.

12.9   Driver Contains I/O: Automatically Check

Now that the driver has both the expected and actual values available, we can automate the comparison of the two Strings. Prog1205 gives the code. Note how the expression expected.equals(actual) checks the two Strings for equality. The hardcopy looks like this:

```
Complex(0,0)     should be 0      is 0     OK
Complex(0,5)     should be 5i     is 5i    OK
Complex(3,0)     should be 3      is 3     OK
Complex(3,5)     should be 3+5i   is 3+5i  OK
Complex(3,-5)    should be 3-5i   is 3-5i  OK
Complex(0,-5)    should be -5i    is -5i   OK
Complex(3,1)     should be 3+i    is 3+i   OK
Complex(3,-1)    should be 3-i    is 3-i   OK
Complex(0,1)     should be i      is i     OK
Complex(0,-1)    should be -i     is -i    OK
```

If the actual value ever differs from the expected value, then the tag *** FAILURE *** will signal the mismatch.

Prog1205.java   **Driver Contains Input and Expected Output: Automatic Check**

```java
// Written by Barry Soroka
//
// Tests method toString of class Complex.
// Driver contains input & expected output.
// Automatically check expected & actual output.
//
import java.io.*;
import java.util.Scanner;
/////////////////////////////////////////////////////////////////////////////
class Prog1205
{
//----------------------------------------------------------------------------
   public static void main (String [] args) throws Exception
   {
      testToString(0,0,"0");
      testToString(0,5,"5i");
      testToString(3,0,"3");
      testToString(3,5,"3+5i");
      testToString(3,-5,"3-5i");
      testToString(0,-5,"-5i");
      testToString(3,1,"3+i");
      testToString(3,-1,"3-i");
      testToString(0,1,"i");
      testToString(0,-1,"-i");
   }
//----------------------------------------------------------------------------
   private static void testToString ( int real, int imag, String expected )
   {
      String actual = (new Complex(real,imag)).toString();

      String tag;
      if ( expected.equals(actual) ) tag = "OK";
      else                           tag = "*** FAILURE *** ";

      System.out.println("Complex(" +
                         real + "," +
                         imag + ")\tshould be " +
                         expected + "\tis " +
                         actual + "\t" +
                         tag);
```

```
    }
//- - - - - - - - - - - - - - - - - - - - - - - - - - - - - - - - - - - - - - - - - - - - - -
} // end class Prog1205
//////////////////////////////////////////////////////////////////////////////
class Complex
{
// Same code as Prog1201
}
//////////////////////////////////////////////////////////////////////////////
```

Test your skill with Exercises 12–17 through 12–19.

12.10   Reporting Options

Given a set of test cases, there are three ways to approach reporting the results of our tests:

1. Just print a single yes or no depending on whether our code for Complex meets the specifications. This approach is acceptable when the answer is yes, but it gives us no clue as to what might be wrong if the answer is no. Debugging is helped if we know which cases passed and which cases failed.
2. List every test case and state whether the code passes the test. Prog1205 implements this approach. We have information to help us if debugging is needed.
3. List only those cases that fail the test.

Test your skill with Exercises 12–20 through 12–26.

12.11   static **Automatic Test Method**

Prog1205.java has one remaining drawback: The driver is separate from the code to be tested. Each time we need to run the tests, we need to locate the special driver and compile it with class Complex.

Let's merge the testing code with the code of the class to be tested. We'll take the former main method and turn it into a static method—tester()—which will execute the test cases that were formerly found in main. Any static methods that were called by the `main` method in driver `Prog1205` will become `static` methods in the class `Complex`. `Prog1206` shows the code.

Prog1206.java   static Automatic Test Method

```java
// Written by Barry Soroka
//
// Tests method toString of class Complex.
// static automatic test method
//
import java.io.*;
import java.util.Scanner;
//////////////////////////////////////////////////////////////////////////////
class Prog1206
{
//-------------------------------------------------------------------------
    public static void main ( String [] args ) throws Exception
    {
        Complex.tester();
    }
//-------------------------------------------------------------------------
} // end class Prog1206
//////////////////////////////////////////////////////////////////////////////
class Complex
{
    private int real;
    private int imag;
//-------------------------------------------------------------------------
    public Complex ( int real, int imag )
    {
        this.real = real;
        this.imag = imag;
    }
//-------------------------------------------------------------------------
    public static void tester()
    {
        testToString(0,0,"0");
        testToString(0,5,"5i");
        testToString(3,0,"3");
        testToString(3,5,"3+5i");
        testToString(3,-5,"3-5i");
        testToString(0,-5,"-5i");
        testToString(3,1,"3+i");
        testToString(3,-1,"3-i");
```

```
         testToString(0,1,"i");
         testToString(0,-1,"-i");
      }
//--------------------------------------------------------------------------
   private static void testToString ( int real, int imag, String expected )
   {
      String actual = (new Complex(real,imag)).toString();

      String tag;
      if ( expected.equals(actual) ) tag = "OK";
      else                           tag = "*** FAILURE *** ";

      System.out.println("Complex(" +
                         real + "," +
                         imag + ")\tshould be " +
                         expected + "\tis " +
                         actual + "\t" +
                         tag);
   }
//--------------------------------------------------------------------------
   public static Complex read ( PrintStream ps, Scanner sc )
   {
      if ( ps != null ) ps.println("Reading a complex number ...");
      if ( ps != null ) ps.print("Enter the real part:      ");
      int real = sc.nextInt();
      if ( ps != null ) ps.print("Enter the imaginary part: ");
      int imag = sc.nextInt();
      return new Complex ( real, imag );
   }
//--------------------------------------------------------------------------
   public String toString ()
   {
      if ( imag == 0 ) return real + "";

      String iString = Math.abs(imag) + "i";
      if ( Math.abs(imag) == 1 ) iString = "i";

      if ( real == 0 && imag > 0 ) return iString;
      if ( real == 0 && imag < 0 ) return "-" + iString;

      if ( imag > 0 ) return real + "+" + iString;

      return real + "-" + iString;
   }
```

```
//------------------------------------------------------------------
   public boolean equals ( Complex that )
   {
      return this.real == that.real
             &&
             this.imag == that.imag;
   }
//------------------------------------------------------------------
   public Complex add ( Complex z )
   {
      return new Complex ( real + z.real , imag + z.imag );
   }
//------------------------------------------------------------------
   public Complex sub ( Complex z )
   {
      return new Complex ( real - z.real , imag - z.imag );
   }
//------------------------------------------------------------------
   public Complex times ( Complex z )
   {
      int a1 = real, b1 = imag;
      int a2 = z.real, b2 = z.imag;
      return new Complex ( a1*a2-b1*b2, a1*b2+a2*b1 );
   }
//------------------------------------------------------------------
}
//////////////////////////////////////////////////////////////////
```

The sole statement in method `main` of the test driver (`Prog1206`) is

```
Complex.tester()
```

which invokes the `tester` method to try the test cases and report the results.

Note that the test method is now an integral part of class `Complex`. We don't have to worry about losing some separate driver file—it's become a `static` method within `Complex`—and we can test `Complex` any time we want simply by invoking the `tester` method. This completes our development of four tactics for using test cases to judge the suitability of prospective implementations of a class. Each tactic is a step more useful than the one before.

Another way to test is to build the test code into a main method in each class.

Test your skill with Exercises 12–27 through 12–31.

12.12   Testing the times Method of Class Complex

Prog1207 shows the code that performs automatic testing of the times method of class Complex. This code detects three types of failures:

1. The result is not what we expected. We've been testing this in our code for toString.
2. The receiver is changed.
3. The parameter is changed.

For the second and third failures listed, the times method is supposed to compute the product of the receiver and parameter. It's not supposed to change the receiver, but it certainly has the power to do so.

Prog1207.java   Tests the times Method of Class Complex

```
// Written by Barry Soroka
//
// Tests the times method of class Complex.
// Driver contains input & expected output.
// Automatically check expected & actual output.
// Automatically check that the receiver and parameter have not been changed.
//
import java.io.*;
import java.util.Scanner;
//////////////////////////////////////////////////////////////////////////////
class Prog1207
```

```
{
//---------------------------------------------------------------------------
    public static void main ( String [] args ) throws Exception
    {
        testTimes1(1,1,2,-1,3,1);
    }
//---------------------------------------------------------------------------
    private static void testTimes1 ( int a1, int b1,
                                     int a2, int b2,
                                     int a,  int b   )
    {
        Complex receiver = new Complex(a1,b1);
        Complex oldReceiver = new Complex(a1,b1);

        Complex parameter = new Complex(a2,b2);
        Complex oldParameter = new Complex(a2,b2);

        Complex expected = new Complex(a,b);

        Complex actual = receiver.times(parameter);

        if ( !actual.equals(expected) )
        {
            System.out.println("\n*** FAILURE *** Method times of class Complex");
            System.out.println("   Unexpected result!");
            System.out.println("   Receiver = " + oldReceiver);
            System.out.println("   Parameter = " + oldParameter);
            System.out.println("   Expected =  " + expected);
            System.out.println("   Actual =    " + actual);
        }

        if ( !receiver.equals(oldReceiver) )
        {
            System.out.println("\n*** FAILURE *** Method times of class Complex");
            System.out.println("   Receiver has been changed!");
            System.out.println("   Receiver = " + oldReceiver);
            System.out.println("   Parameter = " + oldParameter);
            System.out.println("   Receiver before =  " + oldReceiver);
            System.out.println("   Receiver after  =  " + receiver);
        }

        if ( !parameter.equals(oldParameter) )
        {
            System.out.println("\n*** FAILURE *** Method times of class Complex");
```

```
        System.out.println("    Parameter has been changed!");
        System.out.println("    Receiver = " + oldReceiver);
        System.out.println("    Parameter = " + oldParameter);
        System.out.println("    Parameter before =  " + oldParameter);
        System.out.println("    Parameter after  =  " + parameter);
      }
    }
//-----------------------------------------------------------------
} // end class Prog1207
/////////////////////////////////////////////////////////////////////////////
class Complex
{
// Same code as Prog1201
}
/////////////////////////////////////////////////////////////////////////
```

Test your skill with Exercises 12–32 through 12–35.

12.13 Coding Tips

This section includes advice that will help you write better code with less aggravation. These tips are common sense, but were learned at the cost of countless frustrating hours. Although you'll be armed with this advice *now*, you probably won't assimilate it all at once. You should re-read this section every month or so, because you may learn something new each time.

Keep the Specification In Front of You

How else can you be sure that you're solving the correct problem? I once encountered a desperate student who couldn't get his program to work correctly. "Where's the spec?" I asked. He didn't have it with him, and it turned out that he was trying to solve a problem that was twice as hard as the one I had assigned. Human memory is not infallible.

Breaks Can Be Helpful

Sometimes—often—you can't write a program at a single sitting. You'll reach a point of diminishing returns. But you can refresh yourself by taking a break and doing something totally different than the programming problem at hand:

- Take a nap.
- Play a piano—just mindlessly run scales.
- Take a walk or toss a ball.
- Do something right-brained.

Sometimes the answer will simply appear in your mind while you're doing the nonprogramming activity. Eureka![4]

Programming Is Not Supposed to Be Trial and Error

Some students "program" by randomly mutating and rearranging statements in hopes of getting a program to do what it's supposed to do. This is not a good strategy for people; it takes too long.[5] Good programmers understand their nonworking programs well enough to pinpoint the probable locations of bugs.

Keep Checkpoints of Working Programs As You Move Along

Every once in a while, make a copy of the files involved in your current programming project. Then, if you seriously wound your code, you can retreat to a prior version that was less buggy.

For example, suppose you come home from a concert and it's 4 A.M. and you're all excited and you think you know how to get your program running. You sit down and proceed to edit your only copy of the half-working program. Sometimes you'll get it to work, but often you'll ruin your one and only copy, and you have to go back to square one.

I know this because I've done this, and I've learned from my experience. Now, before I sit down to change a working or half-working program, I make a read-only copy, and only then do I start modifying the code. I used the same checkpoint strategy for writing the book that you're now reading:

> **Version control system**
> Software that ensures that each member of a programming group is working with the latest version of the software pieces.

Every morning and afternoon, I made a copy of the text so that I could get back to a decent version in case I accidentally trashed the file I was working on.

When you program as a professional you will probably encounter *version control systems,* which assist in keeping track of multiple versions of developing software.

Don't Write All the Code at Once

If you write all the code at once, you may encounter so many error messages that you can't determine where to start debugging. You should always start

---

[4] I hate it when the answer comes to me when I'm somewhere that I can't write it down.

[5] On the other hand, it's a feasible strategy for *machines.* Within artificial intelligence, there's a field called genetic algorithms (or evolutionary programming), which uses mutation and rearrangement to "write" programs. The operations are done by a computer program that is writing *another* computer program. Humans are out of the loop.

with existing code that compiles and runs, and you should add new code incrementally. If bugs appear, you can localize them to the code most recently added. Programmers receive a lot of criticism from compilers; you should try to get as many *kudos* as you can. Start with a shell such as `Blank.java`, which compiles and runs. You'll always be starting from code that works!

Implement a Large Program in Well-Defined Steps

As the number of programs you read and write increases, you'll be able to look at the problem specification and identify independent capabilities that can be implemented sequentially. You'll sketch a working shell of the program and you'll add capabilities one at a time. This sequential implementation allows the following:

- You'll always have a working program.
- If bugs appear, they are due to the code most recently added.

Step-by-step implementation allows you to write programs that are more complicated than those you could write if you tried to write all the code at once.

Order of Implementation Within a Class

When implementing a class, you should generally start by writing the constructors. Without constructors, you can't test anything else. You should then implement `toString` or other printing methods; without these, you can't see the effects of other methods. In fact, you can't even see if the constructors are working. Implement *simple* methods first—you'll receive positive reinforcement, which will help you over the disappointments that will come when you're implementing more difficult methods.

The 80–20 Rule

This "rule" describes how effort is distributed in the course of producing artifacts such as computer programs. If you look at the total development of a program, you'll find that the first 20% of the effort produces a program that meets 80% of the specs; the remaining 80% of the effort is spent *polishing* the program so that it fulfills the remaining 20% of the requirements.[6]

80–20 can work in our favor. With 20% of the effort, you can have a *working model* of the program; you'll feel that you've accomplished a lot. The remaining effort goes to adding or refining capabilities in an incremental fashion. Thus, a larger program can feel more achievable.

---

[6] The fraction 90–10 is often used as well.

12.14 Debugging

Error Messages

When you're compiling a program, pay attention only to the *first* error message. All the others may simply be side effects of that first error. You've probably seen this phenomenon when you've forgotten to declare a variable: The compiler cites you every time you use that undeclared variable. Adding the one declaration makes the other error messages go away.

Many error messages are not very descriptive: They tell you that *something* is wrong, but they don't specifically tell you *what* is wrong. Psychology talks about stimulus–response pairs. The mistake is the stimulus, and the error message is the response. After seeing enough mistake–message pairs, you will come to associate some messages with the mistakes that elicit them. When you're learning new parts of Java—or any new language, for that matter—you ought to spend some time intentionally causing errors so that you'll see what error messages are produced.

Print Statements and the Paradox of Debugging

In the early days we programmed in machine language, and there was no compiler to spot our errors and give us messages. A defective program either bombed or produced the wrong answer. The only way to debug was to insert print statements, which told us the state of the program as it executed. Now we have compilers to spot us, but at times we still use print statements, such as when a compiler-approved program fails. For example, we might print the value of a variable every time a particular statement is executed. We might print the values of *several* variables, and we should label each value so we know what's being shown.

Here's the paradox. We see a sequence of values of variables. How can we know whether the sequence is correct? Well, we need to be able to predict the sequence by *simulating* the program by hand. (This is also called *tracing* or *hand-tracing*.) We need to know what to expect.

We can't write or debug a program for a calculation unless we can do that calculation *by hand*, but if we can do the calculation by hand, then why are we writing a computer program for it?

The paradox is resolved because we need to hand-trace the computation for only a few simple cases. Once we know the code works properly, we can use the program on hundreds or thousands or zillions of cases.

Debugging with Conditional Print Statements

In debugging, the conventional print statement has the typical form

```
System.out.println("i " + i);
```

which prints the value of i whenever the statement is encountered. Once the program is debugged, we don't want to see the debugging lines in the output. Lines such as this

```
i 5
i 6
. . .
```

are no longer needed.

There are several approaches for turning off the diagnostic printouts:

1. We can *delete* the `println` statement. This achieves our goal, but what if another bug appears later? We may find ourselves adding the `println` statement back into the code.

2. We can *comment out* the `println` statement by putting "//" at the beginning of the line:

```
//    System.out.println("i " + i);
```

Again, this achieves our goal, and we can *uncomment* the statement if we need to do some further debugging in future. But commenting and uncommenting become onerous when there are *many* diagnostic statements in a program.

3. We can make the execution of the `println` statement *dependent on a specific variable* whose value we set at the top of the program. Several versions are described in the following paragraphs.

We can use a `boolean` variable to control whether diagnostic statements are executed:

```
boolean debugging = true;
. . .
if ( debugging ) statement1;
. . .
if ( debugging ) statement2;
. . .
if ( debugging ) statement3;
. . .
```

By changing the value of the variable `debugging`, we can turn all the diagnostic statements on or off; one statement controls the execution of many others.

We may want to have several sets of debugging statements that can be turned on and off independently:

```
boolean debugging1 = true;
boolean debugging2 = false;
...
if ( debugging1 ) statement1;
...
if ( debugging2 ) statement2;
...
if ( debugging1 || debugging2 ) statement3;
...
if ( debugging1 && debugging2 ) statement4;
...
if ( !debugging1 ) statement5;
...
if ( debugging1 && !debugging2 ) statement6;
...
```

 Test your skill with Exercise 12–36.

We may want to define several *levels* of debugging, as shown here:

```
int debuggingLevel = 2;
...
if ( debuggingLevel == 1 ) statement1;
...
if ( debuggingLevel >= 3 ) statement2;
...
if ( debuggingLevel >= 2 ) statement3;
...
if ( debuggingLevel >= 1 ) statement4;
...
if ( debuggingLevel == 2 ) statement5;
...
if ( debuggingLevel >= 1 ) statement6;
...
```

 Test your skill with Exercises 12–37.

Debugging Is Not a Monotonic Process

Sometimes a bug will appear and we'll "fix" it, only to have it reappear later. This is summarized in the following table:

Program Version	Test Case 1	Test Case 2
n	OK	Fails
n+1	Fails	OK

Very complicated programs are very hard—if not impossible—to debug. Sometimes we just drive the bugs into hiding, where they lurk, waiting for the most inopportune time to reappear.

12.15   Seeking Help: How to Document Errors

From time to time, your own resources will prove insufficient to understand why a program

- doesn't compile (a compile-time error);
- bombs (a run-time error); or
- gives the wrong answer (a logical error).

When this happens, you'll need to seek the help of other programmers. However, you can't just walk into someone's office and start talking about how the code didn't do what you wanted. You need to document the error so that others can help you.

Folktales Are Not Error Reports

If all you have is an oral report about how a program behaved or misbehaved, you're presenting a *folktale*. Human memory is fallible, and computers are unforgiving, so it's likely that a simple oral report omits crucial information about what happened—information *required* in order to debug your program. No one will believe you if you don't have proper documentation.

Experts can't help you if you come in with a folktale. They'll suggest something and you'll say, "I tried that, but it still gave me an error." You must be able to replicate the error. Experts will blame you and your memory before they'll blame the program.

Characteristics of a Good Error Report

First, *the error must be repeatable*. Often, when my expert demanded a demonstration, the error didn't appear! Sometimes, writing an error report seems to fix the error.[7]

Second, *the code should be short*. Cut out extraneous parts of the code until you have a small program that demonstrates the problem. Sometimes, just isolating the error shows you where you've made the mistake. Experts don't want to look at a 500-line program when the problem can be demonstrated in 25 lines.

A good error report has the following pieces:

- minimal code that produces the error.
- lists of inputs that produce the error.
- copies of data files involved in producing the errors.
- hardcopy of the compile or the test run.

12.16   Learning Novel Language Constructs

No course in programming can teach you *everything* about the language being used. Sooner or later, you'll want or need to use a language construct, or a class or method, that is unfamiliar. Here are some suggestions to help you succeed in that situation.

Write Small Test Programs

When you're trying a new part of a language, write small programs to test your understanding. Your first program involving arrays should be very small, so you can get the feedback of doing it right. Don't start out with a 100-line program—you won't be able to tell where you've gone wrong. It's easier to pinpoint your misunderstanding in a short program than in a long one. The long program has lots of code that doesn't really involve the feature you're trying out.

Don't Throw Out Bad Code Until You Understand It

If you get an error that you don't understand, keep the code until you find out what you're doing wrong. Suppose it's the night before a homework assign-

---

[7] This phenomenon is similar to others, such as when your car doesn't make the nasty noise when you get it to the mechanic, or when the pain goes away while you're sitting in the physician's waiting room.

ment is due, and you can't get Java's "Feature X" to work for you. A reasonable strategy is to produce a working program by trying another approach. However, if you never learned why Feature X wasn't working for you, then you'll have a gap in your knowledge of Java—and Feature X is bound to be needed at some point.

12.17   Keep the Interface but Improve the Implementation

The interface of a class is the set of methods it provides to the outside world. It's a contract between the class-writer and the class-user. If you change the *interface*, then you'll break the programs that use your class. On the other hand, you can change the *implementation* as much as you want, provided that the interface remains unchanged. Good reasons to change an implementation are to make methods faster or to use less memory for a computation. Regression testing can be used to prove that the code still works as advertised.

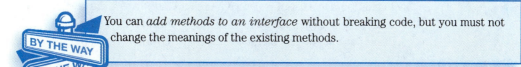

You can *add methods to an interface* without breaking code, but you must not change the meanings of the existing methods.

12.18   Style Sheets

You've learned that there's more than one way to solve a problem, and that codes that look different from each other can do the same thing. Nonetheless, some equivalent code looks better or is easier to understand than other code.

Style sheet   The coding conventions of a company or a programming group—that are created to improve readability.

A *style sheet* enforces consistency in the *optional* features of a program—variable names, indentation and white space, required comments, and so forth. Style sheets make different coders' programs look similar, and this makes it easier for one person to read and revise code written by another person.

This text uses the style sheet given in Appendix 1, which also includes two sample programs in the specified style. Most industrial style sheets are longer and more prescriptive than this one. On the job, you have no choice—you must obey the client's style sheet or else! Your nightmare comes true when you're working on projects for two different clients and each requires its own idiosyncratic and incompatible style sheet. To avoid mistakes, you should re-read the style sheet before turning in any assignment. After a while, the rules of the style sheet will become second nature.

Chapter Summary

- Faulty software can cause great damage.
- We should select test cases even before we write the code.
- We should use test cases at decision points and in all ranges of the test space.
- Poorly chosen test cases can deceive us into thinking that software works correctly.
- Regression testing means that we test a comprehensive suite of test cases every time we alter the code.
- We can type in test cases or we can build them into a driver.
- We can visually verify program outputs or we can have the code compare the actual outputs to a list of expected (required) outputs.
- A testing regime should report the cases for which the software fails.
- A `static` automatic test method is called to perform regression testing of a class.
- Keep the specification in front of you when you are coding.
- Periodic breaks can improve your productivity.
- Keep checkpoints of programs during the coding process.
- Implement a program in a series of well-defined steps, adding capabilities incrementally.
- For a class, implement constructors first, then `toString`, then simple methods, and then more complicated methods.
- Well-chosen `print` statements can aid in debugging.
- Rather than delete the diagnostic `print` statements, it may be wiser to comment them out or to control them with `boolean` variables.
- Debugging is not a monotonic process: Fixing one bug may "unfix" another bug.
- A good error report must include code that reliably repeats the error.
- A program error should be documented with the least possible amount of code.
- Don't throw out bad code until you understand it.

Terminology Introduced in This Chapter

regression testing
style sheet
version control system

Exercises

Exercise 12–1. Recall the problem where we converted an `int` grade to a `char` grade. List the appropriate test cases.

Exercise 12–2. Consider the class `Fraction`, which we have previously studied. Write the chart of test regions for its constructor and `toString` method.

Exercise 12–3. Consider the class `ZooShipment`, which we have previously studied. Write the chart of test regions for its `toString` method.

Exercise 12–4. Consider the class `Rectangle`. Which values are invalid?

Exercise 12–5. Consider a class `Car` that models automobiles. It has instance variables

```
int year
String make
int engineWeight
int totalWeight
```

What are good test cases for class `Car`?

Exercise 12–6. Attendees at a sales meeting are to break into pairs for an afternoon session. Consider a class `SalesPerson` with instance variables

```
String name
String city
```

`Pair` objects have instance variables

```
SalesPerson s1
SalesPerson s2
```

Members of a *legal* `Pair` must come from different cities.
What are good test cases for this problem? Provide code.

Exercise 12–7. Create a flawed version of the code for class `Complex` by mildly mutilating the `toString` method. Demonstrate the (mis)behavior of your flawed code. An ideal flawed version of `Complex` should produce the correct `toString` output for all but a few regions in the test space.

Exercise 12–8. Using `Prog1202`, enter every test case from the table of test cases for `Complex` in Section 12.3. Observe the output from a correct and a flawed implementation of `Complex`. Compare the outputs.

Exercise 12–9. For class `Fraction`, write and run a tester similar to the one described in Section 12.6. Test it with both a correct and a flawed implementation of the constructor.

Exercise 12–10. For the `toString` method of class `ZooShipment`, write and run a tester similar to the one described in Section 12.6. Test it with both a correct and a flawed implementation of `toString`.

Exercise 12–11. Observe the output of `Prog1203` from a correct and a flawed implementation of `Complex`. Compare the outputs.

Exercise 12–12. For class `Fraction`, write and run a tester similar to the one described in Section 12.7. Test it with both a correct and a flawed implementation of the constructor.

Exercise 12–13. For the `toString` method of class `ZooShipment`, write and run a tester similar to the one described in Section 12.7. Test it with both a correct and a flawed implementation of `toString`.

Exercise 12–14. Observe the output of `Prog1204` from a correct and a flawed implementation of `Complex`. Compare the outputs.

Exercise 12–15. For class `Fraction`, write and run a tester similar to the one described in Section 12.8. Test it with both a correct and a flawed implementation of the constructor.

Exercise 12–16. For the `toString` method of class `ZooShipment`, write and run a tester similar to the one described in Section 12.8. Test it with both a correct and a flawed implementation of `toString`.

Exercise 12–17. Observe the output of `Prog1205` from a correct and a flawed implementation of `Complex`. Compare the outputs.

Exercise 12–18. For class `Fraction`, write and run a tester similar to the one described in Section 12.9. Test it with both a correct and a flawed implementation of the constructor.

Exercise 12–19. For the `toString` method of class `ZooShipment`, write and run a tester similar to the one described in Section 12.9. Test it with both a correct and a flawed implementation of `toString`.

Exercise 12–20. Modify `Prog1205` to implement Approach 1 of Section 12.10.

Exercise 12–21. Modify `Prog1205` to implement Approach 3 of Section 12.10.

Exercise 12–22. Modify `Prog1205` to request a *debug mode*, whereby the user can specify whether to use Approach 1, 2, or 3 of Section 12.10.

Exercise 12–23. For the constructor and `toString` method of class `Fraction`, write and run a tester that uses Approach 1 of Section 12.10. Test it with both a correct and an incorrect implementation of `toString`.

Exercise 12–24. For the constructor and `toString` method of class `Fraction`, write and run a tester that uses Approach 3 of Section 12.10. Test it with both a correct and an incorrect implementation of `toString`.

Exercise 12–25. For the `toString` method of class `ZooShipment`, write and run a tester that uses Approach 1 of Section 12.10. Test it with both a correct and an incorrect implementation of `toString`.

Exercise 12–26. For the `toString` method of class `ZooShipment`, write and run a tester that uses Approach 3 of Section 12.10. Test it with both a correct and an incorrect implementation of `toString`.

Exercise 12–27. Recall the three approaches in Section 12.10 used for reporting test results. `Prog1206` uses Approach 2 (for each test case, report *yes* or *no* as appropriate). Implement the `tester` method with Approach 1: Report just one *yes* or *no* depending on whether the implementation is correct.

Exercise 12–28. Recall again the three approaches for reporting test results. `Prog1206` uses Approach 2 (for each test case, report *yes* or *no* as appropriate). Implement the `tester` method with Approach 3: Report only those test cases that fail the test.

Exercise 12–29. Implement the `tester` method for class `Complex` with an `int` parameter that specifies which of the three reporting approaches of Section 12.10 should be taken: 1, 2, or 3.

Exercise 12–30. Same as Exercise 12–29, but using the constructor and `toString` method of class `Fraction`.

Exercise 12–31. Same as Exercise 12–29, but using the `toString` method of class `ZooShipment`.

Exercise 12–32. Take `Prog1207` and mangle `times` so that it elicits the first type of failure described in Section 12.12.

Exercise 12–33. Take `Prog1207` and mangle `times` so that it elicits the second type of failure described in Section 12.12.

Exercise 12–34. Take `Prog1207` and mangle `times` so that it elicits the third type of failure described in Section 12.12.

Exercise 12–35. Write similar code to `Prog1207` to test the `add` method of class `Fraction`. Test it.

Exercise 12–36. Consider the code:

```
if ( debugging1 ) statement1;
...
if ( debugging2 ) statement2;
...
if ( debugging1 || debugging2 ) statement3;
...
if ( debugging1 && debugging2 ) statement4;
...
if ( !debugging1 ) statement5;
...
if ( debugging1 && !debugging2 ) statement6;
...
```

Which diagnostic statements are executed for each of the following cases?

debugging1	debugging2	*Diagnostic statements executed*
true	true	
true	false	
false	true	
false	false	

Exercise 12–37. Consider the code:

```
if ( debuggingLevel == 1 ) statement1;
...
if ( debuggingLevel >= 3 ) statement2;
...
if ( debuggingLevel >= 2 ) statement3;
...
if ( debuggingLevel >= 1 ) statement4;
...
if ( debuggingLevel == 2 ) statement5;
...
if ( debuggingLevel >= 1 ) statement6;
...
```

Which diagnostic statements are executed for each of the following cases?

debuggingLevel	Diagnostic statements executed
0	
1	
2	
3	
4	

CHAPTER THIRTEEN

Loops and Files

Chapter Objectives

- Appreciate the characteristics of different data collections.
- Use the read-process pattern to scan through the elements of a disk file.
- Use the `while` loop.
- Learn a variety of algorithms for working with the elements of disk files.
- Implement a `Section` as a file of `Student`s.
- Learn how to mark the end of a file with a sentinel value.
- Use the `for` loop.
- Use GUI dialog boxes.

In previous chapters, we have written programs that processed a fixed number of items:

- Read and print the first *three* `ZooShipment`s in a file.
- Sum the first *five* `Fraction`s in a file.

Now we will learn to write programs that *iterate* operations over a *variable number* of data items. For example:

- Read and print *all* the `ZooShipment`s in a file.
- Read, print, and sum the `Fraction`s in a file *until* the sum exceeds 3/1.

Notice that the last two programs don't process a fixed number of items; they process all of the items in a file or they process as many items as are required to meet a given criterion. Consider the first program:

Read and print *all* the `ZooShipments` in a file.

- If the file is empty, then *nothing* is printed.
- If the file contains *one* `ZooShipment`, then *one* item is printed.
- If the file contains *two* `ZooShipments`, then *two* items are printed.

The number of iterations depends on the *data*—it's not specified in the program code itself.

Programming languages—including Java—provide a *looping* mechanism so that programs can apply a set of instructions again and again until some *exit criterion* has been met. In this chapter, we will learn Java's iteration statements—`while` and `for`—and we will apply them to a wide variety of common programming problems. You will learn approximately two dozen programming patterns, which you will apply repeatedly during your programming career. You must learn each pattern, and you must recognize when it should be used. By the end of this chapter you will have an extensive arsenal of tactics for solving programming problems.

> **Pattern**   A group of problems solved in a similar way.

13.1   Collections and Their Characteristics

> **Collection**   A group of values using a single name.

This chapter is our first foray beyond single objects and into *collections* of objects. Java permits a wide variety of collections, each of which can be characterized by its position along the axes discussed below.

Where Stored

Is the data stored on disk? In memory? In various sites across the Web?

Redundant vs. Nonredundant

Is the data stored uniquely in a single place? Or are several copies of the data maintained at different sites? In databases, crucial information is often maintained in several copies at multiple sites. This buys survivability of the data, but it imposes a price: The sites must be kept *synchronized*.

Fixed vs. Variable Size

Some collections require that their size be declared in advance, and they allow no growth. Other collections are allowed to shrink and grow as required by the amount of data they are asked to contain.

Homogeneous vs. Heterogeneous

> **Homogeneous**   All elements are of the same type.
> **Heterogeneous**   Elements are of different types.

Some collections require that all the data be of the same type (e.g., all `Complex` or all `Fraction`). Other collections allow us to store items of different types in the same collection.

Objects vs. Primitive Datatypes

Some collections can store *objects* but not *primitive datatypes*. Other collections can contain *both* objects and primitive datatypes.

Duplicates

> **Set**   A collection where order is unimportant and where duplicates are not permitted.

Some collections allow us to store multiple copies of an element. Other collections—for example, `Sets`—do not allow duplicates. Another example is a `Section` of `Students`: A `Student` may not register for the same course twice.

Order

Some collections maintain their elements in a user-specified order. Other collections, such as `Sets`, ignore the order of the elements.

Access

> **Random access**   We can request elements in any order.

Some collections require that elements be accessed in a specific sequential order—for example, from front to rear. Other collections allow *random access* where we can access elements in arbitrary order.

13.2 A Selection of Collections

In the course of your studies, you will encounter a wide variety of collections, including the following:

File. You have been using files since you started working with computers. They're kept on disk, and they will be the first collection that we study.

Array. An array is a fixed-length collection of items with identical type. Chapter 14 will examine how Java provides arrays. In particular, we will transfer most of the algorithms from this chapter (using *files*) to the next chapter (using *arrays*).

> **Array**   A fixed-length collection.

Vector. You have encountered vectors in the math courses you've taken. Frequently, we talk about vectors of fixed length—3-vectors, for example—and we've studied mathematical operations on such vectors—the *dot product* and the *cross product*, for example. The Java libraries define vectors differently—a `Vector` is a collection of `Objects` that can grow and shrink to accommodate a varying number of items. Because a `Vector` contains `Objects`, it may contain `Objects` of any type. Thus, a `Vector` can contain, for example, any combination of `Fractions` and `Complex` numbers and `ZooShipments`.

> **Vector**   A collection that grows to accommodate the number of elements involved.

Linked List. This data type represents a *chain* of items. Each item has a successor and a predecessor, and we operate on the entire linked list by proceeding from its head to its tail. This datatype is appropriate for problems for which we don't know exactly how many items will be in a collection.

> **Linked list**   A chain of items.

Set. A set is like an array or a list except that *no element may appear more than once*. In conventional mathematical notation, {a,b,c} is a set, but {a,b,b} is not. Similarly, {a,b} is the same set as {b,a}.

Tree, Heap, Hash Table. These are examples of more advanced data structures, which store items in more complicated ways. They are useful in organizing large collections of data, and you will study these in CS 2.

13.3 An Initial Set of Programming Patterns

A *pattern* is a set of similar programming problems and their solutions. Consider, for example, the following problem:

> Given a File of ints, how many are negative?

This is an example of the pattern:

> Given a *collection* of *some-type*, how many *fulfill some criterion*?

The set includes problems involving *different collections*, such as:

Given a File of ints, how many are negative?

Given an array of ints, how many are negative?

Given a Set of ints, how many are negative?

Given a Tree of ints, how many are negative?

The set also includes problems involving *different types of items* and *different criteria*, such as:

Given a File of ints, how many are negative?

Given a File of ints, how many are positive?

Given a File of Strings, how many are the empty String?

Given a File of Strings, how many are uppercase?

Given a File of Complex, how many are 0?

Given a File of Students, how many got As?

Given a File of Students, how many failed?

Thus, a single pattern represents an infinite variety of programming problems.

NOTE

Once we know how to write the Java code for one instance of a pattern, we can modify our code to handle any other instance of that pattern.

NOTE A major goal of this course is to teach you an initial set of programming patterns, known and used by all working professional programmers. You must learn these patterns, recognize when to apply them, and know how to adapt the code for a specific problem.

Some patterns have simple and obvious programming solutions. For example, some students think the following problem is easy to solve:

Given a File of ints, how many are negative?

Here's the algorithm for solving that problem:[1]

1. Set a counter to 0.
2. Are we at the end of the File? If so, then the counter is our answer.
3. Otherwise, read an int.
4. If it's negative, then increment the counter and go to Step 2.

Other patterns require algorithms that are more complex and less obvious. For example:

Given a File of ints, print out the int that occurs most frequently.

Or,

Given a File of ints, print out the three largest ints.

By the end of CS 2, you will have learned how to solve most of the programming problems that you'll encounter on the job. In this text, we begin with the easier patterns and work our way toward more complicated patterns.
Here's an initial set of patterns:

1. Given a collection, print its items to the monitor.
2. Given a collection, report the number of items in the collection.
3. Given a collection, compute the sum of the items.
4. Given a collection, compute the average value.
5. Given a collection, does it contain a specific item?
6. Given a collection, do *all* items meet some criterion?
7. Given a collection, do *any* items meet some criterion?
8. Given a collection, how many times does a given item appear in the collection?

---

[1] Is this the solution *you* proposed?

9. Given a collection, are the items in ascending order?

10. Given a collection, generate a new collection in which each element is related to the corresponding element of the incoming collection.

We'll add more patterns later in the text.

Test your skill with Exercise 13–1.

13.4   Files as Collections

Most patterns apply to a variety of collections and a variety of item types. Our first pattern, which is

Given a collection, print its items to the monitor.

can be applied to different *collections*, such as File, array, Vector, Set, and Tree, and to different *item types*, such as String, int, double, Complex, and Fraction.

We'll begin our study of Pattern 1 by using *File* as the collection. Two things are notable:

1. Files are *not* random access. If we want the tenth element in a File, then we must read through the first nine items in order to get the tenth.

2. Files contain *Strings*. Every line of a File is a String, and every call to nextLine brings in the next line in the affected File.[2] On the other hand, we can convert some Strings into numbers—ints and doubles—and we can write static read methods to read user-defined objects from Strings in a given File.

Consider a file containing the following Strings:

```
2
3
0
1
1
-5
```

---

[2]   To be entirely accurate, we should say *Scanner* rather than *File*.

Depending on how we read it, File foo can be interpreted in several ways:

- As a File of *Strings*: "2", "3", "0", "1", "1", "-5".
- As a File of *ints*: 2, 3, 0, 1, 1, -5.
- As a File of *Complex*: 2+3i, i, 1-5i.

The *meaning* of a File depends on the method being used to read it:

- Applying nextLine to foo results in a stream of Strings.
- Applying nextInt to foo results in a stream of ints.
- Applying Complex.read(...) to foo results in a stream of Complex.

Moreover,

- Applying nextDouble to foo results in a stream of doubles.

13.5   The while Loop

Java provides several control structures for looping. We will study the while statement first.

Syntactically, a while loop looks like this, where *condition* is a *boolean expression*:

```
while ( condition ) statement
```

and it has the flowchart shown in Figure 13–1. The loop executes instructions in the following order:

Is *condition* true? If so, continue. Otherwise exit.

Figure 13–1
Flowchart for
while

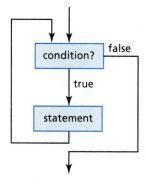

Execute *statement*.

Is *condition* true? If so, continue. Otherwise exit.

Execute *statement*.

. . .

If *condition* is initially `false`, then the loop is *never* entered, and *statement* is never executed. If *condition* ever *becomes* `false`, then Java exits the loop; otherwise, it continues looping forever. Recall the infinite loop that we used in earlier chapters:

```
while ( true ) statement
```

This is a `while` loop where the condition—`true`—can never become `false`. Hence, it acts as an infinite loop.

> **Test your skill with Exercises 13–2 through 13–6.**

13.6   The Read-Process Loop

In this section, we'll present the Java code that solves the problem

Given a `File` of `Strings`, print the `Strings` to the monitor,

which is an example of Pattern 1:

Given a collection of items, print the items to the monitor,

where the *collection* is a `File` and the *items* have type `String`. Let's think about a program that could solve this problem.

It will certainly have a *loop*, since it needs to read an unknown number of `Strings` from the `File`. We've seen *infinite* loops before, but the loop in the current problem must *terminate appropriately* after we've read all the `Strings` in the `File`.

We want to stop the loop when we've reached the end of the `File`. So, how do we know if we're at the end of a file? Here's Java's answer:

Class `Scanner` contains a method `hasNext` which, when applied to a `Scanner`, returns `true` or `false` depending on whether there's another token in the input stream. If we're reading from a file and `hasNext` returns `false`, then we've reached the end of the file.

`Prog1301.java` presents the code to solve our problem. The first few statements read the filename and set up the appropriate `Scanner` `sc`. Then come the statements that do the actual looping:

```
String s;

while ( sc.hasNext() )
{
    s = sc.nextLine();
    System.out.println(s);
}
```

This is an example of a *read-process loop*. Here's the structure:

Loop as long as there's more to process:

- Read another item from the `Scanner`.
- Print the item.

The `while` loop acts in this manner:

1. Are we at the end of the file? If so then exit.
2. *Read*: Read a `String` from the file.
3. *Process*: Print that `String`.
4. Go back to Step 1.

Each time around the loop, a new `String` is read from the file. The loop exits when that `String` is `null`. In solving *other* patterns, we will use the read-process loop, but the process part will be tailored for the specific task at hand.

Prog1301.java   **Print a File to the Terminal**

```
// Written by Barry Soroka.
//
// Read each line of a file & print it to the terminal.
//
import java.io.*;
import java.util.Scanner;
///////////////////////////////////////////////////////////////////////////
class Prog1301
{
//--------------------------------------------------------------------------
    public static void main (String [] args) throws Exception
    {
        Scanner kb = new Scanner(System.in);

        System.out.print("Enter name of file to be shown: ");
```

```
    String filename = kb.nextLine();

    Scanner sc = new Scanner(new File(filename));

    String s;

    while ( sc.hasNext() )
    {
        s = sc.nextLine();
        System.out.println(s);
    }

  }
//-----------------------------------------------------------------------
} // end class Prog1301
///////////////////////////////////////////////////////////////////////
```

Test your skill with Exercises 13–7 through 13–9.

NOTE

The empty file is *not* a special case. The loop is never entered because `hasNext` returns `false`. We don't need special code to handle the case of an empty file!

13.7   Print the Complex Numbers in a File

In Section 13.6 we studied a read-process loop that read through all the lines in a file, printing each to the monitor. Now we'll use a read-process loop to solve a similar problem:

> Given a `File` of `Complex`, print them to the monitor.

This is an example of Pattern 1, where the *collection* is a `File` and the *items* have type `Complex`.

Here's the code we used in `Prog1301` for reading `String`s:

```
while ( sc.hasNext() )
{
    String s = sc.nextLine();
    System.out.println(s);
}
```

The code for looping through a file of Complex is similar:

```
while ( sc.hasNext() )
{
    Complex z = Complex.read(null,sc);
    System.out.println(z);
}
```

The code is given in Prog1302.java.

Prog1302.java   Print a File of **Complex**

```java
// Written by Barry Soroka.
//
// Given a file of Complex, print each Complex to the monitor.
//
import java.io.*;
import java.util.Scanner;
//////////////////////////////////////////////////////////////////////////////
class Prog1302
{
//---------------------------------------------------------------------------
    public static void main (String [] args) throws Exception
    {
        Scanner kb = new Scanner(System.in);

        System.out.print("Enter name of file of Complex: ");
        String filename = kb.nextLine();

        Scanner sc = new Scanner(new File(filename));

        while ( sc.hasNext() )
        {
            Complex z = Complex.read(null,sc);
            System.out.println(z);
        }
    }
//---------------------------------------------------------------------------
} // end class Prog1302
//////////////////////////////////////////////////////////////////////////////
class Complex
{
    private int real;
    private int imag;
//---------------------------------------------------------------------------
    public Complex ( int real , int imag )
    {
```

```
          this.real = real;
          this.imag = imag;
      }
// -------------------------------------------------------------------

   public String toString ()
   {
       if ( imag == 0 ) return real + "";

       String iString = Math.abs(imag) + "i";
       if ( Math.abs(imag) == 1 ) iString = "i";

       if ( real == 0 && imag > 0 ) return iString;
       if ( real == 0 && imag < 0 ) return "-" + iString;

       if ( imag > 0 ) return real + "+" + iString;

       return real + "-" + iString;
   }
// -------------------------------------------------------------------

   public boolean equals ( Complex that )
   {
       return this.real == that.real
             &&
             this.imag == that.imag;
   }
// -------------------------------------------------------------------

   public static Complex read ( PrintStream ps, Scanner sc )
   {
       if ( ps != null ) ps.println("Reading a complex number ...");
       if ( ps != null ) ps.print("Enter the real part: ");
       int real = sc.nextInt();
       if ( ps != null ) ps.print("Enter the imaginary part: ");
       int imag = sc.nextInt();
       return new Complex ( real, imag );
   }
// -------------------------------------------------------------------

   public Complex add ( Complex that )
   {
       return new Complex ( this.real + that.real , this.imag + that.imag );
   }
// -------------------------------------------------------------------

   public Complex sub ( Complex that )
   {
       return new Complex ( this.real - that.real , this.imag - that.imag );
   }
```

```
//------------------------------------------------------------
    public Complex times ( Complex that )
    {
        int a1 = this.real, b1 = this.imag;
        int a2 = that.real, b2 = that.imag;
        return new Complex ( a1*a2-b1*b2, a1*b2+a2*b1 );
    }
//------------------------------------------------------------
} // end class Complex
////////////////////////////////////////////////////////////////
```

As noted in Chapter 6, using a `static read` method protects the code from overdependence on the current format of the input file. We've always used a `static read` method to remove our code from having to know the exact way in which a `Complex` is represented in a file. Therefore, we are protected from future changes in the format of `Complex` files. Right now, we're representing 3 + 5i as two integers, each on its own line:

        3
        5

But, some future redesign of a system might store that same `Complex` as two integers *on the same line*:

        3 5

We want to keep details on a need-to-know basis, and our programs do not need to know the exact file format for a `Complex`. They'll run flawlessly once they are recompiled with the new code for class `Complex`.

Test your skill with Exercises 13–10 through 13–12.

13.8 Patterns for Counting

In this section, we will study and solve problems that involve counting some or all items in a collection. Examples are

Count the number of lines in a file.

and

Given a file of `int`s, report the number of odds and evens.

We'll start with the first one.

Prog1303.java shows the code that reads a filename and counts the number of lines in the file. We declare a local variable count, which we'll start at 0; then we'll increment it each time we read another line from the file. The read-process loop is this:

```
while ( sc.hasNext() )
{
    String s = sc.nextLine();
    count++;
}
```

It reads line after line of the file until it reaches the end of the file. For every line, it performs a process—it increments count.

Prog1303.java   Count the Lines in a File

```
// Written by Barry Soroka.
//
// Count the number of lines in a file.
//
import java.io.*;
import java.util.Scanner;
////////////////////////////////////////////////////////////////////////////////
class Prog1303
{
//-------------------------------------------------------------------------------
    public static void main (String [] args) throws Exception
    {
        Scanner kb = new Scanner(System.in);

        System.out.print("Filename? ");
        String filename = kb.nextLine();

        Scanner sc = new Scanner(new File(filename));

        int count = 0;

        while ( sc.hasNext() )
        {
            String s = sc.nextLine();
            count++;
        }

        System.out.println("File \"" +
                            filename +
```

```
                              "\" contains " +
                              count +
                              " lines.");
    }
//--------------------------------------------------------------------------
} // end class Prog1303
//////////////////////////////////////////////////////////////////////////
```

Note that we started `count` at `0`, which is the natural starting value for *counting*. Our code produces a count of `0` when the file is empty; this is the number of lines in the empty file. Note that we did not need to write any special code to handle the empty file.

Test your skill with Exercise 13–13.

Now let's go on to a slightly more complicated problem.

Given a File of `ints`, Report the Number of Odds and Evens

Let's think about this problem before we explore the code.

First, we're examining a file of `ints` instead of a file of arbitrary `Strings`. This results in a read-process loop such as this:

```
while ( sc.hasNext() )
{
    int n = sc.nextInt();
    // insert appropriate statements here
}
```

Second, our program will be using *two* counters—one for the even `ints` and one for the odd `ints`—and this means that the setup for the loop will contain the following statements:

```
int nOdd = 0;
int nEven = 0;
```

Similarly, our process will test the `int` and increment the appropriate counter depending on whether `n` is even or odd:

```
if ( n%2 == 0 ) nEven++;
else            nOdd++;
```

Putting it all together, we get `Prog1304.java`.

Prog1304.java **Count Odd and Even ints**

```java
// Written by Barry Soroka.
//
// Given a file of ints, report the number of odds & evens.
//
import java.io.*;
import java.util.Scanner;
///////////////////////////////////////////////////////////////////////////////
class Prog1304
{
//------------------------------------------------------------------------------
    public static void main (String [] args) throws Exception
    {
        Scanner kb = new Scanner(System.in);

        System.out.print("Filename? ");
        String filename = kb.nextLine();

        Scanner sc = new Scanner(new File(filename));

        int nOdd = 0;
        int nEven = 0;

        while ( sc.hasNext() )
        {
            int n = sc.nextInt();
            if ( n%2 == 0 ) nEven++;
            else            nOdd++;
        }

        System.out.println(nOdd + " odds");
        System.out.println(nEven + " evens");
    }
//------------------------------------------------------------------------------
} // end class Prog1304
///////////////////////////////////////////////////////////////////////////////
```

 Test your skill with Exercises 13–14 through 13–21.

13.9 Patterns for Accumulating

Now let's study problems that involve *accumulating*—computing either a *sum* or a *product*. The simplest problem we'll consider is this:

Given a file of ints, compute the sum,

which asks us to add together *all* of the ints in a file. A variant of this problem would request accumulating only *some* of the items in the file:

Given a file of ints, compute the sum of the *odd* ints.

Sometimes we'll want to accumulate not the item itself but some function of the item—its square, its cube, its square-root, or whatever. A typical problem is this:

Given a file of `int`s, compute the sum of the squares of the `int`s.

We can combine selection and function to get problems such as this:

Given a file of `int`s, compute the sum of the squares of the odd `int`s,

where we ask to sum the *squares* of only the *odd* `int`s.

If we expand our horizons beyond `int`s, we reach problems that involve *user-defined objects*. Here are just a few of the problems we can ask about files of `Complex` numbers:

Given a file of `Complex`, compute the sum.

Given a file of `Complex`, compute the sum of the squares.

Given a file of `Complex`, compute the sum of the real parts.

Given a file of `Complex`, compute the sum of those that have positive real parts.

All of these problems have similar Java solutions because all of these problems are related by the pattern for accumulating.

Now for Some Code

`Prog1305.java` is the code that solves the simplest problem:

Given a file of `int`s, compute the sum.

Let's analyze this program: We need to accumulate the sum of all the `int`s in the file, so we need a variable into which we'll add each `int`. The initial sum—and the sum of the `int`s in an empty file—is `0`. Thus we get the line

```
int sum = 0;
```

Then we have a read-process loop, which goes through all the lines of the file using `nextInt` to produce a new `int` n each time around. Inside the loop we have the statement

```
sum += n;
```

which does the work of adding into `sum` each `int` that is read. After the loop terminates, we print the result of our accumulation:

```
System.out.println("sum = " + sum);
```

Prog1305.java   Compute the Sum

```
// Written by Barry Soroka.
//
// Given a file of ints, compute the sum.
//
import java.io.*;
import java.util.Scanner;
///////////////////////////////////////////////////////////////////////////////
class Prog1305
{
//-----------------------------------------------------------------------------
    public static void main (String [] args) throws Exception
    {
        Scanner kb = new Scanner(System.in);

        System.out.print("Filename? ");
        String filename = kb.nextLine();

        Scanner sc = new Scanner(new File(filename));

        int sum = 0;

        while ( sc.hasNext() )
        {
            int n = sc.nextInt();
            sum += n;
        }

        System.out.println("sum: " + sum);
    }
//-----------------------------------------------------------------------------
} // end class Prog1305
///////////////////////////////////////////////////////////////////////////////
```

 | **Test your skill with Exercises 13–22 through 13–25.** |

Products and Multiplication

Sometimes we want the *product* of a collection rather than its *sum*. For example, suppose we want a program to solve the problem

> Given a file of `ints`, compute their product.

`Prog1306.java` shows the code required. Only minor changes have been made to transform `Prog1305` (which computes the *sum*) into `Prog1306` (which computes the *product*):

- The variable `sum` has been changed to the variable `product`. The name of the accumulator should accurately reflect its purpose: one is a sum and the other is a product.

- The accumulation operator has been changed from + to $*$.
- The initial value of the accumulator has been changed from 0 to 1. These are the identity elements for addition and multiplication, respectively: $0 + x \to x$ and $1 \cdot x \to x$. If you start the product at 0, then it will always be 0, no matter what you multiply into it. So we need to start product at 1.

Thus we have the following read-process loop for computing the product of the ints in a file:

```
int product = 1;     ←

while ( sc.hasNext() )
{
    int n = sc.nextInt();
    product *= n;     ←
}
```

Only the two indicated lines have changed from computing the sum to computing the product.

Prog1306.java   Compute the Product

```
// Written by Barry Soroka.
//
// Given a file of ints, compute the product.
//
import java.io.*;
import java.util.Scanner;
////////////////////////////////////////////////////////////////////////////
class Prog1306
{
//----------------------------------------------------------------------------
    public static void main (String [] args) throws Exception
    {
        Scanner kb = new Scanner(System.in);

        System.out.print("Filename? ");
        String filename = kb.nextLine();

        Scanner sc = new Scanner(new File(filename));

        int product = 1;

        while ( sc.hasNext() )
        {
            int n = sc.nextInt();
```

```
        product *= n;
    }


    System.out.println("product: " + product);
  }
//-----------------------------------------------------------------------------
} // end class Prog1306
/////////////////////////////////////////////////////////////////////////////////
```

> The sum of the `int`s in the empty file is 0. The product is 1.

NOTE

HOLD YOUR HORSES

Note that once `product` becomes 0, it can never become non-0. A better program than `Prog1306` would stop reading the file once a 0 is found. If, for example, we have a file of 1 million `int`s and the first `int` is 0, then we can save a lot of time if we stop reading the file after the first `int` is read.

Test your skill with Exercise 13-26.

Accumulating Less Than All of the Items

Consider the problem:

> Given a file of `int`s, compute the sum of the *odd* `int`s.

Its solution requires only a tiny modification to `Prog1305`: Instead of *always* adding the integer into the `sum`, we now add the integer to the `sum` *only if the integer is odd*, so the `while` loop becomes this:

```
int product = 1;

while ( sc.hasNext() )
{
    int n = sc.nextInt();
    if ( n%2 != 0 ) product *= n;
}
```

We guard the accumulation statement with the requirement that n be odd.

Test your skill with Exercises 13–27 through 13–35.

Using More Than One Accumulator

Sometimes we're given a collection and we're asked to compute more than one value. For example,

> Given a file of ints, compute both the sum and product of the ints.

Or,

> Given a file of ints, compute the sum of the odd ints and the sum of the even ints.

One approach might be to go through the collection *twice*—once computing the first value and then computing the second value—but we'll examine code that looks at the collection only once.

Let's consider the first problem:

> Given a file of ints, compute both the sum and product of the ints.

Prog1307.java is its solution. Notice that we declare and initialize *two* accumulators

```
int sum = 0;
int product = 1;
```

and that, for each integer we find, we *add* it to sum and we *multiply* it to product:

```
int n = sc.nextInt();
sum += n;
product *= n;
```

Thus, we use the *process* part of the read-process loop to do more than one thing.

Prog1307.java   Compute Sum and Product

```
// Written by Barry Soroka.
//
// Given a file of ints, compute the sum and the product of the ints.
//
import java.io.*;
import java.util.Scanner;
////////////////////////////////////////////////////////////////////////////
```

```
class Prog1307
{
//---------------------------------------------------------------------------

   public static void main (String [] args) throws Exception
   {
      Scanner kb = new Scanner(System.in);

      System.out.print("Filename? ");
      String filename = kb.nextLine();

      Scanner sc = new Scanner(new File(filename));

      int sum = 0;
      int product = 1;

      while ( sc.hasNext() )
      {
         int n = sc.nextInt();
         sum += n;
         product *= n;
      }

      System.out.println("sum:     " + sum);
      System.out.println("product: " + product);
   }
//---------------------------------------------------------------------------
} // end class Prog1307
///////////////////////////////////////////////////////////////////////////
```

The second problem,

> Given a file of ints, compute the sum of the odd ints
> and the sum of the even ints,

is solved by Prog1308.java. We have *two* accumulators, appropriately initialized,

```
      int sumE = 0;
      int sumO = 0;
```

and we use the process part of the loop to update the appropriate accumulator for the current integer:

```
      int n = sc.nextInt();
      if ( n%2 == 0 ) sumE += n;
      else            sumO += n;
```

Prog1308.java   Sum of Odd and Sum of Even

```java
// Written by Barry Soroka.
//
// Given a file of ints,
// compute the sum of the odd ints
//     and the sum of the even ints.
//
import java.io.*;
import java.util.Scanner;
//////////////////////////////////////////////////////////////////////////////
class Prog1308
{
//---------------------------------------------------------------------------
    public static void main (String [] args) throws Exception
    {
        Scanner kb = new Scanner(System.in);

        System.out.print("Filename? ");
        String filename = kb.nextLine();

        Scanner sc = new Scanner(new File(filename));

        int sumE = 0;    // the sum of the even ints
        int sumO = 0;    // the sum of the odd ints

        while ( sc.hasNext() )
        {
            int n = sc.nextInt();
            if ( n%2 == 0 ) sumE += n;
            else            sumO += n;
        }

        System.out.println("even sum: " + sumE);
        System.out.println("odd sum:  " + sumO);
    }
//---------------------------------------------------------------------------
} // end class Prog1308
//////////////////////////////////////////////////////////////////////////////
```

I have used white space to align a variety of things in Prog1308. In the comment, I wrote:

```java
// compute the sum of the odd ints
//     and the sum of the even ints.
```

The alignment of the phrase "the sum of the" helps to accentuate the fact that this program computes two things of equal importance. Then, in the if-else statement, I used white space to align the *actions*:

```
if ( n%2 == 0 ) sumE += n;
else             sumO += n;
```

Finally, in the `println` statements, I have used white space to line up the output:

```
System.out.println("even sum: " + sumE);
System.out.println("odd sum:  " + sumO);
```

so that typical output would be

```
even sum: 28
odd sum:  13
```

These are examples of how white space can make your code and its output more readable.

 Test your skill with Exercises 13–36 through 13–39.

13.10   Computing the Average

When we compute the average of a collection, we need to compute two other quantities first: (1) the number of items, and (2) the sum of the items. Consider the problem:

> Given a file of `ints`, compute the average.

This has the straightforward solution shown in `Prog1309`. We establish two accumulators—`count` and `sum`—and, as we spin through the `ints` in the file, we increment the counter and we add each new element into the `sum`. We force floating-point division by putting `1.0` at the front of the expression `1.0*sum/count`. We could also have written `(double)sum/count`.

Prog1309.java   **Average**

```java
// Written by Barry Soroka.
//
// Given a file of ints, compute the average.
//
import java.io.*;
import java.util.Scanner;
//////////////////////////////////////////////////////////////////////////////
class Prog1309
{
//--------------------------------------------------------------------------
    public static void main (String [] args) throws Exception
    {
        Scanner kb = new Scanner(System.in);
```

```
        System.out.print("Filename? ");
        String filename = kb.nextLine();

        Scanner sc = new Scanner(new File(filename));

        int count = 0;
        int sum = 0;

        while ( sc.hasNext() )
        {
            int n = sc.nextInt();
            count++;
            sum += n;
        }

        System.out.println("The average is " + 1.0*sum/count);
    }
//----------------------------------------------------------------
} // end class Prog1309
////////////////////////////////////////////////////////////////////////
```

I often encounter another solution to this problem, which is shown in Prog1310. Here we read through the input file *twice*—once to compute count and once to compute sum. This version closes the Scanner and re-uses the name sc in opening a second Scanner for the file. Another approach would open two Scanners—say, sc1 and sc2—and each would maintain its own pointer into the lines of the file. The logic of Prog1310 is impeccable, but it's not very efficient: If the data file contains 1 million items, then

- Prog1309 will read 1 million ints from the file.
- Prog1310 will read 2 million ints from the file.

The difference in performance would be quite noticeable with large files. Prog1309 is preferred over Prog1310.

Prog1310.java **Compute Average, Reading the File Twice**

```
// Written by Barry Soroka.
//
// Given a file of ints, compute the average.
// Read the file twice.
//
import java.io.*;
import java.util.Scanner;
////////////////////////////////////////////////////////////////////////
```

```
class Prog1310
{
//-------------------------------------------------------------------------

    public static void main (String [] args) throws Exception
    {
        Scanner kb = new Scanner(System.in);

        System.out.print("Filename? ");
        String filename = kb.nextLine();

        Scanner sc = new Scanner(new File(filename));

        int count = 0;
        while ( sc.hasNext() )
        {
            int n = sc.nextInt();
            count++;
        }

        sc.close();

        sc = new Scanner(new File(filename));

        int sum = 0;
        while ( sc.hasNext() )
        {
            int n = sc.nextInt();
            sum += n;
        }

        System.out.println("The average is " + 1.0*sum/count);
    }
//-------------------------------------------------------------------------
} // end class Prog1310
/////////////////////////////////////////////////////////////////////////
```

The Average int in the Empty File

In earlier sections of this chapter, I've insisted that the sum of the ints in the empty file is 0 and the product is 1. What's a reasonable value for the *average* of the ints in the empty file? The sum is 0. The number of ints is 0. So the average should be 0/0, which should generate an error, and the user who tries to compute the average of an empty collection *deserves* an error. We're at the mercy of how Java handles expressions like 0/0. It's reasonable to expect Java to generate something like a DivideByZeroException, and that would halt the program. However, if you run Prog0311 with the empty file, you'll see this dialog:

```
G:\>java Prog1309
Filename? empty
The average is NaN
```

NaN is Java's way of printing a floating-point value that isn't legal. We won't explore NaN any further in CS 1.

> **HOLD YOUR HORSES**
>
> Java also has symbols Infinity and -Infinity to stand for the very positive and very negative floating-point numbers that arise from expressions such as 1.0/0.0 and -1.0/0.0. We won't explore these symbols in CS 1.

Test your skill with Exercises 13–40 through 13–43.

13.11 More About nextInt and nextLine

In Section 7.22 we examined the interaction of nextInt and nextLine. We saw that a nextLine immediately after a nextInt returns the remainder of the line containing the int. For a line containing *only* an int, the nextLine returns the empty String.

We often work with data files containing alternating lines of ints and Strings. For example, a file might look like this:

```
3
zebra
2
lion
. . .
```

If we read this with the method sequence nextInt, nextLine, nextInt, . . . , we observe the following:

- nextInt reads 3.
- nextLine reads the empty String.
- nextInt throws an InputMismatchException because it's being asked to process zebra as an int, which it certainly is not.

To correctly process this data file, we must use the sequence nextInt, nextLine, nextLine, nextInt, and so forth.

- nextInt reads 3.
- nextLine reads the empty String, which we discard.

- `nextLine` reads `zebra`.
- `nextInt` reads `2`.
- ...

We often place a `nextLine` immediately after a `nextInt` in order to discard the remainder of the integer line; this puts us at the front of the next line. We will use this technique in the next section, where we read files of objects representing `Students`.

If a file is entirely numeric, we can omit the `nextLines`. Similarly, if a file is entirely `Strings`, then we can read it successfully using a sequence of calls to `nextLine`.

 | **Test your skill with Exercises 13–44 and 13–45.** |

13.12   Section—Implemented as a File of Students

Earlier in this chapter, we studied patterns that took a file of items and computed (1) a count of the items, (2) the sum or product of the items, and (3) the average of the items. Each pattern was illustrated by a Java `main` method—an application—that contained the appropriate code. Now we'll develop a class `Section`, which will be a collection of `Student` objects. `Section` will provide methods involving all the patterns we have discussed up to this point. Then we will illustrate further patterns by adding the appropriate methods to class `Section`. In Chapter 14, we will confirm the adage

Change the implementation but don't change the interface

by re-implementing `Section` as an *array* of `Students`. All prior code that uses `Section` will continue to operate, even though we will have changed the implementation.

`Prog1311.java` contains three classes: `Prog1311`, `Section`, and `Student`.

Prog1311.java   **Class Section — A File of Students**

```
// Written by Barry Soroka.
//
// class Section -- implemented as a file of Students
//
import java.io.*;
import java.util.Scanner;
/////////////////////////////////////////////////////////////////////////////
class Prog1311
{
//-----------------------------------------------------------------------------
    public static void main (String [] args) throws Exception
```

```
   {
      Scanner kb = new Scanner(System.in);

      System.out.print("\nEnter name of a file of Students: ");
      String filename = kb.nextLine();

      Section sec = new Section(filename);

      System.out.println("\nIn forward order:");
      sec.print(System.out);

      System.out.println("\nThat section contains " +
                         sec.howMany() +
                         " Students.");

      System.out.println("\nThe average grade is " +
                         sec.average());
   }
//---------------------------------------------------------------------
} // end class Prog1311
/////////////////////////////////////////////////////////////////////////
class Section
{
   private String filename;
//---------------------------------------------------------------------
   public Section ( String filename )
   {
      this.filename = filename;
   }
//---------------------------------------------------------------------
   public void print ( PrintStream ps ) throws Exception
   {
      Scanner sc = new Scanner(new File(filename));

      while ( sc.hasNext() )
      {
         Student s = Student.read(null,sc);
         ps.println(s);
      }
   }
//---------------------------------------------------------------------
   public int howMany() throws Exception
   {
      Scanner sc = new Scanner(new File(filename));

      int n = 0;

      while ( sc.hasNext() )
      {
```

```
            Student s = Student.read(null,sc);
            n++;
        }

        return n;
    }
//-------------------------------------------------------------------------
    public double average() throws Exception
    {
        Scanner sc = new Scanner(new File(filename));

        int n = 0;
        int sum = 0;

        while ( sc.hasNext() )
        {
            Student s = Student.read(null,sc);
            n++;
            sum += s.getGrade();
        }

        return 1.0*sum/n;
    }
//-------------------------------------------------------------------------
} // end class Section
/////////////////////////////////////////////////////////////////////////
class Student
{
    private String name;
    private int grade;
//-------------------------------------------------------------------------
    public Student ( String name, int grade )
    {
        this.name = name;
        this.grade = grade;
    }
//-------------------------------------------------------------------------
    public String getName() { return name; }
//-------------------------------------------------------------------------
    public int getGrade() { return grade; }
//-------------------------------------------------------------------------
    public String toString() { return name + " (" + grade + ")"; }
//-------------------------------------------------------------------------
    public static Student read ( PrintStream ps, Scanner sc )
    {
        if ( ps != null ) ps.println("Reading a Student record ...");
```

```
        if ( ps != null ) ps.print("Enter the name: ");
        String name = sc.nextLine();
        if ( ps != null ) ps.print("Enter the grade: ");
        int grade = sc.nextInt(); sc.nextLine();
        return new Student(name,grade);
    }
//- - - - - - - - - - - - - - - - - - - - - - - - - - - - - - - - - - - - - - - - - - - - - - - - - - - -
} // end class Student
////////////////////////////////////////////////////////////////////////
```

The class `Student` describes an object with a `String name` and an `int grade`. Here are its methods:

- `public Student ( String name, int grade )`—a constructor.
- `public String getName()`—a getter.
- `public int getGrade()`—another getter.
- `public String toString()`—formats the `Student` for printing. Typical output is "`john (84)`".
- `public static Student read(. . . )`—this is the usual `static read` method; it returns `null` when it reaches the end-of-file.

Nothing in the class `Student` should be surprising. Note the use of an extra `nextLine` after each `nextInt` in the `read` method. As described in Section 13.11, this discards the rest of the line following the `int` and positions us at the front of the following line.

Class `Prog1311` contains the main method that exercises class `Section`. Let's analyze some statements of `Prog1311`. The first line is

```
        Section sec = new Section(filename);
```

whereby we define a new `Section` by sending the appropriate filename to the constructor. Next comes a statement that prints out the `Students` to the monitor:

```
        System.out.println("\nIn forward order:");
        sec.print(System.out);
```

Because `print` takes a `PrintStream` parameter, we can order a `Section` to print its `Students` to *any* `PrintStream`, including files as well as the monitor. The next statement computes and reports the number of `Students` in the `Section`:

```
        System.out.println("\nThat section contains " +
                            sec.howMany() +
                            " Students.");
```

Finally, we compute and print the average grade of the Students in the Section:

```
System.out.println("\nThe average grade is " +
                   sec.average());
```

Note how I have crafted a program that *uses the methods* of class Section, but I haven't yet *written the code* for Section. This is a common way to design a class: Write a sample program to test the adequacy of the prototypes of the methods that the class will contain.

Let's examine class Section:

- The only instance variable is the String filename. The current implementation of Section refers to the disk file every time it needs to examine the collection of Students in the Section.
- public Section (String filename)—This is the constructor. Note that its sole action is to record its parameter in the instance variable.
- public void print (PrintStream ps) throws Exception—This method uses the pattern we developed in Section 13.7. Note the tag throws Exception. This is required because the print method calls the constructor File(String) which can throw an Exception. We must acknowledge this possibility by adding the throws Exception phrase to the header of print. Similar logic applies to howMany and average.
- public int howMany() throws Exception—This method computes the number of Students using the pattern we developed earlier in this chapter.
- public double average() throws Exception—This method computes the average grade of the Students in the Section using the pattern developed in Section 13.10.

 Test your skill with Exercises 13–46 through 13–51.

13.13   howMany

Previously, we examined the code for a method howMany for class Section:

```
public int howMany()
```

Now we'll examine some other problems within the pattern:

> Given a collection of items, how many satisfy some criterion?

howMany solves this problem for a simple criterion: Does the item *exist* in the collection?

Let's start with the problem:

> Given a Section of Students, how many are *passing* the course?

We want a method with the prototype

```
public int howManyPass()
```

and the code will be this:

```
public int howManyPassed() throws Exception
{
    Scanner sc = new Scanner(new File(filename));

    int n = 0;

    while ( sc.hasNext() )
    {
        Student s = Student.read(null,sc);
        if ( s.getGrade() >= 60 ) n++;
    }

    return n;
}
```

This method is very similar to our previous howMany method; however, this one increments the counter only when the Student under consideration has a grade 60 or above. The previous howMany method *always* incremented. See Prog1312 for the code in context.

Prog1312.java   howManyPassed

```
// Written by Barry Soroka.
//
// class Section -- howManyPassed
//
import java.io.*;
import java.util.Scanner;
//////////////////////////////////////////////////////////////////////////////
class Prog1312
{
//--------------------------------------------------------------------------------
    public static void main (String [] args) throws Exception
    {
        Scanner kb = new Scanner(System.in);

        System.out.print("\nEnter name of a file of Students: ");
        String filename = kb.nextLine();

        Section sec = new Section(filename);


        System.out.println("\nIn forward order:");
        sec.print(System.out);

        System.out.println("\nThat section contains " +
```

```
                              sec.howMany() +
                              " Students.");

         System.out.println("\nHow many passed? " +
                              sec.howManyPassed());
      }
//-------------------------------------------------------------------
} // end class Prog1312
/////////////////////////////////////////////////////////////////////
class Section
{
   private String filename;
//-------------------------------------------------------------------
   public Section ( String filename )
   {
      this.filename = filename;
   }
//-------------------------------------------------------------------
//
// How many Students have grade >= 60 ?
//
   public int howManyPassed() throws Exception
   {
      Scanner sc = new Scanner(new File(filename));

      int n = 0;

      while ( sc.hasNext() )
      {
         Student s = Student.read(null,sc);
         if ( s.getGrade() >= 60 ) n++;
      }

      return n;
   }
//-------------------------------------------------------------------
   public void print ( PrintStream ps ) throws Exception
   {
      Scanner sc = new Scanner(new File(filename));

      while ( sc.hasNext() )
      {
         Student s = Student.read(null,sc);
         ps.println(s);
      }
   }
//-------------------------------------------------------------------
   public int howMany() throws Exception
   {
      Scanner sc = new Scanner(new File(filename));
```

```
      int n = 0;

      while ( sc.hasNext() )
      {
         Student s = Student.read(null,sc);
         n++;
      }

      return n;
   }
//------------------------------------------------------------------------
} // end class Section
///////////////////////////////////////////////////////////////////////////
class Student
{
   private String name;
   private int grade;
//------------------------------------------------------------------------
   public Student ( String name, int grade )
   {
      this.name = name;
      this.grade = grade;
   }
//------------------------------------------------------------------------
   public String getName() { return name; }
//------------------------------------------------------------------------
   public int getGrade() { return grade; }
//------------------------------------------------------------------------
   public String toString() { return name + " (" + grade + ")"; }
//------------------------------------------------------------------------
   public static Student read ( PrintStream ps, Scanner sc )
   {
      if ( ps != null ) ps.println("Reading a Student record ...");
      if ( ps != null ) ps.print("Enter the name: ");
      String name = sc.nextLine();
      if ( ps != null ) ps.print("Enter the grade: ");
      int grade = sc.nextInt(); sc.nextLine();
      return new Student(name,grade);
   }
//------------------------------------------------------------------------
} // end class Student
///////////////////////////////////////////////////////////////////////////
```

 Test your skill with Exercises 13–52 through 13–69.

13.14   any **and** all

In Section 13.13, we studied the code that solved the problem

(a) Given a Section of Students, how many are passing the course?

This problem required that we examine *every* Student in the file. Now, consider the problems

(b) Given a Section of Students, are *any* of them passing the course?

and

(c) Given a Section of Students, are *all* of them passing the course?

How do (b) and (c) differ from (a)?

STOP AND THINK

Problem (a) requires that we look at every Student in the Section. Problems (b) and (c) allow us to abandon the loop without looking at every element:

For pattern	we can stop looping if we find	and the result is:
(b)	any Student who's *passing*	true
(c)	any Student who's *failing*	false

Prog1313.java presents the code for didAnyPass and didAllPass. Both these methods exhibit a loop that can be exited prematurely by a return statement. Here's the relevant loop for didAnyPass:

```
while ( sc.hasNext() )
{
   Student s = Student.read(null,sc);
   if ( s.getGrade() >= 60 ) return true;
}
```

We run down the Students in the file, and if we find any Student who passed, then we exit the loop by returning true. If we get through the entire file without finding anyone who passed, then we return false. The loop for didAllPass is similar.

We will examine several ways to implement the patterns any and all. The one we've just seen is the simplest: When we know that we can exit the loop, we do so by returning the appropriate boolean value.

Prog1313.java   didAnyPass and didAllPass

```
// Written by Barry Soroka.
//
// class Section -- didAnyPass & didAllPass
//
import java.io.*;
import java.util.Scanner;
//////////////////////////////////////////////////////////////////////////////
class Prog1313
{
//-----------------------------------------------------------------------------
    public static void main (String [] args) throws Exception
    {
        Scanner kb = new Scanner(System.in);

        System.out.print("\nEnter name of a file of Students: ");
        String filename = kb.nextLine();

        Section sec = new Section(filename);

        System.out.println("\nIn forward order:");
        sec.print(System.out);

        System.out.println("\ndidAnyPass? " + sec.didAnyPass());
        System.out.println("\ndidAllPass? " + sec.didAllPass());
    }
//-----------------------------------------------------------------------------
} // end class Prog1313
//////////////////////////////////////////////////////////////////////////////
class Section
{
    private String filename;
//-----------------------------------------------------------------------------
    public Section ( String filename )
    {
        this.filename = filename;
    }
//-----------------------------------------------------------------------------
//
// Did any Student have grade >= 60 ?
//
    public boolean didAnyPass() throws Exception
    {
        Scanner sc = new Scanner(new File(filename));

        while ( sc.hasNext() )
        {
            Student s = Student.read(null,sc);
            if ( s.getGrade() >= 60 ) return true;
```

```
       }

       return false;
   }
//--------------------------------------------------------------------
//
// Did all Students have grade >= 60 ?
//
   public boolean didAllPass() throws Exception
   {
       Scanner sc = new Scanner(new File(filename));

       while ( sc.hasNext() )
       {
           Student s = Student.read(null,sc);
           if ( s.getGrade() < 60 ) return false;
       }

       return true;
   }
//--------------------------------------------------------------------
   public void print ( PrintStream ps ) throws Exception
   {
       Scanner sc = new Scanner(new File(filename));

       while ( sc.hasNext() )
       {
           Student s = Student.read(null,sc);
           ps.println(s);
       }
   }
//--------------------------------------------------------------------
} // end class Section
////////////////////////////////////////////////////////////////////////
class Student
{
   private String name;
   private int grade;
//--------------------------------------------------------------------
   public Student ( String name, int grade )
   {
       this.name = name;
       this.grade = grade;
   }
//--------------------------------------------------------------------
   public String getName() { return name; }
//--------------------------------------------------------------------
   public int getGrade() { return grade; }
//--------------------------------------------------------------------
```

```
   public String toString() { return name + " (" + grade + ")"; }
//------------------------------------------------------------------
   public static Student read ( PrintStream ps, Scanner sc )
   {
      if ( ps != null ) ps.println("Reading a Student record ...");
      if ( ps != null ) ps.print("Enter the name: ");
      String name = sc.nextLine();
      if ( ps != null ) ps.print("Enter the grade: ");
      int grade = sc.nextInt(); sc.nextLine();
      return new Student(name,grade);
   }
//------------------------------------------------------------------
} // end class Student
/////////////////////////////////////////////////////////////////////
```

Let's think about the empty Section for a moment. Did anyone *pass* in that Section? No, because we never found a Student who passed. Did *everyone* pass in that Section? Yes, because we found nobody who failed. More generally, the *any* searcher returns false unless it finds an example; the *all* searcher returns true unless it finds a counterexample.

We now turn our attention to problems involving files of *ints*:

> Given a file of ints, are *any* of them even?

and

> Given a file of ints, are *all* of them even?

We'll look at four ways to solve each of these problems. We'll call these the *any* and *all* problems.

Counting

A simple way of solving the problem is to count the total number of *ints*—nAll—and the number of *even ints*—nEven—and then compare the values. If nEven > 0, then *any* is true. If nEven == nAll, then *all* is true. Prog1314.java gives the code for *all*. The downside to this algorithm is that we look at all of the ints in the file even when we don't need to:

- We know that *all* is false as soon as we read any odd int.
- We know that *any* is true as soon as we read any even int.

Thus, if a file begins *odd, even,* . . . , then we know after reading the first element that *all* is false, and we know after reading the second element that *any* is true. Why bother reading the rest of the file?

Prog1314.java   allEven and anyEven

```
// Written by Barry Soroka.
//
// allEven & anyEven on a file of ints -- compare nEvens with nAll.
//
import java.io.*;
import java.util.Scanner;
/////////////////////////////////////////////////////////////////////////////
class Prog1314
{
//----------------------------------------------------------------------------
    public static void main (String [] args) throws Exception
    {
        Scanner kb = new Scanner(System.in);

        System.out.print("Filename? ");
        String filename = kb.nextLine();

        Scanner sc = new Scanner(new File(filename));

        int nAll = 0;
        int nEven = 0;

        while ( sc.hasNext() )
        {
            int n = sc.nextInt();
            nAll++;
            if ( n%2 == 0 ) nEven++;
        }

        System.out.println("allEven? " + (nEven == nAll) );
        System.out.println("anyEven? " + (nEven > 0) );
    }
//----------------------------------------------------------------------------
} // end class Prog1314
/////////////////////////////////////////////////////////////////////////////
```

The empty file contains no even ints. Also, all of the ints it contains are even. So, for the empty file, anyEven returns false, and allEven returns true.

Create and Maintain a boolean Result

This algorithm is illustrated in Prog1315.java. Here is the code, which is directly applicable to the *any* problem:

```
                    boolean anyEven = false;

                    while ( sc.hasNext() )
                    {
                        int n = sc.nextInt();
                        if ( n%2 == 0 ) anyEven = true;
                    }

                    System.out.println("anyEven? " + anyEven);
```

We create a `boolean` variable `anyEven`, and we initialize it to `false`—we haven't seen any even `int`s so far. Then we spin through all the `int`s in the file and, if we find an even `int`, we change `anyEven` to `true`. When we reach the end of the file, we accept the value of `anyEven` as our result. This algorithm is simple to understand, code, and debug, but it's *inefficient* because we read the entire file even if the first `int` is even.

Prog1315.java   allEven and anyEven—Using a boolean

```java
// Written by Barry Soroka.
//
// allEven & anyEven on a file of ints -- update a boolean result.
//
import java.io.*;
import java.util.Scanner;
////////////////////////////////////////////////////////////////////////////////
class Prog1315
{
//----------------------------------------------------------------------
    public static void main (String [] args) throws Exception
    {
        Scanner kb = new Scanner(System.in);

        System.out.print("Filename? ");
        String filename = kb.nextLine();

        Scanner sc = new Scanner(new File(filename));

        boolean allEven = true;
        boolean anyEven = false;

        while ( sc.hasNext() )
        {
            int n = sc.nextInt();
            if ( n%2 != 0 ) allEven = false;
            if ( n%2 == 0 ) anyEven = true;
        }
```

```
        System.out.println("allEven? " + allEven);
        System.out.println("anyEven? " + anyEven);
    }
//---------------------------------------------------------------------
} // end class Prog1315
/////////////////////////////////////////////////////////////////////////
```

Create a Helper Method So That We Can Use the `return` Statement

The two algorithms discussed previously both suffered from reading more `int`s than necessary. We didn't have this problem when we added the methods `didAllPass` and `didAnyPass` to class `Section`; we could use the `return` statement to exit a loop and return the appropriate result once we knew it. Now we'll use a `static` helper function to achieve the same functionality with a file of `int`s. `Prog1316.java` shows the code. We have created a new method

```
        private static boolean allEven ( Scanner sc )
```

which will do the looping, and we'll use the `return` statement to exit early: If we encounter an odd `int`, then we'll return `false`. The loop is very similar to the one we used in `didAnyPass`.

Prog1316.java   allEven—Using a Helper Method

```
// Written by Barry Soroka.
//
// allEven on a file of ints -- use a helper method & the return statement
//
import java.io.*;
import java.util.Scanner;
/////////////////////////////////////////////////////////////////////////
class Prog1316
{
//---------------------------------------------------------------------
    public static void main (String [] args) throws Exception
    {
        Scanner kb = new Scanner(System.in);

        System.out.print("Filename? ");
        String filename = kb.nextLine();
```

```
    Scanner sc = new Scanner(new File(filename));

    System.out.println("allEven? " + allEven(sc));
  }
//-----------------------------------------------------------------
  private static boolean allEven ( Scanner sc )
  {
    while ( sc.hasNext() )
    {
      int n = sc.nextInt();
      if ( n%2 != 0 ) return false;
    }
    return true;
  }
//-----------------------------------------------------------------
} // end class Prog1316
/////////////////////////////////////////////////////////////////
```

This example illustrates the utility of putting our loops into helper methods so that a well-chosen `return` statement can exit the loop and `return` the appropriate result.

> **Test your skill with Exercise 13–70.**

Exit the Loop Early Using the break Statement

`Prog1317.java` shows the loop we'll use for this algorithm:

```
boolean anyEven = false;

while ( sc.hasNext() )
{
    int n = sc.nextInt();
    if ( n%2 == 0 ) anyEven = true;
}

System.out.println("anyEven? " + anyEven);
```

We create a `boolean` variable `allEven`, which will hold the result as we know it so far. Initially, `allEven` is `true`, because we want `allEven` to be `true` for the empty file. As we spin around the loop, we look at the `int`. If it's even, we continue looping; if it's odd, we use the statements

```
                    allEven = false;
                    break;
```

to change the value of the result and to exit the loop.

Prog1317.java   **allEven—Loop with break Statement**

```java
// Written by Barry Soroka.
//
// allEven on a file of ints -- use the break statement to exit early.
//
import java.io.*;
import java.util.Scanner;
////////////////////////////////////////////////////////////////////////////////
class Prog1317
{
//--------------------------------------------------------------------------------
    public static void main (String [] args) throws Exception
    {
        Scanner kb = new Scanner(System.in);

        System.out.print("Filename? ");
        String filename = kb.nextLine();

        Scanner sc = new Scanner(new File(filename));

        boolean allEven = true;

        while ( sc.hasNext() )
        {
            int n = sc.nextInt();
            System.out.println("Just read " + n);
            if ( n%2 != 0 )
            {
                allEven = false;
                break;
            }
        }

        System.out.println("allEven? " + allEven);
    }
//--------------------------------------------------------------------------------
} // end class Prog1317
////////////////////////////////////////////////////////////////////////////////
```

| **Test your skill with Exercise 13–71.** |

Exit the Loop Early Using the Loop Condition

Prog1318.java gives the code for yet another algorithm for computing allEven on a file of ints. The boolean variable allEven is initialized to true and is used to control the loop:

```
while (sc.hasnext() allEven )
{
    ...
    if ( n%2 != 0 ) allEven = false;
    ...
}
```

If we hit the end-of-file, then our final result is true. If we encounter an odd int, then allEven is set to false, and we exit the loop when we check the condition. This algorithm is very efficient, but not so easy to remember.

Prog1318.java   allEven—boolean Variable Exits the Loop Early

```java
// Written by Barry Soroka.
//
// allEven on a file of ints -- exit the loop early.
//
import java.io.*;
import java.util.Scanner;
/////////////////////////////////////////////////////////////////////////////
class Prog1318
{
//-----------------------------------------------------------------------
    public static void main (String [] args) throws Exception
    {
        Scanner kb = new Scanner(System.in);

        System.out.print("Filename? ");
        String filename = kb.nextLine();

        Scanner sc = new Scanner(new File(filename));

        boolean allEven = true;

        while ( sc.hasNext() && allEven )
        {
            int n = sc.nextInt();
            System.out.println("Just read " + n);
            if ( n%2 != 0 ) allEven = false;
        }
```

```
        System.out.println("allEven? " + allEven);
    }
//----------------------------------------------------------------
} // end class Prog1318
////////////////////////////////////////////////////////////////////////////
```

 Test your skill with Exercises 13–72 through 13–76.

13.15 Finding Extremes

Programmers are often asked to find the *largest* or *smallest* element in a collection. We'll start by solving problems like these:

> Given a file of Students, which Student has the *highest* grade?
>
> Given a file of Students, which Student has the *lowest* grade?

and we'll apply the same algorithm to handle problems like these:

> Given a file of Rectangles, find the one with the largest area
>
> Given a file of ints, find the smallest.

Let's think for a moment.

Q: In computing the maximum element, must we look at *all* the elements in the file?

A: Yes. We can never stop early because an unseen element may be larger than the one we currently believe to be the maximum.[3]

Q: What's the largest element in the empty file?

A: Since the empty file contains no elements, it's silly to say that a particular value is the maximum value in the file. As before, we will not write special code to handle the empty file; our code will throw an expected Exception for the empty file.

Our algorithm for computing the *maximum* element in a file is this:

- Grab the first element and hold it aside as the tentative largest element. Let's call it largest.

---

[3] Our answer is slightly different if we know that the elements come from a *finite set*. For example, if we know that 100 is the maximum possible, then we can stop looking for a maximum item as soon as we find one with value 100.

- Look at each of the following elements in the file. If the element is larger than largest, then replace largest with the new maximum value.
- When we exit the loop, largest will be the maximum value in the file.

Prog1319.java gives the code for solving the problem

Given a file of Students, which Student has the highest grade?

and we have added a method to class Section:

```
public Student getStudentWithHighestGrade()
```

Try this on several data files. When you try it on the *empty file*, you'll see

```
G:\1\book\programs\13programs>java Prog1319
Enter name of a file of Students: empty
In forward order:
Exception in thread "main" java.util.NoSuchElementException
        at java.util.Scanner.throwFor(Unknown Source)
        at java.util.Scanner.next(Unknown Source)
        at java.util.Scanner.nextInt(Unknown Source)
        at java.util.Scanner.nextInt(Unknown Source)
        at Student.read(Prog1319.java:90)
        at Section.getStudentWithHighestGrade(Prog1319.java:42)
        at Prog1319.main(Prog1319.java:23)
```

We get a NoSuchElementException because the program executes nextInt at the end of the (empty) file.

Prog1319.java   **Find Student with Highest Grade**

```java
// Written by Barry Soroka.
//
// class Section -- find the Student with the highest grade.
//
import java.io.*;
import java.util.Scanner;
//////////////////////////////////////////////////////////////////////////////
class Prog1319
{
//----------------------------------------------------------------------------
    public static void main (String [] args) throws Exception
    {
        Scanner kb = new Scanner(System.in);

        System.out.print("\nEnter name of a file of Students: ");
```

```
      String filename = kb.nextLine();

      Section sec = new Section(filename);

      System.out.println("\nIn forward order:");
      sec.print(System.out);

      System.out.println("\nStudent with highest grade: " +
                         sec.getStudentWithHighestGrade());
   }
//------------------------------------------------------------------------
} // end class Prog1319
////////////////////////////////////////////////////////////////////////////
class Section
{
   private String filename;
//------------------------------------------------------------------------
   public Section ( String filename )
   {
      this.filename = filename;
   }
//------------------------------------------------------------------------
   public Student getStudentWithHighestGrade() throws Exception
   {
      Scanner sc = new Scanner(new File(filename));

      Student bigStudent = Student.read(null,sc);

      while ( sc.hasNext() )
      {
         Student s = Student.read(null,sc);
         if ( s.getGrade() > bigStudent.getGrade() ) bigStudent = s;
      }

      return bigStudent;
   }
//------------------------------------------------------------------------
   public void print ( PrintStream ps ) throws Exception
   {
      Scanner sc = new Scanner(new File(filename));

      while ( sc.hasNext() )
      {
         Student s = Student.read(null,sc);
         ps.println(s);
      }
   }
//------------------------------------------------------------------------
} // end class Section
```

```
////////////////////////////////////////////////////////////////////////////
class Student
{
   private String name;
   private int grade;
//----------------------------------------------------------------
   public Student ( String name, int grade )
   {
      this.name = name;
      this.grade = grade;
   }
//----------------------------------------------------------------
   public String getName() { return name; }
//----------------------------------------------------------------
   public int getGrade() { return grade; }
//----------------------------------------------------------------
   public String toString() { return name + " (" + grade + ")"; }
//----------------------------------------------------------------
   public static Student read ( PrintStream ps, Scanner sc )
   {
      if ( ps != null ) ps.println("Reading a Student record ...");
      if ( ps != null ) ps.print("Enter the name: ");
      String name = sc.nextLine();
      if ( ps != null ) ps.print("Enter the grade: ");
      int grade = sc.nextInt(); sc.nextLine();
      return new Student(name,grade);
   }
//----------------------------------------------------------------
} // end class Student
////////////////////////////////////////////////////////////////////////////
```

Prog1319 returns the *Student* with the highest grade. What if we don't care about the name and we only want the grade? Then we can write the following method:

```
int bigGrade = Student.read(null,sc).getGrade();

while ( sc.hasNext() )
{
   Student s = Student.read(null,sc);
   if ( s.getGrade() > bigGrade )
   {
      bigGrade = s.getGrade();
   }
}

return bigGrade;
```

What is returned if the `Section` contains more than one `Student` with the highest `grade`?

 **AND THINK**

The current code returns the `name` of the *first* `Student` to have the highest `grade`. All succeeding `Students` with that same `grade` are ignored; the `Student` with the highest `grade` can only be displaced by a `Student` with a *higher* `grade`.

 Test your skill with Exercises 13–77 through 13–86.

In the exercises, you were asked to solve the problems

Given a file of `ints`, print the largest.

and

Given a file of `ints`, print the smallest.

A naïve solution would be to look through the file *twice*: once to find the *largest* `int`, and once to find the *smallest* `int`. You may have guessed—or proved—that we can achieve the same result with a single pass through the file of `ints`. `Prog1320` presents the code. Note that we initialize *two* temporaries to the same value:

```
int lo = sc.nextInt();
int hi = lo;
```

Then, in the loop, we check each value in the file against the temporaries, replacing as necessary:

```
int n = sc.nextInt();
if ( n > hi ) hi = n;
if ( n < lo ) lo = n;
```

Prog1320.java   **Find Largest and Smallest int**

```
// Written by Barry Soroka.
//
// Given a file of ints, print the largest and smallest int.
//
import java.io.*;
import java.util.Scanner;
//////////////////////////////////////////////////////////////////////////////
class Prog1320
{
```

```
//-------------------------------------------------------------------
    public static void main (String [] args) throws Exception
    {
        Scanner kb = new Scanner(System.in);

        System.out.print("Filename? ");
        String filename = kb.nextLine();

        Scanner sc = new Scanner(new File(filename));

        int lo = sc.nextInt();
        int hi = lo;

        while ( sc.hasNext() )
        {
            int n = sc.nextInt();
            if ( n > hi ) hi = n;
            if ( n < lo ) lo = n;
        }

        System.out.println("lo: " + lo);
        System.out.println("hi: " + hi);
    }
//-------------------------------------------------------------------
} // end class Prog1320
///////////////////////////////////////////////////////////////////////////
```

   Test your skill with Exercise 13–87.

13.16   Is a Sequence in Order?

Here's a typical example of this pattern:

Given a file of `ints`, is it in ascending order?

By "ascending," let's allow adjacent elements to be equal.[4] Thus, the following sequences are ascending:

```
[3,6,7,13,20]
[3,3,6,7,13,20]
[3,6,7,7,7,13,20]
[3]
[]
```

---

[4] Mathematicians use the term "*strictly* ascending" to denote ascending sequences where adjacent elements are *not* permitted to be equal.

Note that singletons and the empty sequence are considered to be ascending.

What will the code be like? In general, we're going to be looking at *two adjacent elements*, comparing a previous element (last) against a current element (next). If they're out of order, then we don't need to look at the rest of the file—it's not ascending. If last and next *are* ascending, then we replace last with next and we fill next with the next element in the file. For the sequence [3,6,7,13,20], we'd expect the variables to shift as shown in the following table:

last	next	Sequence Not Yet Seen
		3,6,7,13,20
3	6	7,13,20
6	7	13,20
7	13	20
13	20	

return true

We will also have to watch for the empty and singleton cases, because these will throw Exceptions if we execute nextInt while at the end of the file.

Prog1321 shows the code for the algorithm we have discussed. Note that I'm using a static helper method so that I can cleanly exit loops with the return statement. Here's the code we need to discuss next:

```
if ( !sc.hasNext() ) return true;

int last = sc.nextInt();

while ( sc.hasNext() )
{
    int next = sc.nextInt();
    if ( next < last ) return false;
    last = next;
}

return true;
```

We begin by checking the Scanner. If it has no next element, then it's the empty file, and we return true.[5] Otherwise, we assign a value to last, and we proceed to the loop. For a singleton, we never enter the loop—we fall past the loop to the statement, which returns true. If we enter the loop, then the file contains at least two elements, last and next. If these are out of order, we return false; otherwise, we read another line and go to the top of the loop.

---

[5] For most of the patterns in this chapter, the empty file is *not a special case*. The method isAscending *does* need to treat the empty file as a special case.

Prog1321.java   **Are ints Ascending?**

```java
// Written by Barry Soroka
//
// Given a file of ints, is it in ascending order?
//
import java.io.*;
import java.util.Scanner;
//////////////////////////////////////////////////////////////////////////////
class Prog1321
{
//------------------------------------------------------------------------------
    public static void main ( String [] args ) throws Exception
    {
        Scanner kb = new Scanner(System.in);

        System.out.print("Filename? ");
        String filename = kb.nextLine();

        Scanner sc = new Scanner(new File(filename));

        System.out.println("isAscending? " + isAscending(sc));
    }
//------------------------------------------------------------------------------
    private static boolean isAscending ( Scanner sc )
    {
        if ( !sc.hasNext() ) return true;

        int last = sc.nextInt();

        while ( sc.hasNext() )
        {
            int next = sc.nextInt();
            if ( next < last ) return false;
            last = next;
        }

        return true;
    }
//------------------------------------------------------------------------------
} // end class Prog1321
//////////////////////////////////////////////////////////////////////////////
```

➡️ **Test your skill with Exercises 13–88 through 13–94.**

13.17   Pattern: New File(s)

This section discusses programs that take one input file and generate one or more output files. A typical problem is this:

Given a file of `int`s, generate a new file in which each `int` has been squared.

`Prog1322.java` is the solution. Here is an overview of the code:

- Open the input file for reading.
- Open the output file for writing.
- Loop through the elements of the input file.
  Write the square of the element to the output file.

This pattern can be used or generalized to solve many other problems.

Prog1322.java   Square the ints

```java
// Written by Barry Soroka
//
// Given a file of ints,
// generate another file where each int has been squared.
//
import java.io.*;
import java.util.Scanner;
/////////////////////////////////////////////////////////////////////////////
class Prog1322
{
//-------------------------------------------------------------------------
    public static void main ( String [] args ) throws Exception
    {
        Scanner kb = new Scanner(System.in);

        System.out.print("Filename? ");
        String filename = kb.nextLine();

        Scanner sc = new Scanner(new File(filename));

        System.out.print("Output file? ");
        String outfile = kb.nextLine();

        PrintStream ps = new PrintStream(
                            new FileOutputStream(
                                new File(outfile)));

        while ( sc.hasNext() )
        {
            int n = sc.nextInt();
```

```
            ps.println(n*n);
        }
    }
//-------------------------------------------------------------------
} // end class Prog1322
///////////////////////////////////////////////////////////////////////
```

Test your skill with Exercises 13–95 through 13–103.

13.18   Pattern: Two Files In

This pattern applies to problems that take *two* input files, and there are several variants of the pattern. We'll start with problems involving files of *equal length*, such as

> Given two equal-length files of ints, generate a file whose elements are the sum of the corresponding input elements.

For example, if the input files are *in1* and *in2*, as shown below, then the output file is *out*.

in1	in2	out
2	5	7
-5	13	8
2	-2	0
7	4	11

Prog1323 gives the code that solves this problem. Here's the structure:

- Open the input files for reading.
- Open the output file for writing.
- Loop through the input files, writing the sum of the two incoming elements to the output file.

This pattern assumes that the files are the *same length*; thus, we don't have to worry about one file running out before the other.

Prog1323.java   **Add ints from Two Input Files**

```
// Written by Barry Soroka
//
// Given two equal-length files of ints,
// generate a new same-length file of ints
// where each int is the sum of the two corresponding incoming ints.
//
```

```
import java.io.*;
import java.util.Scanner;
/////////////////////////////////////////////////////////////////////////////
class Prog1323
{
//---------------------------------------------------------------------------
   public static void main ( String [] args ) throws Exception
   {
      Scanner kb = new Scanner(System.in);

      System.out.print("File1? ");
      Scanner sc1 = new Scanner(new File(kb.nextLine()));

      System.out.print("File2? ");
      Scanner sc2 = new Scanner(new File(kb.nextLine()));

      System.out.print("Output file? ");

      PrintStream ps = new PrintStream(
                          new FileOutputStream(
                            new File(kb.nextLine())));

      while ( sc1.hasNext() )
      {
         int n1 = sc1.nextInt();
         int n2 = sc2.nextInt();
         ps.println(n1+n2);
      }
   }
//---------------------------------------------------------------------------
} // end class Prog1323
/////////////////////////////////////////////////////////////////////////////
```

 | **Test your skill with Exercises 13–104 through 13–110.** |

Dot Product

This pattern takes two files and produces a *scalar*—a single element. You may recall the mathematical operation *dot product*, which takes two equal-length lists of ints and produces a single int as the result, according to the formula

$\sum a_i b_i$. For example, if we have files *in1* and *in2*:

in1	4	-3	2
in2	5	2	4

then their dot product is

$$4 \cdot 5 + (-3) \cdot 2 + 2 \cdot 4 = 20 - 6 + 8 = 22.$$

Of course, our program must work for input files of *any length*. Note that *the empty file is not a special case*: The dot product of two empty files is 0, which is what we always get as the sum of *no* elements. Prog1324 shows the code for the dot product pattern.

Prog1324.java   **Dot Product**

```
// Written by Barry Soroka
//
// Given two equal-length files of ints, compute the dot product.
//
import java.io.*;
import java.util.Scanner;
//////////////////////////////////////////////////////////////////////////////
class Prog1324
{
//----------------------------------------------------------------------------
    public static void main ( String [] args ) throws Exception
    {
        Scanner kb = new Scanner(System.in);

        System.out.print("File1? ");
        Scanner sc1 = new Scanner(new File(kb.nextLine()));

        System.out.print("File2? ");
        Scanner sc2 = new Scanner(new File(kb.nextLine()));

        int result = 0;

        while ( sc1.hasNext() )   // files are guaranteed to be equal in length
        {
            int n1 = sc1.nextInt();
            int n2 = sc2.nextInt();
            result += n1 * n2;
        }

        System.out.println("The dot product is " + result);
    }
//----------------------------------------------------------------------------
} // end class Prog1324
//////////////////////////////////////////////////////////////////////////////
```

 | **Test your skill with Exercise 13–111.** |

Are Two Files Equal?

Suppose we say that two files are equal if (1) they have the same number of lines, and (2) corresponding lines are equal. Prog1325 shows how to do this with a helper method `equalScanners`, which takes two `Scanner`s as its parameters. Here is the loop:

```
while ( sc1.hasNext() && sc2.hasNext() )
{
    String s1 = sc1.nextLine();
    String s2 = sc2.nextLine();
    if ( !s1.equals(s2) ) return false;
}
return !sc1.hasNext() && !sc2.hasNext();
```

The loop continues as long as both files are nonempty. If the corresponding `String`s differ, then the method exits the loop by returning `false`. If we get past the loop, then one or more of the `Scanner`s is empty. If they run out simultaneously, then both `sc1.hasNext()` and `sc2.hasNext()` are `false` and we should return `true`. In all other cases, we should return `false`. Hence the closing line:

```
return !sc1.hasNext() && !sc2.hasNext();
```

Prog1325.java   Are Two Files Equal?

```
// Written by Barry Soroka
//
// Are two files equal?
// "Equal" means the same number of lines
// and corresponding lines equal.
//
import java.io.*;
import java.util.Scanner;
//////////////////////////////////////////////////////////////////////////////
class Prog1325
{
//-----------------------------------------------------------------------------

    public static void main ( String [] args ) throws Exception
    {
        Scanner kb = new Scanner(System.in);

        System.out.print("File1? ");
        Scanner sc1 = new Scanner(new File(kb.nextLine()));

        System.out.print("File2? ");
        Scanner sc2 = new Scanner(new File(kb.nextLine()));

        System.out.println("\nFiles equal? " + equalScanners(sc1,sc2));
    }
//-----------------------------------------------------------------------------
```

```
public static boolean equalScanners ( Scanner sc1,
                                       Scanner sc2 )
{
    while ( sc1.hasNext() && sc2.hasNext() )
    {
        String s1 = sc1.nextLine();
        String s2 = sc2.nextLine();
        if ( !s1.equals(s2) ) return false;
    }

    return !sc1.hasNext() && !sc2.hasNext();
}
//-------------------------------------------------------------------
} // end class Prog1325
///////////////////////////////////////////////////////////////////
```

Test your skill with Exercises 13–112 through 13–114.

Is One File a Prefix of Another?

File A is a prefix of file B if (1) A contains no more lines than B, and (2) corresponding lines are equal. Here is a table that shows a variety of test cases and expected results:

A	B	A is a prefix of B?
[3,5,-7]	[3,5,-7]	true
[3,5,-7]	[3,5,-7,2]	true
[3,5,-7]	[3,5,-7,2,4,1,9,3]	true
[3,5,-7]	[3,4,-7]	false
[3,5,-7]	[3,5]	false
[3,5,-7]	[]	false
[]	[]	true
[]	[3,5,-7]	true
[1]	[1]	true
[1]	[1,2]	true
[1,2]	[1]	false
[1,2]	[1,2]	true
[1,2]	[1,2,1]	true

Note that the empty file is a prefix of every file. Prog1326 shows how to implement an appropriate algorithm using a helper function isPrefix, which takes two `Scanners` as parameters. Here is the loop, which is very similar to that of `Prog1324`:

```
while ( sc1.hasNext() && sc2.hasNext() )
{
    int n1 = sc1.nextInt();
    int n2 = sc2.nextInt();
    if ( n1 != n2 ) return false;
}
return !sc1.hasNext();
```

The loop continues as long as both files are nonempty. If corresponding `int`s differ, then the method exits the loop by returning `false`. If we get past the loop, then one or more of the `Scanner`s is empty. If the first file is empty, then we return `true` because all of its `int`s have been matched; otherwise, the second file has exhausted first, leaving `int`s unmatched in the first file, and `isPrefix` returns `false`.

Prog1326.java   Is One File a Prefix of Another File?

```
// Written by Barry Soroka
//
// Is one file a prefix of another?  Both files are files of ints.
//
import java.io.*;
import java.util.Scanner;
//////////////////////////////////////////////////////////////////////////////
class Prog1326
{
//------------------------------------------------------------------------------
    public static void main ( String [] args ) throws Exception
    {
        Scanner kb = new Scanner(System.in);

        System.out.print("File1? ");
        Scanner sc1 = new Scanner(new File(kb.nextLine()));

        System.out.print("File2? ");
        Scanner sc2 = new Scanner(new File(kb.nextLine()));

        System.out.println("\nfile1 is a prefix of file2? " + isPrefix(sc1,sc2));
    }
//------------------------------------------------------------------------------
    public static boolean isPrefix ( Scanner sc1,
                                     Scanner sc2 )
    {
```

```
        while ( sc1.hasNext() && sc2.hasNext() )
        {
            int n1 = sc1.nextInt();
            int n2 = sc2.nextInt();
            if ( n1 != n2 ) return false;
        }
        return !sc1.hasNext();
    }
//-------------------------------------------------------------------------------
} // end class Prog1326
////////////////////////////////////////////////////////////////////////////////
```

Test your skill with Exercise 13–115.

Joining Files

Consider the problem

> Given two files, produce a third file which is the join of the first file with
> the second file.

For example, if

$$in1 = \quad 3 \quad 2 \quad 7 \quad 4$$

and

$$in2 = \quad 6 \quad 1 \quad 2$$

then their *join* is

$$out = \quad 3 \quad 2 \quad 7 \quad 4 \quad 6 \quad 1 \quad 2$$

where the output file contains the elements of the first input file, followed by
the elements of the second input file.

Test your skill with Exercises 13–116 through 13–119.

13.19 Some Miscellaneous Problems

Projection

This pattern describes taking a file of data and producing a new file containing
an item-for-item subset of the data in the input file. You will see this operation
again in an upper-division database course.

Test your skill with Exercise 13–120.

Using Files for Automatic Testing

Recall the class Complex with its intelligent toString method: "3+0i" becomes just "3", and so forth. In Chapter 7, we listed all the special test cases that toString must handle:

real	imag	Result of toString
0	0	0
0	5	5i
3	0	3
3	5	3+5i
3	-5	3-5i
0	-5	-5i
3	1	3+i
3	-1	3-i
0	1	i
0	-1	-i

Let's create a test *file* where each test case becomes three lines:

- the real part;
- the imaginary part; and
- the String expected back from toString.

Here's the beginning of the test file:

```
        0
        0
        0
        0
        5
        5i
        3
        0
        3
        3
        5
        3+5i
        . . .
```

Prog1327 presents a loop that reads each set of triples and tests the available toString method. Every mismatch is reported, and if all tests are passed an appropriate message is printed at end-of-file. Notice that this test file is read with a mixture of nextInts and nextLines. Therefore, we need an extra nextLine to clear the remainder of the line after the Complex has been read.

Prog1327.java   **Automatic Testing of toString for Class Complex**

```java
// Written by Barry Soroka
//
// Automatic test file for method toString in class Complex.
// The file consits of triples:  real part, imaginary part, expected toString.
//
import java.io.*;
import java.util.Scanner;
/////////////////////////////////////////////////////////////////////////////
class Prog1327
{
//-------------------------------------------------------------------------
    public static void main ( String [] args ) throws Exception
    {
        Scanner kb = new Scanner(System.in);

        System.out.print("File of tests for Complex? ");
        String filename = kb.nextLine();

        Scanner sc = new Scanner(new File(filename));

        int nErrors = 0;

        while ( sc.hasNext() )
        {
            Complex z = Complex.read(null,sc); sc.nextLine();
            String expected = sc.nextLine();
            String actual = z.toString();
            if ( !expected.equals(actual) )
            {
                System.out.println("*** Mismatch: " + expected + " vs " + actual);
                nErrors++;
            }
        }

        if ( nErrors == 0 ) System.out.println("\nAll test cases are correct.");
    }
//-------------------------------------------------------------------------
} // end class Prog1327
/////////////////////////////////////////////////////////////////////////////
class Complex
{
    private int real;
    private int imag;
//-------------------------------------------------------------------------
    public Complex ( int real , int imag )
    {
        this.real = real;
```

```
         this.imag = imag;
      }
//-----------------------------------------------------------------
   public String toString ()
   {
      if ( imag == 0 ) return real + "";

      String iString = Math.abs(imag) + "i";
      if ( Math.abs(imag) == 1 ) iString = "i";

      if ( real == 0 && imag > 0 ) return iString;
      if ( real == 0 && imag < 0 ) return "-" + iString;

      if ( imag > 0 ) return real + "+" + iString;

      return real + "-" + iString;
   }
//-----------------------------------------------------------------
   public boolean equals ( Complex that )
   {
      return this.real == that.real
             &&
             this.imag == that.imag;
   }
//-----------------------------------------------------------------
   public static Complex read ( PrintStream ps, Scanner sc )
   {
      if ( ps != null ) ps.println("Reading a complex number ...");
      if ( ps != null ) ps.print("Enter the real part:      ");
      int real = sc.nextInt();
      if ( ps != null ) ps.print("Enter the imaginary part: ");
      int imag = sc.nextInt();
      return new Complex ( real, imag );
   }
//-----------------------------------------------------------------
   public Complex add ( Complex that )
   {
      return new Complex ( this.real + that.real , this.imag + that.imag );
   }
//-----------------------------------------------------------------
   public Complex sub ( Complex that )
   {
      return new Complex ( this.real - that.real , this.imag - that.imag );
   }
//-----------------------------------------------------------------
   public Complex times ( Complex that )
   {
      int a1 = this.real, b1 = this.imag;
      int a2 = that.real, b2 = that.imag;
```

```
        return new Complex ( a1*a2-b1*b2, a1*b2+a2*b1 );
    }
//-------------------------------------------------------------------
} // end class Complex
///////////////////////////////////////////////////////////////////////
```

 Test your skill with Exercises 13–121 through 13–123.

13.20 Generating Integer Sequences with `while`

Up to this point, we have been using `while` to loop through *files*. Now we'll examine ways of using `while` loops to solve problems involving *sequences of integers*.

HOLD YOUR HORSES

Many of these problems are better solved with the `for` loop, which we will learn later in this chapter.

Print "`hello`" Five Times

Here's the code:

```
int i = 0;

while ( i < 5 )
{
    System.out.println("hello");
    i++;
}
```

This is the pattern that guarantees that we do something exactly n times:

```
int i = 0;

while ( i < n )
{
    desired action
    i++;
}
```

If you hand-trace the loop, you'll see that i goes through the values 0,1,2,3,4 for a total of five values. It's easy to get `while` wrong, so you should select and memorize a pattern that guarantees the performance you want.

> **Test your skill with Exercises 13–124 and 13–125.**

From Low to High

These problems have the following form: Repeat something with variable i having the values lo, . . . , hi. Here's the pattern:

```
int i = lo;

while ( i <= hi )
{
    desired action
    i++;
}
```

Let's examine the particular problem: *Print the ints from 20 to 25*. Using the pattern, we have:

```
int i = 20;

while ( i <= 25 )
{
    System.out.print(i + " ");
    i++;
}
```

This prints the desired sequence: 20 21 22 23 24 25.

　　`while` loops are very fragile. Using the wrong relational operator is a common error. Let's see what happens if we use "<" instead of "<=":

```
int i = 20;

while ( i < 25 )
{
    System.out.print(i + " ");
    i++;
}
```

This loop produces the sequence 20 21 22 23 24, which omits the desired final value 25.

NOTE

OBO is shorthand for off by one, a common error when using while loops.

Skipping Numbers

We often want loops to skip numbers, as in this problem: *Print the odd numbers from 1 to 100*. There are several ways to solve this problem. A brute-force approach would be:

```
int i = 1;

while ( i < ... )
{
    if ( i%2 != 0 ) System.out.print(i + " ");
    i++;
}
```

This code looks through all the integers in the range [1,100] and prints the number only if it's odd. Another approach would be:

```
int i = 1;

while ( i < ... )
{
    System.out.print(i + " ");
    i += 2;
}
```

which increments i by 2 so that we *only* see the odd numbers. Yet another approach would be:

```
int i = 0;

while ( i < 49 )
{
    System.out.print(2*i+1 + " ");
    i++;
}
```

which relies on transforming the sequence [0,1,2,. . . ,49] into the sequence [1,3,5,. . . ,99]. This last approach is prone to error, so be careful when you use it.

Test your skill with Exercises 13–126 through 13–128.

Backward

Consider the problem: *Print the integers from 100 down to 1.* Here's a straightforward implementation:

```
int i = 100;

while ( i >= 1 )
{
    System.out.print(i + " ");
    i--;
}
```

This pattern is fairly safe to use because we start with the largest int and we keep going as long as we're >= the smallest int. Another approach is:

```
int i = 1;

while ( i < 101 )
{
    System.out.print(101-i + " ");
    i--;
}
```

which relies on transforming the sequence [1,2,3,. . . ,100] to the sequence [100,99,98,. . . ,1].

Test your skill with Exercise 13–129.

13.21   Signaling End-of-File with a Sentinel

The first programming languages did not have a nice way of detecting end-of-file—if a program read beyond the end of a file, it might retrieve some other file's data or it might generate an error. Programmers developed a way to use files despite these difficulties, though. After the data of a file, they put a value that

Sentinel   A value used as a signal.

could not occur in that data set. We call this value a *sentinel*. -1 might be a good sentinel for a file of numerical grades.[6] Prog1328 shows how we can use a while loop to print and

---

[6]   But not always. I had a friend who turned in a paper that received a grade of 95, less 120 for lateness, giving a final score of -25.

count the `ints` in a file, where end-of-file is signaled by the sentinel -1. A typical file might be [82,73,45,62,91,-1]. The "empty file" contains just the sentinel: [-1]. Sometimes we use more generic sentinels:

```
while ( i >= 0 )
```

stops when a grade is negative, whereas

```
while ( i != -1 )
```

stops when a grade is exactly -1.

Prog1328.java   Using a Sentinel Value

```java
// Written by Barry Soroka
//
// Stop reading when a sentinel value is encountered.
//
import java.io.*;
import java.util.Scanner;
//////////////////////////////////////////////////////////////////////////////
class Prog1328
{
//----------------------------------------------------------------------------

    public static void main ( String [] args ) throws Exception
    {
        Scanner kb = new Scanner(System.in);

        System.out.print("File of ints (ending with sentinel -1): ");
        String filename = kb.nextLine();

        Scanner sc = new Scanner(new File(filename));

        int i = sc.nextInt();
        int count = 0;

        while ( i != -1 )
        {
            System.out.println(i);
            count++;
            i = sc.nextInt();
        }

        System.out.println("File contained " + count + " ints.");
    }
//----------------------------------------------------------------------------
} // end class Prog1328
//////////////////////////////////////////////////////////////////////////////
```

Modern programming languages obviate the need to put sentinels at the ends of files, but you may encounter legacy code and legacy files that *do* use sentinel values.

Test your skill with Exercises 13–130 through 13–134.

13.22 More about while

We need while loops when we don't know in advance how many times we will be repeating a body of code. A typical usage is this: Read and sum ints until the sum hits or exceeds 100. Prog1329 gives the code. Note how sum < 100 is given as the condition guarding the loop.

Here is a more general loop structure, which lets us exit by causing the condition to become false:

```
boolean done = false;
while ( !done )
{
    ...
    if ( condition ) done = true;
    ...
}
```

Prog1329.java   **Read ints Until . . .**

```
// Written by Barry Soroka
//
// Read ints until the sum hits or exceeds 100.
//
import java.io.*;
import java.util.Scanner;
//////////////////////////////////////////////////////////////////////////////
class Prog1329
{
//----------------------------------------------------------------------------
    public static void main ( String [] args ) throws Exception
    {
        Scanner kb = new Scanner(System.in);

        int sum = 0;

        while ( sum < 100 )
        {
```

```
        System.out.print("Enter an int: ");
        sum += kb.nextInt();
        System.out.println("sum: " + sum);
    }
  }
//------------------------------------------------------------------------
} // end class Prog1329
//////////////////////////////////////////////////////////////////////////
```

    Test your skill with Exercises 13–135 through 13–138.

13.23 The for Loop

Consider the problem:

Given a file of Students and a non-negative integer n, read and print the first n Students in the file.

We could write this with a while, but instead we'll use a for loop. The general rule is as follows:

NOTE

Use for when you know exactly how many times you'll execute the loop body. This is a *definite* loop.

Use while when you don't know how many times you'll be executing the loop. This is an *indefinite* loop.

Prog1330 gives the code that solves the problem. Here's the crucial statement:

```
for ( int i = 0 ; i < n ; i++ )
    System.out.println(Student.read(null,sc));
```

The for statement has the form

```
for ( initialization ; condition ; increment ) body
```

where *initialization*, *condition*, *increment*, and *body* have the roles shown in Figure 13–2. Note that *condition* must be a *boolean expression*. For our particular loop, we have the correspondences:

Figure 13–2
Flowchart for the
FOR statement

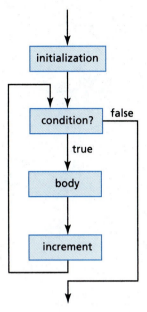

Initialization	`int i = 0`
Condition	`i < n`
Increment	`i++`
Body	`System.out.println(Student.read(null,sc));`

We create a variable i and we initialize it to 0. We keep entering the loop as long as i < n. Each time around we increment i by 1. This is the pattern that performs the body exactly n times—the variable i enters the loop with values 0, 1, 2, . . . , n-1—a total of n times. *Memorize this pattern!* It guarantees performance of the loop exactly n times. There are many ways to alter this pattern, most of them to its detriment:

Initialization	Condition	Effect
i = 0	i < n	n iterations
i = 1	i < n	n-1 iterations
i = 1	i <= n	n iterations
i = 0	i <= n	n+1 iterations

Note that two of the mangled loops exhibit OBO (off-by-one) errors. Note also that if n <= 0, then the loop is never entered at all. This is as it should be, since the user is requesting 0 or fewer iterations.

Prog1330.java   Print n Students Using a for Loop

```java
// Written by Barry Soroka
//
// Print n Students from a file of Students -- using for.
//
import java.io.*;
import java.util.Scanner;
////////////////////////////////////////////////////////////////////////////////
class Prog1330
{
//------------------------------------------------------------------------------
    public static void main ( String [] args ) throws Exception
    {
        Scanner kb = new Scanner(System.in);

        System.out.print("\nEnter name of a file of Students: ");
        String filename = kb.nextLine();

        Scanner sc = new Scanner(new File(filename));

        System.out.print("How many lines to print? ");
        int n = kb.nextInt();

        for ( int i = 0 ; i < n ; i++ )
            System.out.println(Student.read(null,sc));
    }
//------------------------------------------------------------------------------
} // end class Prog1330
////////////////////////////////////////////////////////////////////////////////
class Student
{
    private String name;
    private int grade;
//------------------------------------------------------------------------------
    public Student ( String name, int grade )
    {
        this.name = name;
        this.grade = grade;
    }
//------------------------------------------------------------------------------
    public String getName() { return name; }
//------------------------------------------------------------------------------
    public int getGrade() { return grade; }
//------------------------------------------------------------------------------
    public String toString() { return name + " (" + grade + ")"; }
//------------------------------------------------------------------------------
    public static Student read ( PrintStream ps, Scanner sc )
    {
```

```
if ( ps != null ) ps.println("Reading a Student record ...");
if ( ps != null ) ps.print("Enter the name: ");
String name = sc.nextLine();
if ( ps != null ) ps.print("Enter the grade: ");
int grade = sc.nextInt(); sc.nextLine();
return new Student(name,grade);
}
//- - - - - - - - - - - - - - - - - - - - - - - - - - - - - - - - - - - - - - -
} // end class Student
/////////////////////////////////////////////////////////////////////
```

Test your skill with Exercises 13–139 through 13–145.

Why Not Use while?

Recall the problem that introduced the for loop:

> Given a file of Students and a non-negative integer n, read and print the first n Students in the file.

Here is the code that solves it using while:

```
int i = 0;
while ( i < n )
{
    System.out.println(Student.read(null,sc));
    i++;
}
```

and here's the code using for:

```
for ( int i = 0 ; i < n ; i++ )
    System.out.println(Student.read(null,sc));
```

I think that the for loop is easier to understand because it puts all the loop parameters in a single Java phrase—they're easy to see when they're all in one place.

The Dangers of for

I mentioned that for is good for definite loops and while is good for *indefinite* loops. Actually, the for statement can do anything that while can do, and it can do many other fancy things, too. I'm restricting how we use `for` in order to make code easier to write, debug, read, and maintain.

HOLD YOUR HORSES

If you have a C++ background, you may have used the `for` statement in all its complexity. Humor me. Use the simple form of `for`.

Local Variables

Recall our loop with the `for` statement

```
for ( int i = 0 ; i < n ; i++ )
```

By saying *int* i = 0, we are declaring a variable i *local to the* `for` *loop*. However, if we have a variable i outside the loop, then we can't declare i in the initialization phrase or inside the loop. On the other hand, we might have code such as this:

```
int i = 5;
. . .
for ( i = 0 ; i < n ; i++ )
```

where the `for` loop uses the variable i declared outside the `for`.

Test your skill with Exercise 13–146.

Some Special Cases

Beware! A common error is to put a semicolon directly after the control phrase of a `for`:

```
for ( whatever );
```

This results in the `for` governing an *empty statement*, and nothing gets done.
    A useful form of `for` is

```
for(;;) whatever
```

because `for(;;)` acts as the controller of an *infinite loop*.

Test your skill with Exercise 13–147.

13.24   End-of-File

So far, we've seen two ways that programmers can detect the end of input data files:

1. We can use Java's end-of-file reporting mechanism, which turns `has-Next()` `false` when we've reached the end of the file. Here's a typical file of five `Student`s:

```
Sally
100

John
82

Sue
95

Bill
43

Rob
67
```

(The dark lines don't occur in the file; I've drawn them here to separate the `Student`s.)

1. We can put a *sentinel value* at the end of the file, and we can check for it as we loop through the file. Here's a sample file of five `Student`s that terminates with `xyz` (which presumably is not a `Student`'s name):

```
Sally
100

John
82

Sue
95

Bill
43

Rob
67

xyz
97
```

Now I'll introduce a *third* method:

3. At the top of the file, we can put the *number* of items contained in the file. As an example of this approach, here is the same file of Students for which the top line is the number of Students in the file:

5
Sally 100
John 82
Sue 95
Bill 43
Rob 67

Again, the dark lines don't occur in the file itself—I've drawn them here to show the integer 5 at the top and the five Student records that follow it. Prog1331 is the code that reads data files of the form above. The crucial lines are:

```
int n = sc.nextInt();

for ( int i = 0 ; i < n ; i++ )
    System.out.println(Student.read(null,sc));
```

The first statement reads the first line of the file and converts it into an integer n. The for loop then spins through the n Students in the file, reading and printing each of them.

Prog1331.java   **First Line Tells File Length**

```
// Written by Barry Soroka
//
// Print a file of Students
// where the first line of the file is the number of Students which follow.
//
import java.io.*;
import java.util.Scanner;
/////////////////////////////////////////////////////////////////////////////
class Prog1331
{
//-------------------------------------------------------------------------
    public static void main ( String [] args ) throws Exception
```

```
   {
      Scanner kb = new Scanner(System.in);

      System.out.print("\nEnter name of a file of Students: ");
      String filename = kb.nextLine();

      Scanner sc = new Scanner(new File(filename));

      int n = sc.nextInt(); sc.nextLine(); // move to the next line


      System.out.println("\nThis file contains  " + n + " Students:");

      for ( int i = 0 ; i < n ; i++ )
         System.out.println(Student.read(null,sc));
   }
//-------------------------------------------------------------------------
} // end class Prog1331
/////////////////////////////////////////////////////////////////////////////
class Student
{
   private String name;
   private int grade;
//-----------------------------------------------------------------------
   public Student ( String name, int grade )
   {
      this.name = name;
      this.grade = grade;
   }
//-----------------------------------------------------------------------
   public String getName() { return name; }
//-----------------------------------------------------------------------
   public int getGrade() { return grade; }
//-----------------------------------------------------------------------
   public String toString() { return name + " (" + grade + ")"; }
//-----------------------------------------------------------------------
   public static Student read ( PrintStream ps, Scanner sc )
   {
      if ( ps != null ) ps.println("Reading a Student record ...");
      if ( ps != null ) ps.print("Enter the name: ");
      String name = sc.nextLine();
      if ( ps != null ) ps.print("Enter the grade: ");
      int grade = sc.nextInt(); sc.nextLine();
      return new Student(name,grade);
   }
//-----------------------------------------------------------------------
} // end class Student
/////////////////////////////////////////////////////////////////////////////
```

Only recently have programming languages provided for the automatic detection of end-of-file. Before that, programmers used sentinel values, or put the number of lines at the top of each data file. FORTRAN provided the first language-based method for end-of-file detection. Here is a FORTRAN statement that reads a variable X:

```
READ(5,500,END=1000) X
```

If end-of-file occurs, control transfers to line 1000 of the Fortran program. Notice how much things have changed: We no longer have line numbers and we no longer jump to arbitrary lines in a program. It may seem primitive to use sentinels or to put the number of records at the top of a file, but these methods *work*, and you may encounter them in legacy code. Many "modern" language constructs will one day seem primitive, too.

13.25   Reading the Same File Twice

Earlier, we implemented class Section as a disk file of Students, and we added new methods as we studied new algorithms. Let's consider the problem:

Given a Section, print the Students with grade above average.

We will solve this by implementing the following method:

```
public void printAboveAverageStudents(PrintStream)
```

The code and its driver are given in Prog1332.
The new method is not very efficient. It spins through the file *once* in order to compute the average:

```
double average = this.average();
```

and then it spins through the file a *second* time in order to compare each Student against the average grade:

```
if ( s.getGrade() > average ) System.out.println(s);
```

The algorithm will always require looking at the data *twice*. When this is done with *files* the process can be very costly. In Chapter 14 we will learn how to keep collections in *arrays*, which are stored in memory rather than on disk.

Prog1332.java   **Print Students Who Are Above Average**

```
// Written by Barry Soroka
//
// class Section -- printAboveAverageStudents.
//
import java.io.*;
```

```
import java.util.Scanner;
/////////////////////////////////////////////////////////////////////////////
class Prog1332
{
//---------------------------------------------------------------------------
    public static void main (String [] args) throws Exception
    {
        Scanner kb = new Scanner(System.in);

        System.out.print("\nEnter name of a file of Students: ");
        String filename = kb.nextLine();

        Section sec = new Section(filename);

        System.out.println("\nIn forward order:");
        sec.print(System.out);

        System.out.println("\nAverage is: " + sec.average());

        System.out.println("\nAbove Average Students:");
        sec.printAboveAverageStudents(System.out);
    }
//---------------------------------------------------------------------------
} // end class Prog1332
/////////////////////////////////////////////////////////////////////////////
class Section
{
    private String filename;
//---------------------------------------------------------------------------
    public Section ( String filename )
    {
        this.filename = filename;
    }
//---------------------------------------------------------------------------
    public void printAboveAverageStudents ( PrintStream ps ) throws Exception
    {
        double average = this.average();

        Scanner sc = new Scanner(new File(filename));

        while ( sc.hasNext() )
        {
            Student s = Student.read(null,sc);
            if ( s.getGrade() > average ) System.out.println(s);
        }
    }
//---------------------------------------------------------------------------
    public void print ( PrintStream ps ) throws Exception
    {
        Scanner sc = new Scanner(new File(filename));
```

```
      while ( sc.hasNext() )
      {
         Student s = Student.read(null,sc);
         ps.println(s);
      }
   }
//-----------------------------------------------------------------------
   public double average() throws Exception
   {
      Scanner sc = new Scanner(new File(filename));

      int n = 0;
      int sum = 0;

      while ( sc.hasNext() )
      {
         Student s = Student.read(null,sc);
         n++;
         sum += s.getGrade();
      }

      return 1.0*sum/n;
   }
//-----------------------------------------------------------------------
} // end class Section
/////////////////////////////////////////////////////////////////////////
class Student
{
   private String name;
   private int grade;
//-----------------------------------------------------------------------
   public Student ( String name, int grade )
   {
      this.name = name;
      this.grade = grade;
   }
//-----------------------------------------------------------------------
   public String getName() { return name; }
//-----------------------------------------------------------------------
   public int getGrade() { return grade; }
//-----------------------------------------------------------------------
   public String toString() { return name + " (" + grade + ")"; }
//-----------------------------------------------------------------------
   public static Student read ( PrintStream ps, Scanner sc )
   {
      if ( ps != null ) ps.println("Reading a Student record ...");
      if ( ps != null ) ps.print("Enter the name: ");
      String name = sc.nextLine();
      if ( ps != null ) ps.print("Enter the grade: ");
```

```
        int grade = sc.nextInt(); sc.nextLine();
        return new Student(name,grade);
    }
//-------------------------------------------------------------
} // end class Student
///////////////////////////////////////////////////////////////////
```

13.26   GUI: JOptionPane and Dialog Boxes

Java provides three predefined dialog boxes, which make it easy to write GUI programs. All three are invoked by using the appropriate `static` method of class `JOptionPane`.

- `JOptionPane.showInputDialog(String)` displays the `String` and waits for the user to enter a `String` and click either "OK" or "Cancel." The entered `String` is returned as the result of the call to `showInputDialog`. This is useful when we want to prompt for some input.
- `JOptionPane.showMessageDialog(null,String)` displays the given `String` and waits for the user to click "OK." This is useful when we want to give the user some information.
- `JOptionPane.showConfirmDialog(null,String)` displays the given `String` and allows the user to choose from "Yes," "No," and "Cancel." This allows the user to provide confirmation of a pending action. The result is returned as an integer. "Yes" returns `JOptionPane.YES_OPTION`. "No" returns `JOptionPane.NO_OPTION`. "Cancel" returns `JOptionPane.CANCEL_OPTION`. We needn't be concerned with the actual numerical values used for these options—we can compare the returned value with the constants just described.

`Prog1333.java` is an application that uses all three dialog boxes. First, the user enters a `String`. Then the program displays that `String` all in uppercase and all in lowercase. Finally, the program asks whether the user wants to try again.

Prog1333.java   **Dialog Boxes**

```
// Written by Barry Soroka
//
// Tests dialog boxes.
//
import java.io.*;
import javax.swing.*;
///////////////////////////////////////////////////////////////////
class Prog1333
```

```
      {
//--------------------------------------------------------------------------------------
      public static void main (String[] args)
      {
          int again = JOptionPane.YES_OPTION;

          while (again == JOptionPane.YES_OPTION)
          {
              String s = JOptionPane.showInputDialog("Enter a String: ");

              JOptionPane.showMessageDialog(null,"Lowercase is \"" +
                                            s.toLowerCase() + "\"\n" +
                                            "Uppercase is \"" +
                                            s.toUpperCase() + "\"");

              again = JOptionPane.showConfirmDialog(null,"Do Another?");
          }
      }
//--------------------------------------------------------------------------------------
} // end class Prog1333
//////////////////////////////////////////////////////////////////////////////////////
```

Test your skill with Exercise 13–148.

13.27 GUI: Graphics and Loops

Our graphics programs thus far included only straight-line code. Now that we know the loops—while and for—we can write more complicated graphics programs.

Test your skill with Exercises 13–149 through 13–154.

Chapter Summary

- Collections aggregate many data values into a single entity.
- A given pattern may apply to several collections. For example, given a collection of ints, compute the sum of the ints.
- Files are an example of a collection.
- Files are not random access.
- Files contain Strings.
- The while loop repeats a group of statements as long as some boolean condition is true.
- A read-process loop is a while loop that applies a set of statements against all the elements of a file.

- Algorithm: Print the `Complex` numbers in a file.
- Algorithm: Count the `Complex` numbers in a file.
- Algorithm: Report the number of odd and even `int`s in a file.
- Algorithm: Sum the `Complex` numbers in a file.
- Algorithm: Sum the odd `int`s in a file.
- Algorithm: Given a file of `int`s, sum the odd `int`s and sum the even `int`s.
- Algorithm: Compute the average of the `Complex` numbers in a file.
- We can implement a `Section` as a file of `Student`s.
- By using a `static read` method with `null` for the `PrintStream` argument, we can read the elements of a file without printing prompts.
- Algorithm: How many `Student`s are in a `Section`?
- Algorithm: Given a `Section`, how many `Student`s are passing the course?
- Algorithm: Given a `Section`, are *any* `Student`s passing the course?
- Algorithm: Given a `Section`, are *all* `Student`s passing the course?
- Algorithm: Given a `Section`, what is the highest grade?
- Algorithm: Given a `Section`, are the grades in ascending order?
- Algorithm: Given a file of `int`s, generate a new file for which every `int` has been squared.
- Algorithm: Given two equal-length files of `int`s, generate a new file whose elements are the sums of the corresponding input elements.
- Algorithm: Given two `Section`s, are they equal, element for element?
- We can generate sequences of `int`s using `while` loops.
- We can signal the end of a file by using a *sentinel* value—a value that cannot be valid.
- The `for` loop is used to perform a set of statements a precise number of times.
- Use `for` when you know how many times a loop should be performed; otherwise, use `while`.
- The GUI method `showInputDialog` requests a `String` from the user.
- The GUI method `showMessageDialog` displays a `String` for the user to acknowledge.
- The GUI method `showConfirmDialog` requires that user click "Yes," "No," or "Cancel."

Terminology Introduced in This Chapter

array	linked list	set
collection	pattern	`Vector`
heterogeneous	random access	
homogeneous	sentinel	

Exercises

Exercise 13–1.   Consider the following set of patterns:

1) Given a collection, print its items to the monitor.
2) Given a collection, report the number of items in the collection.
3) Given a collection, compute the sum of the items.
4) Given a collection, compute the average value.
5) Given a collection, does it contain a specific item?
6) Given a collection, do *all* items meet some criterion?
7) Given a collection, do *any* items meet some criterion?
8) Given a collection, how many times does a given item appear in the collection?
9) Given a collection, are the items in ascending order?
10) Given a collection, generate a new collection in which each element is related to the corresponding element of the incoming collection.

For each of the problems below, identify the appropriate pattern from the list above. If no pattern applies to the problem, say so.

a. Given an array of `int`s, create a new array in which every `int` has been squared.
b. How many times does the space character occur in a `String`?
c. Given a `File` of `Complex`, compute the average.
d. Given a `File` of `Complex`, generate a new `File` of `Complex` where each number in the original file has been negated.
e. Given a `File`, does it contain the `String` `"frank"`?
f. Given a `File` of `int`s, compute the sum of the odd `int`s and the sum of the even `int`s.
g. How many times does the space character occur in a `File`?
h. Given a `File` of `Complex`, compute the sum.
i. How many negative numbers are in a given `File` of `int`s?
j. How many blank lines are in a given `File`?
k. Given an array of `String`s, does it contain the `String` `"frank"`?
l. Given an array of `String`s, create a new array in which every `String` has been converted to uppercase.

Exercise 13–2.   What is printed by each of the following pieces of code?[7]

a.
```
int n = 0;
while ( n < 4 )
{
    System.out.println(n);
    n++;
}
```

---

[7] Our goal here is to learn how *while* works, not to become experts at *all* loops involving numbers. We'll turn our attention to loops involving `String`s, `Complex`, and so forth, next. But numbers are good for the first few exercises using `while`.

b.
```
int n = 0;
while ( n < 4 )
{
   n++;
   System.out.println(n);
}
```

c.
```
int n = 8;
while ( n > 0 )
{
   System.out.println(n);
   n-=2;
}
```

d.
```
int n = 8;
while ( n > 0 )
{
   n-=2;
   System.out.println(n);
}
```

Exercise 13–3.   Consider the code in `Prog1334.java`. Suppose we apply this to a file containing the following three lines:

```
first
second
third
```

What do you think will be printed? What does Java actually do?

Prog1334.java
```
// Written by Barry Soroka
//
// For an exercise.
//
import java.io.*;
import java.util.Scanner;
//////////////////////////////////////////////////////////////////////////////
class Prog1334
{
   //----------------------------------------------------------------------
```

```
    public static void main (String [] args) throws Exception
    {
        Scanner kb = new Scanner(System.in);

        System.out.print("Enter name of file to be displayed: ");
        String filename = kb.nextLine();

        Scanner sc = new Scanner(new File(filename));

        String s;

        s = sc.nextLine();

        while ( true )
        {
            System.out.println(s);
            s = sc.nextLine();
        }
    }
//--------------------------------------------------------------------------
} // end class Prog1334
////////////////////////////////////////////////////////////////////////////
```

Exercise 13–4. Consider the code in `Prog1335.java`. How does this program differ from that in Exercise 13–3? Compile and run the program. What happens?

Prog1335.java

```
// Written by Barry Soroka
//
// For an exercise.
//
import java.io.*;
import java.util.Scanner;
////////////////////////////////////////////////////////////////////////////
class Prog1335
{
//--------------------------------------------------------------------------
    public static void main (String [] args) throws Exception
    {
        Scanner kb = new Scanner(System.in);

        System.out.print("Enter name of file to be displayed: ");
        String filename = kb.nextLine();

        Scanner sc = new Scanner(new File(filename));
```

```
    String s;

    s = sc.nextLine();

    while ( false )
    {
        System.out.println(s);
        s = sc.nextLine();
    }
  }
//--------------------------------------------------------------------------
} // end class Prog1335
////////////////////////////////////////////////////////////////////////////
```

Exercise 13–5.   Create an *empty* text file. Write a Java program that opens that file and attaches the Scanner sc to it. Execute the following lines:

```
String s = sc.nextLine();
System.out.println(s);
```

What happens?

Exercise 13–6.   Create a file with the following three lines:

```
first
second
third
```

Write a Java program that opens that file and attaches the Scanner sc to it. Execute the following lines:

```
System.out.println(sc.nextLine());
System.out.println(sc.nextLine());
System.out.println(sc.nextLine());
System.out.println(sc.nextLine());
```

What happens?

Exercise 13–7.   Consider Prog1301.java. What parts of the code run and don't run when the data file is empty?

Exercise 13–8.   Modify `Prog1301.java` so that it reads as follows:

```
String s;

while ( sc.hasNext() )
{
    System.out.println(s);
    s = sc.nextLine();
}
```

What have we changed? Does the code run normally? How does this error show itself at run-time?

Exercise 13–9.   Modify `Prog1301.java` so that it reads as follows:

```
String s;

while ( sc.hasNext() )
{
    System.out.println(s);
}
```

What have we omitted? Does the code run normally? How does this error show itself at run-time?

Exercise 13–10.   The class `Car` models automobiles, and each `Car` has a `String make`, `String model`, and `int year`. In a file of `Car`s, each `Car` is represented by three consecutive lines; for example, a 1975 Toyota Tercel would be represented by the following lines:

```
1975
Toyota
Tercel
```

Write a program that reads the name of a file of `Car`s and then prints each `Car` to the monitor. Be sure to test your code with

1) an empty file—the program should not contain special code for this case.
2) a singleton—a file with only one `Car`.
3) a general file containing two or more `Car`s.

Design an appropriate `toString` method for class `Car`.

Exercise 13–11.   The class `Person` models living people, and each `Person` has a `String name` and `int age`. In a file of `Person`s, each `Person` is represented by two consecutive lines; for example, if Kevin is age 23, then he would be represented by the following lines:

```
Kevin
23
```

Write a program that reads the name of a file of `Person`s and then prints each `Person` to the monitor. Be sure to test your code with

1) an empty file—the program should not contain special code for this case.
2) a singleton—a file with only one `Person`.
3) a general file containing two or more `Person`s.

Exercise 13–12.   Modify the program from Exercise 13–11 so that you only print the `name`s of `Person`s with `age >= 21`. Test your code with an appropriate set of files and defend your choices.

Exercise 13–13.   Use `Prog1303` on a variety of different text files. Be sure to apply `Prog1303` to the code file `Prog1303.java` itself—after all, a computer program can also be viewed as a simple file of `String`s.

Exercise 13–14.   Apply `Prog1304` to a variety of test files. Your goal is to verify that the program is correct. Defend your choice of test files.

Exercise 13–15.   Consider a class `Student`, where each `Student` has a `String name` and an `int grade`. The data for each `Student` is laid out on two lines. For example, if Kevin has grade 78, then his record in a data file would be

```
Kevin
78
```

A passing grade must be `>= 60`. Write a program that reads the name of a file of `Student`s and then reports the number of `Student`s who passed. Typical output would be the following, where what the user types is underlined:

```
% javac HowManyPassed
Enter the name of a file of Students: foo
13 passed
```

Test your code on an appropriate set of test files. Defend your choice of test files.

Exercise 13–16. Modify your program from Exercise 13–15 so that it reports how many passed, how many failed, and the total number of Students. Typical output would be the following, where what the user types is underlined:

```
% javac PassFail
Enter the name of a file of Students: foo
13 passed
 4 failed
17 total
```

Test your code on an appropriate set of test files. Defend your choice of test files.

Exercise 13–17. Modify your program from Exercise 13–15 so that it reports the frequency of each letter grade, using the following table:

A	B	C	D	F
≥ 90%	≥ 80%	≥ 70%	≥ 60%	< 60%

Typical output would be the following, where what the user types is underlined:

```
% javac Distribution
Enter the name of a file of Students: foo
 2 A
 4 B
 8 C
 8 D
 6 F
28 total
```

Test your code on an appropriate set of test files. Defend your choice of test files.

Exercise 13–18. Write a program that requests the name of a file of EggShipments and reports how many EggShipments are in the file. Typical output would be the following, where what the user types is underlined:

```
% javac CountEggShipments
Enter the name of a file of EggShipments: foo
That file contains 12 EggShipments.
```

Test your code on an appropriate set of test files. Defend your choice of test files.

Exercise 13–19. Write a program that solves the following problem: Given a file of Rectangles, compute the number that are *squares*.

Exercise 13–20. Write a program that solves the following problem: Given a file of Rectangles, compute the number that are *thin*, where *thin* means that length > 2 * width.

Exercise 13–21. Write a program that solves the following problem: Given a file of Complex, compute the number of entries that are purely real, the number that are purely imaginary, and the number that are mixed.

Exercise 13–22. Write a program that solves the following problem: Given a file of Complex, compute the sum. Suppose that the file Complex3 contains the following lines:

```
2
3
0
1
1
-5
```

Here are some typical test runs, where what the user types is underlined:

```
% javac SumComplex
Enter the name of a file of Complex: empty
sum: 0
% javac SumComplex
Enter the name of a file of Complex: Complex3
sum: 3-i
```

Test your code on an appropriate set of test files. Defend your choice of test files.

Exercise 13–23. Recall the class Rectangle, where each instance has an int length and an int width. In a file, a Rectangle is represented by two lines, each containing an int. For example, the lines

```
5
3
```

represent a Rectangle with length 5 and width 3. Write a program that solves the following problem: Given a file of Rectangles, compute the sum of their areas.

Exercise 13–24. Consider the class Quadratic, which represents quadratic polynominals in *x*. Mathematically, these polynomials have the form

$$ax^2 + bx + c$$

The sum of the polynomials

$$a_1 x^2 + b_1 x + c_1$$

and

$$a_2 x^2 + b_2 x + c_2$$

is

$$(a_1 + a_2)x^2 + (b_1 + b_2)x + (c_1 + c_2)$$

Write the code for class `Quadratic`, including a `static read` method. Describe how you are representing `Quadratic`s in a text file. Your class must include a method `Quadratic add(Quadratic)` that computes the sum of two quadratic polynomials. Write a program that solves the following problem: Given a file of `Quadratic`s, compute the sum. Test your code on an appropriate set of test files. Defend your choice of test files.

Exercise 13–25. Recall the class `EggShipment`. Write a program that solves the following problem: Given a file of `EggShipment`s, compute the sum. Test your code on an appropriate set of test files. Defend your choice of test files.

Exercise 13–26. Write a program that solves the following problem: Given a file of `Complex`, compute the product. Here are some typical test runs, where what the user types is underlined:

```
% javac ProductComplex
Enter the name of a file of Complex: empty
product: 1
% javac ProductComplex
Enter the name of a file of Complex: Complex3
product: 7+17i
```

Test your code on an appropriate set of test files. Defend your choice of test files.

Exercise 13–27. Write a program that solves the following problem: Given a file of `int`s, compute the product of the *odd* `int`s. Test your code on an appropriate set of test files. Defend your choice of test files.

Exercise 13–28. Write a program that solves the following problem: Given a file of `int`s, compute the product of the *positive* `int`s. Test your code on an appropriate set of test files. Defend your choice of test files.

Exercise 13–29. Write a program that solves the following problem: Given a file of `Complex`, compute the sum of those whose real part is 0. Suppose that the file `Complex3` contains the following lines:

```
2
3
0
1
1
-5
```

Here are some typical test runs, where what the user types is underlined:

```
% javac SumComplex1
Enter the name of a file of Complex: empty
sum: 0
% javac SumComplex1
Enter the name of a file of Complex: Complex3
sum: 3-i
```

Test your code on an appropriate set of test files. Defend your choice of test files.

Exercise 13–30. Recall the class `Rectangle`. Write a program that solves the following problem: Given a file of `Rectangles`, compute the sum of the areas of those that are *squares*. Test your code on an appropriate set of test files. Defend your choice of test files.

Exercise 13–31. Recall the class `Rectangle`. Write a program that solves the following problem: Given a file of `Rectangles`, compute the sum of the areas of those that are *not* squares. Test your code on an appropriate set of test files. Defend your choice of test files.

Exercise 13–32. Recall the class `Rectangle`. Write a program that solves the following problem: Given a file of `Rectangles`, compute the sum of the areas of those with area > 20. Test your code on an appropriate set of test files. Defend your choice of test files.

Exercise 13–33. Recall the class `Quadratic`, which represents quadratic polynomials of the form $ax^2 + bx + c$. Write a program that solves the following problem: Given a file of `Quadratics`, compute the sum of those that have no x^2 term. These polynomials have $a = 0$. Test your code on an appropriate set of test files. Defend your choice of test files.

Exercise 13–34. Recall the class `Quadratic`, which represents quadratic polynomials of the form $ax^2 + bx + c$. Modify your code to include a method `int valueAt(int)`, which computes the value of the polynomial at the specified integer value. For example, if q is the polynomial $3x^2 - x + 5$, then `q.valueAt(2)` should return

$$3 \cdot 2^2 - 2 + 5 = 3 \cdot 4 + 3 = 12 + 3 = 15$$

Write a program that solves the following problem: Given a file of `Quadratics`, compute the sum of those that have negative values at $x = 5$. Test your code on an appropriate set of test files. Defend your choice of test files.

Exercise 13–35. Recall the class `EggShipment`. Write a program that solves the following problem: Given a file of `EggShipments`, compute the sum of the shipments that have an odd number of eggs. Test your code on an appropriate set of test files. Defend your choice of test files.

Exercise 13–36. Write a program that solves the following problem: Given a file of `ints`, compute the sum of the `ints` and the product of the `ints`.

Exercise 13–37. Write a program that solves the following problem: Given a file of `ints`, compute the sum of the *even* `ints` and the product of the *odd* `ints`.

Exercise 13–38. Write a program that solves the following problem: Given a file of `Complex`, compute the sum and the product of the numbers.

Exercise 13–39. Write a program that solves the following problem: Given a file of `Rectangle`, compute the sum of the areas and the sum of the perimeters.

Exercise 13–40. Write a program that solves the following problem: Given a file of `Complex`, compute the average.

Exercise 13–41. Write a program that solves the following problem: Given a file of `Rectangle`, compute the average area and the average perimeter.

Exercise 13–42. Write a program that solves the following problem: Given a file of `Strings`, compute the average line length.

Exercise 13–43. Write a program that solves the following problem: Given a file of `EggShipment`, compute the average.

Exercise 13–44. If a file is entirely numeric, why can we omit `nextLine` method calls?

Exercise 13–45. We have seen several types of data files that were entirely numeric. What did these files represent?

Exercise 13–46. How does the compiler respond if you remove the `throws Exception` tags from the methods of class `Section`?

Exercise 13–47. Add to class `Section`:

```
public void printPassing(PrintStream)
```

which prints `Student`s who are passing.

Exercise 13–48. Add to class `Section`:

```
public void printFailing(PrintStream)
```

which prints `Student`s who are failing.

Exercise 13–49. Add to class `Section`:

```
public void printGradeInRange(lo,hi,PrintStream)
```

which prints `Student`s with `grade` in the range `[lo,hi]`.

Exercise 13–50. Add to class `Section`:

```
public String getNames()
```

which gloms together all of the `names`, separated by a new-line `char`.

Exercise 13–51. Add to class `Section`:

```
public double getAveragePassingGrade()
```

which returns the average `grade` of `Student`s who passed.

Exercise 13–52. Add to class `Section`:

```
public int howManyFailed()
```

which returns the number of `Student`s who failed.

Exercise 13–53. Add to class `Section`:

```
public int howManyInRange(int lo,int hi)
```

which reports how many `Student`s have `grade` in the range `[lo,hi]`.

Exercise 13–54. Add to class `Section`:

    public int howManyWerePerfect()

which reports how many `Student`s have `grade` 100.

Exercise 13–55. Add to class `Section`:

    public void printHistogram(PrintStream)

which prints the number of A-B-C-D-F grades.

Exercise 13–56. Write a program: Given a file and a `String`, how many times does the `String` occur as a line in the file?

Exercise 13–57. Write a program: Given a file and a `String`, how many times does the `String` occur as a prefix to a line in the file?

Exercise 13–58. Write a program: Given an `int` and a file of `int`s, how many times does the given `int` occur in the file?

Exercise 13–59. Write a program: Given an `int` and a file of `int`s, how many `int`s in the file are larger than the given `int`?

Exercise 13–60. Write a program: Given a file of `int`s and a range `[lo,hi]`, report how many of the `int`s are in that range.

Exercise 13–61. Write a program: Given a `Complex` and a file of `Complex`, how many times does the given `Complex` occur in the file?

Exercise 13–62. The modulus of the `Complex` number $a + bi$ is $\sqrt{a^2+b^2}$. Write a program: Given a `Complex` and a file of `Complex`, how many `Complex` in the file have modulus larger than that of the given `Complex`?

Exercise 13–63. Write a program: Given a file of `Complex` and a range `[lo,hi]`, report how many of the `Complex` have modulus in that range.

Exercise 13–64. Write a program: Given a file of `Rectangle`s and an `int`, how many have an area equal to the `int`?

Exercise 13–65. Write a program: Given a file of `Rectangle`s and an `int`, how many have an area greater than the `int`?

Exercise 13–66. Write a program: Given a file of `Rectangles` and a range `[lo,hi]`, report how many of the `Rectangles` have an area in that range.

Exercise 13–67. Write a program: Given a file of `Cars` and a `String`, how many `Cars` have this `String` as their `make`?

Exercise 13–68. Write a program that asks for (1) the name of a file of `ZooShipments`, and (2) a `String` representing a `species`, and that reports the number of animals of that `species` in the file of `ZooShipments`.

Exercise 13–69. For a given application, a data file contains alternating records of `ZooShipments` and `Strings` representing a person's name. Each `ZooShipment` belongs to the person whose name follows it.

Write a `main` method that reads (1) the name of a data file, and (2) the name of a person, and then prints out the total number of animals owned by that person according to the given file.

Exercise 13–70. Write the method

```
private static boolean anyEven ( Scanner sc )
```

which corresponds to the `allEven` method in `Prog1316.java`, but which returns `true` if and only if the file of `ints` contains *any* even `int`.

Exercise 13–71. Modify the algorithm in `Prog1317.java` to compute `anyEven` for a file of `ints`.

Exercise 13–72. Modify the algorithm in `Prog1318.java` to compute `anyEven` for a file of `ints`.

Exercise 13–73. Add to class `Section` a method

```
public boolean containsStudent(Student)
```

Exercise 13–74. Add to class `Section` a method

```
public boolean containsName(String)
```

Exercise 13–75. Add to class `Section` a method

```
public boolean containsBStudents()
```

which returns `true` or `false` depending on whether or not any `Student` in the Section has a `grade` in the range `[80,89]`.

Exercise 13–76.   a.   Given a file and a `String`, does the file contain that `String`?
　　　　　　　　　　b.   Given a file and a `String`, are all the lines of the file equal to the `String`?

c.   Given an `int` and a file of `int`s, does the file contain that `int`?

d.   Given an `int` and a file of `int`s, are all the `int`s equal to the given `int`?

e.   Given a file of `Rectangle`s and an `int`, how many `Rectangle`s have an area greater than the `int`?

f.   Given a file of `Rectangle`s and an `int`, do all the `Rectangle`s have an area smaller than the `int`?

g.   Given a file of `EggShipment`s and an `EggShipment`, does any shipment in the file match the given one?

h.   Given a file of `EggShipment`s and an `EggShipment`, do all the shipments in the file match the given one?

i.   Given a file of `Car`s and a `String`, do all the `Car`s have this make?

j.   Given a file of `Car`s and an `int`, how many of the `Car`s have this year?

k.   Given a file of `Person`—with name and age—how many `Person`s have reached the legal drinking age of 21?

Exercise 13–77.   Add to class `Section`:

```
public Student getStudentWithLowestGrade()
```

Exercise 13–78.   Add to class `Section`:

```
public int getLowestGrade()
```

Exercise 13–79.   Add to class `Section`:

```
public String getNameOfLowest()
```

Exercise 13–80.   Given a file of `Rectangle`s, find the one with the largest area.

Exercise 13–81.   Given a file of `Rectangle`s, find the one with the smallest area.

Exercise 13–82.   Given a file of `Rectangle`s, find the largest area.

Exercise 13–83.   Given a file of `Rectangle`s, find the smallest area.

Exercise 13–84.   Given a file of `Rectangle`s, find the one with the largest area but not greater than 20.

Exercise 13–85.   a.   Given a file of `Complex`, find the one with the largest modulus.

b.   Given a file of `Complex`, find the one with the smallest modulus.

c.   Given a file of `Complex`, find the largest modulus.

d.   Given a file of `Complex`, find the smallest modulus.

e.   Given a file of `Complex`, find the one with the largest real part.

f.   Given a file of `Complex`, find the one with the smallest real part.

g.   Given a file of `Complex`, find the largest real part.

h.   Given a file of `Complex`, find the smallest real part.

Exercise 13–86.   a.   Given a file of `int`s, print the largest.

b.   Given a file of `int`s, print the smallest.

Exercise 13–87. Given a file of `Complex`, print the numbers with the largest and smallest moduli. Use a single loop.

Exercise 13–88. Given a file of `ints`, are they in descending order?

Exercise 13–89. Given a file of `ints`, describe their order: ascending, descending, or other.

Exercise 13–90. Recall the code for a `Section` of `Students`. Add a method

```
public boolean hasGradesAscending()
```

Exercise 13–91. Recall the code for a `Section` of `Students`. Add a method

```
public boolean hasGradesDescending()
```

Exercise 13–92. Given a file of `Complex`, are they in ascending order by modulus?

Exercise 13–93. Given a file of `Complex`, are they in descending order by modulus?

Exercise 13–94. Given a file of `Rectangles`, are they in ascending order by area? By perimeter? By `length`?

Exercise 13–95. Given a file of `ints`, generate a new file in which each `int` has been doubled.

Exercise 13–96. Given a file of `ints`, generate a new file that contains only the odd `ints` from the input file.

Exercise 13–97. Given a file of `ints`, generate two new files—one containing the evens and one containing the odds.

Exercise 13–98. Given a file, generate a new file containing all the nonblank lines of the input file. Consider a line to be blank if it is empty or if it contains only spaces.

Exercise 13–99. Given a file of `Rectangles`, generate a new file containing only those `Rectangles` that are squares.

Exercise 13–100. Given a file of `Rectangles`, generate a new file in which each `Rectangle`'s linear dimensions—`length` and `width`—have been doubled.

Exercise 13–101. If $a + bi$ is `Complex`, then its *conjugate* is $a - bi$. Given a file of `Complex`, generate a new file in which each `Complex` has been converted to its conjugate.

Exercise 13–102. Given a file of `Strings`, generate a new file in which each line is the numerical length of the corresponding line in the input file. For example, if the input file is

```
alpha
xy
beta
```

then the output file is

```
5
2
4
```

Exercise 13–103. A data file consists of pairs of lines, where each pair has an `int` on the first line and a `String` on the second. For example,

```
2
hello
3
ab
0
hello
1
x
```

Write a program that reads such files and produces output files with half the number of lines, but each output line comes from an input pair by self-concatenating the `String` the `int` number of times. For the preceding file, the output file would be

```
hellohello     ← 2 of "hello"
ababab         ← 3 of "ab"
               ← 0 of "hello"
x              ← 1 of "x"
```

Exercise 13–104. Given two equal-length files of `int`s, generate a file whose elements are the product of the corresponding input elements.

Exercise 13–105. Given two equal-length files, generate a file whose elements are the concatenation of the corresponding input lines. For example:

in1	in2	out
"ab"	"cde"	"abcde"
""	"ab"	"ab"
"ab"	""	"ab"
""	""	""

Exercise 13–106. Given two equal-length files of `ints`, generate a file with `boolean` values—if two corresponding input values are `n1` and `n2`, then the output value is `n1 < n2`.

Exercise 13–107. Given two equal-length files of `ints`, generate a file with `boolean` values—if two corresponding input values are `n1` and `n2`, then the output value is `n1 == n2`.

Exercise 13–108. Given two equal-length files, generate a file with `boolean` values—if two corresponding input values are `s1` and `s2`, then the output value is `s1.equals(s2)`.

Exercise 13–109. There are two input files of equal length. The first file is a file of nonnegative `ints`. The second file is a file of `Strings`. The output file consists of `Strings` that are generated by repeatedly self-concatenating the `String` by int times. If the `int` is 0, then the output `String` is the empty `String`. Here's an example of two input files and the expected output:

in1	in2	out
0	`"a"`	`""`
1	`"a"`	`"a"`
2	`"a"`	`"aa"`
3	`"a"`	`"aaa"`
0	`"abc"`	`""`
1	`"abc"`	`"abc"`
2	`"abc"`	`"abcabc"`
3	`"abc"`	`"abcabcabc"`
0	`""`	`""`
1	`""`	`""`
2	`""`	`""`
5	`"17"`	`"1717171717"`

Exercise 13–110. Write a program that adds files of `ints` when the lengths of the files are *different*. Unmatched values are simply copied to the end of the output file. For example:

```
[2,3,4] + [1,7,6,5] → [3,10,10,5]
[2,3,4] + [7]       → [9,3,4]
[2,3,4] + []        → [2,3,4]
[7] + [2,3,4]       → [9,3,4]
[] + [2,3,4]        → [2,3,4]
```

Exercise 13–111. Write a program that solves the following problem: Given a file of `ZooShipments` and an equal-length file of `double`, interpret the `double` as the price per animal, and calculate the total cost of the input file.

For example, the following is a typical `ZooShipment` file and a typical price file:

3	2	8	4
tiger	worm	sheep	tiger

| 2100.0 | 0.45 | 300.0 | 2000.0 |

Your program must compute the total cost as

```
3*2100.0 + 2*0.45 + 8*300.0 + 4*2000.0
= 6300.0 + 0.90 + 2400.0 + 8000.0
= 16700.90
```

Notice that it's possible for two different `ZooShipments` to have the same `species` but different prices.

Exercise 13–112. Write a program for reporting equality of files, without using a helper method. How readable is your code?

Exercise 13–113. Add to class `Section`:

```
public boolean equals(Section)
```

Exercise 13–114. Write a program that compares two files, line by line, reporting either (a) that the files are equal, or (b) that they differ, noting the first line number at which they differ and printing the two lines that differ.

Exercise 13–115. Write a program that tests whether one file is a prefix of another file, without using a helper method. How readable is your code?

Exercise 13–116. Write a program that asks for the names of two files and creates a file that joins them.

Exercise 13–117. Write a program that asks for the names of two `Sections` and produces the file that joins them.

Exercise 13–118. Write a program that joins two files of `Rectangles`.

Exercise 13–119. Given three equal-length files of `ints` (symbolically a, b, and c), produce a file of `booleans` where each value reports whether $a_i + b_i = c_i$.

Exercise 13–120. Given a file of ZooShipments, produce a new file containing just the species.

Exercise 13–121. Design a similar test file for the toString method of class ZooShipment. Write a main method with a loop that uses the test file to automatically test ZooShipment.

Exercise 13–122. Design a similar test file for the constructor and method toString of class Fraction. Write a main method with a loop that uses the test file to automatically test Fraction.

Exercise 13–123. Suppose that a file of ints represents a polynomial in x. Element 1 is a_0, element 2 is a_1, element 3 is a_2, and so forth. For example, the file [6,-1,0,2] represents $6 - x + 2x^3$. Write a program that reads (1) the name of a file of ints, and (2) the value of x, and computes the value of the represented polynomial evaluated at the given value of x. For example, the polynomial [6,-1,0,2] evaluated at $x = 3$ is

$$6 - 3 + 2 \cdot 3^3 = 3 + 2 \cdot 27 = 3 + 54 = 57$$

Exercise 13–124. Write and test a while loop that prints the ints from 0 to 100.

Exercise 13–125. Write and test a while loop that prints the first 10 powers of 2.

Exercise 13–126. Write and test a while loop that prints the sequence [0,3,6,9,. . . ,300].

Exercise 13–127. Write and test a while loop that prints the sequence [1,4,7,10,. . .] ending at or below 100.

Exercise 13–128. Write and test a while loop that prints the sequence [0.0, 0.1, 0.2, . . . , 1.0].

Exercise 13–129. Write and test a while loop that prints integers, beginning at 100 and counting downward by 7—100,93,86,79,. . . . Don't go below 0.

Exercise 13–130. Devise a sentinel system for files of Complex. Write a program that computes the sum of the Complex in such a file.

Exercise 13–131. Devise a sentinel system for files of Students. Write a program that computes the average grade in such a file.

Exercise 13–132. Devise a sentinel system for files of Rectangles. Write a program that prints the Rectangles in such a file.

Exercise 13–133. Devise a sentinel system for files of ZooShipments. Write a program that reads a species and computes the total number of animals with that species in such a file.

Exercise 13–134. Write a program that reads and sums ints until it sees the sentinel value 999.

Exercise 13–135. Write a program that reads and concatenates `String`s until the length of the accumulated `String` is 50 or greater.

Exercise 13–136. Write a program that reads and sums `Complex` until the sum equals 0.

Exercise 13–137. Write a program that reads and sums `Fractions` until the sum is 10/1 or greater.

Exercise 13–138. Write a program that reads `Rectangles` and sums their area until the area is 500 or greater.

Exercise 13–139. Write a program that reads (1) the name of a file, and (2) a nonnegative integer n, and then prints the first n `String`s in the file.

Exercise 13–140. Write a program that reads (1) the name of a file of `Complex`, and (2) a nonnegative integer n, and then prints the sum of the first n `Complex` in the file.

Exercise 13–141. Write a program that reads (1) the name of a file of `Fractions`, and (2) a nonnegative integer n, and then computes the sum of the first n `Fractions` in the file.

Exercise 13–142. Write a program that reads (1) the name of a file of `Rectangles`, and (2) a nonnegative integer n, and then computes the sum of the areas of the first n `Rectangles` in the file.

Exercise 13–143. Write a program that reads a `String` and prints each `char` of the `String` on a separate line. (This cries out for a `for` loop because we know exactly how many `char`s are in the `String`.)

Exercise 13–144. Write a program that reads a `String` and computes how many `char`s are uppercase, lowercase, and other.

Exercise 13–145. Write a program that reads the name of a file and computes the total number of `char`s in each of the following categories: uppercase, lowercase, and other.

Exercise 13–146. Write a short program that proves that changes to i inside the statement

```
for ( i = 0 ; i < n ; i++ ) ...
```
change the value of an i declared outside the `for` loop.

Exercise 13–147. Locate a program where we used

```
while ( true ) ...
```

and change it to

```
for(;;) ...
```

Does it behave as expected?

Exercise 13–148. Using the `JOptionPane` dialog boxes, write an application that selects a number at random in the range [0,100] and allows the user to make repeated guesses until the number has been guessed.

Exercise 13–149. Draw a bull's-eye using concentric circles with alternating colors. Use `showInput-Dialog` boxes to read the number of rings and the desired ring width.

Exercise 13–150. Draw a bull's-eye using concentric circles with alternating colors. Use a `showInput-Dialog` box to read the number of rings desired. Adjust the ring width to fit a window of reasonable size.

Exercise 13–151. Draw a bull's-eye using concentric *squares* with alternating colors. Use a `show-InputDialog` box to read the number of "rings" desired. Adjust the ring width to fit a window of reasonable size.

Exercise 13–152. Draw an asterisk with n spokes. Use a `showInputDialog` box to read the number of spokes desired.

Exercise 13–153. Figure 13–3 shows a series of lines connecting points on intersecting horizontal and vertical lines:

    (0,0) connects to (10,50)
    (0,10) connects to (20,50)
    (0,20) connects to (30,50)
    (0,30) connects to (40,50)
    (0,40) connects to (50,50)

Figure 13–3
Race Car

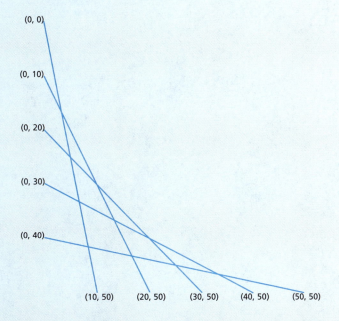

Write an application that draws n lines connecting the corresponding points on the left edge and bottom edge of the current window. Read n from a showInputDialog box.

Exercise 13–154. For the purposes of this exercise, a *command file* consists of text lines that command the renaming or deletion of disk files. A *rename command* consists of three lines:

```
rename
oldName
newName
```

Its effect is to change the name of the specified file. A *delete command* consists of *two* lines:

```
delete
filename
```

and its effect is to delete the specified file. A command file may contain any number of commands in any order.

Write a program that requests the name of a command file and then reads and executes the commands in the file.

CHAPTER FOURTEEN

Arrays

Chapter Objectives

- Learn the syntax and semantics of arrays in Java.
- Read elements from files into arrays.
- Work with class `MyString`, which represents `String`s as arrays of `char`s.
- Explore the space of methods which involve `MyString`s.
- Take algorithms that work with files and adapt them to work with arrays.
- Investigate algorithms enabled by arrays.
- Implement `Section` as an array of `Student`s.
- Understand shallow copying and deep copying.
- Use parameters passed via the command line.
- Use two-dimensional arrays of numbers, `char`s, and `boolean`s.
- Draw a GUI checkerboard.

The previous chapter introduced the concept of a *collection*, and we used *file* as our first example of a collection. We studied a wide variety of problems involving collections, and we saw that most problems fit into one of a few tens of patterns. You are now quite competent at studying a problem, determining the appropriate pattern, and producing Java code to solve the problem. This chapter will introduce a second kind of collection—the *array*—and we will see that we can solve problems involving arrays by adapting the patterns we previously learned for solving problems involving files.

We'll begin by studying the basics of arrays—creating them and filling them. Then we'll define a class `MyString`, which will represent a `String` as an array of char, and we'll implement for MyString most of the methods that Java supplies for class String. Finally, we will take our class Section and re-implement it using an array of Student, and we will translate all our prior Section methods to use the array representation.

14.1   Arrays as Collections

In Chapter 13, we learned that files are collections of Strings, and that access to elements in a file is not random access: To get to the tenth String in a file, we need to look at the first String, and then the second String, and then the third String, and so forth.

Now let's look at the features of arrays as collections.

1. Arrays may contain either objects or primitive datatypes. We can have arrays of ints and we can have arrays of Students.
2. Within an array, all of the elements are the same type. We can have arrays of ints and arrays of Students, but we can't have an array containing both ints and Students. Arrays are *homogeneous* rather than *heterogeneous*.
3. When an array is created, its length is fixed. We will always have that exact number of elements in the array; it can't grow or shrink.
4. If we know the name of an array, we can get its length. The length of an array is a public constant—public because it can be requested from outside, and constant because it cannot be altered.
5. The positions in an array are numbered 0, 1, ..., length-1. This is also the numbering used for positions within Strings. Position numbers are also called *indices* (singular *index*) or *subscripts*.

> **Index (subscript)**   Indicates a particular cell of an array.

14.2   An Array of Three ints

Declaring

We'll start our study of arrays by working with an array containing three integer values. The statement

```
int[] a;
```

is the declaration that, henceforth, the variable a may only point to arrays of ints. The empty brackets—[]—turn type "int" into type "array *of* int." Similarly, we can declare arrays of other types, both primitive and object:

```
String [] args;
Student [] students;
```

The declaration does not give any value to a by initialization or assignment; it merely restricts the type of object to which a may point. Later, a may point to an array of 3 ints or an array of 5 ints, but a may not point to an int, a Student, or an array of Students.

Allocating

We allocate our array by means of the statement

```
a = new int[3];
```

which makes a point to an array with positions for three ints. This statement grabs for a the appropriate amount of memory to store three ints. We could have joined our first two statements into the single statement

```
int [] a = new int[3];
```

which both declares and allocates array a. The positions are indexed as 0,1,2. Note that we have not yet filled the slots of *a* — we have merely asserted that there are three of them. The situation can be illustrated like this:

where the slots are a[0], a[1], and a[2]. The expression a.length will evaluate to 3. As a is assigned to different arrays of ints, the value of a.length will change appropriately.

Test your skill with Exercise 14-1.

Filling

We use assignment statements to fill the slots of array `a`:

```
a[0] = 7;
a[1] = 3;
a[2] = 9;
```

The only legal subscripts are $0, 1, \ldots, length-1$. The array is now:

```
     0  1  2
a →[ 7 | 3 | 9 ]
```

Accessing

We can access the elements of an array by using subscript notation. For example:

```
a[2] = 2*a[2];
a[0] = a[0] + a[1];
```

We can print out the values in the array by writing

```
System.out.println(a[0]);
System.out.println(a[1]);
System.out.println(a[2]);
```

or we could use a loop:

```
for ( int i = 0 ; i < 3 ; i++ )
    System.out.println(a[i]);
```

Suppose we make `a` point to an array of five `int`s. We would have to alter the `for` loop to handle the new situation. A number embedded in code is called a *magic number* because it must be changed if the problem changes. Note that we could have avoided the magic number if we'd written

```
for ( int i = 0 ; i < a.length ; i++ )
    System.out.println(a[i]);
```

ArrayIndexOutOfBoundsException

If our code requests access to a nonexistent array element, then Java raises the ArrayIndexOutOfBoundsException. You'll get lots of these. Since our array a has three elements, the following statements will raise an Exception:

```
a[-1] = 7;
a[3] = 2;
```

Test your skill with Exercise 14-2.

14.3   **An Array of 10 ints**

Consider the problem:

Construct an array of ints, length 10, where each element is the square of its subscript.

followed by:

Print the elements of the array, separated by spaces.

followed by:

Compute and print the sum of the elements of the array.

The desired array will be:

```
[0,1,4,9,16,25,36,49,64,81]
```

and the desired output is:

```
0 1 4 9 16 25 36 49 64 81
sum: 285
```

Here's an initial approach to the code:

```
int a[] = new int[10];

for ( int i = 0; i < 10 ; i++ ) a[i] = i*i;

for ( int i = 0; i < 10 ; i++ )
   System.out.print(a[i]+ " ");
System.out.println();

int sum = 0;
for ( int i = 0; i < 10 ; i++ ) sum += a[i];
System.out.println("sum: " + sum);
```

Note that 10 is a magic number in this situation. If the problem spec changes so that it requires an array of length 12, then we have to replace 10 by 12 in four different places! That's an invitation to error—inevitably, we find ourselves changing some of the values and forgetting to change some others. Redundancy in code invariably leads to such errors.

We will eliminate the magic number 10 by using a constant MAX:

```
final int MAX = 10;

int a[] = new int[MAX];

for ( int i = 0; i < MAX ; i++ ) a[i] = i*i;

for ( int i = 0; i < MAX ; i++ )
    System.out.print(a[i]+ " ");
System.out.println();

int sum = 0;
for ( int i = 0; i < MAX ; i++ ) sum += a[i];
System.out.println("sum: " + sum);
```

Now, we can change the array size simply by changing 10 to 12 in a single line of code.

OBO (Off-By-One)

OBO errors are very common. Consider the code

```
for ( int i = 0; i < a.length ; i++ )
    System.out.print(a[i]+ " ");
```

which prints the elements in array a. How many ways can we go wrong? Consider the following table:

Statement	Effect
for (int i = 0; i < a.length ; i++)	Perfect.
for (int i = 1; i < a.length ; i++)	Misses a[0].
for (int i = 0; i <= a.length ; i++)	Illegally touches a[a.length].

You should memorize the pattern we've been using for stepping through the elements of an array. Just repeat it and adjust it as necessary.

There's a shortcut for allocating and initializing an array. Consider the code:

```
int [] a = new int[3];
a[0] = 7;
a[1] = 3;
a[2] = 9;
```

An equivalent statement is

```
int [] a = {7,3,9};
```

TRY IT OUT

Can we have an array of `length` 0? Try

```
int[] a = new int[0];
```

What is its `length`?
Is a the same as `null`?
What is the shortcut for allocating and initializing this array?

14.4 Given a File of `ints`, Read Them into an Array

This problem is somewhat tricky because arrays cannot grow and shrink. Once we allocate an array we can fill it, but once it's full we can't add any further elements. In this section, we'll examine several ways of solving the problem.

Read the File Twice

One approach is this:

- Read through the file, counting the `ints`.
- Allocate an array of precisely the correct size.
- Read through the file again, putting each `int` into its appropriate place in the array.

Prog1401 gives the code for this solution. It reports the *squares* of the ints that were read. This is just a quick proof that we converted the file's Strings into ints. It's straightforward but inefficient because of having to read the disk file twice.

Prog1401.java   Read **ints** into an Array—Read Twice

```
// Written by Barry Soroka
//
// Given a file of ints, read them into an array --
// Read the file twice.
//
import java.io.*;
import java.util.Scanner;
////////////////////////////////////////////////////////////////////////////
class Prog1401
{
//--------------------------------------------------------------------------
    public static void main (String [] args) throws Exception
    {
        Scanner kb = new Scanner(System.in);

        System.out.print("I read ints from a file to an array.");

        System.out.print("\nFilename? ");
        String filename = kb.nextLine();

        Scanner sc = new Scanner(new File(filename));

        int n = 0;
        while ( sc.hasNext() )
        {
            sc.nextInt();
            n++;
        }

        System.out.println("\nRequired length: " + n);

        int [] a = new int[n];

        sc = new Scanner(new File(filename));
        for ( int i = 0 ; i < n ; i++ ) a[i] = sc.nextInt();

        System.out.println("\nThe squares of the ints are:");
        for ( int i = 0 ; i < n ; i++ ) System.out.print(a[i]*a[i]+" ");
        System.out.println();
    }
//--------------------------------------------------------------------------
} // end class Prog1401
////////////////////////////////////////////////////////////////////////////
```

Grow the Array By One Cell Each Time

Our second solution will go through the file only once, and we'll maintain an array containing precisely the number of ints we've read so far. Prog1402 gives the code. We start with an array of 0 elements:

```
int [] a = new int[0];
```

Each time we read a new int, we expand a to hold it. Let's examine the loop that goes through the file. When we get a new element, we need to produce a new array with size 1 greater than the current array. We start by allocating the bigger array:

```
int[] newA = new int[a.length + 1];
```

Then we copy the ints from a to newA. There are a.length of them:

```
for ( int i = 0 ; i < a.length ; i++ ) newA[i] = a[i];
```

Finally, we make a point to the new array:

```
a = newA;
```

Now that we've got an array with a single slot unused at the end, we fill that unused slot by putting the newest int at the end of the array:

```
a[a.length-1] = sc.nextInt();
```

As before, this program prints the *squares* of the ints that were read.

Prog1402.java   **Read ints into an Array—Grow One Cell at a Time**

```java
// Written by Barry Soroka
//
// Given a file of ints, read them into an array --
// Start with an array of size 0 and grow it as needed.
//
import java.io.*;
import java.util.Scanner;
/////////////////////////////////////////////////////////////////////////////////
class Prog1402
{
//-----------------------------------------------------------------------------
    public static void main (String [] args) throws Exception
    {
        Scanner kb = new Scanner(System.in);

        System.out.print("I read ints from a file to an array.");
```

```
        System.out.print("\nFilename? ");
        String filename = kb.nextLine();

        Scanner sc = new Scanner(new File(filename));

        int [] a = new int[0];

        while ( sc.hasNext() )
        {
            int[] newA = new int[a.length + 1];
            for ( int i = 0 ; i < a.length ; i++ ) newA[i] = a[i];
            a = newA;

            a[a.length-1] = sc.nextInt();
        }

        System.out.println("\nThe squares of the ints are:");
        for ( int i = 0 ; i < a.length ; i++ ) System.out.print(a[i]*a[i]+" ");
        System.out.println();
    }
//-------------------------------------------------------------------------------
} // end class Prog1402
///////////////////////////////////////////////////////////////////////////////
```

The downside to `Prog1402` is that it spends a lot of time copying array elements from the current array into the one which is 1 cell larger. Would it be more efficient if we doubled the size of the array each time we filled it? We can do this, but it requires that we keep more data; instead of a full array, we now have a partly filled array with a counter that tells how many cells are currently in use.

Allow a Partly Filled Array

`Prog1403` offers another solution to reading `ints` from a file into an array. This program tracks the `ints` by means of *two* variables:

- `a`—an array of `ints`.
- `used`—an `int` that tells us how much of `a` has been filled.

The variable `used` has two meanings:

    1. It tells us *how many* slots have been filled.
    2. It tells us *where* to insert the next `int`.

Hence, if `used == a.length`, then

    1. we've inserted `a.length` `ints` into `a`, meaning that it's full, and
    2. the next slot to receive an `int` would have index `a.length`. But that's not a legal slot, since the slots are numbered `0,1,2,....,a.length-1`. So we must grow the array before trying to save the next `int`.

Prog1403.java   **Read `ints` into an Array—Double the Array As Needed**

```java
// Written by Barry Soroka
//
// Given a file of ints, read them into an array --
// Start with an array of size 0 and grow it as needed --
// Double the array when it gets full.
//
import java.io.*;
import java.util.Scanner;
//////////////////////////////////////////////////////////////////////////////
class Prog1403
{
//----------------------------------------------------------------------------
    public static void main (String [] args) throws Exception
    {
        Scanner kb = new Scanner(System.in);

        System.out.print("I read ints from a file to an array.");

        System.out.print("\nFilename? ");
        String filename = kb.nextLine();

        Scanner sc = new Scanner(new File(filename));

        int [] a = new int[0];
        int used = 0;

        while ( sc.hasNext() )
        {
            // Is the array full?
            if ( used == a.length )
            {
                int[] newA = new int[2*a.length + 1];
                for ( int i = 0 ; i < used ; i++ ) newA[i] = a[i];
                a = newA;
            }
            a[used] = sc.nextInt();
            used++;
        }

        System.out.println("\nThe squares of the ints are:");
        for ( int i = 0 ; i < used ; i++ ) System.out.print(a[i]*a[i]+" ");
        System.out.println();
    }
//----------------------------------------------------------------------------
} // end class Prog1403
//////////////////////////////////////////////////////////////////////////////
```

In the prior solution, we grew the array by only one cell each time it became full. If we always double the array size, using the formula

```
length' ← 2*length
```

then an initial array of length 0 would never get any bigger. So we'll use the formula

```
length' ← 2*length + 1
```

This formula *always* grows the array—even a size 0 array will grow. Another approach would start with a larger but empty array:

```
int[] a = new int[5];
int used = 0;
```

Test your skill with Exercises 14-3 through 14-5.

14.5   Passing Arrays and Array Elements

Inside a program, there are two basic schemes for using an array:

1. The array is *full*, and its `length` can be requested as needed.
2. The array is *not full*, and the number of full slots is stored in a separate variable, for example `used`.

If we want a method to print out an array, then we'll need *two* methods, one for each of the schemes listed. For the full array, we have

```
public static void print(int[])
```

and for the array that is not full, we have

```
public static void print(int[],int).
```

The complete code is

```
public static void print( int[] a )
{
   for ( int i = 0 ; i < a.length; i++ )
      System.out.println(a[i]);
}
```

and

```
public static void print( int[] a, int used )
{
   for ( int i = 0 ; i < used; i++ )
      System.out.println(a[i]);
}
```

What Can We Change?

Suppose we pass an array to a method. What can we change?

- Can we change the values of individual slots? *Yes.*
- Can we change the values of all the slots? *Yes.*
- Can we make the variable point to another array? *No.*
- If we pass an array element to a method, can the method change that element? *No.*

Prog1404 proves these points.

Prog1404.java   Passing an Array As a Parameter

```
// Written by Barry Soroka
//
// When you pass an array, you pass a pointer to an array of slots.
// What can a receiving method change?
//
import java.io.*;
////////////////////////////////////////////////////////////////////////////
class Prog1404
{
   //-------------------------------------------------------------------------
```

```
    public static void main (String [] args) throws Exception
    {
        BufferedReader kb = new BufferedReader(
                            new InputStreamReader ( System.in ));

        int[] a = {1,2,3};
        System.out.println("\nInitial array:");
        print(a);
        System.out.println("\nIncrementing a[0]:");
        f(a);
        print(a);
        System.out.println("\nSquaring the elements:");
        square(a);
        print(a);
        System.out.println("\nTrying to replace an array in a method:");
        g(a);
        print(a);
        System.out.println("\nTrying to change an element by passing a[i]:");
        h(a[0]);
        print(a);
    }
//----------------------------------------------------------------------
//
// f(a) -- increments the first element of array a
//
    public static void f ( int[] a )
    {
        a[0]++;
    }
//----------------------------------------------------------------------
//
// g(a) -- tries to change the value of a
//
    public static void g ( int[] a )
    {
        a = new int[5];
    }
//----------------------------------------------------------------------
//
// h(int) -- tries to change the value of an int parameter
//
    public static void h ( int n )
    {
        n = 13;
    }
```

```
//-----------------------------------------------------------------------
//
// square(a) -- squares the elements of array a
//
   public static void square ( int[] a )
   {
      for ( int i = 0 ; i < a.length ; i++ ) a[i] = a[i]*a[i];
   }
//-----------------------------------------------------------------------
   public static void print ( int[] a )
   {
      System.out.println();
      for ( int i = 0 ; i < a.length ; i++ ) System.out.print(a[i] + " ");
      System.out.println();
   }
//-----------------------------------------------------------------------
} // end class Prog1404
//////////////////////////////////////////////////////////////////////////
```

We allocate and initialize array a, and it prints

```
1 2 3
```

Then we pass a to the following method:

```
public static void f ( int[] a )
{
   a[0]++;
}
```

On returning, it prints

```
2 2 3
```

proving that method f has altered the first element of its parameter. Then we pass a to this method:

```
public static void square ( int[] a )
{
   for ( int i = 0 ; i < a.length ; i++ )
   {
      a[i] = a[i]*a[i];
   }
}
```

On returning, it prints

```
4 4 9
```

which proves that method `square` was able to change *all* of the elements in the incoming array. Next we send a to the method

```
public static void g ( int[] a )
{
    a = new int[5];
}
```

which tries to make a point to a new array of length 5. On return, a prints

```
4 4 9
```

showing that *method g did not change where a is pointing*. The statement

```
a = new int[5];
```

does create a new array, and it *does* make its parameter point to this new array, but the linkage is lost when the method exits. Inside the method, a is treated as a local variable, which goes away when we exit the method. The association of a with the three-element array has not been altered by the assignment inside the method.

Finally, the statement

```
h(a[0])
```

invokes the method

```
public static void h ( int n )
{
    n = 13;
}
```

but, on return, a still prints

```
4 4 9
```

The call h(a[0]) is translated so that *the value of* a[0] is sent to method h. Inside the method, the parameter n is treated as a *local* variable, which is changed by the assignment statement, but this new value is lost when we exit the method.

> **NOTE**
>
> In general, if you pass a *reference* as a parameter, then the receiver can change the slots of the object being sent. If you pass a *primitive datatype*, then the receiver can't change it.

Returning an Array from a Method

Consider Prog1405 and its method

```
public static int[] growBy1 ( int[] a )
```

Notice that the return type is int[], meaning that this method returns an array of ints as its result. In particular, growBy1 takes in a full array of ints and returns an array that contains the same ints as the parameter array, but which has *one more cell* at its end. The first statement allocates the array to be returned:

```
int[] result = new int[a.length + 1];
```

Then the method copies all the values from the parameter a to result:

```
for ( int i = 0 ; i < a.length ; i++ )
    result[i] = a[i];
```

Finally, the method returns the array that has been constructed. Thus, arrays can be used just like objects or primitive datatypes: They can be parameters and they can be return values.

Prog1405.java   Return an Array

```java
// Written by Barry Soroka
//
// Read ints from the keyboard and store them in a growing array.
//
import java.io.*;
import java.util.Scanner;
/////////////////////////////////////////////////////////////////////////////
class Prog1405
{
//--------------------------------------------------------------------------
    public static void main (String [] args) throws Exception
    {
        Scanner kb = new Scanner(System.in);

        int[] a = {};

        while ( true )
        {
            print(a);
            System.out.print("\nEnter an int: ");
            int n = kb.nextInt();
            a = growBy1(a);
            a[a.length-1] = n;
        }
    }
//--------------------------------------------------------------------------
    public static int[] growBy1 ( int[] a )
    {
        int[] result = new int[a.length + 1];
        for ( int i = 0 ; i < a.length ; i++ ) result[i] = a[i];
        return result;
    }
//--------------------------------------------------------------------------
    public static void print ( int[] a )
    {
        System.out.println();
        for ( int i = 0 ; i < a.length ; i++ ) System.out.print(a[i] + " ");
        System.out.println();
    }
//--------------------------------------------------------------------------
} // end class Prog1405
/////////////////////////////////////////////////////////////////////////////
```

14.6   **Class** MyString**—Array of** char

In this section we will begin to develop class MyString; its instances represent Strings by storing an array of char. After introducing the class, we will apply various patterns to implement many of the methods that Java provides for class String, plus more methods that Java doesn't provide. Although many programmers will use class String and its methods without thinking about how they work, computer scientists must also know how to implement each method from scratch.[1]

Prog1406 contains (1) a driver and (2) our initial implementation of class MyString. Let's study the driver. After creating a Scanner kb, it reads a MyString:

```
MyString s = MyString.read(System.out,kb);
```

We have encapsulated all the details of MyString. The user doesn't know how a MyString is read or how it's stored. The next statement reports the MyString:

```
System.out.println("You entered the MyString \"" + s
                        + "\".");
```

The code concatenates a MyString with two Strings—this means that MyString provides a toString method. We can print MyStrings without knowing their internal details. The last statement of the driver prints the length of the MyString:

```
System.out.println("Its length is " + s.length());
```

Based on this analysis of the driver, we now know that MyString must contain at least the following methods:

```
public static MyString read ( PrintStream ps,
                                      Scanner sc )
public String toString()
public int length()
```

---

[1] This is another checkpoint where you can test whether and how much you want to be a CS major. If you are happy just using the methods of the API, then CS will be a stretch for you. If you don't like writing all the mini-methods we'll write for MyString, then CS is not for you.

Prog1406.java   Class **MyString**

```java
// Written by Barry Soroka
//
// Introduces class MyString -- Represent a String as an array of char.
//
import java.io.*;
import java.util.Scanner;
//////////////////////////////////////////////////////////////////////////////
class Prog1406
{
//----------------------------------------------------------------------------

    public static void main (String [] args) throws Exception
    {
        Scanner kb = new Scanner(System.in);
        MyString s = MyString.read(System.out,kb);
        System.out.println("You entered the MyString \"" + s + "\".");
        System.out.println("Its length is " + s.length());
    }
//----------------------------------------------------------------------------
} // end class Prog1406
//////////////////////////////////////////////////////////////////////////////
class MyString
{
    private char [] a;
//----------------------------------------------------------------------------
//
// MyString ( String s )
//
// Constructs a MyString from a String
//
    public MyString ( String s )
    {
        this.a = new char[s.length()];
        for ( int i = 0 ; i < s.length() ; i++ )
        {
            this.a[i] = s.charAt(i);
        }
    }
//----------------------------------------------------------------------------
//
// MyString ( char[] a )
//
// Constructs a MyString from a full array of char
```

```
//
   public MyString ( char[] a ) { this.a = a; }
//---------------------------------------------------------------
//
// MyString ( char[] a, int used )
//
// Constructs a MyString from an unfilled array of char
//
   public MyString ( char[] a, int used )
   {
      this.a = new char[used];
      for ( int i = 0 ; i < used ; i++ ) this.a[i] = a[i];
   }
//---------------------------------------------------------------
   public int length () { return a.length; }
//---------------------------------------------------------------
   public static MyString read ( PrintStream ps, Scanner sc )
   {
      if ( ps != null ) ps.print("Enter a String: ");
      String s = sc.nextLine();
      return new MyString(s);
   }
//---------------------------------------------------------------
   public String toString ()
   {
      String result = "";
      for ( int i = 0 ; i < a.length ; i++ )
      {
         result += a[i];
      }
      return result;
   }
//---------------------------------------------------------------
} // end class MyString
/////////////////////////////////////////////////////////////////////////
```

14.7 Primitive Methods for MyString

Now we will analyze the basic MyString methods defined in Prog1406. The sole instance variable is an array of char:

```
private char[] a;
```

This means that `MyString` is always keeping a *full* array of `char`. On the positive side, this means that we have only one instance variable. On the negative side, this means that adding even a single `char` to an existing `MyString` will require creating a new array and copying `chars` from the old array to the new one. As we implement more and more methods, we will see the consequences of our decision to store a full array of `char`.

Constructors

`MyString` provides three constructors. The first takes a `String` and makes a `MyString` from it:

```
public MyString ( String s )
{
    this.a = new char[s.length()];
    for ( int i = 0 ; i < s.length() ; i++ )
    {
        this.a[i] = s.charAt(i);
    }
}
```

First we create an array of the appropriate length, and then we copy the `chars` from the `String` to the array.

The second constructor accepts a full array of `chars` and uses this as the value of the instance variable:

```
public MyString ( char[] a ) { this.a = a; }
```

Note that this constructor shares the same array between the instance variable and the source variable in the caller. We may sometimes want to copy rather than share the array.

<table>
<tr><td>**Test your skill with Exercise 14-6.**</td></tr>
</table>

The third constructor accepts an *unfilled* array of `char`, plus an `int` that specifies the number of slots that are filled:

```
public MyString ( char[] a, int used )
{
    this.a = new char[used];
    for ( int i = 0 ; i < used ; i++ ) this.a[i] = a[i];
}
```

The constructor creates a new array of char, precisely n chars long, and then copies the chars from the parameter a to the instance variable a.

Test your skill with Exercise 14-7.

length

The length method for MyString simply returns the length of the array of char.

static read

Class MyString provides the expected static read method:

```
public static MyString read ( PrintStream ps, Scanner sc )
{
    if ( ps != null ) ps.print("Enter a String: ");
    String s = sc.nextLine();
    return new MyString(s);
}
```

We prompt, if necessary, and we read a String. This is passed to the constructor MyString(String), and we return the MyString that is created.

toString

The toString method is straightforward. First we create a variable in which to accumulate the result:

```
String result = "";
```

Then we loop through the array, and we concatenate each char, in turn, to the result:

```
for ( int i = 0 ; i < a.length ; i++ )
{
    result += a[i];
}
```

When that's done, we simply return result.

14.8 A Taxonomy of MyString Methods

In the sections that follow, we will implement a wide variety of methods for class MyString. Some will be solved in the text and some will be given for homework. Some of these methods are the same as methods found in Java's class String, and others are not found in the API at all.

We can better understand the space of all MyString methods by organizing the methods in a table—a taxonomy, if you will. How should we organize this table?

A method has *incoming parameters* and an *outgoing result*. Input parameters can be:

- empty—no input parameters, as in length().
- char—as in containsHowMany(char).
- int—as in substring(int) or substring(int,int).
- MyString—as in equals(MyString).

Outgoing results can be:

- boolean—as in isPalindrome().[2]
- char—as in charAt(int).
- int—as in length().
- MyString—as in trim() or concat(MyString).
- String—as in toString().

Here is a table into which we can place each MyString method with respect to its incoming parameters and outgoing results:

		PARAMETER(S)			
		none	**char**	**int**	**MyString**
RESULT	boolean	isPalindrome()			
	char			charAt(int)	
	int	length()	containsHowMany(char)		
	MyString	trim()		substring(int) substring(int,int)	concat(MyString)
	String	toString()			

I have already indicated the positions of the methods described. Methods in the same cell will, typically, use similar array-handling techniques.

 Test your skill with Exercises 14-8 through 14-10.

---

[2] A palindrome is the same forward and backward. For example, radar is a palindrome, but palindrome is not.

14.9   equals

This method has the prototype

```
public boolean equals ( MyString )
```

and it returns `true` only if both `MyString`s—the receiver and the parameter—are "equal" in the sense that (1) they have the same `length`, and (2) corresponding characters are equal.

`Prog1407` gives a driver and the code for method `equals`. Let's examine the method. The first line

```
public boolean equals ( MyString that )
```

sets up the familiar variables `this` and `that`. The code will be quite parallel. We first check for the negative case, where the `length`s are not the same:

```
if ( this.length() != that.length() ) return false;
```

An alternative statement is this:

```
if ( this.a.length != that.a.length ) return false;
```

Now we know that the two `length`s are the same, so we can proceed into a `for` statement, which will loop through the two arrays. We can exit, returning `false`, if we ever find a mismatch:

```
for ( int i = 0 ; i < this.length() ; i++ )
{
    if ( this.a[i] != that.a[i] ) return false;
}
```

If we get to the end of the arrays without detecting a mismatch, then we execute the final statement:

```
return true;
```

We've seen logic like this in Chapter 13, where we compared two files for equality.

Prog1407.java   boolean equals(MyString)

```
// Written by Barry Soroka
//
// MyString -- add method boolean equals(MyString).
//
import java.io.*;
import java.util.Scanner;
```

```
//////////////////////////////////////////////////////////////////////////////
class Prog1407
{
//------------------------------------------------------------------------------

    public static void main (String [] args) throws Exception
    {
        Scanner kb = new Scanner(System.in);

        MyString s1 = MyString.read(System.out,kb);
        MyString s2 = MyString.read(System.out,kb);

        System.out.println("\ns1: \"" + s1 + "\"");
        System.out.println("\ns2: \"" + s2 + "\"");

        System.out.println("\ns1.equals(s2): " + s1.equals(s2));
        System.out.println("\ns2.equals(s1): " + s2.equals(s1));
    }
//------------------------------------------------------------------------------
} // end class Prog1407
//////////////////////////////////////////////////////////////////////////////
class MyString
{
    private char [] a;
//------------------------------------------------------------------------------

    public boolean equals ( MyString that )
    {
        if ( this.length() != that.length() ) return false;

        for ( int i = 0 ; i < this.length() ; i++ )
        {
            if ( this.a[i] != that.a[i] ) return false;
        }

        return true;
    }
//------------------------------------------------------------------------------
// More code is included!  See Prog1406.
//------------------------------------------------------------------------------
} // end class MyString
//////////////////////////////////////////////////////////////////////////////
```

Test your skill with Exercise 14-11.

Here's another way to write the `equals` method:

```
public boolean equals ( MyString that )
{
    char[] a1 = this.a;
    char[] a2 = that.a;

    if ( a1.length != a2.length ) return false;

    for ( int i = 0 ; i < a1.length ; i++ )
    {
        if ( a1[i] != a2[i] ) return false;
    }

    return true;
}
```

The statements

```
char[] a1 = this.a;
char[] a2 = that.a;
```

allow us to reference the two arrays—a1 and a2—while ignoring `this` and `that`. Study the two programs and form your own opinion as to which is easier to read.

Check for Exceptions/Negative Examples

The preceding code returns `false` as soon as any deviation from equality is detected:

```
if ( this.a.length != that.a.length ) return false;
```

Let's see what happens if we write the `if` condition as

```
if ( this.a.length == that.a.length ) ...
```

We get the following correct and working code:

```
public boolean equals ( MyString that )
{
    if ( this.length() == that.length() )
    {
        for ( int i = 0 ; i < this.length() ; i++ )
        {
            if ( this.a[i] != that.a[i] ) return false;
        }
        return true;
    }
    else return false;
}
```

Notice that the `for` loop is now indented one extra level, and the `return false` statement has been separated from its condition by eight lines! The code is correct, but it's much harder to understand than the code we saw initially.

> **Test your skill with Exercises 14-12 and 14-13.**

14.10   Concatenating Arrays

Consider the method

```
public MyString concat ( MyString that )
```

which returns the concatenation of two `MyString`s. Here's the programming logic that we'll use:

Let the two `array`s be `a1` and `a2`:

```
char[] a1 = this.a;
char[] a2 = that.a;
```

Then the size of the two `array`s will be `n1` and `n2`:

```
int n1 = a1.length;
int n2 = a2.length;
```

Now we've set up variables that will make the code easy to read and write. Let's use `newA` as the name of the array of the resulting `MyString`, and specify that `newA` must have length `n1+n2`:

```
char[] newA = new char[n1+n2];
```

First, we must copy `char`s from `a1` to `newA`. Here's the correspondence of the slots:

```
newA[0] ← a1[0]
. . .
newA[n1-1] ← a1[n1-1]
```

and the required code is:

```
for ( int i = 0 ; i < n1 ; i++ ) newA[i] = a1[i];
```

Then we must copy `chars` from a2 to newA. Here's the correspondence of the slots:

```
newA[n1]     ← a2[0]
newA[n1+1]   ← a2[1]
  . . .
newA[n1+n2-1] ← a2[n2-1]
```

and the required code is:

```
for ( int i = 0 ; i < n2 ; i++ )
    newA[n1+i] = a2[i];
```

Be sure that you understand why this `for` loop performs the copying required. Finally, we create and return the appropriate `MyString`:

```
return new MyString(newA);
```

Prog1408 gives the code plus a driver.[3]

Prog1408.java   MyString concat(MyString)

```java
// Written by Barry Soroka
//
// MyString -- add method MyString concat(MyString).
//
import java.io.*;
import java.util.Scanner;
/////////////////////////////////////////////////////////////////////////////
class Prog1408
{
//-------------------------------------------------------------------------

   public static void main (String [] args) throws Exception
   {
      Scanner kb = new Scanner(System.in);

      MyString s1 = MyString.read(System.out,kb);
      MyString s2 = MyString.read(System.out,kb);

      System.out.println("\ns1: \"" + s1 + "\"");
      System.out.println("\ns2: \"" + s2 + "\"");

      System.out.println("\ns1.concat(s2): \"" + s1.concat(s2) + "\"");
      System.out.println("\ns2.concat(s1): \"" + s2.concat(s1) + "\"");
   }
```

---

[3]   To emphasize the `concat` method, I have put it at the top of class `MyString`, violating the style sheet.

```
//- - - - - - - - - - - - - - - - - - - - - - - - - - - - - - - - - - - - - - - - - - - - - - - - - - - - -
} // end class Prog1408
//////////////////////////////////////////////////////////////////////////////
class MyString
{
    private char [] a;
//- - - - - - - - - - - - - - - - - - - - - - - - - - - - - - - - - - - - - - - - - - - - - - - - - - - - -
    public MyString concat ( MyString that )
    {
        char[] a1 = this.a;
        char[] a2 = that.a;

        int n1 = a1.length;
        int n2 = a2.length;

        char[] newA = new char[n1+n2];

        for ( int i = 0 ; i < n1 ; i++ ) newA[i] = a1[i];

        for ( int i = 0 ; i < n2 ; i++ )
            newA[n1+i] = a2[i];

        return new MyString(newA);
    }
//- - - - - - - - - - - - - - - - - - - - - - - - - - - - - - - - - - - - - - - - - - - - - - - - - - - - -
// More code is included!  See Prog1406.
//- - - - - - - - - - - - - - - - - - - - - - - - - - - - - - - - - - - - - - - - - - - - - - - - - - - - -
} // end class MyString
//////////////////////////////////////////////////////////////////////////////
```

 Test your skill with Exercises 14-14 and 14-15.

14.11   Index, Contains, How Many

In this section we will study MyString methods, which handle the following related problems:

- Given a MyString and a char, what is the index of the *leftmost* occurrence of the char?
- Given a MyString and a char, what is the index of the *rightmost* occurrence of the char?
- Does a MyString contain a given char?

- Given a MyString and a char, how many times does that char occur in the MyString?

> **NOTE** The empty MyString is not a special case for any of these patterns. The code that works on the general case will also work, without change, on the empty MyString, and will return the appropriate value.

Index

The method int indexOf(char) returns the index of the leftmost position at which char occurs. If char does not occur in the receiving MyString, then we need to return some special value that indicates this. Following the indexOf method in class String, we'll return -1.[4] The method int lastIndexOf(char) is similar, but it returns the index of the *last*, or *rightmost*, occurrence of char.

The algorithm for indexOf is straightforward:

- Walk down the array from the first char (index 0) to the last char (index a.length-1).
- If we find the char, then we return the index.
- If we get to the end of the array without finding char, then we return -1.

Here's the code:

```
public int indexOf ( char c )
{
    for ( int i = 0 ; i < a.length ; i++ )
        if ( a[i] == c ) return i;
    return -1;
}
```

Notice how we return -1 if we fall past the for loop.

The corresponding algorithm for lastIndex is as follows:

- Walk down the array from the last char (index a.length-1) to the first char (index 0).

---

[4] Some languages return the length of the String, which also signals a nonexistent position.

- If we find the `char`, then we return the index.
- If we reach the front of the array without finding `char`, then we return `-1`.

Here's the code:

```
public int lastIndexOf ( char c )
{
    for ( int i = a.length - 1 ; i >= 0 ; i-- )
        if ( a[i] == c ) return i;
    return -1;
}
```

The only difficulty with this code is that we must get the loop to look at the array elements in the right order, starting and stopping correctly. It's easy to get it wrong.

Here's a different algorithm for `lastIndexOf`:

```
public int lastIndexOf ( char c )
{
    int result = -1;
    for ( int i = 0 ; i < a.length ; i++ )
        if ( a[i] == c ) result = i;
    return result;
}
```

We keep a variable `result`, initially set to `-1`, and we walk down the array from front to rear. Any time we find `char`, we change `result` to the new index. When the loop is finished, `result` is either `-1` (no `char` found) or it's the index of the *last* occurrence of `char`.

Q: Why is this algorithm inefficient?

STOP AND THINK

A: Suppose that `char` occurs at the far right of the array. Then the first algorithm would look at this position *first* and would immediately return `a.length-1` without looking at any other elements of the array. The second algorithm would start at the front and would traverse the entire array before locating the rightmost occurrence of `char`. To magnify the consequences, suppose that the array contains 1 million `char`s:

- Algorithm 1 would look at only *one* `char`.
- Algorithm 2 would look at all *1 million* `char`s.

`Prog1409.java` gives the code for `indexOf` and `lastIndexOf`. These may come in handy for implementing some other methods later.

Prog1409.java   indexOf and lastIndexOf

```
// Written by Barry Soroka
//
// MyString -- adds int indexOf(char)
//                  int lastIndexOf(char)
//
import java.io.*;
import java.util.Scanner;
/////////////////////////////////////////////////////////////////////////////
class Prog1409
{
//---------------------------------------------------------------------------
   public static void main (String [] args) throws Exception
   {
      Scanner kb = new Scanner(System.in);

      while ( true )
      {
         MyString s = MyString.read(System.out,kb);
         System.out.print("Enter a char:   ");
         char c = kb.nextLine().charAt(0);
         System.out.println("\"" + s + "\".indexOf('" + c + "') ->      " +
                            s.indexOf(c));
         System.out.println("\"" + s + "\".lastIndexOf('" + c + "') -> " +
                            s.lastIndexOf(c));

      }
   }
//---------------------------------------------------------------------------
} // end class Prog1409
/////////////////////////////////////////////////////////////////////////////
class MyString
{
   private char [] a;
//---------------------------------------------------------------------------
   public int indexOf ( char c )
   {
      for ( int i = 0 ; i < a.length ; i++ )
         if ( a[i] == c ) return i;
      return -1;
   }
//---------------------------------------------------------------------------
   public int lastIndexOf ( char c )
   {
```

```
      for ( int i = a.length - 1 ; i >= 0 ; i-- )
         if ( a[i] == c ) return i;
      return -1;
   }
//---------------------------------------------------------------------------
// More code is included!  See Prog1406.
//---------------------------------------------------------------------------
} // end class MyString
///////////////////////////////////////////////////////////////////////////
```

Contains

A typical method of this pattern has prototype contains(char), which reports whether the receiving MyString contains a specified char. We'll look at two ways to implement contains.

The first implementation is this:

```
public boolean contains ( char c )
{
   for ( int i = 0 ; i < a.length ; i++ )
      if ( a[i] == c ) return true;
   return false;
}
```

We see a loop very similar to that of indexOf:

- We walk down the array.
- If we find the char, we return true.
- If we get to the end of the array without finding char, then we return false.

A second implementation takes advantage of the previously written indexOf method:

```
public boolean contains ( char c )
{
   return this.indexOf(c) != -1;
}
```

If this contains c, then it must have an index other than -1.

Test your skill with Exercises 14-16 through 14-19.

How Many

The prior pattern reported whether a receiving MyString contained *any* occurrences of a given char, and the result was true or false. Moreover, we didn't need to look at the entire array; we could return true as soon as we discovered any occurrence of the char.

The next pattern reports more information—namely, how many of the specified char are in the receiving MyString. This pattern requires that we look at the *entire* array, since we need to know the total number of times the char occurs. Here's the code:

```java
public int howMany( char c )
{
    int result = 0;
    for ( int i = 0 ; i < a.length ; i++ )
        if ( a[i] == c ) result++;
    return result;
}
```

That's straightforward.

Prog1410.java gives the code for contains and howMany.

Prog1410.java   contains and howMany

```java
// Written by Barry Soroka
//
// MyString -- adds boolean contains(char)
//                    int howMany(char)
//
import java.io.*;
import java.util.Scanner;
//////////////////////////////////////////////////////////////////////////////
class Prog1410
{
//-----------------------------------------------------------------------------
    public static void main (String [] args) throws Exception
    {
        Scanner kb = new Scanner(System.in);

        while ( true )
        {
            MyString s = MyString.read(System.out,kb);
```

```
            System.out.print("Enter a char:    ");
            char c = kb.nextLine().charAt(0);
            System.out.println("\"" + s + "\".contains('" + c + "') -> " +
                               s.contains(c));
            System.out.println("\"" + s + "\".howMany('" + c + "') ->  " +
                               s.howMany(c));

        }
    }
//------------------------------------------------------------------------
} // end class Prog1410
////////////////////////////////////////////////////////////////////////
class MyString
{
    private char [] a;
//------------------------------------------------------------------------
    public boolean contains ( char c )
    {
        for ( int i = 0 ; i < a.length ; i++ )
            if ( a[i] == c ) return true;
        return false;
    }
//------------------------------------------------------------------------
    public int howMany( char c )
    {
        int result = 0;
        for ( int i = 0 ; i < a.length ; i++ )
            if ( a[i] == c ) result++;
        return result;
    }
//------------------------------------------------------------------------
// More code is included!  See Prog1406.
//------------------------------------------------------------------------
} // end class MyString
////////////////////////////////////////////////////////////////////////
```

 Test your skill with Exercises 14-20 through 14-23.

14.12 MyString **in,** MyString **out—Same Length**

Methods in this section convert one MyString into another. We'll consider three problems:

- MyString replace(char,char)—Returns a new MyString in which all occurrences of the first char have been changed to the second char. For example,

    "hello there".replace('e','a') → "hallo thara"

- MyString replaceCharAtIndex(int,char)—Returns a new MyString in which the char at the specified position has been changed to the specified char.
- MyString reverse()—Returns a new MyString in which the order of the chars has been reversed.

Note that the resulting MyStrings are the *same length* as the receiving MyStrings. A later section will examine problems in which the resulting MyStrings are a different length than the receiving MyStrings—for example, take a MyString and return a new MyString in which every instance of a given char has been deleted.

The code for these methods is gathered in Prog1411.java.

Prog1411.java   Replace and Reverse

```
// Written by Barry Soroka
//
// Prog1411.java
//
// MyString -- adds MyString replace(char,char)
//                  MyString replaceCharAtIndex(int,char)
//                  MyString reverse()
//
import java.io.*;
import java.util.Scanner;
/////////////////////////////////////////////////////////////////////////////
class MyString
{
   private char [] a;
//---------------------------------------------------------------------------
   public MyString replace ( char c1, char c2 )
   {
      char[] result = new char[a.length];
      for ( int i = 0 ; i < a.length ; i++ )
         if ( a[i] == c1 ) result[i] = c2;
         else              result[i] = a[i];
      return new MyString(result);
   }
//---------------------------------------------------------------------------
```

```
   public MyString replaceCharAtIndex ( int n, char c )
   {
      char[] result = new char[a.length];
      for ( int i = 0 ; i < a.length ; i++ )
         if ( i == n ) result[i] = c;
         else          result[i] = a[i];
      return new MyString(result);
   }
//-------------------------------------------------------------------
   public void reverse ()
   {
      int n = a.length;
      for ( int i = 0 ; i < n/2 ; i++ )
      {
         char temp = a[i];
         a[i] = a[n-1-i];
         a[n-1-i] = temp;
      }
   }
//-------------------------------------------------------------------
// More code is included!  See Prog1406.
//-------------------------------------------------------------------
} // end class MyString
/////////////////////////////////////////////////////////////////////////
```

Replace

This pattern produces a new MyString in which every occurrence of a given char has been replaced by another given char. Here's the code:

```
   public MyString replace ( char c1, char c2 )
   {
      char[] result = new char[a.length];
      for ( int i = 0 ; i < a.length ; i++ )
         if ( a[i] == c1 ) result[i] = c2;
         else              result[i] = a[i];
      return new MyString(result);
   }
```

We begin by allocating the array for the result. Then we step down the receiver's array, copying or replacing each char as appropriate. Finally, we return a new MyString using the array we've created.

This method has an analog that changes the receiving MyString rather than returning a new one:[5]

```
public void replace ( char c1, char c2 )
{
    for ( int i = 0 ; i < a.length ; i++ )
        if ( a[i] == c1 ) a[i] = c2;
}
```

Q: Can both these methods be defined in class MyString simultaneously?

 **AND THINK**

A: No. The two methods have different *prototypes*:

```
public MyString replace ( char c1, char c2 )
public    void    replace ( char c1, char c2 )
```

but they have the exact same *signature*:

```
replace ( char c1, char c2 )
```

Overloaded methods must differ in *signature*. Hence, these two methods cannot be defined in class MyString simultaneously.

Let's look at how they differ. The first version produces a new MyString and leaves the original MyString untouched. Consider the code:

```
MyString s1 = new MyString("hello there");
MyString s2 = s1.replace('e','a');
System.out.println(s1);
System.out.println(s2);
```

The printed output is

```
hello there
hallo thara
```

---

[5] We can even imagine a replace method that both changes the receiving MyString and produces a new MyString. I can't think of when this would be useful, though.

We can see that the original `MyString` has not been changed.

By contrast, we would invoke the second version of `replace` with dialog like this:

```
MyString s1 = new MyString("hello there");
s1.replace('e','a');
System.out.println(s1);
```

and the printout would show

```
hallo thara
```

which indicates that the original `MyString` has been changed.

Study carefully these two versions of `replace`. When we're designing methods for a new class, we will often have to decide between (1) changing an existing object, and (2) generating a new and changed object.

Test your skill with Exercises 14-24 through 14-26.

replaceCharAtIndex

This method returns a new `MyString` in which the `char` at a specified index has been changed:

```
public MyString replaceCharAtIndex ( int n, char c )
{
    char[] result = new char[a.length];
    for ( int i = 0 ; i < a.length ; i++ )
        if ( i == n ) result[i] = c;
        else          result[i] = a[i];
    return new MyString(result);
}
```

We create an array for the `result`, and we copy from the receiver to the `result` *except at the specified index*, where we copy the specified alternate `char`.

Test your skill with Exercises 14-27 and 14-28.

Reverse

The basic structure of the `reverse` method is this:

```
public MyString reverse ()
{
```

```
int n = a.length;
char[] result = new char[n];
for ( int i = 0 ; i < n ; i++ )
    result[i] = a[?];
return new MyString(result);
}
```

We'll have a new array to hold the `result`, and we'll copy `chars` from `a` to `result`. The major question is: *What element of `a` is supposed to fill position `i` of `result`?* Let's look at how the indices align:

result[0]	should get	a[n-1]	The last element becomes the first.
result[1]	should get	a[n-2]	
result[2]	should get	a[n-3]	
. . .	. . .	. . .	
result[n-2]	should get	a[1]	
result[n-1]	should get	a[0]	The first element becomes the last.

So, what's the formula that takes the `result` index `i` and computes the appropriate receiver index? Since $0 \rightarrow$ n-1 and $1 \rightarrow$ n-2, let's guess that the formula is $f(i) = n - 1 - i$. Does it work for the later indices?

$$f(n-2) = n - 1 - (n - 2) = 1 \qquad \text{OK!}$$
$$f(n-1) = n - 1 - (n - 1) = 0 \qquad \text{OK!}$$

So the incomplete line of Java should be this:

```
for ( int i = 0 ; i < n ; i++ ) result[i] = a[n-1-i];
```

Study how we solved this problem: In copying between `arrays`, we will often need to compute indices in this fashion.

Reversing in Place

Suppose we had wanted a method

```
public void reverse()
```

which reverses the receiving `MyString`. A naïve approach would adapt our previous code directly:

```
public void reverse ()
{
    int n = a.length;
    for ( int i = 0 ; i < n ; i++ )
        a[i] = a[n-1-i];
    return new MyString(result);
}
```

 Test your skill with Exercise 14-29.

A problem arises because we replace a char, and when we come back later we expect it to have its original value. We can avoid problems by *swapping* the two values and walking only halfway up the MyString. This is as though we were folding the array in half, as shown in Figure 14–1. The code is this:

> **Swapping**   Reversing the values of two variables or cells.

```
public void reverse ()
{
    int n = a.length;
    for ( int i = 0 ; i < n/2 ; i++ )
    {
        char temp = a[i];
        a[i] = a[n-1-i];
        a[n-1-i] = temp;
    }
}
```

Figure 14–1
Reversing in
Place: Folding an
Array

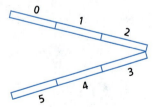

(a) Folding a six-element array

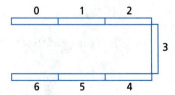

(b) Folding a seven-element array

Note the characteristic code for swapping the values of two variables, say, p and q:

```
char temp = p;
p = q;
q = temp;
```

Another way to reverse a MyString is to create a new (reversed) array and then replace the array within the MyString. Here's the code:

```
public void reverse ()
{
    int n = a.length;
    char[] newA = new char[n];
    for ( int i = 0 ; i < n ; i++ )
        newA[i] = a[n-1-i];
    a = newA;
}
```

   Test your skill with Exercise 14-30.

14.13   Add a char at the Front or Rear

The prior section examined problems that took a MyString and produced another MyString with the same length. Now we will examine algorithms that take a MyString and return a Mystring with a *different* length—sometimes longer and sometimes shorter. In the current section, we'll study the following problem:

Given a MyString and a char, produce a new MyString where the char has been added to the front or rear.

The resultant MyStrings are one larger than the receiving MyStrings. Prog1412 gives the code for both methods.

Prog1412.java   **Add a char at the Front or Rear**

```
// Written by Barry Soroka
//
// MyString -- adds MyString addCharAtFront(char)
//             MyString addCharAtRear(char)
//
import java.io.*;
import java.util.Scanner;
///////////////////////////////////////////////////////////////////////////////
class Prog1412
{
    //-----------------------------------------------------------------------
```

```java
    public static void main (String [] args) throws Exception
    {
        Scanner kb = new Scanner(System.in);

        while ( true )
        {
            System.out.print("\nEnter a MyString: ");
            MyString s = MyString.read(null,kb);
            System.out.print("Enter a char: ");
            char c = kb.nextLine().charAt(0);
            System.out.println("addCharAtFront gives \"" +
                                s.addCharAtFront(c) + "\"");
            System.out.println("addCharAtRear gives  \"" +
                                s.addCharAtRear(c) + "\"");
        }
    }
//-------------------------------------------------------------------------
} // end class Prog1412
/////////////////////////////////////////////////////////////////////////////
class MyString
{
    private char [] a;
//-------------------------------------------------------------------------
    public MyString addCharAtFront ( char c )
    {
        int n = a.length;
        char[] newA = new char[n+1];
        newA[0] = c;
        for ( int i = 0 ; i < n ; i++ ) newA[i+1] = a[i];
        return new MyString(newA);
    }
//-------------------------------------------------------------------------
    public MyString addCharAtRear ( char c )
    {
        int n = a.length;
        char[] newA = new char[n+1];
        for ( int i = 0 ; i < n ; i++ ) newA[i] = a[i];
        newA[n] = c;
        return new MyString(newA);
    }
//-------------------------------------------------------------------------
// More code is included!  See Prog1406.
//-------------------------------------------------------------------------
} // end class MyString
/////////////////////////////////////////////////////////////////////////////
```

When we add a char at the rear, we allocate newA, an array that is one larger than a, and we copy all the chars from a to newA:

```
for ( int i = 0 ; i < n ; i++ ) newA[i] = a[i];
```

This leaves empty the last slot of newA, and we fill it with the statement:

```
newA[n] = c;
```

Finally, we create a new MyString containing newA.

Adding a char at the *front* is similar, except that we put the new char into the *first* slot of newA:

```
newA[0] = c;
```

and, when we copy, we must copy *with an offset*:

```
for ( int i = 0 ; i < n ; i++ ) newA[i+1] = a[i];
```

which produces the desired effect

```
newA[1] = a[0];
newA[2] = a[1];
newA[3] = a[2];
. . .
newA[n] = a[n-1]
```

 Test your skill with Exercises 14-31 and 14-32.

14.14 Deleting chars

Consider the problem:

> Given a MyString, return a new MyString
> from which all the space characters have been deleted.

We'll study four different implementations of the method

```
public MyString deleteSpaces()
```

1: Count Nonblank chars

Our first implementation involves the following steps:

- We'll walk through a, computing the number of nonblank chars:

```
int n = 0;
for ( int i = 0 ; i < a.length ; i++ )
    if ( a[i] != ' ' ) n++;
```

- Then we'll allocate newA, destined for the result. Clearly, the length of newA is n, the number of nonblank chars in a.

```
char [] newA = new char[n];
```

- We're going to be copying chars from a to newA. We'll index through a with the indices [0,1,2,. . . . ,a.length-1], but we'll be filling newA slots with indices [0,1,2,. . . . ,n]. Because newA may contain fewer chars than there are in a, we probably won't have a one-to-one correspondence between the sets that index newA and a. Therefore, we'll have a variable next that tells us where to drop the next nonblank char from a:

```
int next = 0;
```

- Now we walk through a, copying nonblank chars into the appropriate slots of newA, incrementing next each time:

```
for ( int i = 0 ; i < a.length ; i++ )
    if ( a[i] != ' ' )
    {
        newA[next] = a[i];
        next++;
    }
```

- Finally, we create and return the new MyString:

```
return new MyString(newA);
```

Prog1413 contains the code and a test driver.

Prog1413.java   deleteSpaces—**Algorithm 1**

```
// Written by Barry Soroka
//
// MyString -- MyString deleteSpaces() --
//
//    Count the non-blanks, allocate the exactly sized result array,
//    copy non-blank chars.
//
import java.io.*;
import java.util.Scanner;
```

```
////////////////////////////////////////////////////////////////////////////////
class Prog1413
{
//------------------------------------------------------------------------
   public static void main (String [] args) throws Exception
   {
      Scanner kb = new Scanner(System.in);

      while ( true )
      {
         System.out.print("\nEnter a MyString: ");
         MyString s = MyString.read(null,kb);
         System.out.println("deleteSpaces takes \"" + s +
                            "\" to \"" +
                            s.deleteSpaces() + "\"");
      }
   }
//------------------------------------------------------------------------
} // end class Prog1413
////////////////////////////////////////////////////////////////////////////////
class MyString
{
   private char [] a;
//------------------------------------------------------------------------
   public MyString deleteSpaces()
   {
      int n = 0;
      for ( int i = 0 ; i < a.length ; i++ )
         if ( a[i] != ' ' ) n++;

      char [] newA = new char[n];
      int next = 0;
      for ( int i = 0 ; i < a.length ; i++ )
         if ( a[i] != ' ' )
         {
            newA[next] = a[i];
            next++;
         }

      return new MyString(newA);
   }
//------------------------------------------------------------------------
// More code is included!  See Prog1406.
//------------------------------------------------------------------------
} // end class MyString
////////////////////////////////////////////////////////////////////////////////
```

2: Create a Full-Sized `array` for the Result

`Prog1414` shows a second implementation of `deleteSpaces()`. To hold the result we allocate `newA`, which is the same size as `a`. We keep a counter—`next`—which tells us where to put the next nonblank `char`. After walking through `a`, we know that positions 0 through `next-1` of `newA` contain `chars` destined for the result. Finally, we create the `MyString` to return by using the constructor

```
public MyString(char[],int)
```

via

```
return new MyString(newA,next);
```

Prog1414.java   deleteSpaces — Algorithm 2

```java
// Written by Barry Soroka
//
// MyString -- MyString deleteSpaces() --
//
//    Generate a full-size non-full result array.
//
import java.io.*;
import java.util.Scanner;
/////////////////////////////////////////////////////////////////////////////
class Prog1414
{
//-------------------------------------------------------------------------
   public static void main (String [] args) throws Exception
   {
      Scanner kb = new Scanner(System.in);

      while ( true )
      {
         System.out.print("\nEnter a MyString: ");
         MyString s = MyString.read(null,kb);
         System.out.println("deleteSpaces takes \"" + s +
                     "\" to \"" +
                     s.deleteSpaces() + "\"");
      }
   }
//-------------------------------------------------------------------------
} // end class Prog1414
/////////////////////////////////////////////////////////////////////////////
```

```
class MyString
{
   private char [] a;
//------------------------------------------------------------
   public MyString deleteSpaces()
   {
      char [] newA = new char[a.length];

      int next = 0;
      for ( int i = 0 ; i < a.length ; i++ )
         if ( a[i] != ' ' )
         {
            newA[next] = a[i];
            next++;
         }

      return new MyString(newA,next);
   }
//------------------------------------------------------------
// More code is included!  See Prog1406.
//------------------------------------------------------------
} // end class MyString
////////////////////////////////////////////////////////////////////////
```

3: Grow the Result Array As Needed

In this implementation, we'll create an empty array of char and we'll "grow" that array as we add each new nonblank char. Prog1415 gives the code and a driver. We start with:

```
char[] newA = new char[0];
```

which creates the initial, empty result array. Then we must loop through all the chars of a. If the current char is nonblank, then we enter the body of the if statement. We're going to "grow" newA by creating newerA, which is one longer, and then we'll make newA point to newerA. We allocate the larger array:

```
char[] newerA = new char[newA.length+1];
```

and we copy all the chars from newA to newerA:

```
for ( int j = 0 ; j < newA.length ; j++ )
   newerA[j] = newA[j];
```

Then we fill the last slot of `newerA` with the newly found nonblank `char`:

```
newerA[newA.length] = a[i];
```

and we make `newA` point to the longer array that we've created:

```
newA = newerA;
```

Finally, we call the appropriate constructor to generate a new `MyString` from the array `newA`:

```
return new MyString(newA);
```

Prog1415.java   deleteSpaces — Algorithm 3

```java
// Written by Barry Soroka
//
// MyString -- MyString deleteSpaces() --
//
//    Start with an empty result array and grow it as required.
//
import java.io.*;
import java.util.Scanner;
////////////////////////////////////////////////////////////////////////////
class Prog1415
{
//----------------------------------------------------------------------------
    public static void main (String [] args) throws Exception
    {
        Scanner kb = new Scanner(System.in);

        while ( true )
        {
            System.out.print("\nEnter a MyString: ");
            MyString s = MyString.read(null,kb);
            System.out.println("deleteSpaces takes \"" + s +
                        "\" to \"" +
                        s.deleteSpaces() + "\"");
        }
    }
//----------------------------------------------------------------------------
} // end class Prog1415
////////////////////////////////////////////////////////////////////////////
class MyString
{
    private char [] a;
//----------------------------------------------------------------------------
```

```
public MyString deleteSpaces()
{
    char[] newA = new char[0];

    for ( int i = 0 ; i < a.length ; i++ )
        if ( a[i] != ' ' )
        {
            char[] newerA = new char[newA.length+1];
            for ( int j = 0 ; j < newA.length ; j++ ) newerA[j] = newA[j];
            newerA[newA.length] = a[i];
            newA = newerA;
        }
    return new MyString(newA);
}
//-------------------------------------------------------------------------
// More code is included!  See Prog1406.
//-------------------------------------------------------------------------
} // end class MyString
/////////////////////////////////////////////////////////////////////////
```

4: Use String—Danger!

Prog1416 gives the code for a fourth implementation of deleteSpaces(). This version has the fewest lines of Java:

```
String result = "";
for ( int i = 0 ; i < a.length ; i++ )
    if ( a[i] != ' ' ) result += a[i];
return new MyString(result);
```

This version simply tacks nonblanks at the end of a String variable. The code is very readable because:

- we don't need to compute the size of a new array to be allocated and filled, and
- we don't need to compute how the index in one array maps to the index in another array.

These tasks were explicitly handled in the previous implementation, but all the work is now being handled "behind the scenes" because "growth" is built into Strings. Somebody else wrote all the relevant code so that we can use Strings without thinking about the hidden issues.

Prog1416.java   deleteSpaces—Algorithm 4

```java
// Written by Barry Soroka
//
// MyString -- MyString deleteSpaces().
//
//   Accumulate non-blank chars with a String.
//
import java.io.*;
import java.util.Scanner;
//////////////////////////////////////////////////////////////////////////////
class Prog1416
{
//----------------------------------------------------------------------------
    public static void main (String [] args) throws Exception
    {
        Scanner kb = new Scanner(System.in);

        while ( true )
        {
            System.out.print("\nEnter a MyString: ");
            MyString s = MyString.read(null,kb);
            System.out.println("deleteSpaces takes \"" + s +
                            "\" to \"" +
                            s.deleteSpaces() + "\"");
        }
    }
//----------------------------------------------------------------------------
} // end class Prog1416
//////////////////////////////////////////////////////////////////////////////
class MyString
{
    private char [] a;
//----------------------------------------------------------------------------
    public MyString deleteSpaces()
    {
        String result = "";
        for ( int i = 0 ; i < a.length ; i++ )
            if ( a[i] != ' ' ) result += a[i];
        return new MyString(result);
    }
//----------------------------------------------------------------------------
// More code is included!  See Prog1406.
//----------------------------------------------------------------------------
} // end class MyString
//////////////////////////////////////////////////////////////////////////////
```

NOTE

For the purpose of this chapter, do not use `String`s and their "hidden" capabilities. The purpose of this chapter is to learn how to use *arrays*, including allocating, growing, and indexing.

Test your skill with Exercises 14-33 through 14-40.

14.15 substring

This section presents an implementation of the two-parameter `substring` method for `MyString`s. We will follow the conventions of the `substring` method for class `String`, so our prototype will be:

```
public MyString substring ( int first, int lastPlusOne )
```

`Prog1417` gives the code and a driver. Let's analyze the code. We begin by computing the length of the result:

```
int n = lastPlusOne - first;
```

and we create an array to hold the result:

```
char[] result = new char[n];
```

Let's look at how the indices align:

result[0]	should get	a[first]
result[1]	should get	a[first+1]
result[2]	should get	a[first+2]
. . .	. . .	. . .
result[n-2]	should get	a[first+n-2]
result[n-1]	should get	a[first+n-1]

The last of these assignments can be written as

```
result[n-1] should get a[first+(lastPlusOne-first)-1]
```

which is what we expected:

```
result[n-1] should get a[lastPlusOne-1].
```

Here's the code that copies the desired part of a:

```
for ( int i = 0 ; i < n ; i++ )
    result[i] = a[i+first];
```

Finally, we create and return a new `MyString`:

```
return new MyString(result);
```

Prog1417.java   MyString substring(int,int)

```
// Written by Barry Soroka
//
// MyString -- adds MyString substring(int,int)
//
import java.io.*;
import java.util.Scanner;
////////////////////////////////////////////////////////////////////////////////
class Prog1417
{
//-----------------------------------------------------------------------------
    public static void main (String [] args) throws Exception
    {
        Scanner kb = new Scanner(System.in);

        while ( true )
        {
            System.out.print("\nEnter a MyString: ");
            MyString s = MyString.read(null,kb);
            System.out.print("Enter 1st int for substring: ");
            int i1 = kb.nextInt();
            System.out.print("Enter 2nd int for substring: ");
            int i2 = kb.nextInt(); kb.nextLine(); // clear to the end of the line
            System.out.println("substring(" + i1 + "," + i2 + ") takes \"" + s +
                            "\" to \"" +
                            s.substring(i1,i2) + "\"");
        }
    }
//-----------------------------------------------------------------------------
} // end class Prog1417
////////////////////////////////////////////////////////////////////////////////
class MyString
{
    private char [] a;
//-----------------------------------------------------------------------------
    public MyString substring ( int first, int lastPlusOne )
    {
        int n = lastPlusOne - first;
        char[] result = new char[n];
        for ( int i = 0 ; i < n ; i++ )
```

```
            result[i] = a[i+first];
         return new MyString(result);
   }
//----------------------------------------------------------------
// More code is included!  See Prog1406.
//----------------------------------------------------------------
} // end class MyString
////////////////////////////////////////////////////////////////////////////
```

Test your skill with Exercise 14-41.

14.16   trim

In this section, we will write a method for MyString that acts like the trim method of Java's class String—trim returns a copy of the receiving MyString *except* that all leading and trailing spaces have been removed. Prog1418 presents the code and a driver.

Prog1418.java   MyString trim()

```
// Written by Barry Soroka
//
// MyString -- adds MyString trim().
//
import java.io.*;
import java.util.Scanner;
////////////////////////////////////////////////////////////////////////////
class Prog1418
{
//----------------------------------------------------------------
   public static void main (String [] args) throws Exception
   {
      Scanner kb = new Scanner(System.in);

      while ( true )
      {
         System.out.print("\nEnter a MyString: ");
         MyString s = MyString.read(null,kb);
         System.out.println("trim takes \"" +
                            s +
                            "\" to \"" +
                            s.trim() + "\"");
```

```
      }
   }
//-------------------------------------------------------------------------------
} // end class Prog1418
//////////////////////////////////////////////////////////////////////////////////
class MyString
{
   private char [] a;
//-------------------------------------------------------------------------------
   public MyString trim()
   {
      int firstNonBlank = this.firstNonBlank();
      if ( firstNonBlank == -1 ) return new MyString(new char[0]);
      int lastNonBlank = this.lastNonBlank();
      int length = lastNonBlank - firstNonBlank + 1;
      char[] newA = new char[length];
      for ( int i = 0 ; i < length ; i++ )
         newA[i] = a[i+firstNonBlank];
      return new MyString(newA);
   }
//-------------------------------------------------------------------------------
   public int firstNonBlank()
   {
      for ( int i = 0 ; i < a.length ; i++ )
         if ( a[i] != ' ' ) return i;
      return -1;
   }
//-------------------------------------------------------------------------------
   public int lastNonBlank()
   {
      for ( int i = a.length - 1 ; i >= 0 ; i-- )
         if ( a[i] != ' ' ) return i;
      return -1;
   }
//-------------------------------------------------------------------------------
// More code is included!  See Prog1406.
//-------------------------------------------------------------------------------
} // end class MyString
//////////////////////////////////////////////////////////////////////////////////
```

trim works by creating a new MyString, which goes from the first nonblank char of a to the last nonblank char. To make the code more readable, I've defined helper methods `firstNonBlank()` and `lastNonBlank()`, both of which return `int`s. If no nonblank `char` is found, then they return `-1`. The code for these methods should be obvious at this point.

How shall we assemble these methods into `trim`? We start by finding the first nonblank `char`:

```
int firstNonBlank = this.firstNonBlank();
```

If *no* nonblank `char` is found, then we have an empty `MyString`, or one that consists entirely of spaces. The appropriate response is to return a `MyString` with zero `char`s:

```
if ( firstNonBlank == -1 )
    return new MyString(new char[0]);
```

If we know that we've got at least one nonblank `char`, then let's compute the index of the *last* nonblank char:

```
int lastNonBlank = this.lastNonBlank();
```

The resulting `MyString` has the following length:

```
int length = lastNonBlank - firstNonBlank + 1;
```

so we create an array to hold exactly that number of `char`s:

```
char[] newA = new char[length];
```

We proceed to copy that number of `char`s from `a` to `newA`, starting at position `firstNonBlank` of `a`:

```
for ( int i = 0 ; i < length ; i++ )
    newA[i] = a[i+firstNonBlank];
```

Finally, we create and return a new `MyString`, which uses `newA`:

```
return new MyString(newA);
```

 Test your skill with Exercises 14-42 and 14-43.

14.17 isPrefixOf

Consider the method

```
public boolean isPrefixOf ( MyString that )
```

where `Prog1419` presents the code and a driver. Let's examine the code. First, we isolate the arrays and the `lengths` to make our code easier to read:

```
char[] a1 = this.a; int n1 = a1.length;
char[] a2 = that.a; int n2 = a2.length;
```

If `a1` is longer than `a2`, then `a1` can't possibly be a prefix of `a2`:

```
if ( n1 > n2 ) return false;
```

Now we know that `a1` is no longer than `a2`, so we can walk down `a1` and compare it, `char` by `char`, against `a2`:

```
for ( int i = 0 ; i < n1 ; i++ )
    if ( a1[i] != a2[i] ) return false;
```

If we ever find a mismatch, then the prefix predicate is certainly `false`. If we get all the way to the end of `a1` without finding a mismatch, then the predicate is `true`. By this logic, the empty `MyString` is a prefix of all other `MyStrings`. Try the code!

Prog1419.java   isPrefixOf(MyString)

```
// Written by Barry Soroka
//
// MyString -- boolean isPrefixOf(MyString)
//
import java.io.*;
import java.util.Scanner;
//////////////////////////////////////////////////////////////////////////////
class Prog1419
{
//----------------------------------------------------------------------------
   public static void main (String [] args) throws Exception
   {
      Scanner kb = new Scanner(System.in);
```

```
        while ( true )
        {
            System.out.print("\nEnter a MyString: ");
            MyString s1 = MyString.read(null,kb);
            System.out.print("Enter a MyString: ");
            MyString s2 = MyString.read(null,kb);

            System.out.println("s1 = \"" + s1 + "\"");
            System.out.println("s2 = \"" + s2 + "\"");
            System.out.println("s1.isPrefixOf(s2) --> " + s1.isPrefixOf(s2));
        }
    }
//-------------------------------------------------------------------------
} // end class Prog1419
////////////////////////////////////////////////////////////////////////////
class MyString
{
    private char [] a;
//-------------------------------------------------------------------------
    public boolean isPrefixOf ( MyString that )
    {
        char[] a1 = this.a; int n1 = a1.length;
        char[] a2 = that.a; int n2 = a2.length;

        if ( n1 > n2 ) return false;

        for ( int i = 0 ; i < n1 ; i++ )
            if ( a1[i] != a2[i] ) return false;

        return true;
    }
//-------------------------------------------------------------------------
// More code is included!  See Prog1406.
//-------------------------------------------------------------------------
} // end class MyString
////////////////////////////////////////////////////////////////////////////
```

Test your skill with Exercises 14-44 through 14-53.

14.18   Section—Implemented as an Array of Student

In Chapter 13 we implemented a Section as a *file* of Students. In this chapter, we'll re-implement Section as an *array* of Students. We will change the *implementation* but not the *interface*, so any programs that used the file implementation will run, without change, using the array implementation.

When storing items in an array, we have two options:

1. Keep the array *full at all times*. (This is what we did in class MyString.)
2. Allow the array to be *only partially full*. This requires an integer variable used, which tells us (a) how many slots are used and (b) where to insert the next value in adding to the array.

Because we used option 1 for MyString, we'll use option 2 for Section. Now, because the array will only be partially full, we'll need to decide how much to grow it when it becomes full. We'll use the formula

```
newLength ← 2 * oldLength + 1
```

In Prog1420, we have taken Prog1313 and replaced the *file*-based Section with an *array*-based Section. The driver is identical between the two programs and the output of the two programs are identical. This is an example of keeping the interface while changing the implementation.

Prog1420.java   Section as an Array of Students

```java
// Written by Barry Soroka.
//
// class Section -- implemented as an array of Students
//
// Same driver as Prog1313 which worked with a file of Students.
//
import java.io.*;
import java.util.Scanner;
//////////////////////////////////////////////////////////////////////////////
class Prog1420
{
//----------------------------------------------------------------------------
    public static void main (String [] args) throws Exception
    {
        Scanner kb = new Scanner(System.in);

        System.out.print("\nEnter name of a file of Students: ");
        String filename = kb.nextLine();

        Section sec = new Section(filename);

        System.out.println("\nIn forward order:");
        sec.print(System.out);

        System.out.println("\nThat section contains " +
                        sec.howMany() +
                        " Students.");

        System.out.println("\nThe average grade is " +
                        sec.average());
```

```
        }
//------------------------------------------------------------------------
}  // end class Prog1420
////////////////////////////////////////////////////////////////////////////
class Section
{
    private Student [] a;
    private int used;
    private static final int INIT_SIZE = 20;
//------------------------------------------------------------------
    public Section ( String filename ) throws Exception
    {
        Scanner sc = new Scanner(new File(filename));

        a = new Student[INIT_SIZE];
        used = 0;

        while ( sc.hasNext() )
        {
            Student s = Student.read(null,sc);

            if ( used == a.length )
            {
                Student[] newA = new Student[2*a.length+1];
                for ( int i = 0 ; i < used ; i++ ) newA[i] = a[i];
                newA[used] = s;
                used++;
                a = newA;
            }
            else
            {
                a[used] = s;
                used++;
            }
        }
    }
//------------------------------------------------------------------
    public void print ( PrintStream ps )
    {
        for ( int i = 0 ; i < used ; i++ )
        {
            ps.println(a[i]);
        }
    }
//------------------------------------------------------------------
    public int howMany() { return used; }
//------------------------------------------------------------------
    public double average ()
```

```
      {
         int sum = 0;

         for ( int i = 0 ; i < used ; i++ )
         {
            Student s = a[i];
            sum += s.getGrade();
         }

         return 1.0 * sum / used;
      }
//------------------------------------------------------------------
} // end class Section
//////////////////////////////////////////////////////////////////////
class Student
{
   private String name;
   private int grade;
//------------------------------------------------------------------
   public Student ( String name, int grade )
   {
      this.name = name;
      this.grade = grade;
   }
//------------------------------------------------------------------
   public String toString ()
   {
      return name + " (" + grade + ")";
   }
//------------------------------------------------------------------
   public String getName() { return name; }
//------------------------------------------------------------------
   public int getGrade() { return grade; }
//------------------------------------------------------------------
   public void setGrade( int newGrade ) { grade = newGrade; }
//------------------------------------------------------------------
   public static Student read ( PrintStream ps, Scanner sc )
   {
      if ( ps != null ) ps.println("Reading a Student record ...");
      if ( ps != null ) ps.print("Enter the name: ");
      String name = sc.nextLine();
      if ( ps != null ) ps.print("Enter the grade: ");
      int grade = sc.nextInt(); sc.nextLine();
      return new Student(name,grade);
   }
//------------------------------------------------------------------
} // end class Student
//////////////////////////////////////////////////////////////////////
```

Let's examine the array implementation of Section. The instance variables are as follows:

```
private Student [] a;
private int used;
private static final int INIT_SIZE = 20;
```

The first two lines declare the array and the index of the next open slot. The final variable INIT_SIZE is the size of an initial array; this will be used in the constructor that reads Students from a file. INIT_SIZE is static because the same variable will serve for all instances of class Section. There's no need for each Section object to have its own slot for this variable.

public Section(String)

This constructor begins by opening a Scanner to the given file and initializing an array a and index used. As long as more Students remain in the file, the loop reads the next Student and assigns it to the next open slot in a. If the array is full—used == a.length—then a new, longer array is created, the values are copied, and the new array is substituted for the old one. When the loop is finished, array a contains exactly used entries.

print

This is straightforward code that walks forward through the array, printing each Student as it goes along:

```
for ( int i = 0 ; i < used ; i++ )
{
    ps.println(a[i]);
}
```

Unlike the file implementation, we don't need to spin through the *file* to get the values—they're stored in memory in the array a.

howMany

This method returns used. There's no need to consult the file here, either!

average

We walk down the array and compute the sum of the grades:

```
int sum = 0;
for ( int i = 0 ; i < used ; i++ )
```

```
        {
            Student s = a[i];
            sum += s.getGrade();
        }
```

Then we compute and return the average:

```
        return 1.0 * sum / used;
```

Unlike the file version of `Section`, we always have the *count* in a variable. We don't need to compute it as we go through the file.

14.19 More Constructors and printInReverse

Just as with `MyString`, we will want to have some additional constructors as shown in `Prog1421.java`.

Prog1421.java **More Constructors Plus printInReverse**

```java
// Written by Barry Soroka
//
// Section -- printInReverse(PrintStream)
//
import java.io.*;
import java.util.Scanner;
//////////////////////////////////////////////////////////////////////////
class Prog1421
{
//------------------------------------------------------------------------
    public static void main (String [] args) throws Exception
    {
        Scanner kb = new Scanner(System.in);

        System.out.print("\nEnter name of a file of Students: ");
        String filename = kb.nextLine();

        Section sec = new Section(filename);

        System.out.println("\nIn forward order, students are:");
        sec.print(System.out);

        System.out.println("\nIn reverse order, students are:");
        sec.printInReverse(System.out);
    }
//------------------------------------------------------------------------
} // end class Prog1421
//////////////////////////////////////////////////////////////////////////
```

```
class Section
{
   private Student [] a;
   private int used;
   private final int INIT_SIZE = 20;
//------------------------------------------------------------------
   public Section ( Student[] a )
   {
      this.a = a;
      used = a.length;
   }
//------------------------------------------------------------------
   public Section ( Student[] a, int used )
   {
      this.a = a;
      this.used = used;
   }
//------------------------------------------------------------------
   public Section ( String filename ) throws Exception
   {
      Scanner sc = new Scanner(new File(filename));

      a = new Student[INIT_SIZE];
      used = 0;

      while ( sc.hasNext() )
      {
         Student s = Student.read(null,sc);

         if ( used == a.length )
         {
            Student[] newA = new Student[2*a.length+1];
            for ( int i = 0 ; i < used ; i++ ) newA[i] = a[i];
            newA[used] = s;
            used++;
            a = newA;
         }
         else
         {
            a[used] = s;
            used++;
         }
      }
   }
//------------------------------------------------------------------
   public void print ( PrintStream ps )
   {
```

```
        for ( int i = 0 ; i < used ; i++ )
        {
            ps.println(a[i]);
        }
    }
//-----------------------------------------------------------------

    public void printInReverse ( PrintStream ps )
    {
        for ( int i = used-1 ; i >= 0 ; i-- )
        {
            ps.println(a[i]);
        }
    }
//-----------------------------------------------------------------
} // end class Section
/////////////////////////////////////////////////////////////////
class Student
{
    private String name;
    private int grade;
//-----------------------------------------------------------------

    public Student ( String name, int grade )
    {
        this.name = name;
        this.grade = grade;
    }
//-----------------------------------------------------------------

    public String toString ()
    {
        return name + " (" + grade + ")";
    }
//-----------------------------------------------------------------

    public String getName() { return name; }
//-----------------------------------------------------------------

    public int getGrade() { return grade; }
//-----------------------------------------------------------------

    public void setGrade( int newGrade ) { grade = newGrade; }
//-----------------------------------------------------------------

    public static Student read ( PrintStream ps, Scanner sc )
    {
        if ( ps != null ) ps.println("Reading a Student record ...");
        if ( ps != null ) ps.print("Enter the name: ");
        String name = sc.nextLine();
        if ( ps != null ) ps.print("Enter the grade: ");
```

```
      int grade = sc.nextInt(); sc.nextLine();
      return new Student(name,grade);
   }
//--------------------------------------------------------------------
} // end class Student
/////////////////////////////////////////////////////////////////////
```

public Section (Section[] a)

This takes a full array of Students and creates a Section from it. The created array will be full:

```
      this.a = a;
      used = a.length;
```

public Section (Student[] a, int used)

This takes a partly full array of Students and creates a Section:

```
      this.a = a;
      this.used = used;
```

The Section array will be exactly the same size and exactly as full as the parameter array.

printInReverse

Unlike the file implementation of Section, traversing an array *backward* is as easy as traversing it *forward*:

```
      for ( int i = used-1 ; i >= 0 ; i-- )
      {
         ps.println(a[i]);
      }
```

> **Test your skill with Exercises 14-54 through 14-59.**

14.20   **Adding** Students **to a** Section

Prog1422 presents a driver and the code that adds a Student to a given Section. For this example, we will change the receiving *Section* rather than generate a new Section:

```
      public void addStudentAtRear ( Student s )
```

rather than

```
public Section addStudentAtRear ( Student s )
```

There are two possibilities—array a either is or isn't full. If it *is* full, then we need to "grow" it:

```
Student[] newA = new Student[2*a.length+1];
for ( int i = 0 ; i < used ; i++ ) newA[i] = a[i];
newA[used] = s;
used++;
a = newA;
```

Otherwise, we simply drop the new Student into place:

```
a[used] = s;
used++;
```

Prog1422.java   addStudentAtRear(Student)

```java
// Written by Barry Soroka
//
// Section -- void addStudentAtRear(Student)
//
import java.io.*;
import java.util.Scanner;
//////////////////////////////////////////////////////////////////////
class Prog1422
{
//----------------------------------------------------------------------

    public static void main (String [] args) throws Exception
    {
        Scanner kb = new Scanner(System.in);

        System.out.print("\nEnter name of a file of Students: ");
        String filename = kb.nextLine();

        Section sec = new Section(filename);

        System.out.println("\nIn forward order, students are:");
        sec.print(System.out);

        System.out.println();
        Student s = Student.read(System.out,kb);

        sec.addStudentAtRear(s);

        System.out.println("\nIn forward order, students are:");
        sec.print(System.out);
    }
//----------------------------------------------------------------------
```

```
} // end class Prog1422
///////////////////////////////////////////////////////////////////
class Section
{
   private Student [] a;
   private int used;
   private final int INIT_SIZE = 20;
//-----------------------------------------------------------------
   public void addStudentAtRear ( Student s )
   {
      if ( used == a.length )      // a is full
      {
         Student[] newA = new Student[2*a.length+1];
         for ( int i = 0 ; i < used ; i++ ) newA[i] = a[i];
         newA[used] = s;
         used++;
         a = newA;
      }
      else
      {
         a[used] = s;
         used++;
      }
   }
//-----------------------------------------------------------------
// More code is included!  See Prog1421.
//-----------------------------------------------------------------
} // end class Section
///////////////////////////////////////////////////////////////////
class Student
{
// More code is included!  See Prog1421.
} // end class Student
///////////////////////////////////////////////////////////////////
```

 Test your skill with Exercises 14-60 through 14-62.

14.21 Finding Extrema in Section

In Chapter 13, we learned how to find the maximum or minimum int in a file of ints. Now we're able to tackle similar extrema problems for a Section as implemented with an array of Students. We'll examine the extremum problem in three steps, beginning with:

Find the highest grade of any Student in the Section.

This result is unambiguous: Given a `Section`, there is a unique `int` that is the highest `grade`. But what if we want to find the *Student* with the highest `grade`? That sounds like this problem:

> Find a `Student` with the highest `grade` in the `Section`.

But what if the highest `grade` is shared by two or more `Students`? Which `Student` should be returned as the result of the method? This leads to our third problem:

> Find *all* `Students` with the highest `grade` in the `Section`.

The result of this question is itself a `Section`, namely a `Section` of `Students` who share the highest `grade` in the receiving `Section`.

Prog1423 presents the code and a driver.

Prog1423.java   Methods Involving the Highest Grade

```
// Written by Barry Soroka
//
// Section -- add int getHighestGrade()
//            Student getStudentWithHighestGrade()
//            Section getStudentsWithHighestGrade()
//
import java.io.*;
import java.util.Scanner;
/////////////////////////////////////////////////////////////////////////
class Prog1423
{
//-------------------------------------------------------------------
    public static void main (String [] args) throws Exception
    {
        Scanner kb = new Scanner(System.in);

        System.out.print("\nEnter name of a file of Students: ");
        String filename = kb.nextLine();

        Section section = new Section(filename);

        System.out.println("\nIn forward order, students are:");
        section.print(System.out);

        int hi = section.getHighestGrade();
        System.out.println("\nhighest grade: " + hi);

        System.out.println("\nStudent with highest grade: " +
                        section.getStudentWithHighestGrade());

        Section hiSection = section.getStudentsWithHighestGrade();
        System.out.println("\nIn forward order, students are:");
        hiSection.print(System.out);
    }
```

```
//-------------------------------------------------------------------
} // end class Prog1423
///////////////////////////////////////////////////////////////////////
class Section
{
   private Student [] a;
   private int used;
   private final int INIT_SIZE = 20;
//-------------------------------------------------------------------
   public int getHighestGrade()
   {
      if ( used == 0 )
      {
         throw new Error("\n*** Attempt to find the highest grade in " +
                         "an empty Section ***\n");
      }

      int hi = a[0].getGrade();

      for ( int i = 0 ; i < used ; i++ )
         if ( a[i].getGrade() > hi ) hi = a[i].getGrade();
      return hi;
   }
//-------------------------------------------------------------------
   public Student getStudentWithHighestGrade()
   {
      if ( used == 0 )
      {
         throw new Error("\n*** Attempt to find the Student with the highest " +
                         " grade in an empty Section ***\n");
      }

      Student hiStudent = a[0];

      for ( int i = 0 ; i < used ; i++ )
      {
         if ( a[i].getGrade() > hiStudent.getGrade() )
         {
            hiStudent = a[i];
         }
      }

      return hiStudent;
   }
//-------------------------------------------------------------------
   public Section getStudentsWithHighestGrade()
   {
      int hiGrade = this.getHighestGrade();

      Student[] hiStudents = new Student[a.length];
```

```
    int hiUsed = 0;

    for ( int i = 0 ; i < used ; i++ )
    {
        if ( a[i].getGrade() == hiGrade )
        {
            hiStudents[hiUsed] = a[i];
            hiUsed++;
        }
    }

    return new Section(hiStudents,hiUsed);
    }
//-------------------------------------------------------------------------
// More code is included!   See Prog1421.
//-------------------------------------------------------------------------
} // end class Section
///////////////////////////////////////////////////////////////////////////
class Student
{
// More code is included!   See Prog1421.
} // end class Student
///////////////////////////////////////////////////////////////////////////
```

getHighestGrade

This code is straightforward:

```
        int hi = a[0].getGrade();
        for ( int i = 0 ; i < used ; i++ )
            if ( a[i].getGrade() > hi ) hi = a[i].getGrade();

        return hi;
```

getStudentWithHighestGrade

We want to return the *Student*, not just the grade, so we'll keep aside a variable hiStudent instead of a variable hiGrade. Our tracking variable is a Student, but the predicate concerns grade—a single slot of the Student. Otherwise, the logic of this method is what we've seen before:

```
        Student hiStudent = a[0];

        for ( int i = 0 ; i < used ; i++ )
        {
            if ( a[i].getGrade() > hiStudent.getGrade() )
            {
```

```
        hiStudent = a[i];
    }
}

return hiStudent;
```

What if two or more Students share the high grade? Which Student will the method return? The result will be different if we scan the array from front to rear rather than rear to front. Our next version of the extremum problem will return *all* Students who have the high grade.

getStudentsWithHighestGrade

First we call getHighestGrade to get hiGrade, the value of the highest grade. Then we create an array for the result:

```
Student[] hiStudents = new Student[a.length];
int hiUsed = 0;
```

The result can never include more Students than we started with, so we can make the result array hiStudents the same length as a. We'll be working with a nonfull array, so we set the index hiUsed to 0.

Next we scan down a, looking at each Student. If the Student has the high grade, then we add the Student to the result array hiStudents. Once we've looked at all the Students, we send hiStudents to a constructor that creates a Section, which we return as the value of the method.

> **Test your skill with Exercise 14-63.**

14.22 Sharing and Copying

The paragraphs that follow discuss the downside of sharing data structure, and then we'll examine the use of a copy() method to avoid unwanted effects.

We'll start by defining a method that increments the grade of every Student in a Section. No grade will be permitted to go above 100. Here's the code:

```
public void increment()
{
    for ( int i = 0 ; i < used ; i++ )
    {
        int grade = a[i].getGrade();
        if ( grade < 100 ) grade++;
```

```
                                 a[i].setGrade(grade);
                      }
                  }
```

Now we'll examine three versions of a program that copies or shares an array between two `Sections`. Our goal is to make `section2` an independent copy of `section1`.

Version 1: Full Sharing

Consider a driver that begins by declaring and filling `section1`. Let's assume that `section1` contains the following `Students`:

section1 →	Sally 100	Rico 82	Bill 43

Next we do a complete share with `section2`:

```
Section section2 = section1;
```

which produces the diagram

section1 → section2 →	Sally 100	Rico 82	Bill 43

Because `section1` and `section2` are pointing to the same `Object`, anything we do to `section1` will also be done to `section2`.

Suppose we apply the `increment()` method to `section1`:

```
section1.increment();
```

We now have the diagram

section1 → section2 →	Sally 100	Rico 83	Bill 44

This is an example of *sharing*. We have not achieved our goal of making `section2` an independent copy of `section1`.

Version 2: Shallow Copy—Use Separate Arrays

This version improves on Version 1 because we make `section1` and `section2` point to different arrays. We'll introduce a `copy` method in class `Section`:

```
public Section copy()
{
    Student[] result = new Student[used];
    for ( int i = 0 ; i < used ; i++ )
        result[i] = a[i];
    return new Section(result);
}
```

This method creates a copy of a `Section` by allocating a new array and copying the elements from the receiver to the result. Suppose that we have filled `section1`:

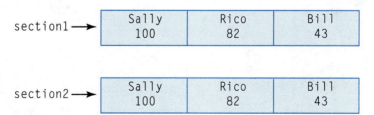

We'll create `section2` with `copy()` rather than the assignment operator:

```
Section section2 = section1.copy();
```

This results in the diagram

section1 ⟶

Sally	Rico	Bill
100	82	43

section2 ⟶

Sally	Rico	Bill
100	82	43

Now let's increment `section1`:

```
section1.increment();
```

Did this change `section2` as well?

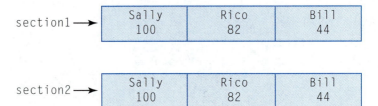

Here's the diagram *after* the increment operation:

The change to section1 has caused the same change in section2. Why?

Our diagrams have been misleading. We drew this:

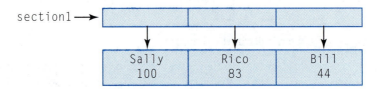

but we really meant this:

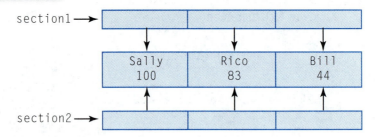

The array inside section1 is an array of *references* to individual Students, and, when we create the new array for section2, we end up populating it with the same references we had in section1. We call this a *shallow copy*. The memory diagram is this:

Shallow copy   Copies share data structure.

When we use the references in section1 to change the Students, we find that section2 is pointing to the Students that we've just changed! We made a *copy* of the array, but we're still *sharing* the Student objects.

Version 3: Deep Copy—Use copy() in Class Student

> **Deep copy** Copies are entirely independent and have no shared data structure.

The next step toward full copying is to make copies of the Students when we copy a Section. In class Student, we'll provide the method:

```
public Student copy()
{
    return new Student(name,grade);
}
```

When applied to a Student, this creates a viable, independent copy:

- name is a String, and Strings are immutable, so it's okay to share them.
- grade is an int, and int is a primitive datatype, so it's not a reference variable.

In class Section, we will alter the copy method so that it fills the new array with references to *copies* of the Students involved:

```
public Section copy()
{
    Student[] result = new Student[used];
    for ( int i = 0 ; i < used ; i++ )
        result[i] = a[i].copy();
    return new Section(result);
}
```

Let's examine how the copy and increment code will perform when using copy() in both Student and Section. We begin with section1:

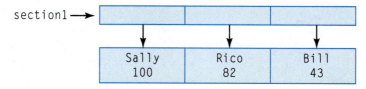

Then we request

```
Section section2 = section1.copy();
```

which produces:

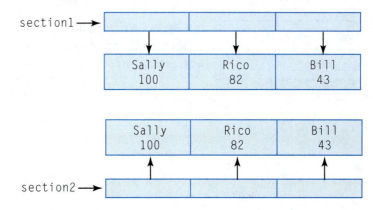

Note that nothing is shared between section1 and section2. When we execute

```
section1.increment();
```

we change only section1, and we get the following diagram:

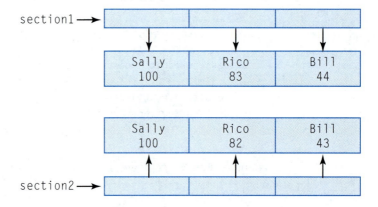

Thus, we have achieved a perfect copy and we've avoided undesirable sharing. Prog1424 gives the code and a driver.

Prog1424.java **Deep Copy for Section**

```java
// Written by Barry Soroka
//
// Section -- read section1
//            section2 = section1.copy();  // make copies of Students, too
//            section1.increment()
//            only section1 is changed!
//
import java.io.*;
import java.util.Scanner;
/////////////////////////////////////////////////////////////////////////////
class Prog1424
{
//----------------------------------------------------------------------------
   public static void main (String [] args) throws Exception
   {
      Scanner kb = new Scanner(System.in);

      System.out.print("\nEnter name of a file of Students: ");
      String filename = kb.nextLine();

   // Read section1.
      Section section1 = new Section(filename);
      Section section2 = section1.copy();

      System.out.println("\nIn forward order, section1:");
      section1.print(System.out);
      System.out.println("\nIn forward order, section2:");
      section2.print(System.out);

   // Increment grades in section1.
      section1.increment();

      System.out.println("\n----------------------------------------------");
      System.out.println("\nIn forward order, section1:");
      section1.print(System.out);
      System.out.println("\nIn forward order, section2:");
      section2.print(System.out);
   }
//----------------------------------------------------------------------------
} // end class Prog1424
/////////////////////////////////////////////////////////////////////////////
class Section
{
   private Student [] a;
   private int used;
   private final int INIT_SIZE = 20;
//----------------------------------------------------------------------------
```

```
    public Section copy()
    {
        Student[] result = new Student[used];
        for ( int i = 0 ; i < used ; i++ ) result[i] = a[i].copy();
        return new Section(result);
    }
//--------------------------------------------------------------------
//
// void increment()
//
// Increment each grade, but don't exceed 100.
//
    public void increment()
    {
        for ( int i = 0 ; i < used ; i++ )
        {
            int grade = a[i].getGrade();
            if ( grade < 100 ) grade++;
            a[i].setGrade(grade);
        }
    }
//--------------------------------------------------------------------
    public Section ( Student[] a )
    {
        this.a = a;
        used = a.length;
    }
//--------------------------------------------------------------------
    public Section ( Student[] a, int used )
    {
        this.a = a;
        this.used = used;
    }
//--------------------------------------------------------------------
    public Section ( String filename ) throws Exception
    {
        Scanner sc = new Scanner(new File(filename));

        a = new Student[INIT_SIZE];
        used = 0;

        while ( sc.hasNext() )
        {
            Student s = Student.read(null,sc);

            if ( used == a.length )
```

```
        {
            Student[] newA = new Student[2*a.length+1];
            for ( int i = 0 ; i < used ; i++ ) newA[i] = a[i];
            newA[used] = s;
            used++;
            a = newA;
        }
        else
        {
            a[used] = s;
            used++;
        }
    }
}
```
//--
```
    public void print ( PrintStream ps )
    {
        for ( int i = 0 ; i < used ; i++ )
        {
            ps.println(a[i]);
        }
    }
```
//--
```
} // end class Section
```
//
```
class Student
{
    private String name;
    private int grade;
```
//--
```
    public Student copy()
    {
        return new Student(name,grade);
    }
```
//--
```
    public Student ( String name, int grade )
    {
        this.name = name;
        this.grade = grade;
    }
```
//--
```
    public String toString ()
    {
        return name + " (" + grade + ")";
    }
```

```
//-----------------------------------------------------------------
   public String getName() { return name; }
//-----------------------------------------------------------------
   public int getGrade() { return grade; }
//-----------------------------------------------------------------
   public void setGrade( int newGrade ) { grade = newGrade; }
//-----------------------------------------------------------------
   public static Student read ( PrintStream ps, Scanner sc )
   {
      if ( ps != null ) ps.println("Reading a Student record ...");
      if ( ps != null ) ps.print("Enter the name: ");
      String name = sc.nextLine();
      if ( ps != null ) ps.print("Enter the grade: ");
      int grade = sc.nextInt(); sc.nextLine();
      return new Student(name,grade);
   }
//-----------------------------------------------------------------
} // end class Student
/////////////////////////////////////////////////////////////////
```

copy **and** clone

We will often provide a copy method for nontrivial classes. There's something similar in Java—a cloneable interface and a clone method—but they're beyond the scope of CS 1.

14.23   Keep and Delete

Keep is a pattern where we take a Section and keep only those Students who meet some criterion. *Delete* is the corresponding pattern, whereby we delete all those Students who meet some criterion. These patterns are similar to some we've seen earlier, so we'll move directly to exercises.

 Test your skill with Exercise 14-64.

14.24   Order!

Now let's examine some problems that involve the *order* of the Students in a Section. A first set of questions involves a single Section:

Given a Section, are the Students in ascending order by grade?

Given a Section, are the Students in ascending order by name?

We call such Sections *ordered* or *sorted*. Another question involves a Section and a *Student*:

> Given an ordered Section, insert a Student at the appropriate spot.

You may wonder how these Sections came to be sorted. In Chapter 20 we'll take a first look at *sorting*, and you'll study it in much more detail when you get to CS 2.

isAscendingByGrade()

A Section is in order by grade if every consecutive pair is nondescending. That means we want to verify, in general, that

```
a[i].getGrade() <= a[i+1].getGrade().
```

We have two questions to answer in writing the code:

- When is this formula applicable and what do we do when it's not?
- What does the for statement look like, so that we don't access nonexistent array elements?

If the Section contains fewer than two Students, then we can't apply the comparison test. We'll simply return true—an empty Section or a singleton Section will be considered sorted. We made the same decision when working with files in Chapter 13. So, the predicate will contain the statement:

```
if ( used < 2 ) return true;
```

In general, what pairs of Students do we want to compare? We want to test

> a[0] against a[1]

then

> a[1] against a[2]

then

> a[2] against a[3]

and so on, up to

> a[used-2] against a[used-1].

Note that we can't compare

> a[used-1] against a[used]

because there is no element a[*used*]! The array only goes from a[0] up to a[used-1]. This tells us how to write the limits of the for loop, and we have:

```
for ( int i = 0 ; i < used-1 ; i++ )
{
    if ( a[i].getGrade() > a[i+1].getGrade() ) return false;
}
```

Note that I've written the test so that a *pair-out-of-order* results in returning false. Once we've found a pair-out-of-order, there's no need to test any other pairs.

If we get through the loop without finding any pairs-out-of-order, then the Section is sorted, and we return true.

Prog1425 presents the code and a driver.

Prog1425.java   isAscendingByGrade()

```
// Written by Barry Soroka
//
// Section -- add isAscendingByGrade.
//
import java.io.*;
import java.util.Scanner;
//////////////////////////////////////////////////////////////////////////
class Prog1425
{
//----------------------------------------------------------------------
    public static void main (String [] args) throws Exception
    {
        Scanner kb = new Scanner(System.in);

        System.out.print("\nEnter name of a file of Students: ");
        String filename = kb.nextLine();

        Section section = new Section(filename);

        System.out.println("\nIn forward order, students are:");
        section.print(System.out);

        System.out.println("\nisAscendingByGrade? " +
                        section.isAscendingByGrade());
    }
//----------------------------------------------------------------------
} // end class Prog1425
//////////////////////////////////////////////////////////////////////////
class Section
{
    private Student [] a;
```

```
   private int used;
   private final int INIT_SIZE = 20;
//-----------------------------------------------------------------
   public boolean isAscendingByGrade()
   {
      if ( used < 2 ) return true;
      for ( int i = 0 ; i < used-1 ; i++ )
      {
         if ( a[i].getGrade() > a[i+1].getGrade() ) return false;
      }
      return true;
   }
//-----------------------------------------------------------------
// More code is included!  See Prog1421.
//-----------------------------------------------------------------
} // end class Section
/////////////////////////////////////////////////////////////////////
class Student
{
// More code is included!  See Prog1421.
} // end class Student
/////////////////////////////////////////////////////////////////////
```

 Test your skill with Exercises 14-65 through 14-69.

insertInOrderByGrade(Student)

Our next method involving sorted Sections will take a Student and insert it into the correct position in the order. Our prototype is this:

```
public Section insertInOrderByGrade ( Student s )
```

We'll create a new Section as the result of the insertion.

There are several ways to implement this method; I've chosen one that seems clear and readable. It's not the most efficient method—I'll leave that study to CS 2.

Let's trace how we would insert 35 into the following array of ints:

0	1	2	3	4	5	6
10	15	15	20	30	40	50

First we'll determine *where* 35 should go. This partitions the array into a *prefix* and a *suffix*. Part of the array is the prefix and goes *before* 35:

0	1	2	3	4
10	15	15	20	30

and the rest of the array—the suffix—goes *after* 35:

	5	*6*
	40	50

We'll create a result array that contains the prefix, 35, and the suffix:

0	*1*	*2*	*3*	*4*	*5*	*6*	*7*
10	15	15	20	30	35	40	50

In implementing this method, there may be special problems when the new Student goes at the beginning of the array or after the end.

Prog1426 presents the code and a driver for this method. The method has six steps:

1. Determine the length of the prefix.
2. Allocate the new array, newA, one slot longer than the incoming array a. Create an index newUsed that indicates where to put the next element into newA.
3. Copy the prefix into newA.
4. Insert the new Student s into newA.
5. Copy the suffix into newA.
6. Create and return a new Section using newA and newUsed.

You should be able to see how these steps perform the required operation. A major phase of programming is to analyze a problem into operations that solve it. The next phase involves implementing the operations in the language required—Java, for us.

Prog1426.java insertInOrderByGrade

```
// Written by Barry Soroka
//
// Section -- adds Section insertInOrderByGrade(Student)
//            where the receiving Section is ordered.
//
import java.io.*;
import java.util.Scanner;
////////////////////////////////////////////////////////////////////////////
class Prog1426
{
//--------------------------------------------------------------------------
    public static void main (String [] args) throws Exception
    {
```

```
        Scanner kb = new Scanner(System.in);

        System.out.print("\nEnter name of a file of Students: ");
        String filename = kb.nextLine();

        Section section = new Section(filename);

        while ( true )
        {
            System.out.println("\nIn forward order, students are:");
            section.print(System.out);

            System.out.println();
            Student s = Student.read(System.out,kb);

            section = section.insertInOrderByGrade(s);
        }
    }
//------------------------------------------------------------------
} // end class Prog1426
////////////////////////////////////////////////////////////////////
class Section
{
    private Student [] a;
    private int used;
    private final int INIT_SIZE = 20;
//------------------------------------------------------------------
    public Section insertInOrderByGrade ( Student s )
    {
    // Determine the length of the prefix.
    //            (Before which element should s go?)

        int prefixSize = -1;
        for ( int i = 0 ; i < used ; i++ )
        {
            System.out.println("Testing a[" + i + "]");
            if ( s.getGrade() < a[i].getGrade() )
            {
                prefixSize = i;
                break;
            }
        }
        if ( prefixSize == -1 ) prefixSize = used;

    // Allocate the array and pointer for the result:

        Student[] newA = new Student[used+1];
        int newUsed = 0;

    // Copy the prefix to newA:

        for ( int i = 0 ; i < prefixSize ; i++ )
```

```
        {
            newA[newUsed] = a[i];
            newUsed++;
        }

    // Insert s into newA:

        newA[newUsed] = s;
        newUsed++;

    // Copy the suffix to newA:

        for ( int i = prefixSize ; i < used ; i++ )
        {
            newA[newUsed] = a[i];
            newUsed++;
        }

    // Create and return the new Section:

        return new Section(newA,newUsed);
    }
//--------------------------------------------------------------------
// More code is included!  See Prog1421.
//--------------------------------------------------------------------
} // end class Section
////////////////////////////////////////////////////////////////////
class Student
{
// More code is included!  See Prog1421.
} // end class Student
////////////////////////////////////////////////////////////////////
```

Now, let's see how these steps are implemented in the code.

1. Determine the length of the prefix.
   A `for` loop compares s with the elements of a. If we find that

   ```
   s.getGrade() < a[i].getGrade()
   ```

   then we know that the `prefixSize` is `i`. If s has a higher grade than *all* the elements of a, then `prefixSize` must be set to `used`. We detect this condition by initializing `prefixSize` to `-1`; if it's never changed, then s goes at the end of the array. Here's the code:

   ```
   int prefixSize = -1;
   for ( int i = 0 ; i < used ; i++ )
   {
   ```

```
            if ( s.getGrade() < a[i].getGrade() )
            {
                prefixSize = i;
                break;
            }
        }
        if ( prefixSize == -1 ) prefixSize = used;
```

2. Allocate the new array, newA, one slot longer than the incoming array a. Create an index newUsed, which indicates where to put the next element into newA.

```
        Student[] newA = new Student[used+1];
        int newUsed = 0;
```

(That's shorter to say in Java than in English!)

3. Copy the prefix into newA.

```
        for ( int i = 0 ; i < prefixSize ; i++ )
        {
            newA[newUsed] = a[i];
            newUsed++;
        }
```

Note how we use newUsed as an index that continuously points to the next available slot as it moves through newA.

4. Insert the new Student s into newA.

```
        newA[newUsed] = s;

        newUsed++;
```

5. Copy the suffix into newA.

```
        for ( int i = prefixSize ; i < used ; i++ )
        {
            newA[newUsed] = a[i];
            newUsed++;
        }
```

At the end of this step, newUsed is exactly the length of newA.

6. Create and return a new Section using newA and newUsed.

```
        return new Section(newA,newUsed);
```

The most difficult part of writing this method was breaking it into steps that (1) solve the problem, and (2) can be effectively and clearly written in Java.

 | **Test your skill with Exercises 14-70 and 14-71.** |

14.25   String [] args

After studying arrays in this chapter, we can finally understand part of the boilerplate of every static main method—String [] args. This declares args to be an array of Strings, and the Java run-time system allocates args and fills it with all of the command line arguments. Prog1427 displays this array of command line arguments:

```
public static void main ( String [] args ) throws Exception
{
    System.out.println("Number of arguments: " + args.length);
    for ( int i = 0 ; i < args.length ; i++ )
        System.out.println("arg[" + i + "]: " + args[i]);
}
```

It treats args as an array. How does Java fill it? Here is hardcopy of a typical run:

```
G:\> java Prog1427 a "b c" 45.7
Number of arguments: 3
arg[0]: a
arg[1]: b c
arg[2]: 45.7
```

Java breaks the command line into String tokens. The space character separates tokens; the exception is that double quotes can surround Strings that include spaces. All elements of args are Strings, and we can use parseInt or parseDouble to convert Strings to ints or doubles as required.

Prog1427.java   **Command-Line Arguments**

```
// Written by Barry Soroka
//
// Use command-line arguments.
//
import java.io.*;
//////////////////////////////////////////////////////////////////////
class Prog1427
```

```
{
//-------------------------------------------------------------------

   public static void main ( String [] args ) throws Exception
   {
      System.out.println("Number of arguments: " + args.length);
      for ( int i = 0 ; i < args.length ; i++ )
         System.out.println("arg[" + i + "]: " + args[i]);
   }
//-------------------------------------------------------------------
} // end class Prog1427
///////////////////////////////////////////////////////////////////
```

14.26   Array Indexing in Other Languages

Java indexes arrays with the integers 0, 1, ..., length-1. Other languages—Pascal and Ada, for example—have indexed arrays in other ways.

Some languages start the indexing at 1 instead of 0. Some languages allow arrays to be indexed by *any continuous enumeration*:

    3, 4, 5, 6, ..., 20

or

    'a', 'b', 'c', 'd', ..., 'z'

Usually, the language provides a shortcut for describing the index set. The preceding examples might be specified as 3..20 or 'a'..'z'.

Another approach to indexing allows the user to specify any ordered set of indices. For example, it might be useful to index an array by the months of the year:

    { JAN,FEB,MAR,APR,MAY,JUN,
      JUL,AUG,SEP,OCT,NOV,DEC }

Then we could have statements such as:

    summerTotal = a[JUN] + a[JUL] + a[AUG];

That statement is eminently readable.

In the course of your career, you'll see many different schemes for indexing arrays. This section is just an introduction to the possibilities.

14.27 Multidimensional Arrays

In previous chapters, we worked with *one*-dimensional arrays. Values were laid out, one after another, in a single line, indexed by 0, 1, 2, and so forth. Now we will examine *multi*dimensional arrays, and in particular *two*-dimensional arrays. A 2-D array is like a table or a matrix, with values laid out in rows and columns. Specifying a particular location requires *two* numbers, not just one. Numeric matrices often represent real-world data such as maps of temperature, weather, and elevation. Matrices of other primitive datatypes are also useful. Three-dimensional arrays correspond to piles of 2-D arrays, and we can visualize them in three-space. Arrays with more than three dimensions cannot be visualized as 3-D objects.

> **Matrix**   A two-dimensional array.

14.28 2-D Array Basics

Let's review how we work with 1-D arrays before looking at the comparable operations on 2-D arrays.

We declared a 1-D array with a statement such as this:

```
int[] a1;
```

and we initialized it by saying

```
a1 = new int[5];
```

This creates an array of length 5. We filled a particular location with a statement such as

```
a1[2] = 17;
```

and we referenced this location with statements such as

```
System.out.println(a1[2]);
```

The mechanics of 2-D arrays are similar, except that we need to specify *two* dimensions instead of just one. We declare a 2-D array with a statement like

```
int[][] a2;
```

where the two sets of brackets indicate that a2 has two dimensions. The statement

```
a2 = new int[2][3];
```

creates an array with two rows and three columns. It has the structure

where I have indicated the indices of the rows (horizontals) and columns (verticals). As usual for Java, we begin indexing with 0. We can fill the array with statements such as these:

```
a2[0][0] = 7;
a2[0][1] = 3;
a2[0][2] = 4;
a2[1][0] = 1;
a2[1][1] = 6;
a2[1][2] = 3;
```

which results in the array

We can print this array using nested loops:

```
for ( int row = 0 ; row < 2 ; row++ )
{
    for ( int col = 0; col < 3 ; col++ )
        System.out.print(a2[row][col] + "\t");
    System.out.println();
}
```

producing

```
7        3        4
1        6        3
```

Note that we need to do a println at the end of each row.

Given a rectangular matrix m, we can determine its dimensions:

- m.length is the number of rows.
- m[0].length is the number of columns.

> **Test your skill with Exercises 14-72 through 14-74.**

14.29 2-D Arrays of Numbers

We have seen how to create, initialize, and print arrays of integers. Let's look at a few other operations.

Addition

If a and b are m × n arrays, then the m × n array c is their sum if and only if

    c[i][j] == a[i][j] + b[i][j]

for i = 1, ... , m and j = 1, ... , n. *Difference* is defined similarly.

> **Test your skill with Exercise 14-75.**

Identity Matrices

A square matrix a is an *identity matrix* if and only if

$$a[i][j] = \begin{cases} 1 & when\ i = j \\ 0 & otherwise \end{cases}$$

For example, $\begin{bmatrix} 1 & 0 \\ 0 & 1 \end{bmatrix}$, $\begin{bmatrix} 1 & 0 & 0 \\ 0 & 1 & 0 \\ 0 & 0 & 1 \end{bmatrix}$, and $\begin{bmatrix} 1 & 0 & 0 & 0 \\ 0 & 1 & 0 & 0 \\ 0 & 0 & 1 & 0 \\ 0 & 0 & 0 & 1 \end{bmatrix}$ are identity matrices.

> **Test your skill with Exercises 14-76 through 14-79.**

Diagonal Matrices

A square matrix a is a *diagonal matrix* if and only if $a_{ij} = 0$ when $i \neq j$.

For example, $\begin{bmatrix} 2 & 0 \\ 0 & 3 \end{bmatrix}$ and $\begin{bmatrix} 7 & 0 & 0 \\ 0 & 1 & 0 \\ 0 & 0 & 6 \end{bmatrix}$ are diagonal matrices.

> **Test your skill with Exercises 14-80 and 14-81.**

Transpose of a Matrix

If `a` is an m $\times$ n matrix, then its *transpose* `b` is an $n \times m$ matrix where $b_{ij} = a_{ji}$.

For example, the transpose of $\begin{bmatrix} 7 & 3 & 4 \\ 1 & 6 & 3 \end{bmatrix}$ is $\begin{bmatrix} 7 & 1 \\ 3 & 6 \\ 4 & 3 \end{bmatrix}$. If `a` is a *square* matrix,

then its transpose has its elements flipped about the main diagonal (upper left to lower right).

Test your skill with Exercises 14-82 and 14-83.

Symmetric Matrices

A square matrix `a` is a *symmetric matrix* if and only if $a_{ij} = a_{ji}$ for all i and j. For example,

$$\begin{bmatrix} 5 & 2 & 1 & 4 \\ 2 & 3 & 7 & 5 \\ 1 & 7 & 1 & 6 \\ 4 & 5 & 6 & 8 \end{bmatrix}$$

is symmetric.

Test your skill with Exercises 14-84 and 14-85.

14.30   2-D Arrays of `char`

Drawing with `char`s

We can use a 2-D array of `char`s as a canvas on which we can draw rough images. We can draw geometrical shapes using particular `char`s as "colors," and, with enough shapes, we can draw interesting pictures.

Test your skill with Exercise 14-86.

Gray-Scale Pictures with `char`s

Using a fixed-width font such as Courier New, most monitors and printers allow us to draw "pixels" of varying darkness.

We can approximate a gray-scale picture with a suitably chosen finite set of chars. You have probably seen a block drawing of Abraham Lincoln that uses only a few gray levels and a few hundred pixels.[6]

In the old days, I used *impact printers* and I was able to print several lines of chars on top of each other. This provided even greater control of the pixel darkness. 'M' on top of 'N' on top of 'W' on top of 'Z' is a very dark blotch, indeed.

Conway's Game of Life

John H. Conway[7] invented a one-person game in which a 2-D array of 0s and 1s simulates a living system. Cells labeled 1 are alive; cells labeled 0 are dead. The board changes from generation to generation according to a set of rules. The goal of the game is to discover patterns that change the cells in interesting ways, or to find rules that cause interesting changes in the cells over generations.

The most typical rules are these:

- If a live cell has two or three live neighbors, it survives to the next generation.
- If a live cell has less than two live neighbors, it is dead in the next generation due to loneliness.
- If a live cell has more than three live neighbors, it is dead in the next generation due to overcrowding.
- If a dead cell has exactly three live neighbors, it comes to life in the next generation.

Search the Web for "game of life" and you will discover numerous sites with information about the game and with actual applets that allow you to experiment with patterns and rules.

> **Test your skill with Exercise 14-87.**

---

[6] Harmon, L. (1973). The recognition of faces. *Scientific American* 229(5):71–82. Also, check the Web for "domino portraits."

[7] Gardner, M. (1970). Mathematical games: The fantastic combinations of John Conway's new solitaire game "life." *Scientific American* 223(4):120–123.

14.31   **2-D Arrays of** `boolean`

Consider the directed graph shown in Figure 14–2. We can represent this as a square array of `boolean`:

	0	1	2	3	4
0	`false`	`true`	`false`	`false`	`true`
1	`true`	`false`	`true`	`true`	`false`
2	`false`	`false`	`false`	`true`	`false`
3	`false`	`false`	`true`	`false`	`true`
4	`false`	`false`	`false`	`false`	`true`

Consider the element `[i][j]`. It will be `true` if and only if there's a link *from* node i *to* node j. If you compare the graph with the array, you'll find that we have a 1-to-1 correspondence between the links and the `true` values. We call this the *adjacency array* for the graph.

> **Adjacency array**   A boolean array that indicates which nodes connect to which others in a graph.

In later CS courses, you'll learn how to work with adjacency arrays to answer questions like:

- Can we get from node i to node j in a single hop?
- Can we get from node i to node j in two hops?
- Can we get from node i to node j at all?
- What nodes can we get to from node i in n hops?
- What nodes can we reach from node i?

Figure 14–2
A Directed Graph

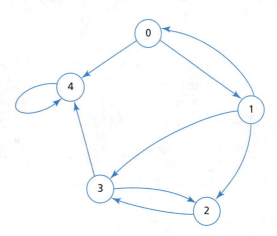

14.32   Computing Array Addresses

As we learned in Chapter 1, the memory of a computer is a 1-D array where each cell has a specific address. When a Java program involves a 2-D rectangular array, the cells of that array can be mapped onto a 1-D array of physical memory cells. *Array addressing* is the math that takes us between 2-D addresses and 1-D addresses.

> **Array addressing**   Computing how the cells of a multidimensional array map onto the linear array of actual memory cells.

As an example, let's consider a 2 × 3 array and how it maps onto a 1-D array of six cells:

n	r	c
0	0	0
1	0	1
2	0	2
3	1	0
4	1	1
5	1	2

Here are the formulas involved in array addressing:

- Going from (r,c) to n, we have the formula

```
n = r * NC + c
```

where NC is the number of columns.
- Given n, we can find (r,c) via the following formulas:

```
r = n / NC
c = n % NC
```

Notice that the number of *rows* is not involved in the calculations for array addressing.

 Test your skill with Exercise 14-88.

14.33   Ragged Arrays

Previously, we used the statement

```
int[][] a2 = new int[2][3];
```

Figure 14–3
Ragged Arrays

a.

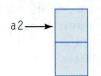

b.

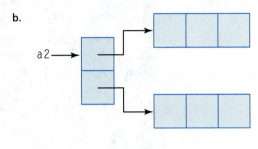

c.

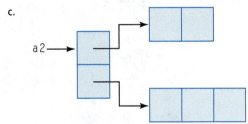

to create a 2 × 3 array. This was actually shorthand for the following statements:

```
int[][] a2 = new int[2][];
a2[0] = new int[3];
a2[1] = new int[3];
```

The first statement creates the structure shown in Figure 14–3(a), where `a2` points to a structure with two slots that we can fill in later. The second and third statements change the structure to Figure 14–3(b), where each row has three slots, which we can fill with `int`s. This illustrates how Java maintains 2-D arrays. There's an array of rows, where each row points to a 1-D array of column values.

Now, since each row points to its own linear array, we might ask: Can different rows have different lengths? Yes! The statements

```
int[][] a2 = new int[2][];
a2[0] = new int[2];
a2[1] = new int[3];
```

Ragged array   A nonrectangular array—rows don't all have the same length.

produce the *ragged array* shown in Figure 14–3(c).

Ragged arrays are not used very often, but they illustrate how Java maintains multidimensional arrays internally.

Test your skill with Exercise 14-89.

14.34 GUI: Regular Polygons

Prog1428.java is an application that draws a regular polygon with n sides, where n is read as a command line argument. For example, to draw a pentagon, use the command line

```
java Prog1428 5
```

Prog1428.java   **Display a Regular Polygon**

```java
// Written by Barry Soroka
//
// Display a regular polygon.
//
import java.io.*;
import java.awt.*;
import javax.swing.*;
////////////////////////////////////////////////////////////////////////
class Prog1428
{
//----------------------------------------------------------------------
    public static void main (String[] args) throws Exception
    {
        JFrame frame = new JFrame ("Polygon");
        frame.setDefaultCloseOperation (JFrame.EXIT_ON_CLOSE);

        MyPanel mp = new MyPanel( Integer.parseInt(args[0]) );
        frame.getContentPane().add(mp);
        frame.pack();
        frame.setVisible(true);
    }
//----------------------------------------------------------------------
} // end class Prog1428
////////////////////////////////////////////////////////////////////////
class MyPanel extends JPanel
{
    private int n;
    private int[] x;
    private int[] y;
```

```
//- - - - - - - - - - - - - - - - - - - - - - - - - - - - - - - - - - - - - - - - - - - - - - - - - - - - -
   public MyPanel ( int n )
   {
      this.n = n;
      x = new int[n];
      y = new int[n];

      int xCenter = 100;
      int yCenter = 100;

      int radius = 50;

      for ( int i = 0 ; i < n ; i++ )
      {
         x[i] = xCenter + (int)(radius * Math.cos(i*2.0*Math.PI/n));
         y[i] = yCenter + (int)(radius * Math.sin(i*2.0*Math.PI/n));
      }

      setBackground(Color.WHITE);
      setPreferredSize(new Dimension(200,200));
   }
//- - - - - - - - - - - - - - - - - - - - - - - - - - - - - - - - - - - - - - - - - - - - - - - - - - - - -
   public void paintComponent ( Graphics page )
   {
      super.paintComponent(page);
      page.drawPolygon(x,y,n);
   }
//- - - - - - - - - - - - - - - - - - - - - - - - - - - - - - - - - - - - - - - - - - - - - - - - - - - - -
} // end class MyPanel
//////////////////////////////////////////////////////////////////////////
```

I use an array to store the coordinates of the vertices, and I use Java's draw-Polygon to connect the coordinates I have stored in the arrays x and y.

     Test your skill with Exercises 14-90 and 14-91.

14.35   GUI: Checkerboard

Prog1429.java displays a checkerboard. Nested loops generate values of (row,col) and we draw a black square if row+col is odd. Here is a depiction of (row,col) for the checkerboard:

(0,0)	(0,1)	(0,2)	(0,3)	(0,4)	. . .
(1,0)	(1,1)	(1,2)	(1,3)	(1,4)	. . .
(2,0)	(2,1)	(2,2)	(2,3)	(2,4)	. . .
(3,0)	(3,1)	(3,2)	(3,3)	(3,4)	. . .
(4,0)	(4,1)	(4,2)	(4,3)	(4,4)	. . .
. . .	. . .	. . .	. . .	. . .	. . .

Here is the sum, row+col:

0	1	2	3	4	. . .
1	2	3	4	5	. . .
2	3	4	5	6	. . .
3	4	5	6	7	. . .
4	5	6	7	8	. . .
. . .	. . .	. . .	. . .	. . .	. . .

Notice how squares with *odd* sums run the alternate diagonals of the checkerboard.

Prog1429.java   Display a Checkerboard

```
// Written by Barry Soroka
//
// Display a checkerboard.
//
import java.io.*;
import java.awt.*;
import javax.swing.*;
/////////////////////////////////////////////////////////////////////////////
class Prog1429
{
//-------------------------------------------------------------------------
    public static void main (String[] args) throws Exception
    {
        JFrame frame = new JFrame ("Polygon");
        frame.setDefaultCloseOperation (JFrame.EXIT_ON_CLOSE);

        frame.getContentPane().add(new MyPanel());
        frame.pack();
        frame.setVisible(true);
    }
//-------------------------------------------------------------------------
} // end class Prog1429
/////////////////////////////////////////////////////////////////////////////
class MyPanel extends JPanel
```

```
{
   private int n;
   private int[] x;
   private int[] y;
//------------------------------------------------------------------
   public MyPanel()
   {
      setBackground(Color.WHITE);
      setPreferredSize(new Dimension(400,400));
   }
//------------------------------------------------------------------
   public void paintComponent ( Graphics page )
   {
      final int SIDE = 20;   // box size
      super.paintComponent(page);
      for ( int row = 0 ; row < 8 ; row++ )
         for ( int col = 0 ; col < 8 ; col++ )
            if ( (row+col)%2 != 0 ) page.fillRect(row*SIDE,col*SIDE,SIDE,SIDE);
   }
//------------------------------------------------------------------
} // end class MyPanel
//////////////////////////////////////////////////////////////////////////
```

 | **Test your skill with Exercises 14-92 through 14-97.**

Chapter Summary

- Arrays are an example of a collection.
- Arrays are random-access.
- Arrays are stored in memory, not on disk.
- A variable is declared to be an array using the syntax *type*[] *varName* for example, int[] a.
- An array is created using the syntax new *type*[*arrayLength*]—for example, new int[5].
- The positions in an array of length 10 are 0, 1, 2, . . . , 9.
- An off-by-one error occurs when we perform an array operation one time more or one time fewer than we need. Such OBO errors are very common.
- *Algorithm:* Given a file of ints, read them into an array.
- When working with arrays, there are two major schemes: (1) keep the array full at all times, and (2) keep the array partially full, but maintain a count of how many elements are currently valid.
- We can pass an array or an array element to a method.

- If we pass an *array element* to a method, changes made within the method are lost upon return.
- If we pass an *array* to a method, changes to elements made within the method are kept upon return.
- The return type of a method can be an array.
- Instances of class `MyString` represent `String`s as arrays of `char`s.
- `MyString` methods can involve no parameters as well as parameters of type `char`, `int`, and `MyString`.
- `MyString` methods can have no return value or can return `boolean`, `char`, `int`, `MyString`, or `String`.
- Given the range of parameters and return types, we can identify numerous methods that involve `MyString`s.
- Most algorithms involving files can be adapted to work with arrays.
- Arrays enable a host of new algorithms.
- *Algorithm:* Concatenate two `MyString`s, producing a third `MyString`.
- *Algorithm:* Given a `MyString` and a `char`, produce a new `MyString` where the `char` has been added to the *front* of the `MyString`.
- *Algorithm:* Given a `MyString` and a `char`, produce a new `MyString` where the `char` has been added to the *rear* of the `MyString`.
- *Algorithm:* Given a `MyString`, produce a new `MyString` where all the space `char`s have been deleted.
- *Algorithm:* Given a `MyString`, produce a specified substring.
- We can implement `Section` as an array of `Student`s, maintaining a partially full array and a counter.
- Previously, we developed a variety of methods for working with `Section` implemented as a *file* of `Student`s. These methods can be adapted to work with arrays of `Student`s.
- *Algorithm:* Given an array of `Student`s, print them in reverse order.
- When copying a `Section`, a shallow copy shares data structure with its original.
- With a deep copy, no data structure is shared between original and copy.
- *Algorithm:* Given a `Section` and a `Student`, produce a new `Section` where the `Student` has been inserted in ascending order by grade.
- In our boilerplate, `String [] args` referred to an array of the tokens present on the command line, which invoked the Java program. Thus, `args[0]` refers to the first token, `args[1]` refers to the second token, and so forth. We can access these tokens and use them within the `main` method.
- Some other languages index arrays differently than Java does.
- A 2-D array is declared as *type*`[][]` *varName*—for example, `int[][] a`.

- An array is created using the syntax new*type*[*arrayLength1*]-[*arrayLength2*]—for example, `new int[5][3]` has five rows and three columns.
- 2-D arrays of numbers can represent numeric matrices.
- 2-D arrays of `char`s can represent pictures.
- The Game of Life is a simulation of artificial life using a 2-D array of `char`s.
- 2-D arrays of `boolean`s can represent graphs.
- 2-D arrays can be *ragged*—they need not be rectangular.
- We can use the GUI to display graphical representations of 2-D arrays.

Terminology Introduced in This Chapter

adjacency matrix	matrix	subscript
array addressing	ragged array	swapping
deep copy	shallow copy	

Exercises

Exercise 14-1.   What do you think is printed by the statements below? What does Java actually print?

```java
int [] a = new int[3];
System.out.println(a.length);
a = new int[5];
System.out.println(a.length);
a = new int[0];
System.out.println(a.length);
```

Exercise 14-2.   Write a program that declares an array a of five `int`s:

```java
int [] a = new int[5];
```

Write a loop that requests an `int` and attempts to assign 0 to the corresponding element in a. Note which values are legal and which give `Exception`s.

Exercise 14-3.   Write a method

```java
private static int[] readArray(Scanner)
```

that returns a full array of the `int`s in the specified `Scanner`.

Exercise 14-4. Write a method

```
private static Student[] readArray(Scanner)
```

that returns a full array of the Students in the specified Scanner.

Exercise 14-5. Write a method that reads ints from the user and puts them into an array, stopping at the sentinel value 999.

Exercise 14-6. Write a driver that demonstrates that the constructor

```
public MyString ( char[] a ) { this.a = a; }
```

shares the array between the driver and the MyString:

- Create and fill a variable a that holds an array of char.
- Create a MyString using that variable.
- Print the MyString.
- Change any slot in the variable a in the driver.
- Print the MyString.
- Did the MyString change?

Exercise 14-7. Study the constructor

```
public MyString ( char[] a, int n )
```

Does data sharing occur between the parameter array and the constructed MyString?

Exercise 14-8. For each of the following MyString methods, identify the cell in the table of Section 14.8 to which it belongs:

```
addCharAtFront(char)          howManyVowels()
addCharAtRear(char)           indexOf(char)
allAre(char)                  isPrefixOf(MyString)
anyAre(char)                  isSubstringOf(MyString)
commonCharacters(MyString)    isSuffixOf(MyString)
containsAny(char)             lastIndexOf(char)
```

```
containsDigit()                    lastNonBlank()
containsVowel()                    matches(int,char)
delete(char)                       mostFrequentChar()
deleteSpaces()                     replace(char,char)
deleteUpperCaseChars()             replaceCharAtIndex(int,char)
deleteVowels()                     reverse()
equals(MyString)                   subtract(MyString)
equalsIgnoreCase(MyString)         toLowerCase()
firstNonBlank()                    toUpperCase()
howManyUpperCaseChars()
```

Exercise 14-9. Identify further methods for the class `MyString`. Try to fill in some of the empty or poorly populated cells in the table given in Section 14.8.

Exercise 14-10. Which `MyString` methods have counterparts in class `String`? Which do not?

Exercise 14-11. How does the `equals` method differ from the `equals` method of class `Object` with respect to how they handle `MyString`s? *Hint:* Run your driver *without* defining your own `equals` method; it will default to the `equals` method of class `Object`. Which `equals` method implies the other?

Exercise 14-12. Write the method

```
boolean equalsIgnoreCase(MyString)
```

Exercise 14-13. Recall our class `MyString`. The sole instance variable is an array of `char`. Add a method

```
public boolean match(MyString)
```

that considers the two `MyString`s and returns `true` if and only if the two `MyString`s are of equal `length` and are equal, character for character, with the exception that a '?' in *either* `MyString` counts as a wild card that matches any character in the corresponding position of the other `MyString`. The `MyString`s may be any `length`, including 0. For example:

MyString Represents	MyString2 Represents	Result of match
"abc"	"ab"	false
""	""	true
"abc"	"abc"	true
"abc"	"aeb"	false
"ab?"	"abd"	true
"a?c"	"adc"	true
"ab"	"a"	false
"ab"	"a?"	true

Exercise 14–14.   Write a method `duplicate` which, when applied to a `MyString`, returns a new `MyString`, twice as long, containing two copies of the receiver, one after the other.

Exercise 14–15.   Write a method

```
public MyString sprinkle ( MyString )
```

that takes two equal-length `MyString`s and returns a new `MyString` in which the `char`s of the two `MyString`s have been interspersed. For example,

```
"abc".sprinkle("123") → "a1b2c3"
```

Your method should throw an `Error` if the two `MyString`s are not equal in `length`.

Exercise 14–16.   Add to `MyString`:

```
boolean containsIgnoreCase(char)
```

that returns true if the receiving `MyString` contains the specified `char` in either upper- or lowercase. You may want to write a helper method `toUpperCase(char)`.

Exercise 14–17.   Add to `MyString`:

```
boolean containsDigit()
```

that returns `true` only if the receiving `MyString` contains a `char` from the set [0123456789].

Exercise 14–18.   Add to `MyString`:

```
boolean containsVowel()
```

which returns `true` only if the receiving `MyString` contains a `char` from the set `[aeiouAEIOU]`.

Exercise 14-19.   Add to `MyString`:

```
boolean containsAny(MyString)
```

which returns `true` only if the receiving `MyString` contains *any* `char` from the parameter `MyString`.

Receiver	Parameter	Result
"hello there"	"bag"	false
"hello there"	"brag"	true
"hello there"	""	false
""	"bag"	false
""	""	false

You don't need a nested loop. You can solve this using an appropriate helper method.

Exercise 14-20.   Add to `MyString`:

```
int howManyIgnoreCase(char)
```

which returns the number of times `char` appears in the `MyString` in either upper- or lowercase.

Exercise 14-21.   Add to `MyString`:

```
int howManyVowels()
```

which returns the number of `char`s in the `MyString` that come from the set `[aeiouAEIOU]`.

Exercise 14-22.   Add to `MyString`:

```
int howManyUpperCaseChars()
```

which returns the number of uppercase `char`s in the `MyString`.

Exercise 14-23.   Add to `MyString`:

```
int howMany(MyString)
```

which returns the total number of `char`s in the receiving `MyString` that occur in the parameter `MyString`.

Receiver	Parameter	Result
`"hello there"`	`""`	0
`"hello there"`	`"e"`	3
`"hello there"`	`"eb"`	3
`"hello there"`	`"reb"`	4
`""`	`"bag"`	0
`""`	`""`	0
`"hello there"`	`"ee"`	3

You don't need a nested loop. You can solve this using an appropriate helper method.

Exercise 14-24. Add to `MyString`:

```
public MyString toUpperCase()
```

with behavior analogous to the same method defined for `String`.

Exercise 14-25. Add to `MyString`:

```
public MyString replaceDigits(char)
```

which returns a new `MyString` in which every digit—0123456789—has been replaced by the specified `char`.

Exercise 14-26. Add to `MyString`:

```
public MyString replace ( MyString s1, MyString s2 )
```

The parameters must have the same `length` and they represent a translation. For example,

```
MyString s1 = new MyString("abcdefghijklmnopqrstuvwxyz");
MyString s2 = new MyString("bcdefghijklmnopqrstuvwxyza");
```

The translation is: Every `'a'` in the receiver becomes a `'b'` in the output, and so forth. If a `char` in the receiver is not mentioned in `s1`, then it continues, unchanged, to the result. Historically, this particular translation is known as a *Caesar cipher* because the Roman general Julius Caesar used this code to hide his messages from the enemy.

Exercise 14–27.   Add to `MyString`:

```
public void replaceCharAtIndex ( int n, char c )
```

which, for a given `MyString`, replaces the `char` at the specified position.

Exercise 14–28.   Add to `MyString`:

```
public MyString blackout(char)
```

which returns a new `MyString` in which *every other char*—beginning with the first—has been replaced by the specified `char`.

Exercise 14–29.   Write a program that tests the first `reverse` method given under "Reversing in Place" in Section 14.14. Fill out the table:

MyString	Reverses To
" "	
"a"	
"ab"	
"aa"	
"abc"	
"aba"	
"abcd"	

Explain why you get the results you do.

Exercise 14–30.   Consider a method `maxSoFar`, which takes a `MyString` and produces another `MyString` where the `char` in each position is the largest of the `chars` *at or before* that position in the `MyString`. For example, `"abdafehg"` would become `"abddffhh"`. Write two different forms of `maxSoFar`:
a. One that alters the receiving `MyString` and returns type `void`.
b. One that returns a new `MyString` containing the computed values.

Exercise 14–31.   Write and test the following methods for class `MyString`:

```
public void addCharAtFront ( char c )
public void addCharAtRear ( char c )
```

Unlike the versions previously discussed, these methods *change the receiving MyString*—they don't return a new `MyString`.

Exercise 14-32. Write and test the following methods:

```
private static int[] addAtFront(int[],int)
private static int[] addAtRear(int[],int)
```

Exercise 14-33. Add to MyString:

```
public MyString deleteChar(char)
```

which returns a MyString from which the specified char has been deleted.

Exercise 14-34. Add to MyString:

```
public static MyString deleteChar(MyString, char)
```

Exercise 14-35. Add to MyString:

```
public MyString deleteUpperCaseChars()
```

Exercise 14-36. Add to MyString:

```
public void deleteUpperCaseChars()
```

Exercise 14-37. Add to MyString:

```
public MyString deleteVowels()
```

Exercise 14-38. Add to MyString:

```
public void deleteVowels()
```

Exercise 14-39. Add to MyString:

```
public MyString deleteDigits()
```

Exercise 14-40. Add to MyString:

```
public void deleteDigits()
```

Exercise 14-41. Add to class MyString:

```
public MyString substring(int)
```

with behavior that matches substring(int) of class String.

Exercise 14-42.   Write the method

```
public MyString trimLeft()
```

which removes leading spaces.

Exercise 14-43.   Write the method

```
public MyString trimRight()
```

which removes trailing spaces.

Exercise 14-44.   For class `MyString`, write the method

```
public boolean isSuffixOf(MyString)
```

Exercise 14-45.   For class `MyString`, write the method

```
public boolean isSubstringOf(MyString)
```

If `s1` is a substring of `s2`, then `s1` is a prefix of some suffix of `s2`. For example

`"llo"`	vs.	`"hello there"`	converts to
`"llo"`	vs.	`"ello there"`	converts to
`"llo"`	vs.	`"llo there"`	returns true

or

`"abc"`	vs.	`"ababe"`	converts to
`"abc"`	vs.	`"babe"`	converts to
`"abc"`	vs.	`"abe"`	converts to
`"abc"`	vs.	`"be"`	returns false

The last line, `"abc"` vs. `"be"`, returns `false` because `a1` is longer than `a2`, so `a1` can't be a `substring` of `a2`.

Exercise 14-46.   A `MyString` is a *palindrome* if it reads the same forward and backward. For example, the following are palindromes: `radar`, `madam`, `eve`.
Write a method

```
public boolean isPalindrome()
```

that returns `true` if and only if the receiving `MyString` is a palindrome.

Exercise 14-47. Add to class `MyString` a method

```
public MyString rotate1()
```

that returns a new `MyString` which is the same as the receiver *except* that the first `char` has been moved to the rear. For example, if we apply `rotate1` to the `MyString` `"hello there"`, we get the new `MyString` `"ello thereh"`.

Exercise 14-48. Add to class `MyString` a method

```
public void rotate1()
```

that rotates the receiving `MyString` as described in the previous problem.

Exercise 14-49. Add to class `MyString` a method

```
public void rotate(int)
```

that rotates the receiving `MyString` the specified number of times.

Exercise 14-50. Add to class `MyString` a method

```
public MyString twin()
```

that returns a new `MyString` in which every `char` has been "twinned." For example, if we apply `twin` to the `MyString` `"n17A"`, we get the new `MyString` `"nn1177AA"`.

Exercise 14-51. Add to class `MyString` a method

```
public MyString triple()
```

that returns a new `MyString` containing, in order: (1) the incoming `MyString`, (2) the lowercase of it, and (3) the uppercase of it. For example, if we apply `triple` to the `MyString` `"DaRT"`, we get the new `MyString` `"DaRTdartDART"`.

Exercise 14-52. Add to class `MyString` a method

```
public MyString deleteDoubles()
```

that returns a new `MyString` in which any adjacent doubles (or triples or quads or ...) have been compressed into a single `char`. For example, if we apply `deleteDoubles` to the `MyString` `"abbcddde"`, we get the new `MyString` `"abcde"`.

Exercise 14-53. Add the following method to class `MyString`:

```
public MyString insertMyStringAtIndex(MyString s, int i)
```

This method inserts the `MyString` `s` into the receiving `MyString` between the `char`s at positions `i` and `i+1`. Throw an `Error` if `i` is negative or is greater than the length of the receiving `MyString`.

Exercise 14-54. Write a method

```
public void printInReverse(PrintStream)
```

for class `Section` as implemented with a *file*.

Exercise 14-55. Write a method

```
public void printAboveAverageStudents(PrintStream)
```

Exercise 14-56. Write a method

```
public void printPassingStudents(PrintStream)
```

where "passing" means `grade ≥ 60`.

Exercise 14-57. Write a method

```
public void printFailingStudents(PrintStream)
```

where "failing" means `grade < 60`.

Exercise 14-58. Write a method

```
public void printStudentsWithGradeInRange(int,int,PrintStream)
```

Exercise 14-59. Write a method

```
public void printEveryOtherStudent(PrintStream)
```

Exercise 14-60. Write the method

```
public void addStudentAtFront(Student)
```

Exercise 14-61. Write the method

```
public void addStudentsAtRear(Student[]).
```

The parameter is an array full of `Student`s. Add them at the rear of the `Section`.

Exercise 14-62. Write the method

```
public void addStudentsAtFront(Student[])
```

The parameter is an array full of `Student`s. Add them at the front of the `Section`.

Exercise 14-63. Write the methods

a. `public int getLengthOfLongestNames()`
b. `public String[] getLongestNames()`
c. `public Student getStudentWithLongestName()`
d. `public Section getStudentsWithLongestName()`

Exercise 14-64. For class `Section`, write the methods:

a. `public Section deleteFailingStudents()`
b. `public Section keepEveryOtherStudent()`
c. `public Section deletePassingStudents()`
d. `public Section keepStudentsInRange(int,int)`
e. `public Section keepStudentsWithNamesInRange(char,char)`

Try writing some of these in the form:

```
public void dropFailingStudents()
```

Exercise 14-65. For class `Section`, write the method

```
boolean isStrictlyAscendingByGrade()
```

where *strictly ascending* means that adjacent elements are not allowed to be equal.

Exercise 14-66. For class `Section`, write the method

```
boolean isAscendingByName()
```

Exercise 14-67. For class `Section`, write the method

```
boolean isStrictlyAscendingByName()
```

Exercise 14-68. Write a program that determines whether an array of `Complex` is in ascending order by modulus.

Exercise 14-69. Write a program that determines whether an array of `Fraction`s is in ascending order.

Exercise 14-70. For class `Section`, write a method

> `Section insertInOrderByName(Student).`

Exercise 14-71. Write a method `insertInOrderByGrade(Student)` that is more efficient than the method previously described. In particular, write your method so that you only look through the incoming array *once*.

Exercise 14-72. Write a method

> `public static boolean isSquare ( int[][] )`

that takes a rectangular matrix and determines if it's square.

Exercise 14-73. Write a class `M33` that represents a 3 × 3 integer matrix. Include a constructor

> ```
> public M33 ( int a00, int a01, int a02,
>              int a10, int a11, int a12,
>              int a20, int a21, int a22 )
> ```

that creates the specified `M33`. Include a `toString` method that returns the three-line representation.

Exercise 14-74. Write a method

> `public void display ( int[][] )`

that prints a rectangular matrix.

Exercise 14-75. Add to class `M33` the methods

> `public M33 add(M33)`

and

> `public M33 sub(M33)`

that compute, respectively, the sum and difference of two `M33`s.

Exercise 14-76. Add to class `M33` a method

```
public boolean isIdentity()
```

which returns `true` if and only if the receiving `M33` is an identity matrix.

Exercise 14-77. Write a method

```
public static boolean isIdentity ( int[][] )
```

that returns `true` if and only if the parameter is an identity matrix. Note that a matrix must be *square* in order to be an identity matrix.

Exercise 14-78. Add to class `M33` the method

```
public static M33 identityMatrix()
```

that returns a 3×3 identity matrix.

Exercise 14-79. Write a method

```
public static int[][] identityMatrix ( int n )
```

that returns an $n \times n$ identity matrix.

Exercise 14-80. Add to class `M33` a method

```
public boolean isDiagonal()
```

that returns `true` if and only if the receiving `M33` is a diagonal matrix.

Exercise 14-81. Write a method

```
public static boolean isDiagonal ( int[][] )
```

that returns `true` if and only if the parameter is a diagonal matrix. Note that a matrix must be *square* in order to be an identity matrix.

Exercise 14-82. Add to class `M33`

```
public M33 transpose()
```

that returns an `M33`, which is the transpose of the receiving `M33`.

Exercise 14-83.   Write a method

```
public static int[][] transpose ( int[][] )
```

that returns the transpose of its parameter.

Exercise 14-84.   Add to class M33 a method

```
public boolean isSymmetric()
```

that returns `true` if and only if the receiving M33 is a symmetric matrix.

Exercise 14-85.   Write a method

```
public static boolean isSymmetric ( int[][] )
```

that returns `true` if and only if the parameter is a symmetric matrix.

Exercise 14-86.   Implement a class Picture with the following constructor and methods:

- `public Picture ( int nr, int nc, char background )` creates a Picture
  with an nr × nc array of `char`, with the initial background value.
- `public void rectangle (int rlo, int rhi, int clo, int chi, char
  color)` draws a rectangle of the specified `color` in cells with row value in the
  range [rlo,rhi] and column value in the range [clo,chi].
- `public void circle (double rc, double cc, double radius, char
  color)` draws a circle of the specified `color` with the specified center and
  `radius`. A reasonable algorithm would test each pixel on the canvas. If the pixel is
  within `radius` of the center, then it gets colored appropriately.

Write a driver that tests class Picture by drawing a reasonably complex scene, such
as a locomotive with body, wheels, and smoke.

Exercise 14-87.   Implement a version of Conway's Game of Life, using the rules given above. The class
Board should have the following methods:

- `public Board ( int nr, int nc )` creates a board with nr × nc cells. All cells
  are initially dead.
- `public void print()` prints a board so that we can see the current pattern.
- `public void set ( int r, int c )` turns on (makes live) the cell (r,c).

- `public void reset ( int r, int c )` turns off (makes dead) the cell (r,c).
- `public Board next()` takes an existing `Board` and returns the `Board` corresponding to the next generation.

Write a driver that tests your class. Typically, start with a 50 × 50 board having a 10 × 10 solid live square in its center. Print out various boards as you move from generation to generation. Label each board with its generation number.

Exercise 14-88. Implement a class `Sim2D` that simulates a 2-D rectangular array with a 1-D array. Your class should have at least the following methods:

- `public Sim2D ( int nr, int nc )` sets up the mapping and allocates a 1-D array with nr*nc cells.
- `public void put ( int r, int c, int value )` stores `value` in the cell that corresponds to (r,c).
- `public int get ( int r, int c )` retrieves the value stored in the cell (r,c).
- `public String toString()` returns a `String` that, when printed, shows the familiar 2-D form of the array.
- `public Sim2D add(Sim2D)` returns the result of adding two `Sim2D`s.
- `public static Sim2D identityMatrix(n)` returns a simulated n × n identity matrix.
- `public boolean isIdentity()` returns `true` if and only if the simulated array is an identity matrix.

Write a driver that tests your class `Sim2D`.

Exercise 14-89. In your prior courses in math, you've encountered Pascal's triangle:

```
                    1
                 1     1
              1     2     1
           1     3     3     1
        1     4     6     4     1
     1     5    10    10     5     1
  1     6    15    20    15     6     1
1     7    21    35    35    21     7     1
  . . .
```

Among other things, the numbers correspond to the coefficients of the $x^i y^{n-i}$ term of the binomial expansion of $(x + y)^n$. A new row is formed from the prior row by the following rules:

- The first element is 1.

- The last element is 1.
- The elements in between are formed by summing the two numbers above them in the row above.

Write a main method that creates and prints a ragged array, which represents Pascal's triangle to any given depth.

Exercise 14-90. Write an application that draws a regular star with n vertices. Take n as a command line argument.

Exercise 14-91. Write an application that graphs a 1-D function $f(x)$. Experiment to determine the optimum number of x-values to use. Store the values of $f(x)$ in an array. Determine the range of the function and scale your graph so that the function fits.

Exercise 14-92. Add lines between the squares of the checkerboard of Prog1429. There should be nine horizontal lines and nine vertical lines, and the squares—filled or empty—should be 20 × 20 pixels.

Exercise 14-93. Write a graphics application that visualizes an n × m array of 0s and 1s. The 0s should display as empty squares, and the 1s should display as filled squares. Test your code on a variety of patterns.

Exercise 14-94. Write a graphics application that displays an n × m grid on the screen. When the mouse is clicked inside a square, display the row and column of the clicked square.

Exercise 14-95. Write a graphics application that visualizes an n × m array of 0s and 1s. When the mouse is clicked inside a square, invert that binary value—0 becomes 1, or 1 becomes 0. The value in the array should change, and the color of the square—filled or empty—should be inverted.

Exercise 14-96. Add a next button that takes a visualized n × m array and produces the next generation according to the rules of the Game of Life. Both the screen and the array should change.

Exercise 14-97. Add a run button that takes a visualized n × m array and steps through future generations according to the rules of the Game of Life. Both the screen and the array should change.

Exercise 14-98. Write and test a method

```
public static int nEqual(int[],int[])
```

that reports the number of positions at which the two arrays are equal.

Exercise 14–99.   Write and test a method

```
public static int nEqual(String[],String[])
```

that reports the number of positions at which the two arrays are equal.

Exercise 14–100.   Add to class `Section`:

```
public Section get3AStudents()
```

that creates a new `Section` containing three A `Student`s from the receiving `Section`.

Exercise 14–101.   Add to class `Section`:

```
public Section getABCStudents()
```

that creates a new `Section` containing, in order, an A `Student`, a B `Student`, and a C `Student`.

Exercise 14–102.   Write a `static` method that prints elements from an array of `int`s until their sum reaches or exceeds 30.

Exercise 14–103.   Given a file of text—including digits—compute the distribution of the digits 0123456789. Use an array of length 10 to store the frequencies.

Exercise 14–104.   Write code that takes an array of `int`s and generates two arrays, one of *positive* `int`s and one of *negative* `int`s. Ignore the 0s.

Exercise 14–105.   Write code that takes an array of `String`s and generates three arrays:
a. `String`s beginning with uppercase letters
b. `String`s beginning with lowercase letters
c. `String`s beginning with nonletters

Exercise 14–106.   Write a method for class `Section` that generates two new `Section`s, one for the passing `Student`s and one for the failing `Student`s.

Exercise 14–107.   A `Vector` is a data structure where elements can be randomly accessed, but new elements are always added at the end. Using an array of `int`, implement a class `MyVector` with the following methods:

- Constructor `MyVector()`—Creates an empty `MyVector`.
- `public int size()`—Returns the current size of the receiving `MyVector`.
- `int elementAt(int)`—Returns the element at a designated position. Positions are numbered beginning with 0.
- `void addElement(int)`—Adds the given element at the *end* of the `MyVector`.
- `MyVector copy()`—Returns a copy of the receiving `MyVector`.

Exercise 14-108. Repeat Exercise 14-107, but work with `MyVector`s containing `Students` or `Complex` or `Fractions` or `Strings`.

Exercise 14-109. Recall the class `Complex`, which we implemented with instance variables `real` and `imag`. Re-implement `Complex` to store these values in an array of length two.

Exercise 14-110. Write a `static` method that takes two equal-length arrays of `Strings` and returns an array of `Strings`—of the same length—in which each element is the concatenation of the corresponding items in the parameter arrays. For example, if the input arrays are

"apple"	"nap"	"Ara"

and

"sauce"	"kin"	"gorn"

then the returned array should be

"applesauce"	"napkin"	"Aragorn"

Exercise 14-111. Write the code for the class `M3Vector` that models mathematical 3-vectors. The sole instance variable should be an array of three `ints`. Implement at least the following methods:

a. A constructor that takes three `ints`. For example,

```
M3Vector v1 = new M3Vector(2,7,3);
```

b. A `toString` method with output such as this:

```
v1.toString() → "(2,7,3)"
```

c. An `add` method that returns the sum of a receiving `M3Vector` and a parameter `M3Vector`. For example,

```
M3Vector v2 = new M3Vector(6,5,4);
v1.add(v2).toString() → "(8,12,7)"
```

d. A `dot` method that computes the dot product of a receiving `M3Vector` and a parameter `M3Vector`. The usual mathematical formula applies: $a \cdot b = \sum_i a_i b_i$. For example,

$$(2,7,3) \cdot (6,5,4) \rightarrow 2 \cdot 6 + 7 \cdot 5 + 3 \cdot 4 \rightarrow 12 + 35 + 12 \rightarrow 59$$

```
v1.dot(v2) → 59
```

Other possible methods are scalar multiply, scalar add, scalar subtract, and cross product.

Exercise 14-112. Consider a class `Polynomial`, which represents polynomials of a single variable up to the fourth power—x^4. The sole instance variable of a `Polynomial` is an array of `double`, size 5. Each element of the array represents the coefficient of the `Polynomial` at the corresponding power:

element 0 is the coefficient of the x^0 term,
element 1 is the coefficient of the x^1 term,

. . .

element 4 is the coefficient of the x^4 term.

Thus, the polynomial $3.0 - 1.0x + 2.0x^2$ would be represented by the array:

3.0	–1.0	2.0	0.0	0.0

Give the Java code for the class `Polynomial`. Include a constructor that takes five `double`s as its parameters. These are the coefficients of the terms, as previously described. Include the method

```
public Polynomial add ( Polynomial p )
```

which computes the sum of two `Polynomial`s. Include the method

```
public double eval ( double x )
```

which computes the value of the `Polynomial` at this value of x. For our example above, `eval(3.0)` returns `18.0` because:

```
3.0 - 1.0 x + 2.0 x²
= 3.0 - 1.0 * 3.0 + 2.0 * (3.0)²
= 3.0 - 3.0 + 2.0 * 9.0
= 18.0
```

Exercise 14-113. A `Set` is a data structure that contains elements subject to the following rules:

- The order of the elements is not important.
- Within a `Set`, duplicates are not permitted.

Write and test the code for class `Set`, which represents sets of `int`s. Include the following methods:

- `static Set emptySet()`—Returns an empty `Set`.
- `Set add(int)`—Returns a `Set` that is equal to the receiving `Set`, except that the given `int` has been added as a new element in the `Set`.
- `Set delete(int)`—Returns a `Set` that is equal to the receiving `Set`, except that the specified `int` is deleted, if possible.
- `boolean contains(int)`—Determines whether the given `int` is a member of the receiving `Set`.
- `boolean equals(Set)`—Determines whether two `Set`s are equal.
- `Set union(Set)`—Computes the union of two `Set`s.
- `Set intersect(Set)`—Computes the intersection of two `Set`s.
- `Set difference(Set)`—Computes the set difference of two `Set`s.
- `static Set makeSet(int[])`—Takes an array of `int`s and produces the corresponding `Set`. Duplicates are eliminated.

CHAPTER FIFTEEN

Interfaces and Polymorphism

Chapter Objectives

- Understand interfaces in Java.
- Use Java's `Comparable` interface.
- Sort arrays of `Comparable` objects.
- Define and use the `Talker` interface.
- Understand and use polymorphism.
- Pass methods to other methods using Java's interface mechanism.
- Produce tables and bar graphs.
- Use Java's `MouseListener`, `MouseMotionListener`, and `KeyListener` interfaces to produce interactive GUI programs.

In this chapter and the next, we will learn two techniques with which the class designer can specify how classes are related. In this chapter we study *interfaces*, which enable us to stipulate that classes are related because they all offer a particular set of methods. In Chapter 16 we study *inheritance*, which is a way to specify that classes are related because one class inherits methods and/or instance variables from another. Interfaces and inheritance facilitate software development because they allow and encourage code reuse.

15.1 The Two Meanings of "Interface"

Java uses the word "interface" in two ways. These ways may appear different, but are actually quite similar.

In previous chapters, *interface* meant the set of public methods offered by a class. We stressed the difference between *interface* and *implementation* by stating that the same interface can be implemented in many different ways. We have a proverb: *Change the implementation, but don't change the interface.* We are free to reimplement a class using faster or different algorithms. So long as we preserve the interface, code that *uses* the changed class will run unchanged.

In the new meaning, *interface* describes a set of public methods that may be offered by any number of classes. A class is said to *implement an interface* if it publicly offers all of the methods listed for that interface.

Both uses of the word *interface* refer to the *public methods offered by a class or classes*.

15.2 Musical Instruments and the `CanPlayNotes` Interface

Consider the set of musical instruments that produce a continuum or a discrete set of musical pitches.[1] The interface `CanPlayNotes` might refer to any instrument that implements the method

```
public void play ( Pitch )
```

Notice that different instruments can implement this method in different ways:

- `Xylophone`—strike the appropriate key with a mallet.
- `Violin`—finger appropriately and then bow or pluck.
- `Flute`—finger appropriately and then blow air.
- `Piano`—strike the appropriate key with a finger.

Because each of these instruments provides the capability of playing a note, we say that they are related by the interface `CanPlayNotes`. In later sections, we'll see how such common functionality can be exploited in software development.

15.3 The `Comparable` Interface

`Comparable` is a built-in interface. If a class implements `Comparable`, then its elements have a *defined ordering*. The sole method required by interface `Comparable` is

```
int compareTo(Object)
```

---

[1] This excludes percussion instruments such as drums.

which takes two objects of the class and reports how they are ordered. We will shortly discuss the type of the parameter—Object—but for the moment, let's present the following definition:

If o1 and o2 are objects, then the following table shows the correspondence between the result of compareTo and the ordering of o1 and o2.

o1.compareTo(o2) < 0	**corresponds to**	o1 < o2
o1.compareTo(o2) == 0	**corresponds to**	o1 = o2
o1.compareTo(o2) > 0	**corresponds to**	o1 > o2

Prog1501 reads two Students, compares them with compareTo, and then prints the result. The first line of class Student has been changed:

```
class Student implements Comparable
```

It declares, clearly, that class Student implements the Comparable interface. This *requires* that class Student implement a method compareTo with the following prototype:

```
public int compareTo ( Object o )
```

Prog1501.java   Making **Students Comparable**

```
// Written by Barry Soroka
//
// Class Student implements Comparable.
// Read two Students and print the result of compareTo.
//
import java.io.*;
import java.util.Scanner;
import java.util.Arrays;
/////////////////////////////////////////////////////////////////////////////
class Prog1501
{
//-----------------------------------------------------------------------------
   public static void main ( String [] args ) throws Exception
   {
      Scanner kb = new Scanner(System.in);

      while ( true )
      {
         System.out.println();
         Student s1 = Student.read(System.out,kb);
         Student s2 = Student.read(System.out,kb);
```

```
                int compare = s1.compareTo(s2);
                System.out.println("\ns1.compareTo(s2) --> " + compare);
        }
    }
//--------------------------------------------------------------------------------
} // end class Prog1501
////////////////////////////////////////////////////////////////////////////////
class Student implements Comparable
{
    private String name;
    private int grade;
//--------------------------------------------------------------------------------
    public Student ( String name, int grade )
    {
        this.name = name;
        this.grade = grade;
    }
//--------------------------------------------------------------------------------
    public int compareTo ( Object o )
    {
        Student that = (Student) o;
        return ( this.grade - that.grade );
    }
//--------------------------------------------------------------------------------
    public String toString ()
    {
        return name + " (" + grade + ")";
    }
//--------------------------------------------------------------------------------
    public static Student read ( PrintStream ps, Scanner sc )
    {
        if ( ps != null ) ps.println("Reading a Student record ...");
        if ( ps != null ) ps.print("Enter the name: ");
        String name = sc.nextLine();
        if ( ps != null ) ps.print("Enter the grade: ");
        int grade = sc.nextInt(); sc.nextLine();
        return new Student(name,grade);
    }
//--------------------------------------------------------------------------------
} // end class Student
////////////////////////////////////////////////////////////////////////////////
```

| | **Test your skill with Exercise 15–1.** |

Now let's examine the implementation of compareTo inside class Student:

```
public int compareTo ( Object o )
{
   Student that = (Student) o;
   return ( this.grade - that.grade );
}
```

Notice two things:

- First, although we plan to compare Students, the parameter of the compareTo method has type *Object*. This is required by Java's definition of the Comparable interface. Students *are* Objects, so we don't need to do anything special when we invoke compareTo. However, we plan to compare the *grades* of the two Students, so we'll need to cast the Object to type Student before we can ask for its grade. The generic Object doesn't have a slot for grade, but once we cast it, we can access the grade.
- Second, we need to return an int, which reflects the *order* of the two Students according to the table we saw in the preceding definition. If the receiver Student has a higher grade than the parameter Student, then we want to return a positive int—direct subtraction of the two grades will work. It also works for the case where the two Students are considered equal (we're ignoring the name in our compareTo method). In addition, it works when the receiver is *less* than the parameter, because in that situation subtracting the grades will produce a negative number.

The driver of Prog1501 reads two Students, passes them to compareTo, and prints the result:

```
int compare = s1.compareTo(s2);
System.out.println("\ns1.compareTo(s2) --> " + compare);
```

Here are some sample runs:

Student s1	Student s2	Result
bill (98)	sue (80)	18
bill (98)	sally (100)	-2
bill (98)	annie (98)	0

As expected, compareTo is subtracting the grade of the parameter from the grade of the receiver, producing an integer result. These examples are consistent with the definition of compareTo, but I think the numbers are a bit hard to understand.

Prog1502 adds the code that interprets the results of compareTo:

```
int compare = s1.compareTo(s2);
System.out.print("\n" + s1);
if      ( compare > 0 ) System.out.print(" is greater than ");
else if ( compare < 0 ) System.out.print(" is less than " );
else                    System.out.print(" equals ");
System.out.println(s2);
```

Here's what is printed for the cases we tried above:

Student s1	Student s2	Prints out
bill (98)	sue (80)	bill (98) is larger than sue (80)
bill (98)	sally (100)	bill (98) is less than sally (100)
bill (98)	annie (98)	bill (98) equals annie (98)

Prog1502.java   Comparable Students

```
// Written by Barry Soroka
//
// Class Student implements Comparable.
// Read two Students, call compareTo,
// and print the relationship between the Students.
//
import java.io.*;
import java.util.Scanner;
import java.util.Arrays;
//////////////////////////////////////////////////////////////////////////////
class Prog1502
{
//----------------------------------------------------------------------------
   public static void main ( String [] args ) throws Exception
   {
      Scanner kb = new Scanner(System.in);

      while ( true )
      {
         System.out.println();
         Student s1 = Student.read(System.out,kb);
```

```
        Student s2 = Student.read(System.out,kb);
        int compare = s1.compareTo(s2);

        System.out.print("\n" + s1);
        if      ( compare > 0 ) System.out.print(" is greater than ");
        else if ( compare < 0 ) System.out.print(" is less than " );
        else                    System.out.print(" equals ");
        System.out.println(s2);
     }
  }
//-----------------------------------------------------------------------
} // end class Prog1502
/////////////////////////////////////////////////////////////////////////
class Student implements Comparable
{
   private String name;
   private int grade;
//-----------------------------------------------------------------------
   public Student ( String name, int grade )
   {
      this.name = name;
      this.grade = grade;
   }
//-----------------------------------------------------------------------
   public int compareTo ( Object o )
   {
      Student that = (Student) o;
      return ( this.grade - that.grade );
   }
//-----------------------------------------------------------------------
   public boolean equals ( Student that )
   {
      return this.name.equals(that.name)
             &&
             ( this.grade == that.grade );
   }
//-----------------------------------------------------------------------
   public String toString ()
   {
      return name + " (" + grade + ")";
   }
//-----------------------------------------------------------------------
   public static Student read ( PrintStream ps, Scanner sc )
   {
      if ( ps != null ) ps.println("Reading a Student record ...");
```

```
      if ( ps != null ) ps.print("Enter the name: ");
      String name = sc.nextLine();
      if ( ps != null ) ps.print("Enter the grade: ");
      int grade = sc.nextInt(); sc.nextLine();
      return new Student(name,grade);
   }
//--------------------------------------------------------------------
} // end class Student
////////////////////////////////////////////////////////////////////////
```

Sometimes you will find it useful to define methods like isLessThan, isGreaterThan, and isEqualTo:

```
      public boolean isLessThan ( Student that )
      {
          return this.compareTo(that) < 0;
      }

      public boolean isEqualTo ( Student that )
      {
          return this.compareTo(that) == 0;
      }

      public boolean isGreaterThan ( Student that )
      {
          return this.compareTo(that) > 0;
      }
```

By defining and using these predicates, we can relieve the user from having to think about the integers returned by compareTo. This can make the code more readable.

Note that something is strange about the method isEqualTo: If Student s1 is Bill (98) and Student s2 is Sue (98), then s1.isEqualTo(s2) returns true. On the one hand, they *are* equal with respect to grade. On the other hand, they are clearly *not* equal if we were to require equality of *both* name and grade—an equals method would check *both* of the instance variables.

 Test your skill with Exercise 15–2.

15.4   Sorting Arrays of Comparable Objects

Once we have defined an interface, we can write methods that perform useful work on any item that implements that interface. Our particular example will be with class Student, which implements Comparable. The Java API provides a method, `sort`, which can sort an array of any class that implements `Compa-rable`. In particular, it can sort an array of `Students`. The method is overloaded, and the version we'll study is found in the built-in class `Arrays`:

```
sort(Object[] a, int fromIndex, int toIndex)
```

This sorts part of an array of `Objects`, beginning at position `fromIndex` and ending in the position before `toIndex`. Of course, the `Objects` must implement interface `Comparable`.

Prog1503 provides the relevant code for class `Student` and class `Section`, and a driver to test them. Here's the method that sorts the array of `Students` in a `Section`:

```
public void sort()
{
    Arrays.sort(a,0,used);
}
```

This sorts the entire array `a`, from position 0 to position `used-1`.

Prog1503.java   Using **Arrays.sort** on an Array of Students

```java
// Written by Barry Soroka
//
// Make class Student implement Comparable.
// Use Arrays.sort to sort an array of Students.
//
import java.io.*;
import java.util.Scanner;
import java.util.Arrays;
//////////////////////////////////////////////////////////////////////////////
class Prog1503
{
//------------------------------------------------------------------------------
    public static void main ( String [] args ) throws Exception
    {
        Scanner kb = new Scanner(System.in);

        System.out.print("\nEnter name of a file of Students: ");
        String filename = kb.nextLine();

        Section section = new Section(filename);

        System.out.println("\nIn forward order, students are:");
        section.print(System.out);

        System.out.println("\nNow sorting ...");
```

```
         section.sort();

         System.out.println("\nIn forward order, students are:");
         section.print(System.out);
      }
//------------------------------------------------------------------------
} // end class Prog1503
////////////////////////////////////////////////////////////////////////
class Section
{
   private Student [] a;
   private int used;
   private final int INIT_SIZE = 20;
//------------------------------------------------------------------------
   public void sort()
   {
      Arrays.sort(a,0,used);
   }
//------------------------------------------------------------------------
   public Section ( Student[] a )
   {
      this.a = a;
      used = a.length;
   }
//------------------------------------------------------------------------
   public Section ( Student[] a, int used )
   {
      this.a = a;
      this.used = used;
   }
//------------------------------------------------------------------------
   public Section ( String filename ) throws Exception
   {
      Scanner sc = new Scanner(new File(filename));

      a = new Student[INIT_SIZE];
      used = 0;

      while ( sc.hasNext() )
      {
         Student s = Student.read(null,sc);

         if ( used == a.length )
         {
            Student[] newA = new Student[2*a.length+1];
            for ( int i = 0 ; i < used ; i++ ) newA[i] = a[i];
            newA[used] = s;
            used++;
```

```
                a = newA;
           }
           else
           {
                a[used] = s;
                used++;
           }
        }
    }
//-----------------------------------------------------------------
    public void print ( PrintStream ps )
    {
        for ( int i = 0 ; i < used ; i++ )
        {
            ps.println(a[i]);
        }
    }
//-----------------------------------------------------------------
} // end class Section
/////////////////////////////////////////////////////////////////////
class Student implements Comparable
{
    private String name;
    private int grade;
//-----------------------------------------------------------------
    public Student ( String name, int grade )
    {
        this.name = name;
        this.grade = grade;
    }
//-----------------------------------------------------------------
    public int compareTo ( Object o )
    {
        Student that = (Student) o;
        return ( this.grade - that.grade );
    }
//-----------------------------------------------------------------
    public boolean equals ( Student that )
    {
        return this.name.equals(that.name)
                &&
                ( this.grade == that.grade );
    }
//-----------------------------------------------------------------
    public String toString ()
```

```
   {
      return name + " (" + grade + ")";
   }
//------------------------------------------------------------------------
   public static Student read ( PrintStream ps, Scanner sc )
   {
      if ( ps != null ) ps.println("Reading a Student record ...");
      if ( ps != null ) ps.print("Enter the name: ");
      String name = sc.nextLine();
      if ( ps != null ) ps.print("Enter the grade: ");
      int grade = sc.nextInt(); sc.nextLine();
      return new Student(name,grade);
   }
//------------------------------------------------------------------------
} // end class Student
//////////////////////////////////////////////////////////////////////////
```

In Chapter 19 we'll write our own code for sorting. Our only purpose in using Java's built-in sort routines is to illustrate how interfaces can be used.

 Test your skill with Exercises 15–3 through 15–6.

15.5 Comparing Objects on More Than One Attribute

Sometimes we want to sort an array of `Objects` based on more than one attribute. For example, we might want to sort `BankAccounts` based first on `name` and then on `accountNumber`. The sort functions of modern spreadsheets generally allow the user to sort on a variety of attributes, with a choice for each of *sort ascending* versus *sort descending*.

 Test your skill with Exercises 15–7 through 15–12.

15.6 Sorting Arrays of Primitive Datatypes

In Sections 15.4–15.5, we've seen how Java's `sort` methods can sort arrays of items from classes that implement the `Comparable` interface. Java has over-loaded the `sort` method so that we can also sort arrays of *primitive datatypes* such as `int`. For example, suppose we define an array of `int`s such as this:

```
int[] a = { 3, 1, 4, 1, 5, 9 };
```

The following statement allows us to sort this array using the same syntax we used before:

```
Arrays.sort(a,0,a.length);
```

Test your skill with Exercise 15–13.

15.7   Defining Our Own Interface—Talker

For our first interface, let's think about some classes that represent creatures that talk—Dog, Cat, Human, and Mime.[2] Each of these classes implements an interface Talker, which contains the single method

```
public void talk ( PrintStream ps )
```

The following code defines the new interface:

```
/////////////////////////////////////////////////
interface Talker
{
    public void talk ( PrintStream ps );
}
/////////////////////////////////////////////////
```

The keyword interface defines this as an interface rather than a class, and whatever prototypes occur in its scope are required of any class that implements Talker. We give the *prototype* of method talk, but we omit the *body* of the method—we put a semicolon directly after the prototype. (Note that the Style Sheet used by this text requires that interface definitions be surrounded by rows of slashes, in the same manner as class definitions.)

Now we need to add the required methods to the classes, which will implement Talker. Dog and Cat will use the default constructor:

```
/////////////////////////////////////////////////////////////////////////////
class Dog implements Talker
{
//---------------------------------------------------------------------
    public void talk ( PrintStream ps ) { ps.println("Woof!"); }
```

---

[2] Mimes don't speak, of course, but we'll consider silence another form of talking.

```
//---------------------------------------------------------------
}
///////////////////////////////////////////////////////////////////
class Cat implements Talker
{
//---------------------------------------------------------------
   public void talk ( PrintStream ps ) { ps.println("Meow!"); }
//---------------------------------------------------------------
}
///////////////////////////////////////////////////////////////////
```

Here is the code for class `Human`:

```
///////////////////////////////////////////////////////////////////
class Human implements Talker
{
   private String name;
//---------------------------------------------------------------
   public Human ( String name ) { this.name = name; }
//---------------------------------------------------------------
   public void talk ( PrintStream ps )
   {
      ps.println("My name is " + name + ".");
   }
//---------------------------------------------------------------
}
///////////////////////////////////////////////////////////////////
```

Each instance of `Human` has a `name`, which is set when the instance is created. Notice that the `talk` method uses the `name`. Implementing the interface requires that we provide a `talk` method with the specified prototype, but inside that method we can put any legal code that we want.

Here is the code for `Mime`:

```
///////////////////////////////////////////////////////////////////
class Mime implements Talker
{
   private String name;
//---------------------------------------------------------------
   public Mime ( String name ) { this.name = name; }
//---------------------------------------------------------------
   public void talk ( PrintStream ps )
   {
```

```
    ps.println("");
  }
//--------------------------------------------------------------------
}
////////////////////////////////////////////////////////////////////
```

It's quite similar to the code for `Human`, but because `Mimes` don't speak, the `talk` method prints only a blank line.

Test your skill with Exercises 15–14 and 15–15.

15.8   **Variables of Type** `Talker`

Previously, we saw that a class that implements `Comparable` can be sorted by Java's built-in method `Arrays.sort`. Now we have defined our own interface, `Talker`. It makes no sense to *sort* it, so the question arises: What *can* we do with it?

Let's start by examining the legal statement

```
Talker t;
```

This says that, from now on, the variable `t` may only refer to instances of classes that implement interface `Talker`. Thus, `t` can refer to a `Dog` or a `Cat` or a `Human` or a `Mime`. This is news. Compare this to the statement

```
Scanner sc;
```

which restricts variable `sc` to objects from the class `Scanner`. The variable `t` is not restricted to objects of a single class; it can refer to an instance of *any* class that implements `Talker`.

Thus, the following Java statements are legal:

```
t = new Dog();
t = new Cat();
t = new Mime("Marcel");
t = new Human("Ashton");
```

and the variable `t` may refer to an object from any class that implements `Talker`. We will say that any such object *is* a `Talker`.

We can also use the statement

```
t.talk()
```

which sends the `talk()` message to the object to which `t` refers. This statement is legal because `t` can refer *only* to `Talker`s, and all `Talker`s must provide a method `talk()`. The previous four-line program can be modified as follows:

```
t = new Dog();
t.talk();
t = new Cat();
t.talk();
t = new Mime("Marcel");
t.talk();
t = new Human("Ashton");
t.talk();
```

and we'll observe the output:

```
Woof!
Meow!

My name is Ashton.
```

Notice the blank line produced by the `Mime Marcel`.

15.9   Arrays of Type `Talker`

We have seen how a single variable can refer to any object that implements `Talker`. We can also declare an *array* of `Talker`:

```
Talker[] a  = new Talker[5];
```

where each element of `a` must refer to some object that implements `Talker`. The elements of `a` don't all have to refer to objects from the same *class*. The following code is legal:

```
t[0] = new Dog();
t[1] = new Cat();
t[2] = new Human("Bill");
t[3] = new Mime("Marcel");
t[4] = new Human("Sue");
```

Arrays of this sort are useful in gathering together objects from classes that are related, because they all provide the same method—`talk()`, in the current case.

CanPlayNotes

At the beginning of this chapter, we discussed an interface `CanPlayNotes`, which described classes that contained a `play(Pitch)` method. We can have an array of such instruments:

```
CanPlayNotes[] quartet = new CanPlayNotes[4];
quartet[0] = new Violin(...);
quartet[1] = new Violin(...);
quartet[2] = new Viola(...);
quartet[3] = new Cello(...);
```

Shapes

Another example involves shapes. Classes `Rectangle`, `Square`, `Circle`, and `Polygon` are related because they all provide a method

```
public double area()
```

If we define an interface `ClosedCurve` with method `area()`, then we can create an *array* of `ClosedCurve` with references to any of the classes named above. Of course, these classes may also have other methods in common—`getLocation()`, `grow()`, `shrink()`, `move(...)`, and `rotate(...)` are good examples.

15.10 Polymorphism

In previous sections we've seen how a variable can refer to instances of different classes, provided that the classes are related by an `interface`. Typical code is:

```
Talker t;
t = new Dog();
t = new Cat();
t = new Mime("Marcel");
t = new Human("Ashton");
```

We use the word *polymorphism* to describe this phenomenon. The adjective is *polymorphic*, which comes from the Greek words meaning "many-shaped."

We saw how an *array* can contain references to objects from different classes provided that they all implement the same interface. Here's the code we developed:

```
Talker[] a  = new Talker[5];
a[0] = new Dog();
a[1] = new Cat();
a[2] = new Human("Bill");
a[3] = new Mime("Marcel");
a[4] = new Human("Sue");
```

Our next step is to use a `for` loop to step through the elements of a polymorphic array:

```
for ( int i = 0 ; i < 5 ; i++ )
    a[i].talk(System.out);
```

As `i` moves from `0` to `4`, `a[i]` will always refer to an object that implements `Talker`, but `a[i]` will refer to objects from *different classes*. Because `a[i]` implements `Talker`, the statement

```
a[i].talk(System.out)
```

> **Early binding** When the compiler can determine the method that is being used in a statement.
> **Polymorphism** When a variable can refer to instances of several different classes.
> **Late binding** When we can determine which method is used only at run-time.

will always be legal, but it will invoke *different talk methods* depending on the class of the object to which `a[i]` refers.

This has consequences on compiling. At compile-time, we can often look at the name of a method and determine the exact Java code to which it refers. We call this *early binding*. Not so with statements involving polymorphism! Consider the statement

```
a[i].talk(System.out)
```

`a[i]` can refer to an instance coming from one of several classes, and each has its own `talk` method. We don't know the exact code that will be invoked. Only at run-time will we know the type of the object to which `a[i]` refers. *Polymorphism* is often used to refer to this *late binding* phenomenon. The compiler produces code that determines, at run-time, which class is under scrutiny and which method needs to be invoked.

Here's the `for` loop we've been discussing:

```
for ( int i = 0 ; i < 5 ; i++ )
    a[i].talk(System.out);
```

It produces the following output:

```
Woof!
Meow!
My name is Bill.

My name is Sue.
```

`Prog1504` presents the code for the example we've just discussed.

Prog1504.java   **Interface Talker**

```java
// Written by Barry Soroka
//
// Interface Talker and polymorphism.
//
import java.io.*;
import java.util.*;
/////////////////////////////////////////////////////////////////////
class Prog1504
{
//-------------------------------------------------------------------
    public static void main (String [] args) throws Exception
    {
        final int MAX = 5;

        Talker [] t = new Talker[MAX];

        t[0] = new Dog();
        t[1] = new Cat();
        t[2] = new Human("Bill");
        t[3] = new Mime("Marcel");
        t[4] = new Human("Sue");

        for ( int i = 0 ; i < MAX ; i++ )
            t[i].talk(System.out);
    }
//-------------------------------------------------------------------
} // end class Prog1504
/////////////////////////////////////////////////////////////////////
interface Talker
{
    public void talk ( PrintStream ps );
}
/////////////////////////////////////////////////////////////////////
class Dog implements Talker
{
```

```
//-------------------------------------------------------------------
//    public Dog() {}
//-------------------------------------------------------------------
   public void talk ( PrintStream ps ) { ps.println("Woof!"); }
//-------------------------------------------------------------------
}
/////////////////////////////////////////////////////////////////////
class Cat implements Talker
{
//-------------------------------------------------------------------
//    public Cat() {}
//-------------------------------------------------------------------
   public void talk ( PrintStream ps ) { ps.println("Meow!"); }
//-------------------------------------------------------------------
}
/////////////////////////////////////////////////////////////////////
class Human implements Talker
{
   private String name;
//-------------------------------------------------------------------
   public Human ( String name ) { this.name = name; }
//-------------------------------------------------------------------
   public void talk ( PrintStream ps )
   {
      ps.println("My name is " + name + ".");
   }
//-------------------------------------------------------------------
}
/////////////////////////////////////////////////////////////////////
class Mime implements Talker
{
   private String name;
//-------------------------------------------------------------------
   public Mime ( String name ) { this.name = name; }
//-------------------------------------------------------------------
   public void talk ( PrintStream ps )
   {
      ps.println("");
   }
//-------------------------------------------------------------------
}
/////////////////////////////////////////////////////////////////////
```

More Polymorphism

Let's examine a similar problem. Consider the code:

```
for ( int i = 0 ; i < 5 ; i++ )
    System.out.println(a[i]);
```

As i goes around the loop, a[i] may refer to objects from different classes for every value of i, and the run-time system must invoke the correct toString method. In Chapter 16, we'll learn that this form of polymorphism is due not to interfaces but to *inheritance*, another way by which classes may be related.

> **Test your skill with Exercises 15–16 through 15–19.**

15.11   Before Polymorphism (The Olden Days)

Before the advent of polymorphism, each programmer had to track the type of every object in an array. Instead of today's code

```
for ( int i = 0 ; i < 5 ; i++ )
    a[i].talk(System.out);
```

programmers had to write:

```
for ( int i = 0 ; i < 5 ; i++ )
{
    if      ( a[i] is a Dog ) invoke the talk method of class Dog;
    else if ( a[i] is a Cat ) invoke the talk method of class Cat;
    else if ( a[i] is a Human ) invoke the talk method of class Human;
    else if ( a[i] is a Mime ) invoke the talk method of class Mime;
}
```

If a programmer needed to add a new class with method Talk, he or she needed to add another if statement. Today, we need merely to add the implements Talker phrase to the header of the class, and the correct talk method will automatically be used when the talk message is sent to an object of the new type.

15.12   Multiple Interfaces—Scanner **and** Printer

A class may implement *more than one interface*. As a basis for discussion, let's assume a class `Image`, which represents a 2-D image such as a photograph or a page of text. Interface *Printer* applies to a device that, with a method `print`, takes an `Image` and prints it:

```
//////////////////////////////////////////////////////////////////////////
interface Printer
{
//-------------------------------------------------------------------------
   public void print(Image im);
//-------------------------------------------------------------------------
}
//////////////////////////////////////////////////////////////////////////
```

The relevant method is `print`. Interface *Scanner* applies to a device that, with a method `scan`, captures and returns an `Image`:

```
//////////////////////////////////////////////////////////////////////////
interface Scanner
{
//-------------------------------------------------------------------------
   public Image scan();
//-------------------------------------------------------------------------
}
//////////////////////////////////////////////////////////////////////////
```

A *Copier* possesses both of these abilities: It can scan the page or photograph presented, and it can print the `Image` it acquires. The header of class `Copier` is:

```
class Copier implements Printer, Scanner
```

which illustrates how we describe a class that implements more than one `interface`. Here is a sketch of the code for class `Copier`:

```
//////////////////////////////////////////////////////////////////////////
class Copier implements Printer, Scanner
{
```

```
//-----------------------------------------------------------------
   public void print ( Image im )
   {
       appropriate action
   }
//-----------------------------------------------------------------
   public Image scan()
   {
       appropriate action
       return new Image();
   }
//-----------------------------------------------------------------
   public void copy()
   {
       print(scan());
   }
//-----------------------------------------------------------------
   public void copyN (int n)
   {
       Image im = scan();
       for ( int i = 0 ; i < n ; i++ ) print(im);
   }
//-----------------------------------------------------------------
}
/////////////////////////////////////////////////////////////////////
```

The `copy` method uses `scan` to acquire an `Image`, and then uses `print` to produce the copy:

```
public void copy()
{
    print(scan());
}
```

The method `copyN` can be used to produce multiple copies of a single original:

```
public void copyN (int n)
{
    Image im = scan();
    for ( int i = 0 ; i < n ; i++ ) print(im);
}
```

Prog1505 gathers all the classes and interfaces for this example. Note that this code compiles even though it's only a sketch of a full implementation.

Prog1505.java   Interfaces Scan and Print

```
// Written by Barry Soroka
//
// Multiple interfaces -- Scan and Print.
//
import java.io.*;
//////////////////////////////////////////////////////////////////////////
class Prog1505
{
//-------------------------------------------------------------------------
   public static void main (String [] args) throws Exception
   {
   }
//-------------------------------------------------------------------------
} // end class Prog1505
//////////////////////////////////////////////////////////////////////////
class Image {}
//////////////////////////////////////////////////////////////////////////
interface Printer
{
//-------------------------------------------------------------------------
   public void print(Image im);
//-------------------------------------------------------------------------
}
//////////////////////////////////////////////////////////////////////////
interface Scanner
{
//-------------------------------------------------------------------------
   public Image scan();
//-------------------------------------------------------------------------
}
//////////////////////////////////////////////////////////////////////////
class Copier implements Printer, Scanner
{
//-------------------------------------------------------------------------
   public void print ( Image im )
   {
     // insert appropriate action
   }
//-------------------------------------------------------------------------
   public Image scan()
```

```
   {
      // insert appropriate action
      return new Image();
   }
//------------------------------------------------------------------
   public void copy()
   {
      print(scan());
   }
//------------------------------------------------------------------
   public void copyN (int n)
   {
      Image im = scan();
      for ( int i = 0 ; i < n ; i++ ) print(im);
   }
//------------------------------------------------------------------
}
////////////////////////////////////////////////////////////////////
```

Test your skill with Exercises 15–20 and 15–21.

15.13   Passing Methods Using Interfaces

An important but not obvious category of programming involves *passing one method to another method*. For example, we might want to have one method draw a *graph* of another method—the input to the graphing method is *itself* a method, namely a method that represents a function such as $f(x)$. Similar methods can create a table of values, perform numerical integration, or find the roots of a given equation.

The Interface

Prog1506 provides the code and a driver for taking a method and printing a table of values. We start by defining an interface Function1D, which represents a 1-D function:

```
////////////////////////////////////////////////////////////////////
interface Function1D
{
//------------------------------------------------------------------
   public int valueAt ( int i );
//------------------------------------------------------------------
} // end interface Function1D
////////////////////////////////////////////////////////////////////
```

Every class that implements this interface must provide a method

```
public int valueAt ( int i );
```

which takes one `int` and returns another. This is how we represent a function.

Prog1506.java   Passing One Method to Another Using an Interface

```java
// Written by Barry Soroka
//
// Using an interface to pass one method to another method --
// print a table of values.
//
import java.io.*;
/////////////////////////////////////////////////////////////////////////
class Prog1506
{
   private static final int MAX = 5;
//------------------------------------------------------------------------
   public static void main ( String [] args ) throws Exception
   {
      SquareFunction sq = new SquareFunction();
      makeTable(sq,"Square");
      CubeFunction cu = new CubeFunction();
      makeTable(cu,"Cube");
   }
//------------------------------------------------------------------------
   private static void makeTable ( Function1D f, String label )
   {
      System.out.println("\nTable for function " + label);
      for ( int i = 0 ; i < MAX ; i++ )
      {
          System.out.printf("%3d %8d\n",i,f.valueAt(i));
      }
   }
//------------------------------------------------------------------------
} // end class Prog1506
/////////////////////////////////////////////////////////////////////////
class SquareFunction implements Function1D
{
//------------------------------------------------------------------------
   public int valueAt ( int i ) { return i*i; }
//------------------------------------------------------------------------
} // end class SquareFunction
/////////////////////////////////////////////////////////////////////////
```

```
class CubeFunction implements Function1D
{
//-------------------------------------------------------------------
    public int valueAt ( int i ) { return i*i*i; }
//-------------------------------------------------------------------
} // end class CubeFunction
///////////////////////////////////////////////////////////////////////
interface Function1D
{
//-------------------------------------------------------------------
    public int valueAt ( int i );
//-------------------------------------------------------------------
} // end interface Function1D
///////////////////////////////////////////////////////////////////////
```

Creating a Table

Class `Prog1506` defines `MAX`

```
        private static final int MAX = 5;
```

This specifies the number of rows to be printed in the table. Then we have a helper function, `makeTable`, which takes two parameters:

- An object `f`, which implements `Function1D`. This object contains a method `valueAt(int)`, which represents a 1-D integer function.
- A `String`, which will be printed at the top of the table of values.

Inside `makeTable`, we find the code for a loop:

```
        for ( int i = 0 ; i < MAX ; i++ )
        {
            System.out.println( i + "\t" + f.valueAt(i) );
        }
```

For each integer value `i` from 0 to `MAX-1`, `makeTable` calls `f.valueAt(i)` to compute the value of function `f` at the specified value. Each row of the table contains i and $f(i)$.

Defining 1-D Functions

`Prog1506` presents two classes that represent 1-D functions: `SquareFunction` and `CubeFunction`. Their code is as follows:

```
///////////////////////////////////////////////////////////
class SquareFunction implements Function1D
{
//------------------------------------------------------------
    public int valueAt ( int i ) { return i*i; }
//------------------------------------------------------------
} // end class SquareFunction
///////////////////////////////////////////////////////////
class CubeFunction implements Function1D
{
//------------------------------------------------------------
    public int valueAt ( int i ) { return i*i*i; }
//------------------------------------------------------------
} // end class CubeFunction
///////////////////////////////////////////////////////////
```

Both of these classes implement `Function1D` and provide the appropriate method

```
public int valueAt(int)
```

The Driver

The driver in `Prog1506` calls `makeTable` twice: once for `SquareFunction` and once for `CubeFunction`:

```
SquareFunction sq = new SquareFunction();
makeTable(sq,"Square");
CubeFunction cu = new CubeFunction();
makeTable(cu,"Cube");
```

You may find this code inefficient because every possible instance of `Square-Function` will be identical; ditto for `CubeFunction`. However, it's not difficult to envision classes containing more than one function:

- `Quadratic (3,-2,7)` might represent $f(x) = 3x^2 - 2x + 7$.
- `int[] a = {4,-2,3,1,7}` and `Polynomial(a)` might represent $4 - 2x + 3x^2 + x^3 + 7x^4$.

Output

Here's the output of `Prog1506`:

```
Table for function Square

0            0

1            1

2            4

3            9

4            16


Table for function Cube

0            0

1            1

2            8

3            27

4            64
```

We have successfully produced tables for $f(x) = x^2$ and $f(x) = x^3$!

Test your skill with Exercises 15–22 and 15–23.

15.14   Bar Graphs

In Section 15.13, we used an interface in order to write a method that could take another method and produce a table of its values. Now we'll examine the use of an interface in order to pass a method to another method, which in turn produces *bar graphs*—values that will be represented by a sequence of plus signs ("+"). `Prog1507` presents the code and a driver.

Prog1507.java   **Histogram**

```java
// Written by Barry Soroka
//
// Pass a Quadratic using interface Function1D --
// print a histogram -- truncate to available width.
//
import java.io.*;
//////////////////////////////////////////////////////////////////////////////
class Prog1507
```

```
{
   private static final int MAXROWS = 20;
   private static final int MAXWIDTH = 60;
//------------------------------------------------------------------
   public static void main ( String [] args ) throws Exception
   {
      Quadratic q = new Quadratic(0.0,12.65,-0.666);
      makeGraph(q);
   }
//------------------------------------------------------------------
   private static void makeGraph ( Function1D f )
   {
      for ( int i = 0 ; i < MAXROWS ; i++ )
      {
         System.out.printf("%5.1f %5.1f",(double)i,f.valueAt(i));
         int width = (int)f.valueAt(i);
         if ( width > MAXWIDTH ) width = MAXWIDTH;
         if ( width < 0 ) width = 0;
         for ( int j = 0 ; j < width ; j++ ) System.out.print("+");
         System.out.println();
      }
   }
//------------------------------------------------------------------
} // end class Prog1507
//////////////////////////////////////////////////////////////////////
class Quadratic implements Function1D
{
   private double a0, a1, a2;
//------------------------------------------------------------------
   public Quadratic ( double a0, double a1, double a2 )
   {
      this.a0 = a0;
      this.a1 = a1;
      this.a2 = a2;
   }
//------------------------------------------------------------------
   public double valueAt ( double x ) { return a0 +  a1*x + a2*x*x; }
//------------------------------------------------------------------
} // end class Quadratic
//////////////////////////////////////////////////////////////////////
interface Function1D
{
//------------------------------------------------------------------
   public double valueAt ( double x );
```

```
//---------------------------------------------------------------------------
} // end interface Function1D
///////////////////////////////////////////////////////////////////////////
```

The main program contains the driving code:

```
Quadratic q = new Quadratic(0.0,12.65,-0.666);
makeGraph(q);
```

Note that the interface has been changed so that it uses *doubles*:

```
interface Function1D
{
//----------------------------------------------------
   public double valueAt ( double x );
//----------------------------------------------------
} // end interface Function1D
```

The code for class `Prog1507` relies on two `static` variables. `MAXROWS` is the number of rows in the graph:

```
private static final int MAXROWS = 20;
```

`MAXWIDTH` is the number of columns allowed for the bar graph:

```
private static final int MAXWIDTH = 60;
```

The method `makeGraph` takes one parameter—an object `f`, which implements `Function1D`. For each row in the loop, our code first prints x and $f(x)$, both formatted. Then we compute the number of plus signs we'll print for this row:

```
int width = (int)f.valueAt(i);
```

We *clip* this number into the range [0, `MAXWIDTH`]:

```
if ( width > MAXWIDTH ) width = MAXWIDTH;
if ( width < 0 ) width = 0;
```

Finally, we print the sequence of plus signs and we terminate the row:

```
for ( int j = 0 ; j < width ; j++ )
    System.out.print("+");
System.out.println();
```

Here is the output of `Prog1507`:

```
0.0    0.0
1.0    12.0+++++++++++
2.0    22.6++++++++++++++++++++++
3.0    32.0++++++++++++++++++++++++++++++++
4.0    39.9+++++++++++++++++++++++++++++++++++++++
5.0    46.6++++++++++++++++++++++++++++++++++++++++++++++
6.0    51.9+++++++++++++++++++++++++++++++++++++++++++++++++++
7.0    55.9+++++++++++++++++++++++++++++++++++++++++++++++++++++++
8.0    58.6++++++++++++++++++++++++++++++++++++++++++++++++++++++++++
9.0    59.9+++++++++++++++++++++++++++++++++++++++++++++++++++++++++++
10.0   59.9+++++++++++++++++++++++++++++++++++++++++++++++++++++++++++
11.0   58.6++++++++++++++++++++++++++++++++++++++++++++++++++++++++++
12.0   55.9+++++++++++++++++++++++++++++++++++++++++++++++++++++++
13.0   51.9+++++++++++++++++++++++++++++++++++++++++++++++++++
14.0   46.6++++++++++++++++++++++++++++++++++++++++++++++
15.0   39.9+++++++++++++++++++++++++++++++++++++++
16.0   31.9++++++++++++++++++++++++++++++++
17.0   22.6++++++++++++++++++++++
18.0   11.9+++++++++++
19.0   -0.1
```

 Test your skill with Exercises 15–24 through 15–26.

15.15 GUI: The `MouseListener` Interface

In prior chapters, we have seen several interfaces involving GUI:

- `ActionListener` had method `actionPerformed` and watched for completion of a `JTextField` or selection of a radio button.
- `ItemListener` had method `itemStateChanged` and watched for selecting and deselecting check boxes.

The programs in the following GUI section illustrate the use of three other interfaces: `MouseListener`, `MouseMotionListener`, and `KeyListener`.

Prog1508.java is an application that interacts with the mouse. Whenever the user clicks the mouse, a circular green spot is left on the panel.

Prog1508.java   **Mouse Press Makes a Spot**

```java
// Written by Barry Soroka
//
// Display a new spot each time the mouse is pressed.
//
import java.awt.*;
import java.awt.event.*;
import javax.swing.*;
/////////////////////////////////////////////////////////////////////////////
class Prog1508
{
//------------------------------------------------------------------------
   public static void main (String[] args)
   {
      JFrame frame = new JFrame ("Polygon");
      frame.setDefaultCloseOperation (JFrame.EXIT_ON_CLOSE);

      MyPanel mp = new MyPanel();

      frame.getContentPane().add(mp);
      frame.pack();
      frame.setVisible(true);
   }
//------------------------------------------------------------------------
} // end class Prog1508
/////////////////////////////////////////////////////////////////////////////
class MyPanel extends JPanel
{
   private Point[] points;
   private int n;
//------------------------------------------------------------------------
   public MyPanel()
   {
      points = new Point[100];
      int n = 0;

      addMouseListener ( new DotsListener() );

      setBackground(Color.BLACK);
      setPreferredSize(new Dimension(400,400));
   }
//------------------------------------------------------------------------
   public void paintComponent ( Graphics page )
   {
```

```
        final int SIZE = 4;
        super.paintComponent(page);
        page.setColor(Color.YELLOW);

        for ( int i = 0 ; i < n ; i++ )
            page.fillOval( points[i].x-SIZE, points[i].y-SIZE, SIZE*2, SIZE*2 );
    }
//-----------------------------------------------------------------------------
//////////////////////////////////////////////////////////////////////////////
private class DotsListener implements MouseListener
{
//-----------------------------------------------------------------------------
    public void mousePressed ( MouseEvent event )
    {
        points[n] = event.getPoint();
        n++;
        repaint();
    }
//-----------------------------------------------------------------------------
    public void mouseClicked ( MouseEvent event ) {}
//-----------------------------------------------------------------------------
    public void mouseReleased ( MouseEvent event ) {}
//-----------------------------------------------------------------------------
    public void mouseEntered ( MouseEvent event ) {}
//-----------------------------------------------------------------------------
    public void mouseExited ( MouseEvent event ) {}
//-----------------------------------------------------------------------------
} // end class DotsListener
//////////////////////////////////////////////////////////////////////////////
} // end class MyPanel
//////////////////////////////////////////////////////////////////////////////
```

The interface `MouseListener` requires provision of five methods:

1. `void mousePressed(MouseEvent)`, which is activated when the left mouse button is pressed.
2. `void mouseClicked(MouseEvent)`, which is activated when the left mouse button is pressed and released.
3. `void mouseReleased(MouseEvent)`, which is activated when the left mouse button is released.
4. `void mouseEntered(MouseEvent)`, which is activated when the mouse enters the component (e.g., `JPanel`).
5. `void mouseExited(MouseEvent)`, which is activated when the mouse leaves the component.

In Prog1508.java we have provided all five methods, but only mousePressed has a nonempty body. Notice that MyPanel maintains an array of Points. A Point is a Java object with two public[3] instance variables—x and y—and it stands for a point in 2-D space. We "turn on" the DotsListener with the statement

```
addMouseListener(new DotsListener())
```

When the mouse is pressed, the mousePressed method is called. It gets the Point at which the mouse was clicked, stores the Point in the next location of the Points array, and orders a repaint of the screen. The paintComponent method runs through the elements of Points, drawing a small green circle at each Point. After 100 mouse presses, we encounter an ArrayIndexOutOf-BoundsException because we try to store the 101st Point in an array with room for only 100 Points.

Test your skill with Exercises 15–27 through 15–31.

15.16   GUI: The MouseMotionListener Interface

This interface has two methods:

1. void mouseMoved(MouseEvent), which is activated whenever the mouse is moved.
2. void mouseDragged(MouseEvent), which is activated whenever the mouse is moved *while the left mouse button is depressed.*

We can get the Point to which the mouse has been moved or dragged by requesting getPoint() of the argument.

Prog1509.java is an application that draws a "rubber-band line" from a central point to wherever the mouse is dragged.

Prog1509.java   Rubber-Band Line

```
// Written by Barry Soroka
//
// Display a rubber-band line from a center point.
//
import java.awt.*;
import java.awt.event.*;
```

---

[3] This should be rare. Instance variables are usually private.

```java
import javax.swing.*;
//////////////////////////////////////////////////////////////////////////////
class Prog1509
{
//---------------------------------------------------------------------------

    public static void main (String[] args)
    {
        JFrame frame = new JFrame ("Rubber Band");
        frame.setDefaultCloseOperation (JFrame.EXIT_ON_CLOSE);

        MyPanel mp = new MyPanel();

        frame.getContentPane().add(mp);
        frame.pack();
        frame.setVisible(true);
    }
//---------------------------------------------------------------------------
} // end class Prog1509
//////////////////////////////////////////////////////////////////////////////
class MyPanel extends JPanel
{
    private Point point1;
    private Point point2;
//---------------------------------------------------------------------------
    public MyPanel()
    {
        point1 = new Point(200,200);
        point2 = point1;

        LineListener listener = new LineListener();

        addMouseMotionListener(listener);

        setBackground(Color.BLACK);
        setPreferredSize(new Dimension(400,400));
    }
//---------------------------------------------------------------------------
    public void paintComponent ( Graphics page )
    {
        super.paintComponent(page);

        page.setColor(Color.YELLOW);
        page.drawLine( point1.x, point1.y,
                       point2.x, point2.y );
    }
//---------------------------------------------------------------------------
//////////////////////////////////////////////////////////////////////////////
private class LineListener implements MouseMotionListener
{
//---------------------------------------------------------------------------
```

```
   public void mouseDragged ( MouseEvent event )
   {
      point2 = event.getPoint();
      repaint();
   }
//--------------------------------------------------------------------------
   public void mouseMoved ( MouseEvent event ) {}
//--------------------------------------------------------------------------
} // end class LineListener
///////////////////////////////////////////////////////////////////////////
} // end class MyPanel
///////////////////////////////////////////////////////////////////////////
```

     Test your skill with Exercises 15–32 through 15–38.

15.17   GUI: The KeyListener Interface

Prog1510.java is an application that uses the arrow keys ($\leftarrow$, $\rightarrow$, $\uparrow$, and $\downarrow$) to move a spot around the screen. The KeyListener interface requires three methods:

1. void keyPressed(KeyEvent), which is triggered when a key is pressed.
2. void keyReleased(KeyEvent), which is triggered when a key is released.
3. void keyTyped(KeyEvent), which is triggered when a key is pressed and released.

Prog1510 has empty bodies for keyReleased and keyTyped.

Prog1510.java   Arrow Keys Move a Spot

```
// Written by Barry Soroka
//
// Use arrow keys to walk a spot around a panel.
//
import java.awt.*;
import java.awt.event.*;
import javax.swing.*;
///////////////////////////////////////////////////////////////////////////
class Prog1510
{
//--------------------------------------------------------------------------
   public static void main (String[] args)
   {
      JFrame frame = new JFrame ("Direction Keys");
```

```
            frame.setDefaultCloseOperation (JFrame.EXIT_ON_CLOSE);

            MyPanel mp = new MyPanel();

            frame.getContentPane().add(mp);
            frame.pack();
            frame.setVisible(true);
        }
//-----------------------------------------------------------------------------
} // end class Prog1510
///////////////////////////////////////////////////////////////////////////////
class MyPanel extends JPanel
{
    private int x, y;
    private final int JUMP = 6;
    private final int WIDTH = 500;
    private final int HEIGHT = 500;
//-----------------------------------------------------------------------------
    public MyPanel()
    {
        x = WIDTH/2;
        y = HEIGHT/2;

        addKeyListener(new DirectionKeyListener());

        setBackground(Color.BLACK);
        setPreferredSize(new Dimension(WIDTH,HEIGHT));
        setFocusable(true);
    }
//-----------------------------------------------------------------------------
    public void paintComponent ( Graphics page )
    {
        final int SIZE = 8;
        super.paintComponent(page);
        page.setColor(Color.YELLOW);
        page.fillOval(x,y,SIZE,SIZE);
    }
//-----------------------------------------------------------------------------
///////////////////////////////////////////////////////////////////////////////
private class DirectionKeyListener implements KeyListener
{
//-----------------------------------------------------------------------------
    public void keyPressed ( KeyEvent event )
    {
        switch ( event.getKeyCode())
        {
            case KeyEvent.VK_UP:    y -= JUMP; break;
            case KeyEvent.VK_DOWN:  y += JUMP; break;
            case KeyEvent.VK_LEFT:  x -= JUMP; break;
```

```
      case KeyEvent.VK_RIGHT:  x += JUMP; break;
   }
   repaint();
}
//-------------------------------------------------------------------
   public void keyTyped ( KeyEvent event ) {}
//-------------------------------------------------------------------
   public void keyReleased ( KeyEvent event ) {}
//-------------------------------------------------------------------
} // end class DirectionKeyListener
///////////////////////////////////////////////////////////////////////
} // end class MyPanel
///////////////////////////////////////////////////////////////////////
```

Class `KeyEvent` contains constant codes for every available key. `Prog1510` uses the following keys:

Key	KeyEvent **Constant**
↑	VK_UP
↓	VK_DOWN
←	VK_LEFT
→	VK_RIGHT

Test your skill with Exercises 15–39 through 15–41.

Chapter Summary

- An interface is a set of methods that are provided by a class that implements the interface.
- Java's `Comparable` interface requires a method `int compareTo(Object)`. The result indicates which is the larger of the receiving object and the parameter object.
- Class `Arrays` provides the `sort` method for sorting arrays of `Comparable` objects.
- `Arrays.sort` can also sort arrays of primitive datatypes.
- The `Talker` interface requires `void Talk(PrintStream)`.
- `Dog`, `Cat`, `Human`, and `Mime` implement interface `Talker`.
- We can declare a *variable* to be of type `Talker`. During the course of a program, a variable may refer to any object that is an instance of a class that implements `Talker`.

- We can declare an *array* to be of type `Talker`. An array's elements may be drawn from different classes, provided that each such class implements the `Talker` interface.
- Polymorphism indicates that:
  1. a variable may reference objects of different classes during the course of a program.
  2. an array can contain elements drawn from different classes.
  3. the method used by a given statement will differ over the course of a program, depending on the class of the receiving object.
  4. the need to test the class of an object before sending it a message is eliminated.
- A class may implement more than one interface.
- A `Copier` implements the `Scanner` and `Printer` interfaces.
- A graphing method takes a method and draws its graph. A table-making method takes a method and prints a table of values.
- The interface mechanism is used to pass one method to another method.
- The GUI `MouseListener` interface watches for mouse clicks.
- The GUI `MouseMotionListener` interface watches for mouse motions.
- The GUI `KeyListener` interface watches for keys to be pressed.

Terminology Introduced in This Chapter

early binding
late binding
polymorphism

Exercises

Exercise 15–1. Remove the `compareTo` method from class `Student` in `Prog1501`. Does it compile? If not, what is the error message trying to tell us? How clear is the message?

Exercise 15–2. Write and test the code that implements an ordering of `Students` based on the `name` instance variable.

Exercise 15–3. Modify `Prog1503` so that it sorts `Students` by `name`.

Exercise 15–4. If $a + bi$ is `Complex`, then its modulus (magnitude) is $\sqrt{a^2 + b^2}$. Write a program that sorts an array of `Complex` based on modulus.

Exercise 15–5. Make class `Fraction` implement `Comparable`. Write a program that sorts an array of `Fraction`.

Exercise 15–6.   Make class `Rectangle` implement `Comparable` so that one `Rectangle` is larger than another if its area is greater. Write a program that sorts an array of `Rectangle`.

Exercise 15–7.   Suppose that class `Person` has instance variables `String firstName` and `String lastName`. Write a `compareTo` method for class `Person` that gives priority to `lastName`, but in the case of a tie, uses `firstName` as a tie-breaker. For example, presented with the array on the left, sort would convert it to the array on the right.

Before Sort		After Sort	
firstName	*lastName*	*firstName*	*lastName*
Bill	Rivers	Sally	Block
Sue	Block	Sue	Block
Sam	Rivers	Ravi	Nehru
Ravi	Nehru	Bill	Rivers
Sally	Block	Sam	Rivers

Exercise 15–8.   Suppose that class `Address` has instance variables `int houseNumber` and `String street`. Write a `compareTo` method for class `Address` that gives priority to `street`, but in the case of a tie, uses `houseNumber` as a tie-breaker. For example, presented with the array on the left, sort would convert it to the array on the right.

Before Sort		After Sort	
houseNumber	*street*	*houseNumber*	*street*
2000	Park Avenue	562	Heber
566	Heber	566	Heber
1954	Park Avenue	1222	Kearns
1425	Kearns	1425	Kearns
562	Heber	1954	Park Avenue
1222	Kearns	2000	Park Avenue

Exercise 15–9.   Sort `BankAccount` by `name` and then by `accountNumber`.

Exercise 15–10.   Sort `Complex` first by `real`, then by `imag`.

Exercise 15–11.   Sort `Complex` first by `magnitude`, then by `real`.

Exercise 15–12.   Sort `Complex` first by `magnitude`, then by `imag`.

Exercise 15–13. Write and run the Java code that proves that `Arrays.sort` can sort an array of `ints`.

Exercise 15–14. Interface `Talker` requires a method

```
public void talk ( PrintStream ps )
```

Must we specify the name of the `PrintStream` variable? Is the following statement legal?

```
public void talk ( PrintStream )
```

Exercise 15–15. Interface `Talker` requires a method

```
public void talk ( PrintStream ps )
```

Must we use this same variable name when we implement `talk` inside a class?

Exercise 15–16. Consider classes that represent real estate `Parcels` in a city. Classes include `Restaurant`, `Bank`, `GasStation`, `Residence`, and `Retailer`. These have various instance variables, including `Address`. Interface `Parcel` requires the methods

```
public double getSquareFootage()
public int getAddress()
```

Write the code and show the polymorphism.

Exercise 15–17. Consider classes that represent `UnitItems`—things you buy in integer quantities. Interface `UnitItem` requires a method `public double getCost()`, which tells the cost of a single item. Classes include `Television`, `VCR`, `DVDPlayer`, and `VideoGameBox`. Write code for a method `static double totalCost(UnitItem[])`. Show the polymorphism.

Exercise 15–18. Class `UnitItemPurchase` contains slots for `UnitItem` and `quantity`. Interface `UnitItem` requires the method `public double getCost(int)`, which tells the cost of a given number of this product. Note that the formula is not necessarily `unitPrice * quantity`; there may be price breaks for higher `quantity`. Write `static double totalCost(UnitItemPurchase[])`. Show the polymorphism.

Exercise 15–19. Interface `Shape` requires the methods

```
double area()
double perimeter()
```

The following classes implement `Shape`: `Circle`, `Rectangle`, and `Square`. Write code that includes the interface and classes. Write a method

```
double area(Shapes[])
```

that computes the total area of an array of `Shapes`. Show the polymorphism.

Exercise 15–20. A `ToasterOven` is a device with the capabilities of both a `Toaster` and an `Oven`. Write Java code to represent the appropriate interfaces and the class `ToasterOven`.

Exercise 15–21. An `AmphibiousVehicle` is a device with the capabilities of both a `Truck` and a `Boat`. Write Java code to represent the appropriate interfaces and the class `AmphibiousVehicle`.

Exercise 15–22. Alter `Prog1506` to use floating-point numbers:

```
public double valueAt(double).
```

Print the following tables:

	sin (degrees)	cos (degrees)	tan (degrees)	exp	log	sqrt
From	0.0	0.0	0.0	0.0	1.0	0.0
To	180.0	180.0	180.0	5.0	100.0	10.0
Step	10.0	10.0	10.0	0.1	1.0	0.2

Insert blank lines to make the tables more readable. For example, consider `exp`. Put a blank line after 0.9, 1.9, 2.9, 3.9, and 4.9. Use `printf` to align the columns.

Exercise 15–23. Alter `Prog1506` to use a class `Polynomial` for which an `array` of `doubles` represents the coefficients of the polynomial. Display tables for the following functions:

a. $f(x) = 2 - 5x + 3x^2$
b. $f(x) = x^4$
c. $f(x) = x$
d. $f(x) = 7$

Exercise 15–24. Alter `Prog1507` so that values are *scaled* rather than *clipped*. Thus, if the values are in the range `[lo, hi]`, then the lengths of the bars should be scaled so that the allowed `MAXWIDTH` is never exceeded. Use a function for which scaling and clipping lead to very different bar graphs.

Exercise 15–25. Write a method that takes a `Function1D` and the endpoints of an interval and computes a root of the function.

Exercise 15–26. Write a method that takes a `Function1D` and the endpoints of an interval and computes the integral of the function in that interval.

Exercise 15–27. Modify `Prog1508` so that it deposits spots whenever the mouse is released.

Exercise 15–28. Modify `Prog1508` so that it deposits spots whenever the mouse is clicked.

Exercise 15–29. Modify `Prog1508` so that it deposits outlines of small rectangles whenever the mouse is pressed.

Exercise 15–30. Modify `Prog1508` so that it deposits two spots whenever the mouse is pressed. One spot should appear at the position of the mouse; the other should appear at some fixed offset away from the mouse. This program will give the appearance of drawing spots with two coupled brushes.

Exercise 15–31. Modify `Prog1508` so that it uses the `drawString` method to report the number of spots that have been positioned.

Exercise 15–32. Write an application that draws the trail along which the mouse has been dragged and then deposits a pixel whenever the `mouseDragged` method is triggered.

Exercise 15–33. Write an application that draws two parallel trails whenever the mouse has been dragged. This will simulate using coupled brushes.

Exercise 15–34. Write an application that draws a small solid circle whenever the mouse has been dragged. This will simulate painting with a fat, round brush.

Exercise 15–35. Write an application that draws a small solid rectangle whenever the mouse has been dragged. This will simulate painting with a rectangular brush.

Exercise 15–36. Write an application that draws a rubber-band rectangle with a fixed corner in the center of the window.

Exercise 15–37. Write an application that allows the mouse to drag a circle around the window.

Exercise 15–38. Write an application that draws a circle with a fixed center but with a radius that drags with the mouse. *Note:* You can compute the radius of the desired circle by computing the distance from the mouse to the center of the circle. Given the center and radius, you can easily compute the bounding box of the required circle.

Exercise 15–39. Modify `Prog1510` so that the spot always stays on the drawing canvas.

If it moves off to the . . .	It reappears at the . . .
right	left
left	right
top	bottom
bottom	top

This makes the drawing surface simulate a torus (donut) where the spot never vanishes from the surface.

Exercise 15–40.   Modify `Prog1510` so that the arrow keys leave a trail as the spot moves around the screen.

Exercise 15–41.   Combine `Prog1508` and `Prog1510` so that the arrow keys move a spot incrementally, and a mouse press moves the spot to the place where the mouse was pressed.

Inheritance and Class Hierarchies

C hapter 15 described interfaces, a system whereby classes are related because they offer the same methods for use to the world outside. Now we examine *inheritance*, a system whereby classes are related because a child class inherits data and methods from a parent class. Both the interface and inheritance mechanisms allow for *polymorphism*, a phenomenon whereby a single Java statement may invoke different methods at runtime based on the actual type of a receiving variable. Both interface and inheritance encourage *code reuse*—a good software practice.

> **Inheritance** Where one class is a subclass of another class, using the methods and instance variables of the parent class.

Having learned the mechanics of inheritance and polymorphism, we will apply those mechanisms to real-world problems. We'll develop class hierarchies in the form of *trees*; these trees represent groups of classes related by inheritance. This chapter includes our first exercises based on a real-world problem that is then broken down into the hierarchy of classes that represents it. (You'll study this process in much greater detail in higher-level CS courses.)

16.1 Has-a and Is-a Relationships

has-a

> **has-a** The relationship between two classes, where the first class has instance variables that are instances of the second class.

The *has-a* relationship occurs when instances of one class have an instance variable that is filled by an instance of another class. For example, because we have the code structure

```
class Student
{
    private String name;
    private Date dateOfBirth;
    ...
}
```

we say that

> a Student *has-a* String for its name

and

> a Student *has-a* Date for its dateOfBirth.

In terms of UML diagrams, we have

Student
String name Date dateOfBirth ...
...

We might similarly observe that

> a Person has-a String for its name

and

> a Car has-a Person for its owner.

We can have similar *has-a* statements that don't involve two *classes* in the relationship:

A Complex has-an int for its instance variable real.
A Complex has-an int for its instance variable imag.
A Student has-a double for its gpa.
A Car has-an int for its year.

is-a

Class B has the *is-a* relationship to class A if every instance of B is also an instance of class A. For example,

a Student is-a Person

> **is-a**   An inheritance relationship between two classes.
> **Parent, superclass, base class**
> The class on which a subclass depends.
> **Child, subclass, derived class**
> An extended class that inherits from a superclass.

because every Student object has all the instance variables that belong to a Person object. Moreover, Students may have instance variables of their own that are not found in Persons—for example, major, gpa, classList, transcript, and advisor. The *is-a* relationship indicates *inheritance*: The child class *inherits* the instance variables and methods of the parent class. There are multiple terms to describe the classes involved in inheritance:

parent—superclass—base class

versus

child—subclass—derived class.

(Note that different authors often use different terminologies.)

A typical UML diagram would look like this

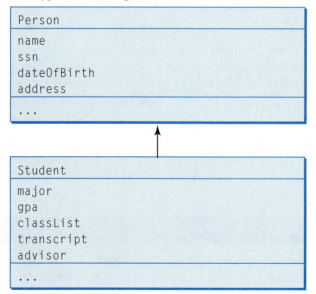

where the arrow indicates *inheritance*: Every Student is-a Person and inherits all the instance variables and methods belonging to class Person.

The rest of this chapter introduces the mechanics of Java's inheritance mechanism.

Test your skill with Exercise 16–1.

16.2 extends

Java uses the keyword `extends` to indicate that two classes are related by inheritance. For example, we write

```
class Student extends Person
{
    ...
}
```

to tell Java that the instance variables and methods of class `Person` are automatically inherited by instances of class `Student`.

Test your skill with Exercise 16–2.

Probable Issues

At this point you should be able to spot two probable issues in any scheme for inheritance:

- What methods and variables of the parent can the child see? Does the parent have the capability of making some things *invisible* to its children?
- What if the child wants to add a method or variable with the same name as a method or variable of the parent? Is this forbidden? If it's allowed, has the child lost the ability to see the corresponding method or variable of the parent?

We'll see that Java has addressed both of these issues, providing considerable flexibility in how much gets inherited from parent class to child class.

16.3 Inheritance Promotes Software Reuse

Inheritance promotes the reuse and adaptation of old software to new purposes. Suppose we need a new class and we already have an old class with *most* of the properties we need. Instead of writing the entire new class from scratch, we'll extend the old class and add on the additional properties and methods required by the new class. This can make writing the new class considerably easier.

Consider, for example, the class `PrintStream`, which provides the methods `print`, `printf`, and `println`. Prog1601 shows the program that writes the `String` `hello` to the file `foo`. It uses the following lines to accomplish the task:

```
PrintStream ps = new PrintStream(
                      new FileOutputStream(
                          new File("foo")));
ps.println("hello");
```

The user needs to refer to classes `File` and `FileOutputStream` as well as `PrintStream`. This is a large and undesirable cognitive burden.

Prog1601.java   **Write a String to File foo**

```
// Written by Barry Soroka
//
// Write a String to the file "foo".
//
import java.io.*;
//////////////////////////////////////////////////////////////////////////////
class Prog1601
{
//----------------------------------------------------------------------------
   public static void main ( String [] args ) throws Exception
   {
      PrintStream ps = new PrintStream(
                          new FileOutputStream(
                              new File("foo")));
      ps.println("hello");
   }
//----------------------------------------------------------------------------
} // end class Prog1601
//////////////////////////////////////////////////////////////////////////////
```

It would be preferable to have the following code achieve the same effect:

```
BetterPS bps = new BetterPS("foo");
bps.println("hello");
```

The user creates and uses a `BetterPS`—a better `PrintStream`—and the code removes the need for the user to think about `Files` and `FileOutputStreams`. Clearly, `BetterPS` has much in common with `PrintStream`, in that we want it to handle `print`, `printf`, and `println` statements. In fact, `BetterPS` includes all the capabilities of `PrintStream`, but has an additional constructor that takes a filename.

Instead of writing all new code for `BetterPS`, we'll piggyback on the existing class `PrintStream`.

Our approach will be this: Start with an existing class and define a derived class that has the data and methods of the base class *plus* the additional data and methods required for the new problem.

Note that I have presented the program using `BetterPS` *even though I've not yet written the code that implements it*. This follows the methodology presented in Chapter 12 for testing a new class by using its methods in a sample program before finalizing the prototypes and writing the code. This sort of previsualization is an important skill in solving problems that require computer programming.

Here is a partial UML diagram that shows the relationship between `PrintStream` and `BetterPS`:

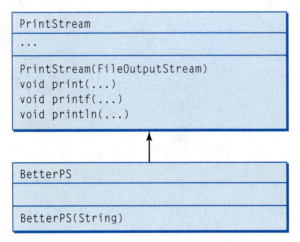

Notice that, since *every* `BetterPS` *is a* `PrintStream`, the methods `print`, `printf`, and `println` will be applicable to every `BBR`.

`Prog1602` presents the code for `BetterPS`, our better `PrintStream`. Let's examine some details of this code.

Prog1602.java   Using BetterPS

```
// Written by Barry Soroka
//
// Write a String to the file "foo" using a BetterPS rather than a PrintStream.
//
import java.io.*;
```

```
///////////////////////////////////////////////////////////////////////////
class Prog1602
{
//--------------------------------------------------------------------------
   public static void main ( String [] args ) throws Exception
   {
      BetterPS bps = new BetterPS("foo");
      bps.println("hello");
   }
//--------------------------------------------------------------------------
} // end class Prog1602
///////////////////////////////////////////////////////////////////////////
class BetterPS extends PrintStream
{
//--------------------------------------------------------------------------
   public BetterPS ( String filename ) throws Exception
   {
      super ( new FileOutputStream (
                 new File ( filename )));
   }
//--------------------------------------------------------------------------
} // end class BetterPS
///////////////////////////////////////////////////////////////////////////
```

The opening line is as expected:

> class BetterPS extends PrintStream

This ensures that the methods of `PrintStream` will be available to instances of `BetterPS`.

The constructor `BetterPS(String)` takes a filename, makes a `FileOutput-Stream` from it, and passes that to the parent's constructor `PrintStream(File-OutputStream)`. The keyword `super` specifies the corresponding constructor in the *superclass* `PrintStream`. The user of our new constructor knows only that it takes a `String` and returns a `BetterPS`—the details of the operation are hidden.

> **super**   Keyword that calls up the corresponding method or variable of the superclass.

Why Not Modify the Existing Class?

Couldn't we just take the code for the existing class, make a copy, and alter it to suit our new needs?

Often, the source code for an existing class—e.g., `PrintStream`—is simply not available. We have the Java byte code for the class, but our license did not include the source code. Even if we do have the source code, it may be difficult to understand, and modifying the code may *break* a well-debugged class.

In addition, code would be duplicated and bloated because both `PrintStream` and `BetterPS` would need the code for `print`, `printf`, and `println`. Duplicating code creates a maintenance nightmare: When a bug is discovered in a duplicated method, we have to fix it in two places!

It's safer to use the existing class and build a subclass that extends it.

16.4   Inheriting Data from a Parent Class

Consider the class hierarchy represented by the following UML diagram:

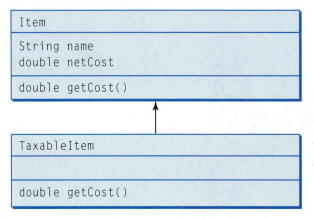

> **Class hierarchy**   The "family tree" of classes in a problem.

`netCost` is declared in the parent class and used in both parent and child. The cost of a basic `Item` is simply its `netCost`. The cost of a `TaxableItem` is its `netCost` plus 8.25% tax.

`Prog1603` gives the code for this situation. Notice the instance variables for class `Item`:

```
protected String name;
protected double netCost;
```

> **Protected**   Can be seen by subclasses

These involve a new visibility modifier: `protected`. This is midway between `public` and `private`, and is summarized in the following table:

`public`	Visible to all classes
`protected`	Visible to this class and to all of its children
`private`	Visible only in this class

Because `name` and `netCost` are `protected`, they can be directly accessed and changed in the subclass `TaxableItem`.

Prog1603.java   Inheriting an Instance Variable

```java
// Written by Barry Soroka
//
// class TaxableItem inherits data netCost from class Item
//
import java.io.*;
/////////////////////////////////////////////////////////////////////////
class Prog1603
{
//--------------------------------------------------------------------------
    public static void main ( String [] args ) throws Exception
    {
        Item item1 = new Item("soup",1.29);
        Item item2 = new TaxableItem("tissue",1.89);

        System.out.printf("item1 costs %6.2f\n",item1.getCost());
        System.out.printf("item2 costs %6.2f\n",item2.getCost());
    }
//--------------------------------------------------------------------------
} // end class Prog1603
/////////////////////////////////////////////////////////////////////////
class Item
{
    protected String name;
    protected double netCost;
//--------------------------------------------------------------------------
    public Item ( String name, double netCost )
    {
        // omitted -- code for validating name and netCost
        this.name = name;
        this.netCost = netCost;
    }
//--------------------------------------------------------------------------
    public double getCost() { return netCost; }
//--------------------------------------------------------------------------
} // end class Item
/////////////////////////////////////////////////////////////////////////
class TaxableItem extends Item
{
//--------------------------------------------------------------------------
    public TaxableItem ( String name, double netCost )
    {
        super(name,netCost);
    }
//--------------------------------------------------------------------------
```

```
   public double getCost() { return netCost * ( 1.0 + 0.0825 ); }
//-------------------------------------------------------------------------
} // end class TaxableItem
///////////////////////////////////////////////////////////////////////////////
```

Test your skill with Exercises 16–3 and 16–4.

Normally, the constructor for class `Item` would include code for *validating* `name` and `netCost`. (An empty `String` is not a valid `name`, and a negative number is not a valid `netCost`.) To make the code simpler, I have omitted the validation code from `Prog1603`.

As expected, the constructor for `TaxableItem` calls the constructor of the parent class `Item`:

```
super(name,netCost);
```

Because `TaxableItem` uses the constructor for `Item`, we won't have to repeat any validation code: The parameters of the `TaxableItem` constructor would be validated by the `Item` constructor. This is a good example of code reuse.

Notice that both `Item` and `TaxableItem` have `getCost` methods. For `Item`, we have

```
public double getCost() { return netCost; }
```

and for `TaxableItem` we have

```
public double getCost() { return netCost * ( 1.0 + 0.08 ); }
```

Override When a method in a child class has the same signature as a method in the parent class.

When the `getCost` message is sent to an *Item*, it uses the first definition; when `getCost` is sent to a *TaxableItem*, it uses the second definition, which *overrides* the first.

You should run this code to verify that it outputs the following:

```
G:\> java Prog1603
item1 costs   1.29
item2 costs   2.04
```

Test your skill with Exercises 16–5 and 16–6.

Notice the following two statements in `Prog1603`:

```
Item item1 = new Item("soup",1.29);
Item item2 = new TaxableItem("tissue",1.89);
```

Although both `item1` and `item2` are references to `Items`, it is perfectly valid to assign a `TaxableItem` to `item2` because `TaxableItem` is a subclass of `Item` and *every `TaxableItem` is also an `Item`*. When Java evaluates the expression `item1.getCost()`, it knows that `item1` is an `Item`, so it uses the first definition of `getCost`. When it evaluates `item2.getCost()`, it knows that `item2` is the *more specific* `TaxableItem`, and it uses the corresponding second definition of `getCost`. Thus, *the method used is dependent on the actual type of the object being referenced, not the type of the reference itself*—otherwise, both calls to `getCost` would use the definition found in class `Item`.

As you discovered in Exercise 16–3, the instance variable `name` could have been made `private` without affecting `Prog1603`. However, it would have prohibited the mention of variable `name` in class `TaxableItem`, so that neither reference nor assignment would be possible. This is sometimes desirable, as it allows us to encapsulate all the code using `name` in the single class `Item`. We'll soon discuss this further.

16.5   Adding Data in a Subclass

`Prog1604` illustrates some further aspects of inheritance, using the classes that correspond to the following UML diagram:

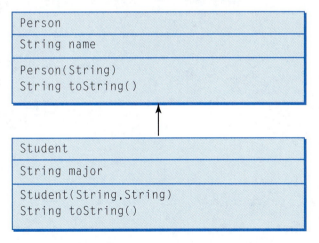

Prog1604.java   Class **Student extends Person**

```
// Written by Barry Soroka
//
// class Student extends Person
//
```

```java
// Subclass adds new data.
// Class and subclass have individual toString methods.
//
import java.io.*;
/////////////////////////////////////////////////////////////////////////////
class Prog1604
{
//----------------------------------------------------------------------------
   public static void main ( String [] args ) throws Exception
   {
      Person bill = new Person("bill");
      Student sue = new Student("sue","physics");
      System.out.println(bill);
      System.out.println(sue);
   }
//----------------------------------------------------------------------------
} // end class Prog1604
/////////////////////////////////////////////////////////////////////////////
class Person
{
   protected String name;
//----------------------------------------------------------------------------
   public Person ( String name )
   {
      // omitted -- code for validating name
      this.name = name;
   }
//----------------------------------------------------------------------------
   public String toString() { return name; }
//----------------------------------------------------------------------------
} // end class Person
/////////////////////////////////////////////////////////////////////////////
class Student extends Person
{
   private String major;
//----------------------------------------------------------------------------
   public Student ( String name, String major )
   {
      super(name);
      // omitted -- code for validating major
      this.major = major;
   }
//----------------------------------------------------------------------------
   public String toString()
```

```
    {
        return name + " (" + major + ")";
    }
//-------------------------------------------------------------------
} // end class Student
/////////////////////////////////////////////////////////////////////
```

A Person has a name, but a Student has both a name and a major. The Student's name is defined and validated in class Person, but the Student's major is defined and validated locally, in class Student. As expected, Person offers

```
    protected String name;
```

so that name can be used by the toString method of class Student. The variable major is declared private, since we don't intend to create subclasses of Student.

As expected, the statement

```
    super(name);
```

indicates that the constructor for Student uses the constructor of class Person to validate the name variable.

Student includes a toString method, which overrides that of Person—a String representing a Student must include both a name *and* a major. This toString directly accesses the name variable defined in Person:

```
    public String toString()
    {
        return name + " (" + major + ")";
    }
```

This access is possible because name is declared protected in class Person. As we discussed in the previous section, this *also* allows methods of class Student to *change* the value of name. This is not always desirable. A simple statement of the form

```
    name = "";
```

can wipe out the validation performed by the constructor of class Person. Likewise, suppose that Person maintains name in an *encrypted* form so as to discourage outsiders from hacking files containing Person objects. Then, in order to print name, both class Person and class Student would need to contain the algorithm for decrypting `names`. This duplication of code makes maintenance harder. The next section discusses how we can encapsulate code involving `name` in the single class `Person`.

16.6 Encapsulating Data and Using Overridden Methods

Data that is `protected` can be changed by any subclass of the defining class. However, as discussed previously, this can have its drawbacks. We now examine `Prog1605`, which shows how to keep data `private` and still print it out in a subclass. We do this by using an overridden `toString` method.

Prog1605.java Superclass Keeps a Variable **private**

```java
// Written by Barry Soroka
//
// class Student extends Person
//
// Subclass toString uses superclass toString.
// Data name is private.
//
import java.io.*;
/////////////////////////////////////////////////////////////////////////////////
class Prog1605
{
//--------------------------------------------------------------------------------
    public static void main ( String [] args ) throws Exception
    {
        Person bill = new Person("bill");
        Student sue = new Student("sue","physics");
        System.out.println(bill);
        System.out.println(sue);
    }
//--------------------------------------------------------------------------------
} // end class Prog1605
/////////////////////////////////////////////////////////////////////////////////
class Person
{
    private String name;
//--------------------------------------------------------------------------------
    public Person ( String name )
    {
        // omitted -- code for validating name
        this.name = name;
    }
```

```
//-------------------------------------------------------------------------
   public String toString() { return name; }
//-------------------------------------------------------------------------
} // end class Person
/////////////////////////////////////////////////////////////////////////////
class Student extends Person
{
   private String major;
//-------------------------------------------------------------------------
   public Student ( String name, String major )
   {
      super(name);
      // omitted -- code for validating major
      this.major = major;
   }
//-------------------------------------------------------------------------
   public String toString()
   {
      return super.toString() + " (" + major + ")";
   }
//-------------------------------------------------------------------------
} // end class Student
/////////////////////////////////////////////////////////////////////////////
```

Class *Person* contains the method

```
   public String toString() { return name; }
```

and class *Student* contains the method

```
   public String toString()
   {
      return super.toString() + " (" + major + ")";
   }
```

The expression `super.toString()` calls the `toString` method of the superclass `Person`, returning a `String` containing the name of the `Person`. Student's `toString` then adds the `major`, in parentheses.

NOTE Using the prefix `super` allows a subclass to use a method that it has - overridden.

Notice that `name` now has visibility `private` in class `Person`. The subclass cannot access this variable; it can use the variable only by means of methods provided in class `Person`. This encapsulation ensures that no subclass of `Person` can accidentally or maliciously change the value of `name`.

In summary, this example illustrates (1) using a method that has been overridden, and (2) privatizing sensitive data so that it cannot be corrupted by methods in a subclass.

Test your skill with Exercise 16–7.

16.7 Overriding an Instance Variable

Consider the following UML diagram:

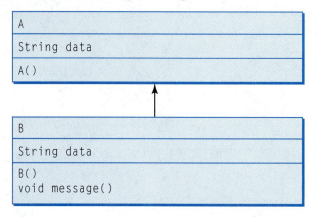

Both the superclass and the subclass have an instance variable `data`. Prog1606 shows how class `B` can access both of these variables:

> `data` refers to the instance variable defined in class `B`.

> `super.data` refers to the instance variable defined in class `A`.

There is no confusion.

Prog1606.java   **Overriding an Instance Variable**

```
// Written by Barry Soroka
//
// Illustrates overriding an instance variable.
//
import java.io.*;
/////////////////////////////////////////////////////////////////////////////
class Prog1606
```

```
{
//------------------------------------------------------------------
   public static void main (String[] args)
   {
      B b = new B();
      b.message();
   }
//------------------------------------------------------------------
} // end class Prog1606
//////////////////////////////////////////////////////////////////
class A
{
   protected String data;
//------------------------------------------------------------------
   public A() { data = "A's data"; }
//------------------------------------------------------------------
} // end class A
//////////////////////////////////////////////////////////////////
class B extends A
{
   private String data;
//------------------------------------------------------------------
   public B()
   {
      super();
      data = "B's data";
   }
//------------------------------------------------------------------
   public void message()
   {
      System.out.println("B has data:       " + data);
      System.out.println("B has super.data: " + super.data);
   }
//------------------------------------------------------------------
} // end class B
//////////////////////////////////////////////////////////////////
```

Shadowing   When a child class defines a variable with the same name as a variable in the parent class (i.e., the overriding of variables).

Most authors call this phenomenon *shadowing* a variable, but it seems to me that it's no different than *overriding* a method. Both use the prefix `super.` to reach back to the overridden element.

You cannot say `super.super.data` in Java.
A class may look only *one* level up.

16.8   `Object` **Is at the Top of All Hierarchies**

We have seen how classes can extend other classes, and how this chain of classes forms a *hierarchy* of classes. `Object` is the class at the top of all hierarchies; *if a class doesn't explicitly extend some other class, then it's assumed to extend `Object`.* This explains why `toString` and `equals` are available to all classes, even if they're not defined. They're inherited from `Object` if not explicitly overridden. `Object` defines very generic versions of these methods:

- `toString` returns a `String` such as `Complex@9fb827`. This is the name of the class; the name includes an @-sign and the memory address at which the object is stored.
- `equals` compares two objects using the `==` operator, returning `true` only if the two references point to the same memory address.

16.9   **Polymorphism Using Inheritance**

We encountered polymorphism in Chapter 15, where we defined it to mean that a given Java statement might use one or another method depending on the binding of a variable *at run-time.* (The compiler cannot determine which method to use *at compile-time.*)

A similar phenomenon is observed with inheritance. The simplest example is this:

```
Item item;
item = new Item("soup",1.29);
System.out.println(item.getCost());    ← statement 1
item = new TaxableItem ("tissue",1.89);
System.out.println(item.getCost());    ← statement 2
```

where statements 1 and 2 are syntactically identical but invoke different `get-Cost` methods. Java applies the method associated with the most specific class applicable to the receiver.

Another example is given in `Prog1607`, which is a modification of `Prog1603`. Here we create an array of `Item`s, and then fill some of the slots with `Item`s and some with `TaxableItem`s. Inside the loop, the expression `items[i].getName()` always invokes the same method, but the expression `items[i].getCost()` does not. The latter statement invokes the different `getCost` methods of `Item` or `TaxableItem`, depending on the type of `items[i]` at run-time.[1]

---

[1]   Note that, within a `printf` control string, `%s` directs `printf` to print a `String` argument.

Prog1607.java   Polymorphism Using Inheritance

```java
// Written by Barry Soroka
//
// Demonstrates polymorphism with inheritance, using an array of Items.
//
import java.io.*;
import java.text.*;
////////////////////////////////////////////////////////////////////////////
class Prog1607
{
//----------------------------------------------------------------------------
    public static void main ( String [] args ) throws Exception
    {
        final int MAX = 4;
        Item [] items = new Item[MAX];

        items[0] = new Item("soup",1.29);
        items[1] = new TaxableItem("tissue",1.89);
        items[2] = new TaxableItem("cleanser",2.18);
        items[3] = new Item("bacon",4.13);

        for ( int i = 0 ; i < MAX ; i++ )
        {
            System.out.printf("%s costs %5.2f\n",items[i].getName(),
                                              items[i].getCost() );
        }
    }
//----------------------------------------------------------------------------
} // end class Prog1607
////////////////////////////////////////////////////////////////////////////
class Item
{
    private String name;
    protected double netCost;
//----------------------------------------------------------------------------
    public Item ( String name, double netCost )
    {
        // validation code omitted here
        this.name = name;
        this.netCost = netCost;
    }
//----------------------------------------------------------------------------
    public String getName() { return name; }
//----------------------------------------------------------------------------
```

```
   public double getCost() { return netCost; }
//---------------------------------------------------------------------------
} // end class Item
/////////////////////////////////////////////////////////////////////////////
class TaxableItem extends Item
{
//---------------------------------------------------------------------------
   public TaxableItem ( String name, double netCost )
   {
      super(name,netCost);
   }
//---------------------------------------------------------------------------
   public double getCost() { return netCost * ( 1.0 + 0.08 ); }
//---------------------------------------------------------------------------
} // end class Shape
/////////////////////////////////////////////////////////////////////////////
```

This sort of polymorphism is also called *dynamic dispatch* and *late binding*.

Test your skill with Exercise 16–8.

16.10   Miscellaneous Topics

This section touches on some miscellaneous topics concerning inheritance.

Use the Parent's Constructor to Validate Parental Variables

Consider the case where class SubClass extends class SuperClass. When we create an instance of SubClass, some of its data is defined and validated by SuperClass, and some of its data is defined and validated by SubClass. Don't replicate the validation code found in SuperClass's constructor.

Don't Confuse Overriding with Overloading

Overriding occurs when a method in a subclass has the same signature as a method in the superclass. *Overloading* occurs in a single class when two methods have the same name but different parameters (i.e., different signatures).

Single versus Multiple Inheritance

Some classes appear to inherit from *two or more parents*. An AmphibiousVehicle inherits properties from both Truck and Boat. A SeaPlane inherits properties from both Plane and Boat. A Minivan inherits properties from both Car and Truck. This phenomenon is known as *multiple inheritance*.

Some languages—notably C++—implement *multiple inheritance*, allowing a class definition to specify that it inherits from two or more super-classes. This leads to conflicts when two or more of the superclasses define a method with the same prototype: Which method should the derived class use?

> **Multiple inheritance**   A class inherits from two parents. Java allows only single inheritance.
> **Single inheritance**   A class may have one and only one parent class.

Java avoids this conflict by restricting itself to *single inheritance*, but it achieves the goals of multiple inheritance through the use of interfaces. Recall that the *class* Copier implements the *interface* Scanner and the *interface* Printer. No conflicts can occur.

Inheritance and Interface Are Orthogonal

It's legal to say

```
class A extends B implements C
```

to indicate that class A participates in inheritance with class B and also implements the interface C.

The final Modifier

The final modifier has three different uses. Each restricts our ability to change the item being modified:

- final makes a variable constant.
- final prevents a method from being overridden in a subclass.
- final makes a class nonextendable.

The String and Scanner classes are final and cannot be extended.

   Test your skill with Exercises 16–9 and 16–10.

How Programs Were Written Before Polymorphism

Before polymorphism, many method calls were tangled nests of multiway branching, each branch calling the method appropriate for a different class.

Consider a graphics program involving the class hierarchy for Shape, as shown in Figure 16–1. Each class has its own draw method for making itself visible in a scene. The method associated with Square executes faster than the method associated with Polygon, so we want to use Square's draw method instead of Polygon's draw method when we're confronted with a Square.

In the old days, we would have written the following code inside a generic draw method:

```
if      ( this is a Square )    invoke Square's draw method
else if ( this is a Rectangle ) invoke Rectangle's draw method
else if ( this is a Triangle )  invoke Triangle's draw method
else if ( this is a Polygon )   invoke Polygon's draw method
else if ( this is a Circle )    invoke Circle's draw method
else if ( this is an Ellipse )  invoke Ellipse's draw method
else                            throw Error("Shape not recognized")
```

and we'd have similar code inside methods for move, grow, shrink, change-Color, and so forth.

Each time we added a new Shape, we had to add the appropriate else-if statement to every multiway branch in the program. Errors were plentiful.

Now, with polymorphism, we can add a new Shape by extending one of the existing classes. We can add special code for handling the new Shape, or we can allow it to inherit the methods defined in its parent method. A statement

Figure 16–1
A Hierarchy of Shapes

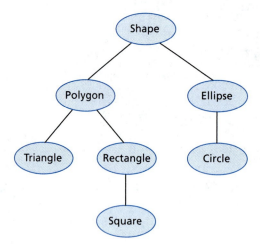

involving the draw method will execute the appropriate draw method without us modifying any code outside the definition of the new class.

16.11   Implementing BetterPS as a Composition

Previously, we defined BetterPS as a *subclass* of PrintStream. This section presents an alternative implementation of BetterPS using *composition*. With composition, we don't extend the existing class. Instead, we define a new class with the existing class as an instance variable.

> **Composition**   A technique for using a previously defined class by having an instance variable be an instance of that type.

Prog1608 gives the code. Notice that the driver is the same code as in Prog1602—the new class has the exact same interface and semantics as our subclass version of BetterPS. Note, however, that we incorporate PrintStream as an instance variable:

```
private PrintStream ps;
```

The constructor makes ps refer to an appropriate PrintStream. The method println(String) acts as expected, sending the String to the println method of class PrintStream.

Prog1608.java   **BetterPS** Using Composition

```java
// Written by Barry Soroka
//
// Write a String to the file "foo" using a BetterPS rather than a PrintStream.
//
import java.io.*;
/////////////////////////////////////////////////////////////////////////////////
class Prog1608
{
//--------------------------------------------------------------------------------
   public static void main ( String [] args ) throws Exception
   {
      BetterPS bps = new BetterPS("foo");
      bps.println("hello");
   }
//--------------------------------------------------------------------------------
} // end class Prog1608
/////////////////////////////////////////////////////////////////////////////////
class BetterPS
{
   private PrintStream ps;
//--------------------------------------------------------------------------------
```

```
   public BetterPS ( String filename ) throws Exception
   {
     ps = new PrintStream(
            new FileOutputStream(
               new File(filename)));
   }
//-------------------------------------------------------------------
   public void print(String s) { ps.print(s); }
//-------------------------------------------------------------------
   public void print(int n) { ps.print(n); }
//-------------------------------------------------------------------
   // other print methods
//-------------------------------------------------------------------
   public void println(String s) { ps.println(s); }
//-------------------------------------------------------------------
   public void println(int n) { ps.println(n); }
//-------------------------------------------------------------------
   // other println methods
//-------------------------------------------------------------------
   // printf method(s)
//-------------------------------------------------------------------
} // end class BetterPS
/////////////////////////////////////////////////////////////////////////
```

Composition has a major drawback in comparison with subclassing. Note how we must specifically implement `println` for `BetterPS`:

```
   public void println(String s) { ps.println(s); }
```

With *subclassing*, we could automatically fall back on the `println` method of `PrintStream`. In fact, the subclass `BetterPS` inherited *all* of the previously existing methods of `PrintStream`. With *composition*, we have to implement each and every borrowed method individually.

There may be cases where composition is appropriate, but in general it requires more work than subclassing.

16.12 A Hierarchy of `Animals`

Consider the hierarchy of `Animals` shown in Figure 16-2. In this section, we will study how this hierarchy is transformed into Java code. For math and computer science purposes, a tree grows *downward* from its *root*. A node at the bottom fringe of the tree is a *leaf*; other nodes are called *interior nodes*. Nodes with the same parent—e.g., Cat, Dog, and Human—are *siblings*.[2]

Prog1609 gives the code that corresponds to the diagram. As expected, we have class declarations that maintain the hierarchy of the diagram:

```
class Animal
class Dog extends Animal
class Cat extends Animal
class Human extends Animal
class Mime extends Human
```

Similarly, each class has a method with the prototype

```
public void speak()
```

and those in child classes override the corresponding methods in parent classes.

> **Tree**   An organization of nodes, from root to leaves.
> **Root**   The topmost node of a tree, from which all others are descendants.
> **Leaf**   A node at the fringe of a tree.
> **Interior node**   A node inside a tree.
> **Sibling**   A brother or sister node.

Prog1609.java   Polymorphism Using Inheritance

```
// Written by Barry Soroka
//
// Demonstrates polymorphism using inheritance.
//
import java.io.*;
////////////////////////////////////////////////////////////////////////////////
class Prog1609
{
//-----------------------------------------------------------------------------
```

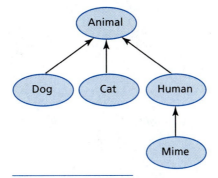

Figure 16–2
Hierarchy of Animals

---

[2]   This is the same term as is used in human genealogy.

```
    public static void main (String [] args) throws Exception
    {
        final int MAX = 7;

        Animal [] animals = new Animal[MAX];
        animals[0] = new Dog();
        animals[1] = new Cat();
        animals[2] = new Human();
        animals[3] = new Dog();
        animals[4] = new Mime();
        animals[5] = new Cat();
        animals[6] = new Animal();

        for ( int i = 0 ; i < MAX ; i++ )
        {
            animals[i].speak();
        }
    }
//-------------------------------------------------------------------------
} // end class Prog1609
///////////////////////////////////////////////////////////////////////////
class Animal
{
//-------------------------------------------------------------------------
    public void speak() { System.out.println("* generic animal noise *"); }
//-------------------------------------------------------------------------
}
///////////////////////////////////////////////////////////////////////////
class Dog extends Animal
{
//-------------------------------------------------------------------------
    public void speak() { System.out.println("woof"); }
//-------------------------------------------------------------------------
}
///////////////////////////////////////////////////////////////////////////
class Cat extends Animal
{
//-------------------------------------------------------------------------
    public void speak() { System.out.println("meow"); }
//-------------------------------------------------------------------------
}
///////////////////////////////////////////////////////////////////////////
class Human extends Animal
{
//-------------------------------------------------------------------------
    public void speak() { System.out.println("hello"); }
```

```
//-------------------------------------------------------------------------
}
/////////////////////////////////////////////////////////////////////////////
class Mime extends Human
{
//-------------------------------------------------------------------------
   public void speak() { System.out.println(); }
//-------------------------------------------------------------------------
}
/////////////////////////////////////////////////////////////////////////////
```

The driver creates an array of `Animal`—`animals`—where the elements are drawn from the classes in the hierarchy. The statement

```
animals[i].speak()
```

demonstrates polymorphism because, at run-time, a different speak method is selected depending on the exact run-time type of `animals[i]`.

`Prog1609` represents a *literal* translation of Figure 16–2 into Java. In the next section we will rewrite this code and change `Animal` into an `abstract` class.

16.13   **Using** abstract **Classes**

Consider `Prog1609`. It makes no sense to create instances of `Animal`. In the current code, the speak method produces a * `generic animal noise` *—there is no obvious default noise made by a generic `Animal`. Suppose we add to `Animal` the instance variable `numberOfLegs`. `Dogs` and `Cats` have four legs, `Humans` and `Mimes` have two legs, and `Snakes` have no legs. However, there's no reasonable value for the `numberOfLegs` of a generic `Animal`.

> **Abstract class**   A placeholder in the class hierarchy. It cannot be instantiated.
> **Concrete class**   A fully formed member of a class hierarchy. It *can* be instantiated.

The class `Animal` is merely a *placeholder* in the hierarchy. It's not meant as a template from which we can create concrete instances. Java acknowledges such placeholders with the modifier `abstract`.

`Prog1610` shows a revised version of the code for the hierarchy of `Animals`. Note that the topmost class is now declared with the statement

```
abstract class Animal
```

This tells Java that `Animal` is a placeholder and that it may not be used to create concrete instances. In the driver, we have commented-out the statement

```
animals[6] = new Animal();
```

because Java won't compile it.

Prog1610.java   An abstract Class

```java
// Written by Barry Soroka
//
// Demonstrates an abstract class.
//
import java.io.*;
///////////////////////////////////////////////////////////////////////////////
class Prog1610
{
//------------------------------------------------------------------------------
    public static void main (String [] args) throws Exception
    {
        final int MAX = 7;

        Animal [] animals = new Animal[MAX];
        animals[0] = new Dog();
        animals[1] = new Cat();
        animals[2] = new Human();
        animals[3] = new Dog();
        animals[4] = new Mime();
        animals[5] = new Cat();
//      animals[6] = new Animal();  // NOT ALLOWED - Animal is abstract!
        animals[6] = new Human();

        for ( int i = 0 ; i < MAX ; i++ )
        {
            animals[i].speak();
        }
    }
//------------------------------------------------------------------------------
} // end class Prog1610
///////////////////////////////////////////////////////////////////////////////
abstract class Animal
{
//------------------------------------------------------------------------------
    abstract public void speak();
//------------------------------------------------------------------------------
}
///////////////////////////////////////////////////////////////////////////////
class Dog extends Animal
{
//------------------------------------------------------------------------------
    public void speak() { System.out.println("woof"); }
//------------------------------------------------------------------------------
}
///////////////////////////////////////////////////////////////////////////////
```

```
class Cat extends Animal
{
//-------------------------------------------------------------------------------
    public void speak() { System.out.println("meow"); }
//-------------------------------------------------------------------------------
}
///////////////////////////////////////////////////////////////////////////////
class Human extends Animal
{
//-------------------------------------------------------------------------------
    public void speak() { System.out.println("hello"); }
//-------------------------------------------------------------------------------
}
///////////////////////////////////////////////////////////////////////////////
class Mime extends Human
{
//-------------------------------------------------------------------------------
    public void speak() { System.out.println(); }
//-------------------------------------------------------------------------------
}
///////////////////////////////////////////////////////////////////////////////
```

 Test your skill with Exercise 16–11.

In class Animal, notice the method defined with the statement

> **Abstract method**   A method that is promised in one class and must be defined in a descendant class.
> **Concrete method**   A normal method, fully defined.

```
abstract public void speak();
```

This is an *abstract method*. It doesn't define a method—it merely makes a *promise* that all the descendants of this class will either (1) contain a concrete method with the prototype

```
public void speak()
```

or (2) will themselves be abstract classes. As required, concrete classes Dog, Cat, Human, and Mime contain concrete definitions of a method with the required prototype.

If a class contains an abstract method, then the class must be abstract. However, a class can be abstract without containing an abstract method. To summarize this section:

- An abstract *class* is a *placeholder* in a class hierarchy.
- An abstract *method* is a *promise*: Descendant classes must either provide a concrete definition or be abstract themselves.

 Test your skill with Exercises 16–12 through 16–16.

16.14 Case Study: Persons in an Organization

In this section we develop a class hierarchy for an organization involving four kinds of Persons:

- Volunteers—They get *thanked*, but they don't get paid.
- Salaried—These people are paid the same amount each week, regardless of how many hours they work. The weeklySalary differs from individual to individual.
- Hourly—They are paid at an hourlyRate, which is different for each individual. They are not paid overtime.
- UnionMembers—They are similar to Hourly workers, but their contract gets them time-and-a-half for hours worked above 40 per week.

Each Person has a pay() method, which has a side effect and a result. The side effect prints an appropriate directive—whom to thank or whom to pay how much. The result is the amount this Person should be paid this week. Prog1611 shows the final code.

Prog1611.java **The Personnel Pay Problem**

```java
// Written by Barry Soroka
//
// The personnel pay problem.
//
import java.io.*;
import java.text.*;
//////////////////////////////////////////////////////////////////////////////
class Prog1611
{
//----------------------------------------------------------------------------
    public static void main ( String [] args ) throws Exception
    {
        final int MAX = 5;
        Person[] personnel = new Person[MAX];

        personnel[0] = new Volunteer("Bill");
        personnel[1] = new Salaried("Sue","111111111",1200);
        personnel[2] = new Hourly("Amber","222222222",10);
        personnel[3] = new UnionMember("Diego","333333333",10);
        personnel[4] = new Volunteer("Trudy");

        ((Hourly)personnel[2]).addHours(10);
        ((Hourly)personnel[3]).addHours(41);
```

```
         double total = 0.0;
         System.out.println();
         for ( int i = 0 ; i < MAX ; i++ )
         {
            total += personnel[i].pay();
         }
         System.out.printf("total = $%7.2f",total);
      }
//------------------------------------------------------------------------------
} // end class Prog1611
////////////////////////////////////////////////////////////////////////////////
abstract class Person
{
   private String name;
//------------------------------------------------------------------------------
   public Person ( String name ) { this.name = name; }
//------------------------------------------------------------------------------
   public String toString() { return name; }
//------------------------------------------------------------------------------
   abstract public double pay();
//------------------------------------------------------------------------------
}
////////////////////////////////////////////////////////////////////////////////
class Volunteer extends Person
{
//------------------------------------------------------------------------------
   public Volunteer ( String name )
   {
      super(name);
   }
//------------------------------------------------------------------------------
   public double pay()
   {
      System.out.println("Thank " + super.toString() + ".");
      return 0.0;
   }
//------------------------------------------------------------------------------
}
////////////////////////////////////////////////////////////////////////////////
abstract class Employee extends Person
{
   protected String ssn;
//------------------------------------------------------------------------------
```

```java
   public Employee ( String name, String ssn )
   {
      super(name);
      this.ssn = ssn;
   }
//----------------------------------------------------------------------
   public String toString() { return super.toString() + " (" + ssn + ")"; }
//----------------------------------------------------------------------
}
////////////////////////////////////////////////////////////////////////////
class Salaried extends Employee
{
   private double weeklySalary;
//----------------------------------------------------------------------
   public Salaried ( String name, String ssn, double weeklySalary )
   {
      super(name,ssn);
      this.weeklySalary = weeklySalary;
   }
//----------------------------------------------------------------------
   public double pay()
   {
      System.out.printf("Pay $%7.2f to %s.\n",weeklySalary, super.toString());
      return weeklySalary;
   }
//----------------------------------------------------------------------
}
////////////////////////////////////////////////////////////////////////////
class Hourly extends Employee
{
   protected double hourlyRate;
   protected double hoursWorked;
//----------------------------------------------------------------------
   public Hourly ( String name, String ssn, double hourlyRate )
   {
      super(name,ssn);
      this.hourlyRate = hourlyRate;
      this.hoursWorked = 0.0;
   }
//----------------------------------------------------------------------
   public void addHours ( double hours ) { hoursWorked += hours; }
//----------------------------------------------------------------------
   public double pay()
```

```
    {
        double amount = hoursWorked * hourlyRate;
        System.out.printf("Pay $%7.2f to %s.\n",amount, super.toString());
        hoursWorked = 0.0;
        return amount;
    }
//------------------------------------------------------------------------------
}
//////////////////////////////////////////////////////////////////////////////
class UnionMember extends Hourly
{
//------------------------------------------------------------------------------
    public UnionMember ( String name, String ssn, double hourlyRate )
    {
        super(name,ssn,hourlyRate);
        this.hoursWorked = 0.0;
    }
//------------------------------------------------------------------------------
    public double pay()
    {
        double amount = hoursWorked * hourlyRate;
        if ( hoursWorked > 40 ) amount += 0.5 * (hoursWorked - 40) * hourlyRate;
        System.out.printf("Pay $%7.2f (includes overtime) to %s.\n",
                            amount,
                            super.toString());
        hoursWorked = 0.0;
        return amount;
    }
//------------------------------------------------------------------------------
}
//////////////////////////////////////////////////////////////////////////////
```

We represent the organization by an array of Persons. Each week we will loop through the array, sending the message pay() to each Person. We will total the results to obtain the total cost of the payroll. As a side effect, each call to pay will also result in printing an appropriate directive for the person involved—"thank . . ." or "pay . . . ".

Let's consider each class of Person, giving typical Java code and the expected output. The subsections describe what we want the code to do. We will write the Java code for all the classes in a later section; for now we are designing our desired output before committing ourselves to specific Java code.

Volunteer

The statement

```
Volunteer v = new Volunteer("Bill");
```

creates a `Volunteer` named `Bill`. No other data is involved. The statement

```
System.out.println(v.pay());
```

should result in the following output:

```
Thank Bill.
0.0
```

The side effect of `pay()` is the line `Thank Bill`. The result of `pay()` is `0.0`.

Salaried

These are created by statements such as

```
Salaried s = new Salaried("Sue","1111111111",1200);
```

where we give the `name`, the `ssn`, and the `weeklySalary`. The statement

```
System.out.println(s.pay());
```

should result in the output

```
Pay $1200.00 to Sue (1111111111).
1200.0
```

The `Pay` directive is a command to the bookkeeper to write a check to Sue for the specified amount.

Hourly

Consider the Java code

```
Hourly h = new Hourly("Amber","222222222",12);
h.addHours(30);
System.out.println(h.pay());
```

which illustrates the use of an `Hourly` worker. The constructor takes the `name`, `ssn`, and `hourlyRate`. Within the `Hourly` object, there's an accumulator—`hoursWorked`—which starts at 0. The method `addHours` adds to the number of `hoursWorked` until such time as `pay()` is invoked. We want to see the output

```
Pay $ 360.00 to Amber (222222222).
360.0
```

where 360 = 30*12. After the weekly payment, `hoursWorked` is reset to 0.

UnionMember

These workers are paid time-and-a-half for hours over 40 per week. Consider the code

```
UnionMember u = new UnionMember("Diego","333333333",10);
u.addHours(41);
System.out.println(u.pay());
```

The constructor for `UnionMembers` takes the same parameters as the constructor for `Hourlys`, and the `addHours` method functions identically. The difference will come when `pay()` is invoked, producing the output

```
Pay $ 415.00 (includes overtime) to Diego (333333333).
415.0
```

Notice that the output includes the phrase `(includes overtime)`, which is absent from the `Pay` line for `Hourlys`.

16.15 Creating a Class Hierarchy

Figure 16–3 shows the UML for the four classes we identified in the previous section. We will merge these into a class hierarchy appropriate to this problem, resulting in a tree.

Our approach will be to merge boxes that share compatible data and methods, producing a tree with more levels. This approach is *bottom-up*: We start with the leaves of the tree, produce the interior nodes, and then eventually, the root. A *top-down* approach is also feasible. More than one methodology can produce a reasonable class hierarchy for this problem.

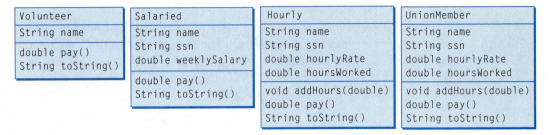

Figure 16–3
Initial Diagram

Step 1

Our first merge will involve Hourly and UnionMember—we'll make UnionMember a subclass of Hourly.[3] They have identical instance variables and toString, but they have different pay methods. We see that UnionMember *extends* Hourly, and we have Figure 16–4. The addHour method is inherited by UnionMember.

Step 2

Salaried and Hourly have a lot in common. They both have instance variables name and ssn, and their toString methods both return Strings resembling Amber (222222222). Let's create a parent class—Employee—which contains the common elements.

Step 3

Figure 16–5 shows the new situation. Notice that Volunteer and Employee both have the instance variable name. Volunteer has a toString composed of name, and Employee has a toString involving both name and ssn. They don't have the same toString, but they can both use a parent's toString if it involves name. We'll create a new parent node—Person—which contains the common elements.

Finally

We have Figure 16–6, which shows a four-level class hierarchy for the organization payroll problem. Now we must translate this diagram from UML to Java.

---

[3] Alternatively, we could make Hourly a subclass of UnionMember.

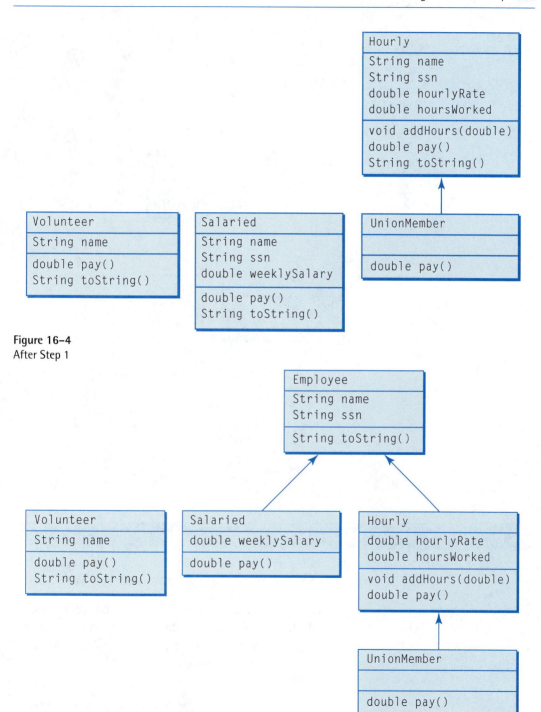

Figure 16–4
After Step 1

Figure 16–5
After Step 2

Figure 16–6
Final Diagram

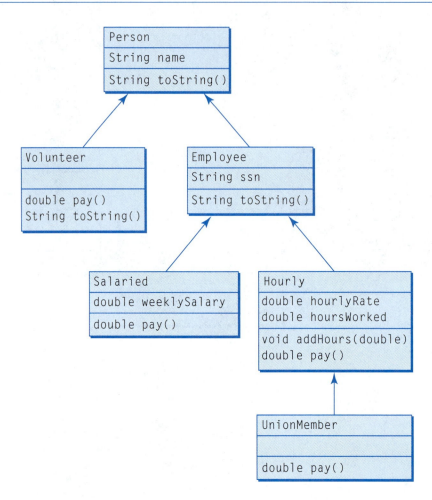

16.16   From UML to Java Code

Prog1611 gives the code for class Person and its subclasses. Each class matches the corresponding box in the UML diagram (Figure 16–6).

Person   This is an abstract class, and it serves as a placeholder at the top of the class hierarchy. I've made name private, because no class below this needs to access or change it. toString returns the name for those methods that need it. pay is an abstract method, which will be made concrete in the classes below.

Volunteer   A concrete class, fleshing out the pay method. Nothing else is novel.

Employee   This is an abstract class and serves as the root of the subtree containing Salaried, Hourly, and UnionMember. It maintains the instance variable ssn for the classes listed below, and its toString returns a String containing the name and ssn of the Employee queried.

Salaried   A concrete class. Note the instance variable weeklySalary, and how the constructor uses super to set up name and ssn but sets weeklySalary in the subclass. pay is a concrete method that prints the appropriate line and returns weeklySalary.

Hourly   A concrete class, but it has UnionMember as a subclass. The constructor uses the constructor for Employee to establish name and ssn, but hourlyRate and hoursWorked are set here. Note that hourlyRate and hoursWorked are *protected*—they are shared with subclass UnionMember. addHours performs as expected. pay prints out the appropriate text line, returns the proper amount, and resets hoursWorked to 0.

UnionMember   A concrete class and a leaf of the tree. It uses the constructor for Hourly because they have the same instance variables. It prints, computes, and resets as expected.

Driver   Prog1611 gives a driver that uses polymorphism to solve our initial problem—we have an array of Persons, and we apply the pay method down the line, producing the appropriate output:

```
Thank Bill.
Pay $1200.00 to Sue (111111111).
Pay $ 100.00 to Amber (222222222).
Pay $ 415.00 (includes overtime) to Diego (333333333).
Thank Trudy.
total = $1715.00
```

Notice the lines that add hours to the Hourly and UnionMember:

```
((Hourly)personnel[2]).addHours(10);
((Hourly)personnel[3]).addHours(41);
```

We need to *cast* the elements of personnel into the appropriate, more specific type before sending the addHours messages. If we don't, we'll get an error message. To the compiler, personnel[2] and personnel[3] are *Persons*, and *Person* does not have an addHours method. However, both are Hourly, and Hourly provides the addHours method.

   Test your skill with Exercises 16–17 through 16–21.

16.17 Observations on Class Hierarchies

Put common features as high in the hierarchy as possible. This reduces the amount of code that manipulates that feature. Recall how we put `name` in class `Person`; this kept `name`-manipulating code to a minimum. Ditto for `ssn`, `hourlyRate`, and `hoursWorked`.

Designing a hierarchy is an art, not a science. A given problem may be represented by several different hierarchies. It's not obvious why one hierarchy should be preferred over another one.

16.18 GUI: `FlowLayout`

This GUI describes *layout managers*—how we can position the graphic elements that we add onto containers such as `JPanel`s. We'll study two layout managers, `FlowLayout` and `BorderLayout`. Other layout managers, such as `GridLayout` and `BoxLayout`, are more complicated and beyond the scope of this text.

> **Layout manager** A scheme for adding items to panels.

By default, containers use `FlowLayout`. With `FlowLayout`, new items are added at the right side of current objects until the line overflows. Items past the end of one line are put onto the next line.

Consider `Prog1612.java`. We explicitly set the layout of `panel` with the `setLayout` method. The horizontal gap between adjacent elements—`Hgap`—is set to 20 pixels. The vertical gap between adjacent lines—`Vgap`—is set similarly. Five buttons are added to `panel`. The window is shown in Figure 16–7, with the five buttons laid out in a horizontal row. When we resize the window, we see Figure 16–8

Figure 16–7
Initial Layout

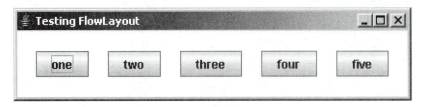

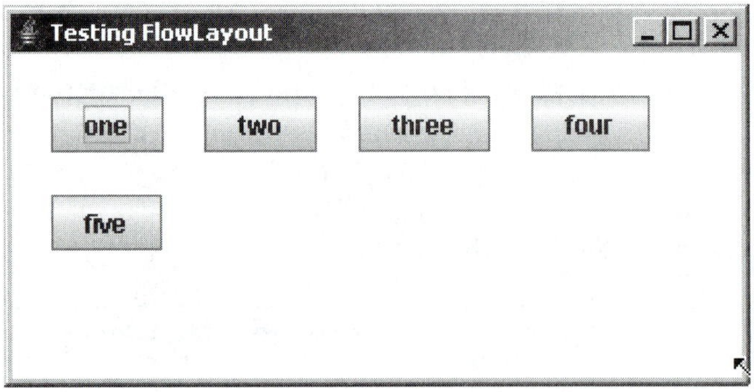

Figure 16–8
After Narrowing the Window

Figure 16–9
After Resizing

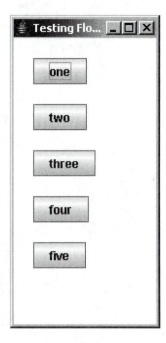

and Figure 16–9; the lines are narrowed so that they fit in the window, producing more lines as required.

Prog1612.java   FlowLayout

```
// Written by Barry Soroka
//
// Plays with FlowLayout.
//
import java.awt.*;
import java.awt.event.*;
import javax.swing.*;
///////////////////////////////////////////////////////////////////////////////
class Prog1612
{
//-------------------------------------------------------------------------
    public static void main (String[] args)
    {
        JFrame frame = new JFrame ("Testing FlowLayout");
        frame.setDefaultCloseOperation (JFrame.EXIT_ON_CLOSE);

        JPanel panel = new JPanel();
        FlowLayout fl = new FlowLayout(FlowLayout.LEFT);
        panel.setLayout(fl);
        panel.setBackground(Color.WHITE);
```

```
        fl.setHgap(20);
        fl.setVgap(20);

        JButton b1 = new JButton("one");
        JButton b2 = new JButton("two");
        JButton b3 = new JButton("three");
        JButton b4 = new JButton("four");
        JButton b5 = new JButton("five");

        panel.add(b1);
        panel.add(b2);
        panel.add(b3);
        panel.add(b4);
        panel.add(b5);

        frame.getContentPane().add(panel);
        frame.pack();
        frame.setVisible(true);
    }
//-------------------------------------------------------------------------
} // end class Prog1612
/////////////////////////////////////////////////////////////////////////////
```

> **Test your skill with Exercises 16–22 and 16–23.**

16.19   GUI: BorderLayout

BorderLayout divides the screen into five regions—north, south, east, west, and center—as shown in Figure 16–10. When the window is resized, the regions flex as illustrated in Figure 16–11: The center becomes, and the north, south, east, and west regions hug the edges of the window.

Prog1613.java shows the code used to produce Figures 16–10 and 16–11. We set the layout of panel to be BorderLayout(5,5):

- The first parameter is the horizontal gap, in pixels, between west and center and between center and east.
- The second parameter is the vertical gap, in pixels, below north and above south.

Figure 16–10
Initial Layout

Figure 16–11
After Resizing

We add a component to one of the five panes using the add method with a second parameter selecting the appropriate pane. We use one of five static constants defined in class BorderLayout: CENTER, NORTH, SOUTH, EAST, or WEST.

Prog1613.java   BorderLayout

```java
// Written by Barry Soroka
//
// Plays with BorderLayout.
//
import java.awt.*;
import java.awt.event.*;
import javax.swing.*;
/////////////////////////////////////////////////////////////////////////////
class Prog1613
{
//-----------------------------------------------------------------------------
   public static void main (String[] args)
   {
      JFrame frame = new JFrame ("Testing BorderLayout");
      frame.setDefaultCloseOperation (JFrame.EXIT_ON_CLOSE);
      frame.setSize(500,500);

      JPanel panel = new JPanel();
      BorderLayout layout = new BorderLayout(5,5);
      panel.setLayout(layout);
      panel.setBackground(Color.RED);
```

```
    JButton b1 = new JButton("center");
    JButton b2 = new JButton("north");
    JButton b3 = new JButton("south");
    JButton b4 = new JButton("east");
    JButton b5 = new JButton("west");

    panel.add(b1,BorderLayout.CENTER);
    panel.add(b2,BorderLayout.NORTH);
    panel.add(b3,BorderLayout.SOUTH);
    panel.add(b4,BorderLayout.EAST);
    panel.add(b5,BorderLayout.WEST);

    frame.getContentPane().add(panel);
    frame.pack();
    frame.setVisible(true);
  }
//-----------------------------------------------------------------------
} // end class Prog1613
/////////////////////////////////////////////////////////////////////////////////
```

 | **Test your skill with Exercises 16–24 through 16–26.** |

Chapter Summary

- Class B has the *has-a* relationship with class A when an instance variable of class B is of type A.
- Class B has the *is-a* relationship with class A when every instance of class B is automatically an instance of class A.
- We say that A is the parent class, superclass, or base class and B is the child class, subclass, or derived class.
- UML diagrams can show the *is-a* relationship between classes.
- Java's extends keyword indicates that one class is a subclass of another class.
- Inheritance promotes software reuse.
- Java provides *single inheritance*; i.e., a class may have only one superclass.
- BetterPS is a subclass of PrintStream, which provides a constructor that facilitates writing to a disk file.
- A child class can directly access parent variables if they are labeled with the visibility modifiers public or protected.
- A protected variable can be seen by subclasses of the defining class.
- super(*arguments*) is a call to the constructor of the superclass.
- The parent's constructor often is used to validate instance variables defined in the parent class.
- A subclass definition can define methods and variables that are not found in the superclass.
- If a child class method has the same signature as a parent class method, then we say the method has been *overridden*.

- A child class can access an overridden method by using the prefix `super.` with the method name.
- If a child class variable has the same name as a parent class variable, then we say that the variable has been *shadowed*.
- A child method can interact with `private` variables of the parent class only via methods provided by the parent class. This encapsulation is often helpful.
- `Object` is at the top of all class hierarchies. If a class does not name a specific superclass, then it inherits methods from class `Object`.
- Unless overridden, every class inherits the methods `toString` and `equals` from class `Object`.
- Polymorphism means that a variable of type `A` can refer to an instance of type `A` or to an instance of any class that inherits from type `A`.
- Polymorphism also means that an array of type `A` can contain elements referring to instances of type `A` or instances of any class that inherits from type `A`.
- Polymorphism using inheritance eliminates having to test a variable for its exact type. Instead, the correct method will be chosen automatically from the methods defined up and down the class hierarchy.
- The `Animal` hierarchy includes `Dog`, `Cat`, `Human`, and `Mime`.
- An `abstract` class is a placeholder in a hierarchy; it cannot be instantiated.
- The `Person` hierarchy includes `Volunteer`, `Salaried`, `Hourly`, and `UnionMember`. `Person` is an abstract class.
- We can construct a class hierarchy from a description of the classes involved.
- Common features should be placed as far up the class hierarchy as possible.
- A given problem domain may be represented by more than one class hierarchy.
- GUI layout managers dictate where successive items are added to a panel.
- In `FlowLayout`, items are added to the right of the current items until they spill over to the next line.
- In `BorderLayout`, items are added in screen areas labeled as `CENTER`, `NORTH`, `SOUTH`, `EAST`, and `WEST`.

Terminology Introduced in This Chapter

abstract class	has-a	`protected`
abstract method	inheritance	root
base class	interior node	shadowing
child class	is-a	sibling
class hierarchy	layout manager	single inheritance
composition	leaf	subclass
concrete class	multiple inheritance	`super`
concrete method	override	superclass
derived class	parent class	tree

Exercises

Exercise 16–1.   Consider the following situation:

- A `Vehicle` **has** `fuelCapacity`, `fuelOnBoard`, `serialNumber`, `passengerCapacity`, **and** `netWeight`.
- A `Car` *is-a* `Vehicle` **with additional properties** `tireWear`, `licensePlate`, **and** `trunkCapacity`.
- A `Plane` *is-a* `Vehicle` **with the additional property** `numberOfPropellers`.
- A `Boat` *is-a* `Vehicle` **with the additional property** `draft`.
- A `SailBoat` *is-a* `Boat` **with the additional property** `numberOfSails`.
- A `MotorBoat` *is-a* `Boat` **with the additional property** `horsePower`.

Draw the UML diagram that relates these classes.

Exercise 16–2.   Consider Exercise 16–1. Give the `class-extends` statements that would appear in a file containing the definitions of `Vehicle` and its subclasses.

Exercise 16–3.   Change the visibility of `name` to `private` in class `Item` in `Prog1603`. Does the code still compile? Why or why not?

Exercise 16–4.   Change the visibility of `netCost` to `private` in class `Item` in `Prog1603`. Does the code still compile? Why or why not?

Exercise 16–5.   Modify class `TaxableItem` in `Prog1603` so that it has a `static` variable `taxRate`. The initial `taxRate` should be 8.25%. Add a method

```
public static void setTaxRate(double)
```

that changes the `taxRate`. Write a driver that demonstrates that your code performs as required.

Exercise 16–6.   Take `Prog1603` and add a subclass `DiscountedItem` to class `Item`. Such items have an instance variable `discount`, which is the percent by which they are discounted. `DiscountedItem`s are not taxed. Their constructor has the prototype

```
public DiscountedItem(String,double,double)
```

for which the second `double` parameter is the discount. Write a driver that demonstrates that your code performs as required.

Exercise 16–7.   Implement and test the classes corresponding to the following UML diagram, which represents bank accounts:

Account
String name String accountNumber
Account(String,String) String toString()

↑

SavingsAccount
double balance
SavingsAccount(String,String,double) void deposit(double) void withdraw(double) String toString()

The result of toString for Account should be this:

```
03425
Bill Smith
```

The result of toString for SavingsAccount should be this:

```
03425
Bill Smith
$245.19
```

Exercise 16–8.   Consider a hierarchy of one-dimensional functions:

Polynomial $f(x) = \sum_{i=0}^{n} a_i x^i$

Quadratic $f(x) = ax^2 + bx + c$

Linear $f(x) = ax + b$

Constant $f(x) = c$

These correspond to the following UML diagram:

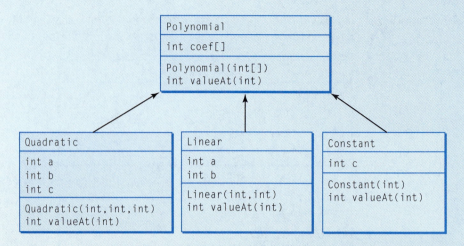

Write a method `makeTable(Polynomial[])`, which makes a columnar table of the functions represented in the array of `Polynomial` it's given. Write a driver that tests your `makeTable` method. Indicate where polymorphism is demonstrated in your code. For example, if `makeTable` gets an array of the functions $f(x) = 2x + 3$ and $f(x) = x^2 - 1$, then a table of the values `f(x)` for $x \in \{1,2,3,4,5\}$ would be:

```
1        5        0
2        7        3
3        9        8
4       11       15
5       13       24
```

Exercise 16–9. Why is the `String` class `final`?

Exercise 16–10. Why is the `Scanner` class `final`?

Exercise 16–11. Starting with `Prog1610.java`, try to create an instance of the `abstract` class `Animal`. What message does Java give?

Exercise 16–12. What message does Java give when you put an `abstract` method inside a class which is not, itself, declared `abstract`?

Exercise 16–13. An `abstract` method cannot be defined as `final`. Why?

Exercise 16–14. An `abstract` method cannot be defined as `static`. Why?

Figure 16–12
Animal Hierarchy

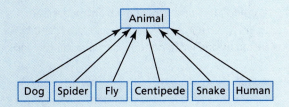

Exercise 16–15. Consider the class hierarchy shown in Figure 16–12. `Animal` is to be an `abstract` class. The following table gives the number of legs for each `Animal`.

Animal	# of Legs
Dog	4
Spider	8
Fly	6
Centipede	100
Snake	0
Human	2

`getNumberOfLegs()` should be an `abstract` method for class `Animal`. Implement this class hierarchy in Java. Provide a method that takes an array of `Animal`s and returns the total number of legs.

Exercise 16–16. Draw the diagram that relates the following classes: `Animal`, `Quadruped`, `Biped`, `Insect`, and `Other`. Add nodes at the leaves of the tree; include `Centipede`, `Millipede`, `Snake`, `Cow`, `Human`, `Giraffe`, and `Gorilla`. Convert your diagram to Java, providing a method `getNumberOfLegs()`. Provide a method that takes an array of `Animal`s and returns the total number of legs.
Note that we also might have solved this problem *without* a class hierarchy. We could have defined class `Animal` in this way:

```
Animal
String species
int numberOfLegs
...
...
```

Exercise 16–17.   Consider the problem domain introduced in Section 16.14 involving `Employee`, `Hourly`, `Person`, `Salaried`, `UnionMember`, and `Volunteer`. Practice creating the class hierarchy and writing the Java code without consulting the text.

Exercise 16–18.   Add a *vacation days* facility to this hierarchy. For each `Person`, keep count of the number of vacation days, add some each payday, debit some when vacation is taken, and report the count when requested.

Exercise 16–19.   Develop a class hierarchy for `Person` by working *top-down* rather than *bottom-up*.

Exercise 16–20.   Consider a hierarchy of 2-D `Shapes`. A `Point` describes the (*x, y*) coordinates of a point in the plane. The color of a `Shape` is specified by an instance of the class `Color`. Every `Shape` has a center, which is a `Point`, and an angle of rotation, which describes how much the `Shape` is rotated from some standard orientation. Each `Shape` also has a color. The following methods apply to `Shapes`:

- `area()` returns the area of a `Shape`.
- `draw()` puts the `Shape` on top of a 2-D canvas.
- `moveTo(Point)` moves the `Shape` to another position.
- `rotateBy(double)` rotates the `Shape`.
- `setColor(Color)` changes the color of a `Shape`.

Here are some individual shapes:

- `Rectangle` has `length` and `width`.
- `Square` has a `side`.
- `Circle` has a `radius`.
- `Ellipse` has a `majorAxis` and a `minorAxis`.

What other classes and properties should exist in a graphics system? Write a driver that demonstrates polymorphism using an array of `Shapes`. Write a method that takes an array of `Shapes` and that also

- determines if there are any *red* `Shapes` in the array.
- computes the total area of the `Shapes` in the array.

Exercise 16–21.   For the `Shape` hierarchy, what are the advantages and disadvantages of the following hierarchies?

- Hierarchy 1 separates circularly symmetric Shapes from those that are not circularly symmetric:

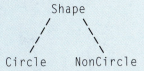

- Hierarchy 2 views Circle as a special case of Ellipse:

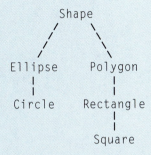

Exercise 16–22. Modify Prog1612 to demonstrate Hgap and Vgap.

Exercise 16–23. Modify Prog1612 to use a loop to produce 24 buttons on the panel. Resize the window so that buttons are positioned eight across, six across, four across, and two across. Notice how the number of lines increases appropriately.

Exercise 16–24. What happens if you add *several* buttons into a single pane of a BorderLayout?

Exercise 16–25. Consider BorderLayout. What happens to a region if you add nothing?

Exercise 16–26. Write an application that uses BorderLayout to read a String (center), and display it in uppercase (north) and in lowercase (south).

CHAPTER SEVENTEEN

Exceptions

Chapter Objectives

- Use Java's Exception handling mechanism.
- Understand the data presented when an Exception is raised.
- Use the Exception mechanism to trap invalid input.
- Define our own Exceptions as needed.

At last we will examine the pesky throws Exceptions that have hounded us throughout this book!

Exceptions exploit our ability to *expect the unexpected*. Exceptions represent unusual situations from which we may be able to recover. Remember how a noninteger caused nextInt to bomb? In this chapter, we'll learn how to protect our code so that an unwanted InputMismatchException will no longer bomb our program: We'll be able to keep reading Strings until we get one that represents an integer.

Exception and Error are similar. Both are subclasses of Throwable, but unlike Exceptions, Errors represent grave conditions from which we do not expect to be able to recover.

Associated with Exceptions are the keywords throw, catch, try, and finally, and the common English word *handle*. In this chapter we will examine the mechanics and uses of Exceptions in Java.

17.1 Exceptions We've Already Encountered

Throughout this book, we've seen Exceptions. Our first program contained the phrase

```
public static void main ( String [] args ) throws Exception
```

by which we made the required acknowledgment that the code within the program was capable of generating an Exception.

When we learned about files, we discovered that we were subject to FileNotFoundExceptions in a variety of circumstances:

- If we tried to open a nonexistent file for reading.
- If we tried to delete a nonexistent file.
- If we tried to write to a file that was protected as read-only.

Later in the text we found that:

- we encountered the InputMismatchException when nextInt encountered a noninteger;
- with arithmetic came ArithmeticExceptions such as *divide by zero*;
- NumberFormatExceptions came when we tried to convert a noninteger String to an int by means of Integer.parseInt; and
- when we learned arrays, we found ArrayIndexOutOfBoundsException.

Now we will learn how to recover from situations that throw these and other Exceptions.

17.2 Anatomy of an Exception

Consider Prog1701, in which we generate an Exception by means of the statement

```
System.out.println(1/0);[1]
```

---

[1] Some compilers do not compile a program that contains this statement. They do some *precompilation* to convert constant expressions, such as 2/3, into their equivalent 0. But 1/0 would generate an error at run-time, and some compilers do us the favor (?) of rejecting the expression at compile-time. It may still be possible to get the desired Exception by using the statements int zero = 0; System.out.println(1/zero);.

At run-time, the output is this:

```
Exception in thread "main" java.lang.ArithmeticException:
/ by zero
          at Prog1701.main(Prog1701.java:12)
```

We can understand this in pieces:

- An Exception occurred in method main.
- The Exception was an ArithmeticException.
- In particular, it was division by zero (/ by zero).
- It was generated by the statement at line 12 of Prog1701.java.

This information is helpful for debugging.

Prog1701.java   **Divide-by-Zero Exception**

```
// Written by Barry Soroka
//
// Throw a divide-by-zero Exception.
//
import java.io.*;
////////////////////////////////////////////////////////////////////////////
class Prog1701
{
//--------------------------------------------------------------------------

    public static void main ( String [] args ) throws Exception
    {
        System.out.println(1/0);
    }
//--------------------------------------------------------------------------
} // end class Prog1701
////////////////////////////////////////////////////////////////////////////
```

Call stack trace   A trail of all the methods from main down to where an Exception is raised.

The line at Prog1701.main ... is part of a *call stack trace* whereby Java reports what specific methods called other methods from main down to whatever method contained the offending statement. Exceptions don't concern *classes*—they concern *methods*.

17.3 Divide by Zero with a Deeper Stack

Prog1702 is a program in which main calls f calls g calls h, which throws an ArithmeticException because of division by zero. Here's the output:

```
Exception in thread "main" java.lang.ArithmeticException:
/ by zero
        at Prog1702.h(Prog1702.java:19)
        at Prog1702.g(Prog1702.java:17)
        at Prog1702.f(Prog1702.java:15)
        at Prog1702.main(Prog1702.java:12)
```

As expected, the call stack trace reflects the sequence of four method calls: main → f → g → h.

Prog1702.java   **A Deeper Call Stack**

```
// Written by Barry Soroka
//
// Divide by 0 with a deeper stack.
//
import java.io.*;
/////////////////////////////////////////////////////////////////////////////
class Prog1702
{
//---------------------------------------------------------------------------
    public static void main ( String [] args ) throws Exception
    {
        f();
    }
//---------------------------------------------------------------------------
    private static void f() { g(); }
//---------------------------------------------------------------------------
    private static void g() { h(); }
//---------------------------------------------------------------------------
    private static void h() { System.out.println(1/0); }
//---------------------------------------------------------------------------
} // end class Prog1702
/////////////////////////////////////////////////////////////////////////////
```

Prog1703 expands this example by having f, g, and h print messages upon entry and exit. We also have an option as to whether we want h to throw an

Exception. Here's the output when we *don't* throw the Exception. What the user types is underlined:

```
G:\>java Prog1703
Do you want an Exception? (y/n)n
Enter method f ...
   Enter method g ...
      Enter method h ...
      Hello from method h!
      Exit method h
   Exit method g
Exit method f
```

Notice how we go down through the methods, then produce the expected Hello line, and then exit back up the call stack.

Prog1703.java   **Exceptions Interrupt Normal Control Flow**

```java
// Written by Barry Soroka
//
// Divide by 0 -- How control flow is interrupted.
//
import java.io.*;
import java.util.Scanner;
///////////////////////////////////////////////////////////////////////////////
class Prog1703
{
//-----------------------------------------------------------------------------
   public static void main ( String [] args ) throws Exception
   {
      Scanner kb = new Scanner(System.in);

      System.out.print("Do you want an Exception? (y/n)");
      char answer = kb.nextLine().charAt(0);
      if ( answer == 'y' || answer == 'Y' ) f(true);
      else                                  f(false);
   }
//-----------------------------------------------------------------------------
   private static void f ( boolean b )
   {
      System.out.println("Enter method f ...");
      g(b);
      System.out.println("Exit method f");
   }
```

```
//--------------------------------------------------------------------
   private static void g ( boolean b )
   {
      System.out.println("  Enter method g ...");
      h(b);
      System.out.println("  Exit method g");
   }
//--------------------------------------------------------------------
   private static void h ( boolean b )
   {
      System.out.println("    Enter method h ...");
      if ( b ) System.out.println(1/0);
      else     System.out.println("    Hello from method h!");
      System.out.println("    Exit method h");
   }
//--------------------------------------------------------------------
} // end class Prog1703
//////////////////////////////////////////////////////////////////////
```

Here's the output when h *does* throw an Exception:

```
G:\>java Prog1703
Do you want an Exception? (y/n)y
Enter method f ...
  Enter method g ...
    Enter method h ...
Exception in thread "main" java.lang.ArithmeticException:
/ by zero
        at Prog1703.h(Prog1703.java:38)
        at Prog1703.g(Prog1703.java:31)
        at Prog1703.f(Prog1703.java:24)
        at Prog1703.main(Prog1703.java:17)
```

We see the entry messages from f, g, and h. However, the normal progress of the computation is completely disrupted by the divide-by-zero Exception: We don't take the normal exits of *any* of the methods we've entered.

17.4   Exceptions Are Objects

Exceptions are *objects*. As objects, they have constructors and methods that can be used in Java code. Additionally, Exceptions can be thrown by explicit statements in a program. We'll examine catching in the next section, and throwing in Section 17.9. Beyond that, we'll learn how to create and throw our own Exceptions.

Constructors

We can create an Exception with the constructor Exception(String). The String is a message that travels with the Exception as it moves along the road of its handling.

The constructor Exception() creates an Exception without a textual message.

Methods

We will use three methods that are associated with Exceptions. The method

```
String getMessage()
```

allows us to see the message that was wrapped up at the creation of an Exception. The method

```
void printStackTrace()
```

prints the call stack trace, which was trapped at the time the Exception was thrown.

We saw both of these methods in use in the dialogs shown in the previous section: When the Java Virtual Machine received the unhandled divide-by-zero Exception, it printed the result of getMessage() and it called printStack-Trace() to print the stack trace.

Exceptions also have a toString method, which prints the name of the Exception and the message, if any.

17.5 try and catch

The try-catch structure is used to handle Exceptions. The syntax is this:

```
try
{
    statements which may generate an Exception
}
catch ( Exception e )
{
    statements which handle the Exception
}
```

The `try` block encloses the statements that may generate the `Exception`, and the `catch` keyword introduces the *type* of `Exception` being caught and the statements that handle it. Within the `catch` block, e refers to the `Exception` that was thrown and caught, so that we can apply the `Exception`-specific methods, if desired. (Sometimes we merely want to *catch* the `Exception` without investigating its innards.)

> `catch` To intercept an `Exception`.
> **handle** To catch and process an `Exception`.

Prog1704 shows code that traps an anticipated divide-by-zero `Exception`. Within the `try` block we have a statement that will throw an `Exception`:

```
System.out.println(1/0);
```

The `catch` block is empty—we will *catch* this `Exception`, but we won't do anything with it. Notice that this code is the same as that in Prog1701, except that we are *handling* the `Exception` instead of *ignoring* it. When Prog1701 was executed, we had the dialog:

```
G:\>java Prog1701
Exception in thread "main" java.lang.ArithmeticException:
/ by zero
        at Prog1701.main(Prog1701.java:12)
G:\>
```

When Prog1704 executes, we see the following:

```
G:\>java Prog1704
G:\>
```

It's as though the `Exception` never happened at all! Remember this: When you catch an `Exception`, your program does not necessarily bomb.

Prog1704.java   **try and catch**

```
// Written by Barry Soroka
//
// Catches an Exception.
//
import java.io.*;
/////////////////////////////////////////////////////////////////////////////
class Prog1704
{
//---------------------------------------------------------------------------
    public static void main ( String [] args ) throws Exception
```

```
    {
        try
        {
            System.out.println(1/0);
        }
        catch ( Exception e )
        {
        }
    }
//- - - - - - - - - - - - - - - - - - - - - - - - - - - - - - - - - - - - - - - - - - - - - - - - - - - - - - -
} // end class Prog1704
//////////////////////////////////////////////////////////////////////////////
```

We must be careful when we `catch Exception`s. Consider the following analogy: A symptom indicates an underlying disease. If we make the symptom disappear, it doesn't mean that the disease has gone away. An `Exception`, like a symptom, indicates an underlying problem. If we catch the `Exception` we hide the symptom, but the underlying problem has not gone away.

When we catch an `Exception`, we have a responsibility to properly handle the problem that threw it. A `try-catch` block creates a "sandbox" in which the code is free to `throw` an `Exception` because we promise to `catch` it. Throwing the `Exception` no longer terminates the program.

Now let's insert statements into the `catch` block to learn more about the `Exception`. First, let's simply print it out, using the `toString` method:

```
        System.out.println(e);
```

`Prog1705` contains the complete program. Here's the dialog:

```
        G:\>java Prog1705
        java.lang.ArithmeticException: / by zero
        G:\>
```

As we can see, the `toString` method of an `Exception` consists of the name of the `Exception`, a colon (":"), and the message wrapped in the `Exception`.

Prog1705.java   **Catching a Divide-by-Zero Exception**

```
// Written by Barry Soroka
//
// Catches an Exception.
//
import java.io.*;
```

```
/////////////////////////////////////////////////////////////////////////////
class Prog1705
{
//---------------------------------------------------------------------------
    public static void main ( String [] args ) throws Exception
    {
        try
        {
            System.out.println(1/0);
        }
        catch ( Exception e )
        {
            System.out.println(e);
        }
    }
//---------------------------------------------------------------------------
} // end class Prog1705
/////////////////////////////////////////////////////////////////////////////
```

 Test your skill with Exercise 17–1.

Prog1706 tests toString, getMessage, and printStackTrace. Inside the catch we find the lines

```
System.out.println(e);
System.out.println("message is \"" + e.getMessage() + "\"");
e.printStackTrace();
```

which generate the output

```
java.lang.ArithmeticException: / by zero
message is "/ by zero"
java.lang.ArithmeticException: / by zero
        at Prog1706.main(Prog1706.java:14)
```

The first line comes from toString. The second line displays the message. The third and fourth lines show the call stack trace, headed automatically by the result of toString.

Prog1706.java   **Methods Applicable to Exceptions**

```
// Written by Barry Soroka
//
// Catches an Exception.
//
```

```java
import java.io.*;
/////////////////////////////////////////////////////////////////////////////
class Prog1706
{
//---------------------------------------------------------------------------
   public static void main ( String [] args ) throws Exception
   {
      try
      {
         System.out.println(1/0);
      }
      catch ( Exception e )
      {
         System.out.println(e);
         System.out.println("message is \"" + e.getMessage() + "\"");
         e.printStackTrace();
      }
   }
//---------------------------------------------------------------------------
} // end class Prog1706
/////////////////////////////////////////////////////////////////////////////
```

17.6   A Fail-Safe Reader of Integers

Consider Prog1707. This program uses a static method readInt(Scanner) to read an integer from the specified Scanner. Here's what happens when the user enters a noninteger:

```
G:\>java Prog1707
Enter an int: hello
Exception in thread "main" java.util.InputMismatchException
        at java.util.Scanner.throwFor(Unknown Source)
        at java.util.Scanner.next(Unknown Source)
        at java.util.Scanner.nextInt(Unknown Source)
        at java.util.Scanner.nextInt(Unknown Source)
        at Prog1707.readInt(Prog1707.java:19)
        at Prog1707.main(Prog1707.java:13)
```

The illegal input has caused nextInt to throw an InputMismatchException, and the program has bombed.

Prog1707.java   **Reading an int**

```java
// Written by Barry Soroka
//
import java.io.*;
import java.util.Scanner;
//////////////////////////////////////////////////////////////////////////////
class Prog1707
{
//-----------------------------------------------------------------------------
   public static void main (String[] args) throws Exception
   {
      Scanner kb = new Scanner(System.in);
      System.out.print("Enter an int: ");
      int n = readInt(kb);
      System.out.println("You entered " + n);
   }
//-----------------------------------------------------------------------------
   private static int readInt ( Scanner sc )
   {
      return sc.nextInt();
   }
//-----------------------------------------------------------------------------
} // end class Prog1707
//////////////////////////////////////////////////////////////////////////////
```

Let's improve this program so that an `InputMismatchException` will be caught and handled. In particular, we'll tell the user that the input was wrong, and we'll prompt for another integer in order to give the user another try. `Prog1708` is the code. Here is hardcopy of a typical run:

```
G:\>java Prog1708
Enter an int: hello
Invalid input.  Try again: 3.17
Invalid input.  Try again: 8
You entered 8
```

Each time we enter invalid input, the program rejects it and asks us to try again, going back to the top of the loop.

Prog1708.java   **Catching Invalid ints**

```java
// Written by Barry Soroka
//
import java.io.*;
```

```
import java.util.*;
import java.util.Scanner;
/////////////////////////////////////////////////////////////////////////////
class Prog1708
{
//----------------------------------------------------------------------------
    public static void main (String[] args) throws Exception
    {
        Scanner kb = new Scanner(System.in);
        System.out.print("Enter an int: ");
        int n = readInt(System.out,kb);
        System.out.println("You entered " + n);
    }
//----------------------------------------------------------------------------
    private static int readInt ( PrintStream ps, Scanner sc )
    {
        int result = 0;
        boolean gotAnInt = false;

        while ( !gotAnInt )
        {
            try
            {
                result = sc.nextInt();
                gotAnInt = true;
            }
            catch ( InputMismatchException e )
            {
                sc.nextLine();
                ps.print("Invalid input.  Try again: ");
            }
        }
        return result;
    }
//----------------------------------------------------------------------------
} // end class Prog1708
/////////////////////////////////////////////////////////////////////////////
```

Notice how the nextInt statement has been put into a try block inside a while loop. If nextInt is successful, then the control variable gotAnInt is turned to true, and we'll exit the try block and return the integer result. If nextInt fails, throwing an InputMismatchException, the Exception will be caught and handled. We execute a nextLine to clear all the input on the current line, then we print a new prompt and return to the top of the loop.

Notice how Prog1708 requires the statement

```
import java.util.*;
```

This is because InputMismatchException is defined in the library java.util, and it won't be recognized unless we specifically include that part of the API.

> **Test your skill with Exercises 17–2 through 17–4.**

17.7 Multiple catch Blocks

It's possible that the code inside a try block can generate different kinds of Exceptions. Consider the code

```
File f = new File(filename);
Scanner sc = new Scanner(new File(filename));
return Integer.parseInt(sc.nextLine());
```

This can generate *different* Exceptions for *different reasons*:

- If filename is not a valid filename for this operating system, then File will throw a FileNotFoundException.
- If filename is not the name of an *existing* file, then Scanner will throw a FileNotFoundException.
- If the first line of the file is not a valid int, then parseInt will throw a NumberFormatException.

Consider a method readIntFromFile that takes a String—a hypothetical filename—and returns the int on the first line of that file. (Of course, it's possible that the first line is *not* a valid int.) Prog1709 gives the code. If anything goes wrong, then readIntFromFile will print an informative message and return 0. Notice the *three* catch blocks that follow the try block:

```
try { ... }
catch ( FileNotFoundException e ) { ... }
catch ( NumberFormatException e) { ... }
catch ( Exception e ) { ... }
```

Each catch block catches its specific Exception and prints the corresponding message. In this way, we can use Java's try-catch mechanism to handle code that can generate different kinds of Exceptions.

Java is pretty smart about this. Let's put the last catch block first, producing

```
try { ... }
catch ( Exception e ) { ... }
catch ( FileNotFoundException e ) { ... }
catch ( NumberFormatException e) { ... }
```

Java gives the errors

```
Prog1709.java:36: exception java.io.FileNotFoundException has
already been caught
        catch ( FileNotFoundException e )
        ^
Prog1709.java:41: exception java.lang.NumberFormatException
has already been caught
        catch ( NumberFormatException e )
        ^
2 errors
```

because Java knows that `FileNotFoundException` and `NumberFormatException` are subclasses of `Exception`. We must always put general `Exceptions` *after* specific `Exceptions`.

Prog1709.java   **Multiple catch Blocks**

```
// Written by Barry Soroka
//
// A try block with multiple catch blocks.
//
import java.io.*;
import java.util.Scanner;
///////////////////////////////////////////////////////////////////////////
class Prog1709
{
//-------------------------------------------------------------------------
   public static void main ( String [] args ) throws Exception
   {
      Scanner kb = new Scanner(System.in);

      while ( true )
      {
         System.out.print("\nName of a file whose first line is an int? ");
         System.out.println("readIntFromFile returned " +
                        readIntFromFile(kb.nextLine()));
      }
   }
//-------------------------------------------------------------------------
```

```
   private static int readIntFromFile ( String filename )
   {
      try
      {
         File f = new File(filename);
         Scanner sc = new Scanner(new File(filename));
         return Integer.parseInt(sc.nextLine());
      }
      catch ( FileNotFoundException e )
      {
         System.out.println("A FileNotFoundException occurred, returning 0.");
         return 0;
      }
      catch ( NumberFormatException e )
      {
         System.out.println("NumberFormatException occurred, returning 0.");
         return 0;
      }
      catch ( Exception e )
      {
         System.out.println("Some other Exception occurred, returning 0.");
         return 0;
      }
   }
//-------------------------------------------------------------------
} // end class Prog1709
///////////////////////////////////////////////////////////////////////////
```

 Test your skill with Exercises 17–5 through 17–7.

17.8 finally

Sometimes we have code that needs to be done no matter what happens in a try block. Perhaps we need to close files or close network connections. The finally block was created to facilitate such cleanup. After all the catch blocks—if any—we can put a finally block, which has the syntax

```
finally
{
   // finally block statements
}
```

The code in a `finally` block is *always* performed. Even if a statement in a `try` or `catch` block is a `throw`, `return`, `break`, or `continue`, the code in the `finally` block is performed before the `throw`, `return`, `break`, or `continue` is executed.

> **Test your skill with Exercises 17–8 through 17–10.**

17.9   Where Can an Exception Be Handled?

We have seen the mechanics of handling `Exceptions` with the `try`, `catch`, and `finally` constructs. Now let's see how the mechanism can be *used*.

An `Exception` can be handled in one of three ways:

1. We can ignore it.
2. It can be handled locally, in the method where the `Exception`-generating statement occurs.
3. It can be handled elsewhere.

We'll look at these three possibilities in order.

Ignoring an Exception

If an `Exception` reaches a method and we don't include code to handle it, then the `Exception` automatically moves upward—*propagates*—to the method that originally called *this* method. This propagation continues until the `Exception` is caught, or until the `Exception` reaches the Java Virtual Machine. If the `Exception` reaches the JVM, then the `Exception` and the stack trace are printed, and the program halts. We saw this behavior when we examined `Prog1702`.

> **Propagate**   To let an `Exception` be handled higher up in the call stack.

Handling an Exception Where It Occurs

This corresponds to (1) putting a `try` block around a statement that is capable of throwing an `Exception`, and (2) putting an appropriate `catch` block after the `try` block. This `catches` the `Exception` and handles it locally (i.e., where it occurs).

Note that we can `throw` an `Exception` from inside a `catch` block. `Prog1710` gives an example. The statement

```
System.out.println(1/0)
```

generates an `ArithmeticException`, which is handled locally by the following `catch` block:

```
catch ( ArithmeticException e )
{
    System.out.println("f caught an ArithmeticException");
    throw e;
}
```

throw To raise or propagate an `Exception`.

This block prints out a message and then `throws` the same `Exception` upward, to the method that originally called this one. In the current case, the `Exception` reaches the JVM and the program bombs. Here's the output:

```
C:\>java Prog1710
f caught an ArithmeticException
Exception in thread "main" java.lang.ArithmeticException:
/ by zero
        at Prog1710.f(Prog1710.java:19)
        at Prog1710.main(Prog1710.java:12)
```

We can clearly see the message printed by the `catch` block and the lines printed by the JVM.

Prog1710.java   **Catching an Exception Locally**

```
// Written by Barry Soroka
//
// Catching an Exception locally.
//
import java.io.*;
/////////////////////////////////////////////////////////////////////////////
class Prog1710
{
//----------------------------------------------------------------------------
    public static void main ( String [] args ) throws Exception
    {
        f();
    }
//----------------------------------------------------------------------------
    private static void f()
```

```
      {
         try
         {
            System.out.println(1/0);
         }
         catch ( ArithmeticException e )
         {
            System.out.println("f caught an ArithmeticException");
            throw e;
         }
      }
   }
//-----------------------------------------------------------------------
} // end class Prog1710
///////////////////////////////////////////////////////////////////////
```

Handling an Exception Elsewhere

Instead of ignoring an Exception or handling it locally, we can handle the Exception in a method *other than* the method in which it is thrown. Prog1711 gives an example. Method f calls method g, which throws a divide-by-zero Exception. Method g doesn't handle the error, but a try block in method f encloses the call to g. Now, when the Exception is thrown, it passes out of g but is caught by the catch block of f.

Prog1711.java   **Catching an Exception Higher Up in the Call Stack**

```
// Written by Barry Soroka
//
// g throws an ArithmeticException; f catches it.
//
import java.io.*;
///////////////////////////////////////////////////////////////////////
class Prog1711
{
//-----------------------------------------------------------------------
   public static void main ( String [] args ) throws Exception
   {
      f();
   }
//-----------------------------------------------------------------------
   private static void f()
   {
      try
```

```
        {
            g();
        }
        catch ( ArithmeticException e )
        {
            System.out.println("f caught an ArithmeticException");
        }
    }
//------------------------------------------------------------------------
    private static void g()
    {
        System.out.println(1/0);
    }
//------------------------------------------------------------------------
} // end class Prog1711
/////////////////////////////////////////////////////////////////////////
```

17.10   **Defining Our Own** Exceptions

Defining a new class often entails defining a new set of Exceptions. The new class provides the user with a new set of capabilities, but similarly, an entirely new set of Exceptions may be appropriate. Rather than simply bombing, we can give the class-user the ability to handle an Exception in a manner appropriate to the program involved.

For example, SectionFullException may be thrown if we attempt to add a Student to a Section that is full. The class-user has several options for handling this:

- Ignore it, leading to abnormal program termination.
- Reject the Student's request to add.
- Enlarge the size of the Section.

You might think that we could avoid this problem by writing the statement

```
        if ( sec.isNotFull() ) sec = sec.addStudent(s);
```

but some other process may add a Student in the time between the isNotFull test and the addStudent call, and an Exception would result.

Here are some other examples of Exceptions that arise from classes we might define:

- NonRegisteredStudentException might be thrown if we try to delete a Student from a Section in which the Student isn't actually registered.
- DualEnrollmentException might be thrown if a Student tries to enroll in the same Section *twice*.
- IllegalDepositException might be thrown if there's an attempt to deposit a *negative* amount into a BankAccount.

A Stack of ints

> **Stack**   A data structure that processes items in the order *last-in first-out* (LIFO).

Let's design our own Exceptions for the data structure known as a *stack*, which operates like a stack of dinner plates on the shelf of a cabinet. A stack has operations *push* and *pop* that, respectively, add a plate to the top of the stack and take the top plate *off* the top of the stack. This is called a *last-in first-out* (LIFO) regime, because the most recently pushed element is the first to be brought out by a pop operation.

There are two possible Exceptions:

- The shelf can be *full*, and there won't be room to *push* another plate on the top of the stack. This is called *stack overflow*.
- The shelf can be *empty*, and there won't be a plate to get with the *pop* operation. This is called *stack underflow*.

You'll learn more about stacks and other data structures in CS 2.

Let's work with a stack of ints. We'll have the following constructor and methods:

- Stack() will create a new Stack. New Stacks are initially empty. We'll create Stacks with a maximum capacity of *three* ints.
- void push(int) will add an int to the top of the Stack. If the Stack is full, we expect this method to throw an Exception.
- int pop() will remove and return the int from the top of the Stack. If the Stack is empty, we expect this method to throw an Exception.

Prog1712 gives an implementation of class Stack and a driver to test it. The program tests either overflow or underflow, depending on user input. If we test *overflow*, we have the dialog:

```
G:\>java Prog1712
Test (f)ull case or (e)mpty case? f
```

```
Exception in thread "main" java.lang.ArrayIndexOutOfBoundsException
        at Stack.push(Prog1712.java:45)
        at Prog1712.main(Prog1712.java:25)
```

If we test *underflow*, we have the dialog:

```
G:\>java Prog1712
Test (f)ull case or (e)mpty case? e
Exception in thread "main" java.lang.ArrayIndexOutOfBoundsException
        at Stack.pop(Prog1712.java:51)
        at Prog1712.main(Prog1712.java:29)
```

In the exceptional cases, Java has halted program execution and has given us an error message. However, the message doesn't tell us what caused the Exception, or whether it was a case of overflow or underflow. We know only that some array indexing problem occurred.

Prog1712.java   **No Special Exceptions for a Stack of ints**

```java
// Written by Barry Soroka
//
// Stack of int -- no special Exceptions.
//
import java.io.*;
//////////////////////////////////////////////////////////////////////////////
class Prog1712
{
//------------------------------------------------------------------------------
   public static void main ( String [] args ) throws Exception
   {
      Stack stack = new Stack();

      BufferedReader kb = new BufferedReader(
                          new InputStreamReader(System.in));

      System.out.print("Test (f)ull case or (e)mpty case? ");
      char testType = kb.readLine().toLowerCase().charAt(0);

      if ( testType == 'f' )
      {
         stack.push(3);
         stack.push(7);
         stack.push(4);
         stack.push(8);    // pushes onto a full Stack
      }
```

```
      else
      {
         int i = stack.pop();    // pops an empty Stack
      }
   }
//------------------------------------------------------------------------
} // end class Prog1712
////////////////////////////////////////////////////////////////////////////
class Stack
{
   private int[] a;
   private int used;
   private static int MAX = 3;
//------------------------------------------------------------------------
   public Stack() { a = new int[MAX]; used = 0; }
//------------------------------------------------------------------------
   public void push ( int n )
   {
      a[used] = n;
      used++;
   }
//------------------------------------------------------------------------
   public int pop()
   {
      int result = a[used-1];
      used--;
      return result;
   }
//------------------------------------------------------------------------
} // end class Stack
////////////////////////////////////////////////////////////////////////////
```

Custom Exceptions for the Stack of ints Problem

We can improve on Prog1712 by defining our own Exceptions to be thrown exclusively by Stack operations. Prog1713 gives the code. Here's the definition of StackOverflowException:

```
////////////////////////////////////////////////////////////////////////////
class StackOverflowException extends Exception
{
//------------------------------------------------------------------------
```

```
        public StackOverflowException ( String message ) { super(message); }
        //------------------------------------------------------------------
    } // end class StackOverflowException
    ///////////////////////////////////////////////////////////////////////
```

New `Exceptions` extend existing `Exceptions`, and the constructor uses `super` to access the existing constructor.

Prog1713.java   Special **Exceptions** for a Stack of ints

```java
// Written by Barry Soroka
//
// Stack with its own Exceptions.
//
import java.io.*;
///////////////////////////////////////////////////////////////////////////
class Prog1713
{
//-----------------------------------------------------------------------
    public static void main ( String [] args ) throws Exception
    {
        Stack stack = new Stack();

        BufferedReader kb = new BufferedReader(
                            new InputStreamReader(System.in));

        System.out.print("Test (f)ull or (e)mpty ? ");
        char testType = kb.readLine().toLowerCase().charAt(0);

        if ( testType == 'f' )
        {
            stack.push(3);
            stack.push(7);
            stack.push(4);
        }
        else stack.pop();
    }
//-----------------------------------------------------------------------
} // end class Prog1713
///////////////////////////////////////////////////////////////////////////
class Stack
{
    private int[] a;
```

```
   private int used;
   private static int MAX = 2;
//-----------------------------------------------------------------------
   public Stack() { a = new int[MAX]; used = 0; }
//-----------------------------------------------------------------------
   public void push ( int n ) throws Exception
   {
      if ( used == MAX )
      {
         throw new StackOverflowException("Trying to push " + n);
      }
      a[used] = n;
      used++;
   }
//-----------------------------------------------------------------------
   public int pop() throws Exception
   {
      if ( used == 0 )
      {
         throw new StackUnderflowException();
      }
      int result = a[used-1];
      used--;
      return result;
   }
//-----------------------------------------------------------------------
} // end class Stack
///////////////////////////////////////////////////////////////////////////
class StackUnderflowException extends Exception
{
//-----------------------------------------------------------------------
   public StackUnderflowException() { super(); }
//-----------------------------------------------------------------------
} // end class StackUnderflowException
///////////////////////////////////////////////////////////////////////////
class StackOverflowException extends Exception
{
//-----------------------------------------------------------------------
   public StackOverflowException(String message) { super(message); }
//-----------------------------------------------------------------------
} // end class StackOverflowException
///////////////////////////////////////////////////////////////////////////
```

Now we need the syntax that `throws` a `StackOverflowException`, when needed, from the `push` method:

```
if ( used == MAX )
    throw new StackOverflowException("Trying to push " + n);
```

We create a new `StackOverflowException`, incorporating the message we want, and then `throw` it.

`Prog1713` has the same driver as `Prog1712`. Here's the dialog we see in case of overflow:

```
G:\>java Prog1713
Test (f)ull case or (e)mpty case? f
Exception in thread "main" StackOverflowException: Trying to push 4
        at Stack.push(Prog1713.java:43)
        at Prog1713.main(Prog1713.java:24)
```

Notice that the `Exception` tells us that *overflow* has occurred—not just an array index out of bounds—and we even get to see the element we were trying to push at the time the `Exception` was thrown.

Here's the dialog we see in case of underflow:

```
G:\>java Prog1713
Test (f)ull case or (e)mpty case? e
Exception in thread "main" StackUnderflowException
        at Stack.pop(Prog1713.java:53)
        at Prog1713.main(Prog1713.java:26)
```

Again, the `Exception` name tells us that *underflow has occurred*—not just an array index out of bounds.

Note that the headers of both `push` and `pop` require the phrase `throws Exception` because we are explicitly throwing `Exceptions` in their bodies.

> **Test your skill with Exercises 17–11 and 17–12.**

17.11   **Checked versus Unchecked** Exceptions

Java partitions `Exceptions` into two groups: checked and unchecked.

Checked Exceptions must be *handled* in the method where they can occur, or they must be *acknowledged* in the header line with the keyword `throws` (as in `throws`

> **Checked** Exception   Must be handled or acknowledged.

Exception). We have seen one checked `Exception`: `File` can throw `FileNot-FoundException`—a subclass of `Exception`—which we have acknowledged with `throws Exception`.

> **Unchecked** Exception   Can be ignored.

Unchecked `Exception`s do not require handling or acknowledgment. These include `ArithmeticException`, `ArrayIndexOutOfBoundsException`, `NumberFormatException`, and `InputMismatchException`. Why does Java require that some `Exception`s be explicitly acknowledged in the code while others are not? Java is trying to help us write better code by pointing out situations—`FileNotFound`, for example—where we ought to be taking care of all circumstances in order to produce bulletproof programs.

If we handle a checked `Exception` locally, then we don't need to acknowledge it with a `throws` clause. Consider `Prog1714`. Both `f` and `g` contain the same statement

```
Scanner sc = new Scanner(new File(filename));
```

which can throw an `IOException`. Method `f` must explicitly acknowledge `throws IOException` because it doesn't `catch` and handle the `Exception`. Method `g` handles `IOException` locally, and it does *not* require a `throws IOException` clause.

Prog1714.java   **Local Handling versus throws IOException**

```
// Written by Barry Soroka
//
// "throws IOException" isn't needed if we handle it locally.
//
import java.io.*;
import java.util.Scanner;
/////////////////////////////////////////////////////////////////////////////
class Prog1714
{
//-------------------------------------------------------------------------
   private static void f ( String filename ) throws IOException
   {
        Scanner sc = new Scanner(new File(filename));
   }
//-------------------------------------------------------------------------
   private static void g ( String filename )
   {
      try
```

```
        {
            Scanner sc = new Scanner(new File(filename));
        }
        catch ( IOException e )
        {
        }
    }
//----------------------------------------------------------------------
} // end class Prog1714
//////////////////////////////////////////////////////////////////////
```

Chapter Summary

- We encountered numerous Exceptions.
- An unhandled Exception causes a program to bomb, printing some information about why and where the Exception was raised.
- Exceptions present an Exception name, a message, and a call stack trace.
- The call stack trace allows us to know the method in which an Exception was raised and the path from main to the offending method.
- Exceptions are objects.
- The class Exception provides the methods getMessage() and printStack-Trace().
- The try-catch structure allows us to catch and handle Exceptions.
- Suspect code is put in the try block.
- If an Exception is raised, the catch blocks are scanned for the one that matches the Exception.
- Java executes the code in the first catch block that matches the Exception.
- We can write a readInt method that reads Strings from the user until a valid int is entered. The Exception-handling mechanisms catch non-ints and prompt the user to enter more input.
- Multiple catch blocks may follow a try block. Only the code in the first matching catch block is executed.
- A finally block contains code that should be executed under all circumstances, regardless of whether an Exception is raised.
- An Exception can be handled in the method in which it is raised.
- An Exception can be handled further up the call stack.
- A catch block can perform some processing and then throw the Exception for further handling.
- Defining our own Exceptions allows our classes to notify the user when abnormal situations occur. The user can handle the Exceptions appropriately.

- A *checked* Exception must be handled in the method in which it can be raised, or the method must explicitly acknowledge the possibility of the Exception with a throws clause in the header.
- An *unchecked* Exception does not have to be handled or acknowledged.

Terminology Introduced in This Chapter

call stack trace	handle	throw
catch	propagate	unchecked Exception
checked Exception	stack	

Exercises

Exercise 17–1. Modify Prog1705 by replacing the println statement inside the try block with

```
throw new Exception();
```

This will throw an Exception containing no message. What does its toString look like? Does it have a dangling colon?

Exercise 17–2. Modify Prog1708 by commenting out the line that imports java.util.*. What error message do you get?

Exercise 17–3. Write a method

```
private static String readExistingFilename()
```

that keeps reading Strings from the user until it receives the name of an *existing* file. Then, return that String.

Exercise 17–4. Write a program that reads the name of a file and computes the number of lines in the file that represent integers. Use Integer.parseInt to parse complete lines read from the file. Use Java's Exception mechanism to detect when a given line is not a valid int.

Exercise 17–5. For Prog1709, prove that the NumberFormatException block can be placed before the FileNotFoundException block. Why is this possible?

Exercise 17–6.   Give code for which two `catch` blocks are triggered by the same `Exception`. Prove that only the first `catch` block is executed.

Exercise 17–7.   Does Java permit a `try` block to have two `catch` blocks for the exact same `Exception`? Prove it.

Exercise 17–8.   Write Java code that proves that the `finally` block is always performed, even if the `try` or `catch` block contains a `return` statement.

Exercise 17–9.   Can a `try` block have *two* `finally` blocks? Prove it.

Exercise 17–10.   Can a `catch` block follow a `finally` block? Prove it.

Exercise 17–11.   Write a driver that uses class `Stack` of `Prog1713`, and that appropriately `catches` the custom `Exceptions` when they are thrown.

Exercise 17–12.   Write a method

```
public static void checkDate(String)
```

that examines `Strings` and determines if they represent valid dates in the form *month*/*day*/*year*, such as *1/25/1903* or *10/3/1843*. Clearly, an alleged date can be invalid for many different reasons:

String	Reason It's Not Valid
3/14/3abc	Invalid year
a/22/2003	Invalid month
13/14/2003	Invalid month
3/hello/2003	Invalid day
3/99/2003	Invalid day

Your `checkDate` method should use `indexOf('/')` to break the `String` apart, and should use `Integer.parseInt` to convert a `String` to an `int`, if possible. Throw `Exceptions`— `IllegalMonthException`, `IllegalDayException`, and `IllegalYearException`—to signify the result of `checkDate`.

CHAPTER EIGHTEEN

Recursion

Chapter Objectives

- Understand the nature of recursion.
- Use recursion to solve problems.
- Hand-trace a recursive call to determine its result.
- Have Java tell us how a recursive call is progressing.
- Define recursive methods for class MyString.
- Appreciate when recursion should be used.

Simply put, *recursion* is what's happening *when a method calls itself*, such as when method f calls method f, or when method f calls method g, which, in turn, calls method f. It's the result of a *circle of calls*. Many computations can be written as recursions, and sometimes the recursive definition is the most natural definition. We'll build on these themes as we go along.

Recursion, recursive   When a method calls itself.

18.1   You've Seen Recursion Before

In your prior studies, you've seen some mathematical examples of recursion, and you may have encountered some other recursions that correspond to problems in the real world.

Almost everyone has seen the recursive definition of *factorial*:

$$0! = 1$$
$$n! = n \cdot (n - 1)!$$

where "!" stands for "factorial." This can also be written as

$$fac(0) = 1$$
$$fac(n) = n \cdot fac(n - 1)$$

Base case When the recursion stops.
Recursive step When the method calls itself.
Fibonacci numbers Each number is the sum of the two preceding numbers.

The definition has two pieces. The *base case* is $fac(0) = 1$, which stands for the parameter value for when we get an instant answer without having to make any further function calls. The *recursive step* is $fac(n) = n \cdot fac(n - 1)$, which tells us how to compute the factorial for numbers *other* than that named in the base case. These two pieces—base case and recursive step—will be common to all the recursions we'll study.

Fibonacci numbers are a numerical model of plant and animal growth, and they are defined by the recursion

$$fib(0) = 1$$
$$fib(1) = 1$$
$$fib(n) = fib(n - 2) + fib(n - 1).$$

Note that the definition has *two* base cases: `fib(0)` and `fib(1)`. The first several Fibonacci numbers are $1, 1, 2, 3, 5, 8, 13, 21, 34, 55, 89, \ldots$

Recursion is also used to model a variety of puzzles and games. The *Eight Queens* problem involves positioning eight chess queens on a chess board so that no two of them are attacking each other. The *Towers of Hanoi* puzzle involves moving n graduated disks from one spindle to another without placing a larger disk on top of a smaller disk. Both of these problems have naturally recursive solutions, and some of you may have seen the recursive code in prior courses.

18.2 Recursive Definitions and Closed Forms

In discrete math there are many recursive definitions, such as the following:

$$S(0) = 1$$
$$S(n) = 2 \cdot S(n - 1) + 1$$

When expanded, this sequence looks like this:

$$S(0) = 1$$
$$S(1) = 3$$
$$S(2) = 7$$
$$S(3) = 15$$

$$\ldots$$

We can guess that $S(n)$ has the *closed form* $S(n) = 2^{n+1} - 1$. The closed form is a pure formula that requires no recursion for its calculation—it's faster than using the recursive definition. In your discrete math course, you'll use *mathematical induction* to prove that the recursive definition and the closed form specify exactly the same function.

> **Closed form**   A formula that doesn't involve recursion.

Some recursions have closed forms, whereas others do not. Some closed forms are easy to guess and prove. If we don't have a closed form, then we need to use the recursive definition to compute values of the function when they're needed. The Fibonacci sequence is a good example of a recursive definition that lacks an obvious closed-form equivalent.

18.3   Animating Recursive Factorial

Consider the recursive definition of factorial:

$$fac(0) = 1$$
$$fac(n) = n \cdot fac(n - 1)$$

which consists of a base case and a recursive step, as described in Section 18.1. In this section, we'll examine how a computer uses this definition to compute `fac(4)`. We'll visualize distributing this problem among the members of the class, where each student knows only the recursive definition of `fac`:

- If the student is asked for the base case, `fac(0)`, then the student returns the value `1`.
- If the student is asked for any other case, `fac(n)`, then the recursive step will be implemented by (1) remembering `n`, and (2) passing the request for `fac(n-1)` to another student. When that student returns an answer, then (3) we'll multiply it by the remembered `n` and return the product as the value of `fac(n)`.

Let's see how this works in computing `fac(4)`.

1. Student A receives the request for `fac(4)`. This is not the base case, so Student A remembers 4 and asks Student B to compute `fac(3)`.
2. Student B receives the request for `fac(3)`. This is not the base case, so Student B remembers 3 and asks Student C to compute `fac(2)`.
3. Student C receives the request for `fac(2)`. This is not the base case, so Student C remembers 2 and asks Student D to compute `fac(1)`.
4. Student D receives the request for `fac(1)`. This is still not the base case, so Student D remembers 1 and asks Student E to compute `fac(0)`.

5. Student E receives the request for `fac(0)`. This *is* a base case, so Student E returns 1—without performing another recursive step.

4′. Student D now multiplies 1 times 1 and returns 1 as the value of `fac(1)`.

3′. Student C now multiplies 2 times 1 and returns 2 as the value of `fac(2)`.

2′. Student B now multiplies 3 times 2 and returns 6 as the value of `fac(3)`.

1′. Student A now multiplies 4 times 3 and returns 24 as the value of `fac(4)`.

Notice that each human "computer"[1] has the identical set of instructions—the recursive definition—and each performs only a small problem, but the net result of all their effort is to compute a factorial that was only implicitly present in the definition.

This is a reasonable model of how a recursive computation is performed within a computer. It's easy to see that there is a limit to how big a problem we can perform using this methodology; if we have only 10 "computers," then we can't compute `fac(11)`! *The Java Virtual Machine also has a limit on its stack space*, so it, too, has a limit on what it can compute recursively.

18.4 Infinite Recursion and Stack Frames

A well-behaved recursion like factorial involves a base case and a recursive step. But what if a recursive definition *doesn't* have a base case? Then we have an *infinite recursion*, because the function repeatedly calls itself without ever reaching a termination criterion.

> **Stack overflow** Running out of stack space in which to keep track of recursive calls.

`Prog1801` shows an infinite recursion implemented in Java: method `f` calls method `f` calls method `f` *ad infinitum*. When we compile and execute this code, Java throws an error—a `java.lang.StackOverflowError`—and we see the tail end of a very long call stack trace:

```
at Prog1801.f(Prog1801.java:17)
at Prog1801.f(Prog1801.java:17)
at Prog1801.f(Prog1801.java:17)
at Prog1801.f(Prog1801.java:17)
at Prog1801.f(Prog1801.java:17)
```

---

[1] "Computer" was a military job title during the Second World War. "Computers" were responsible for accepting simple numerical problems and returning the results to those who requested them. Veritable armies of such "computers" were able to provide the U.S. military with much-needed tables to guide the firing of ballistic weapons. Human "computers" may also have been involved in the design of the atomic bombs.

```
at Prog1801.f(Prog1801.java:17)
at Prog1801.f(Prog1801.java:17)
at Prog1801.f(Prog1801.java:17)
at Prog1801.f(Prog1801.java:17)
at Prog1801.f(Prog1801.java:17)
at Prog1801.f(Prog1801.java:17)
```

Because the call stack trace is so long, you may not be able to see the error at the top of the output.

Prog1801.java   Infinite Recursion

```
// Written by Barry Soroka
//
// Demonstrates infinite recursion and stack frames.
//
import java.io.*;
////////////////////////////////////////////////////////////////////////////
class Prog1801
{
//-----------------------------------------------------------------------
   public static void main ( String [] args ) throws Exception
   {
      f();
   }
//-----------------------------------------------------------------------
   private static void f()
   {
      f();
   }
//-----------------------------------------------------------------------
} // end class Prog1801
////////////////////////////////////////////////////////////////////////////
```

Stacks overflow because Java runs out of space in which to keep track of all the method invocations. How deep did this recursion go before Java ran out of stack space? Prog1802 provides the answer. Notice the following lines:

```
private static int depth = 0;
   ...
//-----------------------------------------------------------------------
   private static void f()
```

```
        {
            depth++;
            System.out.println(depth);
            f();
        }
//-----------------------------------------------------------
```

We use `depth` as a counter, and we increment and print it each time `f` is invoked. When we run this program, we get the following output:[2]

```
1
2
3
4
5
6
7
8
9
10
. . .
16635
16636
16637
16638
16639
```

The stack overflows after 16,639 invocations of method `f`.[3]

Prog1802.java   Infinite Recursion, Reporting Each New Stack Frame

```
// Written by Barry Soroka
//
// Infinite recursion -- reports each new stack frame.
//
import java.io.*;
////////////////////////////////////////////////////////////////////////////
class Prog1802
```

---

[2] You may need to capture the output in order to see the largest number. In DOS and Unix, the command `java Prog1802 > foo` captures the sequence of numbers into the file `foo`.

[3] Your mileage may vary. Each Java system has its own limits on the size of the stack.

```
{
   private static int depth = 0;
//-----------------------------------------------------------------
   public static void main ( String [] args ) throws Exception
   {
      f();
   }
//-----------------------------------------------------------------
   private static void f()
   {
      depth++;
      System.out.println(depth);
      f();
   }
//-----------------------------------------------------------------
} // end class Prog1802
/////////////////////////////////////////////////////////////////////
```

For each invocation of f, Java has to remember (1) the parameters of this invocation, and (2) the return address at which to resume execution after a return from the recursive call. We caused a stack overflow when f had no parameters. What happens if we give f a single int parameter? Prog1803 gives the code. The stack overflows after 12,479 calls.

Prog1803.java   **Infinite Recursion—Each Method Call Has a Parameter**

```
// Written by Barry Soroka
//
// Infinite recursion -- reports each new stack frame.
//
import java.io.*;
/////////////////////////////////////////////////////////////////////
class Prog1803
{
   private static int depth = 0;
//-----------------------------------------------------------------
   public static void main ( String [] args ) throws Exception
   {
      f(3);
   }
//-----------------------------------------------------------------
   private static void f(int n)
   {
      depth++;
```

```
      System.out.println(depth);
      f(n);
   }
//- - - - - - - - - - - - - - - - - - - - - - - - - - - - - - - - - - - - - - - - - - - - - - - - - - - - - - - - - -
} // end class Prog1803
//////////////////////////////////////////////////////////////////////////////////////
```

Test your skill with Exercise 18–1.

18.5   Evaluating a Recursive Call with Hand-Tracing

Hand-tracing is a paper-and-pencil mechanism for evaluating the result of an expression involving recursive calls. Consider the method

```
public static int a ( int x, int y )
{
    if ( x == 0 ) return y;
    return 1 + a(x-1,y);
}
```

We'll apply this recursive method to nonnegative parameters x and y. What does it do?

Let's consider a call to a(3,5). This isn't the base case, so it converts to

```
1 + a(2,5)
```

Notice that the second call—a(2,5)—is "smaller" (in the first parameter) than the original call to a(3,5). This is a good sign that the computation is progressing toward the base case, but the second call is still not the base case, so our expression becomes

```
1 + 1 + a(1,5)
```

which in turn becomes

```
1 + 1 + 1 + a(0,5)
```

which *is* the base case, yielding

```
1 + 1 + 1 + 5
```

This simplifies to

8

Put together, the computation is as follows. The action taken in each line is underlined:

```
a(3,5)
1 + a(2,5)
1 + 1 + a(1,5)
1 + 1 + 1 + a(0,5)
1 + 1 + 1 + 5
1 + 1 + 6
1 + 7
8.
```

Recursive method a computes the *sum* of x and y.

Hand-tracing is an important skill. If you can't hand-trace a recursive expression, then you won't be able to *write* and *debug* a recursive method.

> **Test your skill with Exercises 18–2 through 18–6.**

A *palindrome* is a sequence of values that is the same both forward and backward. The following Strings are palindromes: radar, ABBA, and x. Here is the code:

```
public static boolean isPalindrome ( String s )
{
    if ( s.length == 0 ) return true;
    if ( s.length == 1 ) return true;
    if ( s.charAt(0) != s.charAt(s.length()-1) ) return false;
    return isPalindrome(s.substring(1,s.length()-1));
}
```

For its base cases, the isPalindrome predicate returns true for the empty String and true for a String of length 1. If the first and last characters *differ*, then the method returns false. Otherwise, a recursive call is made for the String *without* its first and last characters.

There are a few hand-traces for the isPalindrome method when we use λ to stand for the empty String:

```
radar → ada → d → true
ABBA → BB → λ → true
x → true
reader → eade → ad → false
```

> **Test your skill with Exercise 18–7.**

Hand-Tracing Can Provide Inspiration

By this point, you should have a solid grasp of how to use hand-tracing to compute the value of an expression involving a call to a recursive method.

Hand-tracing can also be used to perform thought-experiments[4], which shed light on how to write a recursive function that performs a specified task.

 Test your skill with Exercises 18–8 through 18–10.

18.6   Making Java Trace for Us

Consider the code for the Fibonacci function, as found in Prog1804:

```
public static int fib ( int n )
{
    if ( n == 0 ) return 1;
    if ( n == 1 ) return 1;
    return fib(n-2) + fib(n-1);
}
```

Prog1804.java   **Fibonacci**

```
// Written by Barry Soroka
//
// The Fibonacci method.
//
import java.io.*;
////////////////////////////////////////////////////////////////////////////////
class Prog1804
{
//---------------------------------------------------------------------------
    public static void main ( String [] args ) throws Exception
    {
        int n = Integer.parseInt(args[0]);
        System.out.println("fib(" + n + ") --> " + fib(n));
    }
//---------------------------------------------------------------------------
    private static int fib ( int n )
    {
        if ( n == 0 ) return 1;
        if ( n == 1 ) return 1;
```

---

[4] AKA *Gedanken* experiments, after the German.

```
            return fib(n-2) + fib(n-1);
    }
//--------------------------------------------------------------------
} // end class Prog1804
//////////////////////////////////////////////////////////////////////
```

Let's modify this code so that:

1. It prints an announcement, including the value of n, whenever a call to fib is initiated.

2. It prints an announcement, including the return value, whenever a call to fib is complete.

3. The announcements are indented to correspond to the depth of the call to fib. A top-level call is at the left margin, indented by 0 spaces; a depth 1 call is indented by 2 spaces; a depth 2 call is indented by 4 spaces; and so on.

Prog1805 gives the code for the modified function.

Prog1805.java　　**Tracing Fibonacci**

```
// Written by Barry Soroka
//
// Tracing Fibonacci.
//
import java.io.*;
//////////////////////////////////////////////////////////////////////
class Prog1805
{
//--------------------------------------------------------------------
    public static void main ( String [] args ) throws Exception
    {
        int n = Integer.parseInt(args[0]);
        System.out.println(fib(n,0));
    }
//--------------------------------------------------------------------
    private static int fib ( int n, int indent )
    {
        for ( int i = 0 ; i < indent ; i++ ) System.out.print(" ");
        System.out.println("--> fib(" + n + ")");
        int result;
        if      ( n == 0 ) result = 1;
        else if ( n == 1 ) result = 1;
        else               result = fib(n-2,indent+2) + fib(n-1,indent+2);
```

```
        for ( int i = 0 ; i < indent ; i++ ) System.out.print(" ");
        System.out.println("<-- fib(" + n + ") returns " + result);
        return result;
    }
//-----------------------------------------------------------------------
} // end class Prog1805
///////////////////////////////////////////////////////////////////////////
```

Note that we have added a parameter to the original prototype

```
public static int fib ( int n )
```

giving us

```
public static int fib ( int n, int indent )
```

This allows us to pass the correct value of the indentation required for this particular call to fib.

The entry announcement is this:

```
for ( int i = 0 ; i < indent ; i++ ) System.out.print(" ");
System.out.println("--> fib(" + n + ")");
```

for which we print lines of the form

```
--> fib(5)
```

to signify that a call has been made to fib for the specified value. Note that the indent parameter controls how far we indent the entry message.

The exit announcement is made at a single exit point for the method. Note that

```
if ( n == 0 ) return 1;
if ( n == 1 ) return 1;
return fib(n-2) + fib(n-1);
```

has become

```
if      ( n == 0 ) result = 1;
else if ( n == 1 ) result = 1;
else               result = fib(n-2,indent+2) + fib(n-1,indent+2);
...
return result
```

By forcing all the returns through the same single return statement, we are able to put the code for the output announcement in a single place. Had we not unified this exit, we would have had to repeat code of the form

```
for ( int i = 0 ; i < indent ; i++ ) System.out.print(" ");
System.out.println("<-- fib(" + n + ") returns " + result);
```

Here is the output of the code for a call to fib(4):

```
G:\>java Prog1805 4
--> fib(4)
  --> fib(2)
    --> fib(0)
    <-- fib(0) returns 1
    --> fib(1)
    <-- fib(1) returns 1
  <-- fib(2) returns 2
  --> fib(3)
    --> fib(1)
    <-- fib(1) returns 1
    --> fib(2)
      --> fib(0)
      <-- fib(0) returns 1
      --> fib(1)
      <-- fib(1) returns 1
    <-- fib(2) returns 2
  <-- fib(3) returns 3
<-- fib(4) returns 5
5
```

Notice that this output shows how the call to fib(4) becomes various other calls—fib(0), fib(1), fib(2), and fib(3).

Some languages (though not Java) have a built-in trace capability. In Lisp and Prolog, we can tell the system to display appropriate information whenever a specified function is entered or left.

> **Test your skill with Exercise 18–11.**

18.7   Recursive Primitives for MyString

In Chapter 14, we described MyString, a class that represented a String as an array of chars. We implemented a host of algorithms for working with MyStrings: some were copies of Java's methods for Strings, and others were of our own design. Now we'll begin our study of a *recursive implementation* of the `MyString` algorithms. Previously in this chapter, we studied recursive methods for working with *numbers*. Now we'll turn our attention to methods that apply recursion to *objects*, namely `MyString`s.

We'll start by defining a few *recursive primitives* that will apply to `MyString`s. Then we'll find that we can write more complicated algorithms using just the primitives, without looking at the underlying array implementation.

Our first primitive is

```
public boolean isEmpty()
```

which returns `true` if and only if the receiving `MyString` represents an empty `String`. This is an important predicate, because we don't want to extract the components of a `MyString` if that `MyString` is empty. In fact, our implementation of the primitives will yield an `Error` if we try to pick apart an empty `MyString`.

The primitive

```
public char head()
```

returns the *first* char of a `MyString`, and

```
public MyString tail()
```

returns *all but* the first char of the receiving `MyString`. These two methods enable us to pick apart a nonempty `MyString`.

The last primitive is

```
public MyString addAtFront(char)
```

which enables us to build up a `MyString` by returning a new `MyString` where the specified char has been added at the front of the receiver.

`Prog1806` shows the code that implements the primitives; all of it should be quite easy to understand. Notice that we are forcing errors if a user tries to take the `head` or `tail` of an empty `MyString`. Here's how we'll work with recursion and `MyString`s:

- We'll never again look at the way the primitives are implemented.
- We'll never write code that touches the underlying array implementation of the `MyString`.
- We'll implement increasingly complicated `MyString` methods by using *only the primitives* and not by working with the instance variable of `MyString`.

Prog1806.java   **Primitive Methods for MyString Recursion**

```
// Written by Barry Soroka
//
// Primitive methods for writing recursive methods for MyStrings.
```

```
//
import java.io.*;
import java.util.Scanner;
/////////////////////////////////////////////////////////////////////////////
class Prog1806
{
//-----------------------------------------------------------------------------
    public static void main (String [] args) throws Exception
    {
        Scanner kb = new Scanner(System.in);

        System.out.println();
        MyString s1 = MyString.read(System.out,kb);
        System.out.println("You entered \"" + s1 + "\"");
        System.out.println("s1.isEmpty() --> " + s1.isEmpty());
        System.out.println("s1.head() --> " + s1.head());
        System.out.println("s1.tail() --> " + s1.tail());
    }
//-----------------------------------------------------------------------------
} // end class Prog1806
/////////////////////////////////////////////////////////////////////////////
class MyString
{
    private char[] a;   // an array of char
//-----------------------------------------------------------------------------
    public MyString ( String s )
    {
        a = new char[s.length()];
        for ( int i = 0 ; i < s.length() ; i++ ) a [i] = s.charAt(i);
    }
//-----------------------------------------------------------------------------
    public MyString ( char[] a ) { this.a = a; }
//-----------------------------------------------------------------------------
    public String toString ()
    {
        String result = "";
        for ( int i = 0 ; i < a.length ; i++ ) result += a [i];
        return result;
    }
//-----------------------------------------------------------------------------
    public static MyString read ( PrintStream ps, Scanner sc )
    {
        if ( ps != null ) ps.print("Enter a String: ");
        return new MyString(sc.nextLine());
    }
//-----------------------------------------------------------------------------
```

```
//
// Recursive primitives
//
//-------------------------------------------------------------------------
    public char head()
    {
        if ( this.isEmpty() )
        {
            throw new Error("Attempt to take the head of an empty MyString.");
        }
        else return a[0];
    }
//-------------------------------------------------------------------------
    public MyString tail()
    {
        if ( this.isEmpty() )
        {
            throw new Error("Attempt to take the tail of an empty MyString.");
        }
        else
        {
            int newLength = a.length - 1;
            char[] result = new char[newLength];
            for ( int i = 0 ; i < newLength ; i++ ) result[i] = a[i+1];
            return new MyString(result);
        }
    }
//-------------------------------------------------------------------------
    public boolean isEmpty() { return a.length == 0; }
//-------------------------------------------------------------------------
    public MyString addAtFront(char c)
    {
        int newLength = a.length + 1;
        char[] result = new char[newLength];
        result[0] = c;
        for ( int i = 0 ; i < a.length ; i++ ) result[i+1] = a[i];
        return new MyString(result);
    }
//-------------------------------------------------------------------------
} // end class MyString
/////////////////////////////////////////////////////////////////////////
```

We'll begin by implementing a few simple MyString methods, and then try
some exercises that ask you to implement other, more complex methods.
Welcome to the world of recursion!

18.8   Recursive Versions of MyString Methods

In this section, we'll develop the code for MyString methods length, equals, and concat. For each, we'll develop the base case(s) and recursive step(s) using a hand-trace to verify our reasoning, and then we'll present the Java code that implements the rules we discover. We can only use the methods isEmpty, head, tail, and addAtFront. We won't look directly at the array of char that is the instance variable of a MyString.

public int length()

As our first nonprimitive, let's develop the code for the length() method of MyString. There are two rules for computing the length:

1. The *base case* is the empty MyString, which has length 0.
2. For all other cases, we have the *recursive step*: The length of a nonempty MyString is one greater than the length of its tail. (The actual char in the head position makes no difference.)

Let's use these rules to compute the length of the MyString "abc":

```
"abc".length() →
1 + "bc".length() →
1 + 1 + "c".length() →
1 + 1 + 1 + "".length() →
1 + 1 + 1 + 0 →
1 + 1 + 1 →
1 + 2 →
3
```

Note the following:

- I'm writing the Strings "abc", "bc", . . . as shorthand; technically, I would need to write longer expressions of the form

  ```
  (new MyString("abc")).length(), . . .
  ```

- I have underlined the next expression that gets evaluated. Recursive expressions are evaluated one operator or one method call at a time.
- At each step of the hand-trace, I apply either the base case or the recursive step.

Eventually, I get the answer I want: the length of "abc" is 3.

Now, having developed the rules and proved them with a hand-trace, we can see the code for method length:

```
public int length()
{
    if ( this.isEmpty() ) return 0;
    return 1 + this.tail().length();
}
```

Notice the expression this.tail().length()—it precisely implements our request to compute the length of the tail of the receiving MyString.

Test your skill with Exercises 18–12 through 18–14.

public boolean equals(MyString)

Our code for equals will use isEmpty, head, and tail to work our way down the receiving and parameter MyStrings, always alert for a mismatch in their heads.

In our array implementation of MyString, we wrote an equals method that checked the lengths of the two arrays as its very first action. We won't do that here: Checking the length with recursion means that *we walk down the length of an entire MyString*. If there's a mismatch in the heads of two very long MyStrings—think millions of chars!—then we don't want to waste time by walking down both MyStrings before we notice the mismatch in their heads. Our code will implicitly check for equality of length as we walk down the MyStrings. We return false if we discover that we've reached the end of one MyString without reaching the end of the other.

Which cases can occur for equals?

First, there's the case for which both the receiver and the parameter are empty MyStrings. In that case, we must have walked all the way down the MyStrings without finding a mismatch, and they both have the same length. We return true.

Second, we may find that one MyString is empty but the other is not. In this case, the MyStrings have *unequal lengths*, and we return false. Now we know that neither MyString is empty, so it's okay to take them apart using head and tail.

Third, if the heads don't match, then we return false, ignoring the rest of the MyStrings.

Fourth, the heads have matched, so we need to test the tails of the two MyStrings.

We can represent these rules in tabular form:

Receiver	Parameter	Action	Reason
""	""	return true	Both are empty; they matched at every position.
""	nonempty	return false	The parameter is longer than the receiver.
nonempty	""	return false	The receiver is longer than the parameter.
"xtail1"	"xtail2"	return "tail1" .equals("tail2")	The heads match—now let's check the tails.
"xtail1"	"ytail2"	return false	The heads don't match—the MyStrings can't be equal.

 Test your skill with Exercise 18–15.

Here's the code for equals:

```
public boolean equals ( MyString that )
{
    if ( this.isEmpty() && that.isEmpty() ) return true;
    if ( this.isEmpty() || that.isEmpty() ) return false;
    if ( this.head() != that.head() ) return false;
    return this.tail().equals(that.tail());
}
```

Notice the second line:

```
if ( this.isEmpty() || that.isEmpty() ) return false;
```

Because we know from the first line that both MyStrings aren't empty, the test

```
this.isEmpty() || that.isEmpty()
```

returns true if one or the other is empty, but not both. This is a fairly standard way of writing the second test of such methods, but a case could be made that the following lines are more readable:

```
if ( this.isEmpty() && !that.isEmpty() ) return false;
if ( !this.isEmpty() && that.isEmpty() ) return false;
```

 Test your skill with Exercise 18–16.

`public MyString concat(MyString)`

The `concat` method will give us an opportunity to use the primitive method `addAtFront(char)`. Let's examine a hand-trace of `concat`:

```
"abc".concat("de") →
"bc".concat("de").addAtFront('a') →
"c".concat("de").addAtFront('b').addAtFront('a') →
"".concat("de").addAtFront('c').addAtFront('b').addAtFront('a') →
"de".addAtFront('c').addAtFront('b').addAtFront('a') →
"cde".addAtFront('b').addAtFront('a') →
"bcde".addAtFront('a') →
"abcde"
```

The rules are:

1. If the receiver is empty, return the parameter.
2. If the parameter is empty, return the receiver.
3. We have two actions:

    a. We need to concatenate the `tail` of the receiver to the parameter. This is a smaller problem, moving us toward the base case.

    b. We need to remember the `head` of the receiver and stick it on the front of the result of the concatenation.

In tabular form, we have:

Receiver	Parameter	Action
`" "`	`"ms2"`	return `ms2`
`"ms1"`	`" "`	return `ms1`
`"xtail"`	`"ms2"`	return `"tail".concat("ms2").addAtFront('x')`

and the code is this:

```java
public MyString concat ( MyString that )
{
    if ( this.isEmpty() ) return that;
    if ( that.isEmpty() ) return this;
    return this.tail().concat(that).addAtFront(this.head());
}
```

   Test your skill with Exercises 18–17 and 18–18.

18.9 Finding Square Roots with Recursive Bisection

In Sections 18.7 and 18.8, we exercised our thinking and programming skills by writing recursive functions for a variety of tasks involving `MyStrings`. Now let's turn our attention to a numerical problem for which we'll compute square roots using a method known as *recursive bisection*. Prog1807 gives the code.

Prog1807.java   **Recursive Bisection**

```
// Written by Barry Soroka
//
// Finds the square root of 2 by recursive bisection.
//
import java.io.*;
import java.util.*;
import java.util.Scanner;
///////////////////////////////////////////////////////////////////////////////
class Prog1807
{
//------------------------------------------------------------------------------
   public static void main (String [] args) throws Exception
   {
      final double TOLERANCE = 0.0001;
      System.out.println(sqrt(2.0,TOLERANCE));
   }
//------------------------------------------------------------------------------
   public static double sqrt ( double x, double tol )
   {
      return sqrt1 ( x, 0.0, x, tol );
   }
//------------------------------------------------------------------------------
   public static double sqrt1 ( double x, double lo, double hi, double tol )
   {
      System.out.printf("%7.4f    %7.4f\n",lo,hi);
      double mid = (lo+hi)/2.0;
      if ( Math.abs(lo-hi) < tol ) return mid;
      if ( mid*mid > x ) return sqrt1(x,lo,mid,tol);
      return sqrt1(x,mid,hi,tol);
   }
//------------------------------------------------------------------------------
} // end class Prog1807
///////////////////////////////////////////////////////////////////////////////
```

The heart of this algorithm is the method

```
private static double sqrt1 ( double x,
                              double lo,
                              double hi,
                              double tol )
```

where

- x is the number for which we seek the square root.
- lo is a lower bound on the square root.
- hi is an upper bound on the square root.
- tol is the proximity we require of lo and hi before declaring the search complete.

sqrt1 proceeds by examining the midpoint of lo and hi—mid:

1. If lo and hi are within the tolerance, then mid is returned as the desired square root.
2. mid*mid is compared with x.
3. If $\sqrt{x}$ is in the interval [lo,mid], then sqrt1 is recursively called for the smaller interval.
4. Otherwise, sqrt1 is called for the interval [mid,hi].

Because hi-lo is always being halved, its width will eventually fall below any required tolerance.

Here's a printout of the successively narrower intervals searched in finding $\sqrt{2}$, where the tolerance is 0.0001:

lo	hi
0.000000	2.000000
1.000000	2.000000
1.000000	1.500000
1.250000	1.500000
1.375000	1.500000
1.375000	1.437500
1.406250	1.437500
1.406250	1.421875
1.414062	1.421875
1.414062	1.417969
1.414062	1.416016
1.414062	1.415039
1.414062	1.414551
1.414062	1.414307
1.414185	1.414307
1.414185	1.414246
1.414215087890625	

We can use this technique to find the square root of a double to any desired precision.

Test your skill with Exercises 18–19 and 18–20.

Ackermann's function plays an important role in the theory of computation, where it was purposely designed so that it would grow very quickly. It takes two nonnegative integer parameters, and it has the following simple mathematical definition:

$$ack(0,n) = n + 1$$

$$ack(m,0) = ack(m - 1,1)$$

$$ack(m,n) = ack(m - 1,ack(m,n - 1))$$

To convince yourself of its complexity, try hand-tracing the early diagonal terms: `ack(0,0)`, `ack(1,1)`, `ack(2,2)`, `ack(3,3)`, ... A Java implementation is given in `Prog1808`.

Prog1808.java   Ackermann's Function

```
// Written by Barry Soroka
//
// Ackermann's function grows very quickly.
//
import java.io.*;
/////////////////////////////////////////////////////////////////////////////
class Prog1808
{
//---------------------------------------------------------------------------
   public static void main ( String [] args ) throws Exception
   {
      int m = Integer.parseInt(args[0]);
      int n = Integer.parseInt(args[1]);
      System.out.println("ack(" + n + "," + m + ") --> " + ack(m,n));
   }
//---------------------------------------------------------------------------
   private static int ack ( int m, int n )
   {
      if ( m == 0 ) return n+1;
      if ( n == 0 ) return ack(m-1,1);
      return ack(m-1,ack(m,n-1));
   }
//---------------------------------------------------------------------------
} // end class Prog1808
/////////////////////////////////////////////////////////////////////////////
```

`ack(4,1)` evaluates to the integer 65,533, which isn't very large. However, its computation overflows the stack on my computer system. Try yours. I routinely implement and test Ackermann's function on each new system I meet.

This is an example of how an algorithm can be easy to define yet extremely difficult to compute. Computer scientists face many real-world problems that fit that description. You will study a variety of these problems in future courses.

18.11   The Fibonacci Method Can Exhaust Our Patience

Recall the code for the Fibonacci series as presented in Prog1804. Some values are easy to get:

```
javac Prog1804 0 → 1
javac Prog1804 1 → 1
javac Prog1804 2 → 2
javac Prog1804 3 → 3
javac Prog1804 4 → 5
javac Prog1804 5 → 8
```

but others will exhaust our patience. On my system, fib(100) takes a very long time to return. Some other value will bring *your* system to its knees.

> **Test your skill with Exercise 18–21.**

What's happening? I don't get a *stack overflow* because *fib(100) never gets past depth 100*. The sluggishness is due to the fact that the system keeps *recomputing* values such as fib(0), fib(1), fib(2), and so forth. Consider the tree shown in Figure 18–1, which computes fib(5). Notice how the subtree for computing fib(3) occurs *twice*. The fib(2) subtree occurs *three* times. This is an illustration of a recursive function that causes problems because of the number of calls, rather than the depth of the recursion.

18.12   Recursion: Past, Present, Future

When Should We Use Recursion

Many problems can be solved with either recursion or with iteration (loops). Both Fibonacci and factorial can be written in two ways. When should we use recursion and when should we use iteration?

NOTE

Use recursion when it makes the code easier to read without sacrificing speed.

Figure 18–1
Call Made by
fib(5)

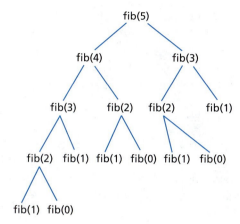

Many problems have recursive definitions, and the code will be more readable if we write it as recursion. Likewise, some recursions *can't* be turned into natural iterations, and these should remain as recursions. The Towers of Hanoi puzzle has a three-line solution using recursion.

Recursion in the Past

At the beginning of the 20th century, mathematicians began discussing how to represent possible computations, and they selected recursive function theory as the means for expressing calculations. This grew into the *theory of computation*, which discusses what problems are solvable or insolvable, and which problems are fundamentally easy or fundamentally difficult. You'll learn more about these topics in an advanced CS course.

Recursion in the Present

Recursion is fundamental to the definition of computer programming languages, and it forms the basis of the algorithms used for parsing and *compiling*. Recursion is used similarly in *natural language processing (NLP)*.

Recursive algorithms are natural for problems involving *graphs* and shortest paths, and these problems arise in real-world scheduling situations such as making pickups from a series of locations distributed over the grid of a city. Similar problems arise in *artificial intelligence (AI)* with mazes and game trees.

Many *data structures* involve recursion in an intimate way—trees and lists are good examples. In CS 2 you will learn recursive algorithms for working with these data structures.

Computer graphics use recursion in the form of *fractals* for supplying textures such as grass, fire, waves, and clouds.

Many problems can be solved with recursive algorithms that can be nicely distributed over a network of *parallel processors*. The supercomputer of the future may be a cloudlike array of smaller computers, joined opportunistically for the purpose of solving fleeting problems. Recursive algorithms often can be distributed quite easily over grids of processors.

Recursion in the Future

We can't be sure what parts of mathematics will be useful for practical computation in the future. In the early 20th century, nobody would have predicted that number theory would be important in daily life. However, most of today's cryptological algorithms depend on number theory for their security. No one knows how big a role recursive functions will play in tomorrow's computations.

This chapter has given you a solid introduction to recursion involving both numbers and objects.

Chapter Summary

- We have seen recursion before in the factorial function.
- Sometimes, recursive computations have closed-form versions that don't require recursion.
- Infinite recursion occurs when a method repeatedly calls itself without provision for stopping.
- Infinite recursions end when the JVM runs out of stack space.
- Recursive methods typically have one or more *base cases* for which the function returns a value without performing more recursion.
- Recursive methods typically have one or more *recursive steps* for which the method calls itself with a slightly diminished parameter.
- Hand-tracing allows us to simulate computation of recursive functions. This is hand-tracing for *analysis*.
- Hand-tracing can also be used to gain insight into how a recursive function should be written. This is hand-tracing for *synthesis*.
- By inserting `print` statements at the entry and exit of a recursive method, we can make Java print a trace of a recursive computation.
- A recursive version of `MyString` has primitives that can be combined with recursion to provide all of the methods we have previously written with iteration.
- `boolean isEmpty()` tells us if a `MyString` is the empty `MyString`. This is a base case for many algorithms.
- `char head()` returns the first `char` of a `MyString`.

- MyString tail() returns all but the first char of a MyString. This is useful for recursive steps.
- MyString addAtFront(char) allows us to build up a result by adding a char to the front of the receiving MyString.
- int length() is a recursive method built from the MyString primitives.
- boolean equals(MyString) is a recursive version of the equals method.
- Many other MyString methods can be built using recursion and the primitives.
- Binary search can be implemented with recursion. We can use it to find square roots of numbers or roots of functions.
- Ackermann's function is a recursive function that grows very quickly.
- The recursive version of the Fibonacci method takes a long time to return results because it often recomputes values that it has previously computed.
- Recursion appears in many CS courses, including Artificial Intelligence, Natural Language Processing, Data Structures, and Computer Graphics.

Terminology Introduced in This Chapter

base case	recursion	stack overflow
closed form	recursive	
Fibonacci numbers	recursive step	

Exercises

Exercise 18–1.   Perform some experiments to see how the maximum depth of an infinite recursion depends on:

  a.   the number of parameters, and
  b.   the size of the parameters (byte vs. short vs. int vs. long).

You'll understand your results much better after you study assembly language. Note that Java systems don't all have the same amount of stack space.

Exercise 18–2.   Do a hand-trace on the following invocations of method a in Section 18.5:

  a.   a(0,7)
  b.   a(2,2)
  c.   a(4,0)

Exercise 18–3.   Consider the following recursive method:

```
public static int m ( int x, int y )
{
    if ( x == 0 ) return 0;
    return y + m(x-1,y);
}
```

Do a few hand-traces to get a feel for how it operates. What does method m do?

Exercise 18–4.   Write the code for a recursive method e that takes two int parameters—x and y—and returns the value of x^y.

Exercise 18–5.   Consider the following recursive method f:

```
private static int f ( int n )
{
    if ( n == 0 ) return 1;
    return 3*f(n-1) + 1;
}
```

which corresponds to the recursive series

$f(0) = 1$
$f(n) = 3 \cdot f(n - 1) + 1$

Write a driver that prints out the first 10 values of the series. What's the closed form of f?

Exercise 18–6.   Consider the Fibonacci function:

$fib(0) = 1$
$fib(1) = 1$
$fib(n) = fib(n - 2) + fib(n - 1)$

Use hand-tracing to compute the following values:

a.   fib(3)
b.   fib(4)
c.   fib(5)

Notice how much extra work is required to compute these values because we need to compute the *same value*—say, fib(2)—many times.

Exercise 18–7.   Give hand-traces for isPalindrome working on the following Strings:

a.   abc
b.   bcdb
c.   exe
d.   noon
e.   abcba

Exercise 18–8.   Consider the following method:

```
public static int mystery ( int n )
{
    if ( n == 0 ) return 0;
    return n + mystery(n-1);
}
```

What does this method compute?

Exercise 18–9. Use hand-tracing to intuit the recursive method that, given n, computes $\sum_{i=0}^{n} i^2$.

Exercise 18–10. Use hand-tracing to intuit the recursive method that, given m and n, computes

$$\sum_{i=m}^{n} i^2.$$

Exercise 18–11. Modify the code of factorial so that it prints a visual trace showing each invocation and leaving of `fac`. Indent each deeper call by increasingly greater amounts.

Exercise 18–12. Test the `length` method on a variety of `MyStrings`, including the `MyString` that represents the empty `String`.

Exercise 18–13. Alter the code for `length` so that Java displays the `MyString` entering each invocation of `length`. Demonstrate your code on a variety of `MyStrings`.

Exercise 18–14. Alter the code for `length` so that Java displays the receiver and the return value for each invocation of `length`. Indent the messages appropriately. Demonstrate your code on a variety of `MyStrings`.

Exercise 18–15. Give the hand-traces for the following calls to `equals`:

Receiver	Parameter
" "	" "
" "	"abc"
"abc"	" "
"abc"	"abc"
"abc"	"ab"
"abc"	"abe"
"abc"	"ebc"
"abc"	"aec"

Exercise 18–16. Add to class MyString a method

```
public int countMatches(MyString)
```

which takes two equal-length MyStrings—*assume they are equal*—and returns the number of positions in which they match. Test this on an appropriate set of test cases.

Exercise 18–17. Using only the four primitive recursive methods from class MyString, add the methods whose prototypes are given below. Perform a test run on a set of representative cases and annotate your output. Provide a hand-trace of the specified case or cases.

    a.   `public boolean isPrefixOf(MyString)`
       `"abc".isPrefixOf("abcdef")`

    b.   `public MyString deleteChar(char)`
       `"beret".deleteChar('e')`

    c.   `public int containsHowMany(char)`
       `"element".containsHowMany('e')`

    d.   `public MyString toUpperCase()`
       `"aBc".toUpperCase()`

    e.   `public boolean containsAny(char)`
       `"abc".containsAny('b')`
       `"abc".containsAny('e')`
       `"".containsAny('e')`

    f.   `public MyString replaceChar(char,char)`
       `"".replaceChar('a','e')`
       `"abc".replaceChar('a','e')`
       `"there".replaceChar('e','f')`

Exercise 18–18. Write a recursive method match that compares two MyStrings, like equals, except that a '?' in a position of either the receiver or the parameter is a *wild card* that can match *any single character*. For example:

Receiver Represents	Parameter Represents	Result
"abc"	"ab"	false
""	""	true
"abc"	"abc"	true
"abc"	"aeb"	false
"ab?"	"abd"	true
"a?c"	"adc"	true
"ab"	"a"	false
"ab"	"a?"	true

Exercise 18–19. Modify `Prog1807` to find $\sqrt{10}$.

Exercise 18–20. A function `f(x)` has a root at x_0 if $f(x_0)$ is 0. We can apply recursive bisection to an interval [`lo`, `hi`] if `f` passes through 0 somewhere in the interval—this means that `f(lo)` is positive while `f(hi)` is negative, or vice versa.
Write the code for a method `rootFind`, which takes four parameters:

- A `Function1D`, as described in Chapter 15.
- The low end of an interval.
- The high end of an interval.
- A tolerance on the width of an interval at which to declare a root.

Your `rootFind` should return a value of `x` that is the center of a small enough interval in which `f` passes through 0.

Exercise 18–21. Using the recursive definition of the Fibonacci sequence, what is the highest term that your computer system can comfortably compute? Use the `long` datatype so that you can avoid integer wraparound as long as possible.

CHAPTER NINETEEN

Numerical and Other Algorithms

Chapter Objectives

- Implement linear search.
- Implement binary search.
- Learn the selection sort algorithm.
- Convert integers to `String`s and vice versa.
- Solve a variety of problems involving numbers and `String`s.
- Use GUI `Timer`s to create animations.

This chapter discusses algorithms involving numbers and `String`s. Some of the algorithms are simple, and some are harder. Among the algorithms discussed will be those for sorting and searching, and for converting between `String`s and integers.

Easy Numerical Problems

The following warm-up exercises are designed to get us thinking about numerical algorithms.

 Test your skill with Exercises 19–1 through 19–7.

19.1   Linear Search

Search is the process by which we look for a specified item in a collection of items. We've seen such processes for files and arrays in methods like `containsAny`. Using that process, we start our search for a specified item at the

Linear search A sequential search through a collection of items.

beginning of the collection. We return `true` if the item is found and `false` if we get through the entire collection without finding it. This is a *linear search*—it starts at the front of the collection and looks at each item as we move through.

Prog1901 gives the code for linear search, along with a driver to test it. Linear search has the following characteristics:

- It's easy to code and debug. The algorithm is simple to write and understand.
- It can work on any collection. It doesn't require that the collection be sorted or be prepared in any way.
- It's not very fast. Imagine searching a dictionary or telephone book by checking entries one at a time, starting from the front.

Technically, we describe linear search as an $O(n)$ algorithm, where "$O(n)$" is read as "order of n." This means that the average time to locate an entry *doubles* if we double the size of the collection. But for small collections, linear search can be quite useful.

Prog1901.java   Linear Search

```
// Written by Barry Soroka
//
// Linear search through an unsorted array.
//
import java.io.*;
import java.util.Scanner;
/////////////////////////////////////////////////////////////////////////////
class Prog1901
{
//--------------------------------------------------------------------------
   public static void main (String [] args) throws Exception
   {
      int[] a = { 27, 17, 15, 31, 85, -6, 2, 3, 43, 57 };

      Scanner kb = new Scanner(System.in);

      while (true)
      {
         System.out.print("\nHere's an array: ");
         for ( int i = 0 ; i < a.length ; i++ ) System.out.print(a[i]+" ");
         System.out.println();

         System.out.print ("\nEnter an int to be found: ");
         int target = kb.nextInt(); kb.nextLine();
```

```
                System.out.print ("                                  "); // line up answer
                if ( linearSearch(a,target) ) System.out.println("found");
                else                          System.out.println("not found");
        }
    }
//-------------------------------------------------------------------------
//
// linearSearch ( int[] a, int target )
//
// Determines whether the target is in the sorted array.
// Uses linear search.
//
    private static boolean linearSearch ( int[] a, int target )
    {
        for ( int i = 0 ; i < a.length ; i++ )
            if ( a[i] == target ) return true;
        return false;
    }
//-------------------------------------------------------------------------
} // end class Prog1901
//////////////////////////////////////////////////////////////////////////
```

The entries in dictionaries and telephone books are not randomly ordered. These collections are prepared by sorting. Given a sorted collection, we can apply *binary search*, which is much faster than *linear search*. We'll study binary search in Section 19.2.

> **Binary search**   Check the entry at the halfway point, and adjust our position accordingly.

 Test your skill with Exercise 19–8.

19.2 Binary Search

Here is a transcript of how I'd use a physical dictionary—a sorted collection—to look up the word "binary":

1. I open the dictionary near its middle to find myself on page 662, which begins with "judge advocate."
2. That's too late into the dictionary, so I open to approximately the middle of the first half of the book. Now I'm on page 214, which begins with "chow."
3. Still too late. I open this section to its middle, finding myself on page 88, which begins with "axon."

4. Now it's too early. I split the second half of this section open and find myself on page 144, "brachium."

5. Too far again. Now I open to page 122, "binocular." I'm pretty close.

6. I turn to the previous page, 121, and find the word "binary."

Except for the last step, this is binary search:

1. We know our target is in the range [lo,hi], so we check the midpoint.

2. If we find the target, then we're done and we report that we found the target.

3. If the target is past the midpoint, then we change the range to be [midpoint+1,hi] and go back to step 1.

4. Otherwise, we change the range to be [lo,midpoint-1], and go to step 1.

Eventually, the range narrows down to a single entry: If it's our target, then we've found it; if not, then the target is not in the collection.

Prog1902 gives the code for binary search of a sorted array of ints.

Prog1902.java **Binary Search**

```
// Written by Barry Soroka
//
// Binary search of a sorted array of ints.
//
import java.io.*;
import java.util.Scanner;
//////////////////////////////////////////////////////////////////////////////
class Prog1902
{
//---------------------------------------------------------------------------
    public static void main (String [] args) throws Exception
    {
        int[] a = { -6, 2, 3, 15, 17, 27, 43, 57, 85 };

        Scanner kb = new Scanner(System.in);

        while (true)
        {
            System.out.print("\nHere's an array: ");
            for ( int i = 0 ; i < a.length ; i++ ) System.out.print(a[i]+" ");
            System.out.println();

            System.out.print ("\nEnter an int to be found: ");
            int target = kb.nextInt(); kb.nextLine();
```

```
            System.out.print ("                              "); // line up answer
            if ( binarySearch(a,target) ) System.out.println("found");
            else                          System.out.println("not found");
        }
    }
//----------------------------------------------------------------------
//
// binarySearch ( int[] a, int target )
//
// Determines whether the target is in the sorted array.
// Uses binary search.
//
    private static boolean binarySearch ( int[] a, int target )
    {
        int lo = 0;
        int hi = a.length -1;
        while ( lo <= hi )
        {
            int mid = ( lo + hi ) / 2;
            if ( a[mid] == target ) return true;
            if ( a[mid] > target ) hi = mid - 1;
            else                   lo = mid + 1;
        }
        return false;
    }
//----------------------------------------------------------------------
} // end class Prog1902
////////////////////////////////////////////////////////////////////////
```

 | **Test your skill with Exercises 19–9 through 19–12.** |

Speed of Binary Search

We have seen that linear search is $O(n)$—double the number of entries means that the average search takes double the time. What's the speed of binary search? There are two ways to think about this.

First, let's consider a collection with 64 entries. This means our initial range is size 64. Let's look at the midpoint. In the worst case, our target will be to either side of this midpoint, in a range of size 32. The next try cuts down the range to size 16. Subsequent tries cut the range to size 8, then to size 4, then to size 2, and finally to size 1. In the worst case, it takes us 7 tries to locate—or not locate—the target. This is almost $\log_2(64) = 6$.

Second, let's suppose that in the worst case a collection of n entries requires $\log_2(n)$ tries to locate a target. Suppose we double the number of entries to be $2*n$. Then we need exactly one try more than $\log_2(n)$, because the first try cuts $2*n$ down to n, and we know that n entries requires $\log_2(n)$ tries, and

$$\log_2(2*n) = \log_2(2) + \log_2(n) = 1 + \log_2(n).$$

Thus, we can conclude that binary search is $O(\log_2(n))$. This is considerably faster than linear search:

Size of Collection	Worst Case Number of Tries Required by O(n)	Worst Case Number of Tries Required by O($\log_2(n)$)
64	64	6
128	128	7
256	256	8
1024	1024	10
2^{20}	1,048,576	20

In CS 2 you will study other sorting schemes and will discuss "big-O" notation in much greater depth.

Beyond Arrays

In daily life, faster search is possible and necessary. Give the following query to your favorite search engine: `"java tutorial"` and `"binary search"`. I got more than 100 responses to this query. It's not likely that the engine had sorted its Web pages by this particular combination of search terms. In CS 2 you'll learn about special data structures that facilitate the indexing and search of large databases such as the collection of all Web pages known to a search engine. Among other structures, you'll learn about *trees* and *hash tables*.

19.3 Sorting

Sorting is one of the most common, and time-consuming, operations. Here are some examples:

- A company must type and organize the information on thousands of physical time cards. Sometimes the data must be sorted by name, sometimes by Social Security Number, and sometimes by mail-stop.

- A Student asks for the names of the other Students in a given Section of a course. The names must be sorted for presentation.
- A Student asks for the departments and course numbers of all open courses that fulfill General Education requirement 2B. The courses are sorted by department and course number.
- A videogame must display the current graphic scene. A large set of polygons must be sorted by distance to determine which are visible and which are not.

A large fraction of computer cycles are spent on sorting, and many different sorting algorithms have been published. Even a small speedup can save a lot of cycles.

In Chapter 15 we saw the built-in method Arrays.sort, which could sort an array of objects provided that the objects all implemented the Comparable interface. The Java API provides several sort methods, and these are used without question by our colleagues in management information systems. As CS majors, however, we must understand how to write a sort algorithm from scratch. In Section 19.4, we'll study one particular sort algorithm—*selection sort*—and we'll talk briefly about some other sorting methods. You'll learn lots more about sorting in CS 2.

19.4   Aside, Swapping

Before we attack the code for selection sort, I want to talk about the process of *swapping* the values of two variables—a process we'll require in selection sort.

Suppose a Java program contains the lines

```
int a = 3;
int b = 5;
```

and we're asked to swap the two values so that a has value 5 and b has value 3. The naïve code for swapping would be this:

```
a = b;
b = a;
```

but this doesn't have the desired effect, as shown in the following hand-trace:

	a	b
initially →	3	5
a = b;		
	5	5
b = a;		
	5	5

Our "swap" caused *both* variables to have the value that b initially had.

True swapping requires a third variable—a temporary—and requires *three* statements:

```
temp = a;
a = b;
b = temp;
```

We can verify the swap by examining the following hand-trace:

	a	b	temp
initially →	3	5	
temp = a;			
	3	5	3
a = b;			
	5	5	3
b = temp;			
	3	5	3

Test your skill with Exercise 19–13.

19.5   Selection Sort

Selection sort   Find the smallest element in each successive slice.

I'm going to illustrate selection sort by doing a hand-trace of its actions on the array containing the following elements:

27   17   15   31   85   -6   2   3   43   57

Here are the main features of selection sort:

- It looks at a *slice* of the array that extends from some element all the way to the right end. Initially, it looks at the entire array.
- The leftmost element of the slice will be replaced by the smallest element in the slice.

- After this replacement, the replaced element is in correct sort order, so the slice to be sorted is one element shorter than it was before.
- The selection-replacement procedure continues until the slice is only one element wide. (That one element is clearly sorted!)

For our sample array, here is the sequence of slices considered by selection sort:

27	17	15	31	85	-6	2	3	43	57
-6	17	15	31	85	27	2	3	43	57
-6	2	15	31	85	27	17	3	43	57
-6	2	3	31	85	27	17	15	43	57
-6	2	3	15	85	27	17	31	43	57
-6	2	3	15	17	27	85	31	43	57
-6	2	3	15	17	27	85	31	43	57
-6	2	3	15	17	27	31	85	43	57
-6	2	3	15	17	27	31	43	85	57
-6	2	3	15	17	27	31	43	57	85

At the end, all of the elements have been put into the correct order, and the last slice consists of the single, sorted element: 85. Notice how the algorithm swaps the *first* element of the slice with the *smallest* element of the slice:

27	17	15	31	85	-6	2	3	43	57

becomes

-6	17	15	31	85	27	2	3	43	57

because -6 is the smallest element in the slice. Notice how 27 has replaced it in the slice, and the slice has become one smaller. When the algorithm processes the slice

-6	2	3	15	17	27	85	31	43	57

it finds that 27 is already the smallest element, so no swap is necessary.

Prog1903 gives the code for selection sort of an array of integers. The structure of this code is *two nested loops*. One loop continuously shortens the slice, and the other loop looks over the slice and finds the index of its smallest element.

Prog1903.java **Selection Sort**

```java
// Written by Barry Soroka
//
// Demonstrates selection sort.
//
import java.io.*;
//////////////////////////////////////////////////////////////////////////////
class Prog1903
{
//-----------------------------------------------------------------------------
    public static void main (String [] args) throws Exception
    {
        final int SIZE = 10;

        int [] a = new int[SIZE];

        a[0] = 27;  a[1] = 17;  a[2] = 15;  a[3] = 31;  a[4] = 85;
        a[5] = -6;  a[6] = 2;   a[7] = 3;   a[8] = 43;  a[9] = 57;

        selectionSort(a);
        System.out.println(); printArray(a);
    }
//-----------------------------------------------------------------------------
    public static void selectionSort ( int[] a )
    {
        for (int i = 0; i < a.length-1; i++)
        {
            // Display the array
            System.out.println(); printArray(a);

            // Locate the smallest element in a[i]..a[length-1]
            int minIndex = i;
            for (int j = i+1; j < a.length; j++)
                if (a[j] < a[minIndex]) minIndex = j;

            // Bring the smallest element to a[i]
            int temp = a[minIndex];
            a[minIndex] = a[i];
            a[i] = temp;
        }
    }
//-----------------------------------------------------------------------------
    public static void printArray ( int[] a )
    {
        for ( int i = 0 ; i < a.length ; i++ )
            System.out.print( iFormat(a[i],4) + " ");
        System.out.println();
    }
```

```
//-------------------------------------------------------------------
   public static String iFormat ( int n, int width )
   {
      String s = n + "";
      for ( int i = 0 ; i < width - s.length() ; i++ ) s = " " + s;
      return s;
   }
//-------------------------------------------------------------------
} // end class Prog1903
/////////////////////////////////////////////////////////////////////
```

Once the smallest element has been found, the code swaps it with the first element in the slice. Note the code:

```
int temp = a[minIndex];
a[minIndex] = a[i];
a[i] = temp;
```

As discussed in Section 19.4, we used a temporary in order to achieve true swapping.

 | **Test your skill with Exercises 19–14 through 19–17.** |

Comparing Sort Algorithms

How do sort algorithms differ? Some are faster than others because they require fewer swaps of elements. Some take up less temporary space than others. Selection sort and bubble sort both require only one temporary variable beyond the array being sorted. Some sort algorithms achieve higher speeds at the price of using large temporary arrays.

> **Bubble sort** Swap adjacent elements if they are out of order.
> **Benchmark test** A task used to time and compare different algorithms and implementations.

Sort algorithms can be compared using *benchmark tests*. Some typical benchmarks:

- An array that is already sorted. Some algorithms require a single pass to confirm it. Naïve selection sort would look at the array several times without doing an exchange before pronouncing the array "sorted."
- An array sorted in *reverse order*. In some sense, this array requires the most effort.
- An array with random elements. This might take an "average" amount of sorting.
- A *mostly sorted* array, produced by taking a sorted array and exchanging just a few pairs of elements. This requires minimal sorting effort.
- An array for which all the elements are the same. This requires almost no sorting effort.

CS 2 will include a thorough study of sorting algorithms and how to compare them.

19.6 Some Predicates with Integers

Recall that *predicates* are methods with `boolean` return types. For example:

```
public static boolean isEven ( int n )
{
    return n == n%2;
}
```

Prime number An integer greater than 1 that is evenly divisible only by itself and 1.

A *prime number* is an integer greater than 1 that is evenly divisible only by itself and 1. The first several prime numbers are 2, 3, 5, 7, 11, 13, and 17. Let's write a Java predicate that returns `true` if and only if its integer argument is prime. The code is:

```
public static boolean isPrime ( int n )
{
    for ( int i = 2 ; i < n ; i++ )
        if ( n%i == 0 ) return false;
    return true;
}
```

My approach is:

I'll check the `int`s, starting at `2`, to see if any of them divides n evenly; if so, then n is not prime and I can exit the method, returning `false`. If I get through all the `int`s without finding an exact divisor for n, then n must be prime, so I return `true`.

Test your skill with Exercises 19–18 through 19–23.

19.7 Converting Integers to `Strings`

In previous chapters, we have formatted numbers using the `printf` method of class `PrintStream` and the `format` method of class `String`. As CS majors, we need to be able to write similar methods from scratch. This section discusses how to do exactly that.

Converting an `int` to a `String` Using Iteration

Suppose we want to write the method

```
public static String intToString ( int n )
```

which uses iteration to convert a nonnegative `int` to a `String`. Here's a table that tracks the changes in two variables—n and `result`—as we go around a loop:

n	n%10	result
		" "
169	9	
		"9"
16	· 6	
		"69"
1	1	
		"169"
0		*Stop!*

`result` starts with the empty `String`, and each time around we concatenate the least significant digit of n—n%10—to the *front* of `result`. In other words, each time around we replace n by n/10. We continue as long as n is nonzero. At the end, we return `result` as the value of the conversion.

The one problem with this algorithm comes when n is initially 0: We want the result to be "0", not the empty `String`. We'll solve this by testing explicitly for 0 and returning "0".

The final code is given, with a driver, in `Prog1904`.

Prog1904.java   **Convert an int to a String**

```
// Written by Barry Soroka
//
// Convert an int to a String.
//
import java.io.*;
import java.util.Scanner;
/////////////////////////////////////////////////////////////////////////////
class Prog1904
{
//-----------------------------------------------------------------------------
    public static void main ( String [] args ) throws Exception
```

```
    {
        Scanner kb = new Scanner(System.in);

        while ( true )
        {
            System.out.print("\nEnter a non-negative int: ");
            int n = kb.nextInt(); kb.nextLine();
            System.out.println("That becomes \"" + intToString(n) + "\"");
        }
    }
//---------------------------------------------------------------------
    public static String intToString ( int n )
    {
        if ( n == 0 ) return "0";

        String result = "";
        while ( n != 0 )
        {
            result = (n%10) + result;
            n /= 10;
        }
        return result;
    }
//---------------------------------------------------------------------
} // end class Prog1904
/////////////////////////////////////////////////////////////////////
```

 | **Test your skill with Exercise 19-24.** |

Converting an `int` to a `String` Using Recursion

Suppose we want to write the method `intToString` using *recursion* instead of iteration:

```
public static String intToString ( int n )
```

Here's a hand-trace of the conversion process for the integer 169:

```
intToString(169) →
intToString(16) + 9 →
intToString(1) + 6 + 9 →
intToString(0) + 1 + 6 + 9 →
"" + 1 + 6 + 9 →
"1" + 6 + 9 →
"16" + 9 →
"169"
```

This has the corresponding Java code:

```
public static String intToString ( int n )
{
    if ( n == 0 ) return "";
    return intToString1(n/10) + (n%10);
}
```

Again, we have a problem when n is initially 0—it returns the empty String instead of "0". We'll solve this by making this code into a *helper method* int-ToString1 and calling it from inside an intToString method that explicitly tests for n == 0. Prog1905 gives the code as well as the same driver we used in Prog1904. The technique of using a nonrecursive method to shield a recursive helper method is useful for many problems.

Prog1905.java Convert an **int** to a **String** Using Recursion

```
// Written by Barry Soroka
//
// Convert an int to a String -- using recursion.
//
import java.io.*;
import java.util.Scanner;
/////////////////////////////////////////////////////////////////////////////
class Prog1905
{
//---------------------------------------------------------------------------
    public static void main ( String [] args ) throws Exception
    {
        Scanner kb = new Scanner(System.in);

        while ( true )
        {
            System.out.print("\nEnter a non-negative int: ");
            int n = kb.nextInt(); kb.nextLine();
            System.out.println("That becomes \"" + intToString(n) + "\"");
        }
    }
//---------------------------------------------------------------------------
    public static String intToString ( int n )
    {
        if ( n == 0 ) return "0";
        return intToString1(n);
    }
//---------------------------------------------------------------------------
    public static String intToString1 ( int n )
```

```
    {
        if ( n == 0 ) return "";
        return intToString1(n/10) + (n%10);
    }
//-------------------------------------------------------------------
} // end class Prog1905
///////////////////////////////////////////////////////////////////////////
```

 Test your skill with Exercises 19–25 through 19–27.

19.8 Parsing Numbers

Java reads `Strings` from the terminal, and we have been converting them into numbers using the built-in methods `parseInt` and `parseDouble`. Now let's see how to implement these methods on our own.

Converting a `String` to an `int` Using Iteration

Consider the `String s = "4157"`. We can convert this to an integer with the following logic

'4'	'1'	'5'	'7'
↓	↓	↓	↓
4	1	5	7
*	*	*	*
10^3	10^2	10^1	10^0
↓	↓	↓	↓
4000	100	50	7

and the sum of these numbers is the integer `4157`.

The only tricky part of this algorithm is determining what power of 10 we want for each digit. Here's a table:

Digit	'4'	'1'	'5'	'7'
Index	0	1	2	3
Power of 10	3	2	1	0

The formula is

```
power = 4 - index - 1
```

which is

```
power = s.length() - index - 1
```

Prog1906 gives the code for a version of parseInt that can parse Strings that represent *nonnegative* integers.

Prog1906.java   Convert a **String** to an **int**

```java
// Written by Barry Soroka
//
// Convert a String to an int.
//
import java.io.*;
import java.util.Scanner;
//////////////////////////////////////////////////////////////////////////////
class Prog1906
{
//-----------------------------------------------------------------------------
   public static void main ( String [] args ) throws Exception
   {
      Scanner kb = new Scanner(System.in);

      while ( true )
      {
         System.out.print("\nEnter a non-negative int: ");
         String s = kb.nextLine();
         System.out.println("That becomes " + parseInt(s));
      }
   }
//-----------------------------------------------------------------------------
// parseInt -- parses Strings representing non-negative ints
//
   public static int parseInt ( String s )
   {
      int result = 0;
      for ( int i = 0 ; i < s.length() ; i++ )
         result += charToInt(s.charAt(i)) * power10(s.length() - i - 1);
      return result;
   }
//-----------------------------------------------------------------------------
// charToInt -- converts a char to the corresponding int -- must be a digit
//
   public static int charToInt ( char c )
   {
      return "0123456789".indexOf(c);
   }
//-----------------------------------------------------------------------------
// power10(int) -- returns the specified power of 10
//
```

```
public static int power10 ( int n )
{
   int result = 1;
   for ( int i = 0 ; i < n ; i++ ) result *= 10;
   return result;
}
//-------------------------------------------------------------------
} // end class Prog1906
///////////////////////////////////////////////////////////////////////////////
```

The helper method `charToInt` uses `indexOf` to convert digits (`'0'`, `'1'`, . . .) from `chars` to `ints`.[1]

 | **Test your skill with Exercises 19–28 through 19–31.** |

19.9   Problems in Number Theory

Ulam's Conjecture

Take a positive integer and apply the following procedure:

1. If the integer is 1, then exit.
2. If the integer is even, then divide it by 2. Go to step 1.
3. If the integer is odd, then multiply by 3 and add 1. Go to step 1.

For example,

$$10 \rightarrow 5 \rightarrow 16 \rightarrow 8 \rightarrow 4 \rightarrow 2 \rightarrow 1$$

and

$$13 \rightarrow 40 \rightarrow 20 \rightarrow 10 \rightarrow 5 \rightarrow 16 \rightarrow 8 \rightarrow 4 \rightarrow 2 \rightarrow 1$$

The mathematician Stanislaw M. Ulam (1909–1984) guessed that this procedure always ends with 1. Nobody can prove it, which is why it's called *Ulam's conjecture*. (If it's ever proven, then we'll have a theorem.)

 | **Test your skill with Exercises 19–32 through 19–36.** |

---

[1] The helper `power10` computes the appropriate power of 10. I was hesitant to use the built-in `Math.pow` because it converts its parameters to `doubles` and it returns a `double` result. I worry about the casting it requires—`power10` is cleaner.

Some Other Integer Problems

> **Test your skill with Exercises 19–37 through 19–41.**

19.10 Easy `String` Problems

In previous chapters, we developed algorithms for various `MyString` problems using both iteration and recursion. In this and the following sections, we will recap those algorithms using `Strings` rather than `MyStrings`, and we'll introduce some new and challenging problems involving `Strings`.

We treat `Strings` and `MyStrings` differently. For example, the `MyString` method

```
public int containsHowMany(char)
```

will become the `String` method

```
public static int containsHowMany(String,char)
```

These differ because `MyString` was our own class. We could add methods to its definition, and these methods were messages that were sent to a receiving `MyString`. `String`, however, is a *built-in* method, and we can't add new methods to its definition. Hence, when we write methods involving `Strings`, we'll need to pass the `String` as a parameter to a `static` method.

You should be able to solve the following exercises without difficulty. Use loops and the `String` methods *charAt* and *concat* (usually just written as "+").

> **Test your skill with Exercises 19–42 through 19–52.**

19.11 Substring and Matching

This section examines some more complicated `String` algorithms.

Using `isPrefix` to Compute `isSubstring`

You should be able to write the method

```
static boolean isPrefix(String,String)
```

using loops.

We can use `isPrefix` to compute `isSubstring`. Consider the problem

```
isSubstring("cde","abcdefg")
```

We'll slide `cde` along `abcdefg` looking for a match where `cde` is the prefix of a substring of `abcdefg`.

- First we'll try `cde` against `abcdefg`. No prefix.
- Then we'll try `cde` against `bcdefg`. No prefix.
- Then we'll try `cde` against `cdefg`. Aha! `cde` *is* a prefix of `cdefg`. Therefore, we can conclude that `cde` is a *substring* of `abcdefg`.

Here's the code:

```
public static boolean isSubstring ( String s1, String s2 )
{
    for ( int i = 0 ; i <= s2.length() - s1.length() ; i++ )
        if ( isPrefix(s1,s2.substring(i)) ) return true;
    return false;
}
```

Each time around the loop, we compute `isPrefix(s1,s2.substring(i))`. If we have a match, then we return `true`.

When do we stop? Let's look at `cdf` versus `abcdefg`. `cdf` is *not* a substring of `abcdefg`, but we'll be able to see how many times we must compare it to `abcdefg`:

0	1	2	3	4	5	6
a	b	c	d	e	f	g
c	d	f				
	c	d	f			
		c	d	f		
			c	d	f	
				c	d	f

The length of `abf` is 3. The length of `abcdefg` is 7. The last index at which we compare the two strings is 4, which is 7 - 3. So we can guess that `s2.length()-s1.length()` is the last index to check. Does this make sense?

- If `s1.length()` increases by 1, then the last index to check must *decrease* by 1.

- If `s2.length()` increases by 1, then the last index to check must *increase* by 1.

So `s2.length()-s1.length()` is correct.

 Test your skill with Exercises 19–53 through 19–55.

19.12   Ciphers

> **Cipher**   A means of hiding the content of a message by replacing characters according to an algorithm.
>
> **Caesar cipher**   A cipher in which each letter is replaced by the letter in the alphabet that follows it.

Julius Caesar developed the first known cipher by shifting each letter in a message to the next one in the alphabet. (`'z'` maps to `'a'` by considering the alphabet to be circular.) Thus, "`hello there`" becomes "`ifmmp uifsf.`" Appropriately, this is called a *Caesar cipher*. It shifts each letter by one, but we can get other ciphers by shifting the letters by two or more. We decipher the message by shifting each letter *backward* by the appropriate amount.

 Test your skill with Exercise 19–56.

> **Substitution cipher**   A cipher for which each character is consistently replaced by some other character, but successive letters do not necessarily have successive replacements.

Shift ciphers are easy to break. The next step up the cryptological ladder involves replacing each `char` with another `char`, but without shifting each `char` by the same amount. These are called *substitution ciphers*. For example, we might have the following table:

a	b	c	d	e	f	g	h	i	j	k	l	m	n	o	p	q	r	s	t	u	v	w	x	y	z
d	k	j	o	q	s	e	p	w	n	a	i	z	t	u	c	y	h	x	v	b	r	g	m	l	f

for which the second row is a *permutation* of the characters `a` through `z`. Using this cipher, the message `hello there` becomes `pqiiu vpqhq`.

 Test your skill with Exercise 19–57.

19.13   GUI: Introducing `Timer`

`Timer` is a class that periodically triggers the `actionPerformed` method of a specified `ActionListener`. `Prog1907.java` is an application that uses a timer to print integers continuously onto `System.out`, one every half-second. We call

```
new Timer(DELAY,new TimerListener())
```

to create a timer instance. The delay is 500 milliseconds between calls to the `actionPerformed` method of the `TimerListener`.

Prog1907.java — Tests the **Timer Class**

```java
// Written by Barry Soroka
//
// Tests the Timer class.  Prints another int at each clock tick.
// Uses an invisible JFrame.
//
import java.awt.*;
import java.awt.event.*;
import javax.swing.*;
//////////////////////////////////////////////////////////////////////////////
class Prog1907
{
//----------------------------------------------------------------------------
    public static void main (String[] args)
    {
        JFrame frame = new JFrame ("Testing Timer");
        MyPanel mp = new MyPanel();
        frame.getContentPane().add(mp);
    }
//----------------------------------------------------------------------------
} // end class Prog1907
//////////////////////////////////////////////////////////////////////////////
class MyPanel extends JPanel
{
    private int n;
    private final int DELAY = 500;
//----------------------------------------------------------------------------
    public MyPanel()
    {
        n = 0;

        Timer timer = new Timer(DELAY,new TimerListener());

        setBackground(Color.BLACK);
        setPreferredSize(new Dimension(100,100));
        timer.start();
    }
//----------------------------------------------------------------------------
    public void paintComponent ( Graphics page )
    {
        super.paintComponent(page);
    }
```

```
//----------------------------------------------------------------------
//////////////////////////////////////////////////////////////////////
private class TimerListener implements ActionListener
{
//----------------------------------------------------------------------
    public void actionPerformed ( ActionEvent event )
    {
        System.out.println(n);
        n++;
    }
//----------------------------------------------------------------------
} // end class TimerListener
//////////////////////////////////////////////////////////////////////
} // end class MyPanel
//////////////////////////////////////////////////////////////////////
```

 | **Test your skill with Exercise 19–58.**

19.14   GUI: An Oscillator

Prog1908.java is an application that displays a spot that oscillates left to right and back again, following a sinusoidal curve. The position of the spot is determined by a formula that uses $\sin(ct)$, where t is the time since the program began and c is a constant. The Timer fires every 100 milliseconds, and the actionPerformed method draws the spot at its new location. DEG_PER_SEC is the number of degrees per second of the sinusoidal motion. EXCURSION is the maximum number of pixels that the spot can deviate from its center position.

Prog1908.java   **1-D Oscillator**

```
// Written by Barry Soroka
//
// 1-D oscillator -- uses a Timer.
//
import java.awt.*;
import java.awt.event.*;
import javax.swing.*;
//////////////////////////////////////////////////////////////////////
class Prog1908
{
//----------------------------------------------------------------------
    public static void main (String[] args)
    {
        JFrame frame = new JFrame ("Oscillator");
        frame.setDefaultCloseOperation (JFrame.EXIT_ON_CLOSE);
```

```
        MyPanel mp = new MyPanel();

        frame.getContentPane().add(mp);
        frame.pack();
        frame.setVisible(true);
    }
//---------------------------------------------------------------------------
} // end class Prog1908
/////////////////////////////////////////////////////////////////////////////
class MyPanel extends JPanel
{
    private int x;
    private int time;
    private final int SIZE = 6;
    private final int DELAY = 100;
    private final double DEG_PER_SEC = 80.0;
    private final int X_CENTER = 150;
    private final int EXCURSION = 100;   // maximum excursion from X_CENTER
//---------------------------------------------------------------------------
    public MyPanel()
    {
        time = 0;
        Timer timer = new Timer(DELAY,new TimerListener());

        setBackground(Color.BLACK);
        setPreferredSize(new Dimension(100+2*EXCURSION,100));

        timer.start();
    }
//---------------------------------------------------------------------------
    public void paintComponent ( Graphics page )
    {
        super.paintComponent(page);

        page.setColor(Color.YELLOW);
        page.fillOval(x-SIZE,50-SIZE,2*SIZE,2*SIZE);
    }
//---------------------------------------------------------------------------
/////////////////////////////////////////////////////////////////////////////
private class TimerListener implements ActionListener
{
//---------------------------------------------------------------------------
    public void actionPerformed ( ActionEvent event )
    {
        time += DELAY;
```

```
      double angle = DEG_PER_SEC * time / 1000.0;
      x = X_CENTER + (int)(EXCURSION * Math.sin(angle*Math.PI/360.0));
      repaint();
    }
//-------------------------------------------------------------------------
} // end class TimerListener
/////////////////////////////////////////////////////////////////////////
} // end class MyPanel
/////////////////////////////////////////////////////////////////////////
```

  Test your skill with Exercises 19–59 through 19–63.

Chapter Summary

- A linear search looks through a collection beginning from the front and proceding element-by-element. Its speed is $O(n)$.
- Binary search can be used on sorted collections. Its speed is $O(\log_2(n))$.
- Sorting is frequently performed.
- Swapping two variables requires a temporary variable.
- Selection sort works by finding the smallest element in slices of an array and swapping that smallest element with the first element in the slice.
- Finding prime numbers and perfect numbers are good problems involving integers.
- We can write code for changing an integer to the corresponding `String`.
- We can write code for changing a `String` to the corresponding integer.
- A cipher is a means of encoding a message by swapping each character into a specified other character.
- A GUI `Timer` object functions as a clock that generates events at equally spaced intervals.
- We can implement GUI animations by using a `Timer` to tell code when to redraw a changing scene.

Terminology Introduced in This Chapter

benchmark test	Caesar cipher	prime number
binary search	cipher	selection sort
bubble sort	linear search	substitution cipher

Exercises

Exercise 19–1. Write a method

```
public static int dot ( int a[], int b[] )
```

that computes the dot product of two equal-length arrays of `int`s using the formula

$$\sum_i a_i b_i$$

.

Exercise 19–2. Write the method

```
public static int fac(int)
```

that computes the factorial of a number *using a loop*. (In Chapter 18 we solved this problem using *recursion*.)

Exercise 19–3. Write a method

```
public static double power ( double x, int n )
```

that uses a loop to compute x^n.

Exercise 19–4. Add to class `Complex`:

```
public Complex power ( int n )
```

which returns the receiver raised to the nth power.

Exercise 19–5. Write a program that computes the first n Fibonacci numbers *using a loop*. (In Chapter 18, we did this computation using *recursion*.) Produce a table that gives the Fibonacci numbers and the ratio of adjacent Fibonacci numbers. This ratio converges to $\frac{1+\sqrt{5}}{2}$, which is called the *Golden Ratio*. Here is typical output for the first 10 Fibonacci numbers:

```
 1    1
 2    1   1.000000
 3    2   2.000000
 4    3   1.500000
 5    5   1.666667
 6    8   1.600000
 7   13   1.625000
 8   21   1.615385
 9   34   1.619048
10   55   1.617647
```

Exercise 19–6.   Suppose a customer opens a bank account with $X at the start of the year. The bank adds 3.75% compound interest to the account at the end of each year. Write a program that determines how many years it takes for the account balance to exceed $100,000. Assume that the customer makes no further deposits or withdrawals.

Exercise 19–7.   Write a program that reads an integer and prints all its divisors.

Exercise 19–8.   Add to class `Section` the method

```
public boolean linearSearch ( String name )
```

which uses linear search to determine whether the `Section` contains a `Student` with this `name`.

Exercise 19–9.   *Instrument* `binarySearch` in `Prog1902` by adding print statements that display `lo`, `hi`, and `mid` and the corresponding array values each time around the loop. Can you see how binary search continuously halves the size of the search interval?

Exercise 19–10.   Add to class `Section` the method

```
public boolean binarySearch ( String name )
```

which uses binary search to determine whether the `Section` contains a `Student` with this `name`. Be sure that the `Student`s are already sorted by `name`.

Exercise 19–11.   Write a main method that finds $\sqrt{2}$ by using binary search.

Exercise 19–12.   Write a main method that uses binary search to locate roots of equations such as $x^3 - 1.8x^2 - 1.1x + 2 = 0$. (That equation has at least one root in the interval [–5, +5].)

Exercise 19–13.   Prove that the following statements swap the values of variables `a` and `b` *without* using a temporary variable:

```
a = a - b;
b = a + b;
a = b - a;
```

Exercise 19–14.   Add to class `Section` the method

```
public void selectionSort()
```

which uses selection sort to put the elements of the `Section` into order by `name`.

Exercise 19–15. Test the speed of selection sort by modifying `Prog1903`. Create and sort arrays of size 1000, 10,000, ... elements. Fill these arrays with random integers in the range 1 to 1,000,000. Use the method `System.currentTimeMillis()` to determine how many milliseconds each sort requires. Once you have found a number of elements with a sorting time of about 100 to 1000 milliseconds, plot the time to sort arrays containing multiples of that number of elements. How does the time required change as you double the number of elements? Triple the number of elements?

Exercise 19–16. Another simple sort is *bubble sort*. The algorithm repeatedly passes over the array, exchanging adjacent elements that are out of order. For our sample array, the first pass would look like this. The adjacent elements that get swapped are underlined:

27	17	15	31	85	-6	2	3	43	57
17	27	15	31	85	-6	2	3	43	57
17	15	27	31	85	-6	2	3	43	57
17	15	27	31	-6	85	2	3	43	57
17	15	27	31	-6	2	85	3	43	57
17	15	27	31	-6	2	3	85	43	57
17	15	27	31	-6	2	3	45	85	57
17	15	27	31	-6	2	3	45	57	85

After the first pass over the array, the "heaviest" element has found its way to the rightmost position in the array. The next iteration performs interchanges on only this slice:

17	15	27	31	-6	2	3	45	57	87

In the worst case, the interchanges continue until the slice width is 1. In better cases, the algorithm will make a complete pass over the array without needing to swap any elements. In that case, the array is sorted.
Implement bubble sort in Java. Modify `Prog1903.java` to use it.

Exercise 19–17. Add to class `Section` the method

```
public void bubbleSort()
```

which uses bubble sort to put the elements of the `Section` into order by `name`.

Exercise 19–18. Modify the code for `isPrime` so that we only search with divisors that are less than or equal to the square root of `n`.

Exercise 19–19. Write a `main` method that reads two integers, `lo` and `hi`, for which `lo < hi`, and prints the prime numbers in the range [`lo`,`hi`].

Exercise 19–20. A *prime pair* is a pair of numbers, n and n+2, such that both n and n+2 are prime. Examples are 3 and 5, 5 and 7, 11 and 13, 17 and 19, and 29 and 31. Write a `main` method that reads two integers, lo and hi, for which lo < hi, and prints the prime pairs in the range [lo,hi].

Exercise 19–21. Write a `main` method that fills in the following table:

lo	hi	# of Primes in This Range
1	1000	
1001	2000	
2001	3000	
. . .	. . .	
49,001	50,000	

Does the density of primes—the number of primes per thousand integers—fall off as we consider increasingly larger integers?

Exercise 19–22. An integer is *perfect* if it is the sum of all its divisors except itself. For example,

6 is perfect because 6 = 1 + 2 + 3.
28 is perfect because 28 = 1 + 2 + 4 + 7 + 14.

Write a `main` method that computes the first four perfect numbers. You needn't search beyond 10,000.

Exercise 19–23. Some integers are the same when they are rotated 180 degrees. Examples are 0, 1, 69, 96, and 101. Write a predicate `isUpsideDownable(int)` that returns `true` if and only if its parameter has this property. Test it by computing rotatable numbers less than 10,000.

Exercise 19–24. Modify `intToString` to correctly handle all integers, including negative integers.

Exercise 19–25. Modify `intToString` in `Prog1905` to correctly handle all integers, including negative integers.

Exercise 19–26. Write a method

```
public static String doubleToString ( double x )
```

that converts a `double` to a `String` with exactly two places to the right of the decimal point, e.g., 19.98732 → "19.99".

Exercise 19–27. Write a recursive method

```
public static String binaryString ( int n )
```

that takes an `int` and produces a `String` that represents it in binary. Your algorithm should be based on the following table:

n	n%2	result
		" "
57	1	
		"1"
28	0	
		"01"
14	0	
		"001"
7	1	
		"1001"
3	1	
		"11001"
1	1	
		"111001"
0		*Stop*

Note: Successive values of n come from `n /= 2`.

Exercise 19–28. Modify `parseInt` in `Prog1906` so that it handles both *signed* and *unsigned* integers. (`"+52"` and `"-735"` are signed integers. `"52"` is an unsigned integer.)

Exercise 19–29. Write an iterative method `parseDouble` that can convert the following sorts of `String`s to `double`s: `"37.814"`, `"1.9e-31"`, `"6.023e23"`.

Exercise 19–30. Write a method `parseBinary` that converts a binary `String`—e.g., `"10111"`—to the corresponding `int`.

Exercise 19–31. Write a method `parseHex` that converts a hexadecimal `String`—e.g., `"2FA"`—to the corresponding `int`.

Exercise 19–32. Implement Ulam's conjecture so that, given an `int`, it reports the values in the chain that terminates with 1. (If you find an `int` for which the procedure does *not* terminate with 1, then you have found the first counterexample.)

Exercise 19–33.   Implement Ulam's conjecture so that, given an `int`, it computes the length of the chain from the given `int` to the final value of 1.

Exercise 19–34.   Write a `main` method which, given integers `lo` and `hi`, determines whether or not Ulam's conjecture holds in the range [`lo`,`hi`].

Exercise 19–35.   Make a two-column table showing an integer and the length of the chain it evokes from Ulam's conjecture. Is there a pattern?

Exercise 19–36.   Write a `main` method which, given integers `lo` and `hi`, produces a table that shows the frequency of the different chain lengths evoked from Ulam's conjecture for integers in the range [`lo`,`hi`].

Exercise 19–37.   Find integer solutions to the equation $3a + 4b + 6c = 120$ with $a, b, c \in [0,25]$. This is a *Diophantine equation*, named for Diophantus of Alexandria (ca. 250 A.D.), one of the founders of algebra.

Exercise 19–38.   Here's another *Diophantine equation*: There's a group of n soldiers. When they march two abreast, there's one left over. When they march three abreast, there are two left over. When they march five abreast, there are four left over. Write a loop that determines the number of soldiers.

Exercise 19–39.   Some numbers are the sum of the factorials of their base 10 digits:

$$1! = 1$$

and

$$2! = 2.$$

Most numbers don't have this property:

$$13 \neq 1! + 3! = 1 + 6 = 7$$

and

$$231 \neq 2! + 3! + 1! = 2 + 6 + 1 = 9.$$

There are exactly four numbers with the property described above. They're all less than 50,000. Write a program that finds them.

Exercise 19–40.   Some integers can be written as the sum of two squares. For instance,

$$50 = 12 + 72.$$

Some integers can be written as the sum of two squares in two different ways. For example,

$$725 = 142 + 232 = 72 + 262.$$

These are the integers we seek. Let's call them "special numbers".

Write a program that finds all special numbers in the range 1... 5000. (Note that $5000 = 50^2 + 50^2$.) For each special number you find, print lines such as:

```
  7        26        725
 14        23        725
```

For the sake of this exercise, we'll allow special numbers to include integers that can be written as the sum of two squares in two or more different ways.

Exercise 19–41.   Find the smallest integer that is the sum of two cubes in two different ways.

Exercise 19–42.   Write a method

```
public static boolean containsAny(String,char)
```

that reports whether the given `char` occurs in the given `String`.

Exercise 19–43.   Write a method

```
public static int containsHowMany(String,char)
```

that reports how many times the given `char` occurs in the given `String`.

Exercise 19–44.   Write a method

```
public static String delete(String,char)
```

that returns a new `String` in which each occurrence of the `char` has been deleted.

Exercise 19–45.   Write a method

```
public static String replace(String,char,char)
```

that returns a new `String` in which each occurrence of the first `char` has been replaced by the second `char`. For example, `replace("hello there",'e','x')` returns the `String` "hxllo thxrx".

Exercise 19–46.   Write a method

```
public static String replace(String s,
                             String oldChars,
                             String newChars)
```

that returns a new `String` in which each occurrence of a `char` in the `String` old-Chars has been replaced by the corresponding `char` in the `String newChars`. For example,

```
replace("hello there",'le','bx')
```

returns the `String "hxbo thxrx"` for which `'l'` has been replaced by `'b'` and `'e'` has been replaced by `'x'`.

Exercise 19–47.   Write a method

```
public static String reverse(String)
```

that returns a `String` that is the reverse of the given `String`.

Exercise 19–48.   Write a method

```
public static boolean isPalindrome(String)
```

that returns `true` if and only if the given `String` is a palindrome (i.e., reads the same forward and backward).

Exercise 19–49.   Write a method

```
public static String reportDoubles(String)
```

that returns a `String` containing any characters that occur twice or more in the given `String`. For example:

```
reportDoubles("baby")  →  "b"
reportDoubles("banner")  →  "n"
reportDoubles("mississippi")  →  "isp"
```

Exercise 19–50.   Write a method

```
public static String reportSequentialDoubles(String)
```

that returns a `String` containing any characters that occur twice or more *in a row* in the given `String`. For example:

```
reportSequentialDoubles("banner") → "n"
reportSequentialDoubles("mississippi") → "sp"
```

Exercise 19–51. Write a method

```
public static boolean isPrefix(String,String)
```

that returns `true` if and only if the first `String` is a prefix of the second `String`.

Exercise 19–52. Write a method

```
public static boolean isSuffix(String,String)
```

that returns `true` if and only if the first `String` is a suffix of the second `String`.

Exercise 19–53. Write a version of `isSubstring` that does not explicitly call `isPrefix`. Instead, use nested loops, computing `isPrefix` implicitly.

Exercise 19–54. Write a method

```
public static boolean match ( String pattern, String s )
```

that considers the two `String`s and returns `true` if and only if they are of equal length and are equal, character for character, with the exception that a `'?'` in the `pattern` counts as a *wild card* that matches any single character in the corresponding position of the `String` s. The `String`s may be any length, including 0. For example:

pattern	s	Result
"abc"	"ab"	false
""	""	true
"abc"	"abc"	true
"abc"	"aeb"	false
"ab?"	"abd"	true
"a?c"	"adc"	true
"ab"	"a"	false
"??"	"ab"	true

How many loops are required?

Exercise 19–55. Write a method

```
public static boolean match ( String pattern, String s )
```

that considers the two Strings and returns true if and only if they are equal, character for character, with the exception that an '*' in the pattern counts as a *wild card* that matches *any number of* chars—including 0 chars—in the corresponding position of String s. The Strings may be any length, including 0. For example:

Pattern	Matches
" "	" "
abc	abc
*	" ",a,ab,abc,...
a*	a,aa,ab,abc,abaca,...
a*c	ac,aac,axc,axyc,axyzc,...
*bc	bc,xbc,xybc,bbc,bcbc,...
*c	c,cc,xc,xyc,xyzc,...
a*b*c	abc,aabc,abbc,acbc,axbc,abxc,axbyc,axybc,...

How many loops are required?

Exercise 19–56. Write a method

```
public static String encipher ( String s, int shift )
```

that takes a message s and enciphers it by shifting each letter by the amount shift. Negative shifts can be used to *de*cipher a message. What does the following message say?

```
ridi uisma kqxpmza miag
```

Exercise 19–57. Write a method

```
public static String encipher ( String message,
                                String replacements )
```

that implements a substitution cipher. The replacements parameter is a String of length 26:

replacements[0] substitutes for 'a';
replacements[1] substitutes for 'b';
...

Test your code by enciphering and deciphering a variety of messages.

Exercise 19–58. (*Raindrops*) Modify `Prog1907` so that it places a spot at a random location on a `JPanel` every half-second.

Exercise 19–59. Experiment with the parameters of `Prog1908`:

- Change the speed of the sinusoidal motion.
- Change the maximum excursion of the moving spot.
- Change the frequency of the graphic update.

Exercise 19–60. Modify `Prog1908` so that `DEG_PER_SEC` is read from a `JTextField`.

Exercise 19–61. Modify `Prog1908` so that the spot moves in *two* dimensions, x and y. Each of the two motions is controlled by an independent sinusoid. Depending on the ratio of the frequencies of the two motions, characteristic 2-D patterns—called *Lissajous figures*—are observed. A frequency ratio of 1:1 draws a circle. Try the ratios 1:2, 1:3, and 2:3.

Exercise 19–62. Modify `Prog1908` to display a graphic pendulum, such as the pendulum of a grandfather clock.

Exercise 19–63. Write an application that simulates a ball bouncing around in a 2-D box. At any given time, the ball's velocity should be one of the following:

x-Velocity	y-Velocity
v	v
v	−v
−v	v
−v	−v

At each clock tick, compute the ball's position and redraw the ball. If a motion would take the ball past one of the walls of the box, reverse its velocity along that dimension.

Style Sheet

Every programming project has a Style Sheet—a set of conventions regarding the optional aspects of Java programming. This appendix presents the Style Sheet used in this text. Programs `Example1` and `Example2` are presented as demonstrations of the style.

1. Classes should be enclosed between rows of slashes:

   `/////////////////////////////////////////////////////////////`

   A row of slashes may be used in no other way. (See the example programs.)

2. Methods should be enclosed between rows of dashes:

   Thus, a row of hyphens will separate the instance variables from the first method in a class. Similarly, a row of hyphens should precede the first method in a class if there are no class or instance variables. A row of hyphens may be used in no other way. (See the example programs.)

3. Class names have the first letters of all words capitalized. For example: `Complex`, `RationalNumber`.

4. Variables, methods, and instances have names for which all words are capitalized *except* the first word. For example: `sum`, `dateLastModified`, `nUpperCase`, `numberOfOddEntries`.

5. Constants are written in all capital letters. Underscores may be used to separate words. For example, `MAX_SIZE`, `E`, `PI`. Underscores are only permitted in constants.

6. Within a class, the order should be: variables, constructors, methods.

7. In general, instance variables should be `private`.

8. Instance variables should be initialized in constructors, *not* in their declarations.

9. Always label instance variables and methods as `public`, `private`, or `protected`.

10. Here is an example of the required indentation scheme:

```
public static void main ( String [] args )
{
   if (a == b)
   {
      System.out.println("They're equal!");
   }
}
```

11. If only a single statement follows an `if` or `else`, then the braces may be omitted:

```
if (cond1) System.out.println();
```

Avoid nested `if` statements; they can become very hard to understand and debug. Multiway branches, such as `if ... else if ... else if ... else,` are an exception.

12. Indent each level by *three spaces*. Do not indent using the TAB key.

13. Names of classes, methods, and instances should reflect the purpose of said classes, methods, and instances.

14. Include your name in a comment near the top of each code file.

15. Hardcopy of Java code, data, and output should be printed using a `fixed-width` font.

16. Avoid wraparound, in which one line spills uncontrolled onto the next line.

Example1.java **Java Style, Simple Example**

```
// Written by Barry Soroka
//
// Example1:  A simple example of the required Java style.
//
import java.io.*;
//////////////////////////////////////////////////////////////////////////////
class Foo
```

```
{
//----------------------------------------------------------------------
   public static void main ( String [] args ) throws Exception
   {
      System.out.println("hello");
   }
//----------------------------------------------------------------------
} // end class Foo
//////////////////////////////////////////////////////////////////////////
```

Example2.java   Java Style, Longer Example

```
// Written by Barry Soroka
//
// Example2:  A more complicated example of the style sheet.
//
import java.io.*;
//////////////////////////////////////////////////////////////////////////
class Name
{
   private String firstName;
   private String lastName;
//----------------------------------------------------------------------
   public Name ( String firstName, String lastName )
   {
      this.firstName = firstName;
      this.lastName = lastName;
   }
//----------------------------------------------------------------------
//
// getInitials()
//
// If the name were "John Doe" then this method would return "JD".
//
   public String getInitials()
   {
      return firstName.substring(0,1) + lastName.substring(0,1);
   }
//----------------------------------------------------------------------
} // end class Name
//////////////////////////////////////////////////////////////////////////
```

Reserved Words

The following identifiers are reserved by Java. They cannot, and should not, be used to name user-defined variables, methods, classes, or interfaces.

abstract	else	interface	switch
assert	enum	long	synchronized
boolean	extends	native	this
break	false	new	throw
byte	final	null	throws
case	finally	package	transient
catch	float	private	true
char	for	protected	try
class	goto	public	void
const	if	return	volatile
continue	implements	short	while
default	import	static	
do	instanceof	strictfp	
double	int	super	

Printable Characters

The following is a list of printable characters and their Unicode values, in decimal. The ASCII values are identical.

32	*space*	56	8	80	P	104	h
33	!	57	9	81	Q	105	i
34	"	58	:	82	R	106	j
35	#	59	;	83	S	107	k
36	$	60	<	84	T	108	l
37	%	61	=	85	U	109	m
38	&	62	>	86	V	110	n
39	'	63	?	87	W	111	o
40	(	64	@	88	X	112	p
41	)	65	A	89	Y	113	q
42	*	66	B	90	Z	114	r
43	+	67	C	91	[	115	s
44	,	68	D	92	\	116	t
45	-	69	E	93	]	117	u
46	.	70	F	94	^	118	v
47	/	71	G	95	_	119	w
48	0	72	H	96	`	120	x
49	1	73	I	97	a	121	y
50	2	74	J	98	b	122	z
51	3	75	K	99	c	123	{
52	4	76	L	100	d	124	|
53	5	77	M	101	e	125	}
54	6	78	N	102	f	126	~
55	7	79	O	103	g		

Operator Precedence

This appendix lists the most widely used of Java's operators and their precedence. Java has more operators than we can learn in a CS 1 course. For information about those we haven't studied, try a reference such as David Flanagan's *Java in a Nutshell*, Fifth Edition (Sebastopol, CA: O'Reilly & Associates, 2005).

The table that follows lists the operators in groups, separated by horizontal lines. Within a group, the operators have equal precedence. Each group has higher precedence than the group that follows it. Associativity—left-to-right (L), or right-to-left (R)—is indicated for each group.

Operator	Description	Associativity
[ ]	array indexing	L
.	object member access	
(*args*)	method invocation	
++	post-increment	
- -	post-decrement	
++	pre-increment	R
- -	pre-decrement	
+	unary plus	
-	unary minus	
!	boolean NOT	
new	object creation	R
(*type*)	casting	

Operator	Description	Associativity
*	multiplication	L
/	division	
%	remainder	
+	addition	L
-	subtraction	
+	String concatenation	
<	less than	L
<=	less than or equal to	
>	greater than	
>=	greater than or equal to	
==	equal	L
!=	not equal	
&	bitwise AND	L
&	boolean logical AND	
^	bitwise exclusive OR	L
^	boolean logical exclusive OR	
|	bitwise inclusive OR	L
|	boolean logical inclusive OR	
&&	boolean conditional AND	L
||	boolean conditional OR	L
? :	conditional operator	R
=	assignment	R
*=	multiply and assign	
/=	divide and assign	
%=	remainder and assign	
+=	add and assign	
-=	subtract and assign	
&=	boolean AND and assign	
|=	boolean OR and assign	

Increment and Decrement Operators

In this text, we introduced i++ and i-- as the *increment* and *decrement* operators, meaning

```
i = i + 1;
```

and

```
i = i - 1;
```

respectively. Java offers two additional forms, ++i and --i. These have the following names:

++i	*pre-increment*
i++	*post-increment*
--i	*pre-decrement*
i--	*post-decrement*

When used as *statements*, both ++i and i++ mean

```
i = i + 1;
```

Similarly, when used as *statements*, both --i and i-- mean

```
i = i - 1;
```

The differences between *pre* and *post* arise when the forms are used as *expressions* such as

```
n = 2 * (i++);
```

or

```
n = 2 * (++i);
```

The following table describes the meanings of the pre- and post-increment and decrement operators when used as expressions:

Expression	Meaning
++i	Increment i and use the new value
i++	Use the current value of i and then increment i
--i	Decrement i and use the new value
i--	Use the current value of i and then decrement i

For example, the code

```
int i = 5;
System.out.println(i++);
System.out.println(i);
```

prints

```
5
6
```

and the code

```
int i = 5;
System.out.println(++i);
System.out.println(i);
```

prints

```
6
6
```

Code involving `--i` and `i--` behaves similarly.

WARNING	It's a rare programmer who hasn't accidentally used `i++` instead of `++i` or vice versa, or who hasn't misinterpreted pre- or post-increment when debugging. It's safest to use them as individual *statements* rather than as parts of *expressions*. Ditto for pre- and post-decrement.

Exercises

APP05–1.   What are the values of `i`, `j`, `k`, `l`, and `m` after execution of the following code?

```
int n = 5;
int i = (n++) + 2*n;
int j = (--n) + 2*n;
int k = (n++) + 2*(--n);
int l = (++n) + 2*(n--);
int m = n;
```

Conditional Operator — ? :

This is Java's only *ternary* operator—it involves *three* items. Its form is:

boolean-expression ? *expression1* : *expression2*

where *expression1* and *expression2* must evaluate to the same type. For example,

```
( n == 0 ) ? "zero" : "non-zero"
```

evaluates to the String "zero" or the String "non-zero", depending on whether n == 0.

The conditional operator can be used in statements such as

```
String title = ( gender == 'm' ) ? "Mr" : "Ms";
```

which is equivalent to

```
String title;
if ( gender == 'm' ) title = "Mr";
else                 title = "Ms";
```

Another use is for console output. Consider the statement

```
System.out.println("There " +
          ((n == 1) ? "is " : "are ") +
          n + " item" +
          ((n == 1) ? "." : "s."));
```

If n is 1, we get:

```
There is 1 item.
```

If n is 5, we get:

```
There are 5 items.
```

The conditional operator is like a compressed `if-else` for which the operator itself returns a value.

Enhanced for Loop

Iterating over all the elements of an array is a fairly common task. Examples are:

```
int a[] = {3,1,4,1,5,9};

for ( int i = 0 ; i < a.length ; i++ )
    System.out.print(a[i] + " ");
System.out.println();
```

and

```
String[] days = { "Monday", "Tuesday",
                  "Wednesday", "Thursday",
                  "Friday" };

for ( int i = 0 ; i < days.length ; i++ )
    System.out.println(days[i]);
```

Java provides the *enhanced for loop* to facilitate this iteration. The preceding for loops can be replaced with the more intuitive statements here:

```
for ( int n : a )
    System.out.print(n + " ");
System.out.println();
```

and

```
for ( String d : days ) System.out.println(d);
```

The colon (":") can be read as "in," producing the apt "for int n *in* a" and "for String d *in* days."

The enhanced for loop also works with many of Java's advanced Collections, including List.

Exercises

APP07–1. Using the enhanced for loop, write the code that computes the average value of an array of ints.

APP07–2. Using the enhanced for loop, write the code that concatenates all the Strings in an array of Strings.

APP07–3. Using the enhanced for loop, write the code that computes the average of the Complex numbers in an array of Complex.

APP07–4. Using the enhanced for loop, write the code that computes the average grade of the Students in a *full* array of Students.

vararg—Variable Length Argument Lists

Java 5 allows a method to take a variable length argument list. This is called the *vararg* or *varargs* feature. Consider the method

```
private static int sum ( int ... ints )
{
    int total = 0;
    for ( int n : ints ) total += n;
    return total;
}
```

Notice the *ellipsis*—the three dots—between int and ints. This tells Java that sum may take any number of int arguments. The arguments are collected into an array of int (called ints here) and the body of the method can reference this array. Java requires that all of the vararg arguments be of the same type.

Typical calls to sum are:

```
System.out.println(sum(1,2,3,4));

System.out.println(sum());
```

The second call illustrates calling sum with *zero* arguments.

The Java compiler implements varargs by collecting the arguments into an array, and we can call sum with an *array* of ints:

```
int[] a = {3,1,4,1};

System.out.println(sum(a));
```

Methods involving varargs may have other parameters in addition to the vararg parameter, but the vararg parameter must come *last*. Here's an example:

```
private static labeledValues ( String label, int ... values )
{
    System.out.println(label);
    for ( int n : values ) System.out.println(n);
}
```

A method may have only one varargs parameter.

Previously, we have seen two API methods that involved varargs:

- Method `printf` of class `PrintStream`.
- Method `format` of class `String`.

Both of these took a variable number of arguments.

Exercises

APP08–1.   Using the varargs feature, write a method that computes the average of the integer arguments it receives.

APP08–2.   Using the varargs feature, write a method that takes any number of `String`s and prints each on its own line.

Enumerated Types—enum

When programming, we often want to define a new type with a specified range of values. In Java, we do this with the enum statement:

```
enum Gender = { M, F };
enum Season = { SUMMER, FALL, WINTER, SPRING };
enum Grade = { A, B, C, D, F };
```

An enum is a special sort of class, which possesses only a fixed number of instances. An enum statement cannot occur within a method; it should appear at the top of a file so that it can be referenced by all the classes within the file.

We access a value by naming the enum and the instance:

```
System.out.println(Season.SUMMER);
```

prints out

```
SUMMER
```

We can use the enhanced for loop to see *all* of the values of an enum:

```
for ( Season s : Season.values() )
    System.out.println(s);
```

prints out

```
SUMMER
FALL
WINTER
SPRING
```

We can use a `switch` statement to branch according to the value of an `enum` variable:

```
Season s = ... ;
switch ( s )
{
    case SUMMER:  // statements for SUMMER
    case FALL:    // statements for FALL
    case WINTER:  // statements for WINTER
    case SPRING:  // statements for SPRING
}
```

Generally, we need to specify both the `enum` and the value—as in `Season.SUMMER`—but, within a `switch`, we need name only the value.

`APP0901.java` shows the use of the `enum` `Gender` to classify `Persons` as M or F, and a loop prints out the names only of those with `gender == F`.

APP0901.java   Using an **enum** for Gender

```java
// Written by Barry Soroka
//
// Using an enum for gender.
//
import java.io.*;
//
enum Gender { M, F }
/////////////////////////////////////////////////////////////////////////////
class APP0901
{
//----------------------------------------------------------------------------
    public static void main ( String [] args ) throws Exception
    {
        Person [] persons = { new Person("artur",Gender.M),
                              new Person("britt",Gender.F),
                              new Person("carol",Gender.F),
                              new Person("david",Gender.M),
                              new Person("emily",Gender.F) };

        // Print out names of Persons with Gender F.
        for ( Person p : persons )
            if ( p.getGender() == Gender.F ) System.out.println(p.getName());
    }
//----------------------------------------------------------------------------
```

```
} // end class APP0901
/////////////////////////////////////////////////////////////////////////
class Person
{
   private String name;
   private Gender gender;
//-----------------------------------------------------------------------
   public Person ( String name, Gender gender )
   {
      this.name = name;
      this.gender = gender;
   }
//-----------------------------------------------------------------------
   public String getName() { return name; }
//-----------------------------------------------------------------------
   public Gender getGender() { return gender; }
//-----------------------------------------------------------------------
} // end class Person
/////////////////////////////////////////////////////////////////////////
```

The enum values are all written in uppercase, to match our convention for constants.

ArrayList

We'll use `APP1001.java` to study `ArrayLists`—a Java datatype that acts like an array of `Objects`, but which allows us to insert and delete items in the middle of the array. `APP1001` maintains a roster of names—`Strings`—and can perform operations on the roster in response to user commands. The following dialog illustrates the commands. What the user types is underlined:

```
G:\>java APP1001
roster is []
```

`APP1001` always displays the current roster before requesting a command from the user. The `help` command lists which commands are available:

```
Command? help
Legal commands are:
    add       Add a name to the end of the roster
    help      Display this message
    quit      Exit the program
  reverse     Reverse the roster
  shuffle     Shuffle the roster
    sort      Sort the roster

roster is []
```

The `add` command allows us to add new names to the end of the roster:

```
Command? add
Enter a name: sue
roster is [sue]
```

```
                        Command? add
                        Enter a name: bill
                        roster is [sue, bill]

                        Command? add
                        Enter a name: debra
                        roster is [sue, bill, debra]

                        Command? add
                        Enter a name: john
                        roster is [sue, bill, debra, john]
```

The reverse command reverses the order of the roster:

```
                        Command? reverse
                        roster is [john, debra, bill, sue]
```

The sort command sorts the roster:

```
                        Command? sort
                        roster is [bill, debra, john, sue]
```

The shuffle command shuffles the order of the names in the roster:

```
                        Command? shuffle
                        roster is [john, bill, debra, sue]
```

The quit command exits the program:

```
                        Command? quit
                        Ending program per your request.
                        C:\>
```

The remaining sections of this appendix explain the code of APP1001.

APP1001.java   Exercising **ArrayList**

```java
// Written by Barry Soroka
//
// Exercises ArrayList.
//
import java.io.*;
import java.util.*;
```

```
//////////////////////////////////////////////////////////////////////////////
class APP1001
{
//------------------------------------------------------------------------------
    public static void main ( String [] args ) throws Exception
    {
        Scanner kb = new Scanner(System.in);

        List<String> roster = new ArrayList<String>();

        while ( true )
        {
            System.out.println("roster is " + roster);
            System.out.print("\nCommand? ");
            String cmd = kb.next();
            if      ( cmd.equalsIgnoreCase("add") )     cmdAdd(kb,roster);
            else if ( cmd.equalsIgnoreCase("help") )    cmdHelp();
            else if ( cmd.equalsIgnoreCase("quit") )    break;
            else if ( cmd.equalsIgnoreCase("reverse") ) cmdReverse(roster);
            else if ( cmd.equalsIgnoreCase("shuffle") ) cmdShuffle(roster);
            else if ( cmd.equalsIgnoreCase("sort") )    cmdSort(roster);
            else
            {
                System.out.println("Sorry, but \"" + cmd +
                                    "\" is not a legal command.");
            }
        }
        System.out.println("Ending program per your request.");
    }
//------------------------------------------------------------------------------
// Prompts for a name & adds it to the end of the roster.
//
    private static void cmdAdd ( Scanner sc, List<String> roster )
    {
        System.out.print("Enter a name: ");
        String name = sc.next();
        roster.add(name);
    }
//------------------------------------------------------------------------------
    private static void cmdHelp()
    {
        System.out.println("Legal commands are:");
        System.out.println("   add      Add a name to the end of the roster");
        System.out.println("   help     Display this message");
```

```
        System.out.println("   quit      Exit the program");
        System.out.println("   shuffle   Shuffle the roster");
        System.out.println("   reverse   Reverse the roster");
        System.out.println("   sort      Sort the roster");
        System.out.println();
    }
//-------------------------------------------------------------------
//
// Reverses a roster.
//
    private static void cmdReverse ( List<String> roster )
    {
        Collections.reverse(roster);
    }
//-------------------------------------------------------------------
//
// Shuffles a roster.
//
    private static void cmdShuffle ( List<String> roster )
    {
        Collections.shuffle(roster);
    }
//-------------------------------------------------------------------
//
// Sorts a roster.
//
    private static void cmdSort ( List<String> roster )
    {
        Collections.sort(roster);
    }
//-------------------------------------------------------------------
} // end class APP1001
/////////////////////////////////////////////////////////////////////
```

The Generic List

List<E> is a *generic* interface, which can be specialized to represent a list of specific types such as List<String> or List<Complex>. E stands for the type of Object for which this List is specialized. A List entity must provide the methods listed in Table APP10–1.

Table APP10–1

`void add(E)` Adds an item at the end of the `List`.

`void add(int,E)` Adds an item at the specified index of the `List`. (Numbering begins with position 0.)

`void clear()` Removes all elements from the `List`.

`E get(int)` Retrieves the element at the specified index.

`int indexOf(E)` Returns the leftmost index at which E occurs in the `List`. Returns -1 if E does not occur in the `List`.

`boolean isEmpty()` Returns `true` if and only if the `List` is empty.

`int lastIndexOf(E)` Returns the rightmost index at which E occurs in the `List`. Returns -1 if E does not occur in the `List`.

`void remove(int)` Removes the element at the specified index.

`int size()` Returns the current size of the `List`.

Implementations of List

There are two principal classes that implement the `List` interface: `ArrayList` and `LinkedList`.

1. The items in an `ArrayList` are stored in adjacent memory locations, providing a compact representation of the `List`. On the other hand, if we insert or delete an element in the middle of the `List`, much copying is required in order to keep the elements adjacent. (We don't do the copying explicitly; Java does it behind the scenes.)

2. The items in a `LinkedList` can be stored in widely separated memory locations. The order is preserved because each item contains a reference to the specific location of the succeeding element. Each item thus requires additional memory to store the pointer, and `LinkedList` provides a noncompact representation of the `List`. On the other hand, inserting or deleting items does not require copying of memory cells as does `ArrayList`. You will study linked lists and Java's `LinkedList` class in a CS 2 course.

APP1001 declares roster to be of type `List`, implemented as an `ArrayList`:

```
List<String> roster = new ArrayList<String>();
```

Because we have declared that roster implements the `List` interface, we can use any of the `List` methods described in Table APP10–1, and all references to `roster` will refer to it as a `List`. Its specific implementation as an `ArrayList` is mentioned only once in the code. We can change the implementation from `ArrayList` to `LinkedList` by changing a single symbol in a single line of code. This is good software practice.

Methods from Interface `Collections`

`List`, `ArrayList`, and `LinkedList` are all nodes in Java's `Collection` hierarchy. This hierarchy is the basis of the *Java Collections Framework*, or JCF. The `Collections` class provides some common methods for working with such items. `APP1001` uses three of the `static` methods of class `Collections`:

1. `void reverse(List<E>)`—reverses a `List`.
2. `void shuffle(List<E>)`—shuffles a `List`.
3. `void sort(List<E>)`—sorts a `List`.

The Structure of `APP1001`

`APP1001` consists of a main loop that (1) displays the current roster, (2) prompts for a user command, and (3) performs a multiway branch based on the entered command. Each command—say, `add`—calls a helper method—`cmdAdd`—that performs the actual work of the command. This keeps the loop lean.

Adding a new command is a threefold process:

1. Add a helper method that does the work of the command. Appropriate arguments are sent along with the call.
2. Add an `else if` line to the main loop, which calls the appropriate helper method.
3. Add a line to the `cmdHelp` method, which describes the new command.

`APP1001` is a robust and flexible structure for an interactive command-line program.

Exercises

APP10–1.   Add a `front` command to `APP1001` that reads a name and adds it to the front of the current `roster`.

APP10–2.   Add a `remove1` command to `APP1001` that reads a name and removes the *first occurrence* of it from the current `roster`.

APP10–3.   Add a `remove` command to `APP1001` that reads a name and removes *all occurrences* of it from the current `roster`.

Wrappers, Boxing, Unboxing

As we have seen in the text, primitive datatypes are distinct from objects: they're created, referenced, and manipulated in distinctly different ways. Except for arrays, Java's collections—such as `ArrayList`s—are aimed at storing *objects*, not primitive datatypes. If we want to store a primitive datatype in an `ArrayList`, we would normally have to enclose it in a *wrapper*.

Every primitive datatype has a corresponding object type, which is called its *wrapper class*:

Primitive datatype	Wrapper
byte	Byte
short	Short
int	Integer
long	Long
boolean	Boolean
char	Character

Integer—a typical wrapper class—contains a variety of methods:

- `Integer(int)` creates an `Integer` object from the given primitive `int`.
- `int intValue()` returns the `int` inside the wrapper.
- `static Integer.parseInt(String)` converts a `String` to the corresponding `int`.
- `static String toBinaryString(int)` creates the binary `String` corresponding to the given `int`.
- `static String toOctalString(int)` creates the octal `String` corresponding to the given `int`.

If we want to store ints inside collections, we would normally spend a lot of statements converting between Integers and ints. For example, consider adding and retrieving an int from an ArrayList of Integers:

```
List<Integer> numbers = new ArrayList<Integer>;
numbers.add(new Integer(5));
int i = numbers.get(0).intValue();
```

Notice how we explicitly convert between Integers and ints.

Java 5 provides two new features to facilitate coding:

1. *Boxing* refers to conversion from an int to an Integer.
2. *Unboxing* refers to conversion from an Integer to an int.

Java performs these operations automatically as needed. Thus, the preceding code becomes more readable:

```
List<Integer> numbers = new ArrayList<Integer>;
numbers.add(5);
int i = numbers.get(0);
```

Java automatically *boxes* the int 5 into an Integer, and it automatically *unboxes* number.get(0)—an Integer—into an int.

The following code uses autounboxing to sum the values inside numbers:

```
int sum = 0;
for ( Integer i : numbers ) sum+= i;
```

Note that we don't need to use intValue().

Another example involves equality testing. Consider the statement x == y. If one of the operands is a primitive and the other is an object, then the object is unboxed and the values are compared.

Java does automatic boxing and unboxing on all the primitive datatypes and their corresponding wrapper classes.

javadoc

javadoc is a program that takes special comments in a Java source file and generates documentation in HTML format. The output has the look and feel of the API documentation with which we are familiar. javadoc is generally distributed along with Java compilers. This appendix is an introduction to javadoc.

Our first step in using javadoc is to make our classes public. Consider Prog1313.java, which introduces a Section as a file of Students. Currently, this file contains three classes:

    1. Prog1313, the driver.
    2. Section, the code for the Section class.
    3. Student, the code for the Student class.

To make these classes *public*, we put each class in a separate file, and we add the public attribute to the class.

We start with a single file such as:

Prog1313.java

```
class Prog1313
. . .
class Section
. . .
class Student
. . .
```

and we end up with *three* files, such as:

Prog1313.java

```
public class Prog1313
. . .
```

Section.java

```
public class Section
. . .
```

Student.java

```
public class Student
. . .
```

Note that the name of the file must be the same as the name of the class inside the file.

We compile the program by issuing three compile statements—one for each source file—and we execute `java` on `Prog1313`, which will find the class files corresponding to all three classes.[1]

Student.java   **Class Student** with *javadoc* **Comments**

```
// Written by Barry Soroka.
//
import java.io.*;
import java.util.Scanner;
///////////////////////////////////////////////////////////////////////////////
/**
 Represents a student with a name and a numeric grade.
 @author Barry Soroka
*/
public class Student
```

---

[1] This book used a single file to hold all three classes because it cut the number of files and compile commands required for the examples.

```
{
   private String name;
   private int grade;
//-------------------------------------------------------------------
/**
 Creates a Student with the specified name and grade.
*/
   public Student ( String name, int grade )
   {
      this.name = name;
      this.grade = grade;
   }
//-------------------------------------------------------------------
/**
 Returns the name of a Student object.
 @return The name of the receiving Student.
 @see #getGrade
*/
   public String getName() { return name; }
//-------------------------------------------------------------------
/**
 Returns the name of a Student object.
 @return The grade of the receiving Student.
 @see #getName
*/
   public int getGrade() { return grade; }
//-------------------------------------------------------------------
/**
 Returns a String that represents the receiving Student.  The complex number 3+5i
 would be represented as <code>(3,5)</code>.
*/
   public String toString() { return name + " (" + grade + ")"; }
//-------------------------------------------------------------------
/**
 Static read method for class Student.
 @param ps PrintStream to which prompts should be sent.  <code>null</code> specifies
 that no prompting is desired.
 @param sc Scanner from which Student data is to be read.
*/
   public static Student read ( PrintStream ps, Scanner sc )
   {
      if ( ps != null ) ps.println("Reading a Student record ...");
```

```
    if ( ps != null ) ps.print("Enter the name: ");
    String name = sc.nextLine();
    if ( ps != null ) ps.print("Enter the grade: ");
    int grade = sc.nextInt(); sc.nextLine();
    return new Student(name,grade);
  }
//-------------------------------------------------------------------
} // end class Student
///////////////////////////////////////////////////////////////////
```

Student.java shows Student as a `public` class with `javadoc` comments mixed with the code. We run `javadoc` with the command

```
javadoc -author Student.java
```

This produces the file Student.html, plus a host of supporting files. When I ran `javadoc` on Student.java, it produced the following files and directory:

```
05/04/21  09:09                685 allclasses-frame.html
05/04/21  09:09                665 allclasses-noframe.html
05/04/21  09:09              4,769 constant-values.html
05/04/21  09:09              4,705 deprecated-list.html
05/04/21  09:09              8,592 help-doc.html
05/04/21  09:09              6,327 index-all.html
05/04/21  09:09              1,211 index.html
05/04/21  09:09              4,835 overview-tree.html
05/04/21  09:09                856 package-frame.html
05/04/21  09:09                  2 package-list
05/04/21  09:09              5,042 package-summary.html
05/04/21  09:09              4,846 package-tree.html
05/04/21  09:09      <DIR>        resources
05/04/21  09:09             11,508 Student.html
05/04/21  09:09              1,231 stylesheet.css
```

If we open Student.html in a browser, we see the Web page shown in Figure APP12–01. This is API-style documentation of the Student class. Let's now examine how Student.java produced this output.

Along with Java code, Student.java contained a variety of documentation comments—"doc comments"—delimited by /** and */. The compiler treats these as comments, but `javadoc` treats them as special text to be used in the HTML file. Doc comments may directly precede any `public` class or `public` method.

As we see in Student.html, the text in a doc comment is used as the textual descriptor of the constructors and methods of the class. Inside doc comments,

Figure APP12–01 Q

Package **Class** **Tree Deprecated Index Help**
PREV CLASS NEXT CLASS   FRAMES   NO FRAMES   All Classes
SUMMARY: NESTED | FIELD | CONSTR | METHOD   DETAIL: FIELD | CONSTR | METHOD

Class Student

```
java.lang.Object
  └ Student
```

```
public class Student
extends java.lang.Object
```

Represents a student with a name and a numeric grade.

Author:
    Barry Soroka

Constructor Summary
Student(java.lang.String name, int grade)   Creates a Student with the specified name and grade.

Method Summary	
int	getGrade() Returns the name of a Student object.
java.lang.String	getName() Returns the name of a Student object.
static Student	read(java.io.PrintStream ps, java.util.Scanner sc) Static read method for class Student.
java.lang.String	toString() Returns a String which represents the receiving Student.

Methods inherited from   class java.lang.Object
clone, equals, finalize, getClass, hashCode, notify, notifyAll, wait, wait, wait

Constructor Detail

Student

Figure APP12–01
(continued)

```
public Student(java.lang.String name,
               int grade)
```

Creates a Student with the specified name and grade.

Method Detail

getName

```
public java.lang.String getName()
```

Returns the name of a Student object.

Returns:
The name of the receiving Student.

See Also:
getGrade()

---

getGrade

```
public int getGrade()
```

Returns the name of a Student object.

Returns:
The grade of the receiving Student.

See Also:
getName()

---

toString

```
public java.lang.String toString()
```

Returns a String which represents the receiving Student. The complex number 3+5i would be represented as (3,5).

Overrides:
toString in class java.lang.Object

---

read

```
public static Student read(java.io.PrintStream ps,
                           java.util.Scanner sc)
```

Figure APP12–01
(continued)

Static read method for class Student.

Parameters:
 ps - PrintStream to which prompts should be sent. null specifies that no prompting is desired.
 sc - Scanner from which Student data is to be read.

Package Class **Tree Deprecated Index Help**
PREV CLASS NEXT CLASS
SUMMARY: NESTED | FIELD | CONSTR | METHOD

FRAMES NO FRAMES All Classes
DETAIL: FIELD | CONSTR | METHOD

tags are special lines that produce text and links in the output file. We see four types of tags in Student.java:

1. @return The name of the receiving Student—produces a **Returns:** statement in the HTML, using the given text.
2. @param ps PrintStream to which prompts are sent—produces a line in the **Parameters:** section that lists the parameter and the given text.
3. @see #getName—generates a link to the specified method in a **See Also:** section of the HTML.
4. @author Barry Soroka—puts a name in the **Author:** section of the HTML.

HTML tags can be used to change the fonts of the text produced by doc comments. The tags <B> ... </B> make the enclosed text **bold**. The tags <code> ... </code> put the enclosed text into a fixed-width font signifying code.
 inserts line breaks.

You can find more information about javadoc on the Sun Microsystems website.

Index